The
SIX WIVES
of
HENRY VIII

Antonia Fraser

WEIDENFELD & NICOLSON
London

First published in Great Britain in 1992
by George Weidenfeld and Nicolson Ltd
Orion Publishing Group Ltd
Orion House
5 Upper St Martin's Lane
London WC2H 9EA

Tenth Impression December 1993

British Library Cataloguing-in-Publication Data
is available on request.

Typeset by Selwood Systems,
Midsomer Norton, Avon
Printed and bound in Great Britain by
Butler & Tanner Ltd, Frome and London

The
SIX WIVES
of
HENRY VIII

ALSO BY ANTONIA FRASER

Mary Queen of Scots
Cromwell, Our Chief of Men
King Charles II
The Weaker Vessel: Woman's lot in seventeenth-century England
The Warrior Queens: Boadicea's Chariot

In the *Kings and Queens of England* series
King James VI of Scotland, I of England

CONTENTS

·CONTENTS·

ILLUSTRATIONS

Between pp. 50–1

Pomegranate badge of Catherine of Aragon (Weidenfeld & Nicolson Archive)
The Madonna of the Catholic Kings by an unknown artist showing Catherine of Aragon's parents (Weidenfeld & Nicolson Archive)
Edward IV, maternal grandfather of Henry VIII (The Royal Collection, © HM The Queen)
Margaret Beaufort, Countess of Richmond, paternal grandmother of Henry VIII (Master and Fellows, St John's College, Cambridge)
Henry VII, father of Henry VIII (Society of Antiquaries of London)
Elizabeth of York, mother of Henry VIII (The Royal Collection, © HM The Queen)
Bust thought to be Henry VIII as a boy, attributed to Guido Mazzoni (The Royal Collection, © HM The Queen)
The young Catherine by Michael Sittow (Kunsthistorisches Museum, Vienna)
The Family of Henry VII with St George and the Dragon by an unknown artist of the Flemish school (The Royal Collection, © HM The Queen)
An early sixteenth-century Flemish tapestry showing the betrothal of Prince Arthur and Catherine of Aragon (President and Fellows, Magdalen College, Oxford)
Stained glass in the chapel at The Vyne, featuring Henry VIII and Catherine of Aragon (National Trust Photographic Library)
Watercolours by Daniel Chandler of stained glass showing King Henry and Queen Catherine (Society of Antiquaries of London)
The palace of Greenwich in the early seventeenth century (National Trust Photographic Library)
Mary, sister of Henry VIII, and her second husband, Charles Brandon, Duke of Suffolk (Courtesy of the Trustees of the Bedford Estate and the Marquess of Tavistock)
Letter from Catherine of Aragon, as Regent of England, describing the victory over the Scots at Flodden in 1513 (British Library)
Contemporary illustration of the tournament held to celebrate the birth of Prince Henry in 1511 (British Library)
Armour made for Henry VIII in his late twenties (Royal Armouries, HM Tower of London)
Medal of Henry VIII, about 1525 (British Museum)

Between pp. 146–7

Badge of Anne Boleyn: crowned falcon accompanied by Tudor roses (Weidenfeld & Nicolson Archive)
Thomas Boleyn, father of Anne Boleyn, by Hans Holbein (The Royal Library, Windsor, © HM The Queen)
Hever Castle, Kent (Courtesy of Lord Astor, Hever Castle)
One of the letters of Henry VIII to Anne Boleyn, written in July 1528 (Weidenfeld & Nicolson Archive)
Petition from Henry VIII to Pope Clement VII concerning a divorce (Weidenfeld & Nicolson Archive)
Design by Holbein for a triumphal arch for the coronation of Anne Boleyn on 1 June 1533 (Weidenfeld & Nicolson Archive)
Henry VIII in his early forties by Joos van Cleeve (The Royal Collection, © HM The Queen)
Anne Boleyn by an unknown artist (National Portrait Gallery)
Miniature of Catherine of Aragon, attributed to Lucas Horenbout (National Portrait Gallery)

– vii –

Catherine of Aragon by an unknown artist (National Portrait Gallery)
Miniature of Anne Boleyn at the age of 25, attributed to Lucas Horenbout (Courtesy of the Duke of Buccleuch and Queensberry)
Anne Boleyn: a drawing by Holbein (The Royal Library, Windsor, © HM The Queen)
Anne Boleyn's bedhead at Hever Castle (Courtesy of Lord Astor, Hever Castle)
Henry Fitzroy, Duke of Richmond (The Royal Collection, © HM The Queen)

Between pp. 242–3

Badge of Jane Seymour (Weidenfeld & Nicolson Archive)
Screen at King's College, Cambridge, showing H and A, for Henry and Anne Boleyn (Courtesy of the Provost and Fellows, King's College, Cambridge)
Announcement of the birth of Elizabeth (British Library)
Clock supposedly given by Henry VIII to Anne Boleyn (The Royal Collection, © HM The Queen)
1534 medal of Anne Boleyn with her motto 'The Moost Happi' (British Museum)
Sixteenth-century view of the Tower of London (British Library)
Henry VIII aged 45 by Holbein (Thyssen-Bornemisza Collection/Bridgeman Art Library)
Elizabeth Seymour, sister of Jane Seymour – incorrectly identified as Katherine Howard in the late nineteenth-century (National Portrait Gallery)
Jane Seymour painted by Holbein about the time of her wedding, 1536 (Kunsthistorisches Museum, Vienna)
John Fisher, Bishop of Rochester (The Royal Library, Windsor, © HM The Queen)
Cardinal Thomas Wolsey (National Portrait Gallery)
Thomas Cranmer by Gerlach Flicke, 1546 (National Portrait Gallery)
Thomas Cromwell by Holbein (Frick Collection, New York)
Holbein's design for a gold cup for Jane Seymour (Ashmolean Museum, Oxford)
Designs for jewellery by Holbein (British Library)

Between pp. 306–7

Badge of Anna of Cleves (Weidenfeld & Nicolson Archive)
Coins of Henry VIII (British Museum)
The Great Gatehouse of Hampton Court Palace (Crown Copyright, Historic Royal Palaces)
Selection of jewels and ciphers designed by Holbein (British Library)
Richmond Palace by Wyngaerde (Ashmolean Museum, Oxford)
The Emperor Charles V (The Royal Collection, © HM The Queen)
Christina of Milan by Holbein (National Portrait Gallery)
François I, King of France (Musée Condé/Giraudon)
James V of Scotland. Artist unknown (National Galleries of Scotland)
Anna of Cleves by Holbein (The Louvre/Giraudon/Bridgeman Art Library)
Chart showing Anna of Cleves's projected journey to England in the autumn of 1539 (British Library)
Dedication on a blank leaf at the back of a Book of Hours, printed in Germany about 1533, given by Anna of Cleves to Henry VIII (Folger Shakespeare Library, Washington)
Anna of Cleves: a contemporary portrait from the workshop of Barthel Bruyn the Elder in Cologne and possibly by Bruyn himself (President and Fellows, St John's College, Oxford)

Between pp. 338–9

Crowned rose badge of Katherine Howard (Weidenfeld & Nicolson Archive)
Window of the Queen of Sheba, King's College Chapel (Courtesy of the Provost and Fellows, King's College, Cambridge – photo Dr H.G. Wayment)
Thomas Howard, 3rd Duke of Norfolk; uncle to both Katherine Howard and Anne Boleyn (The Royal Collection, © HM The Queen)
Detail of the Window of the Queen of Sheba, King's College Chapel (Courtesy of the Provost and Fellows, King's College, Cambridge – photo P.A.L. Brunney)

Henry VIII about 1542. Artist unknown (National Portrait Gallery)

Armour made for Henry VIII in 1540 (Royal Armouries, HM Tower of London)

Edward, Prince of Wales, son of Henry VIII and Jane Seymour (National Gallery of Art, Washington)

Elizabeth, daughter of Anne Boleyn and Henry VIII, aged about 13, attributed to William Scrots (The Royal Collection, © HM The Queen)

Miniature of Mary, daughter of Henry VIII and Catherine of Aragon (Courtesy of Brian Pilkington)

Mary by Holbein (The Royal Library, Windsor, © HM The Queen)

The only known letter by Katherine Howard addressed to 'Master [Thomas] Culpeper' (Public Record Office)

The Chapel of St Peter ad Vincula at the Tower of London (Photo Geoff Langan)

Edward, Prince of Wales, aged about 6 (Kunstmuseum, Basel)

Katherine Willoughby, Duchess of Suffolk, by Holbein (The Royal Library, Windsor, © HM The Queen)

Between pp. 402–3

Badge of Catherine Parr (Weidenfeld & Nicolson Archive)

William Parr, Marquess of Northampton, brother of Catherine Parr, by Holbein (The Royal Library, Windsor, © HM The Queen)

Thomas Seymour, fourth husband of Catherine Parr (National Portrait Gallery)

Henry VIII and his family, painted by an unknown artist in about 1545 (The Royal Collection, © HM The Queen)

Engraving of Henry VIII in his last years by Cornelius Matsuys (The Royal Library, Windsor, © HM The Queen)

Medal of Henry VIII as 'defender of the faith', 1545 (British Museum)

Catherine Parr, attributed to William Scrots (National Portrait Gallery)

A manuscript version of Catherine Parr's *Prayers and Meditations* (Courtesy of the Mayor and Town Council of Kendal – photo Edward Geldard)

Sudeley Castle (Reproduced courtesy of Sudeley Castle)

The slab of marble marking the grave of Catherine of Aragon in Peterborough Cathedral (Courtesy of the Dean and Chapter of Peterborough – photo Helen Drake)

Slab marking the vault beneath the floor of the choir of St George's Chapel, Windsor, in which Jane Seymour and Henry VIII are buried (Courtesy of the Dean and Canons of Windsor)

Plaque in the floor of the Chapel of St Peter ad Vincula, Tower of London, marking the burial place of Anne Boleyn (photo N.W. Jackson)

The tomb of Anna of Cleves on the south side of the High Altar in Westminster Abbey (Courtesy of the Dean and Chapter of Westminster)

Plaque in the floor of the Chapel of St Peter ad Vincula, Tower of London, marking the burial place of Katherine Howard (Photo N.W. Jackson)

The tomb of Catherine Parr in the Chapel of Sudeley Castle (Courtesy of Sudeley Castle)

The Queen's Closet, St George's Chapel, Windsor (Courtesy of the Dean and Canons of Windsor)

Illustration from Thomas Bentley's *Monument of Matrones*, 1582 (British Library)

The Plantagenet Descent of Henry and his Queens

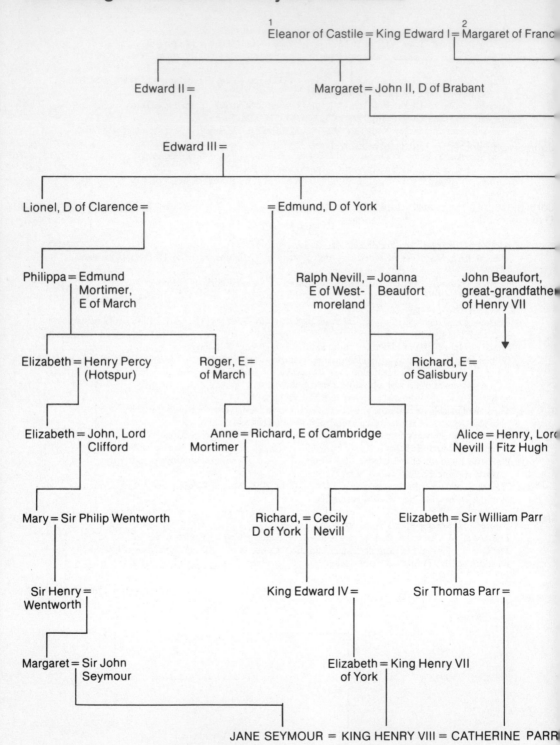

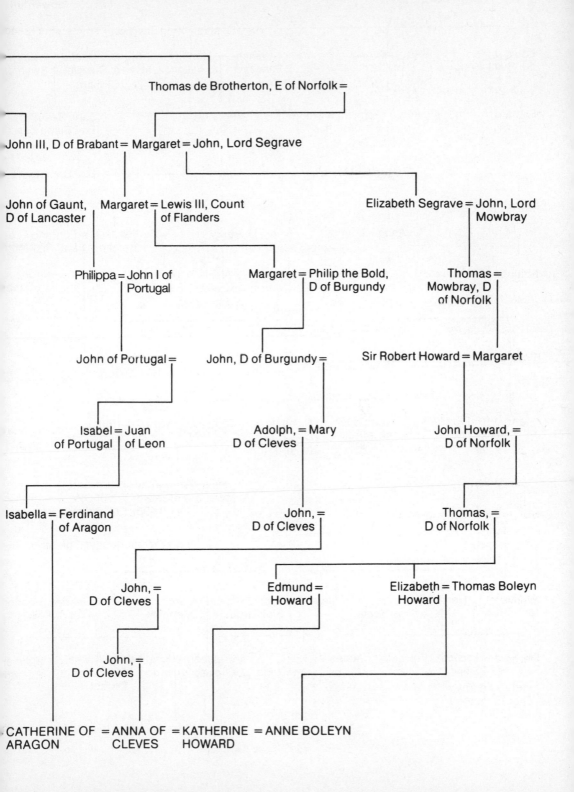

Thomas de Brotherton, E of Norfolk =

John III, D of Brabant = Margaret = John, Lord Segrave

John of Gaunt,
D of Lancaster

Margaret = Lewis III, Count
of Flanders

Elizabeth Segrave = John, Lord
Mowbray

Philippa = John I of
Portugal

Margaret = Philip the Bold,
D of Burgundy

Thomas =
Mowbray, D
of Norfolk

John of Portugal =

John, D of Burgundy =

Sir Robert Howard = Margaret

Isabel = Juan
of Portugal | of Leon

Adolph, = Mary
D of Cleves

John Howard, =
D of Norfolk

Isabella = Ferdinand
of Aragon

John, =
D of Cleves

Thomas, =
D of Norfolk

John, =
D of Cleves

Edmund =
Howard

Elizabeth = Thomas Boleyn
Howard

John, =
D of Cleves

CATHERINE OF = ANNA OF = KATHERINE = ANNE BOLEYN
ARAGON   CLEVES   HOWARD

The Tudors and their Rivals

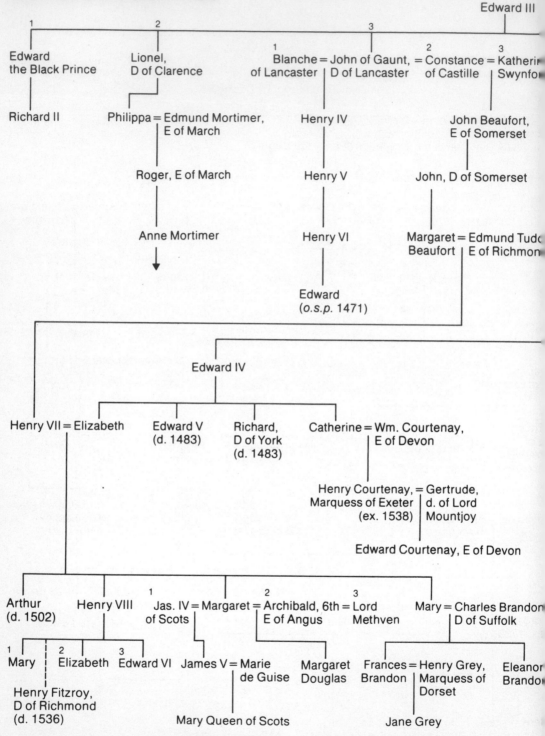

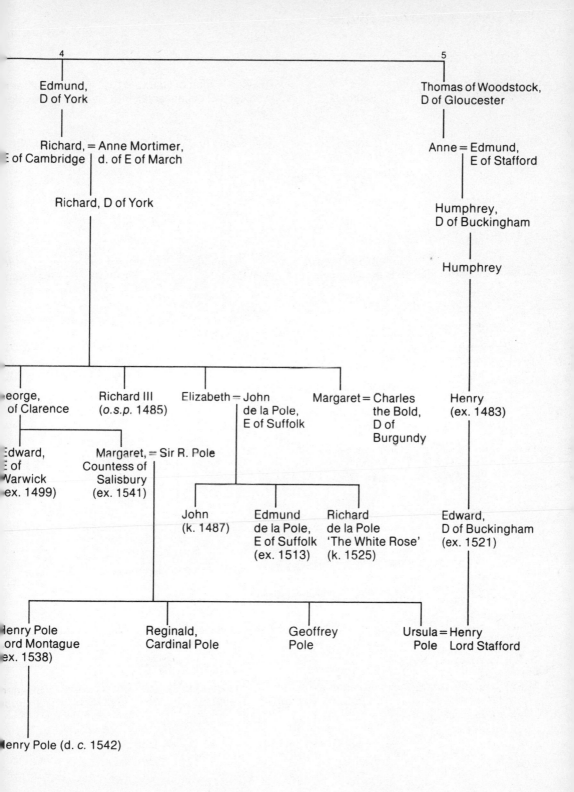

Edmund,
D of York

Thomas of Woodstock,
D of Gloucester

Richard, = Anne Mortimer,
E of Cambridge | d. of E of March

Anne = Edmund,
E of Stafford

Richard, D of York

Humphrey,
D of Buckingham

Humphrey

George,
of Clarence

Richard III
(*o.s.p.* 1485)

Elizabeth = John
de la Pole,
E of Suffolk

Margaret = Charles
the Bold,
D of
Burgundy

Henry
(ex. 1483)

Edward,
E of
Warwick
(ex. 1499)

Margaret, = Sir R. Pole
Countess of
Salisbury
(ex. 1541)

John
(k. 1487)

Edmund
de la Pole,
E of Suffolk
(ex. 1513)

Richard
de la Pole
'The White Rose'
(k. 1525)

Edward,
D of Buckingham
(ex. 1521)

Henry Pole
Lord Montague
(ex. 1538)

Reginald,
Cardinal Pole

Geoffrey
Pole

Ursula = Henry
Pole   Lord Stafford

Henry Pole (d. *c.* 1542)

*For Harold
with love*

PROLOGUE

'Divorced, beheaded, died ... divorced, beheaded, survived ...': you can hear this rhyme, recalling the order of Henry VIII's wives, like an endless respectful susurration on the lips of visitors to the historic places associated with them. So the six women have become defined in a popular sense not so much by their lives as by the way these lives ended. In the same way their characters are popularly portrayed as female stereotypes: the Betrayed Wife, the Temptress, the Good Woman, the Ugly Sister, the Bad Girl and, finally, the Mother Figure. The perils of such stereotyping were once forcibly illustrated to me on a visit to Hever Castle when I listened to a knowledgeable schoolchild pronounce on a presumed portrait of Anna of Cleves: 'That's her, the ugly one.' To which his companion agreed: 'That's right, she's dead ugly' – except that they were both actually looking at a picture of the 'Temptress' Anne Boleyn.

A more sophisticated example is provided by the treatment of the six women in religious terms, given that this was a period when religion and the question of religious reform was the dominant issue in Europe. Catherine of Aragon is crudely assumed to have been a bigoted Catholic, as we should now understand the word (although in her prime distinguished for her patronage of Erasmian humanism – 'the New Learning'); Anne Boleyn displayed strong Protestant tendencies, once again in modern terms, long before the action of Rome in blocking her marriage to the King made her the natural ally of the reformers; Jane Seymour, who has gone down in history as the Protestant Queen, adhered in fact to the old ways in religion; Anna of Cleves, married for her 'Lutheran' connection, was a natural Catholic; Catherine Parr was the true Protestant Queen. The truth – as so often where the female in history is concerned – is both more complicated and more interesting than the legend.

My first aim in writing this book has therefore been to look at the women behind the stereotypes – how far if at all did they deserve such labels? – as well as relating six life stories which are fascinating in themselves, quite apart from the manner in which they ended. With this in mind, I have tried wherever possible, without straining too much, to avoid hindsight. In short, although *we* know Henry VIII will marry six times, we must always remember that he did not.

The early sixteenth century was a time when prophecies were popular and prophets were confident: men and women puzzled over ancient rhymes which might (or might not) be held to have predicted such mighty topics as the fall of Cardinal Wolsey, the split from Rome, and the dissolution of the monasteries. But no one ever predicted that the King would marry six times and, if they had, he would not have believed it. Nor for that matter would any of his six queens have believed the various destinies which lay in store for them, if predicted at birth: not one but two princesses were to die cast off; equally surprisingly, four women of modest enough birth were to become royal consorts; most astonishingly of all (as it would have seemed) two of these apparently unexceptional women were to die a traitor's death.

Lastly, of course, no one could have predicted that the lithe and golden-haired Prince Charming who ascended the throne of England just before his eighteenth birthday in 1509 – 'the handsomest prince in Europe' – would die nearly forty years later, a monster of obesity, with a reputation more like that of Bluebeard than Prince Charming. Let us not forget that the story of the six wives of Henry VIII, with all its elements of sexual drama, pathos, horror, and at times, comedy, filled Europe itself with amazement. The King of France – no stranger himself to extramarital pastimes – was incredulous when told that his brother of England had just repudiated his fourth wife of six months' standing in favour of a nubile little creature of whom no one had ever heard, young enough to be the granddaughter of his first wife. 'The Queen that now is?' enquired François I and on being told that it was, he let out a deep sigh. An indiscreet lady-in-waiting spoke for many when she exclaimed in 1540: 'What a man is the King! How many wives will he have?'

My second aim has been to illumine certain aspects of women's history through the lives of these celebrated exemplars – celebrated in the first place through marriage. But then that is the point. Marriage was the triumphal arch through which women, almost without exception, had to pass in order to reach the public eye. And after marriage followed, in theory, the total self-abnegation of the woman. Here is the contemporary view of marriage plainly expressed by one of those most sympathetic to the situation of women at the time, the Spanish philosopher Juan Luis Vives: 'A wife's love for her husband includes respect, obedience and submission. Not only the traditions of our ancestors but all human and divine laws agree with the powerful voice of nature which demands from women observance and submissiveness.' Yet Vives, unusually, was a public advocate of education for women whom Catherine of Aragon consulted on behalf of her daughter Mary Tudor; in general, Vives' belief that woman was 'a frail thing, and of weak discretion, and may be lightly deceived, which thing our first mother Eve sheweth whom the Devil caught with a light argument' represented the prevailing view.

Even Sir Thomas More, sometimes regarded as a prominent patron of women's learning because he encouraged the education of his daughter Margaret, once expressed the hope that her coming child would resemble her in all but 'the inferiority of her sex'. Behind the liberals Vives and More marched ranks of people, both men and women, who took for granted woman's inferiority – and her subordination to her husband. If this were held to be true of ordinary wives bowing before ordinary husbands, how much more awe-inspiring must the power of a royal husband have been! We are dealing here with six women who were married in turn to the supreme power in the land, the royal head of state and, from 1534, the self-constituted head of the church as well. No wonder Katherine Howard, young and incredulous, was convinced that the omnipotent King (to whom she was married) must be able to overhear the very sins mentioned in the confessional. Catherine Parr, one of the very few women in this period whose works (prayers and meditations) were printed, was explicit on the subject in her *Lamentation of a Sinner*: 'Children of light . . . if they be women married, they learn of St Paul to be obedient to their husbands.'

It is now that the wonderful paradox emerges that makes the study of women's history so fascinating and even exhilarating to those who practise it, not merely a pathetic chronicle of suffering. Rich, feisty characters flourished in this atmosphere of theoretical subjection: one might note that even the naive Katherine Howard was not suggesting that certain sins should not be committed – only that they should not be mentioned in the confessional. The other five wives, as we shall see as the story unfolds, exhibited remarkable degrees of spirit and defiance of which women living in much easier circumstances, legally speaking, might still be proud.

Although this is the story of six very different women (to that extent the varied stereotypes are correct), it is essentially a composite narrative. This reflects the important linkage which existed between the various women whose stories cannot be neatly sealed off in compartments from each other. In terms of court ceremonial, Anne Boleyn waited on Catherine of Aragon before supplanting her, Jane Seymour waited on Anne Boleyn, Katherine Howard on Anna of Cleves, Anne Parr on Katherine Howard thus bringing her sister Catherine into court circles. King Henry certainly did not pass easily from one marriage into another (as a modern serial divorcé may at least hope to do). The stability of his early married life to Catherine of Aragon – nearly twenty years of it, a much longer period than is sometimes realized – gave way to an era of marital tempest in which there were all too often two women alive who either were or had once been Queen of England. If her fate does not compare in poignancy with that of Catherine of Aragon, Anna of Cleves' bizarre and protracted survival at the English court in the honorary role of the King's 'good sister', following her divorce, is certainly one of the odder episodes in the story. We are told of her dancing happily with the queen who had taken her place – Katherine Howard – at the New Year celebrations of 1541, while the old King stumped off to bed to nurse his bad leg.

Other transfers were of course achieved with much less serenity. Jealousy of all types permeates this story, not only the desperate jealousy of the queens who found themselves abandoned but also the sexual jealousy of the King who discovered himself betrayed. Rivalry was also inevitable when the stakes were so high in the great game of marrying the King of England; for the woman concerned, and also for her country if she was a princess and her family if she was a commoner. This is however no reason for a biographer to perpetuate those rivalries nearly five hundred years later. I myself have not felt the need to develop a particular favourite among the six queens – unlike King Henry VIII himself, for whom Jane Seymour remained his 'true wife', the one who was 'entirely beloved', on the grounds that she gave him a son. This partiality extended to having her prominently enshrined after her death as his consort in his vast dynastic portrait of his family, when Catherine Parr was actually the living loyal wife at his side.

I have, on the contrary, attempted to deal with each woman in turn with the sympathy I feel they all deserve for having had the unenviable fate (to my way of thinking) of being married to Henry VIII. At the same time I have tried to practise the detachment which recognizes that this is an eminently modern judgement; not one of the King's six wives married him against her will. I have also hoped to practise that detachment towards the King himself: the gigantic Maypole at the centre of it all round which these women had to dance. But of course this is not his story. It is theirs.

In order to tell the story without unnecessary confusion from the reader's point of view, I have preferred clarity to consistency over the spelling of names, even where this leads to some anomalies. That is to say, I have referred to Catherine, not Katherine, of Aragon throughout, according to modern practice (she herself began life as Catalina in Spain, but used Katherine and the initial K mainly – but not entirely – in England). I have also referred to Catherine Parr, who may have been named for the earlier

Queen; but describe her immediate predecessor as Katherine Howard in order to distinguish her. For the same reason, I have referred to Anna (the name she was known by in her native country), not Anne of Cleves, so that we have only one Queen Anne – Boleyn.

With regard to other foreign forenames, once again I have tried to put the reader's interests first. For example, Margaret of Austria, daughter of the Emperor Maximilian I, married to the Infante Juan of Spain and then Duke Philibert of Savoy, finally Regent of the Netherlands, is referred to throughout her life as the Archduchess Margaret; similarly the sister of the French King François I is always described as Marguerite d'Angoulême, despite marrying in turn the Duc d'Alençon and the King of Navarre. I have also modernized spelling where necessary and dated letters and documents as though the calendar year began on 1 January, as it does now, instead of 25 March, as it did then.

In writing this book, I owe a great deal to the many works of the many scholars acknowledged in the References. I would like to thank Fräulein Bärbel Brodt for translating and advising on material in German related to Anna of Cleves; the Marquess of Salisbury for allowing me to quote from Robert Whittington's Latin panegyric to Anne Boleyn and Mr Richard Murray for translating it; (Lord) Hugh Thomas for discussions on Spanish royal genealogy in the fifteenth century; Dr H. C. Wayment for his expert advice on the heraldry of the queens, depicted in stained-glass windows; the staff of the London Library and the Round Reading Room of the British Library.

I would also like to single out the following who have given me help in many different ways and thank them: Dr Susan Brigden; Mr Lorne Campbell; Ms Enid Davies, Archivist, St George's Chapel; Dr Maria Dowling; Mr Howard Eaton, Administrator for the National Trust, Blicking Hall; Dr Susan Foister; Ph Dr Frantisek Frölich; Mr Tony Garrett; Professor Barbara J. Harris; Mr Richard Hall, Cumberland and Westmorland Antiquarian and Archaeological Society; Mr S. J. Hession, Peterborough Cathedral; Mr Peter Holman; the Rev. George Howe, Vicar of Holy Trinity, Kendal; Mr N. W. Jackson, Yeoman Clerk, Tower of London; Dr Susan E. James; Dr Lisa Jardine; Mr Mark Jones, formerly Keeper of the Department of Coins and Medals, British Museum; Ms Sharon Johnson, Photographic Librarian, Royal Armouries; Dr Rana Kabbani; Dr Peter Le Fevre; Dr Nati Krivatsky, Folger Shakespeare Library, Washington DC; Mr David Lyon, National Maritime Museum; Ms Claire Messenger, Department of Prints and Drawings, British Museum; the Very Reverend Michael Mayne, Dean of Westminster; Mrs E. Nixon, Assistant Librarian, Muniment Room of Westminster Abbey; Mr Richard Ollard; Mr Geoffrey Parnell, Crown Buildings and

Monuments Advisory Group, English Heritage; Mr Brian Pilkington; Mr John Martin Robinson, Librarian to the Duke of Norfolk; Mrs Lynda Shaw, Assistant Keeper of Manuscripts, University of Nottingham; Councillor W. Stewart, Mayor of Kendal and Mr Percy S. Duff, Town Treasurer; Mr David Spence, National Maritime Museum; Mr Steven Tomlinson, Department of Western Manuscripts, Bodleian Library; Mr Simon Thurley, Curator, Hampton Court Palace; Major-General Christopher Tyler, Lieutenant-Governor of the Tower of London; the Very Revd Randolph Wise, former Dean of Peterborough. Perhaps I should add that with the exception of the people specifically named above, I have, as ever, done all my own research, which I regard as one of the pleasures and privileges of my working life.

I am particularly grateful to Jasper Ridley who read the manuscript and made important comments (any errors are of course my own responsibility); my mother Elizabeth Longford who brought her lucid mind to bear upon the book at an early stage; Douglas Matthews for the Index – yet again; Michael Shaw of Curtis Brown; Christopher Falkus and Hilary Laurie of Weidenfeld & Nicolson; and Sonny Mehta of Knopf. As for the wonderful Georgina Gooding, who typed the manuscript and put it on disk, she must be almost as glad as I am that King Henry VIII did not marry one more time. This is a feeling which may also, I suspect, be shared by my family, led by my husband, to whom in recognition of his support my book is justly dedicated. It was my friend Robert Gottlieb, in New York, who suggested this book to me with the uncharacteristically diffident words: 'This may not sound like a good idea, but . . .' Lastly I wish to thank him without whom, I can truthfully say without fear of cliché, the book would never have been written.

Antonia Fraser
All Hallows Eve 1990 – Lady Day 1992

Part I

CATHERINE

of

ARAGON

Chapter 1

ARTHUR'S DEAREST
SPOUSE

My dearest spouse . . . truly those your letters have
rendered me so cheerful and jocund that I fancied I
beheld your highness and conversed with and embraced
my dearest wife.

Arthur Prince of Wales to Catherine of Aragon, 1499

The story begins in Spain. On 16 December 1485, a few months after the historic battle of Bosworth Field at which Henry VII secured the throne of England, a princess Catherine (or Catalina) was born. She had an unusual parentage. Catherine was the daughter of not one but two reigning monarchs, Isabella of Castile and Ferdinand of Aragon – the 'Catholic Kings' as they would be designated by the Pope.[1] There would be many princesses born in Europe around this time, the daughters of mighty kings and dukes of strategically placed territories, whose marital destinies would weave and interweave with Catherine's own. But to Catherine and her three elder sisters had fallen a special fate. Their mother was Queen of Castile in her own right, as well as the consort of the King of Aragon.

Catherine was the youngest child of Isabella and Ferdinand. For the first fifteen years of her life (half the life expectancy of a woman of that time, and as it turned out nearly one third of her own life) she lived under the tutelage of her remarkable mother. For Isabella's unique position as a queen regnant was matched by that combination of a pious character and military achievement which had made her by the 1490s the wonder of Europe. In 1497 a mere queen consort – Elizabeth of York – referred to the 'eminent dignity and virtue by which your said majesty so shines and excels that your most celebrated name is noised abroad and diffused everywhere.'[2] As contemporary Europe was indelibly impressed by the image of Isabella the Catholic, so too was her daughter Catherine.

–9–

As a result, Catherine grew up conscious from her earliest years of the dignity to which she had been born as a daughter – an infanta – of Spain; it was an awareness of being a true royal princess (compared to those of lesser or less established title) which never left her. By the time Catherine was born, the civil war faced by Isabella on her accession to the throne in 1474 was long forgotten. Catherine's childhood image therefore was not only of a king and queen working in harness, but of a flourishing royal family.

Her three elder sisters, Isabel, Juana and Maria were born in 1470, 1479 and 1482 respectively, but the key birth was that of the Infante Juan, born in June 1478 and thus seven years Catherine's senior. Handsome, light-hearted and seemingly robust, it was no wonder that the Infante was adored by his sisters. To his parents also, the birth of the Infante Juan after an eight-year gap was a symbol of God's kindly providence. In Aragon, unlike Castile, the Salic law operated by which a female could not succeed; but Juan could inherit the kingdoms of both his parents. The whole family picture was suffused with the golden glow of a hopeful future.

In the spring of 1485 Queen Isabella found herself pregnant once more. She had already been engaged for four battling years in the so-called *'Reconquista'* of southern Spain from the Moors. Animated in part by crusading Catholic zeal, in part by a different kind of zeal – for territorial aggrandisement – Isabella, no less than Ferdinand, had flung herself into the rigours of campaigning (miscarrying at least one child as a result). Nor did the Queen allow her condition to impede her active involvement in the enterprise on this occasion. High summer saw the capture of Ronda from the Moors. It was not until the autumn that Isabella turned north with the intention of resting at the main Spanish base of Cordoba. But the flooding at Cordoba defeated her – it was an exceptionally wet autumn – and it was finally at Alcalá de Henares, in a castle belonging to the Archbishop of Toledo, that Isabella gave birth to what would prove to be her last child.

The name chosen was significant. Although the Spanish form of Catalina would have been used in Catherine's childhood, she was nevertheless named for an English princess: Catherine of Lancaster, Isabella's grandmother.[3] To the Spanish and Portuguese royal blood which flowed in the veins of Isabella's children was added a strong dose of Plantagenet. (See family tree 1) Isabella herself was descended twice over from John of Gaunt, both from his first marriage to his cousin Blanche of Lancaster and his second to Constance of Castile. (Ferdinand also had a Plantagenet inheritance, descending rather more remotely from a daughter of Henry II.)

The early years of Catherine's childhood were adventurous, and sometimes arduous as her mother's pregnancy had been. Isabella's court was still more than half a movable camp. There were alarms such as an outbreak of fire in the siege-camp, either accidental or the result of a small raid. And Catherine was present on the occasion of another Moorish raid known as 'the Queen's skirmish' when the royal ladies, young and old, knelt in prayer for safety. Nevertheless, whatever the checks, the progress of the *reconquista* was inexorable. Catherine grew up against a background of military success. As a contemporary observed, in a play upon the word Granada: 'the pomegranate is being eaten, grain by grain'.[4] It was shortly after Catherine's sixth birthday that the final triumph came.

In January 1492 Granada, the redoubt of the Moorish kingdom, fell to the Spanish monarchs. Ferdinand and Isabella, their children at their side, rode to the great palace of the Alhambra and took possession of it. The Catholic thanksgiving which followed, where once the ceremonies of Islam had held sway, presaged the most triumphant years of the Spanish monarchy.

These were also the years of Catherine's education. Isabella herself had come to the throne unexpectedly thanks to the accident of her half-brother's death without a legitimate heir. She had been raised in a secluded convent without any of the skills needed by a statesman – male or female – on the European stage. In particular she knew no Latin, and since this was still the language of international diplomacy, had therefore been obliged to learn it as an adult: a traditionally painful task. Thereafter Queen Isabella's own interest in and patronage of learning led to a general revival of classical studies in Spain, while other scholars including Peter Martyr of Anghiers were imported from Italy. Women were not excluded from this renaissance. There were female lecturers in rhetoric at Alcala and Salamanca.

Martyr later boasted: 'I was the literary foster father of almost all the princes, and of all the princesses of Spain'.[5] Celebrated humanists such as the poet Antonio Geraldini and his brother Alessandro also took part in their education. For, where her daughters were concerned, Queen Isabella was determined that they should be given the advantages that had been denied to her. In this she acted not only as a prudent mother but also, in agreement with Ferdinand, as a prudent monarch. Once the male succession was assured, the birth of a princess who through a powerful marriage could act as the ambassadress of her parents, was not seen as a disaster. 'If your Highness gives us two or three more daughters', wrote the Spanish chronicler Hernando de Pulgar to Isabella in 1478, 'in twenty years time you will have the pleasure of seeing your children and grandchildren on all the thrones of Europe.'[6] The birth of Catherine meant that Isabella now had four of these potential envoys. She was determined that they should be well trained.

As a result Catherine studied not only her Missal and the Bible, but also the classics such as Prudentius and Juventus, St Ambrose on St Augustine, St Gregory, St Jerome, Seneca and the Latin historians. She ended by speaking good classical Latin with great fluency. Then a knowledge of both civil and canon law was thought appropriate, as well as of heraldry and genealogy – how important both of these latter were to a Renaissance princess who would take her place in an elaborate world where panoply often symbolized power! The point has been made that Catherine of Aragon in England displayed 'a quality of mind ... which few queens have seriously rivalled'. That was not in itself surprising.[7] She had, after all, been raised at a court where both women and men acknowledged that it was 'a universal condition of mankind to want to know.'[8]

Catherine's intellectual attainments apart, music, dancing and drawing – the traditional and graceful spheres of Renaissance feminine accomplishment – were naturally not ignored. But Queen Isabella also passed on to her daughters another more universal feminine tradition of basic domestic skills, all the more poignant perhaps, since the wives who practised them would be married to kings and archdukes, not merchants and farmers. It was said that the Queen insisted on making all King Ferdinand's shirts. Certainly her daughters were taught to spin, weave and bake: Catherine in turn would see it as both her duty and her right to embroider her own husband's shirts. And Catherine's constant preoccupation with the material side of her husband's comforts – his clean linen while away campaigning, a sudden need of a late night supper of meat provided in her apartments – provides a domestic counterpoint to the regality which she brought to the English court.

There was another personal legacy which Isabella passed to her daughters which had important emotional consequences. It was true that on her accession, Isabella had declared herself – not herself jointly with her husband – *la reina proprietaria*. That is, the 'proprietorship' of the Castilian throne was vested in her own person, even though Ferdinand always acted in effect as co-ruler. Isabella also refused to alter the succession laws in Castile which allowed her eldest surviving daughter to succeed her if she died without a male heir; although in this event Ferdinand, as her second cousin, would actually be the male with the best claim to the throne. But with this strength of public purpose (originating perhaps in the Castilian nobles' irritable refusal to bow to the Aragonese) went a private wifely submission to the husbandly authority of Ferdinand and a profound belief in the divinely ordained nature of all marriages –

and hers, which had brought about the fruitful union of two countries, in particular.

A husband was sent by God. 'It is he, it is he', Isabella is supposed to have cried on her first meeting with Ferdinand, selecting him unerringly from a group of other young gentlemen.[9] A wife, whatever her royal rights, submitted to her husband and was of course bound to him for life; but the same God-given chain which bound her also bound *him*. Two of Isabella's daughters – Juana as well as Catherine – were to show, in their very different ways, an absolute obsession with the husband given to them in the first place for reasons of state, but surely also by the will of God.

Then there was Isabella's personal piety: rigorous, humble, sincere, listening always to the voice of her religious advisers, her confessors, as though to atone once more, as with her husband, by submissiveness in that direction for the august position so unusual in a female which she occupied. Nevertheless it is significant for Catherine's future that the humanist ideal, to be propagated by Erasmus, and later by Catherine's fellow Spaniard Juan Luis Vives, did not call for abandonment of that august position in favour of a convent or monastery. It was considered perfectly possible to lead a truly Christian life within the world, as another kind of vocation.[10]

It is hardly surprising that such a pious woman as Isabella was also chaste. Indeed, it is noticeable that among the princesses of Europe who were descended from Isabella, personal chastity like wifely submission was another characteristic: not for them the hot-running blood of the Tudors – Catherine's future sisters-in-law – who on several occasions allowed their hearts or physical appetites to rule their heads.

Personal chastity, on the other hand, was not the watchword of Catherine's father, Ferdinand, whose deviousness would rapidly become proverbial in Europe (Machiavelli praised his statesmanship in *The Prince*). His amours angered Isabella – as such things generally do – without diminishing her devotion, let alone her feeling for the divinely instituted nature of her marriage. In this respect, of course, Isabella did not offer a unique role model to her growing daughters; on the contrary, she merely followed the accepted pattern of queens, consort or regnant (Isabella being of course both). She might be furious at such things, jealous too on a purely human level; but she would never consider that the position of mistress could or would be converted into that of wife. That to Isabella – or her daughter – was quite unthinkable.

As for Ferdinand himself, his intelligence and his ability to survive were probably his greatest legacies to Catherine. (Although he too was deeply religious, an aspect of his character sometimes ignored in view of the more celebrated piety of Isabella.) There was a streak of unbalance in Isabella's family, coming from her mother, a Portuguese princess, which may have had its origin in depression following childbirth.[11] This would emerge tragically in one of Catherine's sisters, but in Catherine such hysterical feelings were for the most part kept well under control; through all her tribulations she retained Ferdinand's fierce sanity. Catherine, with that strong sense of family inculcated by her upbringing, greatly admired her father: his constant hostility to France, for example, based on the geographic position of his own kingdom of Aragon, was one of his attitudes which certainly formed her own. His deviousness she was trained to see merely as suitable regard for his national interests.

It was to be expected that the marital alliances planned by King Ferdinand for his children would reflect his preoccupation with the neutralization – or better still the encirclement – of France. The key players in this game of dynastic chess, with all Europe as its board, were Burgundy and Austria. In 1477 their houses had been joined by the marriage of Marie of Burgundy, heiress of Charles the Bold, to Maximilian of Austria. The convenient birth of a son and daughter to this royal Habsburg couple, of an age to be matched with a princess and a prince of Spain, put Ferdinand within reach of his most brilliant *coup*. In August 1496 – three years after Maximilian had been elected Holy Roman Emperor – Catherine's sister Juana, not quite seventeen, departed for the Burgundian court to marry the Archduke Philip of Austria; in April the following year her eighteen-year-old brother the Infante Juan was married to the Archduchess Margaret who had been brought to Spain.

But if the Habsburgs were the most august players, they were not the only players in the game. The first marriage arranged by King Ferdinand – that of his eldest daughter Isabel to her cousin, Don Alfonso of Portugal – reflected another perennial preoccupation. As Scotland was to England, so was Portugal to Spain: a neighbour whose geographical proximity made it ever a potential ally or a potential enemy; hence the series of hopefully emollient royal marriages arranged between the two pairs of countries during this period. Nor was the early death of Don Alfonso allowed to prejudice the Portuguese connection: in 1496 Isabel was induced to marry his cousin, King Manuel of Portugal.

Then there was England. At first sight England was a minor power compared to the mighty trio of Spain, France and the Habsburg Empire (as it became); her population, combined with that of Wales, made up a mere two and a half million, compared to the seven and a half million of Castile and Aragon, the fifteen million of France.[12] Nevertheless England enjoyed certain natural advantages in any diplomatic or military game.

Apart from the earlier Anglo-Castilian matches already mentioned, there had once been a question of Queen Isabella herself marrying an English Yorkist prince – Edward IV perhaps or the Duke of Clarence. Once again it was a question of geographical position. Spanish merchants wishing to reach the Netherlands, Burgundian merchants or travellers heading for Spain, needed the protection of English ports if France was barred to them. Furthermore in the 1480s – not so very long after Agincourt in terms of folk memory – France was the hereditary foe of England. Although only Calais remained of the English possessions in France, ancient English claims to French territory and the throne of France itself were still maintained and bellowed forth on appropriate occasions.

The real problem with an English royal marriage, from Ferdinand's point of view, was the shaky nature of the new dynasty. In August 1485, Henry of Lancaster had established himself on the English throne as Henry VII, the first Tudor monarch. It was, in the final analysis, an accession secured at the point of the sword he wielded at Bosworth Field. For there were undoubtedly other individuals with a superior dynastic claim – not only the girl he married, Elizabeth, daughter of Edward IV, but other representatives of the house of York. (See family tree 2)

Even Henry's declared position as the male heir of the house of Lancaster was somewhat dubious on close inspection. It came through his mother, Margaret Beaufort, Countess of Richmond, a descendant of John of Gaunt from his third marriage to his mistress Katherine Swynford (unlike Catherine of Aragon who descended from his first two 'royal' marriages). Margaret's grandfather John Beaufort had actually been born before this Swynford marriage, although subsequently legitimized. Nevertheless Henry VII was careful to make it clear that he did not base his claim to the throne on that of his wife, who as the eldest daughter of Edward IV might be assumed to have inherited the rights of her vanished brothers, known to history as 'the princes in the Tower'. This marriage between Lancaster and York, in the words of the Pope's dispensation, 'willing all such divisions to be put apart',[13] was deliberately delayed until January 1486; and Henry VII did not have his wife crowned for nearly two years, by which time she had given birth to a son and heir.

It was incidentally never suggested that Margaret Beaufort, a strong-willed and formidably learned lady, alive and well in her forties, should actually ascend the throne herself, let alone the younger and more passive Elizabeth of York. Margaret Beaufort's right had simply been transformed, with her enthusiastic support, into that of her 'dearest and only desired joy in this world ...', her 'good King . . . and only beloved son'.[14] England was not Castile, and the English had no precedent of a queen regnant. Although both the houses of York and Lancaster had passed at different points through the female line, the claim of Matilda, daughter of Henry I, to rule in the twelfth century had brought about a civil war with her cousin Stephen. The eventual succession not of Matilda but of her son as Henry II (during her own lifetime) was inconclusive on the subject of female rights.

Henry VII's vulnerability about the real nature of his title to the throne was understandable. But it had awkward consequences for those claimants, particularly those of Yorkist blood, who might fancy that they had a better one. A series of judicial executions of such possible claimants took place – while the King's insecurity was a bloodstained legacy which he would hand on to his son. One must however bear in mind that in addition to genuine Yorkist rivals, Henry VII had also dealt with two pretenders, Lambert Simnel and Perkin Warbeck, early in his reign. With hindsight, it is easy to dismiss the falsity of their claims to represent various Yorkist heirs such as the two princes in the Tower, Edward V and Richard Duke of York, and Edward Earl of Warwick, son of the Duke of Clarence. At the time Duchess Margaret of Burgundy, sister to Edward IV, and thus the putative aunt of these young men, acknowledged them in turn. Warbeck in particular was always termed 'the Duke of York' in English official reports.[15] Worst of all, predatory neighbours, including France and Scotland, backed the pretenders in military action, seeing in the situation something of advantage to themselves. These things were not so easily shrugged off.

As circumstances made Henry VII suspicious, even paranoid, about possible rivals, so Ferdinand of Aragon retained a watching brief towards the Tudor monarchy. The first overtures concerning the marriage of Henry's son Arthur Prince of Wales to Ferdinand's daughter Catherine probably came as early as 1487 when Arthur (born in September 1486) was under a year old, and Catherine not yet two.[16] On the surface there was steady progress. In April 1488 a commission was given to Dr Roderigo Gonzalva de Puebla, a middle-aged Castilian with a decent record of government service in Spain, and an excellent grasp of languages.[17] Together with an assistant, he was to draft a treaty of marriage with the commissioners of the English King.

There was also much courtly rejoicing – particularly on the English side. In July, for example, Henry VII was to be found congratulating Ferdinand and Isabella fulsomely on their latest success against the Moors and hoping that 'the ties of blood' would soon render the friendship which already existed between them even stronger. From London, de Puebla reported that the English King broke into a spontaneous *Te Deum Laudamus* when the subject of the match – and the alliance – came up.[18]

The Spanish reactions were somewhat cooler. It was no part of the policy of Ferdinand, known for good reasons as 'the wily Catalan', to marry one of his well-trained ambassadresses into 'a family which might any day be driven out of England' as he himself wryly put it. Besides, the recent civil wars, the killings after Tewkesbury, had left an impression of English barbarism in the continental mind. When the English began to quibble about terms – matters such as the dowry to be given to Catherine by her parents, or her rights of succession to the throne of Castile – the Spanish commissioners suggested that 'bearing in mind what happens every day to Kings of England, it was surprising that Ferdinand and Isabella should dare give their daughter at all.' De Puebla was confident that the remark had been made 'with great courtesy' so that the English 'might not feel displeasure or be enraged'.[19] But one suspects that they were at least a little put out by such a marked reference to their recent turbulent history.

Nevertheless, for Henry VII, the value of the marriage was sufficient to make it well worth swallowing a polite insult or two. The Treaty of Medina del Campo, which followed in March 1489, was his first major break-through in terms of a European alliance. It was of the essence for Henry that Yorkist pretenders would no longer find refuge on Spanish soil; and both Ferdinand and Henry were relieved to be united against the French in the matter of the struggle over Brittany. Furthermore Henry had secured the promise of a bride for his son, grander than any English consort since that French princess whom Henry V had wed, Catherine de Valois.

Where such royal marital bargains were concerned, however, a promise was a very long way from performance. The great heiress Marie of Bur-gundy, for example, was betrothed no less than seven times before she married Maximilian of Austria. Her daughter the Archduchess Margaret had actually been brought up at the French court as the bride of Charles VIII, before he humiliatingly abandoned her for the sake of another heiress, Duchess Anne of Brittany. This left the high-spirited, witty Margaret able to observe, as she sailed for Spain and the arms of the Infante Juan, that if she perished on the journey, they would be able to record on her tomb that she had been married twice and still remained a maid (*'encore est pucelle'*).[20] In the great dynastic game, formal betrothals, even proxy mar-riages which theoretically allowed a princess to sail for a foreign country already with the status of a wife (as Archduchess Margaret had done) were none of them foolproof moves. Nothing was which allowed an opening through which one of the participants might deftly slip away – if it suited the convenience of his or her country at the time.

Catherine of Aragon was just over three at the time of Medina del Campo. When she learned about the history of her English ancestors – the adventures of the Black Prince, John of Gaunt, from whom she was doubly descended, the great victory at Agincourt – these were not misty legends, but elements in her consciousness of what her own future might be, as

Princess of Wales. Then there were the romantic tales of the court of another Arthur, the legendary king (Queen Isabella's library contained a Spanish version of these stories). Latterday English knights came to the Spanish court on their way to the crusade, just as English archers under Lord Scales had fought during the *reconquista*.[21] All of this – for Catherine could barely have remembered a time before the treaty – contributed to a strong feeling of an English destiny.

At the same time, negotiations for the actual betrothal of the young pair, as provided for at Medina del Campo, were not begun until late 1496, shortly before Catherine's eleventh birthday. At this date, given the various twists and turns of the international situation in the intervening seven years, the marriage currently suited both parties to the treaty. Moreover Dr de Puebla was impressed by the growth of internal stability in England (he would be happier still when Edward Earl of Warwick was executed three years later and he could gleefully report that 'not a drop of doubtful Royal blood remains in England').[22] So that Catherine also grew up with her allegiance to the interests of Spain, those of her own family, strongly implanted. If one accepts the celebrated dictum of the Jesuits, that order founded by Catherine's contemporary (and fellow Spaniard) Ignatius Loyola, concerning the importance of the first seven years of life, then a sense both of an English destiny and of a family allegiance was there virtually from the start.

In January 1497 the young infanta commissioned Dr de Puebla to treat on her behalf for her betrothal. As a result, in the following August Arthur and Catherine were formerly affianced at Woodstock, with de Puebla 'standing in' for Catherine. Despite the practical caveats about royal betrothals already mentioned, in theory this was a solemn and indeed binding ceremony. If such a betrothal *per verba de praesenti* (i.e. one with immediate present effect, as opposed to a betrothal *per verba de futura*, for some future date) was actually consummated, it had the force in church law of a marriage. Of course there was no question of such a consummation with Arthur in England, and Catherine in Spain. But from now on Catherine was officially termed the Princess of Wales.

The betrothal also resulted in a renewed outbreak of affectionate letters between the four royal parents concerned. In December 1497, Henry VII, in thanking Isabella for her recent expressions of love, replied that he simply could not imagine any affection which was deeper or more sincere than his own. The marriage of their respective children would merely secure the everlasting continuance of this splendid friendship. Elizabeth of York, for her part, rejoiced graciously in 'the affinity' as she called it, which made Catherine 'our common daughter'.[23]

One of the vexed questions raised by treaties of marriage between the young royals concerned when, and at what stage of development, the betrothed princess should set out for her fiancé's country. (This in turn related to the matter of the delivery of her dowry – another perennially vexed question, especially where parents such as Ferdinand of Aragon and Henry VII were in dispute; if the one was rapidly becoming a byword for diplomatic trickery, the other was gaining a similarly distasteful reputation for inordinate meanness.) A series of instructions about life at the English court were despatched to the 'Princess of Wales' from her future mother-in-law and the woman who was Queen Mother in all but name, Margaret Beaufort Countess of Richmond. Catherine should attempt to learn French by speaking it with her French-educated sister-in-law, the Archduchess Margaret, in order to be able to converse in that language when she came to England.

The next request was for Catherine to accustom herself to drink wine. 'The water of England', wrote Elizabeth of York sadly, 'is not drinkable, and even if it were, the climate would not allow the drinking of it'.* Meanwhile the King, according to de Puebla, loved to speak, even drool over his little daughter-in-law, in which connection Isabella's pre-eminent reputation received a tribute: 'He said he would give half his kingdom if she [Catherine] were like her mother'.[24] But while Henry was anxious for Catherine's arrival, Dr de Puebla still counselled a diplomatic delay.

Another rival Spanish envoy, Don Pedro de Ayala, a more worldly character than de Puebla, who was ostensibly credited to the court of Scotland, but actually spent his time cutting a dash at the English court, believed on the contrary that Catherine should be despatched as soon as possible. His was a point of view of lofty chauvinism which illustrates the disdain in which rough-hewn England was still held. While acknowledging that 'the manners and way of life of this people in this island' would cause Catherine 'grave inconveniences', he feared that 'the Princess can only be expected to lead a happy life through not remembering those things which would make her less enjoy what she will find here. It would, therefore, still be best to send her directly', he wrote in July 1498, 'before she has learnt to appreciate our [Spanish] habits of life ...'[25]

On Whit Sunday – 19 May – 1499 the first of the wedding ceremonies that were to bind Arthur Prince of Wales and Catherine of Aragon took place about nine o'clock in the morning, after Mass, at Bewdley Palace in Worcestershire. Prince Arthur spoke 'in a loud and clear voice' according to the report of de Puebla, declaring that he was pleased to contract 'an

---

* To drink water was considered to be a horrible fate. People who did not drink wine, drank beer – small beer – most houses having their own brewery.

indissoluble marriage with Catherine Princess of Wales'. He was acting not only out of obedience to the Pope and his father 'but also from his deep and sincere love for the said Princess, his wife'.[26] (The reference to the Pope arose from the papal dispensation that had been granted in order for Arthur to make his vows – he was not yet fourteen and thus below the age of consent.) De Puebla's own role, a conventional one by the standards of the time, was that of the bride; as such he not only took the prince's right hand in his own and was seated at the King's right hand at the subsequent banquet but also inserted the statutory symbolic leg into the royal marriage bed.

Once again there was an outward show of tender, even sentimental rejoicing. And this time the young bride and groom were allowed to play their part: Arthur began to write letters in Latin (their mutual language) to his 'dearest spouse'. There is something touching about these schoolboy missives, no doubt phrased for him, but copied out with evident care, and the elaborate superscription also in his own hand: 'To Princess Katerine [sic], Princess of Wales, Duchess of Cornwall, me plurimi dilecte [the most highly esteemed]'. It is as though, beneath the stately language, the thirteen-year-old boy cannot help being excited at the idea of having such a grown-up relationship. 'Truly those your letters', he wrote, 'traced by your own [hand] have so delighted me and rendered me so cheerful and jocund, that I fancied I beheld your highness and conversed with and embraced my dearest wife.'[27]

But for Ferdinand's part, so little did he trust the bargain – or the bargainer – that he instructed another Spanish envoy in London to watch de Puebla like a hawk, fearing that the doctor had been suborned by Henry VII. He was to keep his ears open for rumours of another match being negotiated for Arthur with a princess of some rival country and at all times Catherine must be styled 'the Princess of Wales'.[28] A further precaution on which Ferdinand insisted, and which de Puebla negotiated for him in the autumn of 1500 was that of a second proxy marriage in England once Arthur had actually reached the age of consent (thus demonstrating Ferdinand's suspicion, not only of Henry VII, but also of the value of a papal dispensation).

In this way yet another 'indissoluble marriage' was contracted between the prince and de Puebla in person, Catherine in spirit, at Ludlow Castle on the borders of Wales, shortly after Arthur's fourteenth birthday. De Puebla reported once more on the high level of respect shown to him as the proxy of the Princess of Wales – 'more than he had ever before received in his life' – as he sat at table on the prince's right hand, and had all the dishes of the banquet presented to him first. Ferdinand and Isabella were equally overwhelmed (at least in public) by the sheer wealth of emotion which they felt for Henry. The usual courtly clichés flowed forth: 'we love him and the Prince of Wales, our son, so much that it would be impossible to love them better' etc, etc.[29] Meanwhile the jockeying for position over the delivery of Catherine's person to England, and the delivery of Catherine's dowry to the English King continued behind the scenes.

It was finally agreed in the course of 1500 that Catherine should commence her journey towards England shortly after her sixteenth birthday. But the royal family of Spain during this last year of Catherine's crucial girlhood was very different from the confident unit in which she had been brought up. Ferdinand and Isabella had been stricken with a series of appalling tragedies no less grievous in personal terms because these family disasters also had the effect of wrecking Ferdinand's European policy.

The first of these was the worst. In October 1497 Catherine's adored brother, the Infante Juan, newly married to the Archduchess Margaret, died after a short illness. 'Thus was laid low the hope of all Spain', wrote Peter Martyr.[30] Queen Isabella never recovered from the blow. She was forty-six. Her health, weakened by her arduous campaignings in the course of her frequent pregnancies, had never been robust. There was now no direct male heir to Aragon, while the Castilian succession passed to Isabella's eldest daughter, Isabel Queen of Portugal. And fate had not finished with the 'Catholic Kings'. Isabel herself died in the summer of the following year at the age of twenty-eight, giving birth to a son Miguel, who for the short span of his existence, his position recognized by the Aragonese, stood to inherit both the thrones of Spain and Portugal.

After the death of the baby Portuguese Prince Miguel, the succession now passed on to the Catholic Kings' second daughter Juana, wife of the Habsburg Archduke Philip of Austria. Juana gave birth to a son, Charles, in February 1500. It became apparent that this infant Habsburg heir was the most likely candidate to succeed to the Spanish throne as well as the empire of his father Maximilian. Miguel's accession would at least have enabled Ferdinand's grandson to unite the Iberian peninsula. But now Ferdinand's son and eldest daughter were dead. And his brilliantly planned dynastic marriages, far from elevating the power of his own royal house, looked like handing over the throne of Spain to the Habsburgs.

The last months of Catherine's residence at her mother's side were melancholy. Even her sister Maria, her senior by three years, was gone: despatched in October 1500 to marry her brother-in-law, the widowed King of Portugal, in yet another effort to preserve this treasured connection. Catherine's stately journeyings north-west across Spain through the summer of 1501 were scarcely more cheerful. There were further delays. A fresh Moorish uprising threatened Ferdinand's farewell to his youngest daughter. Catherine herself suffered en route from something described as 'a low fever',[31] a phrase which covered a multitude of indispositions in modern terms from a form of influenza to a bout of (understandable) adolescent depression.

One of Catherine's last stops, before her embarkation at Corunna on 17 August, was at Santiago de Compostela, where she spent the night in prayer at the hallowed shrine of St James, as so many crusaders had done in the past. But her prayers did not serve to spare her yet another ordeal once she was aboard the ship. A vicious storm in the Bay of Biscay drove her back to the shores of Spain. It was not until the end of September that Catherine was able to re-embark for an England increasingly impatient for her arrival.

Afterwards there would not be wanting chroniclers who would claim that Catherine's troubled future was presaged by these ill-timed winds. Catherine herself was supposed to have observed, in view of the fate of her first marriage, that 'this tempest portended some calamity'. But since storms in the Bay of Biscay were not a rarity, Catherine probably suffered more from 'the fatigue caused by the furious sea', as Henry VII himself phrased it, than from the weight of omens.[32] The second journey was not noticeably calm – the weather around the autumn equinox was always turbulent – but at least it was accomplished. On 2 October 1501 the little fleet designated to escort the Princess of Wales to England arrived at Plymouth Sound.

'The Princess could not have been received with greater joy had she been the Saviour of the World', wrote a member of Catherine's Spanish entourage.[33] This reception began with the spontaneous welcome given by the people of the West Country, who were moved by the gallantry, as well as the charm and dignity, of the young princess. Immediately on setting foot on shore, despite the nature of her ordeal – she had indeed been horribly seasick – and without time to change her clothes, Catherine asked to be taken to a church to give thanks for her safe arrival. (Here was the spirit and training of Queen Isabella.) The English delight with their royal bride – not only the King of Spain's daughter come from across the sea but a princess with the true untainted blood of the Plantagenets in her veins – continued during her progress eastwards towards the English court, currently residing near London at Richmond Palace.

After so many delays and frustrations, King Henry's own excitement equalled that of the subjects who were warming Catherine's heart en route with their loyal acclamations (if she could not understand their words, she could appreciate their sentiment). At the last moment, he decided not to await 'the Princess of Wales' at Richmond, as had been planned, but sally forth to meet her having first taken in tow Prince Arthur, coming from Ludlow. The palace of the Bishop of Bath at Dogmersfield in Hampshire, about forty miles from London, was to be the site of the first encounter. It would be pleasant to see the King's uncharacteristic impetuosity as being inspired by that well-nigh unbearable weight of quasi-paternal affection to which his letters over the years had borne witness. But something more calculating was in fact at the bottom of it all.

What did the Princess of Wales actually look like? Like Doubting Thomas, King Henry needed to see his son's bride with his own eyes, to make sure that she was healthy, nubile – so far as the eye could see, and appearances were held to count for a lot in this respect during this period – and preferably goodlooking as well. The King, who had sent off specially to Spain to request that Catherine's Spanish ladies-in-waiting should be beauties, was not acting purely out of lust of the eye (or mind). The connection between a fair appearance and a good character, like that between a healthy appearance and fertility, was something in which more or less everybody at this time believed. Sending for princesses from afar always brought with it an element of doubt for all the best efforts of ambassadors to inspect the goods (as Arthur had been shown to the Spanish commissioners years before as an apparently wonderfully healthy baby).

But at Dogmersfield, the cries of mutual rapture came to an abrupt halt. For the King was sharply told that at this point there was no question of Catherine being personally inspected. As a high-born Castilian bride, Catherine would remain veiled to both her husband and her father-in-law until the solemn benediction of the final ceremony had been pronounced.* For a moment there was an ugly impasse between the victor of Bosworth Field, the man who had helped himself to the English crown sixteen years earlier and not faltered in resolve since, and a redoubtable Spanish matriarch named Doña Elvira Manuel, whom Queen Isabella had put in charge of Catherine. Doña Elvira was named in the considerable list of Catherine's attendants (which went all the way down to two slaves – probably Moorish prisoners – to attend her as maids of honour) as 'First Lady of Honour and First Lady of the Bedchamber': she was not about to surrender her position now. King Henry on the other hand pointed out that, since Catherine was styled as his daughter-in-law, she was actually an English subject – so that quaint old Castilian customs were of little relevance.

In the end the dispute was solved in favour of Catherine's English future as opposed to her Castilian past (a pragmatic solution one must believe that Queen Isabella and King Ferdinand would have favoured, whatever the scandalized disgruntlement of Doña Elvira). The veil was lifted. Catherine

---

* The use of the veil in this way, unknown in England, was part of the strong Muslim heritage rooted in Spanish culture; unaffected by the fact of a military conquest, grand Spanish ladies were in fact imitating the customs of the sophisticated Muslim courts of the south.

curtsied deeply in a gesture of symbolic obedience to the English King.

How fortunate then that Henry was speedily enchanted by what he saw! There had been no trick, no dissimulation. With a mixture of relief and delight, the King was able to say of Catherine that he 'much admired her beauty as well as her agreeable and dignified manners.' The Prince of Wales obediently followed suit. He had never felt so much joy in his life, he wrote to his parents-in-law a few weeks later, as when he beheld 'the sweet face of his bride'.[34]

Even allowing for tactful hyperbole, it is clear that Catherine, now on the eve of her sixteenth birthday, did have the kind of youthful prettiness and freshness of appearance that charmed observers, not only the family into which she would marry. It was partly a question of her complexion: her naturally pink cheeks and white skin were much admired in an age when make-up – 'paint' – was clumsy in execution, easy to detect and much scorned. Ambassadors abroad, describing princesses to their masters, generally emphasized the tint of the skin, carefully noting whether it was 'painted' or not. A fair complexion like Catherine's was thought to indicate a more serene and cheerful temperament than a 'brown' (sallow) one. Then Catherine's hair was also fair and thick, with a reddish-gold tint, her features neat and regular in a pleasingly shaped oval face.

Perhaps Catherine's fair colouring, so far from the conventional picture of a dark-visaged Spaniard, reminded onlookers of her one-eighth of English blood: Thomas More, eight years Catherine's senior, was one of those who derided Catherine's Spanish escorts as 'ridiculous . . . pigmy Ethiopians, like devils out of hell' in true English xenophobic fashion. But of Catherine herself he wrote that 'there is nothing wanting in her that the most beautiful girl should have.'[35]

If her complexion was her chief beauty, Catherine's chief disadvantage was her lack of height. All the grace of her bearing, inculcated over many years at the Castilian court, could not conceal the fact that she was extremely short, even tiny. Years later a loyal defender had to admit that she was 'in stature somewhat mean', while adding quickly 'but bonarly [bonnie] withal'. She was also on the plump side – but then a pleasant roundness in youth was considered to be desirable at this period, a pointer to future fertility. In contrast Catherine's voice was surprisingly low and 'big-sounding' for a woman; and that no doubt contributed to the impression of gracious dignity she left on all observers, making up for the lack of inches.[36]

Catherine, for her part, might have been less enchanted by the sight of her bridegroom, had her royal training encouraged any but the most dutiful thoughts on that subject. Arthur Prince of Wales was now fifteen, but he was so small and undeveloped that he seemed much younger. He had been born prematurely – by at least a month, probably two – and had never quite recovered from that debilitating start in life. When it came to height, Catherine might be short, but Arthur was half a head shorter still; the longed-for male heir to the house of both York and Lancaster gave the impression of being a mere child – and a delicate child at that.[37] He too was very fair-skinned like his bride, but, without her healthy pink cheeks, the result was a worrying pallor. The magnificent genes of his grandfather Edward IV, that blonde giant, which, coupled with those of his beautiful consort Elizabeth Woodville, would serve to make Arthur's younger brother and sisters the handsomest, most upstanding princes and princesses in Europe, had all passed by the sad little Prince of Wales.

The very name of Arthur, that of the legendary king, might seem to mock this frail youth; but the prince had not in fact been named for the most august of his mythical forebears. The Tudor manipulation of history in this respect was to come later. According to his tutor Bernardus Andreas, Arthur was actually named for a star prominent at his nativity – probably Arcturus, in the wake of the Great Bear.[38] At least the prince had received (like his bride) an excellent classical education. Andreas recorded that he 'had either committed to memory or read with his own eyes and leafed with his own fingers' such authors as Homer, Virgil and Ovid, such historians as Thucydides and Livy. As Latin had been the language of their correspondence, the shy young couple could at least talk in Latin to each other, since Catherine knew no English and Arthur knew no Spanish.

Unfortunately Catherine's pronunciation of Latin, however fluent, turned out to be different from that of King Henry and Prince Arthur, so that she still could not make herself understood.[39] Only the English bishops were able to persevere and make some sort of contact. Nor could the prince and princess even dance together. Their training in this respect – important as it was at any Renaissance court – was once again completely different. So Catherine was content to dance a Spanish dance, while Arthur danced in the English manner with some ladies of the English court.

None of this was felt to matter in the slightest, given that Arthur had at last successfully set eyes on his 'dearest spouse'. By the standards of a royal marriage at the time, it was really already a remarkably happy venture, with the couple roughly the same age, some of the dowry already paid up, the contract virtually completed. In an optimistic mood, King Henry swept his son and daughter-in-law towards London for the last, the very last wedding ceremony at St Paul's.

Chapter 2

THE PRINCESS IN
HIS POWER

*It is clear that the King [Henry VII] thinks he can
do whatever he likes because he holds the princess in his
power ...*

Ferdinand of Aragon to his ambassador in London, 1508

Catherine of Aragon was welcomed in triumph to the City of London on 12 November 1501. Queen Isabella, in her practical way, had requested that not too much money should be spent on her daughter's reception so that the new Princess of Wales should not be 'the cause of any loss to the English ...' but rather 'the source of all kinds of happiness'. A 'substantial part' of the festival, she believed, should be 'the love' King Henry displayed for his daughter-in-law – a love that need cost nothing.[1]

That was not however how Henry VII viewed his coup in capturing at last his Spanish princess. In the state language of the time, triumph needed to be signalled by appropriate pageantry. Plans for the spectacle organized by the City of London had first got under way two years earlier. Six separate scenes greeted Catherine on her journey through the City from Southwark; these were intended to be viewed on two levels. Immediately, the populace were expected to be impressed as well as entertained by the magnificence before their eyes, as with a modern military parade: the monarchy that ruled them was in good shape. But each scene also had a more complex meaning; there were significant allusions to the past, as well as to the glorious future. Catherine watched it all wearing a little hat 'of carnation colour' trimmed with gold lace perched on her flowing hair: there were no more veils.[2]

On London Bridge, it was 'St Katherine', a 'fair young lady' holding the saint's traditional wheel, who greeted her namesake: 'You took this name ... for very trust and love, which name ye registered in the high court above.' (The French princess, Catherine de Valois, bride of Henry

V, had been greeted by similar allusions to the saint and her wheel eighty years before.) But a patriotically British saint, Ursula, daughter of a Christian British king, accompanied St Katherine. In the second scene the princess was identified with Hesperus, the evening star (Hesperia or 'the western land' being a Roman name for Spain), while Arthur became Arcturus, the star of his nativity. The third involved splendid prognostications for a marriage over which the Archangel Raphael and King Alfonso of Castile (from whom both Catherine and Arthur descended) were seen to be presiding.

Subsequent spectacles concentrated on the court of Henry VII, to which Catherine was being welcomed by Arthur, 'your spouse most bounteous'. Humility was not the order of the day. The imagery used involved both Henry and Arthur in comparisons to an even more powerful court, that of the heavenly 'New Jerusalem' to come, with Henry compared to God the Father, and Arthur, as his 'Sun [or Son] of Justice', one of the biblical titles of the coming Christ.[3] More down to earth were the Tudor arms and badges, the red dragon of Wales, the greyhound which betokened Richmond and references to Catherine's own descent from John of Gaunt. Finally 'Honour' addressed Catherine:

> Wherefore Noble Princess, if that ye shall persevere
> With your excellent spouse, then shall ye
> Reign there with us in Prosperity forever.

The marriage took place two days later on 14 November at St Paul's Cathedral to the sound of Spanish trumpeters who had been brought over to give their princess a suitable national send-off. Another Spanish note was struck by the fact that Catherine, like her ladies, wore a mantilla with her stiffly embroidered dress of white and gold, encrusted in jewels. If coming events truly cast their shadow before, then Catherine should have been aware of some tremor as she was escorted up the aisle of the church by her husband's younger brother, Henry Duke of York, her hand in his. He was only ten years old, but with his long legs and broad shoulders had already far outstripped Arthur, five years his senior.

But there is no evidence that she felt any such tremor. On the contrary, all Catherine's concentration was bent on pleasing by her comportment (despite difficulties of language) the man whom she had been trained to accept as her new 'father': Henry VII. Arrangements at the banquet which followed the wedding were significant in this respect. Catherine sat on the right hand of the King. But Prince Arthur sat at a separate children's table with Prince Henry and his sisters, the twelve-year-old

Princess Margaret in cloth of gold and Princess Mary, aged five, in crimson velvet trimmed with fur.

The banquet took place at Baynard's Castle, the historical London residence of the house of York. Here the crown had been offered to Edward IV in 1461, and to Richard III in 1483. It was described by a contemporary as 'not embattled or so strongly fortified castle-like, but far more beautiful for the entertainment of any prince of great estate'; Baynard's Castle had been rebuilt by Henry VII the previous year and was now used largely for state occasions.[4] Lying on the river between Blackfriars and Paul's Wharf (with Thames Street to its north), it was generally reached by water, like most London palaces of this period.

The 'carriage' (transportation) – presumably in a litter – of Catherine and Arthur together down to the river for embarkation after the wedding ceremony cost 12d according to the royal accounts.[5] After this, not only during the banquet itself but for the whole period of official celebration which followed, Arthur was not considered to have any particular role to fulfil. He was certainly far too immature to take any part in the knightly jousts, as his hearty younger brother would rejoice to do in years to come. (And on this occasion, it was Prince Henry who cast off his jacket to dance, unlike Prince Arthur who danced decorously with Lady Cecil; Catherine, as at their first meeting, danced with one of her Spanish ladies.) There was however one exception to Prince Arthur's non-participation in the ceremonies. This was the ceremony of the wedding night which, like the banquet, took place at Baynard's Castle.

The symbolic leg that Dr de Puebla had first placed in the prince's bed over two years earlier at Bewdley Palace was now to be replaced with the real thing. Thus, at the end of the banquet, the Princess of Wales was formally bedded with her husband by a host of courtiers, English and Spanish; the attendants then withdrew to the outer room and they were left to lie there together for the night according to the elaborate rules of this particular ceremony. It is extremely doubtful, however, whether now or at any other time, the princess herself actually enjoyed any greater congress with her young husband than had the good doctor's leg.

By one of those ironic twists of fate to which history is prone, the question of the sexual relationship – if any – between these two innocent adolescents would become of paramount importance nearly thirty years later. By then one of the two had been dead almost as long; the other was facing the most desperate crisis of her life. There is no contemporary record of Prince Arthur's views on the subject and one must surely leave aside the vulgar gossip produced so conveniently many years later by courtiers who manifestly hoped to serve the interests of their master. One is therefore left with Catherine's unwavering assertions, dating from 1502 onwards (not from the late 1520s like the courtiers' tales), that the marriage was unconsummated.

There was however a third person entitled to express a first-hand view on this delicate if vital point (as it turned out to be): Catherine's second husband, Henry VIII. He after all had either found her to be a virgin on their own wedding night (as he used to boast in his youth) or had not. It can be argued that Catherine herself, like Henry's courtiers, was not an unbiased witness. In that case more convincing evidence of non-consummation is provided by the fact that Henry VIII himself in later life never gave Catherine the lie on the subject, when publicly challenged to deny that he had found her 'a maid' when he married her.*

Let us return to that winter of 1501 and the brief months of 'married life' which Arthur and Catherine enjoyed following their ceremonial wedding and bedding at Baynard's Castle. Arthur's physical immaturity and lack of growth – even shorter than his admittedly tiny wife – has already been stressed. This is in itself no proof that he had not reached puberty (although it makes it seem unlikely) and, even if he had not reached it in November, he might have reached it at some point during the next few months. Catherine's story years later in the confessional to Cardinal Campeggio was that they had shared a bed on only seven occasions, and at no time had Arthur 'known' her.[6] But what really stands against the notion of the consummation of the union, all subsequent allegations apart, is that the custom of the time was all against it.

In an age when marriages were frequently contracted for reasons of state between children or those hovering between childhood and adolescence, more care rather than less was taken over the timing of consummation. Once the marriage was officially completed, some years might pass before the appropriate moment was judged to have arrived. Anxious reports might pass between ambassadors on physical development; royal parents might take advice on their offsprings' readiness for the ordeal. The comments sometimes remind one of those breeders discussing the mating of thoroughbred stock, and the comparison is indeed not so far off. The siring of progeny was the essential next step in these royal marriages, so endlessly negotiated.

Where an heiress was concerned, her 'spoiling' by being obliged to have sex and bear children too young might have important consequences. The physique of the great heiress Margaret Beaufort was considered to have been ruined by early childbearing. She bore the future Henry VII when she was only thirteen, and never had any other children in the course of

---

* The courtiers' anecdotal allegations, and Henry's own remarks, will be considered more fully in their proper place in the narrative.

four marriages. Henry survived, but the existence of a single heir was in principle a great risk to any family in this age of high infant mortality, as the shortage of Tudor heirs would continuously demonstrate. Nego-tiations for the marriage of James IV King of Scotland and Arthur's sister Princess Margaret had begun in 1498. The trouble was that the bride was only nine, while the King of Scots was twenty-five. Both Princess Margaret's mother and her grandmother Margaret Beaufort – the latter with an obvious grim interest in the subject – worried about the age gap and pleaded for the marriage ceremony itself to be held off lest consummation follow: 'they fear the King of Scots would not wait, but injure her, and endanger her health.'[7] (They were finally married in 1503 when Princess Margaret was fourteen.)

The health of the bridegroom was taken equally seriously. For instance, it was firmly believed by the Spanish court physicians that Catherine's brother, the Infante Juan, had weakened himself by spending so much time in bed with his wife – with disastrous consequences. Henry Fitzroy Duke of Richmond, illegitimate son of Henry VIII, was married off to Lady Mary Howard when he was fourteen, but the marriage remained unconsummated at his premature death (of tuberculosis) three years later; no doubt it was thought that the act would prove too taxing for one of doubtful health. Mary Howard's brother, Thomas Earl of Surrey, lived with Lady Frances Vere for three years after marriage before con-summation when they were both fifteen.

In the case of Arthur and Catherine, all four parents apparently agreed that nothing should be rushed. Henry VII and Elizabeth of York were anxious to protect their son's health, while Ferdinand and Isabella made it clear that they too would 'rather be pleased than dissatisfied' if con-summation was delayed for some time, in view of Arthur's 'tender age'. These were the instructions relayed to Doña Elvira, which, as a resolute duenna, she could be trusted to carry out.[8]

The plan therefore was for Catherine to remain in London, under the tutelage of her mother-in-law (not forgetting her dominating grand-mother-in-law), while Arthur was to be allowed to continue his growing-up, undisturbed by the distractions of a wife, in the Marches of Wales at Ludlow Castle. But this plan, which had an agreeably human side to it – Catherine would learn to know her new family, and also learn English, before she attempted to forge a proper relationship with her husband – was not carried out. Instead, Catherine Princess of Wales set off for Ludlow in December.

The change of plan, which infuriated the Spaniards, came back to money – that is, the question of Catherine's dowry. The principle of the dowry, for princesses as for other affluent girls of the period, was of payment by the parents now, in return for promise of full financial support from her husband's estate later. Thus Ferdinand had agreed to hand over 200,000 crowns on his daughter's marriage, on condition that Catherine, if widowed, was to receive one-third of the revenues of Wales, Cornwall and Chester. Of the promised 200,000 crowns, however, Ferdinand had so far only delivered half. He suddenly announced that a substantial portion of the remaining sum due – 35,000 crowns – was in fact being consigned in plate and jewels. This was definitely stealing a march on the English King, for whom, like most monarchs of the time, cash was an essential but elusive commodity.

It did not take Henry VII long to come up with a Machiavellian counter-plan: for in this respect Ferdinand and Henry were well-matched players. Supposing the Princess of Wales was sent to Ludlow: the establishment of her household there would inevitably involve the considerable deployment of plate and jewels, commensurate with that status on which the Spaniards were so keen. To do this, she would have to use her own plate. This in turn would make it difficult for the Spanish King to have 'these same, now second-hand jewels and plate' re-emerge as part of the dowry owed to Henry VII.[9] The Spaniards in London – Don Pedro de Ayala in particular – were wise to the plot, without being able to do anything about it.

At least they fought a rearguard action by refusing to take Henry's decision for him, or let their princess do so. The King mused aloud as to whether the princess should depart and confided to de Ayala that his indecision was shared by his Council, some of whom thought it was good for her to go to Ludlow, others not. Next he asked Arthur to persuade Catherine to volunteer to accompany him; Catherine refused. So the King was obliged to consult Catherine herself. At which she swept, metaphorically speaking, another of her deep curtsies, and responded most graciously that she had no other will but the King's own. King Henry's bluff was called. 'With a great show of sorrow' he ordered Catherine to go with her husband.[10] And so to the Marches of Wales, finally, Catherine went, with a considerable Spanish train, including Doña Elvira, as Isabella's watchful surrogate, and a Spanish chaplain.

Ludlow Castle was another historic residence of the house of York – but one with less fortunate connotations than Baynard's Castle. Once the property of Richard Duke of York, father of Edward IV, it had housed Arthur's boy uncles at the time of Edward IV's death in 1483; from here they had set forth for the capital where they would vanish forever into the recesses of the Tower of London. Strategically, however, it was extremely well placed. An imposing stronghold of Norman origin, built on rock, the castle had magnificent views across the valley of the river

Teme to the Clee Hills and the hills of Stretton, and was therefore virtually impregnable; except for the side which abutted the largely English-flavoured town.

At Ludlow, roughly 150 miles from London, Catherine and her Spanish train sat out the winter.[11] Little record remains of this melancholy idyll except that the Welsh dignitaries came to pay their respects to their prince and princess – Ludlow was the capital of the Marches of Wales. These dignitaries included the man Arthur's father called 'Father Rhys' – Sir Rhys ap Thomas, who could remember Henry VII as the Welsh Tudor challenger for the English crown in the age before Bosworth Field. Another encounter with a representative of England's troubled past was of greater significance for Catherine's own future.

The President of the Prince's Council in Wales – the effective ruling instrument – was Sir Richard Pole. A relative of Henry VII on his mother's side, but lacking the royal blood that might encourage indecent ambition, Pole was a convenient protégé. (He had helped organize Prince Arthur's wedding.) Pole's wife Margaret, on the other hand, was a Plantagenet: her long, thin, aristocratic face with its delicate bone structure, narrow lips and aquiline nose was a reminder of the race from which she had sprung. Nor was she a remote relation of the royal family: as the daughter of Edward's murdered brother, the Duke of Clarence, she was first cousin to Queen Elizabeth of York. Following the execution of her brother in 1499 (one of those ruthless deaths by which Henry VII had cleared away unwelcome Yorkist–Plantagenet rivals) Margaret Pole was also Clarence's sole surviving child and heiress. Furthermore she had never been declared illegitimate, as had Elizabeth and her siblings in an effort by Richard III to justify his usurpation by law. (See family tree 2)

For the time being this dangerous inheritance was in abeyance. Henry had deliberately given Margaret in marriage to one whose loyalty he trusted; the Pole sons, who might one day perhaps assume to themselves their mother's claim, were only babies. Far more important at Ludlow was a sturdy friendship which sprang up between two women, not particularly close in age – Margaret Pole was nearly thirty – but sharing, as time would show, the same kind of character. Both had the charm of goodness; both were well-educated, pious, and bookish; both were affectionate, outwardly submissive, inwardly strong.

On the Welsh borders that spring, the weather was notably cold and wet, as a result of which sickness of various types was rife. Towards the end of March 1502 Prince Arthur's fragile health began to give way. The prince may have been suffering from tuberculosis; there was also an outbreak of plague in the neighbourhood, and an epidemic of another scourge of the times known as 'the sweating sickness'. This disease was much feared by contemporaries for its mysterious course: victims did recover but others died 'some within three hours, some within two hours, some merry at dinner and dead at supper', as a chronicle reported it.[12] The sweating sickness seems the most likely explanation, since Catherine also collapsed.

She was still seriously ill on 2 April when Prince Arthur died. He was fifteen and a half, his 'dearest spouse' was now his widow; Catherine of Aragon, at the age of sixteen and three months, had become the Princess Dowager of Wales. If she contemplated her own death during this period of her sickness, Catherine could surely have echoed that wry little epitaph once suggested by her sister-in-law the Archduchess Margaret for herself: she had been married yet *'encore est pucelle'* – still remained a maid.

The news of the death of the Prince of Wales reached the court at Greenwich by messenger late on the following day, 3 April. The Council had the sensitivity to summon King Henry's confessor, a Franciscan Observant friar from the monastery close by the palace to break the news. Henry then sent for the unfortunate boy's mother and broke the news to her himself. Elizabeth of York behaved with great courage; she did not break down, but pointed out that the King's own mother 'had never no more children than him only, and that God by his grace had ever preserved him, and brought him where that he was.'[13] They too had a son, Henry Duke of York, who would shortly take on his brother's title of Prince of Wales, as well as two princesses, Margaret (betrothed to the King of Scots) and six-year-old Mary.

Besides, the Queen added, their family was not necessarily complete: 'we are both young enough'. They were in fact thirty-six and forty-five respectively: the Queen had given birth to a third son, Edmund, who died, only three years previously. Elizabeth of York's confidence in her own fertility was not misplaced; she did in fact conceive again, as she had promised, a month after Arthur's death and gave birth at the beginning of the following February. What she did not foresee was that the child would be a daughter, that the daughter would die, and she herself die too shortly afterwards as a result of her ordeal.

The death of Prince Arthur brought in fact to an end that brief honeymoon period when the Tudor monarchy enjoyed the luxury of having two direct male heirs to the crown, albeit both young. Now only the life of one boy – Prince Henry – served to ward off the nightmare of King Henry VII: the dreaded prospect of further rival pretenders and even civil war itself. Nor were these fears, grounded in the blood-lettings of the past, utterly without foundation in the present. Henry VII, at forty-five with a hard life behind him, had visibly grown old. Was a mere boy to follow him? Subversive gossip reported to King Henry by informers shortly after Prince Arthur's death revealed a lingering attachment to the idea of an *adult* male ruler succeeding, with royal blood enough to justify his claim (as Henry VII himself had done), not a child.

There was for example the twenty-three-year-old Duke of Buckingham, a handsome and imposing figure who had been the most glittering dignitary at Catherine's wedding, his clothes alone costing him £1,500.[14] This display indicated not only Buckingham's vast inherited riches but also his position as the leading grandee – and only duke – in the kingdom, one furthermore who could trace his descent back to Thomas of Woodstock, the youngest son of Edward III. 'Many great personages' in the important English continental base of Calais were said to have agreed that Buckingham was 'a noble man and would be a royal ruler'.

Then there was Edmund de la Pole, Earl of Suffolk, another first cousin to the Queen like Margaret Pole, being the son of Edward IV's sister. He was now the senior male claimant of the house of York; if that old canard about the illegitimacy of all Edward IV's children was resurrected, he had a very good claim indeed. Edmund de la Pole had prudently fled from Henry VII's reach. When the King's informant told him that others had spoken of 'your traitor, Edmund de la Pole' succeeding, this was not the kind of news that made Henry VII feel secure; still less did his informant's ominous postscript: 'none of them spoke of my lord prince' – that is, the ten-year-old Henry.[15]

At Ludlow the prince's Council awaited orders as to the manner of Arthur's funeral, while Catherine languished, sick, in the care of her Spanish attendants. It was not until three weeks later that Arthur's body was taken by torchlight in procession to Ludlow parish church; from there the procession moved on to Bewdley (where Arthur's first proxy marriage to Catherine had been performed). Oxen were needed to draw the 'chariot' bearing the coffin through the mud, on 'the foulest, cold, windy, and rainy day and the worst way [road] I have seen', as one observer wrote.[16] It was ordained from London that the prince should be buried in the nearest cathedral, which happened to be Worcester. At a chantry subsequently raised there, the heraldic allusions of the roses of York and Lancaster, the Beaufort portcullis and Catherine's secondary personal badge of an arrow-sheaf (alternative to the pomegranate) provided a sad echo of the glorious marriage celebrations only six months earlier.

Catherine Princess of Wales had now become a problem of state – in two countries. Elizabeth of York, with characteristic kindness, did despatch a suitably sombre black velvet litter, with valences and fringes also of black made by her own tailor, to bring the princess to London when she should be well enough to travel.[17] Otherwise little thought was spared for the personal feelings of the girl who now found herself convalescent in a country whose language she spoke sparingly if at all, surrounded by possessive Spanish attendants whose intention was to cut her off still further in the name of the honour due to her. Those close to her, whether her natural protectors like her parents or her new protector Henry VII, were a great deal more interested in the practical problems posed by her future, including, of course, the question of her dowry.

The obvious solution was that Catherine should be married – or at least betrothed – to 'the Prince of Wales that now is' as Ferdinand described the young Henry. This occurred to both sets of parents almost immediately. In Spain Isabella and Ferdinand were predictably shocked by the news of Arthur's death; when Ferdinand wrote on 12 May that 'the affliction caused by all their former losses had been revived by it' we may believe that for once there was real sincerity beneath the conventional language of royal condolence: that the deaths of the Infante Juan and Queen Isabel of Portugal were still raw to their parents.[18] Yet once again, an alliance was imperilled as well and in the case of the death of Arthur (whom they had never met) their first thought must be to stabilize the rocking balance of power.

Then there was the question of money, in short supply in Spain so that Ferdinand had never completed the payment of the second half of Catherine's dowry. In theory – Spanish theory – it could all now be beautifully simple. The money already paid for the first marriage could be negotiated to count towards the second; the Anglo-Spanish alliance would remain intact. This renewal of negotiations was not necessarily unwelcome to the English King, since he knew himself to be in a strong position with regard to Spain for two reasons. First, he indubitably did have the widowed Princess of Wales there at the English court. Secondly, Prince Henry, who was only eleven at the end of June 1502, was a ripe candidate to take part in one of those betrothals which could, if necessary, be repudiated once he reached the age of consent. Besides that, it was against nature for Henry VII to return any of the money already paid. Returning then to the question of Catherine's dowry, what would be the proper provisions for the next marriage treaty? At this point, things, theoretically so simple, turned rapidly nasty.

When King Ferdinand, shortly after Arthur's death, set himself to establish whether his daughter's marriage had been consummated or not, he was not interested in her physical wellbeing. The fact was that the Princess Dowager of Wales had the right to demand back the 100,000 crowns paid as the first instalment of her dowry, even before she received the stipulated one-third of the revenues of Wales, Cornwall and Chester, if the marriage had been completed in this respect. But as we have seen, it had almost certainly not. And Doña Elvira swore categorically to that effect. It is important to bear in mind for the future that when Doña Elvira swore so firmly that consummation had not taken place, she was not giving the answer then most convenient to the Catholic Kings in Spain. Nevertheless her version of events convinced King Ferdinand: 'God had taken Arthur to himself too soon'. By the beginning of July 1502 he was quite certain that 'our daughter remains as she was here', i.e. a virgin. On this basis Ferdinand instructed his representative the Duke of Estrada to negotiate for the new marriage.[19]

According to his instructions Estrada was to begin by demanding the return of Catherine to Spain: if the betrothal to Prince Henry did not follow immediately, it would be 'very important for us to have the Princess in our [Spanish] power'.[20] But there is little doubt that this was a mere ploy, and at this point Catherine's departure, leaving behind her dowry, was never seriously contemplated. Far more to the point were Estrada's instructions concerning the princess's maintenance, her own and that of her household. Why was Catherine being obliged to live off portions of her dowry, when she should be supported by the revenues of properties assigned to her for life? Henry VII's meanness in refusing to provide for his daughter-in-law at this point and expecting her to live off Spanish money was intolerable. Ferdinand pointed out that neither his widowed daughter (Isabel of Portugal, following the death of her first husband) nor his widowed daughter-in-law (the Archduchess Margaret) had expected Spanish revenues to support them. The grim process by which Catherine of Aragon was to be ground between the upper millstone of Ferdinand's poverty and the nether millstone of Henry VII's avarice had begun.

The treaty of betrothal between Prince Henry and Catherine was in fact signed the following summer, on 23 June 1503. Ferdinand had his own reasons for needing the English alliance at this point, and under the circumstances Dr de Puebla, his established ambassador in London, secured the best deal possible[21] (although Catherine herself, fed stories on the subject of the doctor by Doña Elvira, was increasingly convinced that he had placed the interests of his long-time patron, the English King, before her own).

This projected match required special permission – a dispensation from the Pope. According to the rules of the church, there was an 'impediment' to it. The marriage of Arthur to Catherine had created an 'affinity' between Catherine and Arthur's brother Henry. It was as though Catherine had become Henry's actual sister, rather than his sister-in-law, through this earlier union: brothers and sisters, being related 'in the first degree col-lateral', were forbidden to marry. (The universal prohibition against parents and children marrying was due to their relationship being 'in the first degree'.)

It was the sexual union between husband and wife, not the marriage ceremony, which was held to create this affinity. As we shall see, a man who had made love to one sister might require a dispensation to marry another, even though no ceremony had been involved in the first (clandestine) relationship. A different kind of dispensation was required in the case of an unconsummated marriage: one on grounds of 'public honesty'. Notwithstanding the lack of consummation, a first marriage had taken place in the public eye: this fact had to be acknowledged before the second marriage was publicly seen to be legitimate (even if it was technically already so). Given that the entire point of such dispensations was to establish a lawful unquestionable marriage, from which – even more importantly – legitimate offspring would flow, more thought was generally given to the future of the second marriage, rather than the facts about the first.

Thus when the Spanish King asked for a dispensation from Rome for Catherine to marry Henry, he asked for, and was granted, a dispensation which referred to the fact that her first marriage had 'perhaps' (*forsitan* in Latin) been consummated. A great deal of trouble would later be caused by this little weasel word 'perhaps'. At the time – with King Ferdinand quite convinced that the marriage had not been consummated, Catherine herself, to say nothing of Doña Elvira, passionate of her denials – what was taking place was clearly a Spanish manoeuvre.[22]

King Ferdinand himself wrote quite frankly on the subject to his ambassador on 23 August 1503. 'It is well known in England that the Princess is still a virgin. But as the English are much disposed to cavill, it has seemed to be more prudent to provide for the case as though the marriage had been consummated ... the dispensation of the Pope must be in perfect keeping with the said clause of the [marriage] treaty.' The nub of his meaning came in the next sentence: 'The right of Succession [that is, of any child born to Catherine and Henry] depends on the undoubted legitimacy of the treaty'.[23] In this way Dr de Puebla also saw himself as able to get the best financial deal over Catherine's dowry; the princess was angry, but he thrust aside her protests as irrelevant. In any case it was Catherine's father who was the prime mover and who, in a sense, betrayed her.

Such a dispensation – for a man to marry his brother's widow – was unusual but it was certainly not unknown. Catherine of Aragon herself could hardly have regarded it as an exceptional state of affairs, since only a short while before her own brother-in-law King Manuel of Portugal had married her two sisters Isabel and Maria in quick succession. (He ended by marrying, as his third wife, the niece of his first two wives.) There were various biblical texts on the subject, one of which – from Leviticus – forbade such a marriage, and one of which – from Deuteronomy – explicitly enjoined it as bounden duty on the part of the second brother. These texts, which like the little word 'perhaps' and the events of the wedding night of two adolescents, were to be analysed exhaustively twenty-five years later, featured little if at all at the time; this was yet another game of power politics, with youthful royal brides and grooms as pawns.*

There were however some significant new pawns on the matrimonial chessboard. Catherine of Aragon's claim, as a princess of Spain, to represent the most powerful alliance available to Henry VII, had been considerably eroded since that original Anglo-Spanish treaty nearly fifteen years earlier. There were, for example, the grandchildren of the Emperor Maximilian, that is, the growing family of his son Philip the Handsome and Catherine's sister Juana: if Charles, Catherine's nephew, born in 1500, was the greatest male matrimonial prize in Europe, his sisters, Eleanor and Isabella, also represented interesting possibilities as brides. Then there was the baby French princess Claude, so far the only child of Louis XII and his wife Anne of Brittany; and the ten-year-old Marguerite d'Angoulême, whose brother François stood to inherit the throne of France (under the Salic law) if King Louis died without a son. Nor was Catherine of Aragon the only widow on the European scene. Catherine's former sister-in-law the Archduchess Margaret, who had gone on to marry Philibert of Savoy, had recently been widowed for the second time.

Catherine of Aragon's matrimonial fate had not been made simpler by the death of her mother-in-law Elizabeth of York in February 1503, a few months before her official betrothal to Prince Henry. On a personal level, she was robbed of a patron whose benevolent presence might have made a considerable difference to the bitter years which followed. Publicly, it meant that Henry VII, a forty-six-year-old widower, had become once again for purposes of diplomacy an eligible bachelor. There was one rumour which reached Spain that the King would now marry his own daughter-in-law.

Officially the Catholic Kings reacted with disgust to such a proposal: 'one never before seen, the mere mention of which offends our ears'.[25] (Quite apart from the May-to-December aspect of the match, King Henry and Catherine were ostensibly related in the first degree.) But there was of course a more worldly aspect to the Catholic Kings' revulsion: Prince Henry would still take precedence in the succession over any son born to Catherine and his father, so that the Spanish princess was likely to end up merely as a king's widow, not as a king's mother, a possible Regent of the country.

---

* Archbishop Warham probably did raise an eyebrow in 1503, on the grounds of Leviticus, but a few years later his objections had apparently been stifled.[24]

'Speak of it as a thing not to be endured', wrote Ferdinand firmly.

This rumour probably had no basis in fact.[26] Yet the mere existence of it (at a time when official negotiations were in progress for Catherine's marriage to the English King's son) illustrates the treacherously shifting nature of matrimonial Europe during this period. Furthermore Ferdinand's disgust at the idea of King Henry as a bridegroom has an ironic ring when one considers his own future behaviour.

October 1504 saw the death of another queen, Catherine's own mother, Isabella. It was Ferdinand's pious hope that she had gone to 'a better and more lasting realm than those she ruled here'.[27] Certainly the unification of the kingdoms of Aragon and Castile had not proved lasting: Isabella's death meant the succession of her daughter Juana and Philip the Handsome, absent in Flanders. King Ferdinand, deprived of the title of 'King of Castile' which he had borne for thirty years, was left struggling gamely to retain effective rulership of his wife's dominions as Governor. In the meantime the separation of Aragon from Castile, with the latter possibly passing into the imperial camp, opened up a whole new set of diplomatic prospects.

Furthermore King Ferdinand was yet another middle-aged widower who had become transformed into an eligible bachelor (in his case, one in need of a male heir to Aragon). Promptly the next year, as a result of the Treaty of Blois made with France, he married Germaine de Foix. Apart from being the niece of the King of France, she was also his own half great-niece. She was eighteen. He was fifty-three.

Such mercurial turnabouts boded ill for Catherine who, physically cut off in the power of England, was unlikely to benefit from them. By the summer of 1505, as the fourteenth birthday of Prince Henry approached (the date at which Catherine might confidently expect their actual marriage to take place), a very different set of rumours was sweeping Europe. King Henry VII was believed to have set his heart on a triple marriage to link his own family to the imperial house of Habsburg. Princess Mary would be betrothed to Charles, the heir to the Habsburgs and to Castile. King Henry himself would wed Charles's twice-widowed aunt, the Archduchess Margaret. And Henry Prince of Wales would be espoused to Charles's sister, Eleanor of Austria, the seven-year-old niece of that nineteen-year-old princess who had hitherto fondly imagined him to be her destined husband.

Under the circumstances, King Henry instigated a ploy which would free his son – if necessary. On 27 June 1505, the day before his fourteenth birthday at which he reached the official age of consent, Henry Prince of Wales formally repudiated his betrothal to Catherine Dowager Princess of Wales and Princess of Spain.

*

Even before this blow fell Catherine's state had become increasingly wretched. Nor had the betrothal two years earlier substantially affected her welfare as might have been hoped: on the contrary it made the pointed requests of King Henry – where was the rest of her dowry? – all the more exigent. Such demands were accompanied by polite but firm refusals to provide anything but minimal maintenance for her himself.

Unhappy households do not run smoothly. For most of the time, the princess was cooped up with Doña Elvira and the rest of her Spanish attendants in Durham House in the Strand, the mediaeval town house of the Bishops of Durham. At least it had agreeable long gardens down to the river; but these were no compensation for the kind of seclusion which Doña Elvira thought appropriate. A series of unpleasant incidents marked the years of Catherine's widowhood, punctuated by a series of departures, which although in some cases relieving the tension, also served to increase her feeling of isolation.

After five years in England, Catherine told her father that she still scarcely spoke English at all.[28] But how was she to learn, guarded by Doña Elvira, ignored or harassed by King Henry? The odd visit to court, the occasional hunting expedition in Windsor Forest was scarcely enough. The first departure was that of Father Alessandro Geraldini, the humanist scholar who had been her tutor in happier days in Spain. He had accompanied her to England as her confessor and principal chaplain. But Father Alessandro was believed to have spread rumours to the effect that Catherine had become pregnant by Prince Arthur: this was to Catherine both at the time and years later quite unforgivable. An indignant Doña Elvira secured Father Alessandro's recall before the end of 1502.

Quite soon the ladies of Catherine's household would have been glad to depart too. They neither enjoyed the restricted life of Durham House, nor relished Catherine's inability to provide them with the kind of dowries a lady-in-waiting to a royal princess could expect. Catherine herself could not think about this failure on her part 'without pangs of conscience'.[29] Yet her father, enmeshed in his own problems in Spain, steadily failed to send her even her own portion, let alone something to distribute. Soon all luxuries, all extras were out of the question. By the spring of 1504 Catherine reported that she did not even have enough money to buy food for herself and her household.

Doña Elvira's departure was not however voluntary. It was the result of a plot which backfired. Doña Elvira's brother, Don Juan Manuel, was a Castilian diplomat in Flanders who was anxious to secure an alliance between the English King and the new rulers of Castile which would effectively draw Henry VII away from the side of Aragon. At the same time, one of the people who could at least in theory ameliorate Catherine's poverty-stricken condition was her elder sister Juana, as heiress to their mother. Catherine was induced to write to her sister, asking Juana to request a meeting at Saint-Omer with Henry VII: that in turn would involve him crossing to Calais, with Catherine as part of his train. Queen Juana would then, remarking her sister's destitution, either remedy it herself or cause the English King to do so.

It was the despised Dr de Puebla who put an end to this plot by appealing passionately to Catherine's first loyalty – which must surely be to her father. Catherine was angry: but she did abandon the project. Doña Elvira was expelled to Flanders, taking with her, incidentally, the Spanish chaplain who had served the princess in the confessional since the departure of Father Alessandro. For the next two years, Catherine would not even have the comfort of being able to make her confession in her own language. Yet increasingly religion, of an austere and self-mortifying nature, was becoming her solace. We know this from a letter sent by the Pope to Henry Prince of Wales dated 20 October 1505, empowering him as her husband (*sic*) to cause her to desist from her vow of rigorous prayer and fasting, abstinence and pilgrimage.[30] Such zeal might distract her from the true purpose of marriage: to wit, the procreation of children. The irony of this letter at this time is obvious; and yet, as with any negotiation where Henry VII was concerned, nothing was plain sailing, not even the prince's repudiation of his bride.

An unscheduled visit to England by Juana and Philip the Handsome – now Queen and King of Castile – took place in January 1506. It brought with it, however, none of the relief that Doña Elvira had predicted would flow from one sister to another. The royal armada, on its way from the Netherlands to Spain, was blown off course by a mighty gale and came to rest at Weymouth. King Philip came to Windsor and was entertained by the court. For a moment, publicly, Catherine of Aragon was able to recapture her Spanish youth: she wore jewels in her hair, and danced with two of her ladies the graceful Castilian dances she had first displayed at Dogmersfield. But the Treaty of Windsor, which followed on 31 January between King Henry and King Philip, was a blatant threat to her future.

England was now ranged with the Habsburg Empire against Aragon. Henry VII even went so far as to hint at assisting Philip against Ferdinand – if Philip had to take possession of Castile by force. In return King Henry was to marry the Archduchess Margaret, and the first stages of the much-desired betrothal of Charles of Austria to Princess Mary were reached. (The princess sang Spanish songs, taught to her by Catherine, at the court entertainment.) Would Prince Henry complete the picture by his betrothal to Charles's sister Eleanor?

Furthermore the sisterly rapport for which Catherine must have hoped never took place. Queen Juana was enchanting to look at (the loveliest of all Isabella's daughters); nevertheless she was both melancholy and hysterical, obsessed at all times with jealousy for her dashing husband and his relationships with other women. For some reason, possibly due to one of her erratic moods, Queen Juana was only brought to Windsor some time after her husband, and Catherine left the court the next day.

The princess's anxiety sharpened. Not only present poverty but ultimate rejection seemed to threaten her. In April 1506 she told her father that she was 'herself all but naked' and that she had asked King Henry 'with tears' for money for food – but without success. And yet the situation was not at all clear cut: King Henry deliberately maintained an ambivalent attitude to the 'betrothal' he had caused his son to repudiate. At the very same time as Catherine's lamentations to Aragon, the young Prince Henry, undoubtedly on his father's orders, was still referring to her (to her brother-in-law King Philip) as 'my most dear and well-beloved consort, the princess my wife'.[31]

Prince Henry's language was reminiscent of Prince Arthur's formal schoolboy missives to his 'dearest spouse' nearly ten years earlier. But there was a difference. Prince Henry actually knew his wife, his 'well-beloved consort', having met her when she first came to England. Furthermore the departure of Doña Elvira together with the King's reluctance to pay for Durham House meant that Catherine spent more time either at court, or shuttled about among the King's other minor palaces. In either situation, she might encounter the royal children. In short, over a number of years Prince Henry (and Princess Mary) had been thrown together with Catherine.

This proximity was not brought about deliberately. It was simply the unwitting consequence of Henry VII's parsimony, and the persistent way he tried to keep up the pressure on Ferdinand to provide the money by in effect persecuting his daughter. The King understood his control over his son to be total. Observers were indeed struck by how Prince Henry existed entirely under the thumb of his father, living in virtual seclusion; the King, either out of fear for his son's safety or from a testy habit of domination, arranged every detail of his life. The following year Catherine was to issue a touching complaint to her father: she had not even been allowed to see 'the Prince her husband' for four months although they were living in the same palace.[32]*

To Henry VII the brusque removal of Catherine from his son's company

---

* Richmond Palace: the vast extent of the Tudor palaces meant they were more small towns than residences; hence the King's ease at keeping Catherine away from the Prince of Wales – each would have their own establishment and household.

was one more manoeuvre (just as King Ferdinand had cynically supported the myth of the consummation of Catherine's marriage). But a relationship based on propinquity had been casually allowed to develop between the handsome boy now rapidly growing into manhood – Prince Henry was sixteen in 1507 – and the unfortunate little princess, an object of sympathy, surely, to any romantic heart. It was to have important consequences.

As for Catherine, it was at about this time that she told Henry VII to his face with a courage that did her credit, that she regarded her marriage to Prince Henry as 'irrevocable'. Of course, duty, religious conviction and training were all on her side – as well as her father's instructions from afar. Yet the fact that the husband under consideration was 'most comely of stature' must surely also somewhere have played its part. 'There is no finer youth in the world than the Prince of Wales', Dr de Puebla told the King of Aragon in October 1507. Prince Henry's startling looks, including his strong athletic limbs 'of a gigantic size' as de Puebla put it, were already beginning to arouse the admiration of those cynically unused to such perfection in princes.[33]

Queen Juana's obsession with her living husband had only a short while more to run. She replaced it with an obsession with his corpse. After Philip died in October 1506, Juana's fragile reason began to collapse; she travelled distractedly from castle to castle, with her husband's unburied body in its coffin as part of her train. Oddly enough, one side effect of her visit to England had been to impress Henry VII with her beauty. She was sole monarch of Castile and without a husband. Was he not after all *still* an eligible bachelor? (The marriage to the Archduchess Margaret never took place; instead she found her true destiny ruling the Netherlands as a sage and respected regent.)

Under the circumstances, there is something pathetic about the English King's efforts to convince himself that the stories of Juana's madness were a Spanish trick to withhold her rights from her. On the other hand Dr de Puebla's hearty endorsement of the same marriage smacks of farce: he took the line that even if the Queen of Castile *was* mad, it would not matter much among the English, given that she had already given birth and would presumably do so again.

Once more the situation was not simple. The question of marriage to Ferdinand's daughter Juana put Henry VII back in possible need of Aragonese help. Even that celebrated matrimonial prize, the Emperor's grandson and heir, Charles of Austria, was equally grandson and heir to Ferdinand. The King of Aragon had it in his power to either support or try to subvert his match with Princess Mary. King Henry also allowed himself to listen to other siren voices telling of bewitching brides with Aragonese connections. There was Ferdinand's niece, Queen Joanna of

Naples, for example, a young widow and a celebrated beauty. Although King Henry loved what he heard about her, he took nothing on trust. Further enquiries must be made: did she paint? Was there hair on her upper lip? He had heard that her breasts were rather big and full and 'trussed somewhat high'. Was her breath sweet? The ambassadors should not trust to the report of others but should get near enough to test the matter for themselves.[34]

None of this relieved the dour atmosphere at the English court. Exotic entertainments were a thing of the past. The marriage celebrations of Catherine and Arthur had proved to be the last – as well as greatest – spectacle of the reign. For all his fantasies of beautiful young brides, the King's real pleasure these days consisted of gambling compulsively at cards or dice with his male courtiers. Money, in one form or another, remained the true mainspring of his actions. When King Ferdinand, his finances improved, did manage to send some of Catherine's missing dowry in July 1507, King Henry responded by rounding on the princess and accusing her of breaking unlawfully into the original portion. His argument went as follows: the jewels and plate she had brought for Prince Arthur had belonged to him and had thus passed to his father on his death; Catherine herself had no right to touch them.

Catherine's stream of letters to her father continued to make pitiful reading.* Food and clothing were the recurring themes. Catherine had only managed to buy two dresses – of plain black velvet – since she came to England from Spain six years earlier, and she had had to sell her bracelets to pay for them. Her officers were in rags. As for food, the situation had only worsened, and there was no way of paying for it except by selling her plate. Surely it was her father's duty 'to succour a young princess who is living in a foreign land without protection'.

Under the circumstances it was hardly surprising that her health gave way, and she suffered persistent attacks of 'low fever' – once again this is as likely to be a form of depression as any other feverish ailment – for which the contemporary remedy of bleeding the patient can only have lowered her resistance still further. In the spring of 1507 she told her sister Queen Juana that she had recovered, and was bearing her adversity with fortitude. But by August, Catherine burst out to her father that 'no woman of whatever station in life' could ever have suffered more. Put against this, King Henry's protestations a month later that he had just sent her £200, so that her servants must have stolen it, and that he loved her so much that

* The originals, in the Egerton MSS, British Library, display the growing strain as her sprawling handwriting gets ever larger and more frantic.[35]

he could not bear the idea of her 'being in poverty' have at the very least a hollow ring.[36]

The unrest in the poverty-stricken household continued. The arrival at last of a Spanish confessor should have made things easier. He came at Catherine's urgent request, due to the difficulty of her making her confession in English. The new arrival was a Franciscan Observant friar, as Queen Isabella's confessor had been; while the Franciscan Observant friary next to the palace at Greenwich also supplied the English royal family with chaplains. Catherine was immediately delighted with him. Unfortunately her circumstances had not combined to make her a good judge of people. Her acute need for support in her intimate circle, if she was to survive at all, inclined her to equate any outspoken loyalty to her interests – as she perceived it – with decency and goodness.

Sometimes this worked well. A new lady-in-waiting, Maria de Salinas, arrived from Spain at some point during this dreadful period. Described by Catherine later as having ever comforted her 'in the hour of trial', Maria de Salinas would prove to be one of Catherine's most devoted friends and servants.[37] A little younger than her mistress, extremely pretty in youth, she was distantly related to Catherine through the Aragonese side of her family; Maria de Salinas's sister Inez, who married a Spaniard living in England, may have been one of Catherine's original ladies-in-waiting. Fidelity was not Maria de Salinas's only good quality: she was also tactful.

The same could not be said of Catherine's new confessor, Fray Diego Fernandez. He was certainly not quite as terrible as the Rasputin figure, 'haughty and scandalous in an extreme manner', painted by his detractors. There were those who found in him 'neither learning, nor appearance, nor manners, nor competency, nor credit'. If this was going altogether too far, then neither was Fray Diego the repository of all wisdom and goodness that Catherine believed him to be, 'the best [confessor] that ever woman in my position had, with respect to his life as well as to his holy doctrines and proficiency in letters'.[38]

In reality Fray Diego was a genuinely cultured man, one who had studied at Salamanca, and risen from a poor background by his efforts. The real trouble was that the friar exercised a most possessive control over all the princess's household arrangements, not only those pertaining to her spiritual welfare. It was a form of power mania that was particularly inappropriate in view of Catherine's delicate relationship with the English court. Yet if Catherine ever dared to question his decisions, he played upon her piety and convinced her that what she was proposing was a sin: he, after all, not she, was in a position to pronounce upon such matters. The Spanish ambassador expostulated that it was an easy game with someone 'so conscientious' as Catherine, to make 'a sin of all acts, of whatever kind they may be, if they displease him'.[39]

There was one notorious incident when it had been arranged for Catherine to ride with Princess Mary to Richmond Palace and join the court. At the last moment Fray Diego intervened on the grounds that Catherine had been sick during the night. 'You shall not go today', he declared. Catherine for once did not give way: riding, particularly with Princess Mary, was a treat and the King had after all sent for her. Even when Fray Diego first announced that to disobey his order would be a mortal sin, the normally submissive Catherine still persisted, demonstrating the depth of her disappointment. But her confessor could not in the end be gainsaid. After an awkward delay, Princess Mary rode off. Catherine stayed behind to find that she was without food, since she had been expected to depart. The King was – understandably on this occasion – 'much grieved'. The next day this allegedly sick girl had to travel in the most humble way (for a princess) attended by three women on horseback, her chamberlain – and Fray Diego – when she could have travelled in comfortable royal style with Princess Mary.[40]

The fleeting gossip that Fray Diego's influence over the princess was due to some kind of sexual misbehaviour can be confidently dismissed. Catherine's piety, her lifelong personal chastity, to say nothing of her oft-expressed consciousness of her own virginity, would have made such an episode unthinkable, indeed quite horrifying to her. But of course from the point of view of the Rasputin figure – Fray Diego – there was absolutely no need of such a dangerous course. Catherine's conscience and her loneliness already made her an easy prey. His expert management of her scrupulous fears provided enough control. All the same, one can understand the reaction of King Ferdinand's new ambassador, Don Gutierre Gomez de Fuensalida, when he groaned: would that 'an honest old confessor' could be found as a substitute for the trouble-making friar.

Fuensalida arrived to replace Dr de Puebla, dismissed at Catherine's request, in 1508. If Catherine thought too highly of Fray Diego, she had always underestimated Dr de Puebla in her obstinate conviction, originally planted by Doña Elvira, that he was the tool of Henry VII. Once again, isolation had not made Catherine a good judge of men. It may be that de Puebla's Jewish blood – he was partly or wholly Jewish – had contributed to Doña Elvira's prejudice, although many of Ferdinand's officials, before the expulsion of the Jews in 1492, were *conversos*, that is, Jews converted to Christianity. The matter was by no means hard and fast in Spanish society after 1492 and could hardly be so (Ferdinand himself – and thus by extension Catherine – had some Jewish blood from his mother Juana Henriquez).[41] It certainly worked against Dr de Puebla, an elderly, middle-class official, with no great social graces. But there was something more: Dr de Puebla provided a convenient scapegoat for Catherine at all times when the real culprit, apart from Henry VII, was her own father for failing to deliver the dowry. Given Catherine's adoration for Ferdinand (in Spain she had been his pet, his youngest and favourite child), blaming Dr de Puebla provided a useful safety valve.

Fuensalida was a very different type of ambassador. He was an aristocrat who arrived from the polished Burgundian court of Flanders, although he had some knowledge of England. Yet Fuensalida fared no better. At least de Puebla had remained on good terms with King Henry, however Catherine had interpreted the relationship; Fuensalida's perpetual pressure on the subject of Catherine's marriage maddened him. From Catherine's point of view, indeed, Fuensalida fared even worse, since he arrived with instructions from Ferdinand that this famous long-delayed match must either take place forthwith – or Catherine must be rescued, with whatever could be obtained of her original dowry and belongings, and brought home. 'It is clear that he [Henry VII] thinks he can do and ask what he likes', wrote Ferdinand, 'because he holds the princess in his power'. Yet still Catherine herself affirmed the 'indissoluble' nature of her second union.[42]

Insult was added to injury – at least from the point of view of the Spaniards – when Henry VII tried to substitute his own marriage to Queen Juana, who remained attractive to him, for the original match between Henry Prince of Wales and Catherine. This way he hoped he could preserve his friendship with Aragon. When Fuensalida pointed out indignantly that the English King was bound by a treaty to marry Catherine of Aragon to his son, Henry VII replied blandly: 'My son and I are free'.[43] It was, to Fuensalida at least and to his master, the death knell of Catherine's marriage.

Catherine denounced Fuensalida in his turn and Fray Diego weighed in once more. There was a ridiculous incident involving one of her ladies, Francesca de Caceres, who received an offer of marriage from a wealthy Italian banker Francesco Grimaldi (who was involved in the complicated arrangements for the eventual payment of Catherine's portion). Doña Francesca, in view of her dowerless state, considered herself fortunate to have secured such a well-set-up bridegroom; but the fact that Fuensalida lodged in Grimaldi's London house made Catherine, encouraged by Fray Diego, detect a conspiracy. Doña Francesca had to leave her household and the wedding took place at Grimaldi's own house.[44]

The fact was that in Fuensalida's opinion the time had come to pack up Catherine's belongings and take the princess away from the English tower, to which, in seven years, no knight had ridden to rescue her. The proxy marriage – the official betrothal – of Princess Mary to Charles of Austria, Prince of Castile, in December 1508 made Henry VII's procrastination over the earlier union seem all the more gratuitous. A furious Fuensalida refused to attend the court celebrations and tried to forbid the princess to do so. Nevertheless, Catherine went, holding her head high. Charles was her nephew, Princess Mary her sister-in-law; proudly, she would observe the conventions. When the twelve-year-old Mary spoke 'the words of matrimony' perfectly and distinctly in French 'without any abashing of countenance, stop or interruption', the touching sight brought tears into the eyes of many observers.[45] But if Catherine was among those who wept, she must also have spared a tear for herself.

In the spring of 1509 Catherine's spirit finally gave way. In a letter to her father of 9 March, she broke down and told him that she could no longer combat the petty persecutions of Henry VII. Only recently he had told her that he was under no obligation to feed either her or her attendants; he added spitefully that her food was being given to her as alms. Her health was recovered since another recent bout of illness; now she wanted to return to Spain and spend the rest of her life serving God.[46] This was the final expression of despair on the part of Queen Isabella's daughter, who had been trained to believe that life on the throne, not in the convent, was the destiny for which God had sent her on earth.

The next month Fuensalida began the process of despatching Catherine's belongings to Bruges. And then, suddenly, Catherine was no longer in King Henry's power. On 21 April, after a short illness, he died.[47] It was almost exactly seven years since the death of Prince Arthur. The spell was broken.

Chapter 3

GOLDEN WORLD

Our natural, young, lusty and courageous ... sovereign
... had taken upon him the regal sceptre ... of this
fertile and plentiful realm of England ... called then
the golden world, such grace of plenty reigned ...

George Cavendish, Life of Wolsey

Six weeks after the death of the old King, on 11 June 1509, the new King, Henry VIII, married Catherine of Aragon in the oratory of the friary church just outside the walls of Greenwich Palace. He was about to be eighteen (on 28 June); she was twenty-three. The ceremony was small and private; Catherine wore white, with her hair long and loose as befitted a virgin bride.[1] Describing the wedding night which followed, King Henry liked to boast that he had indeed found his wife 'a maid'; although years later he would attempt to pass off these boasts as 'jests', there seems little doubt that he made them.[2] Youthful braggadoccio apart, it is understandable that in so far as any lingering doubt remained about his brother's relationship with Catherine, he should wish to settle the matter – as he then thought – once and for all.

On Midsummer Day a more public and splendid celebration of their union took place when, at the orders of the new King, his bride shared in his coronation at Westminster Abbey. Henry VIII may well have deliberately hastened the marriage ceremony in order that Catherine might 'lie the night before the crowning at the Tower'. In this manner, she could accompany him through the City of London in the traditional eve-of-coronation procession to Westminster. Thus Londoners could gaze at their new Queen as she passed by in her litter, 'borne on the backs of two white palfreys trapped in white cloth of gold, her person apparelled in white satin embroidered, her hair hanging down her back, of a very great length, beautiful and goodly to behold, and on her head a coronal, set with many rich stones'.[3]

But the coronation of a queen was more than a good opportunity for loyal subjects to feast their eyes on a great deal of glittering gold and white – and inspect her charms (unless they had witnessed that earlier procession with Prince Arthur eight years previously). It was also a deliberate act of state, one which did not necessarily coincide with marriage to the King: Elizabeth of York, as was noted, had only been crowned nearly two years later, following the birth of a son and heir. Thomas More, in a burst of ecstasy at the hopeful accession of the new monarch, drew attention to Catherine's particular contribution: 'She is descended from great kings'.[4]

In this manner over £1,500 was spent on the Queen's coronation alone: three times as much as had been spent on the wedding celebrations in 1501, and a mere £200 less than was spent on the coronation of the King himself. Two thousand yards of red cloth were needed, and a further 1,500 of the superior scarlet cloth. Careful lists were drawn up of those entitled to wear the Queen's newly devised livery of crimson velvet; while Queen Catherine wore a crown of gold, the border set with six sapphires and pearls, and she carried a sceptre of gold with a dove on top.[5]

Sometimes the ceremony creaked a little, as such things can when traditions are too eagerly preserved. The form used was that of Henry VII, a quarter of a century earlier: thus viscounts were appointed to carry the sceptre and ivory rod in the Queen's procession although there were none in England. Then Lord Grey of Powis was put down to lead the horses of the Queen's litter as Lord Grey of Powis had done in 1485 – but this Lord Grey turned out to be only six years old.[6] These fumblings apart, the sumptuous celebration of a new order was unqualified.

Many stood to gain and a few, very few, to lose. For example numerous Knights of the Bath were created in honour of the coronation: among them was a rising young courtier, called Thomas Boleyn, assiduous and hardworking, and married to a member of the Howard family who had recently presented him with a family of a son and two daughters. The losers were those unpopular symbols of the old King's avarice, his servants Richard Empson and Edmund Dudley who had carried out his financial exactions; they were arrested, charged, and finally executed. These arrests, coupled with an amnesty declared by Henry VIII towards certain fines imposed on the aristocracy by his father, only served to enhance the general atmosphere of rejoicing. Thomas More wrote of the freshness of it all: 'This day is the end of our slavery, the fount of our liberty; the end of sadness, the beginning of joy'.[7]

Nor did the death of old Margaret Beaufort, the new King's grandmother, a few days after the coronation, cause any particular grief; she was judged to be like Simeon, ready to depart, having seen the successful accession of her 'dearest son's' male heir. Stalwart figure as she was, Margaret Beaufort was a relic from the old era of dissension. For Cather-

Catherine of Aragon
m 1509

Pomegranate badge of Catherine of Aragon.

The Madonna of the Catholic Kings *by an unknown artist showing Catherine of Aragon's parents, Ferdinand and Isabella, on either side of the altar with her brother Don Juan.*

Edward IV, maternal grandfather of Henry VIII.

Margaret Beaufort, Countess of Richmond, paternal grandmother of Henry VIII.

Henry VII, father of Henry VIII.

Elizabeth of York, mother of Henry VIII.

Bust thought to be Henry VIII as a boy, attributed to Guido Mazzoni.

The young Catherine.

The Family of Henry VII with St George and the Dragon *by an unknown artist of the Flemish school, c. 1505–9.*

An early sixteenth-century Flemish tapestry showing the betrothal of Prince Arthur and Catherine of Aragon, now in Magdalen College, Oxford.

Stained glass in the chapel at The Vyne, featuring Henry VIII and Catherine of Aragon.

Watercolours by Daniel Chandler of contemporary stained glass showing King Henry and Queen Catherine commissioned by the Society of Antiquaries in 1737.

The palace of Greenwich in the early seventeenth century (the earliest known authentic view).

Mary, sister of Henry VIII, and her second husband, Charles Brandon, Duke of Suffolk.

Letter from Catherine of Aragon, as Regent of England, describing the victory over the Scots at Flodden in 1513 to Henry VIII then in France and sending him the coat of the dead King of Scots. 'In this your grace shall see how I can keep my promise, sending you for your banners a king's coat. I thought to send himself to you but our Englishmen would not suffer it.'

Whose john Glyn nob bringeth in this your grace shal see
yow I can kepe my premys sending you for your baners a kings
cote / I thought to sende hymself vnto you but our englishmen
hertz wold not suffre it / it shuld have been better for hym to

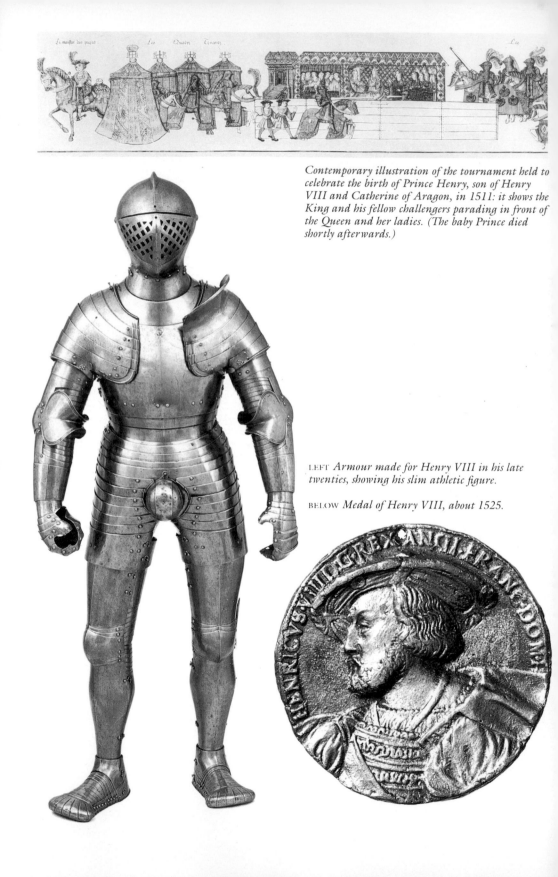

Contemporary illustration of the tournament held to celebrate the birth of Prince Henry, son of Henry VIII and Catherine of Aragon, in 1511: it shows the King and his fellow challengers parading in front of the Queen and her ladies. (The baby Prince died shortly afterwards.)

LEFT *Armour made for Henry VIII in his late twenties, showing his slim athletic figure.*

BELOW *Medal of Henry VIII, about 1525.*

ine's part, she was now not only the sole queen, but unlike Elizabeth of York in the previous reign, the sole queen figure in England.

There was a favourite image in the culture of Catherine's youth, recurring in the romances and histories which filled her mother's library: Fortune's Wheel.* 'We are like pots in a water-wheel ... one up and another down, one full and another empty; it is fortune's law that nothing can continue any long time in one and the selfsame state of being' (here quoted from the famous Spanish novel *La Celestina*, first published in 1499).[8] But Fortune's Wheel, sometimes also taken as an emblem of Christian fortitude, was expected to turn slowly if remorselessly around. Seldom can there have been a more violent revolution of the wheel than that which had brought Catherine of Aragon to her present eminent position. It was barely two months since the old King's death, and not much more than three since Catherine had uttered her cry of desolation, called for her return to Spain 'to serve God' and watched her belongings being despatched by Fuensalida to Bruges. (The ambassador now had the honour of getting them back again.)

Why had this miraculous transformation taken place? One explanation was given by Henry VIII himself in a letter to the Archduchess Margaret as a representative of the Habsburg family. His father, on his deathbed, had begged Henry to go through with the marriage, and the new King had respected his wish. It is true that Henry VIII had indeed been present at his father's deathbed, so it is in theory possible that this surprising last-minute plea took place. In every other way it is extremely unlikely. The new King's explanation was simply a polite way of glossing over the fact that by marrying Catherine he had in effect jilted the Archduchess's niece Eleanor of Austria.

As to Henry VII's own intentions, we must acquit him surely of any sentimental desire to right the wrong he had done over so many years to his daughter-in-law. In December he had secured the vital proxy marriage of Princess Mary to Charles, the Habsburg heir, without surrendering his son. Henry VII died only a month after humiliating Catherine yet again on the subject of her maintenance, with no other evidence of a change of heart.

Another explanation was put forward by Edward Hall in his *Chronicle*, first published in about 1542 (a document throughout which Henry VIII can do no wrong). Hall blamed the King's Council for wishing to hang on to Catherine's dowry (now at last available) and advising him that the marriage would in consequence be 'honourable and profitable to his

---

* For example, Catherine's exact contemporary – also born in 1485 – Hernán Cortés, the conquistador of Mexico, was fond of using it.

realm'; the King 'being young and not understanding the laws of God' agreed.[9] Certainly the securing of Catherine's dowry, compared to the possible need to pay out to the Princess Dowager of Wales, was one possible argument; then there was the current need to secure King Ferdinand of Aragon as an ally against France. Lastly there was the nervous dynastic situation in England, where, if King Henry had died as a result of an accident at one of the coronation tournaments in 1509, it was not at all clear who his heir would be, apart from his sisters, to whom all the old caveats about female succession applied; besides which one was only thirteen, the other married to the King of Scots. An adult bride was far more attractive in terms of founding the new dynasty than, for example, the eleven-year-old Eleanor of Austria, who was not likely to bear children for a number of years.

The truth is more romantic. Although the various arguments given above in favour of the Spanish marriage may also have played their part – especially where the King's counsellors were concerned – they were essentially justifications of a decision which the new King took himself. And he took it originally for reasons of love, not politics, ruled by his heart not his head. After that, it was hardly difficult to find arguments to support a union to which he had been committed officially for six years, one that had many obvious material and diplomatic advantages.

Catherine herself always believed that the only true obstacle to her happiness was Henry VII. She once wrote to her father that 'her marriage would soon be celebrated if the old King were to die' (as Ferdinand told Fuensalida in May 1509). King Ferdinand also reminded Catherine of her own words: that to bring about the marriage 'would be easy' if Henry VII was removed from the scene; a man justly characterized by Ferdinand as 'neither his friend nor hers'.[10] And Catherine's confidence was not misplaced.

All his life King Henry VIII had a happy capacity for falling in love: happy at least from his own point of view, given that he was able to secure the object of his passion with reasonable speed. (Of his six celebrated marriages, four were actually made for love, one for affection, bordering on love; the only marriage which was made for pure reasons of state was an instant disaster.) In the summer of 1509, he was a young man, ardent, chivalrous, moved by the sufferings of the girl he had been brought up to consider his 'most dear and well-loved consort'. It was not difficult to love the graceful, appealing Catherine, with her sweet nature and evident devotion to 'the prince her husband', especially for a young man to whom other opportunities for romance had been sternly denied.

For Henry no less than Catherine had spent his formative years in royal isolation, deprived of female company, obliged to conduct most of his conversations in the presence of his father who guarded his heir as sedulously as Doña Elvira had once brooded over her own charge. Catherine of Aragon was the exception: as his 'consort' (and the Princess Dowager of Wales) she was allowed to spend enough time with him over the years to complain bitterly when the privilege was withdrawn. Prince Henry may even have made Catherine certain promises about the future in the lifetime of his father – this is speculation, although Catherine's assurances to Ferdinand that the marriage would 'soon be celebrated' if Henry VII died, do bear that construction. At the very least Catherine's words suggest confidence in the character and tender feelings of the young prince.

Now the prince had turned into a king and Henry was free. Given the suppression of his youth, it is scarcely a coincidence in psychological terms that Henry VIII's first public action completely reversed the policy of his father over many years: he would marry Catherine of Aragon and abandon Eleanor of Austria. But from Henry's point of view, there was more to the marriage than mere defiance of the parental embargo. Henry VIII was impetuous and he was a romantic: he now had a perfect opportunity to marry his first love and give the fairy story, as it were, a happy ending. When the young King wrote to his father-in-law Ferdinand in the month following his wedding that if he were still free, he would choose Catherine before all others, there is no reason to doubt that in the youthful rapture of the moment, he spoke the truth.[11]

For Queen Catherine, her new life certainly had all the elements of a fairy story, including the presence of a handsome young prince. Never is it more important to get away from the popular stereotype of King Henry VIII – Bluff King Hal, the bloated monarch of the later years – than in considering the man whom Catherine of Aragon married in 1509. If few queens have shown the qualities of mind possessed by Catherine, then few kings have been endowed by nature with such dazzling physical qualities as the young King Henry. It was suggested earlier that Henry and his equally striking fair-haired sisters owed their looks to their maternal York inheritance, not their Lancaster father. Certainly the resemblance between Henry VIII and his grandfather Edward IV is remarkable, if one compares their portraits at the relevant ages. Here was another fine figure of a man, renowned when young for his 'beauty of personage', and his daughter Elizabeth of York inherited his blonde good looks; while Henry VIII's father, with his much darker colouring, narrow face and small beady eyes on which all observers commented, was generally considered by his contemporaries to look more French than English.[12]

No less than Edward IV, Henry VIII had the advantage of looking like a king: or at least the popular ideal of one. (Remember how his cousin the Duke of Buckingham, during that nervous moment after Arthur's death when Henry was only a child, was praised for being 'a noble man' who therefore looked likely to be 'a royal ruler'.) This was an age when the actual bodily presence of the sovereign formed the focus of his court, which was in turn the focus of his country; it was an age, also, when sovereigns still led their people in war. Henry VIII was fortunate in that from his earliest years he excited admiration for having what was deemed to be the perfect princely appearance and bearing.

Thomas More once took Erasmus to visit the royal nursery at Eltham Palace: the Dutch theologian later recalled how the eight-year-old Henry had stood there in the middle of the hall, amid a great retinue of people, 'already with a certain royal demeanour; I mean a dignity of mind combined with a remarkable courtesy.' Adolescence only enhanced the dazzling impression that he made. The awe-struck remarks of Dr de Puebla in 1507 concerning Henry's gigantic limbs were only the first in a long line of similar tributes that he would incur, not only in the flush of youth but late into his twenties. In 1519 for example, when Henry was twenty-eight, the Venetian ambassador Giustinian found him 'extremely handsome; nature could not have done more for him'. He had a beard 'which looks like gold' and a complexion as delicate and fair as a woman's. It was, reported Giustinian, the 'prettiest thing in the world' to see the King playing tennis, 'his fair skin glowing through a shirt of the finest texture'.[13]

Lyrical descriptions like these may perhaps be thought to owe something to the contrast between Henry VIII's appearance and that of most kings. (How few of them actually corresponded to the popular ideal!) When Henry came to the throne, Aragon, the Habsburg Empire and France were all three headed by elderly men in bad health. Of the next generation, Henry's chief rivals were to be the new King of France, François I, and Charles of Austria and Castile, who succeeded his grandfather as the Emperor Charles V in 1519. François I, although tall and well set-up, had a Mephistophelean air, with his long priapic nose, which even the finest painters in the world could never quite disguise. The future Charles V, whatever his mental abilities, was downright clumsy, a hobbledehoy with the unattractive jutting Habsburg lower lip. Under these circumstances, it was perhaps not too difficult for Henry VIII to be 'the handsomest sovereign' Giustinian 'had ever seen'.

Yet where looks were concerned, the English King could have held his own in any company. Apart from his colouring – the golden hair with a glint of red, the blue eyes and fair skin which received universal praise – his build was heroic. The King was six foot two inches tall, with broad shoulders and fine long muscular legs, in an age when men were smaller than they

are today, if not quite as small as is sometimes suggested. His various suits
of armour, now in the armoury of the Tower of London, enable us to be
precise about his measurements (as well as monitoring his increasing girth
over the years). In 1514, for example, the King's armour shows him to
have had a waist of 35 inches and a 42-inch chest: measurements that
substantiate Giustinian's judgement that his whole frame was 'admirably
proportioned'. In short, we should think of Shakespeare's Prince of Wales,
the future Henry V, described to Hotspur rather than Bluff King Hal, in
picturing Henry VIII in the first years of his reign:

> I saw young Harry with his beaver on,
> His cuisses on his thighs, gallantly arm'd,
> Rise from the ground like feather'd Mercury,
> And vaulted with such ease into his seat
> As if an angel dropp'd down from the clouds,
> To turn and wind a fiery Pegasus
> And witch the world with noble horsemanship.

The sheer physical energy of the young Henry VIII, forever leaping,
dancing, riding, hunting, wrestling, tilting, jousting, masking, amazed
the world; like vaulting Harry, he too was constantly bewitching spectators with his agility. A vast love of life and pleasure in all its forms
exuded from him, so agreeable to contemplate in a charming young
man – particularly one who had inherited a prodigious fortune from his
careful father. (Like Henry VII, he thought it good sport to gamble a
good deal of this money away: very often losing to ladies of the court,
where his father had mainly played with his male cronies.) Jewels, splendid
materials, glittering embroideries, robes that were 'the richest and most
superb that can be imagined' all delighted him. As for his counsellors, it
was hardly surprising that they should smile upon their young master in
his lively hedonism; they feared that if they discouraged him, he might
grow 'too hard among his subjects' as his father had done.[14]

Yet for all the King's impatience at any activity which involved staying
still for too long – writing letters for example was never a favourite
pastime – this was no handsome but mindless athlete. Henry VIII, like
his wife Catherine (and like many Renaissance princes and princesses),
had been extremely well educated; he was an avid reader and he had a
naturally quick intelligence; theological debate was an area of real interest.
Music was another passion. In 1515 he was described as being able to
play almost every instrument and composing tolerably; another report
had the King able to sing 'from a book at first sight'. He would leave
behind him a legacy of over thirty songs and instrumental pieces which

he had either composed or arranged himself; most however probably date from early in his reign. While the plangent Masses of John Taverner might provide a reminder of more solemn things, the titles of the King's songs commemorated a carefree time: 'Pastime with good company', 'It is to me a right great Joy', 'The time of youth, O my heart', 'Green groweth the holly' and 'Lusty Youth'.[15]

If it had not been difficult for the innocent Henry to fall in love with Catherine, then it would be positively easy for any woman to love such a man as Henry now was: and Catherine of Aragon was not any woman – she had for many years been his wife in the eyes of God, as she firmly believed. At the same time, where Catherine herself was concerned, she had not escaped unmarked from her seven years' ordeal of hardship and humiliation.

It was not – fortunately – her looks that had suffered. She was after all not yet twenty-four at the time of her marriage; she still possessed all the prettiness that had enchanted her father-in-law when the veil was lifted at Dogmersfield, and now gratified beholders at her coronation. Though tiny, Catherine remained nicely plump rather than heavy (illness and privation had not encouraged her to put on weight). Her two chief assets were her hair and her complexion, both important by the contemporary standards of beauty: her golden-auburn hair (a deeper shade of Henry's own) was seen to be exceptionally thick and 'of very great length' as it flowed down her back beneath her circlet; her pink-and-white colouring continued to ravish observers.[16] If Catherine's appearance lacked the exceptional radiance of her husband's, nevertheless in 1509 she made a delightful impression.

It was the inner woman who bore the marks. Catherine had survived, and, finally, she had won. Her prayers had been answered. Like a medi-aeval saint, she had undergone a series of harrowing experiences, only to prevail; we may assume that her last despairing letter of 9 March was soon forgotten, compared to the years of steadfastness. But these privations were not without effect on her character – how could they be? Catherine of Aragon was stamped as much by her tribulations, as she had been earlier formed by her happy childhood, with its confident picture of a triumphant mother and father. She was no longer the tremulous young girl who had arrived seasick, if still dignified, in England. She was much stronger, of course, as people who surmount adversity generally are if they do not crack. Nevertheless the memories of that dreadful time would remain.

On the one hand they would sustain her in her darkest hour, darker than anything she had yet endured; she was a character tempered with steel. On the other hand these experiences would also convince her that even the most fearful events did – with God's blessing – have a happy ending; more than ever she believed that Henry was not only her lawful but also her destined husband. If Catherine as a girl could summon up her courage, friendless in a foreign country, to tell Henry VII that her marriage was 'irrevocable', and be proved right, she was not likely to change her mind on the subject in the future. Above all, her newly found happiness at the side of her high-spirited eighteen-year-old husband did not forewarn her that high-spirited boys, allowed to have their own way in everything, may turn into wilful monarchs, furious at any frustration of their will; just as charming pink-cheeked girls may turn into sad, stout, middle-aged women.

The depth of her religious devotion, by consoling her, had probably saved her where another princess might have collapsed; but the effect was to give her a somewhat narrow, black-and-white view of morality. Fray Diego had been able to play upon her conscientious nature, taking advantage of it; it did not help that the kind of piety he inculcated was rigid in its application, and did not allow for human change or even for human peccadilloes. Those worldly lessons, so important for court life, most easily learnt insensibly by degrees, had been omitted from Catherine's restricted experience. Under extreme pressure, Catherine of Aragon had not broken; but she had also not learnt how to bend.

For the present the English court spent its time, as Queen Catherine wrote to her father, in 'continuous feasting'. The feeling of renewal on which Thomas More had commented with biblical ecstasy took a practical form in an endless series of tournaments, masques, and ceremonial rejoicing. Wolsey's gentleman-usher, George Cavendish, who wrote his master's life with the help of information from Wolsey himself, summed it up: 'our natural, young, lusty and courageous Prince and sovereign lord ... entering into the flower of pleasant youth, had taken upon him the regal sceptre and the imperial diadem of this fertile and plentiful realm of England ... called then the golden world, such grace of plenty reigned then within this Realm'.[17] In every tournament, King Henry as Sir Loyal Heart or Cœur Vaillant jousted under the colours of his lady, and his Queen. Every public opportunity was taken to blend their initials – H and K with the occasional C – from the mock castles erected for pageants down to the very love-knots on his armour.*

Among the list of jewels deposited in the Tower of London in 1520 were gold goblets, one chased upright with Henry and Catherine knit together about the border; a gold salt cellar ornamented with H and K,

---

* The armour at least has lasted (still to be seen in the Tower of London armoury). The decoration was done by Henry VIII's harness-gilder Paul van Vrelant in about 1514.

and enamelled red roses; a basin of gold, the border similarly garnished with red and white roses as well as H and K, 'given to the King by the Queen'. Hs and Ks were also chased on rich candlesticks for a chantry.[18]

Another present from Catherine to her husband consisted of a pair of 'goodly basins' engraved more formally with the arms of England and Spain. Everywhere Catherine's personal emblems of the pomegranate – not only referring to her upbringing in Granada, but also a fertility symbol – and the arrow-sheaf, jostled with the rampant Tudor roses. This was indeed an age when badges, emblems and personal devices generally were never casual. Windows decorated with arms, mottoes, heraldic displays in every corner of public and private life put forward their ceremonial message (even the royal close-stools had badges on them).[19] Throughout the early years of his reign the King of England demonstrated constantly by material means his pride in his union to the daughter of Spain, and his gallant devotion to his Queen who presided over his court.

Masques – including elaborate disguises which fooled of course absolutely no one – were a passion of the King; as such, they quickly became the passion of the whole court. Everyone joined in, especially the King's young male friends and the numerous jolly girls of fairly good family who had come to court hoping to secure a profitable marriage – and along the way enjoy a good time. One such girl was Bessie Blount, who first came to court in 1513 when she was very young. Bessie was a superb dancer and had a pretty singing voice: excelling everybody 'in all goodly pastimes'. Above all Bessie, with her high spirits and energies which matched the King's own, was fun. Even when she was middle-aged, a visitor described himself as having had 'very good cheer with her'. At Christmas 1514 she was one of the four 'Ladies of Savoy' in blue velvet and gold bonnets who danced opposite four 'Kings from Portugal' – the King was Bessie's partner.[20]

The Queen's role in all this was not so much to be fun – she was in fact heavily pregnant at this particular date – as to be astonished, full of wonder, definitely not recognize the King, suddenly recognize the King, and finally congratulate him with lavish praise. This Catherine of Aragon did very well. It came naturally to her. On this Christmas occasion the Queen was so delighted by the maskers' 'strange apparel' that she invited them to continue the dancing in her own chamber; after which she thanked the King fervently for the wonderful time she had had (as spectator) and kissed him. The next year a band of masked outlaws, all in green and headed apparently by Robin Hood himself, surprised the Queen and her ladies by bursting into her chamber. With unusual presence of mind under the circumstances, the ladies all elected to dance with the strangers instead of having them thrown out; imagine their sheer amazement, then, when the outlaws, unmasked, proved to be the King and his young esquires! Henry asked his wife if the ladies dared to venture into the wood with so many outlaws. Catherine replied – the authentic voice of a good wife – that 'if it pleased him then she was content'.

At the court of King Henry and Queen Catherine there was both a great deal of elaborate formality and ceremonial, and a great deal of chaos. The reforming Eltham Ordinances of 1525–6 indicate graphically the kind of abuses that crept in (as well as providing a clue to the constant need for herbs and perfumes to sweeten the air, as reflected in the royal accounts).[21] After dinner – which should take place from 10 am to 1 pm – and supper – from 4 to 7 pm – the food and drink left over should be given to beggars, instead of being abandoned for flies and vermin; nor were broken meats to be given to dogs. There were indeed to be 'no greyhounds, mastiffs, hounds or other dogs' in the royal palaces, other than a few small spaniels for the ladies (although the numerous instructions against dogs in bedchambers suggest these orders were generally disobeyed). The master cooks should not work naked but should be given clothes. There were to be no naked or vilely dressed scullions.

As for the royal suites, the grooms must get up at 6 am and purge the King's Privy Chamber of all filthiness, so that it can be clean and wholesome when he gets up; while the pages must get up at 7 am and the chambers of the King and Queen must be ready by 8 am. The entrance to the King's chamber must not be clogged up, must be clean, there must be no ale, water, broken meats and so forth left about, nor indeed a crowd of people, so that he can have 'large passage' to the Queen's chamber.

It was according to custom that the King and Queen lived in two parallel households with their own officers.[22] For this reason the presence of a queen was much welcomed after a gap of more than six years, since it substantially increased the amount of places available at court. There was a Dining Chamber where they dined in state; otherwise their respective suites of apartments were mirror images of each other. The layout varied from palace to palace, according to its size but in principle each had a Privy Chamber, a Bed Chamber beyond it, a Raying or Robing Chamber, a Breakfast Chamber, a Closet or Oratory, a Study or Library, and a Jakes or Stool Chamber. These suites were generally on the same floor, with the bedrooms as close together as possible. Queen Catherine's original household contained 160 people, only eight of whom were Spaniards, although these included two important figures from her past – Maria de Salinas whom the King liked (he called a ship after her) and Fray Diego (whom he did not, but who, thanks to Catherine's favour, survived in her service until 1515). Her first Lord Chamberlain was the venerable Earl of Ormonde, a Wars-of-the-Roses veteran, but in May 1512 his role was taken over by William Lord Mountjoy (who married Inez de Venegas, one of the Queen's remaining Spanish ladies). A sophisticated courtier who shared the Queen's own interests, a friend of Erasmus and a lover of humanist learning, Mountjoy would serve her faithfully.

It was a way of life which did not preclude cosiness – the King would bring visitors without warning to dine late in the Queen's chamber (his third large meal of the day) or suddenly decide he needed a meat meal himself, causing her to scurry like any wife proud of her housekeeping, determined not to fail a masculine need. The domesticity of Catherine's life with her ladies was the counterpoint to the Queen's more formal role presiding over tournaments as the official 'lady' of Sir Loyal Heart. A good deal of this free time was spent making and embroidering the King's shirts – often in black and white, the colours of Castile – another activity on which Catherine prided herself and which, like her admiration of his dancing and jousting, cannot have been displeasing to her husband. There was of course no privacy about such a way of life nor did the architecture of the time envisage it.[23] But the mere use of the word in the modern sense implies a concept which would have been quite alien to a sixteenth-century king or queen, let alone their subjects.*

Even the King's natural functions were not performed in private: the role of Groom of the Stool, responsible for the maintenance of the royal close-stool (as well as the King's linen and goods when he travelled) became in consequence one of the most important posts at court, because it involved the ultimate proximity to the King's person.[24] When King Henry VIII decided to make love to his wife, the curtains of his bed were drawn back, his night-robe (or dressing-gown) was sent for, and he was assisted to put it on, and an escort of pages and Grooms of the Bedchamber was summoned to accompany him with torches down the passage to the Queen's chamber (hopefully the passage was not in too filthy a state but one feels the language of the Eltham Ordinances reflects some distasteful royal experiences in this area). In no way was this an inhibiting process: it was the manner in which Henry's ancestors – kings – had behaved, and the way the kings who came after him would behave too.

The evidence indicates that King Henry took that conjugal route with great regularity. He was young and healthy: in the tradition of St Augustine Erasmus declared that the purpose of marriage was not to gratify 'lusts' but to procreate children[25] – but who was to prevent a man doing both at the same time? The King needed heirs; he thus had every reason to make love to his wife with assiduity. (As all monarchs were expected to do, if

---

* Most people were born, lived and died in what would now be considered a crowd: no one had any real privacy – except the occasional state prisoner who did not want it.

humanly possible, during this period; it was the exception, when the King did not 'go unto his wife', which was noted.) In Henry VIII's case, given his original affection for Catherine, and the fact that she was neither old, ugly nor charmless, it was a duty of state, but it was also an agreeable one.

When Thomas More had hailed the Queen at her coronation for the splendour of her ancestry, he had added, 'And she will be the mother of Kings as great as her ancestors'. At first sight, that prophecy seemed very likely to come true. It was a good omen that Catherine of Aragon herself came of notably fertile stock: her mother had produced five surviving children who lived to adulthood, her sister Queen Juana, for all her madness, had a family of six, and her youngest sister Maria of Portugal would give birth to no less than nine children. (To come of a copiously childbearing family was always a point in favour of a woman, since the female, not the male, was believed to determine these matters.) Queen Catherine did in fact conceive her first child with suitable speed after her wedding in June 1509. Four and a half months later the King was able to write to his father-in-law in Spain not only that the Queen was pregnant but 'the child in the womb was alive'.[26]

The 'quickening' of the baby at four months or thereabouts was always an important moment; up till then the midwives were never absolutely sure that they were dealing with pregnancy rather than some other condition. It was not that they did not understand the relevance of a woman's monthly cycle and its stopping; just that hopes of conception were always so desperately keen in high-born ladies that a great deal of unwarranted optimism was encouraged. The quickening of the baby made a hope an established fact.

This baby, a daughter, was stillborn at seven months on 31 January 1510. For some time Catherine did not tell King Ferdinand in Spain, and when she did, she begged him not to be angry with her since 'it has been the will of God'. (Her father, whose only child – a son – by Germaine de Foix had been born and died in March 1509, had been full of good advice for her pregnancy, including the need to desist from writing to him in her own hand.) In any case, by the time Catherine broke the news on 27 May, she was already about seven weeks pregnant, although, by the custom of the time, it was too soon to mention the fact.[27] By the end of September yards of purple velvet were being ordered for 'the King's Nursery'. And joy of joys, a son, named Henry for his father, his grandfather, and a long line stretching backwards of mediaeval royal Henries, was born on 1 January 1511.

The baby prince was christened on 5 January (the Archduchess Margaret was his godmother). It was a measure of his august position that despite being fed at the breast by a wetnurse, Prince Henry was immediately considered to need a carver, a cellarman and a baker and of course there were those who stepped forward immediately, volunteering – for reward – to occupy these onerous posts. At Candlemas, on 2 February, an elaborate tournament took place to celebrate this great event which had, as it seemed, ensured the Tudor succession.

The King as Cœur Loyal with his equally tall cousin Sir Edward Neville as Valiant Desire, William Earl of Devonshire as Bon Valoir and Sir Thomas Knyvet as Joyeux Penser represented the challengers: the Four Knights of the Joust. Chivalrous language surrounded the whole event: the answer to the challenge came in the name of 'Noble Renown, Queen of the realm named Cœur Noble', who has heard of 'the good and gracious fortune of the birth of a YOUNG PRINCE that it hath pleased God to send to her [Queen Catherine] and her husband; which is the most joy and comfort that might be to her and to the most renowned realm of England.'[28] Queen Catherine for her part sat surrounded by her ladies smiling graciously as the King (wearing her colours) thundered down the lists again and again, unhorsing again and again his opponents. At suitable moments she presented the prizes: the King as challenger got one on the second day.

Only a few weeks later, the royal accounts, which had been full of payments for scarlet and crimson velvet for the tournament, were paying merchants for black cloth for the burial of Prince Henry. High-born mourners, ten children of the royal chapel choir and 'nine score poor men' formed part of the torchlight procession of the customary night burial. Prince Henry had lived a mere fifty-two days. The cause of his death was never stated, but then in an age of such high infant mortality, this particular death might be a tragedy, but it was not of itself extraordinary. According to Hall's *Chronicle*, the Queen took it worse than the King: she 'like a natural woman, made much lamentation'; while he 'like a wise Prince, took this dolorous chance wondrous wisely'.[29]

No doubt the King did comfort his Queen, as Hall suggested, so that by 'his good persuasion ... her sorrow was mitigated'. Nevertheless things had not gone according to plan. The world was, momentarily, not quite so golden. It was fortunate for Henry VIII that foreign policy existed to distract him from domestic tragedy; and given that Henry's foreign policy was heavily entwined with that of Catherine's father, fortunate for Catherine that she too could share in the enterprise.

A few months after his accession – in August 1509 – the new King of England received a visit from the ambassador of the King of France. This ambassador, the Abbot of Fécamp (who happened to be extremely fat) got off to a bad start by announcing that he had come to confirm the peace requested of King Louis by King Henry. At this, King Henry turned to his counsellors and demanded: 'Who made this request? *I* ask peace of the King of France who daren't look at me, let alone make war!' And he stormed off to the tiltyard where the Abbot, waddling after him, was at first not even offered a seat.[30]

Henry VIII's natural belligerence towards France was something that struck all observers. It was the Venetian ambassador who drew the obvious corollary: he would shortly invade the country. This belligerence – or martial spirit as it was more flatteringly viewed – was neither surprising in a monarch nor unwelcome to Henry's subjects. King Louis's predecessor, Charles VIII of France, had declared in the 1490s that 'war was the business of kings'.[31] The cultivated Lord Mountjoy expatiating to his friend Erasmus on the wonders of the new reign deliberately contrasted the avarice of Henry VII with his son's heroic ambition: 'Our [new] King is not after gold, or gems, or precious metals, but virtue, glory, immortality.'[32]

War was after all the ultimate tournament, in which an energetic young man could win renown in the eyes of his royal peers, as well as his native court. The idea of a march on France, in theoretical pursuit of ancestral claims, was not even an anachronism: François I of France would lay claim to Italian territory in the name of his Visconti great-grandmother. The anonymous author of the first life of King Henry V – significantly composed between 1513 and 1514 – was simply exploiting these feelings when he suggested that Henry V went to France 'for the recovery of his just and rightful inheritance on that side of the sea'.[33]

King Henry's genuine enthusiasm for war fitted neatly with the more serpentine ambitions of the King of Aragon. The first mutual essay against France occurred in 1512, when some English troops commanded by Henry's cousin the Marquess of Dorset were despatched to Fuenterrabia in the south to aid the Spanish in their attack. Looked at practically, it was a disastrous affair; the English were laid low with fever, or alternatively complained at the lack of English beer; only Ferdinand, intent on making his boundaries safe by grabbing Navarre, benefited. None of this prevented King Henry from setting about the invasion of France himself the following year. By the end of 1513 he had in fact nearly emptied his once replete treasury on the needs of war.

One of the most important of his preparations was to designate the Queen as Regent of the kingdom in his absence. It was a natural step in a sense because before the rise of the King's super-servant, Thomas Wolsey, Catherine was Henry's closest confidante, the one person privy to all his plans, whom he could trust absolutely. But the appointment of the King's consort was by no means automatic in such a situation: so that it was also a tribute to Catherine's intelligence and diplomatic ability which had been well demonstrated in the first years of her husband's reign. Besides, her work was not expected to be purely formal: the King and his Council, wrote Hall, 'forgot not the old Pranks of the Scots, which is ever to invade England whenever the King is out.'[34]

Given that the King's war was undertaken in alliance with Spain, given his confidence in Catherine, how much did his expensive martial foreign policy owe to his wife's 'Spanish' influence? At first sight, the Queen's five-year seniority coupled with her devotion to her father would seem to indicate that she had exercised a considerable sway in directing her husband towards Spain. King Ferdinand would certainly have had it so. In August 1510 he dictated exactly the course his daughter should follow to help his interest. But this view of the Queen's paramount influence is to reckon without two important arguments pointing the other way.

The first concerns Catherine's near fanatical devotion to her husband: duty to him, enjoined by God, came before her duty to her father – and that order of priorities too was enjoined by God. She was indeed so careful in her behaviour in this respect that, by December 1514, the Spanish ambassador to the Provincial of Aragon was complaining that the Queen of England needed some discreet and intelligent person to point her in the right direction – towards the interests of Aragon: 'The Queen has the best intentions, but there is no one to show her how she may become serviceable to her father.' Fray Diego was criticized for telling her (although it should surely be held in his favour) 'that she ought to forget Spain and everything Spanish, in order to gain the love of the King of England and of the English.' Queen Catherine, encouraged also by Maria de Salinas, was said to be so set on this pro-English course that nothing would make her change it.[35]

The second argument against Queen Catherine being the prime mover in all this concerns the character of King Henry himself, a young lion increasingly confident of his own strength. Time would show that the most successful campaigns to influence the King in a particular direction only took place when the King wanted to go in that direction all along. His boyish charm, his respect for his father-in-law, his love for his wife, only concealed the development of his will.

There were some pointers towards this. Before the King went to war, he directed the first 'dynastic' execution of the reign, that of the Yorkist claimant, the Earl of Suffolk: 'your traitor, Edmund de la Pole' as he had once been described to Henry VII. The 'traitor' had languished in the Tower since 1506. His estates were distributed to that upright character Margaret Pole, by now a widow, who was created Countess of Salisbury. In February the next year the Suffolk title was given to Henry's companion in the joust, born plain Charles Brandon – to indicate that the life of the

Yorkist Suffolk title was over. King Henry VIII, no less than King Henry VII, intended to be master in his Tudor house.

In the same way war against France in 1513 suited the King's image of himself, of how a king should behave (and incidentally showed those aged European monarchs that he was a force to be reckoned with). The machinations of King Ferdinand in the south, wanting a pincer movement against France, and the prayers of Queen Catherine, happened to coincide with his own deepest inclinations.

Once the King departed for France in June 1513, the Queen's prayers were chiefly concentrated on his personal safety rather than victory. Thomas Wolsey, currently the King's almoner, made an excellent conduit for her anxious messages since the King himself, as has been noted, found life too short (and exciting) to write letters. She told Wolsey that she would worry all the time about the King's health: there could be no rest for her while the King was so near 'our enemies'. The King led his 'army royall' in the siege of Thérouanne and Tournai (both of which were captured) and the Battle of the Spurs (where the French fled). As a matter of fact he was never anywhere near the front of the action – unlike François I and Charles V, and indeed his own father, Henry VIII never actually fought – but reading the Queen's letters is to get rather a different picture.[36]

On 13 August, she was once again desperately anxious because her husband was so close to the siege of Thérouanne: 'without his health and life' being secured, she wrote, 'I can see no manner of good thing' coming out of the siege. After the Battle of the Spurs, she was at least reassured that the presence of the wise old Emperor Maximilian would restrain her madcap boy: 'I think with the company of the Emperor and with his good counsel, his Grace [Henry] shall not adventure himself so much as I was afeared of before'.

In the meantime, when not worrying about her husband (did he have enough clean linen in France?), the Queen was playing her part as Regent with energy and determination. The Scots – led by the King's brother-in-law James IV – did indeed take the opportunity to indulge in 'the old Pranks' and attacked England's northern border.

In mid-August the Queen wrote to the King: 'I am horrible [*sic*] busy with making standards, banners and badges'. That was a traditional female occupation. But the Queen as her mother's daughter, one who had been brought up around battlefields in her first youth, also put on the mantle of the warrior queen. Peter Martyr, her old professor, heard that 'in imitation of her mother Isabella' Catherine had made a splendid oration to the English captains, told them to be ready to defend their territory, 'that the Lord smiled upon those who stood in defence of their own, and they should remember that English courage excelled that of all other nations.'[37]

The men were said to be 'fired by these words' – which were incidentally delivered in English. To her native Spanish, fluent Latin, and French which had become expert in the years when it was the only language she could speak at the English court, Catherine had now added good or goodish English (although we must naturally picture her speaking it with a strong Spanish accent).

The Queen had intended to go north herself but before she could set out, news was received of the colossal Scottish defeat at Flodden on 9 September. A poem, 'Scotish Feilde', written in celebration of the victory, referred to the hunger and thirst of the English army beneath 'clouds cast up cheerily like castles full high', the beautiful terror of the trumpets, and finally the mass of Scottish dead: 'breathless they lie gaping against the moon.' The flower of the Scottish nobility were among those lying there – and the King of Scots too was killed. His body, so slashed and serrated that it was only recognizable by his coat and cross, was not however left to lie beneath the moon. It was brought down to England, where the Queen at least, in an excess of fervour, would have liked to despatch the body within the coat to Henry VIII in France, as a trophy of war 'but our Englishmen's hearts would not suffer it.' In the event the cross – weighing nineteen ounces, encasing a fragment of the Holy Cross with a bejewelled chain – went to the royal treasure and the Queen sent the King of Scots' coat without the body to France. 'In this your Grace shall see how I can keep my promise', she wrote, 'sending you for your banners a King's coat.'[38]*

The Queen's patriotic pride in her achievement shines through her letters to Wolsey as well as to the King. She was however careful to give credit where it was really due: 'This matter is so marvellous', she wrote to Wolsey, 'that it seemeth to be of God's doing alone.' Then she could not resist adding: 'I trust the King shall remember to thank him for it' (as she herself had done, immediately on hearing the news). Fortunately the King did: a tent of cloth of gold was set up, a sung Mass took place, with a *Te Deum* and a sermon from the Bishop of Rochester, the 'learned and virtuous' John Fisher, who had been chaplain to the King's grandmother Margaret Beaufort. Catherine hammered home the same message to the King personally: referring to 'the great Victory that our Lord hath sent your subjects in your absence', she begged him personally to remember to thank God. 'And I am sure your Grace forgetteth not to do this, which shall be cause to send you many more such great victories, as I trust he shall do.'[40]

The victory of Flodden was in fact a major military event: the Scottish

---

* The emphasis on the King's bloodstained coat – with or without the body inside it – was not as ghoulish as it may seem; this was an age when the identity of even the most celebrated personage was not easy to establish. The King's coat was valuable evidence that it was he, not some senior Scots noble, who had been killed.[39]

threat was removed for a generation by the slaughter of its leaders; the eighteen-month-old James Prince of Scotland who now nominally succeeded to the throne was the nephew of the English King, the Regent was his sister. Compared to this, the Battle of the Spurs won over the French, although part of an expensive campaign, was a purely temporary check, forgotten the next year when the King turned his foreign policy on its head.

Nevertheless Queen Catherine greeted the Battle of the Spurs as though the very reverse was true. 'The victory hath been so great that I think none such hath been seen before', she wrote on hearing the news. All England was rejoicing; and no one rejoiced more than its Queen. As a contemporary *chanson* had it, 'England be glad Thy King hath played his part [against the French]'. There was a second-hand story that Catherine was heard exulting over 'her' Flodden victory, to the detriment of her husband's achievements. 'It was no great thing for one armed man to take another', she was supposed to have remarked, 'but she [Catherine] was sending three captured by a woman; if her husband sent her a captive Duke, she would send him a prisoner King.'[41] This kind of boasting was not only completely out of character, but also contradicted by the tone of the Queen's own letters. If anything, her praise of the King's achievements – a victory so great 'none such hath been seen before' – was almost too fulsome (although Henry VIII may not have found it so) just as Queen Isabella regularly praised King Ferdinand to the skies in public, even for achievements in which she herself could justly have taken pride.

You could perhaps accuse Queen Catherine of a loving wifely bossiness over her husband's religious observance. That did not seem of any great significance at the time. It was after all part of her general quasi-maternal concern for all aspects of his welfare both material and spiritual: from clean linen to a spotless conscience. There is no reason to believe that the King was anything but delighted in 1513 by this feminine devotion which was constantly lavished upon him. And when they were reunited – two victors – it was 'such a loving meeting that every creature rejoiced'.[42]

The next year King Henry, furious at King Ferdinand's cynical self-interest in the recent war, executed a complete diplomatic volte-face. He began to negotiate for the union of his sister Princess Mary to the recently widowed King Louis XII of France. Their proxy marriage took place on 13 August 1514 and Catherine was among those who travelled to Dover in October to see 'the French Queen', as Princess Mary was now known, off on her journey to her new country. Since Princess Mary had been formally betrothed to Charles of Austria for the last six years (although they had never actually met) it was hardly surprising that the Habsburg representatives spoke 'shamefully' of the marriage of 'so fair a lady' and 'so feeble, old and pocky a man.'[43] The Princess was eighteen, her bridegroom fifty-two. True enough, King Louis was in terrible health, but having only two daughters, he was in need of a male heir.

The leader of 'the French Queen's' escort abroad was the thirty-year-old Charles Brandon who had been created Duke of Suffolk the previous spring. Suffolk was one of those big, handsome, straightforward English-men, apparently irresistible to women, whose deepest loyalty was never-theless to his master and friend Henry VIII. In the jousts, they were said to bear themselves 'like Hector and Achilles'. Not particularly intelligent or even subtle – unlike the King – Duke Charles, far more than King Hal, deserved the epithet of 'bluff', conveying as it does both geniality and decency. This bluffness however did not inhibit Suffolk's meteoric rise, aided not only by the King, but also by a series of dubious marital manoeuvres in which Suffolk at least always ended up financially bettered.[44] For example he had been contracted to marry one lady, who became pregnant as a result, jilted her for her aunt twenty years her senior to obtain a large inheritance, then had this marriage invalidated on the grounds of the relationship between aunt and niece, and while keeping the inheritance, went back and married the first lady . . .

One of the women who found Suffolk irresistible was evidently Princess Mary. As she sobbed 'by the waterside' before her departure from Dover, she seems to have extracted some kind of promise from her brother, that if she carried out this distasteful duty of the French marriage to the 'pocky' King Louis for reasons of state, she would be allowed to choose her own bridegroom on his death. The image of Suffolk, glorious in his prime, wielding his great lance with its long wooden shaft again and again in the French wedding tournament, is unforgettable. He was watched by the young Queen, sitting bolt upright, while her husband was too feeble to do more than lie on a day-bed at her side, having attempted, probably without success, to consummate his marriage the night before. When King Louis died on 1 January 1515, the 'French Queen' called in her promise of a more satisfying future. That is, in a flurry of tears, she succeeded in per-suading Suffolk to anticipate any future marriage ceremony and then announced – probably untruthfully – that she was pregnant. To his furious royal master Suffolk was left ruefully explaining: 'you never saw a woman so weep'.[45]

King Henry's anger was not unjustified by contemporary standards. One may discount his promise 'by the waterside' as having been made under emotional duress – rather as Suffolk declared himself obliged to make love to the weeping Mary. His sister's hand in marriage had secured a French alliance; she was now free again, the most beautiful princess in Europe, and her disposal might shortly bring him further advantage. (It was true that the new King of France, François I, might also claim to handle the second marriage of a Queen Dowager of France: at least the secret Suffolk match had put an end to that.) It was however the method by which the new couple, returned to England, finally secured the King's forgiveness that was the most interesting aspect of the whole affair from the point of view of Henry VIII's own character. Thanks to the negotiations of Wolsey, the King received the most abject apologies from both his friend and his sister, making it clear that they had not intended to set up their own will against his – and they also paid a considerable price in the shape of Mary's jewels and plate. On that basis, in view of the King's deep affection for them both, their satisfactory self-abasement, and his own financial advantage, the pair were allowed back to court in the summer.

The French marriage had not been of itself a diplomatic reverse for Queen Catherine: she had never argued publicly in favour of the pro-Aragonese alliance, merely acted as the obvious conduit for negotiations between her husband and father. In Thomas Wolsey, the King had now found a servant whose habits of industry matched his own pattern of work – energetic commands, restless execution – in a magical way; one furthermore who, from his origins as a butcher's son in Ipswich, owed everything to royal advancement, a man with an intellect and judgement that few could rival. But Wolsey did not at this point dictate policy and he did have – for good practical reasons – an excellent relationship with the Queen. Nor did the French alliance mark the end of Catherine's political closeness to the King, who continued demonstrably to value both her loyalty (always a favourite quality of his) and her good sense. It was more that their deepest feelings no longer coincided so exactly in every way; for her, the episode represented a very slight reversal of Fortune's Wheel rather than anything more dramatic.

In other ways their relationship showed every sign of prospering in terms of a happy royal marriage. It was true that the expected heir to replace the baby who died, Prince Henry, had not materialized. Yet the Queen's fertility was not in question: she conceived again in the spring of 1513, just before the King went to France, although she lost the baby in October. (Since there were no preparations for her lying-in, this seems to have been a miscarriage rather than a stillbirth.) In early February 1515, as she told her father, she did give birth to a son at full term: a 'prince which lived not longer after'. Nevertheless it is important not to judge this tale of gynaecological woe by modern standards, let alone with any prejudicial knowledge of the end of the story. It has been estimated that in aristocratic families in England only two out of every five births resulted in living children.[46] With such high infant mortality, the ability to conceive was the important thing. So far, in six years, the Queen had conceived at least four times: she was not yet thirty. And a few months after the death of the second baby prince – in May 1515 – the Queen duly became pregnant again.

Even if the King's boyish passion for the Queen had inevitably given way to something more like respectful fondness, it was not as if his ebullient affections were otherwise engaged. In the first decade of his reign, Henry VIII showed himself to be uxorious rather than otherwise. He certainly had no regular mistress. The various rumours of romantic dalliance at this period – not even too many of them – all seem to involve flirtatious gallantries in the Renaissance fashion: relationships which followed an ardent, high-flown but not necessarily sexual pattern.

Playful incidents were reported concerning the King at the court in Flanders in 1513. The twenty-two-year-old King – a man on the continent without his wife – played his glitteron-pipe and his lute-pipe, and showed his skill in dancing to the Archduchess Margaret. The following August a young girl of the country, Etiennette La Baume, sent a letter to the King, along with a bird, and 'some roots of great value belonging to this country'. She reminded him of their encounter at Lille: 'you named me your page' and 'you spoke many pretty things [*beaucoup de belles choses*] to me'. She went on: 'When we parted at Tournai, you told me, when I married, to let you know and it should be worth to me 10,000 crowns.' It has now pleased her father to marry her off, and she is hoping for the present ... (The records show that Etiennette La Baume married one Jean Neufchatel, seigneur de Marnay, in October 1514: they do not record whether King Henry came up with the money.)[47]

In England earlier there had been an episode in 1510 concerning the two attractive married sisters of the Duke of Buckingham, Lady Elizabeth Fitzwalter and Lady Anne Hastings, both of whom were, thanks to their high rank, ladies-in-waiting to the Queen. It is not clear exactly what took place. There was a rumour that the King wished to make advances to Lady Anne. At all events William Compton, current holder of that important and intimate office, Groom of the Stool, was involved. Possibly he was acting as a go-between for his master; or he may have been another potential lover of Lady Anne. Then Lady Elizabeth Fitzwalter seems to have made trouble for her sister with their mistress, the Queen.[48]

The King's crossness at the behaviour of the Queen's ladies 'insidiously spying out every unwatched moment' may indicate that nothing very much had happened by the time Lord Hastings removed Lady Anne from court. The King then insisted on the Fitzwalters being dismissed. Lastly the Duke of Buckingham, in a proud fury at having his sisters' names bandied about by someone of low birth like Compton, quarrelled with the Groom, was reprimanded by the King, and then sulkily left the palace himself. When the Spanish ambassador, primed with gossip from the Spanish court, tried to lecture Fray Diego on the correct behaviour for the Queen under such circumstances, he was smartly told by the friar that he had got the whole thing wrong. And so perhaps the ambassador had.

At all events, it was a storm in a teacup and as such (with the exception of Buckingham's hauteur) quickly forgotten. It may also be significant that the Queen was pregnant (with the ill-fated first son, Prince Henry) at the time of all this: the pattern of King Henry's 'gallantries', and later of his mistresses, does seem to show that in a thoroughly masculine manner he regarded the pregnancies of his wives – not only Catherine – as a positive justification for seeking consolation elsewhere.*

In sexual matters Henry VIII was certainly quite unlike his grandfather Edward IV, of whom it was said that 'no woman was there anywhere ... but he would importunely pursue his appetite and have her'.[49] He was also quite unlike most monarchs of his time. (The amours of the new King of France were already a byword.) At the beginning of 1516, Catherine was looking forward to the birth of her child, expected in February. Surely this would be the healthy prince who would complete that married happiness, begun so auspiciously at the wish of the young King himself. Against her seven years of hardship in the power of Henry VII, she could balance almost seven years in which good fortune had largely predominated, enthroned at the side of Henry VIII as his honoured consort.

* Sex during pregnancy was in principle frowned upon as being dangerous to the health of mother and baby, although the principle was not always adhered to.

Chapter 4

EXAMPLE OF

WEDLOCK

What family of citizens offers so clear an example of
strict and harmonious wedlock? Where could one find a
wife more keen to equal her admirable spouse?

Erasmus on the English court, 1520

On 18 February 1516, at four o'clock in the morning, Queen Catherine gave birth to a daughter who was named Mary. The labour had been long and hard, although the Queen endeavoured to protect herself against the pangs of childbirth by clutching a holy relic – a girdle – of her patron saint. Whatever the sufferings of the mother, the baby herself was healthy, even robust. Two days later, this new princess, Mary Tudor, was first christened and then, as was the custom, immediately confirmed; Cardinal Wolsey was among her godparents at the font and Margaret Countess of Salisbury 'her godmother at the Bishop' as the second ceremony of confirmation was termed.[1]

As at every birth to every royal lady at this time, 'a prince' had been confidently expected. The arrival of a princess meant that celebrations were suitably scaled down. For example, messengers who brought the – modified – good news to the University of Cambridge received a mere 28s 6d from the proctors, plus some muscadine wine; whereas the messengers who had broken the news of the birth of the short-lived baby prince in 1511 had received both more money – 40s – and more wine. Higher up the social scale, Giustinian, the Venetian ambassador, deliberately took his time in presenting his congratulations to the King (although he would have hastened to do so, he admitted, had the baby been a boy). And when he finally did so, the ambassador made an observation which had the merit of truth perhaps, if not of tact: 'your serenity would have experienced greater satisfaction had it [the baby] been a son.'[2]

But King Henry was in a buoyant mood. 'Sons will follow', he told Giustinian, pointing out that 'the Queen and I are both young'. It was a point of view expressed by a contemporary ballad on the subject of 'this young lady fair':

> And send her shortly a brother
> To be England's right heir.

The official court attitude of optimism for the future was expressed by William Lord Mountjoy, away in France, in his congratulatory letter. He hoped that the birth of the princess would make the King 'as glad a father as ever was ... and after this good beginning to send you many fair children to your grace's comfort and [that of] all your true subjects'.[3]

The King was glad and he was right to be so. There was indeed good cause for rejoicing in the present at the birth of a daughter, leaving aside his cheerful prediction (not an unreasonable one under the circumstances) that sons would follow. Although he continued to hope for a Prince of Wales, King Henry undoubtedly had a new and useful card to play in the universal game of European matrimonial alliances. Recently his resources in this respect had been irritatingly impoverished. His sister, Mary, the former French Queen, now the wife of the Duke of Suffolk, was clearly no longer at his disposal: in fact she gave birth to a son a few weeks after Queen Catherine, to whom the King, standing godfather, gave the name Henry.

The situation regarding the King's elder sister, Queen Margaret of Scotland, was hardly more promising. She had secretly married a Scottish noble, Archibald Douglas Earl of Angus, a year after the death of James IV at Flodden, either for love – he was young and extremely good-looking – or for Douglas's support against the French-backed John Stewart Duke of Albany. The political gambit at least did not work. The Duke of Albany, as the first cousin of the late King, was the next heir to the Scottish throne after James IV's two sons although he had been brought up in France and regarded himself as a subject of the French King; he was a man of great military reputation gained in the Italian campaigns of the French army. Now he secured both the regency of the kingdom and the governorship of the boys from their mother; the younger son subsequently died. Queen Margaret fled to Northumberland (where she

---

* Despite her remarriage, the King's sister continued to be termed 'the French Queen' at the English court, in recognition of her royal status, superior to that of her second husband; but this would be a somewhat confusing term in this narrative, which includes an actual Queen of France. It is equally confusing to term her Mary Tudor in view of the birth of another Mary Tudor, the King's daughter; therefore, for clarity's sake, she will henceforward be termed Mary Duchess of Suffolk although the title was never used in her lifetime.

gave birth to a daughter by Angus, styled Lady Margaret Douglas, in October 1515). In the spring of 1516, Queen Margaret came south and joined the English court at Greenwich in May. So that at the moment of Princess Mary's birth, King Henry's two sisters, where once they had been consorts to influential monarchs, were neither marriageable, nor in any kind of helpful position of power.

We should therefore take care to view Queen Catherine's successful delivery of a healthy princess as it was seen then – including by King Henry himself: not as some kind of failure, but as a piece of good, or at least promising news, from which important diplomatic consequences might flow. Besides, the map of Europe had been radically altered shortly before the birth of Mary. In this new world, King Henry needed every kind of diplomatic asset – a quiverful of princesses could have been employed – if he was to hold his own on behalf of England.

The previous summer – by a treaty of 17 July 1515 – the Duke of Milan, the Pope, King Ferdinand of Aragon and the Emperor Maximilian had joined in a league for the defence of Italy against the predatory claims of the new French King, François I. At the battle of Marignano which followed in September, where the French were victorious over the Swiss, King François fought with great personal bravery; he refused to be daunted although he was struck three times by pikes. King Henry, who had not after all fought personally in France two years earlier for all his wife's fears – and plaudits – was said to be sick with disgust at the news.[4] Certainly the presence of an aggressive young monarch on the French throne – François I was born in 1494 and was thus almost exactly Henry VIII's contemporary – meant rivalry at a personal level. In the public arena, there was a need perhaps to rethink English foreign policy, if England was not to be isolated. But it was the death of Ferdinand of Aragon, on 23 January 1516, which tilted the European balance of power in a new direction.

Queen Catherine, who had written so bravely concerning the tragedies of her babies in the past that it was 'the will of God', never had the opportunity to tell her father that God had at last sent her a healthy child, albeit a daughter. In fact the very news of King Ferdinand's death was kept from the Queen – and thus from public announcement at the English court – in case her grief start her labour prematurely. Although Catherine had not set eyes on her father for over fifteen years – since she left Spain – that fact was not of itself particularly significant by sixteenth-century royal standards; the important point was the primal place he had occupied in her affections.

King Ferdinand had never been a rival to King Henry as the central object of her love. But in considering Catherine's deep feelings for her father, it is worth bearing in mind that these feelings had been those of a childless woman – emotionally frozen in time as a dutiful daughter. Now, symbolically enough, the birth of her own child occurred within a few weeks of her father's death. Henceforward it was the young Princess Mary who would provide the main focus for her mother's hopes and familial loyalties; while Catherine's sense of reverence for the Spanish royal house from which she had sprung transferred to her nephew, Charles of Austria.

This sixteen-year-old youth – whom Queen Catherine had never met – was, however, very far from being the Castilian or Aragonese prince of her imagination, as perhaps she remembered her glamorous brother, the Infante Juan. For one thing, the new King Charles had been educated in Burgundy, largely in the care of its Regent, his aunt, the Archduchess Margaret, and in youth spoke French rather than Spanish. It was understandable that King Ferdinand died in bitterness at the prospect of the dominions for which he had fought so long and hard being inherited by alien descendants. Yet Spanish or not, the train of Charles's inheritance rolled relentlessly onwards. King Ferdinand's death meant that Spain was once more ruled by a single monarchy – provided, that is, that Charles could establish his rights there.

The Treaty of Noyon of 13 August 1516 was, from England's point of view, a cruel indication of the changes in Europe following the death of Ferdinand. For the time being at least, it joined together the King of France and the new King of Aragon and Castile: the one was to be left free to pursue his interests in Italy, the other to consolidate his position in Spain. Furthermore, the aging Emperor Maximilian, Charles's surviving grandfather, also joined in the league. This took Henry VIII further by surprise, who had imagined that the Emperor was on the point of joining him in some kind of anti-French alliance. By the Peace of Cambrai in the following March 1517, the Emperor, Charles and the King of France agreed publicly to go to each other's assistance if attacked, as well as joining in a shared crusade. Further secret agreements presaged the carving-up of Italy.

King Henry was anxious that England should not be left out of this accord. It was in this way that the mere existence of Princess Mary offered possibilities of treaty and alliance.

In other ways, these were years of satisfaction for Queen Catherine. It was true that ambassadors no longer commented on her beauty – rather the reverse. One report went so far as to call her more 'ugly than otherwise'. 'Ugly' was certainly an exaggeration: her bright complexion continued to receive tributes. Another report, written much later, describing Catherine as 'if not handsome, certainly not ugly', was probably nearer the truth. Nevertheless the Queen's numerous pregnancies had not helped her figure, always on the plump side. By now she was unquestionably quite fat, a stout little woman on the wrong side of thirty, compared to her glamorous, athletic husband, six years her junior. This age gap between them, unmentioned at the time of their marriage, began to attract attention: in 1519 Catherine was described as the 'King's old deformed wife' (presumably an allusion to her short, excessively dumpy figure); while Henry himself was called 'young and handsome'.[5]

Queens however were not expected to be great beauties, and as with kings, it was more often a subject of surprised comment if they were (Henry's sister, the lovely, fair-haired, oval-faced Mary comes to mind) than if they were not. Across the Channel, the French Queen Claude, tiny like Catherine, but in this case actually deformed – since birth she had walked with a pronounced limp – was considered to be an excellent match for the new King François, since she was the elder daughter of the previous King Louis XII and his wife, the heiress of Brittany. Queens were expected to provide connections and a rich dowry on marriage, and carry out the functions of consort with requisite dignity thereafter.

All this Queen Catherine did and more. Her dignity was imperturbable. Even at the height of her troubles in the future she would be praised for having 'always a smile on her countenance'. At this date the particular flavour she imparted to the court, not only by her graciousness but by her learning and piety, excited general admiration. It was Erasmus who hailed the court of Henry VIII in 1519 as 'a model of Christian society, so rich in men of the highest attainments that any university might envy it'.[6] The Queen's interest in and patronage of the learning termed humanism was an important part of the process which formed this society, as the books dedicated to her indicated.

Basically humanism involved the use of the recently rediscovered classical texts to enhance religious appreciation, rather than obliterate faith. It proved of natural interest to both the King and the Queen since each was endowed with an excellent classical education, and also, in their different ways, a sincere desire to deepen their own spiritual understanding. Humanistic interests became the hallmark of many courtiers and scholars surrounding the royal couple, including Erasmus (who addressed more letters to Catherine than to any other woman), Thomas Linacre and More (by 1518 More acted in effect as the King's secretary and has been described as the King's 'tame Humanist').[7] The Queen's chamberlain, Lord Mountjoy, had been the pupil of Erasmus, and maintained contact with him ever since. The Queen's physician, Dr Fernando Vittoria, was another humanist.

On 31 October 1517 a priest named Martin Luther, interested in reforming and purifying his church, nailed a list of ninety-five theses to the church
door at Wittenberg: his indignation at the corrupt manner in which the
church sold 'indulgences' – the forgiveness of sins in return for money –
could no longer be contained. He turned out to have put a match to dry
timber. While no one could have foreseen exactly where this particular
forest fire would spread, let alone its extent, it burnt briskly from the first.

In London the Queen discussed the matters raised by Luther with her
confessor from the Spanish Observant friary at Greenwich, Fray Alfonso
de Villa Sancta, who was also a close friend of Thomas More.[8] Villa Sancta
was a good source of enlightenment: he would write various works such as
Problema Indulgentiarum arguing against Luther's position and *De Libero
Arbitrio, adversus Melanchthonem*, printed in 1523, which was dedicated
to the Queen (Philip Melanchthon, professor of Greek at Wittenberg,
supported Luther). Villa Sancta bestowed upon Queen Catherine the title
of *Fidei Defensor* more usually associated with her husband; Henry VIII
received it from the Pope in October 1521, for a work in opposition to
Luther known as *The Defence of the Seven Sacraments*.

Erasmus indeed rated Queen Catherine's scholarship more highly than
that of King Henry: her patronage, he believed, was more consistent. It is
true that Queen Catherine was more unrelievedly serious-minded. King
Henry in his twenties continued to enjoy every aspect of life, from the
dance to the learned argument. The Queen in her thirties no longer
danced – there are many references to her withdrawing early – although
she played her official part fully at state banquets and the reception of
ambassadors. She did after all understand how great occasions should be
managed, none better; one 'great entertainment' the Queen made in the
summer of 1519 at Havering-atte-Bower in Essex, for the King and the
French hostages of the recent war, was described as the 'liberallest' ever
seen and delighted Henry.[9] Nevertheless Catherine was able to maintain
the steady interest in scholars and scholarship that she had inherited from
Queen Isabella with fewer distractions. Altogether, indeed, she had fewer
frivolous interests than Henry. It was another instance of the age gap
between them, if less immediately obvious than the physical difference.

The episode of the so-called 'minions' in 1519 illustrates the fact that
there were really two circles at the court of Henry VIII in its first fifteen-
odd years. There were the fashionable Francophiles, people who were 'all
French in eating, drinking, and apparel, yea, and in French vices and brags'
(in this circle a French-educated English girl might be admired for her
particular graces, as we shall discover). The 'minions' were among these
Francophiles. They consisted of the young bloods of the King's Privy
Chamber, men his age or younger, including Nicholas Carew and Francis

Bryan, who in the opinion of many were too familiar with him. In 1519 they had paid a visit to the French court, following a French diplomatic mission to London. There they had been sufficiently carried away by the French capital to ride through its streets in disguise, throwing eggs, stones and 'other foolish trifles' at the innocent bystanders. They had gone too far. When they returned to dull old London, Cardinal Wolsey seized the opportunity to reform the King's household. The young bloods were reproved and 'four sad [that is sober] and ancient knights' including Sir William Kingston put into the Privy Chamber.[10] Then there was the staider world of the scholars and theologians with connections to Burgundy and the lands of the Empire. The King straddled both these worlds; the Spanish-born Queen, with little in common with the merry ways of the minions, and her intellectual humanist leanings, belonged to the latter.

This early Tudor court was, however, not only noted for men of 'the highest attainments' in Erasmus' phrase: the Queen's genuine taste for learning meant that intellectual interests for women in general became fashionable – at least in the highest ranks of society – as had happened under Queen Isabella in Spain. It was Queen Catherine who encouraged her sister-in-law Mary Duchess of Suffolk to take up the study of Latin again. Margaret Countess of Salisbury, who was appointed Governess of the household of Princess Mary (an important post in terms of court protocol, a significant tribute to her Plantagenet blood), requested a translation of Erasmus' *De Immensa Misericordia Dei* from Gentian Hervet.[11]

The spectacle of a royal lady interesting herself in scholarship was not a novelty in England. In one sense Queen Catherine was merely continuing the tradition of her husband's grandmother, Margaret Beaufort Countess of Richmond: as one patroness died, another took her place. For, encouraged by her chaplain John Fisher, the *grande dame* of the house of Lancaster had continued to make benefactions to universities to the very last. St John's College, Cambridge, for example, was only set up, with the aid of revenues granted by her, in 1511, two years after her death, and opened in 1516. This last-minute timing was unfortunate from the college's point of view: Henry VIII showed himself no sentimentalist where his grandmother's final wishes were concerned, and refused to allow the college any revenues not specifically granted in her will. But Queen Catherine proved more helpful: the college recorded that she 'pardoned us of £50 due unto her' for the transaction which conveyed the lordship of Riddiwell to them.[12]

Catherine in her turn was associated with Queens' College, Cambridge, whose President Robert Beckensaw became her almoner in 1510, and as such was in constant attendance on her. In consequence the Queen has been hailed as 'an active protectress' of the college's rights and studies. Cambridge was conveniently situated en route to the Queen's favourite place of pilgrimage at Walsingham in Norfolk; she may have visited the city in 1518 and 1519, and she certainly stayed there for three days in 1521. The college accounts show expenses occurred in such diverse activities apparently inseparable from a royal visit as cleaning up the streets, rewarding the messenger who brought news of the Queen's arrival and procuring fish for a banquet.[13]

Nor was the Queen indifferent to the claims of another place. When the Bishop of Lincoln reported at court what was going on at Wolsey's new Cardinal College at Oxford (the future Christ Church) in January 1525, he was able to tell the Queen that she was to be 'a participant [beneficiary] of the prayers of the college'. Queen Catherine expressed herself as most grateful to the Cardinal and 'marvellously glad' to hear about the prayers. She visited Oxford in the company of Wolsey, attended the shrine of the eighth-century abbess, St Frideswide, patron of the city, and dined at Merton. When she visited Corpus Christi, still in Wolsey's company, she was received as if she was 'Juno or Minerva' and in return gave them a gift of plate, the so-called Pomegranate Cup.[14]

If in one sense this patronage looked back to the late mediaeval tradition of Margaret Beaufort, in another sense it was very much of its own time: the brief, glittering period of the humanist court in England, whose short time span should not consign it to obscurity. There was however a significant difference in the personal attainments of the two royal ladies. Margaret Beaufort, for all her large library of English and French books, was no classical scholar: in fact she had never been taught Latin, as Fisher observed in a sermon after her death, and could only read the Latin headings in her prayer book.[15]

When Margaret Beaufort interested herself in the question of education – in terms of learning – she was thinking of young gentlemen. Young ladies in her care were taught the domestic arts: Margaret Beaufort, the mother of an only son, never had any practical reason to interest herself in the higher education of girls. But Queen Catherine, as we shall see, would shortly set about the important task of educating a royal daughter, as her mother the great Isabella had done before her. It was an important distinction.

Like her interest in learning, the Queen's piety increased with the years, as happens to most people of a natively religious temperament. Time – and sorrow – would bring about a religious routine which might by many standards be considered excessively severe: the Queen, 'a mirror of goodness', would rise at midnight to be present at the Matins of the friars wearing 'an ordinary mantle', spend most of the morning in her chapel, kneel without cushions, wear the habit of St Francis under her robes ...

but the evidence is that this punishing schedule belongs to a later period.[16]*

The Queen who was for so many years the cheerful consort and 'bed-fellow' of Henry VIII had no need of such austere practices, brought on by desolation. In the contented years of their marriage, Queen Catherine pleased her husband rather than otherwise by her religious observance, whether it was her public love of shrines and pilgrimages, or her private devotions. Henry VIII was no exception to the general rule that a pleasure-loving man is happy to have a devout wife – provided she does not interfere with his pleasures. Like his subjects, therefore, King Henry respected his Queen for her admirable character, for being 'as religious and virtuous as words can express' as the Venetian ambassador put it.[18] To display piety was after all another part of a queen's duty. Ten years earlier Fuensalida had commented on Catherine's natural goodness – then considered a problem because she would not stand up for herself to Fray Diego but now a wonderful enhancement of her role as Queen, quite as relevant to the position she occupied, if not more so, than the question of her fading looks.

With Queen Catherine's goodness went inevitably the question of her charity: the two were inseparable to the mind of the time. Every pious precept of the church enjoined charitable works, every will mentioned charity to the poor. To Catherine of Aragon piety, like charity, came naturally, and it brought her as time would show much popularity among the recipients. Once again this was the ideal of the good Queen – one who gave freely and often to the poor, whose charity was 'not small'.[19]

Then there was her compassion. There are various traditional tales that she introduced lace-making to the midland shires, improved English gardening, introduced superior salad. What is much the strongest in terms of the ideal image of a queen is the story of her intervention for the rioting apprentices on May Day 1517:

> For which, kind queen, with joyful heart
> She heard their mothers' thanks and praise
> And lived beloved all her days.

The Venetian ambassador wrote on 19 May 1517 that 400 prisoners were destined for the gallows, 'but our most serene and most compassionate Queen, with tears in her eyes and on her bended knees, obtained their pardon from His Majesty, the act of grace being performed with great ceremony.'[20] The tradition of the fragile, tender royal female petitioning at the knees of the all-powerful male for clemency, was embedded in

---

* The details come down to us from the account of Jane Dormer, Duchess of Feria, who was born in 1538, two years after Queen Catherine's death, but as a young married woman was in waiting to Catherine's daughter Mary and thus in a position to hear stories about the Queen's last years.[17]

English history, ever since Queen Philippa saved the burgesses of Calais by her pleas to King Edward III.

Royally born, intelligent, pious and gracious, Queen Catherine incarnated in all ways but one – the provision of a male heir – the ideal of the early sixteenth-century consort. In 1518 it looked as though she would remedy her single deficiency. (As has been noted, it was axiomatic not only then but for centuries to come that failure to conceive was the sole responsibility of the female.) Some time in the spring – probably in late February – she became pregnant again. There were rumours on the subject as early as 12 April when Richard Pace, the Secretary of State, wrote to Wolsey: 'It is secretly said the Queen is with child'. He prayed to God 'heartily' that it might be a prince, 'to the surety and universal comfort of the realm'. By 6 June, Giustinian had had the report he had received privately some time ago confirmed by 'a trustworthy person'.[21]

Public announcement of this coming event 'most earnestly desired by the whole kingdom' – Giustinian's words – took place at the beginning of July. Shortly before this, the King had written confidentially to Cardinal Wolsey that he trusted 'the Queen my wife be with child', but that he was very anxious to 'remove her as little as I may now' – not only in principle to protect her pregnancy but because it was one of her 'dangerous times' (presumably the usual date of her period when it was believed a woman was prone to miscarry). On 5 July Pace reported happily to Wolsey that when he arrived at Woodstock, the Queen had 'welcomed him with a big belly'. A *Te Deum Laudamus* sung at St Paul's followed, as the official celebration. By the end of August even the Pope, a fortnight's travel away in Rome, was said to be delighted with the news; in common with the rest of the world, he hoped the baby would be a prince who would be 'the prop of the universal peace of Christendom'.[22]

The timing of this Queen's pregnancy had a particular piquancy since on 28 February 1518 the French Queen had presented her husband with an heir, following the birth of two daughters. Outwardly, the King of England rejoiced and accepted the role of godfather to the Dauphin, named Louis. Inwardly the competitive feelings he harboured concerning King François must have made him relieved that his own wife was pregnant again after a two-year gap. But there was of course another angle to the birth of a French prince, when an English princess of roughly the same age existed – the diplomatic one.

The proposed betrothal of the baby Dauphin of France to the two-year-old Princess Mary of England was the symbolic expression of a new accord

---

* This phrase, gross if graphic to modern ears, was always used to denote pregnancy at this time.

between their respective countries: finally expressed in the Treaty of London of 4 October 1518. This accord was to be England's – or Cardinal Wolsey's – answer to the Peace of Cambrai in March 1517, which had left the country so unpleasantly isolated. The timing is important, because in the usual optimistic conviction that Catherine would shortly give birth to a healthy prince, Mary was not at this point being viewed as the potential heiress to the English throne. The Venetian ambassador, doffing his bonnet solemnly to the two-year-old princess, was assured by her proud father that this was one little girl who never cried. Giustinian delighted Henry by replying that this was because her destiny – to be Queen of France – did not move her to tears.[23] England and France bound themselves together to keep the peace in Europe and Princess Mary was formally affianced to the Dauphin.

The French alliance was Wolsey's dream, not the Queen's; he was now the King's closest confidant on matters of policy, as well as his assiduous servant. The Cardinal (as Wolsey had become in 1515) understood very well how to make his will work in harmony with the King's so that it was difficult at the time – and remains so – to decide how much his French initiatives sprang from the King, and how much they were sprung upon him. But clearly King Henry favoured the treaty as a way of getting back into the European game, while both King and Cardinal – and the French King – seem to have been genuine in their desire for a relaxation of hostilities. An Anglo-French *rapprochement* made sense to both sides, at least in theory, and time would show whether it was workable; while it has been suggested by Wolsey's most recent biographer that the Cardinal also saw in peace an opportunity to dominate Europe which would prove a great deal cheaper than war.[24] The Treaty of London was duly ratified by other European powers, exhausted (like the French) by the fact that war had been waged virtually without cease on European soil for the previous twenty-four years.

As to the Queen's position at this point, obviously her political prestige was always greater when England was pursuing a pro-Spanish policy than when the mood was in favour of France, the hereditary enemy of her family. For the same reason, it was hardly her dearest wish to see her daughter married to a French prince: her Habsburg-Spanish nephew Charles was after all still the most eligible bachelor in Europe. Yet she too seems to have accepted the peaceful aims of the treaty as being genuine.

Then on 18 November tragedy struck. The 'prince' so confidently expected turned out to be a princess – and was born dead.*

---

* The Venetian ambassador Giustinian, always interested in these matters, thought the baby was born a month prematurely, but this does not fit with his own report of 25 October that the Queen was near her delivery time; nor with the fact that there were already rumours of the Queen's pregnancy by mid-April.

Privately, the Queen's grief can only have been compounded by the fact that the dashing Bessie Blount had become pregnant by the King very shortly before her own recent sad experience; although Catherine, with her usual composure, made no comment on the matter. That would indeed have been quite out of character for her. Instead, she attended (with the rest of the court) the festivities that the King arranged to celebrate the birth of the child – by a further cruel irony, a healthy boy.

As was noted in the previous chapter, King Henry had known Bessie Blount for some years: she had been a girl-about-court since 1513 and a favoured royal dancing partner. Bessie Blount was exactly the type of girl described by Anthony Fitzherbert in *The Boke of Husbandrye* of 1523 as being most attractive to men: 'hard of words' yet 'merry of cheer', 'well paced' and 'easy to leap upon', and though 'well stirring under a man', of such 'high metal' that she was forever 'chewing on the bridle'. Bessie had probably stirred under the King's boon companion the Duke of Suffolk as well as a few others although she was still very young.[25]

Bessie had never occupied the favoured position of the acknowledged royal *maîtresse en titre* – any more than anybody else had so far at the English court. The marriage that was secured for her, either shortly before or shortly after the birth of her child, was not a particularly exciting one. She married one Gilbert Talboys, of 'gentle' but not noble family, by whom she proceeded to have other children. It was as though the conception of the royal baby was more of a happy accident in a lighthearted career than the symbol of any great and torrid love affair. After all, by October 1518 the Queen was eight months pregnant: the King could be said to be exercising his prerogative to console himself for these long, theoretically celibate months.

The baby boy was born at the beginning of June 1519. He was given his father's Christian name and the traditional surname of a royal bastard which pointed proudly to his parentage: Fitzroy. It was another mark of official favour that Cardinal Wolsey acted as Henry Fitzroy's godfather, just as he had acted as godfather to the baby's half-sister Mary nearly three and a half years earlier. Thereafter the handsome, healthy, lively boy was 'well brought up, a prince's child'. The King doted on him, but then he also loved his daughter, at that stage a winning and attractive little girl with her father's colouring and the neat regular prettiness of her mother as a child. This acceptance of Henry Fitzroy was not in itself exceptional in an age when noblemen of all sorts, as well as kings, saw it as their duty to make provision for their bastards.[26]

Whatever Queen Catherine's private distress, in public terms the election of her nephew as the Emperor Charles V, about the time of the birth of Henry Fitzroy, meant that Spain was once more a potentially valuable ally for England. The French King had campaigned hard for his own election, following the death of the old Emperor Maximilian in January 1519, spending a great deal of money in the process. François failed; and although he assured the English envoy Sir Thomas Boleyn that he was deeply relieved to find the burden of the great office passing away from him, the sentiments must be taken with a pinch of French salt. The extraordinary extent of the territorial sway of the new Emperor – virtually surrounding France – could not fail to threaten French interests, and at the same time attract the favourable attention of France's new ally England.

It was a situation that Queen Catherine, with her long practice of diplomatic relations with Spain, both official and unofficial, was well placed to exploit. The French alliance sat uneasily with a great many of the English nobility; then there was the position of Princess Mary as the betrothed of the Dauphin. Although it is important to realize that, at the beginning of 1520, hopes of the Queen giving birth to a male heir had by no means been totally abandoned – Catherine was after all only thirty-four – at the same time the princess was now her father's only living legitimate child, without any immediate prospect of another brother (or sister). Matters had been different at the date when the Treaty of London was concluded.

Then there were also unresolved disputes between England and France which ranged from the material, the question of the jewels rightfully belonging to Mary Duchess of Suffolk as Dowager Queen of France, to the political: the vicious way the French had supported the Duke of Albany in Scotland, helping him to supplant Henry's sister Queen Margaret and her husband. To secure a meeting between her nephew and her husband became a prime object of the Queen's diplomacy. It made perfect sense in family terms (she had still never met her sister's son) and it made sense also in terms of an Anglo-Spanish *rapprochement*, perhaps even some kind of closer family alliance.

The Queen's desire to bring about such a meeting became more acute as preparations for a splendiferous formal encounter, on the continent, between the official allies, the Kings of France and England, got under way. In an expansive moment, King Henry (then clean-shaven) vowed to grow a beard, which he would not cut until he had met his brother of France. Curiously enough – but Freud would certainly have understood – the Queen discovered that she disliked his beard, and the vow was not kept. The Field of Cloth of Gold, as this majestic enterprise would be known to history, was the focus of an extraordinary amount of English artistic energy, coupled with English money, throughout the early months of 1520. At the same time the Queen bent *her* energies to persuading the Emperor to visit England in the course of his return journey from Spain, so that at least this Anglo-French jamboree would be to some extent neutralized.

At one point the Queen had assembled her own 'council' – literally her advisers – to confer on the subject of the expedition to France when the King unexpectedly arrived to join them. He asked what was being discussed and was informed. The councillors told him that the Queen had 'made such representations, and shown such reasons against the voyage [to France], as one would not have supposed she would have dared to do, or even to imagine'. But the Queen was not to be the target of an outbreak of the royal rage. On the contrary, according to the author of the report – de la Sauch, the French ambassador, writing on 7 April – 'on this account she is held in greater esteem by the King and his council than ever she was'.[27] In pragmatic terms the unpopularity of the expedition with many of the English nobility was in her favour.

Queen Catherine did not manage to impede the mammoth court progress which started to lumber in the direction of France in late May. That was scarcely within her power; she acted as ever as the petitioner and as such knew her limits, knew when to withdraw. But by the same tactics she did secure the arrival of the Emperor Charles. Contrary winds held him up: those winds that had threatened her own arrival from Spain as a young princess so many years ago. The Emperor landed at Dover on 26 May, the last possible date before the English court embarked. Catherine's political instincts proved correct: the brief meeting between the Emperor and the King of England was highly successful.

The grave, rather clumsy boy, with his long chin and jutting Habsburg lower lip, whom she embraced with rapture at the outskirts of Canterbury, accompanied by a cavalcade of her ladies, presented a diffident air to his magnificent uncle. A long breakfast took place – a family breakfast at which not even Cardinal Wolsey was present – and the subject of the peace of Europe was discussed. (Presumably discussions took place in French since the Emperor did not speak English or Spanish.) It is quite possible – although it cannot be proved since there is no record of the proceedings – that on this occasion the betrothal of Princess Mary to her first cousin Charles was also touched upon.

It is true that the child was at this point officially affianced to the French Dauphin: but no one knew better than these three royal persons the evanescent nature of these betrothals. Unbreakable contracts had been known to melt away with remarkable suddenness when reasons of state demanded it. Charles V's first betrothal had been to Claude of France, now the wife of the French King, when they were both babies. He had recently been betrothed to another infant princess, Louise, first-born child of François I and Queen Claude, at the time of the Treaty of Noyon (she had died in 1518 at the age of three). In between, Charles had for six years been affianced to the elder Mary Tudor, whom he would shortly meet for the first time at the English court as the wife of the Duke of Suffolk.

The two former 'spouses' – they had been joined by a proxy marriage – encountered each other at the ball given for the Emperor at Canterbury in the Archbishop's palace. Charles also attended High Mass in Canterbury Cathedral on Whit Sunday. Otherwise the most conspicuous feature of the Emperor's visit was the modesty and respect that he maintained towards King Henry – a tactful approach to any monarch and King Henry was no exception. By going further and referring to King Henry as his 'good father', Charles V struck a yet more welcome note.[28] (The fact that he was only eight-and-a-half years younger than King Henry made it more rather than less welcome.)

Queen Catherine happily found her faith in this family event fully justified; the theoretical affection she had felt at a distance for her sister's son was now kindled into something far more fervent which she at least was convinced was returned. King Henry for his part found himself in the pleasant position of his father Henry VII, potentially able to play off France and the Empire against each other. He agreed to a further meeting with his nephew, this time on the other side of the Channel, following the Field of Cloth of Gold.

As to the twenty-year-old Emperor, this was how the papal legate summed him up to the Pope: 'this Prince is gifted with good sense and prudence far beyond his years; and indeed he has, I believe, much more in his head than appears in his face'. Charles's preternatural restraint was something that struck many observers. Philip Melanchthon wrote later that 'more glorious and marvellous than all his successes was the Emperor's control of his temper. Never a word or an action was the least overbearing . . .'[29]

In contrast, Queen Catherine had a warm heart and romantic feelings about her Castilian past; while King Henry, no great believer in concealing his own emotions, was pleased by his nephew's flattery. It would not necessarily be easy for the pair of them to read this unprepossessing but subtle and intelligent young man aright.

Compared to the Emperor's perfect manners in referring to King Henry as his 'good father', King François' behaviour towards Henry VIII at the Field of Cloth of Gold was a good deal less satisfactory. It was certainly not deferential. How could it be? And indeed why should it be? With some reason, King François was extremely suspicious of King Henry's possible imperial involvement. They were two sovereigns, two energetic and competitive men in their late twenties – in their prime, one might say – who were equals. And as such they were inevitably rivals. Furthermore they headed two countries, who, for all the treaty that now bound them together, had fought each other with zest as recently as 1513. (Both men had been present at this campaign, although they had never actually met.)

The ballyhoo surrounding the Field of Cloth of Gold should not distract attention from the fact that this was an enormously expensive party which not everybody present enjoyed (as is the case with many enormously expensive parties).[30] The cost of the whole adventure to the English crown has been estimated as £15,000.＊ The total of the King's retinue was officially laid down as just under 4,000 people and just over 2,000 horses; that of the Queen's was to be just over 1,000 people and nearly 800 horses. But of course squires, servants and other hangers-on greatly increased this number.

Queen Catherine was surely among those who did not greatly relish the experience. However, clothed in all the hieratic glory of her rich garments, precious jewels and pearls (which were voted the finest of all), with a Spanish headdress over her famous, still abundant, long hair, she played her part. Besides, she was armed with heartening recollections of the recent amicable visit of her nephew. And King Henry also had the satisfaction of knowing he would meet the Emperor again immediately after the French meeting. It was not exactly loyal behaviour to his French brother king – and ally – but it made good sense in English terms.

For all these subterranean currents, the Field of Cloth of Gold was superb show business. The preparations were wide-ranging enough. On the one hand King Henry was asked to send his 'arming doublet' (in which he jousted) to be measured so that when his brother of France presented him ceremonially with a cuirass, it would fit. On the other hand Sir Richard Wingfield from France sent a special plea to the King as early as March that the ladies chosen to be shipped across the Channel should be selected not only for rank but for beauty, since Queen Claude and Louise of Savoy, François I's mother, were busy searching out 'the fairest ladies and demoiselles that may be found'. Wingfield ventured to add: 'I hope at least, Sir, that the Queen's grace shall bring such in her band that the visage of England, which hath always had the prize, shall not at this time lose the same'.

It is possible that among the fair demoiselles brought along by Queen Claude was a young English girl called Anne Boleyn. She was then in attendance at the French court and spoke excellent French; and since her father, as English ambassador to France, had been responsible for negotiating many of the arrangements, her presence would have made

---

＊ It is notoriously difficult to estimate what such sums might mean in terms of 'today's money' particularly as in an age of inflation such comparisons have a habit of going out of date almost as soon as they are written. It is more illuminating to point out that this was one-seventh of the crown's annual income.[31]

sense.[32] But of this there is no record. What was recorded was the chauvinistic French disappointment with the so-called English beauties (evidently Wingfield had anticipated this all along). They considered them to be well-dressed but hideous; the French were also shocked that the English ladies all drank from the same flask of wine – and furthermore drank from it remarkably often.

In terms of more mundane preparations – although the word mundane is scarcely appropriate – two or three thousand English people worked on producing tents in which the court was to be housed. For provisions there was a mixture of the familiar such as 'the sweet wines of Anjou old King Henry [VII] loved' and exciting new foods like turkey which was just coming into fashion as peacock was going out; turbot and salmon were popular staple dishes. Asparagus was another new delicacy, as were prunes, compared to the more usual pears. No one went short of wine, of whatever quality: fountains flowed with drink, and passersby were encouraged to help themselves from silver goblets.

Naturally heraldic display was of the essence in such an enterprise; both Holbein and Clouet were associated with the designs. Ironically enough, Mary, Henry VIII's sister, who was to play a prominent part in the proceedings, leading the dances for England, used the device of the porcupine which she had adopted for her brief married life to King Louis XII. Another rival beauty present was François I's own sister, Marguerite d'Angoulême, Duchesse d'Alençon. Described by the poet Clément Marot as having the body of a woman, the heart of a man and the head of an angel, Marguerite d'Angoulême fittingly chose as her device a marigold turning towards the sun.[33]

But beneath public display, heraldic and otherwise, lay a deeper concern that the two royal couples of France and England should be treated and treat each other exactly equally in all respects. The geographical situation chosen, a place termed by ancient usage 'the golden vale', lay, appropriately enough, on either side of the boundary between two villages owned by the English and the French respectively: Guines (English since the fourteenth century) and Ardres which belonged to France. Accordingly, precedence was to be given to the French at Guines, where they were guests, and to the English at Ardres, where the French were hosts.

It was convenient for Queen Catherine, who no longer cared to dance at her own court, that her opposite number Queen Claude, although many years younger, was also unable to dance. Convenient but also poignant: for at the age of twenty-one, the French Queen was heavily laden down with her fifth pregnancy, having given birth to a second son Henri Duc d'Orléans the previous June. Queen Claude would give birth to this child on 10 August, and the French, anxious about England's imperial involvement, had used her increasing pregnancy to hurry up proceedings. They had also pointed out that a meeting in July, which might have suited the English better, would have unfortunate consequences since the hot weather would cause the people to drink more (wine) and also show unpleasant tendencies to riot.

Disconcertingly – for the French – the weather was so hot on 7 June, the date when the two kings first encountered each other, that one Italian observer remarked that it could not have been hotter in Rome at St Peter's. Both kings however were on their mettle. They walked together bareheaded, apparently impervious to the blazing sun. Thereafter tournaments, jousts – Henry VIII's armour was decked with the familiar Hs and Ks – ecclesiastical ceremonies and banquets followed upon each other like rounds of an intricate song, where every verse had to be repeated twice over.

If Queen Catherine entertained King François, sitting opposite him under a costly canopy at Guines (Cardinal Wolsey was at one end of the table and Mary Duchess of Suffolk at the other) you might be sure that King Henry was at that very moment dining with Queen Claude at Ardres in rival state. When the two kings were in conclave, then the two queens were busy paying each other visits, or, as on one occasion when ceremonial bordered on farce, praying together at Mass. Unfortunately the question of which queen was first to receive the 'pax' or kiss of peace from the celebrating bishops could never be resolved . . . In the end Queen Catherine and Queen Claude resolved the matter by embracing each other, and abandoning the notion of the kiss of peace altogether.

There were however a few unscheduled happenings, some of which went off more successfully than others. When King François decided to pay a surprise visit – in disguise – to Queen Catherine, this veteran of King Henry's boyish pranks was well able to cope with the situation. She had no difficulty in recognizing him and no difficulty either in graciously pretending not to do so. When King François paid a similar unexpected visit to King Henry, however, the outcome was much less fortunate.

'Come, you shall wrestle with me', he suddenly called to the French King.[34] It was a challenge that no English courtier would have declined; but like Queen Catherine, the courtiers would also have known exactly how to behave. King François however proceeded to throw his brother of England heavily to the ground. The incident was glossed over; but it was one of those seemingly unimportant little moments that lingered in the memory. (At least King Henry beat King François at archery.)

It all ended on 24 June with the protestations of undying friendship common to all international conferences. Cardinal Wolsey, whose role had been a prominent one throughout, hailed the French King's brilliant and beautiful sister as his adopted daughter. King François' mother, the formidable Louise of Savoy, referred to Henry VIII in her turn as her newly adopted son. But King François would go on to use his gorgeously ornamented pavilions and encrusted tents for his military wars; while King Henry for his part set off sharply back to his own English territory of Calais in order to prepare to meet his nephew the Emperor for the second time.

First King Henry rode to Gravelines where he conferred with the Emperor and the Archduchess Margaret. Then he escorted the imperial pair back to Calais, where it was time for another prolonged banquet – it was said to have lasted for four hours – in another specially constructed artificial palace. (Although here the hot weather broke: high winds and torrential rain ruined the structure.) Two days of discussions followed. In spite of the weather, all these talks went well. Charles, mercifully not interested in boisterous wrestling games, continued to display that delightful filial obeisance which had pleased his uncle so much at Canterbury. Besides, there was business to be done – or at least to be discussed. With a duplicity that was perfectly commonplace for the period, King Henry allowed the leisurely talks concerning the marital fate of his daughter Mary to continue, for all her betrothal to the 'fair ... large ... and joyous' Dauphin;[35] just as his father had discussed Henry's own marriage to Eleanor of Austria notwithstanding his proxy marriage to Catherine of Aragon.

These discussions, these possibilities of a Spanish marriage for her daughter, were all a great deal more welcome to Queen Catherine than what had recently transpired against the sumptuous background of the Field of Cloth of Gold. Her political star was rising again. It was in 1520 that Erasmus wrote in praise of the English court: 'What family of citizens offers so clear an example of strict and harmonious wedlock? Where could one find a wife more keen to equal her admirable spouse?'[36] Give or take the odd fling with a Bessie Blount, the birth of a Henry Fitzroy (but royal bastards were nothing new in English history), it did not seem altogether too fulsome a verdict on the marriage of Henry VIII and Catherine of Aragon at the time.

The previous year the King had commissioned a joint tomb for his wife and himself. The execution of the tomb of Henry VII had been entrusted to the Florentine Pietro Torrigiano in 1512. On 5 January 1519 a draft agreement was drawn up for a similar tomb of white marble and black touchstone. It was to cost £2,000 and was to be 'more greater by the fourth part' than the tomb of the King's father. But unlike Henry VII who lay – and still lies – in Westminster Abbey, Henry VIII had chosen Windsor as his resting place. As early as 1517, at a Chapter meeting of the Garter held at Greenwich, he declared that 'when the most high God called him out of the world' he would have his corpse interred at Windsor 'and nowhere else'.[37] In the summer of 1520, there seemed no reason why King Henry and Queen Catherine should not one day occupy this stately tomb at Windsor together.

Chapter 5

WITHOUT AN HEIR
MALE

Should, however, the King of England die without an
heir male, and the Princess Mary become Queen of
England ...

From the marriage treaty between Charles V
and Princess Mary, 25 August 1521

Insidiously, the succession question began to permeate the politics of the English court in the early 1520s. Giving up hope of conception is after all an insidious process in itself, where the various stages of depression are reached gradually. There were encouraging precedents: Elizabeth, wife of Edward IV, was over forty when she gave birth to her twelfth child. Queen Catherine herself certainly did not give up hope immediately, while the King continued to 'lie' with her, according to custom. Her absence on a pilgrimage to Walsingham in February 1521 'to fulfil a vow' (when the Queen visited Cambridge en route) may well have been connected with aspirations in that direction.[1]

Popular speculation is another matter. The obvious could no longer be ignored (even if the speculators wished to do so): supposing the Queen did succeed in becoming pregnant again, what guarantee was there that the result would be a living son?* In this way, optimism about the birth of this future 'prince' gradually waned after 1518 and turned to scepticism. The court, the King, and perhaps last of all the Queen, began to face reality: Henry VIII did not have, and was not likely to have, a legitimate male heir. It is true that within his immediate family circle, in terms of blood, the King did have two nephews, the sons of Queen Margaret and Mary Duchess of Suffolk respectively. But James V, born

---

* In the absence of proper medical evidence, it is impossible to know what caused Queen Catherine's babies to be stillborn; although theories include recurrent toxaemia or chronic renal disease.[2]

in 1512, was still a child, quite apart from the complications of his position as King of Scots; Henry Brandon, son of Mary, was even younger, the same age as Princess Mary.

It was a situation to arouse atavistic uneasiness in a country where memories of civil unrest, rebellions by claimants to the throne, had by no means died away. There were still candidates to cause apprehension. Across the water, for example, Richard de la Pole, a man now in his forties, had for years been supported by the French; known as 'the White Rose', he was the younger brother of the Yorkist Edmund de la Pole executed by Henry in 1513. There were obvious if unspoken fears concerning the King's way of life – and he was never cautious about physical risks, hunting and jousting as energetically as ever. Given that his daughter suffered from the double handicap of being both female and a child, who was to succeed him in the event of some accident? Then there was the more openly discussable question of the succession following the King's death in the fullness of time, when 'the most high God' should call him out of the world, and his corpse would be interred at Windsor.

The very different dynastic maelstrom of the 1530s should not blind us to the fact that in the 1520s – certainly for the first half and even after that in varying forms – the solution sought always involved Princess Mary and her putative husband. It is an important point to grasp in the unfolding of the story of Henry VIII and Catherine of Aragon. For it demonstrates how committed the King was during these years to finding this solution within his long-established marriage to a Queen he respected, if he had not loved her in any romantic sense for many years: a Queen who also happened to be the aunt of the all-powerful Emperor.

One might add a cynical rider to this: Queen Catherine's health was bad and getting worse as she approached her fortieth birthday in December 1525. She herself referred to 'the uncertainty of my life' following a bout of illness.[3] When her own mother died, her father had soon married again to secure a male heir; it was possible that this solution would also be open to King Henry. But this, like the King's unexpected death, was hardly discussable. Certainly at this stage, the only way the King would understand himself as being free to marry again to procure a son was, like other kings of the period, as a widower.

At the beginning of 1521, Princess Mary, aged five in February, was still technically betrothed to the Dauphin of France. More and more, however, King Henry leaned towards what he regarded, understandably, as a more magnificent destiny: her marriage to her first cousin (sixteen years her senior) the Emperor Charles V, the match that had already been tentatively discussed in 1520. The enthusiasm of the Queen in this respect fell upon fertile ground. The single previous example of female succession in English history was that of Henry I settling his dominions on his daughter Matilda; it was a debatable subject since civil war with Matilda's cousin Stephen had followed. What was however incontrovertible was the fact that the eventual succession had gone to Matilda's son and Henry I's grandson, Henry II. In the same way Henry VIII began to encourage dreams of his grandson, the child of Charles V and Mary (naturally such a child would be male), who would preside over a large proportion of the Old World, including England, and a great deal of the so-called New World across the seas.

It is in this dynastic context that the execution of the King's mighty kinsman, Edward Stafford Duke of Buckingham, in May 1521 is most plausibly seen. Buckingham combined royal descent with a great deal of semi-royal state, and a certain loftiness – or arrogance – not inappropriate in a monarch.[4] Indeed, these qualities had made Buckingham the focus of rumours about his suitability to ascend the throne as long ago as 1501, following the death of Prince Arthur – because he was adult and a male. Time had not blunted Buckingham's own proudly held conviction that he was 'a noble man' who would be 'a royal ruler' – given the right circumstances. His disgust at the traducing of his high-born Stafford sisters' reputations – as he saw it – by the low-born William Compton in 1510 has been recorded. Nor for that matter had time done very much to change the circumstances concerning the English succession in the last twenty years. As before, the Duke of Buckingham represented the senior adult male (he was in his early forties) of proper royal descent who lived within England; he also had the public glamour to sustain the role of King. In September 1519, the Venetian ambassador recorded that Buckingham was 'very popular' and 'were the King to die without heirs male, he might easily obtain the crown.'[5] (See family tree 2)

Had Buckingham been wiser, with more of a sense of history and less of his own noble birth, it might have been better to have regarded all this as potentially very dangerous for himself and his family.* Instead, he negotiated, in 1519, exactly that match for his son and heir Lord Stafford best calculated to arouse paranoid suspicions concerning his intentions. Lord Stafford was married off to Lady Ursula Pole, who herself, as the daughter of Margaret Countess of Salisbury, had an all-too-strong dose of Yorkist royal blood. Doubling up royal claims to make one good one was a manoeuvre well understood from the past. In addition, Buckingham

---

* Buckingham was descended from Thomas of Woodstock, the youngest son of Edward III. Buckingham's claim was of course junior to that of the houses of York and Lancaster, descending from Thomas of Woodstock's elder brothers, now combined in the person of Henry VIII.

made his hostility to and even contempt for Wolsey clear (based on Wolsey's pro-French policies, and Wolsey's base birth respectively).

A magnate like Buckingham might have survived a negative attitude to Wolsey, if he had not coupled it with positive indiscretions on the subject of the succession. Following the unwise Pole-Stafford marriage, there was an incident in late 1520 which reached the Star Chamber when the King was much angered by Buckingham's illegal use of livery; that too smacked of the over-mighty subject. Then rumours of certain treacherous conversations, boasts within his family, prophecies of Buckingham's future greatness, to which he himself had unwisely listened, began to spread.

The trouble was that Buckingham had never condescended to woo the King. He had not tried to make himself an amusing member of the young court, and the philosophy of 'pastime and good company' so important to the youthful King meant nothing to him. On the contrary Buckingham was 'high minded', wrote Sir William Fitzwilliam, meaning proud, and – a particularly evocative phrase – he generally spoke 'like a man that were in a rage'.[6] Nor was Buckingham subservient, another way to gain favour. Now the great Duke was trailing his coat: and the fact that it was a magnificent coat, like the coat he had worn at Queen Catherine's first wedding costing £1,500, made this a highly threatening piece of display.

Buckingham was arrested in April 1521, taken to the Tower of London, and executed, after a trial for treason, a month later. Although it used to be thought that all this was a put-up job by Wolsey, the verdict of Buckingham's latest biographer is that the Duke was actually guilty as charged: that is, of treasonable thoughts, although the law on treasonable thoughts – as opposed to deeds – was for obvious reasons somewhat more dubious.[7] The significant fact from the point of view of Henry VIII and his increasing obsession with the succession is that all the charges related to the question of the King dying without a male heir.

Buckingham's titles were now forfeited, his properties including palatial Penshurst and the Gloucester stronghold of Thornbury, went to the Crown, and to rub the lesson in further, the Pole family were penalized too, an early example of the kind of guilt-by-association that was to haunt the later years of the reign. Margaret Countess of Salisbury was demoted from her position as Governess to Princess Mary, although her 'noble birth' and 'many virtues' (and, most importantly, the King's affection for her) allowed her to escape prison. Her eldest son, Lord Montague, was however put in the Tower; Arthur Pole was made to leave the court, and indications were sent to the Signory of Venice, where the twenty-one-year-old Reginald Pole was studying, to the effect that he was no longer *persona grata*. The message was clear enough: whoever actually ruled England following the death of Henry VIII, the descent was to go to one of his own blood, and there were to be no threatening shadows permitted.

For all the efficiency of Buckingham's despatch – with two of his sons-in-law among the peers who condemned him to death – it was an incident that caused some uneasiness at the time; even Hall recorded that the people 'mused' at the reason for it, 'and for truth, till it was known, among them was much speaking'. Bad harvests at home added to a feeling of unrest. In contrast to this, negotiations for Princess Mary's splendid match proceeded apace, affording both the King and Queen much happiness. In August Cardinal Wolsey, at Bruges, negotiated the marriage treaty as part of the 'Great Enterprise' by which Henry and Charles were to make war against François. The wording made it clear that at the very least the possibility that Princess Mary would succeed her father was being envisaged. Dowry arrangements were, as ever, discussed quite fiercely. Along the way, it was stated: 'Should, however, the King of England die without an heir male, and the Princess Mary become Queen of England, the Emperor elect is not entitled to any marriage portion.' Even the text of the treaty that referred to the other possibility – 'If an heir male is born to the King of England, so that the Princess Mary cannot succeed him on the throne' – provided another confirmation of the Princess's position.[8]

So King Henry passed cheerfully into the camp of the Emperor. By 1521 France and the Empire were once more at war in Italy over the Emperor's claim to Milan (which Charles had renounced by the Treaty of Noyon in 1516, when he was a younger, more insecure ruler). In the summer of 1522 King Henry was talking once more about his own ancient claims to France; he referred to himself as the future 'Governor' of France, and saw himself as replacing François I one day, much as his own father had replaced Richard III.[9] In June he declared war on France to enforce his claim to the French throne; an invasion followed three months later and the following year, in September, the Duke of Suffolk would lead an enormous English expedition across the Channel. The English received encouragement from the rebellion of another over-mighty subject inside France, Charles Duc de Bourbon, while the Archduchess Margaret from the Netherlands was expected to provide essential troops and money.

In the meantime the visit of Charles V to England in June 1522 – his second to the country, his third meeting with Henry VIII – constituted a triumphant public occasion for Queen Catherine. (She could hardly have anticipated that it was to be the last purely enjoyable public occasion in her life.) The Emperor arrived with a train of 2,000 courtiers and 1,000 horse at Dover where the King greeted him and showed him his ships, which the Emperor sedulously praised. They travelled on through Canterbury to

Gravesend and thence in barges to Greenwich where the Queen awaited them.

The power of the Emperor was already awesome. By the Treaty of Brussels, Charles V did assign the hereditary Austrian land of the Habsburgs to his younger brother Ferdinand, who had married the daughter of King Louis of Hungary the previous year. But that merely spread the Habsburg influence more widely. A few years later, following the death of his brother-in-law Louis II, King Ferdinand was elected King of Hungary and Bohemia in his place (although Hungary itself was in the power of the Turks). Another sudden death – that of the Medici Pope Leo X in late 1521 – resulted in the election of Charles's former tutor Adrian of Utrecht as Pope Adrian VI. Following his short reign, the election of a second Medici Pope as Clement VII in November 1523 did nothing to diminish the Emperor's ascendancy. For Clement VII was described by the imperial ambassador to the Holy See as entirely Charles V's creature: 'So great is Your Majesty's power, that you can change stones into obedient children'.[10]

Yet here – on 2 June 1522 – was this great Emperor kneeling to Catherine at the doors of Greenwich Palace and asking her blessing: 'for that is the fashion of Spain between Aunt and Nephew'. Queen Catherine knew that the two of them were joined – as she put it later – not only by 'consanguinity' but also by 'love'. Furthermore this omnipotent prince was one day to become the husband of the little girl brought to Greenwich to meet him. At the age of six and a quarter Princess Mary presented her fiancé with gifts of horses and hawks. For his part he viewed her 'with great joy'.[11]

The Emperor and his train were lodged at Bridewell Palace, that new royal dwelling which Henry VIII had begun to construct from 1515 on the south side of Fleet Street, following the fire that had destroyed Westminster. (Although as suitable bedchambers were not yet ready, the Emperor himself actually slept at Blackfriars, with a special gallery, lined with tapestries, built to connect with the new palace.) At Greenwich, which he reached by river, the triumphal arches nearly all bore a couplet celebrating the two monarchs' rival claims as champions of Christendom, the one as Defender of the Faith (the title recently granted to Henry by the Pope) and the other of the church:

> *Carolus, Henricus, vivant defensor uterque*
> *Henricus fidei, Carolus ecclesiae.*

The question of a joint crusade against the Turks, a religious duty theoretically dear to the hearts of Christian monarchs, could surely not be ruled out, even though as Queen Catherine herself succinctly put it to a Spaniard: 'The King of France is the greatest Turk'.[12]

Following the Emperor's visit, the language of the English, including that of Cardinal Wolsey, makes it clear that the idea of the marriage became more attractive rather than less with the passing of time. Above all the dream grandson, ruling over Europe 'as Europe had not been ruled since Roman days', was to be the 'magnificent compensation' to Henry VIII for his son-less state.* Henry now habitually spoke of Charles as his son, and it was specially fortunate that Charles V had in fact no living father to compete with Henry's claims to be his *'bon père'* (as the English King had taken to signing himself). Charles V responded in kind. On 10 May 1522, for example, he promised to do all he could for Henry VIII: 'as much as a good son should do for a father'.[14]

These family endearments were the outward show. The heart of the matter had been expressed by Wolsey two months earlier. He told the Spanish ambassador, who passed it on, that the English people should regard Charles V as 'the heir to the throne of England' should their own King fail to have a son. On 22 March Wolsey cried out histrionically that he hoped to see the Emperor have sons (by Princess Mary) before he himself came to die. By the end of March Wolsey was urging the Spanish envoys to assure the Emperor that 'our hearts are his, and we love him not merely as an old friend and ally, but as the son and heir of this kingdom.'[15]

For Queen Catherine, the imperial marriage promised much and threatened nothing. It certainly aroused no fears of national extinction in her breast. This was not only on account of her own Spanish blood, but also because she had grown up in the firm belief that the marriage of a queen to a king – Isabella of Castile to Ferdinand of Aragon – brought felicitous unity in its wake. Why should not the union of Mary of England and Charles of Spain do the same? Neither the Queen nor the King seem to have paid much attention to the disparity in age between the bridal couple: although it might have occurred to them that Charles V's practical need for an heir would make the waiting-period rather long for him. Princess Mary's twelfth birthday (the minimum age of cohabitation supposing the girl was physically mature enough) was not until February 1528. Queen Catherine dismissed such thoughts in favour of educating her daughter to be Queen of Spain, as once Isabella had educated Catherine to be Queen of England.

In general, Catherine's care for the education of Mary took the form of supervision and appointment of teachers rather than direct teaching.

---

* This is the judgement of Garrett Mattingly, editor of the relevant State Papers, whose detailed studies convinced him that 'the link which bound Henry most firmly to the empire was not the economic interdependence of England and the Netherlands, not the fear of French domination of Europe, not the sentimental tie formed by the fact that Henry was married to the Emperor's aunt, but Charles V's betrothal to the Princess Mary'.[13]

They did however study Latin together, since after Mary was sent to Wales, the Queen referred to it in a letter: 'As for your writing in Latin, I am glad that you shall change from me to Master Federston, for that shall do you much good to learn by him to write aright'. Rather wistfully the Queen asked Princess Mary sometimes to pass on her exercises when Federston had corrected them: 'For it shall be a great comfort to me to see you keep your Latin and fair writing and all.'[16] The Queen's influence was however the paramount one in the process of her daughter's education (the accomplishments of Queen Elizabeth I have often led to those of her half-sister Mary being ignored). The scholar she chiefly consulted – the humanist Juan Luis Vives – was a Spaniard like herself, although he was educated in France and had lived in Flanders.

By 1521 the Queen was already giving Vives a small pension, thanks to the intervention of Sir Thomas More, who had met him at Bruges; 'a common star' was said to link their souls. Vives did not reach England till 1523 and then his experience was somewhat mixed. Holding a Readership at Corpus Christi, Oxford, and residing there for two years, he found both the Oxford climate and the Oxford food trying: 'The sky is full of clouds and storms, sad as it is gray', he wrote on one occasion. 'The food is just repulsive; the air full of diseases, some of them beyond any cure; the digestion here is slow, heavy and painful ... Just before I wrote this letter I had a terrible stomach ache.' On the other hand he enjoyed court life.[17]

Vives also kept up a lively correspondence with the Queen and *The Instruction of a Christian Woman* was dedicated to her. In his preface, Vives explained that he was moved to write it 'by the favour, love and zeal that your Grace beareth to holy study and learning.' He also reminded his 'unique protectress' of her past history: she would recognize her own 'visage and image' in many of the sections, since the Queen had been 'both maid, wife and widow'.[18]

Quite apart from its relevance to Princess Mary, this is an important document. For one thing, its emphasis on the need for real (classical) learning in any female likely to face responsibility – including the upbringing of children – demonstrates the trend introduced into England by the Renaissance princess, Catherine, following the example of her mother. *The Instruction* was finally printed in English in 1540, when it was translated by Richard Hyrde. (It is good to find that the dedication to Catherine of Aragon was still extant – and still anachronistically referred to her as 'queen ... wife unto Henry VIII'.) Hyrde's own preface put forward a persuasive argument: 'For what is more fruitful than the good education and order of women, the one half of all mankind, and that half also whose good behaviour or evil tatches [stains]' affect for better or for worse the other half.[19]

Vives for his part denied that learning had ever made women 'cunning' (i.e. wicked) and appended a long list of learned women from history, all of impeccable moral character. He concluded the list, naturally, with the 'chaste' but well-educated daughters of Queen Isabella. If it is not absolutely certain that Vives taught Princess Mary personally – it may be that his precepts were merely passed on by Thomas Linacre who did – it is clear that the princess was brought up to value her own intellect. Vives also inculcated the study of the domestic arts, praising Queen Isabella for the way she enjoined them upon her daughters – 'the dressing of wool hath ever been an honest occupation for a good woman' – but without seeing the two kinds of education as being mutually exclusive.

At the same time Vives' work reveals the extremely low estimate of the moral nature of women – their sheer inferiority to men – which was current at the time, even among male scholars who believed in their education. Vives wrote eloquently of the need for female obedience, and even more, for female silence. Woman, he wrote, was 'a frail thing, and of weak discretion, and may be lightly deceived, which thing our first mother Eve sheweth whom the Devil caught with a light argument'. This should not be regarded as Spanish intransigence: it was a universal attitude. Even Sir Thomas More, so often praised for his enlightened approach to the education of his daughter Margaret Roper, shared the belief that women were frivolously loquacious by nature. When Margaret was pregnant, he hoped that her coming child would be like its mother in all but sex; and if it did unfortunately prove to be a girl, let the child 'make up for the inferiority of her sex by her zeal to imitate her mother's virtue and learning.'[20]

Such an attitude subtly but steadily affected the whole question of female succession: was one of these inferior creatures to be allowed to rule over a nation of men? Surely not: even supposing she was capable of it. Women were not intended to rule. When God worked mysteriously in allowing a woman to inherit a throne, the obvious answer was to install a man – a husband, a protector – at her side; hence the concentration on a suitable bridegroom for Princess Mary.

In 1524 Queen Catherine commissioned a work on the subject of marriage from Erasmus via her chamberlain Lord Mountjoy. This has sometimes been interpreted as a gesture of despair over her husband's infidelity. It was in fact more likely to have been an intellectual interest of her own, and a help to the preparation of her daughter, for whom marriage certainly lay ahead. Despairing over her husband's infidelity was not how Queen Catherine chose to play her hand. When King Henry replaced Bessie Blount (now married and the mother of his son) with a young woman called Mary Boleyn, Queen Catherine gave no outward sign of annoyance. At the end of her royal fling Mary Boleyn married – on 4 February 1521 – a gentleman of the Privy Chamber called William Carey.[21] The Queen attended the wedding festivities, just as she had graced the celebrations for the birth of Henry Fitzroy.

Mary Boleyn, like Bessie Blount, was still quite young when she married: twenty-two, perhaps.* Like Bessie Blount also, she was a high-spirited, rather giddy girl who enjoyed all the pleasures of the court on offer – including the embraces of the King. When she was fifteen she had gone to the French court in the train of Princess Mary Tudor where she had acquired an extremely wanton reputation. After Carey's death, she would make a second match for love. This was widely regarded as imprudent conduct both in principle and in practice; but she herself declared of this new husband: 'I had rather beg my bread with him than be the greatest Queen in Christendom'.[22]

Despite later rumours to the contrary, none of Mary's children were fathered by King Henry: her daughter Catherine Carey and her son Henry Carey, created Lord Hunsdon by his first cousin Queen Elizabeth, were born in 1524 and 1526 respectively when the affair was over. (We may be sure that Henry Carey would have been acclaimed with the same joy as Henry Fitzroy, if he had been the King's son.) But the affair itself was no mere rumour. Throughout his life King Henry showed a rather touching reluctance to tell a direct lie, due maybe to that tender conscience on which he prided himself. Taxed many years later with having had an affair with *three* Boleyns, two daughters and a mother, the best he could do was to reply shamefacedly: 'Never with the mother'. It was his servant Thomas Cromwell who added sharply: 'Never with the sister either'.[23]

The affair with Mary Boleyn was to have unlooked-for consequences in the future, given that sexual intercourse as well as marriage created an affinity between two people: in the case of two sisters, in the first degree collateral. At the time it was important in that the affair repeated the pattern established by Bessie Blount: here once again was a vivacious young girl, an energetic dancer and masker, taking the fancy of a man with an older, more serious-minded wife, no longer interested in such things. Both Bessie and Mary Boleyn were among the maids of honour at court; there seemed no particular reason why King Henry should not

---

* The birth dates and family order of the Boleyns – about which there has been some dispute – will be discussed in the next chapter.

continue to take his pick from among these willing young women, confident of the resigned acceptance of his Queen.

Presents continued to come from the Emperor in Spain to signify his serious intentions: two mules with crimson velvet trappings and marvellous garnishing of silver and gilt for King Henry, and mules with equally rich trappings but 'after the Spanish fashion' for the Queen.[24] Catherine went on writing lovingly to her nephew and future son-in-law. (He did not answer.) But to the King and Wolsey the manoeuvrability of his daughter was like a valuable golden coin: further bargaining with it would not affect its value, so long as it was not actually given away. In this manner, serious negotiations began between the English and Scots for a very different union: that of Mary and her first cousin on her father's side, the young James V, King of Scots.

This match is certainly one of the more interesting might-have-beens of British island history; would the union of the crowns have been antedated by over fifty years?* For a while it seems to have been a serious option – at least with some of the Scots and a good many of the English.[25] It was certainly an intelligent one.

The Bishop of Dunkeld, for the Scots, predicted that this 'convenient marriage' would 'knit together the realm of Scotland and England, in perpetual love and amity'. Surely all Henry VIII's military glories were not so honourable to him, nor so profitable as was a good peace. As for the English, many of them were realistic enough to see that the accession of a James V to the throne of England, with Mary at his side, would not necessarily lead to the swallowing up of England by Scotland, rather the reverse. James was half-English (unlike the Emperor); through his mother, he was actually the nearest Tudor heir male. He could swear fealty to his uncle in advance, thus settling a vexed question between England and Scotland about England's claim of suzerainty over the Scottish kings; in return for this he would be accepted as the King's next heir. According to this scenario, Princess Mary would not even need to be co-ruler: she would simply provide that same validation by her royal descent (to be passed on to her children) which Elizabeth of York had provided for Henry VII.

But there was a problem. A deep-rooted antipathy existed between the two nations which might cast some doubt on the Bishop of Dunkeld's sanguine prediction. The Scots feared English imperialism, and clung to their ancient connection with France – the Auld Alliance of 1173 – as a means of preserving their independence. The English for their part both

---

* That is to suggest Mary and James V, together, would have succeeded Henry VIII (see family tree 2); while history itself would of course have been robbed of two jewels in its crown: Elizabeth I and Mary Queen of Scots, the daughters of Henry VIII and James V respectively.

disliked and disdained the Scots. The 'old Pranks' of the Scots (that phrase used before Flodden) and their habit of attacking in the north whenever England's foreign commitments made her vulnerable – as in 1513 – led to the dislike. As for the disdain, Sir Ralph Sadler expressed it all too well twenty years later, with the traditional exasperation of a colonial official: 'Under the sun live not more beastly and unreasonable people than here [there] be of all degrees'.[26] Nevertheless for about two years, it seemed that this antipathy could be subordinated to the greater good that the marriage – or at least the prospect of it – would bring to both sides.

King Henry's various planned invasions of France in support of the Emperor gave him a strong motive to try to break up the threatening Franco-Scottish alliance. Queen Margaret had returned to Scotland in the summer of 1517, but her second marriage, to Angus, had now run into trouble. She was anxious to divorce him, and finally succeeded in doing so in 1527 in order to marry Henry Stewart Lord Methven, with whom she was already having an illicit romance. The regent whom the Scots preferred in theory, the Duke of Albany, was not only pro-French, but as much involved in French concerns as those of Scotland; none of his sojourns in Scotland lasted very long. In late 1522, for example, King Henry took advantage of his departure to offer a truce, which mentioned the future marriage of King James and Princess Mary.

Negotiations did not begin in earnest until 1524, when Albany finally departed and King James was twelve. Although King Henry's campaign of 1523 in France had foundered when the Archduchess Margaret failed to provide proper support of troops and money, he was still in theory preparing another invasion – especially if the rebel Duc de Bourbon struck at the French from within. In May 1524 the English signed a new treaty with Bourbon in which he promised to swear allegiance to Henry as King of France, following a successful invasion. The Scots for their part were temporarily exhausted by their French involvement: it had brought them little reward for being ever ready to harry England in the French national interest. In such an atmosphere Wolsey was able to hint at grandiose possibilities. On 2 August 1524, he wrote to Queen Margaret that if her son, herself and the Lords Commissioner of Scotland proceeded 'directly, lovingly and nobly' with the English King it might come about 'that such a marriage may be found for your said son, as never Scots had the like'.

Four weeks later Queen Margaret replied that the Lords Commissioner did indeed desire the match, but they were anxious that their King should be pronounced 'second person' of England, i.e. next in precedence after Henry VIII; James V should also be granted suitable possessions for 'the Prince of the Realm'. No one in England actively denied that these wishes could be granted. Instead, English envoys in Edinburgh wrote admiringly back to Wolsey of the Scottish King's physical grace and accomplishments: they praised his riding and his tilting, his dancing and his singing. Furthermore 'It is our comfort to see and conceive that, in personage favour and countenance, and in all his other proceedings, His Grace resembleth very much to the King's Highness, our Master.' (In his pictures, James V does not really look much like a chip-off-the-old-Tudor-block: so no doubt the envoys were exercising their diplomatic initiative.) In late November a truce between England and Scotland was declared; by December there were Scottish envoys at the English court, protesting of their young King's tender love for his uncle and how he needed help to safeguard his inheritance 'through a proper marriage'. (King Henry duly promised that help.) In January Queen Margaret was writing of 'the perpetual Pax' which this wonderful marriage would bring about between their two countries.[27]

But no such perpetual 'Pax' was destined to be established. Louise of Savoy, the French King's mother, crossly discounted the whole thing from the beginning: the princess, she said, had already been promised to both the Dauphin of France and the Emperor, 'and in like manner they [the English] will break the promise made to the Scots.'[28] But then Louise of Savoy, like the Duke of Albany, wanted the Scottish King as a bridegroom for a French princess. In fact King Henry had not broken his word to the Emperor – except in so far as he had allowed other negotiations for Princess Mary's hand to be conducted, and that, as has been sufficiently stressed already, was scarcely uncommon practice. The truth was the very contrary. The Emperor was now about to break his word to King Henry.

The history of the putative marriage negotiations between James V and Princess Mary are a digression in the story of Catherine of Aragon's marriage – except in so far as they attest further to King Henry's desire to find some solution to the succession involving Catherine's child. But the Emperor's treachery – as it was not implausibly seen in England – was another matter altogether. That was to have an extremely damaging effect on the relationship between Henry and Catherine.

There is no reason to doubt that King Henry's commitment to the imperial marriage had been perfectly serious from the start, for all his 'jousting' with the Scots. This was where his heart lay (as well as Catherine's). At Christmas 1524 Louis de Praet, the imperial ambassador, noting the Scots ambassadors at the English court, enquired pointedly where this left the imperial treaty. Both the King and Cardinal Wolsey assured him that they had no intention of breaking the alliance: the game was simply to prevent James V marrying a French princess.[29] And that seems to have been the truth. The Anglo-Scottish marriage – the perpetual peace mentioned by Queen Margaret – foundered on King Henry's perpetual dazzlement with the idea of his daughter as Empress, and his grandson as Emperor.

The Emperor's colossal victory over the French at Pavia in northern Italy on 24 February 1525 only increased the English King's lust for the alliance. The news of the victory reached the English court on 9 March early in the morning, in the form of a triumphant missive from the Archduchess Margaret describing how 'the whole power of France' had been 'discomfited'. The casualties were enormous. The French King was himself captured. The relative attitudes of England and Scotland to this cataclysmic development may be judged by the fact that the English immediately held a solemn Mass of Thanksgiving; while it was said that in Scotland James V had at once changed his crimson satin clothes for black, 'by which token men judged his French heart'.[30] Best of all, from the purely selfish English point of view, was the news that Richard de la Pole, 'the White Rose', had been killed in battle.

Part of the treaty which was imposed upon the vanquished François I concerned a suggested marriage. Queen Claude had died the previous year at the age of twenty-four, worn out with childbearing (she had borne seven children in eight years, five of whom, including all three sons, survived babyhood). Now François I was to marry Charles V's recently widowed sister Eleanor of Austria, Queen of Portugal.* So two of the three rival kings were to become brothers-in-law, while Henry VIII (as Catherine's husband) was to be their uncle by marriage. In celebration of the future, Eleanor of Austria danced a graceful Spanish dance before the captive French King, her future husband, as Catherine of Aragon had once danced before the English court.

In the meantime, Queen Catherine cried out in ecstasy after the news of Pavia came through. She wrote to her nephew on 30 March to congratulate him, blaming 'the inconstancy and fickleness of the sea' for the fact that she had not received any letters from him in reply to her own – a more hurtful explanation was to hand but she rejected that, while admitting that 'nothing would be so painful as to think that your Highness had forgotten ... your good aunt Catharina.' After all, their relationship based on both 'love and consanguinity' simply demanded 'that we write to each other often.'[31] For the last three years, the thought of her daughter's Spanish marriage had been to Catherine as a lodestar, shedding a brilliant guiding light on a life that was otherwise drifting into a melancholy middle age. Over the previous few years there had been the usual arguments about the

---

* It may be recalled that Eleanor of Austria, now in her mid-twenties, had once been spoken of as a bride for Henry VIII, when he was Prince of Wales; she subsequently married King Manuel I of Portugal who was the widower of two of her aunts.

dowry, the usual dispute about the delivery of the princess to her new country to be educated in the Spanish way as the Cortes (parliament) wished. But she could not believe that the various difficulties raised could not be solved.

Even an experienced negotiator and worldly-wise man like Wolsey could not believe it either. On 30 March 1525, as the wrangling continued, he pointed out indignantly to the Commissioners of the Archduchess Margaret how much of possible English benefit had been sacrificed in favour of the imperial marriage. First, the French had been flatly refused the hand of Princess Mary. Then the Scots, making a similar application, had been rebuffed, even when they had offered to forsake the French alliance, furnish nearly 20,000 men at their own expense for the invasion of France, and furthermore 'to take King Henry for their [feudal] superior' during the minority of King James. It is true that the Commissioners were of the private opinion that the Cardinal did protest a little too much: they doubted whether the Scots had ever made quite such firm offers. (The Scots had not in fact broken off the Auld Alliance.) Nevertheless the English ambassador in Rome assured the Pope on 8 April that King Henry would never bestow the hand of Mary on anyone other than the Emperor Charles. Wolsey himself talked of the magnificent marriage that would one day take place in Rome, and how he himself intended to be present at the festivities.[32]

As late as 20 April the envoys of the Emperor – with what has been described as 'complete effrontery' in view of what was about to happen – were still arguing about the Cortes' desire for Princess Mary to come to Spain, as well as the need for some immediate down-payment. The princess was advised to have Spanish lessons. The English for their part were still making the legitimate point that if the Emperor really sought 'a Mistress' to train the princess 'after the manner of Spain', he could not find a better one in all of Christendom than the mistress the princess now had: 'that is to say, the Queen's grace, her mother, who is coming of this house of Spain, and for the affection she beareth to the Emperor, will nourish her, and bring her up as may be hereafter to his most contention.' Wolsey was still making jocular asides: the King, he said, hoped to deliver his daughter to the Emperor *'en son lit à Paris'*: in his bed in Paris, an allusion to the recent crushing of France at Pavia.[33]

Yet already the composed and secretive Emperor had turned away from the English project. He needed a wife who would satisfy his Cortes and pacify his Spanish subjects; he needed a wife with a large dowry; and lastly, he needed her sooner rather than later, so that he could set about procreating a family. His bride was another first cousin: Isabella of Portugal, daughter of Catherine's sister Maria. She was twenty-three years old, with a splendid dowry from a father who could draw upon the wealth of India;

while her mixture of Portuguese and Spanish blood with its promise of Iberian unity pleased the Cortes. The idea had always appealed to the Emperor. As early as 1522, he had sent a message to Portugal, asking that one infanta should be kept unmarried with him in mind.[34] Charles V was betrothed to Isabella officially in July 1525, having withdrawn from the English match in May, and married her the following year. As it happened, Isabella was also intelligent, mature and sensible; to crown it all, she soon presented Charles V with a male heir (the future Philip II). From the Emperor's point of view, Isabella of Portugal represented an excellent choice.

Matters were a good deal less happy from the point of view of King Henry and Queen Catherine. Regardless of the fact that poor Queen Catherine felt herself quite as betrayed as King Henry (where was that love and consanguinity which bound aunt and nephew so closely together?), the King's terrible frown was turned in the direction of his wife. Indeed, the behaviour of Henry VIII following the Emperor's abandonment of the marriage treaty shows a new aspect of his character: a tendency to lash out when thwarted – not necessarily in the direction of the guilty party – but with the object of relieving his own pent-up wrath.

Publicly, the King's demeanour was as gallant and charming as ever. In March 1524 a most disquieting incident had taken place which, with the succession question unsolved, sent a shiver of apprehension through the court. The King was jousting with the Duke of Suffolk, as they had done so many times before, when by an appalling mischance, his face was left 'clean naked', that is to say, his visor had not been put down, before he started to thunder on his horse in the direction of his opponent. The horror of those watching may be imagined. There were cries of 'Hold, hold' but the King could not hear. Suffolk's lance struck him and King Henry fell heavily to the ground.[35]

His weight was not the problem. (Although the King's armour for the Field of Cloth of Gold four years earlier shows a natural increase of a few inches in girth over that of 1514, his major weight gain lay ahead.) The trouble was that his visor filled with pieces of the splintered lance and it was a miracle that the King's sight was not affected. Suffolk immediately declared that he would never joust against the King again. Henry VIII, however, with princely grace, readily forgave the two men who had handed him his spear without his visor being down: 'no one was to blame but himself'. Despite his shaken state, he proceeded to take a spear and run six courses, in order to reassure the spectators that he had not been hurt.

This kind of magnanimity was not what he displayed to his wife, following the final disappointment of the Anglo-imperial project.

*

Shortly after the imperial envoy Penalosa had the unenviable task of breaking the news of his master's defection, King Henry suddenly arranged the
public exaltation of his six-year-old illegitimate son, Henry Fitzroy. This
exaltation was to be in two parts. The first ceremony, which took place on
7 June, had to do with Henry Fitzroy's installation as a Knight of the
Garter: in St George's Chapel at Windsor, he was given the second stall on
the sovereign's side. Catherine of Aragon watched from the 'Queen's
closet', decorated with her pomegranate badges, overlooking the high altar.
Since Henry Fitzroy had actually been elected on the previous St George's
Day, 23 April, according to the custom of the order, this ceremony was
not in itself quite as ostentatious as what followed.

Two weeks later, the little boy was formally created Duke of Richmond
(the title of Henry VIII's grandmother and generally used to refer to Henry
VII before his accession). To this was joined the dukedom of Somerset and
earldom of Nottingham, equally titles of royal association. Letters patent
gave Richmond precedence over all the dukes already created or to be
created in the future – except those born legitimately of the King's body,
or the body of his legitimate heirs. Large estates were settled upon the new
duke, and in addition he was made Lord High Admiral, Lieutenant-General
North of the Trent, and Warden of All the Marches towards Scotland. To
the north Henry Duke of Richmond would now go, to be brought up in
the elaborate state thought commensurate with his position.

Queen Catherine was furious. Since all her hopes for the future were
now concentrated on her lawfully conceived daughter, she could hardly fail
to feel mortified at this celebration of the male bastard. Yet in the past she
had swallowed similar insults: the public festivities at Henry Fitzroy's birth,
for example, less than a year after her own child had been stillborn. Now
there was a difference. The Queen, after years of dealing with her husband
by diplomatic methods of outward submission, displayed open resentment,
making it clear that she remained strongly dissatisfied with the whole
business.[36]

That meant that the King in his turn was furious: it was not the way that
he was used to his wife behaving, but the novelty of it did not make it any
more agreeable. For over fifteen years, Queen Catherine had seen that
matters ran as smoothly as possible round the King – she retained all her
control of domestic detail – and as a man, a husband and a monarch, he
intended that things should remain that way. It seems likely that his decision
to send Princess Mary, with her own household, away to Ludlow, was
connected with his annoyance with her mother.

How far was the Queen's indignation justified? The first thing one should
note is that her anger recalls the hysterical letters of her unhappy youth as
Princess of Wales. Her health was not good now, as it had not been then,

and it may be that the Queen simply felt too ill to maintain her usual dignified serenity, that much-praised smiling countenance. At the same time, the very fact that the Queen did lose control is in itself a proof that the timing of the two ceremonies was deliberate and she knew it. She was being punished for the treachery of her family.

That still leaves the question of what King Henry actually intended – in terms of the future – by the elevation of his son. One thing he certainly did not intend was the immediate demotion of his daughter Mary. There was one report that the King granted Richmond precedence over 'everybody', but since future 'Dukes' who would be the King's lawful issue were to take precedence over Richmond, according to the deed of creation, Mary's position was clearly not affected. On the contrary, he made a further move to treat Mary as 'Princess of Wales'. She had been tacitly treated as Princess (or Prince) of Wales by outsiders in recent times, although never formally given the title. The confusion of gender – was she perhaps a 'Prince' as her grandmother Isabella had been a 'Catholic King'? – was indeed symbolic of the contemporary notion that female rulership was somehow unnatural. Thus queens and princesses were transformed into honorary kings and princes. Vives, for example, dedicated his *Satellitum* to the young princess in July 1524, with an Epistle headed 'To Mary, Prince of Wales: *Princeps Cambriae*'.[37]

Now Princess Mary was sent to Ludlow, capital of the Marches of Wales, as titular administrator of the Welsh kingdom, even as Arthur Prince of Wales had been despatched. She was given a magnificent household – 165 people with a total of over 300 catered for – suitable to a Prince of Wales; the quasi-royal Margaret Countess of Salisbury, back in favour, was put at its head. Princess Mary thus had both the substance and, informally, the style of 'my lady prince's grace', as the title of her Council called her.[38] But she was never actually created Prince (or Princess) of Wales, and never referred to as such in legal documents.* But to many people, untroubled by the exaltation of the illegitimate son, Princess Mary's removal to Wales was further proof of her eventual succession.

For all the Queen's distress at her departure – Mary's previous households had all been close to the court, allowing frequent visits – Catherine recognized the duty of a princess. Mary, by being constituted her father's delegate (as the new Duke of Richmond was similarly established in the north)

---

* There has never been a Princess of Wales in her own right. Even when it became obvious that Princess Elizabeth, now Queen Elizabeth II, would inherit the throne of her father, George VI, the King would not allow her to be created Princess of Wales, on the grounds that the title belonged exclusively to the wife of the Prince of Wales (as a female, Princess Elizabeth remained merely heiress-presumptive who could in theory be displaced by the birth of a male heir-apparent up until her father's death in 1952).

was following in the tradition by which English kings ruled through the ceremonial installation of their offspring. This was at least a recognition of her daughter's status.

If he did not intend to demote Mary, then what did King Henry intend to signify in the long term by the exaltation of Fitzroy? By establishing his illegitimate son, in one way King Henry was of course merely following well-known precedents: as Arthur Plantagenet, son of Edward IV, had been made Viscount Lisle, and Richard III's bastard Captain of Calais. The marriageability of Henry Fitzroy would undoubtedly be much enhanced if his status was improved – even to the point when a full-blown European princess might be available.

At the same time individual life, including royal life and young life, and above all young royal life, was extremely uncertain, as no one knew better than Henry VIII, heir to the houses of York and Lancaster. It is relevant that of the creations made at the same time as that of Richmond, others also indicated some kind of presence within the royal network. Gilbert Talboys, Richmond's complaisant stepfather, was knighted. But the King's nephew Henry Brandon, son of Mary Duchess of Suffolk, was created Earl of Lincoln; Henry Courtenay Earl of Devon (the King's first cousin, being the son of Elizabeth of York's younger sister) was made Marquess of Exeter. All this constituted a kind of shoring up of the King's family position. By forwarding the handsome, precocious son – his 'worldly jewel' whom he was said to love 'like his own soul' – the King allowed himself a further option for the future, without committing himself to anything more definite.[39]

This vague floating of the idea of Richmond as the King's successor – for it was certainly not more than that, if as much – does however cast some additional light on the King's current attitude to Queen Catherine. Richmond's mother was safely married to the newly knighted Gilbert Talboys; at no point had her claims to a more splendid position than that of the mere mother of the King's bastard ever been considered. If the King contemplated – even for a moment – the eventual acknowledgement of Richmond as his heir male, then the one thing he cannot have been contemplating at this point – even for a moment – was a second wife who would give him a legitimate son.

The autumn of 1525 saw the King and Queen reconciled. The Queen's health got better, as she told Princess Mary in a letter. Of the princess, it was reported to Wolsey that she was 'Surely, Sir, of her age as good a child, as ever I have seen, and of as good gesture and countenance.' Wolsey added compliments to the princess's amiability, and also to her dignified deportment.[40] Indefatigably, the Cardinal wondered whether the thirty-one-year-old widower François I might be a suitable bridegroom for the nine-year-old princess – despite his commitment to Eleanor of Austria. In the north the Duke of Richmond tried to get out of learning Latin in order to go hunting, and exchanged gracious messages and presents with his relations – Queen Margaret and James V – still further north. Attractive (and headstrong) as he was, he was at least out of sight. As her fortieth birthday passed on 16 December 1525 Queen Catherine looked forward to a life of ever greater piety, even more pilgrimages. King Henry, on the other hand, rejoiced with undiminished energy in the court masques, the most glittering festivities of his reign.

It was around this time that the Queen happened to take Vives with her in her barge when she travelled from Richmond Palace to her favourite convent of Syon in order to pray. Vives discoursed on the nature of Fortune's Wheel – that image of fate's twists and turns so beloved of Spaniards. Whereupon the Queen told him that personally, if she had to choose between two extremes, she would choose extreme sadness rather than extreme happiness. In the midst of the greatest unhappiness, she reflected, there was always some consolation, whereas it was all too easy to forget things of the spirit in the midst of great prosperity.[41] It was the kind of remark, innocent, even casual at the time, that people remembered long afterwards and saw as some foreshadowing of the Queen's tragic fate.

Yet at this point Queen Catherine herself had no reason to think that the wheel would sink still lower. She believed that an accommodation had been reached. And then something happened to pull down this carefully constructed and not totally unhappy world around her ears. In the spring of 1526, the King fell in love.

Part II

ANNE BOLEYN

Chapter 6

A FRESH YOUNG
DAMSEL

A fresh young damsel, that could trip and go
To sing and to dance passing excellent
No touches she lacked of love's allurement;
She could speak French ornately and plain . . .

William Forrest, *The History of*
Grisild the Second, on Anne Boleyn

The object of the King's affections was a graceful, black-eyed girl called Anne Boleyn. (She was familiarly addressed as Nan, like most Annes of the time – the modern equivalent being Annie – and her name was sometimes spelt Bullen, hence the bulls' heads that formed part of her family's arms; but uniform spelling was never a sixteenth-century priority.) She was born around 1500 or 1501, probably at Blickling in Norfolk where she certainly spent part of her childhood;* her actual birthday seems to have been at the end of May or in early June.[1] Therefore in the spring of 1526 Anne Boleyn was twenty-five or twenty-six, at any rate in her mid-twenties.

This is the consensus view of a date that can never be known with absolute certainty (like so much about Anne Boleyn). It has corroboration from various sources: Anne is for example described as being in her fifteenth year in 1514 and about twenty in 1521.[2] Although a later birth date has been argued,† 1500/1501 fits with the known pattern of her early life, and its few – very few – genuine signposts. This hesitation and

---

* The words *HIC NATA ANNA BOLEYN* commemorating her birth can be seen in the Great Hall beneath an eighteenth-century portrait relief of her; the Blickling of the Boleyns was replaced by the existing Jacobean building.
† William Camden in his *Annals*, printed in 1615, gave it in a marginal note as 1507: '*Anne Bolena nata MDVII*'. But Hugh Paget, in 'The Youth of Anne Boleyn', has convincingly demonstrated that this is impossible.[3]

confusion on the subject of Anne Boleyn's youth has a simple explanation: here was a comparatively obscure young woman, who suddenly leapt to fame (or notoriety) when she was an adult. A few more years passed, and she became a kind of 'non-person' following her fall. A generation passed: and lo and behold, she was the mother of the reigning sovereign! None of these revolutions of historiographical fortune made it possible to establish the facts of her early life with detachment, supposing anyone had been inclined to do so.

With the ancestry of Anne Boleyn, we are on firmer ground. The family into which she was born was not one of the grandest in the land, but it was by no means inferior. Later it became fashionable to laugh at her self-invented pedigree: for instance, her aunt by marriage, Elizabeth Stafford Duchess of Norfolk (Buckingham's daughter) felt she had the right to do so, given her own impeccable lineage. But that mockery was the product of the violent jealousy Anne Boleyn would arouse on many different levels. In reality, Anne Boleyn was well-born enough to make a claim that she was 'descent of right noble and high thorough regal blood' perfectly legitimate,[4] and only a slightly partial picture.

For Anne Boleyn did also have middle-class – merchant – blood. That came from her great-grandfather, Sir Geoffrey Boleyn, who became Lord Mayor of London in 1457. A wealthy mercer, he bought Blickling Hall in Norfolk (a county where the Boleyns had previously been known for at least 200 years as tenant farmers) and Hever Castle in Kent.[5] From that position, the ascent of the Boleyns was rapid; as with other families around this time, a series of noble marriages transformed them until they had left their mercer origins far behind. Sir Geoffrey Boleyn married as his second wife the daughter and co-heiress of Lord Hoo and Hastings; their son William Boleyn made an even more important match (as it turned out) to Lady Margaret Butler, daughter and co-heiress of the 7th Earl of Ormonde. In turn, the son of this union, Thomas Boleyn, married Lady Elizabeth Howard, eldest daughter of Thomas Howard, 2nd Duke of Norfolk. Therefore Anne Boleyn could number a duke and an earl among her great-grandfathers – as well as a self-made man.

The 'thorough regal blood', which was naturally emphasized by Anne's supporters in order to pre-empt the mercer taint, derived from her mother. Lady Elizabeth Howard was descended from King Edward I and his second wife Margaret of France, whose son Thomas of Brotherton had been made Earl of Norfolk. The Norfolk title then passed through various heiresses, ending with Margaret Mowbray who married Sir Robert Howard; their son John was created the first (Howard) Duke of Norfolk by Richard III in 1483. (See family tree 1)

As it happened, the descendants of Edward I were hardly an exclusive club in England in the early sixteenth century. In a country with a relatively small aristocracy, much intermarried, many noble families could trace their way back to him. The connection, stretching as it does back to the early thirteenth century and Anne Boleyn's seven-times-great-grandfather, may also seem a somewhat remote one. But that is to judge Anne Boleyn's pedigree by twentieth-century standards; in her own time, when royal blood conferred such a mystique upon its owner, even a dash of it was an important advantage to women, with their responsibility of breeding. In particular, the parentage of a woman who might one day bear her husband 'a prince' was an important consideration.

So much for Anne Boleyn's forebears; in practical terms it was also relevant that so many members of her family had important court connections. One way or another, according to their degree, they were royal servants. Sir Geoffrey Boleyn, founder of the family fortunes, had died as long ago as 1463. But another more distinguished great-grandfather, in terms of rank, Thomas Butler 7th Earl of Ormonde, was that veteran of the Wars of the Roses who survived long enough to become Queen Catherine's first Lord Chamberlain in 1509, before he died at a great age in 1515. (Anne herself must therefore have known him.)

Turning to her mother's family, the Howards, their recent history had been chequered. The first (Howard) Duke of Norfolk had been killed in 1485 while supporting Richard III and the dukedom put under attainder; this was not reversed until 1514. But the second Duke, Anne's maternal grandfather, actually secured that reversal by his distinguished military career and a lifetime of service to the crown: his was the victory of Flodden, and the office of Earl Marshal was restored to his family. Therefore, whatever the Howard past – and the Howard future – Anne Boleyn was born into a family that intended to consolidate its position by strong, not exactly disinterested, traditions of loyalty to the monarch. Anne's mother, like her ancient Ormonde great-grandfather, formed part of Queen Catherine's first household. Her mother's brother Thomas Howard, 3rd Duke of Norfolk (but known as the Earl of Surrey from 1514 until his father's death in 1524) had commanded the vanguard against the Scots at Flodden. A long and intricate career in public service – and his own – began with his appointment as Lord High Admiral in 1513.

It is however to the character and accomplishments of Thomas Boleyn that we must look for the most important influence on the career of his daughter Anne. He was a remarkable man. Thomas Boleyn was born in 1477, that is to say, he was fourteen years older than Henry VIII (and about the same age as Sir Thomas More). His appearances at court went back to the marriage of Prince Arthur and Princess Catherine in 1501;

he had escorted the then Princess Margaret to Scotland in 1503 to marry James IV. He was a Squire of the Body at the funeral of Henry VII, and was knighted at the new King's coronation. Sir Thomas Boleyn was an expert jouster and took part in the 1511 tournament to celebrate the birth of the ill-fated baby Prince Henry. His local interests at Blickling and Hever were represented by the fact that he was a joint constable of Norwich Castle and Sheriff of Kent in 1512. So far there was nothing outstanding about this career. But Sir Thomas Boleyn *was* remarkable: he had a talent that set him apart from most of his contemporary Englishmen (and would even make him notable among Englishmen today). This was a talent for languages, and thus, by extension, for diplomacy.

In an age when the role of permanently resident ambassador was in its infancy (individual missions were despatched instead), the existence of any man who could converse easily in the courts of Europe was a boon. Furthermore Sir Thomas was an intelligent man with an intellectual bent: Erasmus, from whom he commissioned works, would call him outstandingly learned: *egregie eruditus*. He was industrious. He did not have the dashing tendencies of another occasional envoy, Suffolk (who had even flirted with the Archduchess Margaret Regent of the Netherlands before Princess Mary successfully brought off her shotgun wedding). He might be 'rather plodding' and 'business-like' but these were not bad qualities in a diplomat; even his main fault of meanness – he was generally described as 'niggardly' – could have its advantages, given the unorthodox manner in which ambassadors were then financed.[6] In short, from his first mission to the court of Archduchess Margaret at Brussels in 1512 (it lasted for about a year and concerned the projected invasion of France) Sir Thomas Boleyn showed himself to have a safe pair of hands.

It was Sir Thomas who was entrusted with the detailed negotiations leading up to the Field of Cloth of Gold, as English ambassador to France from 1519 to early 1520. (He was 'royally' treated at the christening of the French King's second son, Henri Duc d'Orléans in June 1519.) Naturally he was present at the Field of Cloth of Gold itself and went on with King Henry to meet Charles V at Gravelines. Once again it was natural that this expert linguist (he spoke fluent Latin as well as the French that would so much impress foreign ambassadors to England) should be in attendance at the time of Charles V's visit in 1522.

Perhaps this talent of Sir Thomas Boleyn was itself part of a family tradition. His great-uncle, the 6th Earl of Ormonde, although an altogether more expansive character (praised by Edward IV for his 'good breeding and liberal qualities'), was a famous linguist and went on many European missions.[7] Be that as it may, Sir Thomas Boleyn certainly handed on his talent to his daughter Anne, as well as the adaptable intelligence that enabled him to exercise it to his own advantage. (And perhaps he handed on to her, also, something of his determination, concealed beneath a more charming exterior.) It may seem whimsical to select the Boleyn capacity to learn foreign languages as the first link in the long chain of circumstances that would end with Anne Boleyn as Queen of England. Yet in seeking to explain the extraordinary career of this young woman, it is appropriate to concentrate on any single element that marked her out from among her contemporaries (as it had marked her father).

It was as a result of his first mission, to the court of Archduchess Margaret, that Sir Thomas Boleyn was able to arrange for his younger daughter Anne to be educated there. She was now about twelve or thirteen, the minimum age for a *fille d'honneur*, of which there were eighteen. It has sometimes been contended that Anne Boleyn was actually older than her sister Mary, despite the fact that Mary was married before her. But the Boleyn family tradition always made Mary the elder – and indeed more than tradition. In 1597 Mary's grandson Lord Hunsdon would try to claim the earldom of Ormonde by right of his mother's seniority over her sister Anne in a letter to Queen Elizabeth's minister Burghley; this seniority was not contested although in the reign of Anne Boleyn's daughter there were plenty who would have done so, if it had been untrue.[8]

The truth was that the three recorded children of Sir Thomas and Lady Elizabeth Boleyn – Mary, Anne and George – were born very close together, soon after their parents' marriage, and certainly before the death of Sir Thomas's father in 1505. We know this from Sir Thomas's own testimony to Cromwell in the 1530s: 'When I married I had only £50 a year to live on for me and my wife, so long as my father lived, and yet she brought me every year a child.'[9] Perhaps this early experience of poverty coupled with fecundity accounted for Sir Thomas's proverbial meanness: it certainly makes mistakes over the Boleyn family order understandable. Nevertheless, it seems right to make Mary the eldest, born in about 1499, the year after her parents' marriage, then Anne born in 1500 or 1501, and George not later than 1504 (allowing for some of these annually arriving babies not to survive).

While the young Anne Boleyn was at the court of Archduchess Margaret – where she was listed as 'Mademoiselle Boullan' – she wrote her first known letter some time in 1513, back home to her father. It is written in clumsy French, since she was learning the language (although it is still not a bad production for the time, when so few women, outside royalty, could write at all). The letter was headed: 'La Vure', now Terveuren, near Brussels. It begins: '*Monsieur*, I understand by your letter that you wish for me to be a woman of honest reputation when I come to court', that is, when Anne should fulfil her father's ultimate ambition and secure a good place at the English court. In the meantime she found herself in a household that included '*dames et demoiselles d'honneur*' from France and Spain, as well as the Netherlands. Clearly Anne did prosper here, exactly as Sir Thomas had hoped, since an undated letter from the Archduchess Margaret to her father sings her praises – 'I find her so presentable and so pleasant, considering her youthful age, that I am more beholden to you for sending her to me, than you to me . . .'[10]

Even allowing for the politeness of princesses, the excellent impression made by the young Anne Boleyn does much to explain why her father made the effort to send her in the first place. Anne Boleyn at thirteen was quite old enough to have demonstrated a particular brightness, sufficient to convince her father that here was a child worth backing – some kind of star, in terms of parental hopes. She was, for example, of a very different character from her giddy sister Mary; far more intelligent and far more applied. These differences, which the respective courses of their lives would amply demonstrate, would have been sufficiently obvious to the girls' father from their childhood for him to select Anne and not Mary for the proposed post.

From the household of the Archduchess Margaret, Anne Boleyn transferred to that of the King's sister Mary 'the French Queen', when she went to France in the autumn of 1514. She joined her own sister Mary. The manner of Anne's transfer is not clear since only Mary Boleyn would return with 'the French Queen', now Duchess of Suffolk, to England the following year. (Mary Boleyn brought back with her a reputation which might not be exactly 'honest' but which would enable her – no doubt for that very reason – to catch the roving eye of Henry VIII.) Nevertheless Anne Boleyn did join 'the French Queen' at court, and after the latter's departure, Anne stayed on in the household of the new French Queen, Claude. This is unequivocally stated by Anne Boleyn's only contemporary biographer De Carles.[11] Whatever the reason for the absence of her name on Mary 'the French Queen's' original list, it is obvious that it was Anne's linguistic talent, combined with her appealing personality and charming manners, which secured her both posts, the short-lived one in waiting on Queen Mary and the far more important position with Queen Claude. Sir Thomas Boleyn's plan had worked. She fitted in.

Anne Boleyn remained in France for the next six or seven years. She became, in effect, a Frenchwoman, or one who would be regarded as such by an English court, already predisposed to be dazzled by all things French, from clothes to manners. She also conceived a great love of things French, not only the language, which she could speak 'ornately and plain', but French poetry and music.[12] There were other less agreeable aspects of the French court: the lechery of King François, for example, was of a very different degree from the mild jolly affairs indulged in by King Henry. The household of his wife Queen Claude to which Anne was attached was, however – perhaps predictably under the circumstances – extremely strict. Certainly Anne Boleyn learnt the art of pleasing at the French court, but it was the art of pleasing by her wit and accomplishments – sophisticated conversation, rallying remarks, flirtatious allusions, these were her weapons; there was courtly promise perhaps, but no question of fulfilment. When Anne Boleyn returned to England, she was indeed able to do so as 'a woman of honest reputation'; there were then no louche whispers surrounding her name.

Inevitably, Anne Boleyn would have encountered many of the royal personages of Europe during this period, albeit from a comparatively humble position. (As has been noted, she may well have been present at the Field of Cloth of Gold, although her name is not listed.) There are indications, however, that Anne Boleyn did form some kind of friendship with Marguerite d'Angoulême, ten years her senior, the scintillating sister of François I. Anne would imply this in the future, at a time when she badly needed to establish that she was no upstart. She referred to Marguerite in 1534 as 'a Princess whom [she, Anne] hath ever entirely loved.'[13]

Nevertheless, even if the friendship was as warm as Anne Boleyn suggested, it still could not, as is sometimes contended, have infected her with zeal for religious reform. Marguerite d'Angoulême, following her marriage to the King of Navarre in 1525, became the patron of religious reformers; herself a writer, she presided over a brilliant circle which included Rabelais and the poet Clément Marot. But all this lay ahead. The princess whom Anne Boleyn 'entirely loved' was extremely cultured; she also stood for female influence: she was the most powerful woman in France after her mother Louise of Savoy. But she was not as yet interested in religious reform.

Anne Boleyn's recall to England, around 1521, concerned her marriage. Although she was by now about twenty, there was no urgency on the subject in terms of her age: only great heiresses were married off in extreme youth and the Boleyn girls were certainly not heiresses. It was a question of solving a tricky dispute over the Butler-Ormonde inheritance by promoting the marriage of young Montague to young Capulet instead of banning it: in this case represented by James Lord Butler as Romeo and Anne Boleyn as Juliet.

When the old Lord Ormonde died without a son in 1515, he left his two daughters Lady Margaret Boleyn and Lady Anne St Leger (for whom

Anne Boleyn was probably named) as co-heiresses; but the title itself was claimed by a distant cousin, Sir Piers Butler, who became the 8th Earl. As ever, the rights of the female, that is the rights of Lady Margaret deemed to have passed to her son Sir Thomas, were a confused area. As a result, Sir Thomas Boleyn claimed certain properties, and had by no means given up on the Ormonde title itself.

Since the son of Sir Piers was at the English court, and roughly the same age as Anne Boleyn, the marriage of the young couple appeared to promise an equitable solution; Anne Boleyn bringing her Ormonde inheritance rights with her as a dower. In September 1520 King Henry agreed with Anne's maternal uncle, Thomas Howard, then Earl of Surrey, to advocate it. And Sir Thomas Boleyn, probably with some reluctance – since his own fortune was not measurably increased – did bring his daughter back from France.[14] While the matter of her marriage was sorted out, Anne Boleyn was placed in the household of Queen Catherine as a maid of honour. Her first recorded appearance at court was at a masque on 1 March 1522. Eight ladies took part, including Mary Duchess of Suffolk who enacted Beauty and the Countess of Devonshire Honour; Anne Boleyn played the part of Perseverance.

What did she look like, the girl who danced at that masque? In view of the tenuous state of information about her youth, it is a relief to find that here at least there is a strong measure of agreement. We must obviously discount venomous propaganda: stories of a goitre disfiguring her neck and a grotesque array of moles or warts (wens). Such a monstrosity would hardly have won the love of a king (and others). Yet even the most hostile account of Anne Boleyn, printed in 1585, by the Catholic recusant Nicolas Sander, who presumably never saw her since he was nine when she died, does not really go far to contradict the evidence of the portraits and of the more detached contemporary judgements.[15]

Anne Boleyn was not a great beauty. The Venetian ambassador, describing her at a moment when all Europe was avidly interested in this phenomenon at the English court, pronounced her 'not one of the handsomest women in the world'. One of her favourite chaplains gave the opinion that Bessie Blount was better-looking: Anne Boleyn was only moderately pretty.[16]

Some of this lukewarm praise may have been due to the fact that her looks did not accord with the fair-haired, blue-eyed ideal of the time. In theory, dark looks were regarded with suspicion and Anne Boleyn's looks were conspicuously dark: she was 'Brunet' in the word of her admirer, the poet Sir Thomas Wyatt. Blondes like Mary Duchess of Suffolk or, in an earlier generation, the termagant beauty Caterina Sforza were the contemporary ideal. (Remember how Catherine of Aragon's naturally fair prettiness had received approval when she arrived in England.) Beautifying lotions – of which there were a great many – generally involved the whitening of the skin and the lightening of the hair, by the use of such diverse preparations as nettle-seed, cinnabar, ivy leaves, saffron and sulphur.

It would have taken a great deal of saffron and sulphur to lighten Anne Boleyn's olive complexion. That was another element on which commentators agreed, whether they called her colouring 'rather dark' (*fuscula*) or sallow (*subflavo*) 'as if troubled with jaundice', or 'not so whitely as . . . above all we may esteem.' She did have a few moles, although she was hardly disfigured by them on the contrary they acted as beauty-spots. Her hair, thick and lustrous as it might be, was extremely dark (it has been suggested that she owed this colouring to her Irish grandmother).[17] And her eyes were so dark as to be almost black. But then the theory of public admiration was one thing – blondes were supposed to be of cheerful temperament – and the practice of physical attraction was quite another. Clearly in adulthood Anne Boleyn exercised a kind of sexual fascination over most men who met her; whether it aroused desire or hostility, the fascination was there.

The black eyes were sparkling and expressive; and they were set off by those 'dark, silky and well-marked eyebrows' praised by a contemporary Italian work on the beauty of women as 'the gift of Venus'. De Carles, Anne's contemporary biographer, certainly waxed lyrical on the subject: she knew well how 'to use [her eyes] with effect', whether deliberately leaving them in repose or using them to send a silent message which carried 'the secret testimony of the heart'. As a result many became obedient to their power.* More prosaically, the Venetian ambassador called her eyes 'black and beautiful'. Her mouth, described by him as 'wide' (another theoretical disadvantage by the standards of the time), was recorded by Sander as pretty.[19] In her portraits with her slightly pursed lips – maybe to counteract the charge of her mouth being too 'wide' – she has an air both prim and provocative, which was probably near the truth.†

Anne Boleyn was 'of middling stature' (which made her of course a great deal taller than Queen Catherine). She seems to have been quite slight or at any rate not full-breasted – the Venetian ambassador remarked that her bosom was 'not much raised' (fashion made the 'trussing' of breasts up high another preoccupation, as evinced by Henry VII's enquiries about

---

* Even a notorious description which came later – a 'goggle-eyed whore' – made it clear that Anne Boleyn's eyes were a striking feature of her appearance; although the secondary meaning of 'goggle-eyed' was then 'squinting' as well as 'prominent, staring or rolling eyes'.[18]

† A miniature of Anne Boleyn, attributed to Lucas Horenbout, the court painter, and dated about 1526, has recently been plausibly identified as the only contemporary likeness (the portraits are copies of contemporary works): it confirms the beauty of her dark eyes.[20]

Joanna of Aragon). Possibly Anne Boleyn did have a vestigial sixth finger on her left hand, which understandably she took some pains to conceal.* But a much more important aspect of her appearance when she first came to court was her elegant long neck; this, with the deportment she had learned in France – 'your ivory neck is raised upright', wrote a panegyrist – gave her a special grace, especially when dancing, which no one denied. William Forrest, for instance, an author concerned to praise Queen Catherine, testified to Anne Boleyn's 'passing excellent' skill at the dance (so important in a dance-mad court), as also to her pretty singing voice. In short: 'here was [a] fresh young damsel, that could trip and go ...'[22]

The fresh young damsel had other qualities, some more obvious than others at the moment of her arrival back in England. She had 'a very good wit', wrote Cavendish in his *Life of Wolsey*, another source not prejudiced in Anne Boleyn's favour.[23] The phrase, going beyond mere intelligence, carried with it connotations of spirit and adventurousness; in other words, Anne Boleyn was good company. Like many spirited people, she had another more impatient side to her: she would display on occasion a quick temper and a sharp tongue. But of these characteristics, deplored in a woman as much as skill at singing and dancing was prized, there was as yet no sign.

The projected Butler marriage did not prosper. Possibly the innate objections of Sir Thomas Boleyn, who still hoped to secure the Ormonde earldom for himself, were responsible for the blight. As an arranged marriage which failed, it casts no particular light on the character of Anne Boleyn (she played no part in its failure). Anne Boleyn's romantic relationship about the same time with the young Lord Percy, on the other hand, deserves closer inspection. If the exact measure of their intimacy is destined to remain tantalizingly obscure – the same confusion surrounds it as surrounds Anne's youth and for the same reasons – nevertheless it does provide illumination about the young woman who would shortly catch the King's eye.

Henry Lord Percy was the heir to great estates and an ancient name: his father was that northern magnate known as 'Henry the Magnificent', the 5th Earl of Northumberland. There had been talk of a betrothal when he was about fourteen to Lady Mary Talbot, the daughter of the Earl of Shrewsbury, but those negotiations had apparently fallen through. As was

---

* The story comes from the hostile source Nicolas Sander, who simply said she had 'six fingers'; yet there are corroborative details from the sympathetic biography of George Wyatt which make it plausible: that she had 'some little show of [extra] nail' on the side of one of her other fingers, and how Anne Boleyn would try to conceal it.[21] Had she led a more conventional life, however, such a minor blemish would have attracted no attention.

often the custom with such young lordlings, he was currently being educated in the south, in the household of Cardinal Wolsey. Lord Percy was
now about twenty.

His dangerous love affair with Anne Boleyn took place against the
background of the Queen's household where he found the 'fresh young
damsel' in waiting. The danger at this point of course lay in the fact that
Lord Percy was one of the most eligible *partis* in England, who could be
expected to make a most profitable match, whereas Anne Boleyn (with a
brother to inherit her father's modest wealth) was no kind of heiress. Lord
Percy was not the first, nor the last young man to become entangled with
a poor young woman in such a situation.[24] The propinquity of the various
noble households, the close living conditions of the young people, meant
that the education in courtly manners their parents expected them to
receive was often accompanied by other kinds of more exciting instruction.

According to Cavendish, Percy began by going to the Queen's chamber
'for his recreation' and ended by being deeply enamoured of Anne, an
affection which she returned. 'There grew such a secret love between them
that at length they were ensured together' (that is to say, they were bound
together by a promise of marriage or a precontract).[25] Again according to
Cavendish, Cardinal Wolsey put an end to the romance – hence Anne
Boleyn's subsequent hatred of him – at the request of the King (whose
motive was said to be his own predatory intentions in that direction).

Lord Percy put up a spirited defence of his choice, mentioning Anne's
'noble parentage' and royal descent, while contending in any case that he
was free to make his vows 'whereas my fancy served me best'. Lastly, he
mentioned that 'in this matter I have gone so far before many worthy
witnesses that I know not how to avoid myself nor to discharge my
Conscience'. Nevertheless Lord Northumberland was sent for. A secret
conclave took place with the Cardinal, at the end of which the Cardinal
called for 'a cup of wine'. Lord Percy received a furious parental lecture,
the match with Lady Mary Talbot was resurrected in 1522, and in early
1524 he duly married her.

Although Cavendish was wrong to ascribe the King's opposition to the
match to the latter's lustful feelings (1522 is much too early for this), it
seems likely that Henry, together with Wolsey, did oppose it, since it ran
contrary to the Butler-Boleyn marriage which they were concurrently
promoting.* However, what is really important about Cavendish's account

---

* George Cavendish, as another member of Wolsey's household (he was his gentleman-usher),
was an eyewitness to Percy's romance with Anne Boleyn; so that his testimony as to its course is
valuable. But he was not an eyewitness to the King and Cardinal's colloquies on the subject. Thirty
years later – in the 1550s – when he composed his memoir of Wolsey, it was all too easy to elide
the dates and assume Henry VIII had opposed the Percy match out of desire for Anne Boleyn.[26]

is the suggestion of a precontract: 'they were ensured together'. There is other evidence that something of the sort took place. Lord Percy's marriage to Lady Mary Talbot was – perhaps predictably – unhappy; according to Lady Percy in 1532, her husband told her he had been precontracted to Anne Boleyn (which would have made their own marriage invalid). As we shall see, there was a degree of official nervousness over Anne Boleyn's marital status in the testing early years of her relationship with Henry VIII – had she or had she not been precontracted? – and this is most plausibly seen in the context of her romance with Lord Percy.[27]

It does not matter that Lord Percy would himself solemnly swear to the contrary in 1536 before august witnesses – including the Archbishops of Canterbury and York: 'The same [the oath] may be to my damnation if ever there were any contract or promise of marriage between her and me', he declared and he subsequently took the sacrament. These desperate times were very different from the easygoing days of the early 1520s; dalliance with a pretty maid of honour, accompanied perhaps by a promise of marriage, had turned into something that might be construed in a far more alarming light. Lord Percy must be forgiven his blasphemy under duress – as it very likely was.*

How far did Percy's dalliance with Anne Boleyn actually go? As was mentioned in the case of Arthur and Catherine on the subject of pre-contracts, proper sexual consummation meant that a precontract – or formal betrothal – acquired the full validity of a marriage. On the other hand passionate kisses, leading to even more passionate embraces, leading to something that is now termed foreplay and stopping there – meant that it did not. In such a world, technical virginity could become an important issue, long after the event. Yet nothing could be more difficult to establish one way or the other; especially in view of this propinquity of young men and women, none of whom were supervised or guarded in the way a Spanish royal princess like Catherine of Aragon had been. Unless pregnancy settled the issue, absolute certainty on this extremely private subject was impossible. The result was that, human nature being what it is, people swore to the circumstances that suited them in the present, regardless of what had actually taken place in the past.

Anne Boleyn did not get pregnant by Lord Percy, and on balance of probabilities did not completely consummate their relationship. But she did perhaps go quite a long way towards doing so and there was assuredly some kind of promise of marriage whether the promises or the embraces

* Donizetti's opera *Anna Bolena*, with a libretto by Felice Homani, which has Percy (Ricardo) as the romantic tenor, telling the baritone Henry VIII (Enrico) that Anna had long ago been promised to him, and later telling Anna that from her earliest years she has always been his, does therefore have some historical basis in fact, even if Percy's real-life behaviour was less chivalrous.

came first. All this took place without any kind of official sanction. So whatever the truth of its intimacies, the Percy relationship should make us envisage Anne Boleyn as a young woman of considerable resolve by the standards of the time, as well as a certain useful measure of secretiveness. It also seems fair to add the notion of boldness to her known characteristics. She saw her chance and she attempted to take it. She was not content with the destiny to which society had apparently consigned her.

Anne Boleyn's premarital relationship with Sir Thomas Wyatt is a more nebulous affair. There are clues in his poetry (whose significance has been hotly debated), but no solid evidence as to its exact nature, beyond the fact that he was briefly imprisoned in the Tower at the time of her fall, but did not forfeit the King's favour thereafter. Wyatt's grandson George wrote an exculpatory biography of Anne in the 1590s – during her daughter's reign. According to this, Wyatt fell in love with Anne on her return from France, first ravished by 'the sudden appearance of this new beauty' and then even more taken with her 'witty and graceful speech'.[28] The Wyatt family, however, lived in Kent, not far from Hever, and it is possible Wyatt knew Anne as a child: he was a year or two younger than her, roughly the same age as her other 'suitors' James Lord Butler and Henry Lord Percy.

But Wyatt, at the time of his involvement with Anne – some time before he went abroad in early 1526 – was already married. Even though he was separated from his wife, he was still in no sense an eligible match. Whatever the extent of their romance, it belonged to the important but separate tradition of courtly love, conventional if ardent poetical professions, not the more down-to-earth world of the marriage market.

A flirtation along the accepted lines of courtly love is also a far cry from a reciprocated passion, let alone a full-blooded affair. After the fall of Anne Boleyn it was, of course, open season on her reputation. The most scurrilous accusations were shot after her departed shade; the idea of a sexual liaison with Wyatt both before and during her marriage was all too tempting to her accusers. But where Wyatt's poetry can be definitely linked to Anne Boleyn, it speaks of past love and past suffering, not of consummation. In 1532, for example, accompanying Henry VIII and Anne to France, Wyatt referred to himself as having 'fled the fire' that burnt him:

> And now I follow the coals that be quenched
> From Dover to Calais against my mind . . .

A poem written later in his life (after Anne's death) to his new love 'Phyllis' described how he 'did refrain' from 'Her that did set our country in a roar' whom he named as 'Brunet':

The unfeigned cheer of Phyllis hath the place
That Brunet had: she hath and ever shall.

The most celebrated poem by Wyatt associated with Anne Boleyn – a Petrarchan sonnet – has him drawing back from the relationship for fear of an august rival and warning others of the useless pursuit:

Whoso list to hunt: I know where is a hind.
But as for me, alas I may no more:
The vain travail hath wearied me so sore . . .
Who list to hunt . . .
As well as I may spend his time in vain,
And graven with diamonds in letters plain
There is written her fair neck round about:
'*Noli me tangere*, for Caesar's I am,
And wild for to hold, though I seem tame.'

The progress outlined here of fascination followed ultimately by with-drawal is the likely course of Wyatt's relationship with Anne, allowing for a flirtation along the way to enliven court life. C. S. Lewis has described Wyatt as being 'always in love with women he dislikes':[29] witty, provocative Anne Boleyn was probably one of them.

The King's love of Anne Boleyn started with great suddenness, most probably in the jovial atmosphere of Shrovetide 1526.[30] That was the nature of the man. He was now in his thirty-fifth year – a dangerous age, it might be thought – and he had been on the throne for seventeen years, one-half of his life. But although middle-aged by the standards of the time, the King remained capable of boyish enthusiasm and what he at least felt to be boyish desire. He was still energetic, still handsome, his build still athletic rather than corpulent. A miniature of Henry VIII painted at this time shows a new pudginess in the features, and no doubt his hat conceals a receding hairline. However, even five years later, he would be described by the Venetian ambassador as having 'a face like an angel' (if his head was by now 'bald like Caesar's'); 'you never saw a taller or more noble-looking personage', wrote another observer.[31]

Yet for all Henry's fresh vigour, he no longer bore any real relation to the secluded youth who had fallen in love with Catherine of Aragon. That Henry had long ago vanished – except perhaps in the Queen's tender memories. Here was a confident and at times ruthless sovereign, who regarded it as his natural right to have his own way in all things, and did not appreciate it when obstacles appeared in his path. He was inclined to deal harshly with those – male or female – whom he perceived as having perversely placed those obstacles in front of him.

The violence of Henry VIII's passion for his wife's lady-in-waiting is attested by the sequence of love letters that he wrote to her. All are handwritten. Indeed, their very existence is a proof of passion, since the King greatly disliked writing letters and very few other handwritten letters of his have survived with the exception of brief notes to Wolsey.[32] But Anne Boleyn's absence from court from time to time, for a variety of reasons, proved intolerable and drove him to his pen.

There are seventeen letters altogether; none of them are dated. Although various internal references help to place the letters in some kind of order, this can only be approximate: authorities have differed over its details since the first printed edition in England in 1714. Nine are written in French, probably as a security precaution since few Englishmen enjoyed the fluency in the language possessed by both Henry and Anne. The King's letters mysteriously ended up in the Vatican Library in Rome (where they surfaced in the late seventeenth century and still are today)* while Anne Boleyn's replies have disappeared altogether. No doubt – again for reasons of security – the King destroyed them.

Yet for all their textual and dating difficulties, the letters do clarify an important point, beyond the mere existence of the King's passion. These are the letters of a lover who aspires to his 'mistress's' favours – the word did not then necessarily have a sexual connotation, rather a courtly one – but has not yet received them: the pleas of a suitor. In a letter written when Henry had, by his own account, been 'for more than a year, struck with the dart of love' he describes himself as having been poring over Anne's own letters with 'a great agony, not knowing how to understand them'. He beseeches her to let him know her true intentions towards him. He is still not yet sure whether he will fail 'or find a place in your heart and affection'. But if it pleases his mistress to give herself 'body and heart to me, who will be, and has been, your most loyal servant', he promises to forsake all others: 'I will take you for my only mistress', casting out all competitors 'and serving only you'.[34]

Another letter, like the first, written some time before July 1527, bewails

---

* Here they received from an unknown archivist the numbering used ever since: it is definitely not chronological. Theories about the manner in which the King's letters reached Rome are various: possibly a freelance papal spy stole them in 1529 since it does not seem that the papal legate, Cardinal Campeggio, tried to smuggle them out, as was once suggested. Alternatively the letters remained in England: they could for example have remained at Hever, been passed thirty years later by the then owner, the Catholic Edward Waldegrave, to a priest he was sheltering who took them to Rome. This is a theory extended by Jasper Ridley in his edition of the love letters (1988), which is the text (and where necessary, the translation) used here.[33]

his 'mistress's' absence, and complains that he has not heard from her; he has also heard a report that she has changed her mind about him and will not come to court. '[I]t seems a very small return for the great love I bear you, to be kept at a distance from the person and presence of the woman in the world that I value the most ... though this will not distress the mistress as much as the servant. Consider well, my mistress, how greatly my absence from you grieves me; I hope it is not your will that it should be so; but if I heard for certain that you yourself desired it, I could do no other than complain of my ill fortune, and by degrees abate my great folly'.[35]

With the complaints that she has not written – 'you have not been pleased to remember the promise which you made me ... which was that I should hear good news of you' – go those other familiar concomitants of the ardent wooer: the presents. These include venison for which the King was proud to relate he was personally responsible (venison was frequently bestowed as a present at this time): 'I send you by this bearer a buck killed late last night by my own hand, hoping that when you eat it, it will remind you of the hunter'.[36]

All this is the stuff of love – and love letters – which does not alter much down the ages. The endings of the letters (to which lovers so often turn first) are significant. On one occasion, slightly coyly, the King describes himself as 'your servant, who often wishes you were in your brother's place'. (George Boleyn was in the King's Privy Chamber.) The King's actual signature varies: we find H.R., H Rex, Henry R. and Henry Rex; but there are also the conceits so beloved of the sixteenth century: signatures (in French) which read: 'H seeks A.B. no other Rex' or 'Un H Rex changeable'. During this period – before July 1527 – the King also once employed a more elaborate code: 'Thanking you most cordially that it pleases you still to have some remembrance of me. B.N.R.I. de R.O.M.V.E.Z.' before adding 'Henry Rex'. Although its precise meaning has defied scholars (the first letter may actually be an 'O' not a 'B') the ultimate meaning of the signature is clear enough: a passionate but for the time being secret love.[37]

It did not remain secret forever. It was true that the courtly conventions of the time – where the relationship of 'Mistress' and 'Servant' might be playful rather than sexual – did help to mask what was really going on. If the King paid court to a maid of honour, chose her for her dancing, no one could be absolutely sure at first whether she was another Bessie Blount in the making. But this state of affairs could not last long. Anne Boleyn was after all a member of the Queen's household. The cramped conditions, the lack of privacy, have already been stressed; then there was the acute interest inevitably felt by the courtiers (and ambassadors) in every aspect of their sovereign's life.

Outwardly, court life continued much as it had done before. Shrove Tuesday 1527, for example, found the King jousting in a strange gilt harness 'of the new fashion'; 286 spears were broken in the course of the day. At the end of it all there was 'a costly banquet' in the Queen's chamber. To observers, indeed, the King and Queen were still sharing 'one bed and table' as they had ever done – and would do as we shall see for some time after this.[38] Furthermore, the marriage prospects of their child, Princess Mary, were being pursued as actively as ever by Cardinal Wolsey. His first choice, after the debacle with Charles V, had been King François I, despite his commitment to the Emperor's sister, Eleanor of Austria. The French King, taken captive at Pavia, had been allowed to leave Spain in March 1526; but when his commitment to Eleanor proved unbreakable, negotiations were switched in favour of his second son, Henri Duc d'Orléans.

There was an apparent problem here: Princess Mary, despite her intelligence – she was already translating St Thomas Aquinas out of Latin – was not particularly well grown for her age (she had inherited her mother's stature, rather than her father's). In the spring of 1527, she was described as 'so thin, spare and small as to make it impossible [for her] to be married for the next three years'.[39] But whatever the general disappointment at the Princess's slow development – grandsons were obviously not to be expected from her for some time – the problem was by this time more apparent than real.

For even as these French negotiations continued, according to King Henry's later account, the French ambassador to England, the Bishop of Tarbes, cast in doubt the Princess's actual legitimacy. He questioned the ecclesiastical validity of her parents' marriage. But the Bishop's bow at a venture cannot have taken place without strong royal encouragement, since it was otherwise a gross insult to the monarch with whom he was supposed to be fashioning an alliance. (According to another account, it was the English embassy to France which first voiced these doubts: equally surprising in view of the fact that the position of their own princess was thus threatened.)[40] The reality was that Henry VIII was no longer interested in a solution to the succession based on the marriage of his daughter and the eventual succession of his son-in-law (or grandson). The secrecy of his relationship with Anne Boleyn was shortly to be at an end – finally, by his own choice.

For Anne Boleyn, capricious fascinating 'Brunet', was not to be another Bessie Blount, let alone another Mary Boleyn, quickly, easily seduced, pedestrianly married off thereafter. Nor for that matter was she to be another Duchesse d'Étampes. About this time François I began his long affair with his most celebrated mistress, then a maid of honour to his mother Louise of Savoy, which would result in her elevation to the role of duchess and her glamorous if adulterous stardom at the French court. A more solemn destiny was planned for Anne Boleyn.

At some point, the exact moment of which can never be known for certain, but it occurred some little time before May 1527, the King had decided that it was God's will that he should have, as it were, a second chance in life. His conscience told him that he should get rid of his first 'wife' (to whom, it transpired, he had never really been married) and procreate a new family with the aid of a 'fresh young damsel'.

Chapter 7

THE KING AND HIS

LADY

Both the King and his lady, I am assured, look upon
their future marriage as certain, as if that of the
Queen had actually been dissolved. Preparations are
being made for the wedding.

The Spanish Ambassador in London to
Charles V, September 1528

In May 1527 Henry VIII sought a divorce from his Queen. Although the word divorce is generally used concerning the King's 'great matter', what he actually sought was not a divorce in the modern sense of the word, which recognizes that a marriage has taken place before splitting it in two. He wanted a declaration that his marriage to Catherine was invalid (in modern parlance Henry VIII sought an annulment). This would mean not only that Henry was unmarried in 1527 but that he had never been married in 1509. According to this line of argument, therefore, Catherine's status was once more that of the widow of his brother Arthur – the Princess Dowager of Wales – as it should always have been.

At this point it must be appreciated that divorce was by no means such an unthinkable prospect, nor such an uncommon occurrence then as is sometimes supposed. Looking no further than Henry VIII's own family, we find that both his sisters were involved in somewhat murky marriage arrangements. The Duke of Suffolk's ambivalent marital position – two divorces – meant that it was thought necessary to apply to Rome for papal approval for his marriage to Mary in 1515. (Lady Mortimer, one of his ex-wives, was still alive.) It was not until 1528 – thirteen years after the event – that the Suffolks secured a solemn papal confirmation of their union, and a declaration of the legitimacy of Mary's three children by Suffolk; at the same time they secured a confirmation of the legitimacy of Suffolk's children by Lady Mortimer.[1]

But if Suffolk's was a particularly flagrant case of marital muddle, it was hardly unique among the English nobility, where it has been observed that the repudiation of a wife was a 'nearly daily occurrence'; for if the nobles in question were not to have their wives killed, but nevertheless needed to get rid of them for financial or philoprogenitive reasons, they had no option but to discover some flaw in the original marriage contract.[2] Some awkward affinity, some hitherto unsuspected precontract, some incorrectly framed dispensation sufficed to end the unwelcome union. (The situation was the same for women – where they were powerful enough to exploit it.)

The King's elder sister, Queen Margaret of Scotland, was an example of such a powerful woman. When her second marriage to the Earl of Angus failed to please her, she embarked on a complicated plea for divorce, which depended on this Angus marriage having taken place bigamously in the lifetime of her first husband. (In reality Queen Margaret had married Angus in 1514 following the death of James IV at Flodden in 1513.) King Henry indulged in some virtuous – if ironic – denunciations of his elder sister's conduct, putting it down to her 'lusts'. In December 1524 Queen Margaret was described as being 'so blinded with folly . . . as to have her ungodly appetite followed, she doth not care what she doth'. Cardinal Wolsey was asked to persuade her to consider the position of her daughter by Angus, Lady Margaret Douglas. He duly pleaded with the Scottish Queen to refrain out of 'natural love, tender pity and motherly kindness' from 'slanderously' proceeding; for she would 'disdain with dishonour so goodly a creature [Lady Margaret]' and make her daughter 'reputed base-born'.[3] But Queen Margaret did secure her divorce and married Methven in 1527.

Kings also got divorces. Most famously in recent memory, Louis XII had rid himself of his first wife Jeanne de France in order to marry Anne of Brittany and thus absorb this heiress's lands into his own. Jeanne de France had been childless, and she subsequently went into a convent after a humiliating physical examination in front of twenty-seven witnesses, in order for it to be established that she was incapable of bearing children (although she herself maintained the contrary).[4] King Louis duly married Anne of Brittany; Claude, his elder daughter by Anne, married his successor François I.

The dramatic consequences of the divorce of Henry VIII from Catherine of Aragon – its relationship to the English Protestant Reformation – have tended to mask the fact that such a divorce might well have gone through comparatively painlessly if certain circumstances had been different. One of these circumstances was undoubtedly the domination which, as we shall see, Catherine's nephew, Charles V, exercised over the papacy.

But the coincidence of two women of unexpectedly iron character on the scene – Anne Boleyn as well as Catherine of Aragon – was another.

The exact moment when the King began to be afflicted by the scruples of conscience concerning his marriage to Catherine which caused him to question its validity can only be estimated. Afterwards, various official explanations were given for these scruples, none of them particularly satisfactory. As was noted in the previous chapter, the Bishop of Tarbes' remarks could not have proved the sheer revelation Henry afterwards pretended, because no incoming ambassador would have risked such an insult; besides, the Bishop only arrived in England in mid-April. Still less would an English embassy to France, negotiating the marriage of the young Mary, have blackened the status of their own princess.

In another version, it was suggested that King Henry first became troubled by some remarks of his confessor, John Longland Bishop of Lincoln. Once again, it is difficult to believe that any priest in such an intimate relationship to the King would have raised the subject out of the blue. (Nicholas Harpsfield, writing in the reign of Catherine's daughter, claimed to have heard from Longland's chaplain that it was the King who approached Longland 'and never left [off] urging him' rather than the other way round.)[5] Nevertheless, according to this version, at some point previous to May 1527, the King was inspired to look at a certain text in Leviticus (20:21). There he read a verse which explicitly stated – so far as he was concerned – that what he had done in marrying Catherine was against the law of God: 'And if a man shall take his brother's wife, it is an unclean thing: he hath uncovered his brother's nakedness'. After that, God's penalty for breaking the law was equally explicitly spelt out: 'they shall be childless'.

But King Henry was a keen amateur theologian – one knowledgeable enough to have written that study of the sacraments for which the Pope had granted him the title of *Fidei Defensor* in 1521. Furthermore, if not exactly a tyrant liable to punish any presumption with hideous penalties, he had nevertheless not reigned for nearly twenty years without a noticeable increase in his public (and private) displays of anger. The order of things is, therefore, likely to have been rather different.

Let us suppose that the real beginning of it all was like this: that the King's dissatisfaction with his son-less state, dulled into acceptance over the years, flared up again in view of his passion for the young (and presumably nubile) Anne Boleyn.

Much has been made of Anne Boleyn's denial of her sexual favours to the King and his consequent frustration which led him to jettison his marriage – and a good many other things as well – in order to achieve consummation. Certainly she did not allow the King to make love to her (fully) for several years after he first began to pursue her. Although as has been noted over her relationship with Lord Percy, matters were not always absolutely clear cut in this period: 'liberties' of an increasingly intimate nature were probably allowed to the King. Since there was no suggestion that the King had any other mistress, or looked for any other mistress at this point, he cannot have been entirely sexually frustrated. Some form of *coitus interruptus* seems indicated: with the interruption occurring at an increasingly late stage of the proceedings as the years passed.

This made good sense from Anne's point of view as well, and not only in the vulgar sense of stringing along a man in order to preserve his keenness – which might vanish if he were to be satisfied. It also made sense because it kept her in control of her own reproductive processes. Contraception was not a science in the sixteenth century, and for all the methods used (from herbs to primitive forms of stoppage) nothing was guaranteed to be effective.[6] As a result *coitus interruptus* was widely practised. On the one hand Anne Boleyn had the example of Bessie Blount and other imprudent young ladies to warn her; on the other hand she had the experience of at least one romantic relationship – with Lord Percy – to teach her how to manage such things. One should therefore concentrate as much on what Anne Boleyn did offer, as on what she did not – or rather reserved for some future date.

She offered the King hope for the future, but hope that would take a precise form: a son. We cannot know the words with which she implanted this conviction – if indeed the first words were hers not his. But supposing Anne Boleyn did breathe such a promise in her love-talk with the King, it cannot have been difficult for this clever young woman, a keen observer of court life, to find the right ones. Here was a middle-aged man, already the visibly doting father of one son (Henry Fitzroy), even if he was born outside marriage. Henry VIII was a man, what was more, with a considerably older wife, described around this time by an incoming ambassador as 'of low stature, rather stout, very good and very religious', one who had failed to produce even one surviving son. (Although Anne should have been wary of the ambassador's postscript: he found Catherine, plump and pious as she might be, 'more beloved by the Islanders [the English] than any Queen that has ever reigned.')[7]

What is clear, throughout all the intricate and highly confused divorce proceedings that were to follow, is that King Henry himself did believe almost mystically in the coming of this male heir. (His change of attitude regarding his daughter Princess Mary is incomprehensible otherwise.) This conviction did after all happily combine two preoccupations from his own point of view: his long-term, sometimes paranoid feelings about the Tudor succession and his much more recent infatuation with the enchanting Anne Boleyn, 'the woman in the world that I value the most'.[8]

Much later the King would be said to explain it all away by reference to sorcery: he had been bewitched by Anne Boleyn. That was not literally true. She was not a witch – whatever malicious tongues would pretend – and cast no spells and devised no potions with the help of the devil, 'the Enemy of Mankind', to capture the King's love.[9] But in another sense Henry VIII was bewitched: not only by Anne's youth, grace and liveliness, but by the promise she offered of a proper fertile marriage (with sons to follow him – like François I and Charles V); somehow he had been robbed of this.*

Anne Boleyn's personal role is attested by the timing of it all; the crucial fact that the King had never contemplated a divorce before he fell in love with her. Various earlier rumours to the contrary have been found upon investigation to refer to other members of King Henry's family. A story that King Henry was seeking a divorce in the summer of 1514, for example, is clearly baseless since Queen Catherine was pregnant at the time (and as usual 'a prince' was expected).† Up to the mid-1520s, King Henry's attempts to marry Princess Mary to some kind of alternative successor are equally incompatible with a plan for a divorce from her mother. Yet within a year of being struck by 'the dart of love' fired by Anne Boleyn's black eyes, King Henry was taking an active part in the struggle to heave off the coils of his first marriage.

If falling in love was the first step, we return to the King's second step: this was his recourse to Leviticus. Even if his confessor Longland actually pointed him the way to this particular verse, he can only have done so in response to a request or the broadest of hints from the King. The importance of Leviticus was that it chimed, immediately and absolutely, with the King's resentment on the subject of his marriage to Catherine – newly aroused by his relationship with Anne. God had punished him by not giving him what he wanted – a son – so that he, Henry, must have somehow transgressed. Were he in the future to undo the mischief, God would rescind the harsh decision and reward his (newly faithful) servant. The dictates of the King's conscience and the dictates of the King's desire thus happily joined. Both told him to get rid of Queen Catherine.

The remarkable convenience of this coincidence did not mean that the King was insincere. On the contrary, Henry VIII really did believe, from 1527 onwards, that he had erred in God's eyes by marrying Catherine.

---

* Isabella of Portugal, Charles V's wife, gave birth to a son (the future Philip II of Spain) on 21 May 1527: François I had three sons by his first wife.
† It is now supposed that the document in question, listed in an eighteenth-century catalogue of the Vatican Archives, concerned the matrimonial affairs of the King's sister.[10]

This is not to say that the King was literally sincere in every statement he made on the subject: he was after all a politician – a statesman – with a policy to achieve. As we shall see, some of his protestations certainly smack of hypocrisy, as when he declared that he would willingly marry Catherine all over again – if their union turned out not to be sinful after all. But in the mind of King Henry, such a declaration, diplomatic manoeuvres apart, was not hypocritical. He was quite convinced that the union would *not* turn out to be free from sin. God had spoken to him through his conscience and would not let him down now. As the papal legate Cardinal Campeggio would say later: 'an angel descending from heaven would be unable to persuade him otherwise'.[11] When all is said and done, Henry VIII was not the first (or the last) man to equate the law of God with his own deepest wishes.

Unfortunately Queen Catherine was from first to last equally certain in her own conviction that she had been lawfully married to King Henry. Her marriage to Prince Arthur had not been consummated; she had been the virgin bride of Henry VIII; she was now his wife of many years' standing (and the mother of his only legitimate child). Through all the gyrations of popes, ecclesiastical lawyers, churchmen, nobles, politicians in London, in Spain, in Paris, in Bruges, in Brussels, at Rome, every conceivable argument would be offered for the validity or otherwise of this marriage, some of the greatest subtlety, others patently time-serving. In contrast, the positions of the two people who had originally been (or not been) married were at bottom extremely simple. But these two positions were basically opposed to each other.

The King's third step was to set in motion the process that would actually lead to a divorce. In May 1527, Cardinal Wolsey, by virtue of his authority as papal legate (granted to him annually from 1518 and made permanent in 1524), set up an official examination – *inquisitio ex officio* – into the validity of the King's marriage. This was a form of examination established at the Fourth Lateran Council of the church in 1215 by which the accused person or persons could be summoned on grounds of 'public infamy' and a judge could impose a sentence. Wolsey however set up the examination in secret without Queen Catherine herself being informed: this was not in accordance with procedure. In any case what Wolsey learned from this preliminary investigation convinced him that the King's case was not going to be quite so easy as the lovelorn monarch may have supposed.[12]

The King's own conviction that his marriage had been against the law of God was all very well; but there were complications. First, there was the matter of the actual text in Leviticus, which had referred to lack of *children*, rather than lack of sons only. King Henry allowed himself to be convinced that the word had been wrongly translated from the Greek into the Latin of the Bible then commonly used. 'He had heard', he said, 'that the word "*liberis*" – children – should actually have read "*filiis*" – sons.' This view was promulgated in a text about the divorce written by Robert Wakefield in 1527 under his aegis.[13] But it was in fact incorrect.

Even more damaging was a second biblical text in Deuteronomy (25:5–7), which explicitly laid down 'the duty of an husband's brother' towards the latter's childless widow: he 'shall go in unto her, and take her to him to wife' so that his dead brother's name 'be not put out of Israel'; severe penalties were to be imposed upon anyone who failed to do this. This second text posed a great deal of difficulty to anyone relying on the argument that Henry's marriage to Catherine had been against the law of God – as defined by Leviticus – which no Pope had the power to dispense. Not only had Henry behaved towards Arthur's childless widow exactly as ordained by Deuteronomy; but since Deuteronomy – the second book of the law – followed Leviticus, it was arguably a gloss upon the first book. Furthermore, the whole appeal to God's law attacked, by implication at least, papal authority: if a Pope could not tamper with this (superior) law, then there were limitations to what a Pope could do. It also attacked the papal finances: the issuing of dispensations from the law in exchange for payment was a profitable business.

Under the circumstances, Wolsey, as an ecclesiastic and a supporter of papal authority, much preferred to concentrate on the specific question of the dispensation itself (even if it could be argued that Deuteronomy applied to the Jews alone).[14] Wolsey's argument left the power of the Pope to issue dispensations intact but merely questioned whether one particular Pope – Julius II in 1503 – had managed to issue one particular dispensation correctly. But taking the King's case to Rome was fraught with difficulties of its own. The imperial victory at Pavia in 1525 had been followed, in May 1527, with the sacking of Rome by a rabble of imperial troops and the imprisonment of the Pope, Clement VII. The eponymous Vandals themselves could hardly have achieved more destruction, when they sacked Rome in the fifth century, than the wanton obliteration of churches, libraries and works of art that now took place. Owing to the currently beleaguered situation of the Pope, one solution might have been to get the whole body of English bishops to condemn the royal marriage as invalid. Here, however, Cardinal Wolsey – and the King – found themselves up against another stumbling block in the shape of another immovable conscience. John Fisher Bishop of Rochester, holy, learned and highly respected, insisted that the marriage had been valid.

Queen Catherine soon got to hear the humiliating and painful news of this secret enquiry: the imperial ambassador, Don Inigo de Mendoza, was tipped off by an informer and alerted her to the danger. The Queen's immediate reaction was to write off to her nephew the Emperor in Spain to seek his help. She wanted him to remonstrate with the erring Henry on the one hand, and get the Pope to take up her case in Rome on the other. Thus another polarity between the King and Queen was present virtually from the beginning of the 'great matter'. The King was understandably anxious that proceedings should take place in his own country – by virtue of Wolsey's legatine authority or by some other means. The Queen, equally understandably, preferred the prospect of Rome where she expected a fairer hearing.

As for Charles V, he was after all her refuge in time of trouble, as her father had once been, and for all the fiasco of Princess Mary's engagement, she turned to him instinctively now. Queen Catherine employed a servant in her household, Francisco Felipez, for this delicate, urgent mission, and in spite of obstacles placed in his path, he succeeded in reaching Spain.

Like Wolsey, the Queen – no fool – grasped the importance of the 1503 dispensation in all this.[15] If there was a weakness in the structure of her second marriage to be exploited, it lay in the nature of this dispensation, which had referred against her own will to her first marriage as having been '*forsitan*' (perhaps) consummated. King Ferdinand had been a supporter of this weasel word *forsitan*: although he knew perfectly well that his daughter was still a virgin (as he admitted in the letter to his ambassador of 23 August 1503), he thought it wiser at the time to get the widest possible kind of dispensation in order to satisfy the English. A non-consummated marriage, however, required a different kind of dispensation, that of 'public honesty': that is, despite the lack of sexual union, the couple had been publicly supposed to be married and that fact had to be acknowledged by the issuing of a dispensation. This apparently had not been asked for: in any case Queen Catherine asked her nephew to investigate the matter of the 1503 dispensation in Spain and see what emerged.

It is possible that at this point Queen Catherine – and even Wolsey – was under the impression there was some question of the King marrying a French princess: Madame Renée for example, the eighteen-year-old sister of the late Queen Claude. It was on 22 June that the King himself first communicated to his wife his 'scruples' concerning their marriage of nearly twenty years. There was certainly no reference to Anne Boleyn here, only to his conscience. He chose to accost Catherine 'in her closet'; one imagines that he must have dreaded such an interview, and perhaps hoped that the cosy domestic setting would somehow palliate the blow. If so, he was to be disappointed. The King explained as gently as possible to the Queen that certain 'learned and pious men' had come to him and broken the news that they were living in sin. No sooner had he done so than the Queen became overwhelmed with 'great grief' and burst into floods of tears.[16]

His intention was probably to persuade the Queen to withdraw from the court voluntarily: expecting her to be as shocked as he had been by this theological bombshell. But he had mistaken his woman: not for the last time in what became the tragedy of Henry VIII and Catherine of Aragon, the Queen's independent spirit ran contrary to the King's expectations. (Just as Queen Catherine, believing Wolsey not Henry to be responsible for 'the procurement' of the divorce, had mistaken her man; although in her case it was of course far less painful to blame Wolsey than to accept her own husband's responsibility.)* The Queen dried her tears; she was after all not unprepared for this 'bombshell'. Wolsey heard afterwards that she now became 'very stiff and obstinate', affirming that Prince Arthur 'did never know her carnally'. The King and herself were man and wife and always had been. He might send her away but she would never go of her own accord. Furthermore, 'she desired counsel', from Englishmen, as well as 'strangers'. In other words, as Wolsey put it to the King, the Queen took it all most 'displeasantly'.[17]

The summer of 1527 happened to be one of those depressingly wet seasons: it had rained continuously from 12 April to 3 June, and now there was a good deal of sweating sickness about (infection was a persistent concern of the King). There had been failure of the harvest: people starved daily for bread and others were crushed to death as they pressed round the relief breadcarts. In London, strong connections between the court and the city led to the circulation of juicy rumours about the King's private affairs. There was already 'a fame' (a story) abroad that the King intended to get rid of his Queen, since his marriage had proved 'damnable' (that is, theologically condemned), although a French princess rather than Anne Boleyn was believed to be his intended new bride. The Mayor had to be instructed to put an end to such rumours 'upon pain of the King's high displeasure', and a royal letter was read aloud on 15 July, castigating these 'seditious, untrue and slanderous' stories; the city was sharply told to curb its 'wild and insolent demeanour'.[18]

The King's happier moments were spent overseeing a series of treatises on the subject of his divorce of which at least three appeared as early as 1527, including a work called *Librum Nostrum – Our Book*. And then there were his letters to Anne Boleyn when they were temporarily parted: 'My mistress and friend', he wrote, 'seeing I cannot be present in person with you, I send you the nearest thing to that possible, that is, my picture set in

---

* It may have been the news of the enquiry, set up secretly by Wolsey, which originally caused the Queen to think this; a view to which she would have been in any case predisposed.

bracelets ... wishing myself in their place, when it shall please you.'[19] Love was as strong as ever and 'his mistress' was a great deal more agreeable to contemplate than a stiff and obstinate wife. If Henry's own situation could not immediately be resolved, then at least some steps could be taken in the direction of this new marriage by clarifying that of Anne Boleyn.

Cardinal Wolsey, accompanied by the magnificent train he considered his due, went to France in July. His intention was to achieve some kind of new balance in Europe so rudely unbalanced by recent events, in which the Holy City had been sacked and the Pope imprisoned. It was during Wolsey's absence that King Henry despatched his own emissary, Sir William Knight, to Rome to ask for a dispensation concerning a second marriage. From the language of the request, however tortuous, valuable information about the romantic past of Anne Boleyn – and King Henry – can be derived. (It was when Knight called on Wolsey at Compiègne on his way, that the Cardinal had to face the fact that the King's affections were focused on no French princess but in a much less worldly way on his wife's maid of honour.)

It is noticeable in the case of Anne Boleyn what strenuous efforts were made to cover in advance any conceivable problem that might arise in the future concerning her status at the time of her marriage. The dispensation sought seems to have covered both a straightforward matrimonial pre-contract (a betrothal) and a secret contract to marry which was not phys-ically consummated; both of these may well refer to Lord Percy. Since information about these precontracts must have derived from Anne Boleyn herself, it indicates how very confused the average person could be about his or her own situation when private vows some years back had to be translated into the terms of canon law. (Another possibility – easy to understand in view of the high stakes involved – would be that Anne herself maintained a certain discretion in what she revealed.) As for King Henry, his affair with Mary Boleyn was clearly envisaged when a dispensation was sought from 'the first degree of affinity [which could be caused by a relationship with a sister] arising from whatever licit or illicit intercourse'. But it was added: 'as long as she [the bride] is not the widow of the aforesaid [Henry VIII's] brother'.[20]

The dispensation which was finally granted – in December 1527 – did indeed cover a multitude of different situations. Since, however, an explicit condition of the granting was that the King should be free of his first marriage, it was useless for the time being.

As a New Year's present at the beginning of 1528, Anne Boleyn sent the King a 'handsome diamond' and a 'ship' in which a 'lonely damsel' was 'tossed about'. Her accompanying letter, wrote the King, had been 'beautiful'. In return Henry breathed the most ardent vows for the coming year: his motto would be *Aut illic aut nullibi* (either there or nowhere). He vowed to 'out-do' her in his love and fidelity: 'assuring you that henceforth my heart will be dedicated to you alone, and wishing greatly that my body was so too, for God can do it if He pleases; to whom I pray once a day for that end, hoping that at length my prayers will be heard.'[21]

For all the Queen's obstinacy in 1528 it seemed not unlikely that these prayers would be heard. The damsel in her ship would become less lonely; tossed about perhaps by a more delightful kind of storm. The Pope had escaped from his Roman captivity in December; the destruction which had left the Holy City 'a pitiable and mangled corpse', as he put it, filled him with natural bitterness towards the Emperor and the imperial cause generally.[22] After much diplomatic activity, England and France were now officially 'at war' again with the Empire. Although the so-called war was shortlived, none of this boded well for Catherine, whose chief trust, as the Spanish ambassador phrased it to Charles V, was in 'Your Imperial Majesty' (apart from God).

In February, two able envoys, Stephen Gardiner, Wolsey's secretary, and Edward Fox, set out for Rome, hoping to bring back that decretal commission which would enable the King's cause to be tried in England. They bore with them a letter from Cardinal Wolsey, referring in extravagant terms to Anne Boleyn: extolling 'the approved, excellent virtues of the said gentlewoman, the purity of her life, her constant virginity, her maidenly and womanly pudicity, her soberness, chasteness, meekness, humility, wisdom', as well as her 'descent of right noble and high thorough regal blood', her excellent education in 'laudable manners', and last but not least, her 'apparent aptness to the procreation of children'. In short, here was no paramour. The King referred contentedly to the mission of the two men in a letter to Anne: 'which brought to pass, as I trust by their diligence it shall be, shortly you and I shall have our desired end, which should be more to my heart's ease, and more quietness to my mind, than any other thing in this world'.[23]

For Anne Boleyn 1528 was a year when she emerged from the shadows of the Queen's household, the secret object of the King's passion, and demonstrated that there was more to her than a graceful figure, a pair of black eyes – and an ability to speak French. Like Queen Catherine, Anne Boleyn had unexpected depths and strengths; unexpected at least to the male-dominated world in which she lived. For one thing, she had a genuine interest in religion, the kind of reforming religion rapidly becoming fashionable on the continent following Luther as a reaction to the obvious failures and corruptions of the clergy. It was not a taste she shared with King Henry; the ten years' gap in their ages was, in terms of religion, a difference of generation. Although, frustrated by the church, the King might become interested in the politics of ecclesiastical reform, he was a natural 'Catholic' as it might now be termed, and remained so, religiously speaking, for the rest of his life, compared to Anne who might similarly be described as naturally 'Protestant'.*

It is true that the praise heaped upon Anne Boleyn in the second half of the sixteenth century as the prematurely Protestant mother of the Protestant Deborah, Elizabeth I, should be regarded with caution. The slightly sanctimonious figure who emerges from all this, the woman so austere in her household habits, so quick to criticize frivolity among her own maids, would certainly never have captivated Henry VIII and, having captivated him, held him. Nevertheless there is sufficient evidence that Anne was interested in radical booksellers, and by extension, tracts, as early as 1528, to show that this was a genuine aspect to her character from the start, not manufactured for hagiographical reasons later. (Obviously her knowledge of French was an advantage in reading such tracts written abroad; commissioning or obtaining translations was tricky and sometimes dangerous.) Furthermore she did display this interest some time before it was absolutely clear that Rome would cast its weight against the divorce; that is, before she had a vested interest in the tenets of the reformers.[24]

The London of this period – that city so quick to fire up with rumours of changes at court – was a hotbed of 'evangelicals' or would-be religious reformers. Their disgust with the practices of the contemporary clergy focused on matters as diverse as the lack of real celibacy (despite profession of it) and the practice of 'selling' Masses and prayers for the dead. (Wretched people impoverished themselves trying to assure a shorter stay in purgatory for their dead relatives.) The importation of texts and books from abroad was good business. It is possible that Anne Boleyn received her beautiful illuminated copy of *The Pistellis and Gospelles for the LII Sondayes in the Yere in French* (now preserved in the British Museum) from a man called Francis Denham, who ended up in Paris where he associated with 'pestiferous followers of Luther', and specialized in Lutheran tracts as well as the works of French reformists; Denham died of the plague in 1528. As early as 1530 or 1531, Thomas Alwaye, an evangelical who had been prosecuted by Wolsey for acquiring banned books, including the New Testament in English, regarded Anne Boleyn as having already a history of assisting in such situations: 'I remembered how many deeds of pity your goodness has done within these few years ... without respect of

---

* This language is of course anachronistic: it is not possible to talk of Catholics and Protestants in any real sense throughout this period when the distinction was generally between 'reformers' or 'evangelicals', sometimes described as Lutherans, and 'reactionaries'; the words are merely intended to convey a certain disposition of mind.

any persons, as well to strangers and aliens as to many of this land, as well to poor as to rich.'[25]

It was in 1528 that Thomas Garret, the curate of All Hallows Church, Honey Lane, in Oxford, was arrested for selling heretical works to scholars of various different colleges, including Wolsey's new Cardinal College. He recanted and the books concerned were subsequently burnt. At some point however Anne Boleyn interceded with Wolsey for him: 'I beseech your grace with all my heart to remember the parson of Honey Lane for my sake ...' Others were involved: conceivably Anne referred not to Garret but to the rector of the church, Thomas Forman. At all events a connection has been traced between these others and Anne Boleyn in her royal prime; William Betts, for example, became her chaplain, and Nicholas Udall would write coronation verses for her.[26]

There are various stories of Anne Boleyn showing anti-clerical or possibly heretical works to the King. One incident concerns an anti-clerical book by Simon Fish called *A Supplication of the Beggars*, printed at Antwerp in 1528; Anne Boleyn may have received it the same year. The chief target of the *Supplication* was the money wasted by the laity on various allegedly holy purposes ordained by the clergy (when they would have done better to have kept it for themselves). The story goes that Anne Boleyn showed her copy of Fish to the King at the suggestion of her brother; Henry was so delighted with it that he gave help to Fish and his wife.[27]

Still more significant is the story which has Anne Boleyn putting a copy of William Tyndale's *The Obedience of a Christian Man* into the King's hands, with certain passages daintily marked by her fingernail for his attention. Tyndale's English translation of the New Testament (from the Greek) had been printed abroad since the ecclesiastical authorities would not allow him to do so in England. *The Obedience of a Christian Man*, like Fish's *Supplication* first printed in 1528, attacked papal power in favour of that of the secular ruler. Anne Gainsford, a waiting-woman, told George Wyatt (Anne Boleyn's late sixteenth-century biographer) a version of this story in which she, borrowing the book from her mistress, subsequently lent it to her own suitor, George Zouch; whereupon it was snatched away by Richard Sampson, the Dean of the Chapel Royal. Anne Boleyn's reaction was to swear that it would be 'the dearest book that ever dean or cardinal took away' and she got the book back, thanks to the friendly intervention of the King. After that Anne Boleyn induced him 'most tenderly' to read the book. Henry VIII was duly impressed. 'By the help of the virtuous lady ... his eyes opened to see the truth.' He pronounced it a book 'for me and all kings to read'.[28]

Even if these stories have been coloured up to please a later generation, they are not mythic (although even mythic stories – what has been called 'the undergrowth of history' – still tell us something about the character concerned in the popular imagination). Essentially they convey the message that Anne Boleyn was independent enough to be genuinely interested in religious reform; as a result, she used her feminine prerogative of pleading on behalf of reformers from an early stage.

But Anne Boleyn's feminine prerogative was not entirely exercised in these devout matters. To have ignored the claims of her family to greater patronage – under the circumstances – would have been most uncharac- teristic of a sixteenth-century 'Mistress'. That was not how the court worked. Besides, for her, family and friends constituted an important power base; the King's passion was to be beneficial to them all. Or so they hoped. The affair of the new Abbess of Wilton in the spring of 1528, however, showed that the King might be in love, but he still remained the King outside the realm of the affections. (There was a lesson there, perhaps, for Anne Boleyn about the limits of any female domination over Henry VIII; but it was a lesson easily ignored in view of the King's extravagant vows.)

On 24 April 1528 the old Abbess of Wilton, Cecily Willoughby, died. There were about fifty nuns at the convent, and in the past there had been quite a few scandals associated with them. Therefore Wolsey's selection of the Prioress, Dame Isabel Jourdain, an 'ancient, wise and discreet' woman, who was sister to the Abbess of the much better conducted convent of Syon, was a wise move. But the Boleyn faction – as it was beginning to be – had other plans. William Carey, husband of Mary Boleyn, seems to have been the prime mover in what followed: the proposal that his sister Dame Eleanor Carey should be elected instead of Dame Isabel. King Henry duly advanced her claims.

It then transpired that Dame Eleanor was one of those very nuns with some kind of murky past whose lives had brought disrepute to Wilton. At which point the King immediately abandoned his advocacy of Dame Eleanor. His letter to Anne Boleyn on the subject – despite being in his sequence of love letters, and headed 'mine own darling' – is quite firm on the subject. Relating the details of Dame Eleanor's confession – 'two children by two sundry priests' and 'since [then] hath been kept by a servant of the Lord Broke that was' – he went on: 'Wherefore I would not for all the gold in the world clog your conscience nor mine to make her ruler of a house ...' He underlined the question of conscience: 'I trust you would not [wish] that ... for brother nor sister I should so destain mine honour or conscience'.[29]

In general, the King's letters of the summer of 1528 have a more settled tone to them: they are the letters of a lover, but one who is confident that 'the time for which I have waited so long' when he will be transformed

Anne Boleyn
m 1533

Badge of Anne Boleyn: crowned falcon accompanied by Tudor roses.

Thomas Boleyn, father of Anne Boleyn, by Holbein.

Hever Castle, Kent.

One of the letters of Henry VIII to Anne Boleyn, written in July 1528. It begins: 'Mine own sweetheart, these shall be to advertise you of the great elengeness [loneliness] that I find here since your departing …' and ends: 'Written with the hand of him that was, is, and shall be yours by his will. H.R.'

*Petition from Henry VIII to Pope
Clement VII concerning a divorce*

*Design by Holbein for a
triumphal arch for the
coronation of Anne Boleyn on
1 June 1533, showing her
heraldic falcon.*

Henry VIII in his early forties, by Joos van Cleeve.

Anne Boleyn, by an unknown artist.

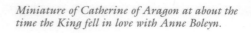
Miniature of Catherine of Aragon at about the time the King fell in love with Anne Boleyn.

Catherine of Aragon by an unknown artist.

Miniature of Anne Boleyn at the age of 25, about the time she attracted the attention of the King: attributed to Lucas Horenbout, it shows a falcon badge at her breast.

Anna Bollein Queen.

Anne Boleyn: a drawing by Holbein now at Windsor Castle.

Henry Fitzroy, Duke of Richmond.

into a husband is approaching; he can thus contain his passion. There was a bad outbreak of sweating sickness once again this summer. Anne Boleyn fell a victim to it.* The King met this challenge by keeping as far away from her company as possible until she was cured. Like many physically very strong men, he was prone to hypochondria. ('We have strengthened ourselves with medicines at our house in Hunsdon', he reported majestically.) 'Wherever I am, I am yours', he wrote to Anne, which covered the situation neatly, along with swearing that he 'would willingly bear half' of her illness.[30] But for him, the exciting news was not so much her health as his work on the matter of the divorce.

In July he had been working so hard on his book *A Glasse of the Truthe* which argued for his marriage to Catherine being against the law of God – for four whole hours on one day alone – that his head ached. His conclusion to this letter gives a glimpse at least of the physical course taken by Henry's dalliance with Anne: 'wishing myself (specially an evening) in my sweetheart's arms, whose pretty ducks [breasts] I trust shortly to kiss.'[31]

In other ways, Anne Boleyn was being coached for her future role as the consort of Henry VIII. Afterwards – long afterwards – it would be declared that she had always been the enemy of Cardinal Wolsey, since he put an end to her romance with Lord Percy. But the evidence of Anne's own letters to Wolsey of this summer is very much against this. In mid-June she wrote a letter which was almost abject in its gratitude. 'I do know the great pains and troubles that you have taken for me, both day and night, [concerning the divorce] is never like to be recompenced on my part, but alonely ... in loving you, next unto the king's grace, above all creatures living.' The King added a postscript: 'The writer of this letter would not cease till she had caused me likewise to set to my hand ...' The would-be lovers signed the letter together: 'By your loving sovereign and friend Henry R.' followed by 'Your humble servant Anne Boleyn'. A few weeks later, Anne Boleyn in thanking the Cardinal for 'a rich present', expressed herself as delighted that he had escaped 'the sweat'. '[A]ll the days of my life,' she wrote, 'I am most bound, of all creatures, next the king's grace, to love and serve your grace; of the which, I beseech you, never to doubt, that ever I shall vary from this thought as long as any breath is in my body.'[32]

Like the Cardinal's adulatory description of Anne Boleyn to Rome – 'the approved, excellent virtues of the said gentlewoman' – Anne's protestation

---

* What would have happened if Anne Boleyn had died of sweating sickness, as many did in the summer of 1528 (including her brother-in-law William Carey), provides a fascinating subject for conjecture. It is possible that the King's conscience would have driven him back to his Queen on the grounds that Anne's death had demonstrated the sinfulness of their relationship; but it seems more likely that Wolsey would have seized his chance to promote the cause of some youthful foreign princess able to bear children.

strikes a tinny note to later ears. But as a matter of fact both Anne and Henry had a great deal to thank Wolsey for in that summer of 1528. Pope Clement VII had been induced to grant a secret decretal commission which appointed Wolsey and another papal legate, Cardinal Campeggio, as joint inquisitors of the King's marriage. Although this was not the full public decretal commission of Wolsey's hopes – it was for the King's eyes only – it was a promising start.

So Cardinal Campeggio started on his journey from Rome to London. It was to be a long-drawn-out journey – he was an elderly man and much troubled with gout – but by the middle of September, the King was able to break the happy news to Anne Boleyn. She for her part had been despatched to her father's castle at Hever in Kent: her radiant presence at court might have been rather tactless at a time when the King was officially bewailing the cruel luck of an invalid marriage. But the King's letters to his 'good sweetheart' conveys his elation. The papal legate – 'which we most desire' – had got as far as Paris. Campeggio's sickness was 'unfeigned'; he himself was 'well-willing' and far from being the pawn of the imperial party. Shortly he would be in Calais and sail for Dover: 'and then, I trust, within a while after, to enjoy that which I have so longed for, to God's pleasure and our both comforts. No more to you, at this present, mine own darling, for lack of time, but that I would you were in mine arms, or I in yours; for I think it long since I kissed you . . .'[33]

Cardinal Campeggio arrived in London on 7 October. The exultation of Henry VIII and Anne Boleyn was undiminished. The Spanish ambassador heard that preparations were being made for their wedding: 'Both the King and his lady, I am assured, look upon their future marriage as certain, as if that of the Queen had actually been dissolved'. At the same time there was a surly public mood concerning these royal dreams of future bliss: 'the people here are much in favour of the Queen', Mendoza told Charles V. Even Hall, writing his *Chronicle* later – in terms entirely favourable to Henry VIII – had to admit that the populace had been woefully wrong-headed at this point: 'being ignorant of the truth and in especial women', they began 'to talk largely and said that the King would for his own pleasure have another wife.' This estimate – which might from some angles seem quite a sensible one – was of course intolerable to Henry VIII. It smacked not only of criticism – a coarse popular indifference to the painful pangs of conscience he was suffering – but worse still of potential obstruction of the royal will. As Mendoza put it: 'nothing . . . annoys this King so much as the idea of not accomplishing his purpose.'[34]

Gout apart – the disease racked him again in London and delayed the start of his work – Campeggio was in many ways an ideal candidate for the post of conciliator in this turbulent situation. He was not only a distinguished lawyer, but a widower with children, who took holy orders after his wife's death; he might be expected to handle the delicate side of this divorce with humanity and care. And there was a delicate side to it: the possibility that the whole divorce, from which Clement VII still shrank, posing as it did an intolerable burden upon him in political terms, might be rendered unnecessary. Why should not Queen Catherine retire to a convent of her own free will and leave the King's marital situation to be sorted out thereafter? With the effective withdrawal of the Queen's opposition, the question of a divorce would take on a new connotation.

At Campeggio's first meeting with Henry VIII, the King had, not surprisingly, rejected another papal notion that Clement VII should grant a fresh dispensation for his marriage to Catherine. A newly valid marriage to Catherine: that was not the way the King's mind tended. But a voluntary withdrawal of the pious Queen into a nunnery was a different matter altogether.

With the permission of the King, Cardinal Campeggio paid a series of three visits to the Queen. (The language they had in common was French which the Queen of course spoke fluently.) Perhaps the most important of these visits, from Catherine's point of view, was that in which she made a full confession to the Cardinal. Under the sacramental oath, she swore that she had been a virgin at the time of her marriage to Henry. According to the Cardinal's report to Rome, she told him she was '*intacta e incorrupta da lui comme venne dal ventre di sua madre*': untouched and unviolated by him (Prince Arthur) as when she came from the womb of her mother.[35] It is impossible to conceive that someone as strictly and straightforwardly pious as Catherine lied at this point and in this way: nor did anyone who knew her – including King Henry – ever seriously maintain so.

But from the point of view of King Henry, it was the Queen's absolute rejection of the proposition that she should enter the nunnery that was the most important aspect of the Cardinal's approach. Campeggio was accompanied by Wolsey. This was 'the expedient' put forward, with the full approval of the Pope: in order to avoid difficulties concerning the succession (which might result in civil discord), 'she should profess in some religious community and take vows of perpetual chastity. That since Her Highness had already reached the third and last period of natural life and had spent the first two setting a good example to the world, she would thus put a seal to all the good actions of her life'. This reasonable proposition – as it seemed to the two men before her – was met at first with 'irritation' by the Queen, especially directed at Wolsey to whom she 'spoke angrily'. But then she 'grew calm'. Recognizing this to be the true crisis of her life – when she had thought herself to have surmounted that true crisis long ago – she answered Campeggio 'with great composure'.[36]

Queen Catherine, too, like King Henry, was not afraid to refer to conscience. She told the papal legate that she held her husband's conscience and honour in more esteem than anything else in the world, before going on to say that she herself entertained no scruple at all about her marriage, 'but considered herself the true and legitimate wife of the King, her husband'. In other words, the Pope's proposal was 'inadmissible'.

It is easy to suggest that Catherine of Aragon really did show a degree of stubbornness in not accepting this solution to what Campeggio called her 'third and last period of natural life'. In material terms, her existence would certainly have been infinitely more comfortable. As to her rank, no one would have been more flatteringly grateful than King Henry: the Queen could have enjoyed an honoured retirement as the revered Mother-figure of the English royal family. It may be argued further that the life she would have led in a convent would not really have been so different from the life of pious practices she was already leading – so appropriate for a middle-aged woman, as Campeggio pointed out. Unfortunately the dictates of conscience may be dismissed as being mere stubbornness by those whom they do not suit, but, as the history of dissidents shows, they cannot so easily be stilled.

Queen Catherine's marriage to Henry was the one absolute certainty in her life, beyond her love of God (and in later years her daughter). For this she had defied Henry VII as a mere girl, unsupported in a foreign country, hardly speaking its language; she was not likely to succumb to Henry VIII now, after twenty years as his consort, and agree for convenience sake – his convenience – that she, a Castilian princess, had been the King's 'harlot' all these years.

Of course jealousy must not be ruled out. Catherine of Aragon was heroic in her stand but she was not a saint – or if she was, saints can be jealous too. To be supplanted by a rival who was not only much younger but also of infinitely lower rank was not easy for the daughter of the 'Catholic Kings' to endure, although she was too clever, and too well-trained to say so. More estimable was her concern for the position of her daughter, Princess Mary.

Afterwards it would be argued that much of King Henry's cruelty to Princess Mary was in revenge for her mother's behaviour, so that if Queen Catherine had voluntarily gone into the convent, Princess Mary would have been much better treated: that is to say (the usual triumphant conclusion of the oppressor) Queen Catherine, not King Henry, was actually responsible for her daughter's sufferings. Would the King have refrained from declaring his daughter a bastard if her mother had been more amenable? It is true that the church did not necessarily demand the bastardization of children of an invalid marriage, when the parents had married in good faith – as Henry and Catherine had undoubtedly done. On the other hand Wolsey's threats to Queen Margaret of Scotland – her daughter would be rendered 'base-born' – showed that it was always a possibility where divorce was concerned. Besides, so long as Princess Mary was allowed to remain legitimate, her claim to the throne would constitute a threat to the children of the second marriage: that was the real danger.

Some clumsy efforts were evidently made by the King's advisers to cope with Princess Mary's ambivalent situation. One of the most extraordinary – yet it seems to have received tacit papal approval – was the weird Pharaonic idea that the half-brother and -sister Princess Mary and Henry Duke of Richmond should be married to each other. This was against canon law (as well as against natural law in most civilizations). Yet the Pope seems to have been inclined to grant a dispensation for such a marriage, on condition that the King would abandon his project of divorce: showing how far the supposedly strict laws of affinity could actually be stretched. Cardinal Campeggio mentioned the subject in a letter to the Pope's secretary of 17 October: Wolsey had told him 'they have thought of marrying her [Mary] with a dispensation of His Holiness to the natural son of the King, if it could be done'. To which Campeggio replied: 'I too had thought of this at first,' as a means of assuring the succession. He went on – assessing Henry VIII's private passion only too correctly – 'but I do not believe this plan would be sufficient to remove the chief desire of the King.'[37]

The idea of the Queen's entry into a convent lingered, at least in the mind of the harassed Pope, for whom the divorce remained an extraordinarily awkward affair. On 28 December, Clement VII was still sending a message to Campeggio to the effect that it would greatly please him if the Queen could be induced to 'enter some religion'; even if such a course might be rather unusual, 'it would involve the injury of only one person'.[38] But in England, King Henry quickly realized – to his rising frustration and rage – that the Queen's convenient disappearance into a convent was no longer an option.

One of the most peculiar elements in the triple relationship of Henry, Catherine and Anne – at least to modern sensibilities – was the way that the routine of the court rolled placidly on, apparently impervious to the storms buffeting the heads of its principals. There is even some doubt as to when conjugal relations between the King and Queen actually stopped. Certainly the King continued to dine in the Queen's chambers, when it suited him, as before. According to Jean du Bellay, the French ambassador, however, in the autumn of 1528 he also continued to spend the night with her: 'till this hour, they have only had one bed and one table'. This official appearance of unity is confirmed by Hall's *Chronicle* which states of the King at this period that he 'dined and resorted to the Queen as he was accustomed'.[39]

Did the King also continue to make love to the Queen, out of royal habit? He was not after all, making love – fully – to Anne Boleyn. This seems less likely. Hall denied it: 'but in no wise he would not [sic] come to her bed'. Cardinal Campeggio also heard in late 1528 that the Queen 'had not had the use of his royal person for more than two years'. Harpsfield's statement that the King 'from the beginning of the divorce suit, did [not] ever use her body' agrees roughly with this. Then there was the question of the Queen's health: in January 1529 Wolsey reported that the King had resolved to abstain from lying with the Queen due to some diseases she had, 'pronounced incurable'.[40]* All this seems to add up to a cessation of physical intimacy between them around 1526, due to a combination of factors, including the King's disinclination and the Queen's health.

But this did not mean that all relations ceased. The terrible formal intimacy of court life – Catherine and no one else was Queen of England – remained. Anne Boleyn now had her own apartments, and her own waiting-women. Yet she too was part of this ritual and had her place in it. There is an anecdote which has Queen Catherine playing at cards with Anne Boleyn, among her other ladies. At some point in the play, the Queen indicated a card and observed pointedly, 'You will not stop till you have your King, Mistress Anne.' The story may or may not be true. If it is true, then it is one of the few instances in which the controlled Queen Catherine allowed herself an ironic comment on the events that were fast overtaking her. But its real importance lies in the glimpse it allows us of the domestic web in which all three, Queen, King and his 'Lady', were caught up. Here was a court where King Henry, according to Campeggio, was openly kissing Anne Boleyn 'and treating her in public as if she was his wife'; yet he was still officially married to Queen Catherine, who theoretically presided over it.[41]

At least the arrival of Campeggio meant that the Queen had to be granted her own legal counsellors: to have denied her that representation would have been to make a travesty out of what was intended to be a serious consideration of a serious case. The bravest and most effective of these would prove to be John Fisher Bishop of Rochester, who had already, the previous year, flung his considerable moral authority behind the Queen's cause when he would not agree that the royal marriage was invalid. Archbishop Warham of Canterbury and Bishop Tunstall of London were made

---

* Presumably of a gynaecological nature, resulting from years of child-bearing, or connected to the menopause.

of more establishment stuff, as their positions indicated. Then there were some foreigners: the Spanish ambassador imported two canon lawyers from Flanders; besides which there was the Queen's Spanish confessor, Jorge de Athequa Bishop of Llandaff, and Juan Luis Vives.

Vives had gone to Bruges in June 1527 – and he remained on good enough terms with King Henry to be commissioned to acquire him a copy of Erasmus' *Adagia*. Queen Catherine had however long sought her favourite scholar's return; she tried to lure his wife Margaret to come to Greenwich with little presents and promises of support. Vives was certainly amongst those who was shocked by the 'stupidity and mad love affair of the King', and impressed by the Queen's resolution: he referred to her 'truly manly strength' (the ultimate accolade of the time), and declared that if the Queen had lived in an age where virtue was properly honoured, 'people would have adored her in a temple as an oracle from above'.

He showed more proper feeling than Erasmus whose letter of consolation was extremely cautious. Erasmus tactlessly recommended to his friend and her chamberlain Lord Mountjoy that the Queen should read a book called *Vidua Christiana* (A Christian Widow): but why should a woman who eminently did *not* consider herself a widow read any such book? Even more tactlessly, Erasmus ventured the quip – but not to Catherine – that divorce was certainly a mistake: better instead to have a Jove with two Junos (by implication, that the King should somehow be allowed to commit bigamy). Yet even Vives, for all the past benefits he had received, for all his admiration of the 'oracle', did not long survive the rival pressures of Wolsey (Vives felt his agents were watching him) and those of the Queen. She became 'furious' with him for insufficient advocacy of her cause and he retreated back to Bruges.[42]

One of the first problems Queen Catherine's advisers had to contend with was that of a so-called 'brief' concerning the original dispensation of 1503. While Pope Julius II's bull for the dispensation had referred to the marriage being 'perhaps' consummated – thus arguably offering no proper dispensation if it had not – the brief was drawn in much wider terms. Its language – referring to 'unnamed other reasons' – envisaged either consummation or non-consummation. A copy of this highly damaging document – from the point of view of the King's case – had arrived from Spain in response to Catherine's original request to Charles V for material relevant to her case. This brief had apparently been obtained for the satisfaction of the dying Queen Isabella.

Naturally Wolsey and the King's advisers immediately queried the authenticity of such a convenient document and demanded that the original be brought from Spain. But if the brief was genuine, then the best case of the King in the eyes of the church – that although the Pope had the power to

dispense marriages, he had not technically managed to dispense this one –
fell to the ground. Queen Catherine resisted for some time sending for the
original, fearing for good reason what would happen to it in England.
When she ostensibly gave in, she made private efforts to cancel the effect
of her public request. The original was never sent, but eventually a fully
notarized and authenticated copy did arrive.[43]*

On the same day as Catherine delivered this brief – 7 November – she
received a visit from her so-called counsellors, Warham and Tunstall, which
would have been absurd if it had not been at the same time menacing.
They came at the request of the King, they said, to report that rumours of
plots against the King's life were abroad, and that if such plots were
successful, the Queen and her daughter would inevitably be suspects.
Catherine reacted indignantly to such laughable charges. She could not
believe that the King gave any credit to them, since she certainly valued
her husband's life more than her own. Then the emissaries' enquiries
descended to a more practical level. It was a matter of this brief. Not only
was the Queen dancing and making merry, encouraging popular support
for her cause – bad enough – but she had kept the brief a secret. Forgery
it might be and probably was, but if she had declared it, the King would
have been saved 'much unease'. The Queen rebutted this charge with equal
vigour. She had not revealed the existence of the brief (which had probably
arrived from Spain about six months previously) because she had not known
it was wanted.[44]

The Queen's personal and legal fight, in such maddening contrast to
the resigned behaviour the King had expected, was paralleled by her
undiminished popularity with 'the Islanders'. Her reputation for virtue and
charity stood her in good stead. Anne Boleyn's long period in the pillory
of the public imagination as 'the bad (younger) woman' who had stolen
the husband of 'the good (older) woman' was beginning: it would only
intensify in years to come. As the French ambassador, du Bellay, noted:
'the people remain quite hardened [against Anne] and I think they would
do more if they had more power'.[45] In a primitive way, it was felt that the
fate of one decent middle-aged woman, being unfairly treated, stood for
all such, however different their social positions; just as Anne Boleyn was
every hussy with designs on another woman's husband.

In November the King took pains to try and pre-empt such irritating
popular manifestations by making a long statement at Bridewell Palace. In
it he praised Queen Catherine to the heights 'as a lady against whom no

---

* Was the convenient brief authentic? Probably yes: King Ferdinand's letter regarding the original
dispensation in the Pope's bull shows how anxious he was to cover every eventuality. Since he was
firmly of the opinion that the marriage had not been consummated, it would have made sense to
have a brief which covered this situation as well.

word could be spoken'. He went on: 'If it be adjudged that the Queen is my lawful wife, nothing will be more pleasant or more acceptable to me, both for the clearness of my conscience, and also for the good qualities and conditions I know her to be in ... besides her noble parentage she is a woman of most gentleness, humility and buxomness; yea, and of all good qualities pertaining to nobility she is without comparison'. In proof of this, he declared unblushingly: 'So that if I were to marry again, I would choose her above all women. But if it be determined in judgement that our marriage is against God's law, then shall I sorrow, parting from so good a lady and loving companion.'[46]

These remarks must have raised a few eyebrows among the attendant courtiers – if anyone had the courage to let their feelings show through. But perhaps they did not, for the French ambassador reported an ugly incident at the end of the speech (Hall, favourable to King Henry, ignores it). All of a sudden, the King became extremely angry. One can imagine the florid complexion darkening, the spreading pink cheeks flushing a deeper shade of red. He shouted that if anyone dared criticize him in the future, he would show who was master: 'There was no head so fine (*si belle*) that he would not make it fly.'[47] There was another lesson here for the future, this time one that was difficult to miss.

Christmas 1528 was spent by Henry VIII and his 'Lady' at the palace of Greenwich; Queen Catherine was also there. But Anne Boleyn was by now lodged in 'a fine apartment close to that of the King'. Greater court, noted the French ambassador, was being paid to her every day 'than has been paid to the Queen for a long time'. As for Catherine, she was evidently depressed and downcast: she displayed 'no manner of countenance and made no great joy of nothing, her mind was so troubled'.[48] If 1528 had not quite brought the successful resolution of his personal life that Henry VIII had confidently predicted in his New Year's letter to Anne Boleyn, then surely 1529 would remedy the deficiency.

Chapter 8

PEOPLE MAY

GRUMBLE

Ainsi sera, groigne qui groigne – That's how it's going
to be, however much people may grumble.

Motto of Anne Boleyn, Christmas 1530

I t was Anne Boleyn's custom (when the occasion was 'fitting') to be
found with a French book in her hand: 'which is useful and necessary
for teaching and discovering the true and straight path of all virtue'.
During the Lenten season of 1529, in particular, she was to be seen at
court reading a French translation of the epistles of St Paul 'in which are
contained the whole manner and rule of a good life'. This vignette of the
King's pious Lady charmed a certain Loys de Brun who recalled it the
following New Year when dedicating a French treatise on letter-writing
to Anne Boleyn.[1]

To others at the court, such a spectacle of radically chic devotions
must have seemed a great deal less charming. Cardinal Campeggio, still
tortured with gout, viewed such goings-on – where would they end? –
with gloom. On 3 April he reported that 'certain Lutheran books, in
English, of an evil sort' were freely circulating at court.[2] It was not a
good omen for the coming tribunal at which the Cardinal, as one of the
two papal legates – Wolsey was the other – had as he saw it a responsibility
to uphold papal authority. When the tribunal opened at the end of May
it did so against a background of general uneasiness, of which 'Lutheran'
resentment at papal authority was one small part. It was however a
resentment that was still only music off stage.

A very different cause for uneasiness lay in the attitude of Queen
Catherine towards the tribunal. On 6 March she had asked the Pope to
take her case to the Curia at Rome, and six weeks later the Emperor also
petitioned the Pope to the same effect. It was not absolutely certain,
therefore, that she would obey the summons to the tribunal, and if so,
how she would conduct herself: would she accept its authority? Nor was

– 156 –

the current frame of mind of the Pope any particular consolation. The two legates, Campeggio and Wolsey, were summoning the tribunal according to the general commission granted by Clement VII the previous year. But with the passage of time, the Pope had once more begun to view the patronage of the Emperor as politically desirable. Florence had been seized by Charles V's troops: now there was a possibility of its being disgorged from the imperial maw. Furthermore the Pope was aware of the need to secure his own personal safety at a moment when the Emperor was master of Italy.

This meant that the two papal legates had in effect divergent interests. Where Cardinal Campeggio needed to deliver a verdict that would not upset the long-term policies of the papacy (whatever they might turn out to be), Cardinal Wolsey needed, more simply, to deliver a verdict in favour of the dissolution of the King's marriage. He must be the King's good servant – not the Pope's – and the verdict of dissolution should prove it.

The tribunal met for the first time on 31 May 1529. The place chosen was the Parliament Chamber of Blackfriars, which was still conveniently joined to Bridewell Palace by that tapestried bridge created for the Emperor Charles V in 1522. Only fragmentary accounts survive of its proceedings – it lasted for nearly two months – and these are sometimes contradictory in their details.* But they do include the reports of Cardinal Campeggio and his secretary Floriano Montini, the contemporary descriptions of the French ambassador Jean du Bellay and the Venetian ambassador Louis Falier; then there is the important testimony of George Cavendish, who was present in attendance on Wolsey (even though he wrote down his recollections many years later).

The procedure to establish the truth was to be inquisitional; in fact, very similar to that of the *inquisitio ex officio* of two years earlier. Only on this occasion both King and Queen were summoned to answer questions: 18 June, three weeks after the opening of the tribunal, was the date chosen. There was still understandable anxiety about the line the Queen would take. Nor was this anxiety allayed by an interview the Queen had with Cardinal Campeggio on 16 June, just before she was due to appear in court.[3] Catherine was now lodged at Baynard's Castle; by a melancholy coincidence it was that palace between Blackfriars and Paul's Wharf, 'beautiful for the entertainment of any prince', where not only the banquet celebrating her marriage to Prince Arthur had taken place in 1501, but also the debatable 'wedding night' which followed.

---

* The best account, piecing them all together (and using one hitherto ignored manuscript in Cambridge University Library – a 'doctored' legatine account) is in H. A. Kelly, *The Matrimonial Trials of Henry VIII*, pp. 75–131, which is the principal basis for this narrative.

On this occasion Queen Catherine 'very solemnly' swore in the presence of her counsellors, Archbishop Warham and Bishop Tunstall, her Spanish confessor, Jorge de Athequa Bishop of Llandaff, and others including notaries, that Prince Arthur had not consummated their marriage during this wedding night or on any other occasion: 'that from the embraces of her first husband she entered this marriage as a virgin and an immaculate woman'.[4] She also formally requested before the notaries that the case should be tried in Rome by the Pope and not by the Pope's legates in England. Two days later she appeared before the tribunal to make another solemn protest which included a complete denial of the tribunal's right to try her case; furthermore, her appearance before it should in no way be construed as accepting its authority, nor as prejudicing her right to take her case to Rome. She duly asked for her protests and various 'provocations' or appeals to be notarized and registered by the court. In return, the legates asked her to appear before them again in three days' time in order to learn their decision.

So that it was on Monday 21 June, in the Parliament Chamber of Blackfriars, that the scene immortalized by Shakespeare took place, when Queen Catherine pleaded with King Henry for her future – in the name of their past.

At the time a large crowd of spectators witnessed the show, which had certainly never been paralleled in the history of 'the Islanders'. Although both King and Queen were seated on chairs under regal canopies of gold brocade – the Queen's slightly lower than that of the King – they seem, from the course of subsequent events, to have been somewhat divided from each other by these spectators. Then there were the two papal legates, in the flowing scarlet of a cardinal's rank. Campeggio's difficulties were compounded by the fact that he understood very little English (it will be remembered that he had discoursed with Catherine in French). Wolsey's difficulties were of another order: although he needed to secure the divorce, and needed also to take the credit for it thereafter, at the same time he did not wish to be pilloried as the instigator of it all.

The King spoke first: at least according to the Venetian ambassador, who wrote his report the next day (Cavendish, recollecting in tranquillity, gives a different order).*[5] His main theme was 'a certain scrupulosity [on the subject of his marriage] that pricked my conscience', and he brought up all over again the manner in which his doubts had allegedly been

---

* Although various different orders are given for the three main speeches of the King, Cardinal Wolsey and the Queen, the main gist in all the accounts does not differ, including the Queen's remarkable dénouement at the end.

raised: the queries of the French ambassador, the Bishop of Tarbes, concerning Princess Mary, and his confessor Longland's pointing to Leviticus. He even repeated his assertion made at Bridewell the previous November that he would willingly take the Queen back as his wife, if the marriage was found to be valid after all: although such an assertion must by now have sounded still more hollow to spectators, in view of the dominating presence at the English court of she whom the French ambassador termed 'the young lady'. Doubtless they bore in mind a useful watchword Norfolk commended to Thomas More, 'By God's body, Master More, *Indignatio principis mors est*': the anger of the prince means death.[6]

It turned out however that not everyone did bear this watchword in mind. There was an incident when the King announced that all his bishops shared his doubts and had signed a petition 'to put this matter in question'. At this point, Bishop Fisher protested violently that he had not signed his name to any such document, and reproached Archbishop Warham for adding his name without authority. The King did not care for this. It was not how these grave, sad proceedings on the subject of his conscience were intended to go forward; with tiresome nit-picking about signatures. 'Well, well', he replied irritably, 'it will make not matter; we will not stand with you in argument herein, for you are but one man'.

King Henry did however take pains to absolve Wolsey from any responsibility in raising the question of divorce. This was a sound tactic: it was after all not Wolsey's conscience which had been pricked in this uncomfortable manner – directly or indirectly by God himself. Wolsey on the contrary was wanted as an impartial judge of the case. And Wolsey, following the King (or, according to Cavendish, preceding him), was equally firm in denying any possible prejudice on his part. He had simply been appointed by the Pope to find out the truth about the marriage. He certainly wanted to assure all those present that he had not been 'the chief inventor or first Mover' in the matter.

Queen Catherine now spoke.[7] According to the French ambassador, she first made an appeal. The King replied along the expected lines – how it was the great love he bore her which had prevented him acting before now, how it was his dearest wish to have the marriage declared valid, and how his desire to keep the case from going to Rome was entirely due to his fear of the Emperor's influence there. (Of these three arguments, the last at least was sincere.) But it was what happened after this which left the deepest impression on the eyewitnesses, from the gouty Cardinal Campeggio straining to understand what was being said in English, to Wolsey's gentleman-usher, Cavendish, whose recollections of the scene would provide the inspiration for Shakespeare over eighty years later.*

Unexpectedly, the Queen left her seat and threading her way through the spectators with some difficulty, reached the King's chair. There she flung herself down at his feet. As Cardinal Campeggio related it, the King immediately raised her up. At which the Queen once more knelt in supplication before him. This left the King with nothing to do but raise her up once more – and listen to her passionate outpourings. Cavendish only remembered her kneeling once before the King, but he gave a summary of her speech. For its true effect, we must imagine her speaking with a strong Spanish accent and in broken English, despite the fluency of Cavendish's summary; we must also remember that voice of hers, surprisingly deep for such a tiny woman; we must bear in mind the courage which brought her to issue this appeal in public (after all, the anger of the prince was death). Even without this, it remains the ultimate expression of loss by a rejected first wife, who had made her husband's life her own and whose only crime had been to grow old before he did.

'Sir,' she began, 'I beseech you for all the love that hath been between us, let me have justice and right, take of me some pity and compassion, for I am a poor woman, and a stranger, born out of your dominion. I have here no friend and much less indifferent counsel.† I flee to you, as to the head of justice within this realm . . .' She went on: 'I take God and all the world to witness that I have been to you a true, humble and obedient wife, ever comfortable to your will and pleasure . . . being always well pleased and contented with all things wherein you had any delight or dalliance . . . I loved all those whom ye loved, only for your sake, whether I had cause or no, and whether they were my friends or enemies.'

Like King Henry, but with, one imagines, more conviction, the Queen was even prepared to be 'put away' if any just cause of law was found against her: 'either of dishonesty [i.e. public honesty] or any other impediment.' She touched also on their shared tragedy: 'By me ye have had divers children, although it hath pleased God to call them from this world'. But it was her challenge on the subject of her virginity which was the most devastating point made to the man before whom she knelt:

---

* Shakespeare in *Henry VIII* (1613) clearly draws – often very closely – on Cavendish's *Life of Wolsey*. His source for Cavendish would not have been the *Life* itself but Holinshed's *Chronicles*, as with much of the historical material he used.

† Compare Shakespeare, *Henry VIII*, Act II, scene IV:

> Sir, I desire you do me right and justice;
> And to bestow your pity on me; for
> I am a most poor woman, and a stranger,
> Born out of your dominions; having here
> No judge indifferent . . .

'And when ye had me at first, I take God to my judge, I was a true maid, without touch of man. And whether this be true or no, I put it to your conscience.' The King did not answer – as he never had (and never would) publicly give her the lie on this intimate but crucial issue.

When she had finished, Queen Catherine rose up, she swept her husband a low curtsy, and leaning on the arm of her gentleman-usher, Griffith Richards, moved slowly out of the court.

The official court crier called after her – three times. At last her nervous usher ventured to say to her: 'Madam, ye be called again.' 'It matters not', replied the Queen, 'this is no indifferent [unprejudiced] court for me. I will not tarry.' And so she left. The women – ordinary women – who had hailed her at her entrance, now greeted her at her departure, 'telling her to care for nothing and other such words'. As du Bellay reported, 'if the matter were to be decided by women' the English King 'would lose the battle'.[8] But of course it was not.

After this the Queen left Baynard's Castle and Bridewell, and went down the river to the palace at Greenwich. (It was a royal residence of which she was particularly fond, for its proximity to the friary of the Franciscan Observants.) Here, a few days after her dramatic plea, Cardinal Wolsey, attended by Cavendish, paid her an evening visit. The Cardinal came at the request of his master to try to persuade the Queen to surrender the whole matter into the King's hands, for otherwise she stood to be 'condemned' by a court of law. Cavendish, along the way, provides us with a glimpse of the Queen's domestic ritual as it continued with apparent placidity: she came out of her Privy Chamber to greet the Cardinal in the Presence Chamber 'with a skein of white thread about her neck', explaining that she had been 'set among my maids at work'.[9]

However, housewifely concerns did not prevent Queen Catherine from answering the Cardinal with some skill. First, the Queen refused to allow the discussion to take place in Latin, which would have effectively barred many of her attendants from following it: 'Nay, good my lord, speak to me in English; although I understand Latin'. She had nothing to hide, let 'all the world' hear what he had to say. Then the Queen refused to consider this request out of the blue from such 'noble wise men as ye be' made to her, 'a poor woman, lacking both wit and understanding' and quite unprepared. Finally, she let the Cardinal into her Privy Chamber. It had been a 'chafing hot' day and the atmosphere evidently did not get much cooler in the interview that followed. Cavendish was left behind in the Presence Chamber, but sometimes could hear the Queen 'speak very loud' although he could not make out exactly what was being said. At the end of this long hot day (the Cardinal had actually been in bed with exhaustion when the King sent him on his mission) nothing had changed. The Queen, 'poor woman' as she might be, was resolute.

On Friday 25 June, the tribunal pronounced the Queen 'contumacious' since she had not appeared as summoned. In her absence, a list of 'interrogations' or articles on the subject of the royal marriage were produced. They ranged from the routine, slightly inane enquiries typical of investigations – the King had to answer whether he and Prince Arthur were brothers, for example – to the graver matter of Catherine's relationship with Arthur. Here it was postulated as an 'Objection' to Catherine's marriage to Henry that this earlier marriage had been consummated 'with carnal *copula*' and that the young couple had lived openly together for some time, until Arthur's death, 'commonly regarded and believed to be man and wife and legitimate spouses'. It seems, however, that when this particular objection was put to King Henry for his signature, the words 'with carnal *copula*' were omitted.[10] Once again the King was not prepared to partake in a direct lie – if such it was.

On 28 June the Queen again refused to appear, although Bishop John Fisher, according to the French ambassador, made an impassioned speech about the validity of the marriage, saying that just as John the Baptist had died in the cause of a marriage, he too would be a martyr. (The difference was that John the Baptist had been martyred for denouncing the marriage of Herod to Herodias as unlawful: whereas John Fisher was willing to die upholding Henry's marriage to Catherine as lawful.)

In the Queen's absence – fortunately for her sensibilities – evidence about that wedding night at Baynard's Castle now twenty-eight years ago was supplied by various courtiers.[11] Not all of it was particularly conclusive: the sixty-year-old Earl of Shrewsbury, for example, supposed that the prince consummated his marriage 'as he [Shrewsbury] did so, being only fifteen and a half when he was married.' The King's cousin, Thomas Grey Marquess of Dorset, had been present when Prince Arthur was escorted to the nuptial bed after his marriage, where 'the lady Catherine' lay under the coverlet 'as is the manner of queens' in that situation. Dorset was sure that the prince 'used the princess as his wife' since Arthur had been 'of a good and sanguine complexion'.

The deposition of Sir Anthony Willoughby was more colourful. By virtue of his father's position as steward of the King's household, he was present both when Prince Arthur was taken to bed and when he emerged from the chamber in the morning. At this point the prince exclaimed: 'Willoughby, bring me a cup of ale, for I have been this night in the midst of Spain.' Later the prince said openly: 'Masters, it is a good pastime to have a wife.' This kind of story was a good deal more to the popular taste than the earnest deposition of the Bishop of Ely which followed: the Bishop had grave doubts about the consummation, since the Queen had so often told him on the testimony of her conscience that she had not been *'carnaliter ... cognita'* (carnally known) by the said Arthur.

Willoughby's deposition did in fact form the basis of a pamphlet wittily entitled *A Glass of the Truth*, printed in September 1532, which had the prince 'demanding and desiring drink incontinently upon his great labours, in the morning very early, to quench his thirst; answer when the question was asked him, "Why, sir, and be ye now so dry?" "Marry, if thou haddest been as often in Spain this night as I have been, I think verily thou wouldst have been much drier" '. Later on in the course of the tribunal, there would be other testimonies to the fact that Arthur and Catherine had lived together as man and wife, sleeping together in the same chamber, and that he had been 'a true and vigorous husband' (evidence was given concerning the prince's ejaculations). But a report of bloodstained bedsheets having been sent to Catherine's parents in Spain (to attest to the loss of her virginity) was never actually produced, although Cardinal Wolsey had threatened to do so.

What is one to make of this evidence, of which the sexual boasting of a teenage boy, remembered over a long passage of time but mysteriously never given currency till this very moment, is the most vivid? The Spanish ambassador would in the future garner quite different testimonies to the effect that Prince Arthur had been impotent. These, if true, do not necessarily rule out the boy making his pathetic boasts; they might even make them more plausible as he attempted to hold his own in the man's world for which he was physically ill-equipped. But the real truth, as this ambassador – Eustace Chapuys – would point out two years later, was that nonconsummation was impossible to prove for certain nearly thirty years later in the case of a woman who had been for twenty years married to another man. The best course was to rely on the Queen's known character: that she was 'so virtuous, devout and holy, so truthful and God-fearing' that she would not lie. This (coupled with King Henry's tortuous attitude to the subject) still remains the best proof.

At the end of the proceedings, on 28 June, the Queen was summoned to appear for 5 July. Although the Queen received the summons at Greenwich three days before, she was absent when the tribunal met. Nor, despite being pronounced contumacious, did she ever appear again before the tribunal, although its proceedings would continue until late July.

The Queen's defence was now being actively mounted with the help of her counsellors, including those in imperial Flanders, in terms of appeals to Rome. The Regent of the Netherlands, the Archduchess Margaret, sent her own appeal: she was of course the Queen's former sister-in-law (through her marriage to the Infante Juan) and had been her friend since those distant days in Spain, meeting her most recently at Gravelines in 1520. But the important link between them was the Emperor: both were his aunts, the Archduchess on his father's side and Queen Catherine on that of his mother; now it suited imperial policy that one powerful aunt was to come to the assistance of another aunt, temporarily (it was to be hoped) down on her luck. In June the imperialists routed the French at Landriano: the Peace of Cambrai between the two countries followed. It was further helpful to Queen Catherine's cause at Rome that the *rapprochement* between Emperor and Pope had continued: finally, by the Treaty of Barcelona, which provided for the marriage of Charles's bastard daughter to the Pope's nephew, the Duke of Parma, they officially came to terms.

Under the circumstances, it was difficult for Clement VII not to advocate (officially transfer) the Queen's case to Rome as she requested. She had been declared contumacious by the English tribunal. Yet her documents showed that she had a strong case; in any case Clement VII was disposed to believe that any fault in the dispensation was purely technical and could be righted since the intention to provide a proper dispensation had evidently been there. (This eminently sensible view reckoned of course without the King's love-driven determination to end the marriage.) In mid-July therefore the Pope agreed to the official transfer of the case.

This news would obviously prove a death blow to the King's high hopes, encouraged by Wolsey, of a summer divorce. Before it reached England, however, there was time for the tribunal to hear a number of detailed legal arguments from both sides. Friday 23 July was the last day on which the tribunal sat. King Henry himself was present, in one of the galleries which overlooked the legates in their scarlet robes. The favourable verdict he had so long awaited did not come. Cardinal Campeggio had learnt the lesson of creative procrastination from Clement VII: he declared that the case was too important to be decided without consultation with the Curia at Rome: unfortunately the Curia was on its (long Italian) summer holiday and he therefore prorogued the tribunal until 1 October. But in any case, the night before, he and his fellow legate Wolsey had heard the news that the Pope intended to advocate the case to Rome. A two-month mixture of theological argument, legal contention and salacious detail (not forgetting the speeches, from the disingenuous to the noble) had ended – and still King Henry was no nearer getting free from his wife.

There was however one manifest consequence of the whole process of the tribunal – and its failure. In the autumn the great Cardinal, and papal legate, Wolsey, fell from power. It was in late September that Queen Catherine informed the new Spanish ambassador 'in a very low tone' that there was no need to present his credentials to Wolsey, for his affairs at present were much embroiled (*en gran brousle*). According to George Cavendish (writing much later, but before the accession of Anne Boleyn's daughter), it was Anne herself who was responsible for striking the decisive blow, having never forgiven Wolsey for his high-handed removal of her eligible lover, Lord Percy. Certainly many contemporaries attributed the Cardinal's disgrace to the influence of 'the Lady'. The French ambassador commented on the new situation at court: 'at the head of all, Mademoiselle Anne'.[12] But this was a pleasantly easy piece of misogyny compared to the rather more onerous task of blaming the King. As Queen Catherine found it less painful to think of it as Wolsey's divorce, so Wolsey himself may have found it easier to accuse the woman than face the man's ingratitude. Yet Anne Boleyn, in turning on the Cardinal, was merely echoing the impatience of her august admirer at failing to get what he wanted; just as she had echoed the King a year previously, in vowing herself that she loved the Cardinal 'next unto the king's grace, above all creatures living' as a result of the pains he was taking to get the divorce.

In political terms, the Cardinal had more powerful enemies: Thomas 3rd Duke of Norfolk, Anne's uncle, and Henry's brother-in-law the Duke of Suffolk, although not in alliance with each other, were both hostile to the prelate. That is, if the King's paranoia was not enough: his conviction that the Cardinal, in all his Byzantine schemes and plots, must have somehow betrayed him since the plots had failed. Showing the fair side of his Janus face, King Henry parted with his servant on the most affable terms, giving no hint of his intentions. The sovereign was visiting Grafton in the course of his autumn progress; now he was on horseback in the courtyard ready to ride out. The previous evening Cavendish had watched the King motion to the Cardinal to replace his cap – a marked sign of favour. The King clattered away; and never saw Wolsey again.

The Cardinal's rise had been long and hard-earned, industry, patience and arduous service accompanying every step. His fall was swift.[13] A series of brutal coups stripped him of his powers, beginning with the Attorney-General on 9 October who charged him with praemunire, that is, exercising his powers of papal legate in the King's realm, thus derogating the King's lawful authority. He was dismissed as Lord Chancellor (Sir Thomas More replaced him) and sentenced to imprisonment. His fortune was stripped from him and all his goods taken 'into the King's hands', in the words of the French ambassador.

For the time being however, the Cardinal was allowed to remain in one of his lesser houses at Esher, from where he wrote a pathetic letter to Thomas Cromwell, formerly his servant, now the King's, about his worsening health: how he had been 'in such anxiety of mind, that this night my breath and wind ... was so short, that I was by space of three hours, as one that should have died'. He hoped to hear 'if the displeasure of my Lady Anne be [some]what assuaged, as I pray God the same may be'. In a sense, his prayer was answered. The King's doctor was sent down to visit him in December and Anne Boleyn too sent him a jewel from her girdle with good wishes for his recovery. But the Cardinal's day was over: he died a year later, on 29 November 1530, on his way to London for trial, having been arrested for high treason three weeks earlier. Whereupon Anne Boleyn's father gave a large banquet including an entertainment which depicted the Cardinal going down to hell, the text of which the Duke of Norfolk had printed.[14]

The autumn of 1529, which saw the disappearance from court of Wolsey, also marked the arrival of a new ally for Queen Catherine. Eustace Chapuys, the incoming Spanish ambassador, was well-equipped to steer the unfortunate woman through the morass of debate and conflict that followed the advocation of the tribunal. Somebody – probably Thomas Cranmer, then a relatively unknown ecclesiastic but with connections to the Boleyn family – had had the idea of transferring the argument from that of law to the realm of theology. This was to be done by appealing to theological scholars at universities throughout Europe to give their opinions. Chapuys was a doctor of canon law and a former ecclesiastical judge in Geneva. He would also fully justify the Emperor's description of him to the Queen as 'a very trusty person, and sure to take up your defence with all fidelity and diligence'.[15]

In 1529 Chapuys was a man of forty, a few years younger than the Queen he would serve so devotedly: about the same age as Thomas Cranmer. For the next sixteen years, with short intervals, he would be posted in England; his reports back to Spain are therefore an extraordinarily important source for the period – provided one bears in mind his natural imperialist bias. Certainly Chapuys developed an excellent intelligence service. He was determined that in this, language should not be a barrier. When he enlarged his staff, recruiting young men from Flanders and Burgundy, he insisted they should learn English. He also employed Catherine's former gentleman-usher, Montoya, who had served twenty years in England and had an excellent command of the language, as his principal secretary. Like Cardinal Campeggio (who went back to Rome at the beginning of October) Chapuys suffered intensely from gout; but with his taste for intrigue, Chapuys turned the disability to good advantage. He would insist on leaning on his English valet Fleming, and got himself another pair of listening English ears as a result. As an efficient spymaster, Chapuys knew the value of maids and other servants, as well as their social superiors at court; and he cultivated the merchant community.

Chapuys also understood the need for tact and charm in diplomacy, particularly where monarchs of tricky temperament were concerned. (He described his mission to England as one of '*toute douceur*' – all sweetness.) His first interview with King Henry took place before he had met Queen Catherine: she warned him that he must not visit her 'without the King's permission'. The King opened with some remarks about 'the discretion or indiscretion of ambassadors' being often the cause of 'the enmities of princes' – but also of their friendships. He then launched into the subject of the controversial brief: Charles V's refusal to send it to England, he said, must mean the Emperor knew it to be a forgery – made with the Queen's knowledge. After that, it was the oft-repeated tale: how the whole divorce had 'no other cause and origin than the peace and tranquillity of his own conscience' (so oft-repeated, in fact, that no doubt by now he believed it).[16] But there was a new element of self-congratulation here.

The King observed how awkward it was for *both* of them – Catherine as well as Henry – not to be able to remarry (*sic*) before going on to praise his own restraint. 'Other princes might not have been so kind'; nobody would have hindered him from adopting such measures 'which I have not taken and never will'. Was he talking of the forcible removal of the Queen from court to a nunnery? It was left sinisterly vague. At this point Chapuys noticed the phenomenon upon which du Bellay had remarked a year previously. As he reflected on the wrongs done to him (and his own goodness in putting up with them) the King's demeanour suddenly changed into something 'so different from the mildness and composure of his former speech'. Recalling that Queen Catherine had recommended flattery as the best method of dealing with the King – his nature was more accessible to persuasion than to threat – the ambassador hastily began to lay it on with a trowel. In his private report on the interview, however, the ambassador wrote (in cipher) that all this about the royal conscience was nonsense: 'the idea of separation originated entirely in his own iniquity and malice'. He also made the gloomiest prognosis about the future: 'The King's passion for the Lady, combined with his obstinacy were such that there was no chance of recalling him by mildness or fair words to a sense of his duty'.[17]

Nevertheless the stalemate over the divorce meant that the King and Queen continued, in a manner of speaking, to live together. The enforced formal relationship did not bring out the best in either of them. Queen Catherine persistently taxed the King on the subject of her virginity at the time of their marriage, which had now become an obsession with her, choosing the opportunities granted to her by state occasions. She even got him in October of 1529 tacitly to agree that she had been a virgin. 'I am content', the King burst out, having listened to her yet again protest that she had been 'a maid' and he knew it. He went on: 'but you are not my wife for all that', since the bull had not dispensed over the impediment of public honesty. (This was true of the original bull, but not of the subsequent brief.) In April 1533 King Henry would airily dismiss any references on his part in the past to his first wife's virginity on their wedding night as being 'spoken in jest, as a man jesting and feasting says many things which are not true.'[18] This was another tacit admission, confirming that there *had* been such references – as Queen Catherine herself constantly maintained – which explain the King's continuing embarrassment on the subject.

What the Queen could not see, would not see, and in any case would never understand, was that all this was now irrelevant. The King had made up his mind that their marriage was against the law of God, and she, by reiterating her complaints, was simply driving him mad with irritation. In July Charles V had written to his aunt that there was every reason to hope that her husband's 'great virtues and magnanimity' would ultimately triumph over his 'scruples';[19] but the King's magnanimity depended increasingly on abasement from the other party. It was certainly not a good plan to irritate King Henry VIII, particularly as the years advanced, since behind irritation lay a colder fury, and out of that would be bred cruelty, which was somehow justified in his mind by the original irritation.

How well the Queen had understood this in her calmer and more rational past! Had she forgotten her own words to Chapuys, about the value of flattery: how the King's nature was more accessible to persuasion than to threat? But now her sense of injustice, aggravated by ill-health, was rapidly getting the better of her judgement. Queen Catherine had descended into being that bane of any man's life, let alone a King's: a nagging wife. It was understandable – but it was not wise.

In 1529 a court dinner to celebrate St Andrew's Day, 30 November, gave Queen Catherine an opening, as she saw it, to upbraid the King for never supping with her privately; as a result, she declared dramatically, she was suffering the pains of purgatory on earth. The King replied ungraciously that she 'had no cause to complain' since she had her own household where she could do as she pleased; as to his visiting her in her apartments and 'partaking of her bed', she ought to know by now that he was not her legitimate husband. They then proceeded to have an argument along familiar lines. When the King alluded complacently to the scholarly opinions of 'innumerable men of probity' which he was collecting in favour of the divorce, the Queen retorted that he had no need of professors to inform him of what he perfectly well knew to be true: *'Il l'avait trouvé pucelle'* (he had found her a maid); and in any case, not only the finest scholars but also the majority of them agreed with her – they would be found to outnumber his supporters by a thousand to one.

In a temper, the King rushed from the room, and went to find consolation from his pretty sweetheart elsewhere in the palace. Anne Boleyn however was in no mood to play that particular role. The King found himself in the yet more disagreeable position of a man caught between a nagging wife and a nagging mistress. In her turn Anne Boleyn snapped at King Henry: 'Did I not tell you that whenever you disputed with the Queen, she was sure to have the upper hand?' Then from anger Anne turned to tears, as she lamented her dismal fate. One day the King would go back to the Queen and abandon her, she wailed: 'I have been waiting long and might in the meanwhile have contracted some advantageous marriage, out of which I might have had issue, which is the greatest consolation in this world, but alas! Farewell to my time and youth spent to no purpose at all'.[20]

There was at least an exciting spice to Anne Boleyn's sharp tongue – courtiers noted that the King and his Lady were always particularly amorous after a row – while hysterical grief could be comforted with kisses and protestations. There is a story about Anne Boleyn exclaiming that she was well aware of the old prophecy that in time a Queen of England would be burnt: but she loved the King so much that she did not fear to pay the price of death, so long as she could marry him. Spitfire as she could be, Anne Boleyn was also uninhibited and demonstrative. The King found this unpredictable creature deeply exciting. There was no excitement to be found in the Queen's reproaches: only frustration.

The evidence of Anne Boleyn's fiery temper, accompanied by some equally combustible words, is sufficiently widespread for it not to be dismissed as the mere fabrication of her enemies. Nor is such a tempestuous nature altogether to her discredit (although in the long term it might not prove wise, like the Queen's eternal complaints). There is on the contrary something splendidly fearless about the way she laid about her with her tongue, often going a great deal further than would be prudent even for the most beautiful and beloved Mistress in the world. After the years of self-restraint and silence imposed upon her both by her place in society and her sex, Anne Boleyn was in a position to defy convention. Roasting the King himself was a further piece of recklessness.*

Naturally, her temper did not diminish as her power increased. In November 1530, Chapuys reported how Anne Boleyn had been seen at a small window which commanded the gallery where the King was granting him an interview, 'overlooking and overhearing all that passed'. At one point the King was sufficiently apprehensive of his Lady's reactions to move nervously into the middle of the room, lest she hear some words that would

---

* An explosive temper (once she was in a position to exercise it) may have been another trait Anne Boleyn inherited from her father; Chapuys reported that in October 1530 the celebrated diplomat slandered the Pope and cardinals in such violent language that he, Chapuys, had to leave the room.[21] But temper in the male was of course (in theory) more acceptable.

offend her. About the same time, Anne Boleyn clashed with the Duchess of Norfolk over the marriage of the latter's daughter (and Anne's first cousin) Lady Mary Howard. She 'used such words to the Duchess' that the latter – Buckingham's daughter and the premier Duchess in England – was nearly dismissed from court.[22]

By the beginning of 1531, Anne was described as being so confident that she was *'brave qu'une lion'*. She told one of Queen Catherine's ladies-in-waiting that she wished all the Spaniards were at the bottom of the sea. When the lady in question reproved her, Anne went further: 'she cared not for the Queen', declared Mistress Anne, 'nor any of her family [household]'. She would rather see Catherine hanged 'than have to confess she was her Queen and mistress'.[23] The lady-in-waiting was duly appalled. But then women as a whole did not warm to Anne Boleyn, regardless of whom they served: she either could not or never cared to build up the nexus of female friendships that Queen Catherine had established. The boldness and independence that enchanted the King – for the present – shocked other women as being dangerously far from the accepted norm.

In Rome it was heard that Anne Boleyn had insulted a gentleman of the King's household in the sovereign's presence, but even then the royal indignation was soon transformed: 'as usual in such cases, their mutual love will be greater than before'.[24] In April, King Henry actually complained to Norfolk – or so the Duke told his wife who told the Queen – that Anne was getting prouder and bolder all the time: she was using language to him that the Queen had never used in her life. Norfolk shook his head and murmured that his wayward niece would be the ruin of the Howards (while continuing to enjoy the privileges that the connection brought). Anne's own attitude to such criticisms is, however, best summed up by the motto she had embroidered on her servants' livery at Christmas 1530: *Ainsi sera, groigne qui groigne* – that's how it's going to be, however much people may grumble.[25]*

Still the King adored her. It is true that every now and then the Lady met her match. In June 1531, she quarrelled with Henry Guildford, Comptroller of the Household, and 'threatened him most furiously', saying that when she became Queen of England, she would have him punished and deprived of his office. Guildford retorted that he would save her the trouble and resigned. He maintained his resignation, despite the King's efforts to dissuade him on the feeble grounds that Guildford 'should not mind women's talk'.[26]

---

* Chapuys reported the Lady as having made a fool of herself by not realizing that the motto was a traditional one of the Burgundian Habsburgs (the second line being *Et vive Bourgogne*). But it has been pointed out that Anne Boleyn could hardly have failed to know this after her service with the Archduchess Margaret; it is more likely that the gesture was one of deliberate bravado.[27]

Some of these explosions must have been provoked, directly or indirectly, by the continued unpopularity of the King's projected new marriage among his subjects of all sorts. People did indeed grumble. Antonio de Guaras, a merchant living in London, wrote: 'It is a thing to note that the common people always disliked her [Anne]'. De Guaras, a Spaniard who may well have come to England with Queen Catherine, is not necessarily an unprejudiced source (although his *Spanish Chronicle* does provide some interesting first-hand accounts of events at this time as well as purveying gossip).[28] However this dislike is confirmed by many others. In August 1530, for example, the Venetian ambassador thought that the people would actually rebel if King Henry married Anne Boleyn and the next year believed a clearly incredible tale of seven or eight thousand women, some of them men in disguise, going to seize the favourite at a villa on the river, but being foiled when she escaped by boat. In 1530, similarly, Chapuys with his care to garner information from outside court circles was reporting 'the wishes of the whole country for the preservation of the marriage and the downfall of the Lady'.[29]

This reaction was not purely snobbery, although of course it played a part: according to the universal law of human nature the people wanted a royal princess to look up to, rather than 'Nan Bullen'; especially since their particular royal princess had made herself so beloved. Beyond that, however, was the fact that Anne Boleyn stood for something in the popular imagination that absolutely everybody distrusted, at least in principle: what Cavendish called 'pernicious and inordinate carnal love'. She was not only Nan Bullen, she was 'Nan Bullen, the mischievous whore' or 'Nan Bullen that naughty paikie' (a word for a common prostitute). And she was 'the King's whore'. No matter how much Wolsey had emphasized the multitude of Anne Boleyn's virtues to Rome, the prevailing attitude to what the King saw in her was better summed up in a phrase in William Forrest's ode: 'This is nought else but Man's sensual mind'.[30]

Naturally no one believed the story that the King had not yet slept with his Mistress. It has been pointed out that 'the commonest scurrilities' against Henry VIII arose out of his association with Anne Boleyn.[31] There were the usual salacious rumours in such situations – that Anne had given birth to several illegitimate children who were being brought up privately. Simon Grynaeus, for example, a professor of Greek at Basle, employed by the King to collect opinions concerning his marriage from the reformed church in Switzerland, had heard this story 'more than once'. He himself was highly sceptical about the King's lack of intercourse, thinking it 'not at all likely', given that Anne Boleyn was 'young [and] good-looking', and the King 'in the vigour of his age'.[32]

Yet carnal love was considered to be the very worst basis for any union.

Affection (clearly distinguished from it), and a wish to carry out God's will and lead a holy life, these were the recommended motives, according to the preachers, and to the 'handbooks' of domestic conduct of the time which incorporated their received thinking. Carnal love was a dangerous and destabilizing element in society. An extreme form of this repugnance was given on Easter Day 1532 by William Peto, head of the Franciscan Observants, who dared to warn the King that if he married Anne Boleyn, the dogs would lick his blood as they had licked Ahab's. As a comparison, it was even less to the King's taste than Bishop John Fisher's to Herod: for Ahab's Queen had been Jezebel, who had stirred him up to do abominable things in the sight of the Lord before his unfortunate end.[33] King Henry was furious and ordered Peto to be placed under house arrest.

At the time, all this was infuriating, rather than actively damaging to the Lady's cause. As the Venetian ambassador put it: 'The more angry people [are] with the King's marriage, the more incensed the King by their presumption'.[34] (This was after all no modern democratic country where an opinion poll was going to vote Anne Boleyn an unsuitable consort – at which point the King would ditch her.) But it might become extremely important if the King's passion for Anne Boleyn ever faded. Then the memories of these presumptuous attacks might return; he would know *now* who to blame for the annoyance he had suffered ... In the meantime, it was not exactly a soothing situation for the focus of the attacks, to whom common women might actually call out insults as she went hunting with the King.

If Anne Boleyn's temper has something rather magnificent about it, at least in theory, her treatment of the Queen she was supplanting is a good deal less attractive. (Her conduct towards Princess Mary – a girl at the beginning of adolescence who watched her world collapse around her – would be even more unsympathetic.) Yet even here, one should at least try to understand the insecurity of her position. Anne created one of her angry scenes when she found one of the servants from the Privy Chamber taking linen along to the Queen, in order that the King should have his shirts made – no doubt for the good sound masculine reason that Catherine had always done so, and he wanted the shirt he knew. On this occasion the King refused to give way and confirmed that the linen was being sent on his instructions.[35] Such jealousy on the part of the Lady seemed highly unreasonable to Queen Catherine's supporters and it lost nothing in the telling. At the same time Anne Boleyn had a point: sewing the King's shirts did have a symbolic significance. Queen Catherine, in continuing to do so, was being allowed by King Henry to assert the rights of a wife.

Equally the Lady's lamentations to the King in the autumn of 1529 on the subject of the 'advantageous' marriage she might have made were certainly not without justification: it was then well over three years since the beginning of their romance, more than a year since the King and his Lady had regarded their marriage as 'certain'; Anne herself was approaching thirty; yet success seemed no nearer.

Between that low point and the high summer of 1531, when Anne felt confident enough to threaten Guildford, her status as a future consort had been officially celebrated to a remarkable degree. At the ball to celebrate Christmas 1529 Anne Boleyn was given precedence in the seating not only over the Duchess of Norfolk, but also over the King's sister, Mary Duchess of Suffolk, which angered both ladies. Shortly before this her father had been created Earl of Wiltshire, and had also received the family earldom of Ormonde which he had long coveted (despite the fact that his cousin Sir Piers Butler had enjoyed the use of it for some years).

Sir Thomas Boleyn's original elevation to Viscount Rochford in 1525 preceded his younger daughter's romance and must be ascribed to his own diplomatic industry. But this latest ennoblement, which meant that his son George Boleyn became Viscount Rochford, and the favourite herself would be described, slightly mysteriously, as 'Lady Anne Rochford', was a clear indication of the way things were intended to go. So the new Lord Wiltshire set off for Europe on a ceaseless round of diplomatic negotiation to smooth the way for the divorce – with the Pope, the Emperor, François I – with the rank suitable to one who might shortly, as a result of these efforts, become the King's father-in-law.

From late 1529 onwards Anne Boleyn would feature heavily in the expenses of the Privy Purse:[36] yards of purple velvet in December to the tune of £180, at the orders of the King; the next year it was lengths of crimson satin, furs to trim her dresses, and fine linen for 'shirts' (smocks) to wear under them and at night. There were payments for the garnishing of Anne Boleyn's desk with gold. While the expenses of her bows and arrows and hunting gloves, and payments to Anne for her 'playing money' (at backgammon, shovel-board, dice or cards) provide in themselves a picture of the life the lovers led together: pleasure-loving and apparently carefree, indoors and out. The King had a passion for gambling: the Privy Purse accounts record wagers on races between dogs, on a performing dog, on a man who could ride two horses at once, on a man who could eat a whole buck. When the Lady's greyhound killed a cow, he paid for that too.

The Lady Anne's insecurity and the gnawing jealousy of Queen Catherine which it brought did however have one unlooked-for consequence. This was the development of a new centre for King and government in London, later to be known as Whitehall.[37] York Place was one of Cardinal Wolsey's palaces which was forfeit to the King at Wolsey's fall. Very soon afterwards King Henry brought his sweetheart on a secret visit to gloat over the rich tapestries and plate with which the Cardinal had graced his magnificent life style, and which had now passed, along with the house itself, to the monarch. As Shakespeare had it:

> You must no more call it York Place, that's past …
> 'Tis now the King's and called Whitehall.

The Lady quickly appreciated that this new royal residence would have one immense advantage: unlike other palaces, as for example Greenwich, it would not contain a series of apartments traditionally accorded to the Queen, which it was very difficult to prevent her occupying as she chose. But at Whitehall,* there was to be no provision made for this awkward *ménage à trois*. This was the genesis of a vast building programme, for which nearby houses including an old leper-house were swept away, so that finally it would extend over more than twenty-three acres. There would be a new gatehouse directly over the main highway between Charing Cross and Westminster (from which royal women would later be able to watch processions). There would be three tennis courts – the 'Brake Great Open Tennis Court', 'Great Close Tennis Court' and 'Small Close Tennis Court', attesting to another passion of the King's. Over £8,000 were spent in one year in constructing this stately complex, with nearly 400 workmen toiling on it, so great was the King's enthusiasm for the project.

'All this has been done to please the Lady', wrote Chapuys, who 'likes better' to have the King stay with her in Whitehall, 'where there is no lodging for the Queen'.[38] There were however elegant apartments for the Lady herself, with her mother, directly beneath those of the King. Thomas Boleyn, Earl of Wiltshire, was also one of the first courtiers to be given his own set of rooms.

Despite all these emoluments for the Lady Anne, symbolic of the King's intentions, it remained Queen Catherine, sick and low-spirited as she might be, who was the target for popular affection. The Queen's health declined throughout 1530. At the end of the year, Chapuys described how Catherine was beginning to lose hope: 'she always fancied that the King, after pursuing his course for some time, would turn away, and yielding to his conscience, would change his purpose as he had done at other times, and return to reason'; now, no longer. Recurrent attacks of fever led to the traditional remedies of bleeding and purgatives, in themselves weakening; Chapuys thought that her patience over her sufferings was coming to an end.[39] Nevertheless she was not – publicly

---

* The new name did not in fact become current until about ten years later; it may have originated in the white ashlar stonework of Wolsey's great hall.

at least – giving way. Still Catherine, when all was said and done, was married to Henry; and she was still the Queen.

The King's appeal to the universities of Europe, the brilliant expedient on which he prided himself, produced in fact an unsurprising result. Most scholars found for their political masters; although in Italy scholars remained divided, despite large sums dispensed by Cranmer and others in bribing them to support the divorce. But the University of Paris produced a positive verdict (for divorce), since François I now viewed the whole affair approvingly as a useful way of making trouble between Henry VIII and Charles V. Spanish universities were negative. The majority opinion in Oxford and Cambridge favoured the King. The stalemate was not relieved.

Practically speaking, the King and Queen were even in a kind of bizarre agreement that the Pope must make up his mind about the validity or otherwise of their marriage. As Catherine wrote to Dr Ortiz, the Emperor's proctor at Rome in April 1530, 'nothing will suffice except a final decision ... Anything else will only bring temporary relief at the cost of greater ills to come.' While the King for his part exploded at the Pope's procrastination in July: 'Never was there any prince handled by a pope as your Holiness treateth us'.[40] Given that two years previously, this same Pope had been prepared to grant a decretal commission to look into the matter, and had changed his mind for political, not doctrinal reasons, this wrath was not without reason. A vast petition, organized by a member of the King's household and signed by numerous peers and churchmen, was sent to Rome appealing to the Pope to act for the sake of peace in England.

Still the Pope hesitated. Lack of pronouncement might heighten the blood pressure of the King in faraway England and deepen the melancholy of his estranged wife, but it did protect the interests of the church because no one power was finally antagonized. There was a new complication: the Pope was worried lest the Emperor manage to insist on a General Council of the church being called to check the growth of Lutheranism in his German dominions: this would deplete his own authority. Hesitation was safety, for the time being.

But the distant King of England was beginning to consider a more radical solution which would make no use of the Pope's authority. He had hinted at the perils of schism in the last few years: how the English people might turn to Lutheranism if their King was not allowed his divorce. Nevertheless a papal blessing upon Henry's second union was still the most convenient answer – because such a union would not then be called in question – and he had after all accepted papal authority freely for the dispensation related to Anne Boleyn. But given that this blessing was being tiresomely withheld, did he really need to acknowledge sovereignty in Rome in such matters?

What indeed was the precise nature of this papal sovereignty? Why did it extend over princes, ordained to rule, surely, by God himself? In December 1530 the Pope requested the dismissal of Anne Boleyn from court – the King called it 'a most outrageous measure' – and in January 1531 expressly forbade the King to marry while the divorce case was *sub judice* in Rome: any children born of such a union would be bastards.[41] In the early church there had been a series of independent provinces: was not a king nowadays sovereign in his own realm, and therefore immune from papal judgements? Particularly ones like these.

The theory of the royal supremacy did not spring from the King's head, fully armed, like the goddess Athena at her birth. The parliament, first convened on 3 November 1529, which was destined in seven years to carry through a religious revolution, started with very different objectives. More, the new Lord Chancellor, was personally bent on trying to eradicate Lutheranism (and Lutheran heretics) whereas the rising star in the King's service, Thomas Cromwell, his secretary from 1530, saw things from the financial angle. For the King's inadequate finances currently presented yet another frustrating problem.

Cromwell, who had previously worked for Cardinal Wolsey, was the son of a wealthy citizen; now about forty-five, assiduous and intelligent, he had been in the past both an attorney and a merchant and even a money-lender. Cromwell saw a way of solving the King's financial difficulties and bringing the clergy into submission by threatening them with a charge of praemunire – the charge that had brought down Wolsey. Chapuys reported indignantly that its whole basis was 'in the imagination of the King' who 'comments and amplifies it at pleasure'. Nevertheless the clergy in convocation in January 1531 trembled before the charge, since they could understand perfectly well what the penalty might be, if not the precise charge. They voted the King £100,000 to cover possible complicity with Wolsey. They also accepted that the King had a new title: 'Supreme Head of the Church and Clergy of England'. Even though the aged Archbishop Warham added the words 'so far as the law of Christ allows' (which if taken seriously, destroyed the whole concept of the title) and Bishop Fisher protested vigorously, it was undeniably a step away from Rome.[42]

Parliament however behaved less cravenly. It refused to ratify the title as it stood. In any case, the King himself was not yet totally committed to the way forward. There was a nasty incident after Bishop Fisher's cook added some noxious white powder to his master's soup – possibly with the aim of harming certain other members of the household whom he did not like; the mixture actually killed some beggars being fed at the house, and made Fisher himself extremely sick. (It was typical of Anne Boleyn's reputation at the time that her family were rumoured to have organized the poisoning:

an accusation for which there was absolutely no evidence.) King Henry however saw his course as clear. He allowed himself the pleasure of demonstrating his horror of such criminal behaviour – and his loyalty to Fisher for all his protests – by having the unlucky cook put slowly to death in boiling oil.

It was left to the two women in the life of Henry VIII to point the true way to the future. Their reactions to his new title of Supreme Head were very different but added up to the same thing. Queen Catherine feared that a man who could do such monstrous things as deny the Pope's authority, might 'one of these days' undertake something 'most outrageous' against her own person. Anne Boleyn, who with her father would be described by Chapuys in March 1531 as more Lutheran 'than Luther himself', was ecstatic. '*La Dame du Roy*' made in fact such 'demonstrations of joy', he wrote, that she might have been admitted to paradise.[43] In short, the people might grumble, but in the words of the motto: *Ainsi sera* – that was how it was going to be.

Chapter 9

HAIL ANNA!

Hail Anna! jewel shining outstandingly gracefully
This year will be joyful and favourable for you.

Robert Whittington, *In praise of the Lady Anna,* 1532

King Henry saw Queen Catherine for the last time in July 1531. Unlike his behaviour towards Wolsey, he did not bid her an affable – if false – farewell. After twenty-two years of marriage there was to be no farewell at all. He merely rode off at dawn from Windsor, where the court was then lodged, to go hunting at Woodstock with the Lady Anne, leaving the unhappy Queen to find out from others that he had gone. But then the King did not necessarily plan this to be a final parting; he did not necessarily plan anything at all at the time, other than a carefree hunting expedition from which the Queen was excluded. It was easier that way. Then, when Catherine wrote him a polite letter of regret – she was generally allowed to ask after his health before he departed on these occasions – exasperation at her nagging could be allowed free rein.

'Tell the Queen', he shouted at her messenger, 'that I do not want any of her goodbyes.' He did not care whether she asked after his health or not since she had caused him no end of trouble, refusing all the reasonable requests of his Privy Council. She might put her trust in the Emperor, but she would find that Almighty God was still more powerful. In any case, he wanted 'no more of her messages'. Queen Catherine, ignoring the prohibition, responded with a long letter rehearsing all the old arguments concerning the validity of their marriage. This brought another explosion from the King: 'It would be a great deal better if she spent her time in seeking witnesses, to prove her pretended virginity at the time of her marriage with him, than in talking about it to whoever would listen to her, as she was doing.'[1] As for sending messages to him, let her stop doing it and mind her own business.

The exasperation of King Henry, like the insecurity of Anne Boleyn, was from his own point of view perfectly understandable: why was Catherine so obstinate when submission would bring her, and all around her, so many benefits? As for the common people, who dared to call out to the King while he hunted at Woodstock, 'Back to your wife!', they were enough to drive anyone to frenzy (was ever a man so tried for following his own conscience?).[2] Furthermore Henry's dig at the Emperor demonstrates how opposition to his will could increasingly be identified as an unpatriotic allegiance to a foreign power.

The early summer of 1531 had after all been occupied by the King in attempting to persuade the Queen to agree to his version of a compromise. There were scratchy moments, but these were not necessarily of his making (as he saw it). At the beginning of May, the King was said to be very gracious at dinner, and then the Queen asked if Princess Mary (who had her separate household under the Countess of Salisbury) could visit them both at Greenwich. Chapuys attributed the King's peremptory refusal – let Princess Mary visit her mother alone – to the influence of the Lady: 'who hates her [the Princess] as much as the Queen, or more so, because she sees the King still has some affection for her'. But this is almost certainly unfair. The fact that the Queen immediately backed away from the suggestion – 'very prudently' in Chapuys' opinion – is significant.[3] Catherine did not want to give credence to the notion that the Princess's parents were separated. In short Princess Mary, like a child in a modern divorce case, was being used by her mother to establish her rights: the King did not need his Mistress to spur him on to refuse them.

But at the end of May, a serious attempt was made by the Duke of Norfolk to induce the Queen to submit to the King's wishes with dignity. Norfolk was a suitable emissary. For all his relationship to Anne Boleyn (or perhaps because of it) he did not approve of his niece's outspoken ways: he admired the Queen and was himself religiously conservative with no leanings to 'Lutheranism'. Chapuys heard that Norfolk told the King's cousin the Marquess of Dorset that it was really 'a thing of the other world' to witness the Queen's courage. To this, Dorset was supposed to have replied that 'no doubt' this courage was due to the Queen's 'own consciousness of the justice and right of her case'.[4]

None of this did any good. The Queen rejected all Norfolk's careful arguments including reminders of the past when King Henry had helped King Ferdinand invade Navarre. She was steady as ever: 'I love and have loved my lord the King as much as any woman can love a man, but I would not have borne him company as his wife one moment against the voice of my conscience.' Now Norfolk described the Queen's arguments as 'foolish'.

When the court at Rome, appointed to try Queen Catherine's suit, opened in June (to be adjourned to October), there were protests from the King's lawyers that he could not be summoned to appear outside of his own realm. The King himself expressed his angry contempt to the papal nuncio in England: he would never agree to the Pope 'being judge in that affair' (the divorce), and as for the Pope's threat of excommunication, 'I shall not mind it, for I care not a fig for all his excommunications.' Let the Pope do what he liked in Rome: 'I will do here what I think best.' At this point, a large delegation of the nobility, headed once more by Norfolk, came to see the Queen at nine o'clock at night to suggest that these proceedings in Rome should be suspended, and a tribunal established on some neutral territory.[5]

This body – about thirty people, including the Duke of Suffolk as well as Norfolk – was no more successful. The Queen, while pretending surprise at the lateness of the hour (although one feels that some hint of such a large-scale impending visit must have reached her in advance), answered composedly enough. Only the Pope who 'has the power of God on earth, and is the image of eternal truth' had the authority to try the case. No matter how fervently the nobles assured her that the King was now, in effect, supreme in all matters spiritual as well as temporal, so that she would do well to entrust her affairs to his hands, she would never give way.

It was against this background that the King's precipitate dawn departure from Windsor accompanied by 'the Grand Enemy' (as Chapuys now called Anne Boleyn) took place. The wrangling – via messengers and letters – which followed merely convinced him that a move which had probably been spontaneous when it was made should be transformed into something more permanent. Orders came that Queen Catherine was to remove, with her household, to one of Cardinal Wolsey's former residences, known as The More, near Rickmansworth in Hertfordshire.

It was an innovatory move rather than a punitive one, in practical terms at least. Although The More was now showing signs of neglect, with its fine gardens 'utterly destroyed', and its magnificent deer park wasted, not so long ago it had been rated by the French ambassador as even finer than Hampton Court, thanks to the Cardinal's embellishments. Nor was the Queen denied the large household to which her status had accustomed her: nearly 200 people in all, with numerous ladies in attendance including her old friend Maria de Salinas, now the widow of Lord Willoughby de Eresby. It was mental anguish that chiefly troubled her, as she signed her letters 'from the More, separated from my husband, without ever having offended him, Katharina, the unhappy Queen', or pleaded to keep her Spanish apothecary and physician: 'They have continued many years with me and (I thank them) have taken great pains with me, for I am often sickly, as the King's grace doth know right well . . .'[6]

However, Catherine preserved her dignity when yet another delegation came on the King's behalf – this time representatives of the clergy and the nobility – to ask her to agree to the resolution of the divorce suit in England. The Queen assembled her entire household and spoke clearly and loudly (the embarrassed messengers had mumbled) so that there could be no doubt about her absolute refusal.

The *ad hoc* nature of the new arrangement is, however, borne out by the fact that the Queen seems to have attended a state dinner as late as November, although she and her husband sat in separate chambers and therefore did not come face to face.[7] When New Year came, with its elaborate and significant ritual of gift-giving and gift-receiving, Queen Catherine hastened to send King Henry the usual rich present – a gold cup – to demonstrate that business was as usual, while King Henry, sharply rejecting the present, was equally concerned to demonstrate that it was not. (But the King subsequently recalled the Queen's messenger, fearing that he would offer the gift again before the whole court; praising its workmanship, the King retained the cup till evening when this danger had passed.)

From The More, Queen Catherine was taken to Bishop's Hatfield, the palace of the Bishop of Ely, and at some point had a sojourn in Hertford Castle; then in the spring of 1533, she was moved to Ampthill in Bedford-shire. This was an impressive castle, with four or five stone towers and a gatehouse said to have been built by Henry IV's brother-in-law, out of the proceeds of the French wars. It stood on a hill, in the centre of an attractive, well-wooded park, and was generally liked for its 'marvellous good health and clean air'; nor was Ampthill in a bad state of repair.[8] So for two years Queen Catherine was kept in seclusion in the country, while King Henry – whether at court, receiving foreign ambassadors, or in the hunting field – attempted to accustom his own and other countries to the idea that the Lady Anne would shortly and inevitably become his true wife.

The time passed by Queen Catherine in the 'clean air' saw another kind of cleansing taking place elsewhere: religious reform, and the concept of the King's supremacy, now had a momentum of its own quite separate from the whole matter of the divorce. In March 1532 a bill for an Act of Conditional Restraint of Annates was introduced into parliament. Hitherto the Pope had received the 'annates' or 'first fruits' of a see after the appointment of a new bishop: that is, its revenues for one year. By the terms of the act the Pope would in future only receive five per cent and if, as a result, he refused to consecrate a bishop, then the consecration would take place without papal consent. But the act was not to be put into force until the King so ordered: Henry now had a useful lever to use against the Pope who would hardly wish to be deprived of this income.

A few days earlier the so-called Supplication against the Ordinaries had emerged (prompted by Cromwell). This was a list of complaints against the church, shared by many English people, from the 'Lutheran' Boleyns to much humbler persons whose lives were bedevilled by the frequent need to pay ecclesiastical fees and tithes or the clergy's unfair use of the weapon of excommunication. While the King at the top of society was able to say proudly that he cared 'not a fig' for all the Pope's excommunications, those lower down could find their lives ruined by such undeserved bans.

Thomas Cromwell, who apart from his administrative and financial abilities, shared the reformist tendencies of the Boleyns, shaped the Supplication into a form in which it was first presented to the King, then passed back to the clergy. In future all clerical legislation would need the royal assent, while past legislation was to be investigated, given that it was now deemed to have sprung from the King's sovereignty (not the Pope's). These radical suggestions were at first rejected by the Convocation of the clergy, under Archbishop Warham. But under threat, the Convocation succumbed. The Submission of the Clergy was made on 15 May 1532. It followed parallel pressure on parliament. The King had menaced a delegation with the suggestion that the members preferred the Pope's authority to his: were they 'but half our subjects, yea, and scarce our subjects?' he demanded.[9] The answer to such a frightening question must be no – if they valued their liberty. (Sir Thomas More, however, resigned as Lord Chancellor the next day.)

Although eight bishops chose to be absent at the moment of submission, and two refused it (Bishop Fisher was ill), clerical opposition to the King's plans was now in effect broken. The death of the aged Warham in August provided a further opportunity for the King to pursue his policies, unimpeded by clerical objections at source, by appointing Thomas Cranmer as the new Archbishop of Canterbury. It was an unexpected appointment: Cranmer's career was not so far sufficiently distinguished to warrant such elevation, although he had worked hard in Europe on the King's cause, following his own suggestion of an appeal to the universities. Cranmer had been made one of the King's chaplains at some date before January 1532 and in this month was appointed ambassador to the court of Charles V. The clue to the appointment therefore must lie not only in Cranmer's manifest desire to serve the King, but also in his intimate association with the Boleyn family. He had probably once been the Boleyn chaplain and may well have lived under the family's roof for about fifteen months from October 1530 onwards.[10]

*

The impending royal visit to his brother of France, and the prospect of a new and amenable Archbishop (marriage surely could not long be deferred), enabled King Henry to take a further bold step in his public presentation of the Lady Anne to the world. The French visit, envisaged as a minor version of the Field of Cloth of Gold, with the French King at Boulogne and the English King on his own ground at Calais, had become a pet project of King Henry. He wanted King François' support to counter-act the Emperor's hostility, and if possible, to overawe the Pope. On the seesaw principle, it was believed that King François viewed King Henry's proposed new marriage with approval, since it was condemned by Charles V. (Although King François had recently married the Emperor's sister Eleanor of Austria, according to the terms of the peace between them following Pavia.)

The French ambassador in England, Jean du Bellay, enjoyed a warm relationship not only with King Henry, but also with the Lady Anne.[11] It was partly on the basis of his master's notional approval, partly because du Bellay expressed these sympathies personally: a friendly French presence at court, where Chapuys was a hostile imperialist one. In his despatches du Bellay boasted of his intimacy, how he was taken hunting by the English King and 'Madame Anne', often finding himself quite alone with King Henry, listening to him discussing his affairs.

Then Madame Anne had given him numerous presents, including hunting clothes, and a hat, a special horn and a greyhound: they would be found side by side, each one with an attendant bowman, waiting for the deer to be driven past. Sometimes it would turn out that du Bellay would be alone not so much with the King as with Madame Anne. His master might wonder at such closeness – was it proper for his ambassador to be *'tant aimé des dames'* (so beloved by the ladies)? – but King François need have no fears. All this was merely to express the growing friendship King Henry felt for him. As for Madame Anne, everything she does 'is entirely by the commandment of the said King' (a significant comment from an observant man who knew both King and Lady well).

It was du Bellay who had the delicate task of getting King François actually to *request* the presence of Madame Anne at the impending cel-ebrations so that he could both see her and *'la festoyer'* (entertain her). Nothing would give his brother King greater pleasure, wrote du Bellay, than if this should seem to be King François' own idea, and after all two such gallant sovereigns would not wish to be together 'without company of ladies'. The task was delicate, not only because of Madame Anne's status – what exactly was it, if it was not that of the King's wife, which it clearly was not? – but also because the new Queen of France was the niece of Queen Catherine.

King Henry expressed himself forcibly to his good friend du Bellay, who duly passed it on: let the (Spanish-Austrian) Queen Eleanor stay away, since he had a personal horror of women dressed *à l'espagnole* (in Spanish dress): to him they looked like devils. This ungallant comment, for which it is not hard to find an explanation, was accompanied by a fervent desire that King François should bring his large family – 'the Children of France' as the princes and princesses were known. He would also welcome King François' sister, Marguerite d'Angoulême, recently married to the King of Navarre; this was a request to which the Lady Anne added her own pleas, claiming that long-established friendship already discussed.

Since the well-brought-up Eleanor of Austria had no intention of receiving the woman who was supplanting her aunt, King Henry's lack of gallantry was probably making a virtue of necessity; he cannot seriously have supposed otherwise. But the Lady Anne's 'friend' Marguerite d'Angoulême did not attend the meeting either. Although the Spanish believed – happily – that this indicated Marguerite's hostility to the divorce, their optimism was probably unfounded. A more likely explanation lies in the match which François I was trying – secretly – to bring off between his second son Henri Duc d'Orléans and the Pope's wealthy niece Catherine de' Medici. Too much affront was not to be given to the Pope's sensitivities.

Meanwhile in England, King Henry took steps to make it clear that whatever the political prudery of the French, the Lady Anne was now his wife in all but name. Indeed, her existing name was to be glorified to fit her new station. On 1 September the Lady Anne Rochford was formally created the Marquess of Pembroke: the expenses of the Privy Purse for that month included payments for her ceremonial robes of silk trimmed with fur. The use of the male title (instead of that of Marchioness) was not in itself significant: the word Marchioness was seldom used at this date, the wife of a Marquess being generally termed 'the Lady Marquess'.[12]* The new Marquess was to be a person of property: she received five manors in Wales, another in Somerset, two in Essex, and five in Hertfordshire including Hunsdon and Eastwick; these were added to the two manors she had already received in 1532 in Middlesex.

The English people, especially the women, might indulge in 'hooting and hissing' when they saw the royal Mistress out hunting – Chapuys thought this caused the King to cancel a hunting trip in the north in July 1532, although the movements of the Scots may have been the real reason – but in Calais the new Lady Marquess was to be accorded every honour. And that was what counted. She was even to wear the royal jewels. The

---

* As Cecily, widow of Thomas Grey, 1st Marquess of Dorset, styled herself Marquess not Marchioness in her will dated 1527.

King sent a message to Queen Catherine asking for them. He got back a tart reply showing that her spirit at least was not broken. Why should she voluntarily surrender the jewels she had worn for so many years as his lawful wife to 'a person who is a reproach to Christendom and is bringing scandal and disgrace upon the King through his taking her to such a meeting as this in France?' Let him send an order and she would obey.[13]

The King duly did so, via a member of his Privy Chamber, which had the force of a royal command. The Queen, in keeping with her policy of submitting to the King's orders in all matters where his authority was lawful, then complied. She sent 'all she had, with which the King was much pleased'. So jewels including twenty rubies and two diamonds 'reserved for my lady Marquess' were handed over. As usual, Anne was blamed for the tactless greed of the request by Queen Catherine's supporters – the favourite was 'making hay while the sun shines', wrote Chapuys.[14] But as usual it was far more likely to have been the King who was the moving spirit in this, such a symbolic rejection of Catherine's title to the position of his Queen.

The fraternal visit between the kings fell into two parts.[15] First King Henry and a large suite arrived in Boulogne on 21 October to be entertained for four days on French territory. The official report of the two kings' first encounter (since the summer of 1520) described 'the lovingest meeting that ever was seen; for the one embraced the other five or six times on horseback; and so did the lords of either party each to other; and so did ride hand in hand with great love the space of a mile.' But King Henry's suite did not include the Lady Marquess of Pembroke or the French royal ladies: all the machinations of the English King could not secure this. Henry did however meet the Children of France – King François' enviable trio of sons – and arranged for his own son, the fourteen-year-old Henry Fitzroy Duke of Richmond to return to the French court at the end of all the festivities, for his further education and general polishing. Anne's turn would come during the subsequent four days spent in Calais: from 25 to 29 October. Here she blossomed: she was treated as the first lady of the English court (the role hitherto occupied by Queen Catherine, or a designated royal deputy such as Henry's sister Mary) and as such opened the dancing with the French King.

King François also watched Anne being presented on his behalf with a fine diamond, by the Provost of Paris, saluting her as she sat graciously and indeed most royally among her bevy of maids of honour. The Lady Marquess also led the masquing after supper accompanied by several ladies, among them 'the Lady Mary', presumably her sister Mary, widow of William Carey,[16] since there is no other mention of the King's daughter being present. All were gorgeously apparelled in cloth of gold and crimson satin, knit with laces of gold, with visors over their faces. Did the French King remark one particular young lady among Anne's entourage, marked out by the exceptional whiteness of her complexion? The names of Anne's maids of honour are not recorded, but it is very likely that a girl called Jane Seymour was amongst them (she was certainly in Anne's service by the following spring);[17] just as Anne Boleyn herself had probably been standing in the wings at the Field of Cloth of Gold twelve years earlier.

For all these demonstrations of affection, for all the loving embraces between monarchs, it would turn out later that King François' candour had left a good deal to be desired. He assured King Henry that he had no intention of marrying his son to the Pope's niece (the marriage took place the next year) and he would later assure the Pope that he had tried to dissuade Henry from marrying Anne (she on the contrary returned from the expedition convinced that France was a firm friend of hers, while Henry believed he would marry her with François' blessing).[18] Such was the essentially tricky nature of the French King. At the time however his charm and geniality left a golden impression.

At Calais King Henry and the Lady Marquess stayed in the exchequer building, a large and commodious place customarily used for visiting dignitaries. Their lodgings were hung with green velvet, and embroideries depicting scenes from Ovid's *Metamorphoses* (a series of mythological stories involving transformations). It has been suggested that it was in Calais in the autumn of 1532 that King Henry, after nearly six years, finally transformed his newly ennobled Mistress into his lover, in the full sense of the word, whether under the stimulus of Ovid or not. (An alternative theory has the Lady Anne receiving her title of Marquess at the beginning of September as a reward for giving way, but the Pembroke title is so clearly linked to the French expedition, where the King wanted Anne to have a proper rank of her own, that this seems less plausible.)[19] The weather which had been very warm on the French coast now turned wet and windy, preventing the King and his Lady sailing for home. That might encourage further speculation that a long indoor sojourn on the continent – the traditional refuge of English honeymoon couples – may have been responsible. King Henry lost 15s gambling to Anne Boleyn: did she perhaps lose more than that to him – her long-prized virginity? Perhaps other payments to a shrine in a wall at Calais and to 'our Lady of Boulogne' betokened the royal gratitude.[20]

The truth can never be known for sure. One can only say with certainty that Henry VIII made love to Anne – fully – some time before the end of 1532. All the rest is speculation. As to the act itself, was it a success after so many years? Did the earth move for them? Once again we have no means of knowing. But common sense leads one to suppose the celebrated 'ultimate conjunction' did not actually represent much sexual novelty for either King or Lady. As has been suggested, matters had probably been going in that direction for some years, with Anne the sole focus of the King's lust, by whatever means she satisfied it.

During this period, however, Anne had remained careful not to become pregnant, since neither she nor the King had any desire to produce a son whose status was arguably extramarital – no better than that of the young Duke of Richmond. (However, her new title was – again significantly – not limited to her heirs born lawfully within marriage.) Now at last, in a newly favourable atmosphere, vigilance in this respect could be relaxed. This was the real difference in their situation: King and putative Queen could now set about conceiving that son and heir, the need for whom was in fact the original *raison d'être* of their relationship, however much the fact had been lost in the mists of romantic declaration on the one hand and conscience-ridden self-justification on the other.

Around the end of the first week of December 1532, the Lady Marquess of Pembroke did become pregnant (this is to assume a nine months' gestation for the baby born the following 7 September). In early January she must have suspected – hoped – as much. As the month wore on, the question of the King's marriage assumed a new urgency. Since royal marriages at this time were small private affairs – like Henry's marriage to Catherine in 1509 – there was nothing unconventional about a quick secret ceremony taking place. 'About St Paul's Day' – 25 January 1533 – in Cranmer's words (who did not however perform the ceremony) the King and the Lady Marquess were married at last.[21]

The news was kept officially secret for the time being, although by the middle of February the Lady Marquess was finding it irresistible to flaunt her pregnant state. She did so in characteristically outrageous fashion – or so it seemed to her detractors. Chapuys reported how the Lady came out of her room, and there and then, 'without rhyme or reason amidst great company', told her former admirer Wyatt of 'a furious hankering to eat apples, such as she had never had in her life before' which had seized her three days previously. 'The King had told her that it was a sign she was pregnant', went on the Lady, 'but she had said it was nothing of the sort.' Then Anne burst out laughing and returned to her room. Almost all the court heard this announcement and according to Chapuys 'most of those present were much surprised and shocked.'[22]

The secrecy had some point to it, quite apart from the fact that the Lady was not yet four months pregnant; as has been noted, that was generally the marker at which point the dangers of early miscarriage or optimistic miscalculation were considered to be over. The truth was that the King, although remarried, was not yet divorced. An Act in Restraint of Appeals was duly passed by a reconvened parliament on 3 February which would enable the matter to be settled in the King's own country, on the grounds that, as the act stated, 'this realm of England is an empire'.[23] (Although it is an example of the wayward pattern of England's relationship with the papacy at this period that, at about the same time, Clement VII himself assented to Cranmer's appointment as Archbishop, and the bulls to consecrate him reached England in March.)

There was a kind of crazy logic to the undivorced King's second marriage. If the original marriage to Catherine had never been valid, then he was still a bachelor, as Anne was a spinster. On the other hand the need for Anne's child to be unquestionably legitimate in the eyes of his subjects meant that this logic was not entirely pursued. (In any case 'public honesty' demanded the dissolution of his marriage to Catherine – to whom he had long been married in the estimation of the world and who had borne him children.) A divorce procedure was still needed. It was planned to take place as discreetly as possible, in the little market town of Dunstable, in Bedfordshire, not far from Ampthill, where the Queen was currently lodged.

At the beginning of April – when Anne was almost exactly four months pregnant – the news was made public, although the actual date of the wedding was tactfully fudged. Rumours were set about that Henry married Anne on St Erkenwald's Day, 14 November, which meant that the ceremony had taken place the day after they returned to Dover from Calais. On 9 April a deputation came to see Queen Catherine at Ampthill and broke the news of the King's marriage to her. The Queen was told the truth: the man she still regarded as her husband had been married to 'the scandal of Christendom' for two months (since Chapuys had suspected Anne was pregnant in February, the Queen probably knew about that too). She was now to be treated as the Princess Dowager – the title she had borne thirty years earlier as Prince Arthur's widow – and formally to be addressed as such.

Human nature being what it is, the news must have come as an appalling disappointment, if not exactly a shock to Catherine. Only two years before, the Queen had convinced herself that if only she could have the King to herself for a short while as things used to be, his great virtues, including his magnanimity, would enable her to win him back, and she wrote as much to the Pope. She had struggled so hard – and was in a sense still struggling, since Rome had not yet reached a decision on her case – that part of her had to believe in her ultimate victory if only to spur on her spirits. Now she had lost. To Catherine, instead of victory, there was the humiliation of another summons: to the ecclesiastical court constituted by Cranmer at Dunstable.

Chapuys, full of indignation at the news of the second marriage, thought that the solution lay in some aggressive action on the part of the Emperor. (Bishop Fisher had urged him to persuade the Emperor that an invasion would save the Christian religion in England.) Given 'the great injury done to Madame, your aunt', he wrote to Charles V, 'you can hardly avoid making war now upon this king and kingdom'. Chapuys convinced himself that such an action would be 'the easiest thing in the world', given that 'the affections of the people' were entirely on the side of Queen Catherine – and, apparently, the Emperor; the Pope 'should invoke the secular arm', that is, call for war. Chapuys further proposed a form of economic sanction, adding that the Scots were eager to help, while the French King would not stir.[24]

But the Emperor decided against such a chivalrous expedition of rescue. The plight of the aging aunt, away in England, was something which did not and never had touched him emotionally; what she had seen as a close family tie had been for him a useful political alliance – or not, according to his needs at the time. On a more immediate level, the Emperor was currently beset with problems, including that of the Turks, ever threatening on his eastern frontiers.

In any case Queen Catherine herself wanted no such action, as she hastened to tell Chapuys. Bloodshed on her behalf was horrifying to contemplate: it would be 'a sin against the law and against my lawful husband of which I shall never be guilty'. Chapuys had to admit that Catherine was so 'overscrupulous that she would consider herself damned eternally were she to consent to anything that might provoke a war.'

Naturally Queen Catherine refused to appear in Dunstable; once more she was declared contumacious as at Blackfriars four years previously. The King was also absent; as a matter of fact he was busy preparing for the coronation of Anne Boleyn, although to read an account of the Dunstable divorce proceedings, you would hardly imagine that to be the case. If his remarriage did at least have a kind of logic to it, no such palliating excuse can be found for the behaviour and language of Archbishop Cranmer in this court.

Here was a man who was very shortly to crown the King's pregnant new wife in London – as he well knew – and yet he actually threatened to excommunicate King Henry if he did not 'put away' Queen Catherine. 'Did you not in fact laugh yourself', wrote Reginald Pole to Cranmer many years later, 'when you made a pretence of all this severity and threatened the King in this way?' But Cranmer had nothing to laugh about at the time; on the contrary, he was extremely wary about his language throughout proceedings since by judging the King himself it was just possible he would encroach on the new doctrine of the royal supremacy. In short, Cranmer's main desire was, in his own words, not to deprive the King of 'his trust in me'.[25]

On 23 May the Archbishop gave his judgement that the marriage of Henry VIII and Catherine of Aragon was invalid. He had asked the King's permission to try the case 'most humbly on my knees', words which the King altered in draft to 'prostrate at the feet of your Majesty'. From Dunstable, Archbishop Cranmer scurried back to Lambeth to place the crown on the head of Anne Boleyn exactly one week later.

The coronation of Queen Anne on 1 June 1533, when she was nearly six months pregnant, represented her apotheosis. This was true, not only because, with hindsight, one can see that it was indeed the high point of her glamorous, adventurous and ultimately ill-fated life. But also because it was intended to be an apotheosis at the time. The coronation of a queen was a solemn and symbolic act, with a significance quite beyond that of mere marriage to a king (generally, as has been noted, done privately). Not every queen was crowned. Those who were 'royally anointed' – a part of the coronation ceremony – were aware of the special sanctity which this conferred. On the day of the Dunstable judgement, Queen Catherine based her refusal to be relegated to the status of Princess Dowager on the fact that she was 'a crowned and anointed Queen'. The year following, Sir Thomas More was careful to make it clear that despite his growing opposition to the King's church policies, he accepted the King's marriage to Anne Boleyn as being part of God's providence, and would neither 'murmur at it nor dispute upon it', since 'this noble woman' was 'royally anointed queen'.[26]

The timing of the consort's coronation varied considerably. Queen Catherine as a princess of Spain had been crowned together with her husband in order to signal the splendour of the new reign. But in general there was a strong link between the ceremony and the production of heirs. In this way Queen Anne's visible fecundity – 'she is now somewhat big with child', admitted Cranmer to the English ambassador to the Emperor's court – made her an appropriate candidate to receive the consort's crown. Hall caught the flavour of this when he wrote in his *Chronicle* that some people judged that God loved this new marriage because 'the new Queen was so soon with child'. (It was, after all, the deaths of his infant sons which had officially convinced King Henry of God's displeasure with his union to his brother's wife.)

A scurrilous story, related by the egregious Chapuys, which had the two Boleyns, father and daughter, quarrelling over the Queen's dress, did at least make the same point. Anne was supposed to have added a panel of cloth to her dress to accommodate her growing figure (maternity clothes as such did not exist). When her father remarked that she should take away the cloth and thank God for the state in which she found herself, Anne, with her usual spirit, retorted that she was in a better plight than he would have wished her to be.[27] More publicly, during the endless relation of processional verses which predicted a golden age when Queen Anne should give birth to a son, it must have been a great comfort to loyal beholders to reflect that this wondrous event was actually likely to take place quite soon.

To prepare for the ceremony, Queen Anne came first from Greenwich to the Tower of London by water as was customary. It was 29 May, the Thursday before Whit Sunday. She was 'apparelled in rich cloth of gold' and escorted by fifty 'great barges, comely beseen', belonging to the various guilds of the City, which had come down to greet her. As a result, Antonio de Guaras, author of the *Spanish Chronicle* – an eyewitness – described how nothing was to be seen for four miles but 'barges and boats all draped with awnings and carpeted, which gave pleasure to behold'. Each barge, according to the official account of the 'Triumph' printed later, contained 'minstrels making sweet harmony'. But theirs must have been an uphill task, for the *Spanish Chronicle* reported that the firing of the artillery was so persistent that 'it verily seemed as if the world was coming to an end'. As a result, there was not a single pane of glass left round the Tower or in the St Katherine's area (where de Guaras lived). 'It seemed as if all the houses must tumble to the ground'.[28]

When Queen Anne reached the Tower of London, King Henry received her 'with loving countenance at the postern by the waters' side' and he kissed her publicly.[29] They spent the next two nights together at the Tower. The ancient structure had recently been the subject of massive repairs, set in motion by Thomas Cromwell in the summer of 1532. Nearly 3,000 tons of Caen stone were needed, and over £3,500 spent with 400 workmen employed; a new gallery was built for the Queen between the King's gallery and the end of the King's wardrobe, and roofs and floors for the Queen's chambers. As with Whitehall, the Queen destined to enjoy all this was Queen Anne, not Queen Catherine. On the Saturday the new Queen was to be taken in a solemn and magnificent procession through the City of London, with elaborate pageantry, to Westminster.

Already there had been some controversy about the arrangements. For example, Queen Anne had insisted on using the royal barge of her predecessor, with its badges stripped off and replaced with her own, for her journey up river. This seems to have been more of a personal gesture on the new Queen's own part (*ainsi sera* – that's how it's going to be) than the previous demand for Queen Catherine's jewels. At any rate, the Duke of Norfolk told Chapuys that the incident had made King Henry very angry, as there were plenty of other barges on the river fit for the purpose; the new Queen's chamberlain Lord Borough received a reprimand.[30]

Of course Norfolk talking to Chapuys was not unprejudiced. He was extremely anxious at this point about the prospect of a Spanish invasion. He also wanted to assure Chapuys along the way that he personally had never favoured the Boleyn marriage – even though it was also in a sense a Howard marriage. (Nor did Norfolk attend the coronation of his niece, since he set off for France immediately before to exert an English diplomatic presence at a meeting of the Pope and King François.) Chapuys, however, was prepared to be philosophical on the subject – there were after all more important issues: 'May God permit that she [Queen Anne] may henceforward be contented with possessing the barge, the jewels and the husband of the Queen', he wrote, 'without attempting also ... the life of the Queen and Princess'.[31]

There is independent evidence – other than the reports of Chapuys or de Guaras, both inevitably sympathetic to Queen Catherine – that the celebrations of the City were not an unalloyed success at the grassroots level such things were supposed to reach. Norfolk earlier questioned whether the City clergy should even be invited to attend since they were in a difficult and critical mood. Then it was customary for the dignitaries of the City to present the new Queen with a substantial financial gift; on this occasion the aldermen went round in person to collect the contributions to inhibit refusal. With unwonted tact, the aldermen also left the Spanish merchants off the list of those paying a household tax towards the gift – no doubt wishing to avoid possible unpleasant arguments, which might rebound on the City if they came to the ears of the King. But the initials H and A, displayed in many combinations as H and K had once been, provided in themselves material for covert satire: HA! HA! sniggered certain disloyal Londoners.[32]

Not a hint of this appeared, of course, in the elaborate pageantry of Saturday's procession. Queen Anne's garb was a mixture of the virginal and the resplendent. Her wonderful long black hair 'hung down' her back like a bride's and she carried some flowers in her hand. But her dress of crimson brocade was encrusted with precious stones, while round her neck she wore 'a string of pearls larger than chick peas', according to de Guaras, and a large jewel 'made up of diamonds of evidently great value.' A robe of royal purple velvet surmounted it all, while her ladies were similarly 'richly clothed in crimson powdered with ermines'.[33]

Queen Anne sat in a litter, with the canopy over her head born by the Barons of the Cinque Ports, at the head of a long procession of nobles and attendants. A long Latin panegyric had been written for Anne by the celebrated grammarian Robert Whittington at the New Year while she was still merely 'the most illustrious and beautiful heroine Lady Anna, the Marquess of Pembroke'.[34] Whittington had indulged in a series of comparisons from the classical world (although the text itself must have been slightly lost on his heroine, who never had an opportunity to learn Latin):

> Hail Anna! jewel shining outstandingly gracefully
> This year will be joyful and favourable for you.
> You will see years, months, and days as happy as
> those which Livia, the consort of Caesar, saw.

And poets were ordered by Whittington to praise Penelope or even Helen no longer since this heroine excelled them both. Now that she was Queen, Christian imagery was added, with St Anne, mother of the Virgin Mary, an obvious prototype, just as St Catherine, martyred with her wheel, had been for Catherine of Aragon.[35]*

Queen Anne's first encounter was with Apollo surrounded by the Nine Muses at Gracechurch Street, in a tableau of Parnassus attributed to Holbein. But at the Cornhill, by Leadenhall, she was greeted by a full-scale pageant of 'the Progeny of St Anne': the Virgin Mary and other Marys in the New Testament. A series of children spoke the verses; one can only hope that their infant charm helped to gloss over the banality of the language. These verses were written by John Leland and Nicholas Udall. Leland was a distinguished antiquary and Udall (an early 'Lutheran' who had been implicated in the affair of heretical bookselling in Oxford in 1528) would become Provost of Eton College the next year and later Headmaster of Westminster School; he also wrote the earliest known English comedy *Ralph Roister Doister*. So that it is kindest to say that these verses did not represent the summit of their respective achievements.[37]

The first child duly compared the Queen to St Anne, ancestress of Christ, and then went on to hope for 'such issue and descent' in 'short space'. The second child saluted the arrival of a white falcon (the crest of the Butler Earls of Ormonde, inherited by Thomas Boleyn and in the case of Anne, crowned) followed by an angel, bearing a 'Crown Imperial' from heaven. The proximity of the pageant to Whit Sunday meant that a further equation could be made between Anne-as-falcon and the arrival of the Pentecostal dove – the Holy Spirit. While Queen Anne's own celebrated virtue was not forgotten:

---

* St Anne had featured strongly in the first known pageantry in honour of a royal consort when Anne of Bohemia, wife of Richard II, accompanied her husband on his solemn entry into London in 1392.[36]

> This gentle bird
> As white as curd...
> In chastity
> Excelleth she

At the Cross in Cheapside ('new-gilt' for the occasion), Queen Anne received the City's 'free gift of honour' – 1,000 marks in gold coin. According to the official version, the Queen then gave 'great thanks both with heart and mind'. (To the Spanish de Guaras, however, her behaviour seemed something less than gracious; a real Queen would have known that she had to turn the purse over to her halberdiers and lackeys, but this lady, being 'a person of low station', kept it.)[38]

At the Little Conduit in Cheapside, a further pageant showed the Judgement of Paris, sixteenth-century version, with Queen Anne, not Venus, receiving the golden apple. The next pageant, at Paul's Gate, was the crucial one since it centred round the Queen's future – and the nation's. Virgins 'costly arrayed' in white, ladies with tablets of silver and gold in their hands, combined to call out messages to her in Latin of which the general theme was: 'Queen Anne prosper! Proceed! and reign!' Under their feet was a long roll on which was inscribed, also in Latin, the real motif of the whole ceremonial: 'Queen Anne when thou shalt bear a new son of the King's blood, there shall be a golden world unto thy people!'

No wonder that the Queen, confident she would bring about this gold world within a few months, called out 'Amen' with a joyful smiling countenance to 200 children on 'a great scaffold' who had recited further 'poet's verses' to her. Whatever the quality of the lines, she had after all witnessed a great deal to give her pleasure during her long procession from the Tower to Westminster, as she turned her face 'from one side to the other' in the traditional gracious mode of royalty, then and now.

On the pavements stood the people (there were orders to keep the horses back so that the crowd should not be trampled on), and from the galleries and windows gazed down the greater folk. It is true that the Spanish merchant remarked on the paucity of loyal cries: the shouts of 'God save you!' which had been the wonted popular expression when 'the sainted queen' (Catherine) passed by. There was another story that King Henry took his wife in his arms at the end of the procession and asked her 'how she liked the look of the City'. To which Queen Anne replied tartly that she liked the look of the City well enough, 'but I saw a great many caps on heads and saw but few tongues'.[39] But after all, for her, such trifling setbacks were insignificant compared to the moment of real glory which was to come.

At eight o'clock the next morning, Queen Anne Boleyn, accompanied by noble ladies 'in their robes of estate' and all the peers of the realm in 'Parliament robes', proceeded to Westminster Abbey. There she received 'her crown' according to the official account 'with all the ceremonies thereof, as thereunto belongeth' from the Archbishop of Canterbury, Thomas Cranmer. Very few of these nobles had cried off out of loyalty to the previous Queen: the Duke of Norfolk, as has been noted, was conveniently absent on the King's business, but the Duke of Suffolk, ever the King's devoted man, acted as High Constable and Steward of the banquet that followed the coronation in Westminster Hall (when the conduit pipe outside ran with wine for the people). The King's semi-royal first cousin, the Marquess of Exeter, did not attend, but in any case he had recently been excluded from court for his support of Queen Catherine; his wife Gertrude, the daughter of Catherine's chamberlain and her Spanish lady-in-waiting Inez de Venegas, was one of Catherine's closest friends. Lord Stafford, son of the executed (and attainted) Duke of Buckingham, paid a fine rather than attend. But these were the exceptions. 'Great jousts' followed the next day; everything was as it used to be (except that the King himself did not joust).

All in all, Henry VIII, as he watched proceedings at the banquet from a gallery in Westminster Hall (monarchs traditionally did not attend the coronation ceremonies and celebrations of their consorts, if performed separately to their own), could feel well pleased. The religious service in the Abbey had not reflected the momentous break with Rome which had recently taken place: why should it, from King Henry's point of view? For one thing, he was conservative in his own piety, seeing no particular merit in 'reformed' rituals for their own sake. As to the royal supremacy, surely he was merely restoring the church to its ancient practices ...

In a bull of 11 July 1533 Pope Clement VII declared Cranmer's judgement void and ordered Henry to put away Anne, adding that any child of theirs would be illegitimate; he also excommunicated the King even if the operation of the excommunication was suspended. None of this materially assisted the cause of Queen Catherine. Only the Emperor could do that now, with troops, and he was not disposed to do so. He would by his influence prevent the Pope from reaching an accommodation with the English King (thus preventing one kind of solution for his aunt, who as a loyal daughter of the church would have had to bow to a papal decision in favour of divorce), but he would not bring about the other kind of solution in her favour. Thus Queen Catherine – or rather the Princess Dowager as she was firmly termed – was stuck in a kind of unhappy limbo. Meanwhile she resisted the change of title following Queen Anne's coronation with the same vigour as before: realpolitik and compromise had no meaning for her.

Hall, in his *Chronicle*, referred contemptuously to this policy: how Catherine 'ever continued in her old song' since 'women love to lose no dignity'. But the impression left on a delegation about this time to Catherine at Ampthill was more of a woman prepared to defend a principle to the death – very likely her own death, since they found Catherine lying miserably on a pallet, since she had pricked her foot and poisoned it on a needle, and was also 'sore annoyed with a cough'.[40] It was Lord Mountjoy, her chamberlain, who was instructed to persuade her to accept her new rank. He was accompanied among others by Griffith Richards, her gentleman-usher, who had accompanied Catherine to the tribunal – and away from it – in 1529.

But Mountjoy was allowed no chance to deploy his arguments. (He must have been a reluctant delegate in the first place: and did in fact resign his post of chamberlain in October, on the grounds that he had sworn an oath in 1512 to serve Catherine 'as Queen', and that to serve her as 'Princess Dowager' now would be breaking it.) The first use of the dreaded title got an emphatic response from Catherine: 'She was not Princess Dowager but the Queen, and the King's true wife'. Then followed what Hall called the 'old song' – her virginity at the time of her marriage to King Henry – followed by the reminder that she was a crowned and anointed Queen, and had by the King lawful issue. The embarrassed delegation pointed out that Anne Boleyn was now 'anointed and crowned' Queen of England.[41] How could there be *two* Queens? Catherine waved this aside – what had that to do with her?

She was similarly dismissive of suggestions that the King was angered by her disobedience. When the delegation suggested she was 'vainglorious' clinging on to the title – where was now the reputation for 'virtue and obedience' for which she been noted? – she replied she would rather disobey the King than disobey God. To threats that the King would confiscate her goods, and worse still, treat the Lady Princess (Mary) harshly as a result of her mother's 'unkindness', Catherine replied magnificently that 'neither for her daughter, family possessions or any worldly adversity or displeasure that might ensue, she would yield in this cause, to put her soul in danger'. She ended by quoting the words of the gospel: 'they should not be feared which have the power of the body, but He only, that hath power of the soul'. The next day, when a written account of the interview was presented to her, she ran through the words 'Princess Dowager' with a pen, and, showing that the charge of vainglory at least had angered her, protested that she would rather be 'a poor beggar's wife, and be sure of Heaven, than to be Queen of all the world'.[42]

Catherine's wits had not deserted her. For all her pleas of weakness –

they must forgive her if she was to 'err in any word', for she was Spanish-born, and without proper legal counsel – she managed to make a good debating point. If, as they asserted, she was not the King's wife, then she could hardly be his subject. For she had only come into the realm to be a royal wife, certainly not as a 'merchandise, nor yet to be married to any merchant'; she was certainly not going to confess to having been 'the King's harlot' for the last twenty-four years. The correct answer to Catherine's point was that King Henry did still have dominion over Catherine as a subject, since she was the widow of his brother; but this was not easy to insist on when dealing with one born a royal princess of another country.

When Thomas Cromwell heard of all this he was moved to exclaim that nature had wronged Catherine in not making her a man. But for her sex, she would have surpassed all the heroes in history![43] Nor should one regard his compliments as insincere, despite the irony of Cromwell pronouncing them, the very man who had helped the King find a way of getting rid of Catherine. In an age when most men and women subordinated themselves to the will of the sovereign, as being part of the natural order, there was still scope to admire those who preferred higher claims: as the fate of other 'dissidents' in the coming years would show.

Meanwhile at court these days, there were indications to encourage Catherine's supporters that all was not well between the King and the new Queen. For many years King Henry had been accustomed to treat the pregnancy of his wife as being a period when a man, deprived of proper comfort at home as it were, could be forgiven a mild flirtation, gallantries that went perhaps a little too far . . . He did not see that Queen Anne Boleyn should take exception to a pattern of behaviour that Queen Catherine of Aragon had in former times so admirably tolerated. The ladies-in-waiting who surrounded the new Queen were just as pretty, just as tempting, as those who had attended Queen Catherine.

But there were crucial differences in the new situation. First, the stakes were now much higher. There was at least a possibility that the King might abandon his wife for love of another, since he had done so once. Thus his passions, fleeting or otherwise, incurred even closer attention from the King-watchers – a category that included almost everyone at court. Secondly, this theoretical possibility, which for all the high-flown language of the coronation, with its chaste white doves and childish cries of 'Queen Anne prosper!', could not be denied, inevitably stirred up the new Queen. She was already prone to fits of jealousy which (unlike Queen Catherine) she made no attempt to control. The King dealt with his tempestuous wife's protests in some sharp exchanges. There was much 'coldness and grumbling' between them. When Queen Anne made use of 'certain words' which he greatly disliked, he told her that she must shut her eyes and endure as those who were better than herself had done. He added, even more unpleasantly, that she ought to know that he could at any time 'lower her as much as he had raised her'.[44]

Yet one should not see this grumbling as more significant than it was at the time. On another level, King Henry's happiness impressed observers, a by-product of the pregnancy in which he rejoiced. Such masculine pride was natural. After fourteen years the King had demonstrated himself once more to be 'a man like other men' (*'homme comme les autres'*), a phrase he had used to Chapuys – three times over – in April. Besides, as a couple Henry VIII and Anne Boleyn had always found rows stimulated their passion. In a few months time – following the birth of their child – they would be lovers all over again. Sir John Russell, an experienced courtier who knew the King as well as anyone, thought that he had never seen his master 'merrier' – not at least for a great while – than he was now. The romantic side to their love still existed. At the beginning of an extremely beautiful *Book of Hours of the Blessed Virgin*, which belonged jointly to King and Queen, Anne wrote suitably enough underneath the scene of the Annunciation:

> By daily proof you shall me find
> To be to you both loving and kind.

Henry himself wrote in French below a figure of Christ wearing the crown of thorns – often used as a symbol of Christian kingship – that if Anne remembered him in her prayers, 'I will never be forgotten because I am yours forever, King Henry'.[45]

Their child was after all certain to be a boy. Everyone knew that. Astrologers predicted it. So did the King's physicians. On 3 September these two bodies of scientific practitioners joined forces to assure the King that the Queen would 'certainly' give him a male heir. Preparations for a celebratory tournament were begun, and for the actual birth 'one of the most magnificent and gorgeous beds that could be thought of' was brought out of the King's treasure room; it had originally come from France as part of the ransom for a captured nobleman.[46] The names proposed were Henry or Edward.

According to custom, Queen Anne took to her chamber in advance, to await the birth of her son. Precedent was extremely important in these matters, even though there had been a change of Queen. Lord Mountjoy, veteran of Queen Catherine's confinements, advised Lord Cobham, Queen Anne's chamberlain, on the correct procedure. The rules to be followed had been laid down in the reign of Henry VII. 'A fair pallet bed' should be set down beside the ornate royal bed for the actual delivery. All the windows save one were to be covered with richly embroidered arras. And 'No man to come into the chamber, save women'.[47]

Queen Anne retired from public view on 26 August, that is to say, about two weeks before the baby was actually born. Obviously, the amount of time spent by queens awaiting their time varied considerably, babies being notoriously unreliable in arriving, but this was not an unusually short period.* Since the date of Henry and Anne's marriage had been antedated in people's minds to 14 November 1532, which gave plenty of time for the lawful conception of a child born any time after mid-August, there was after all no need to pretend this baby was premature.

It was a fine healthy child, born about three o'clock in the afternoon of 7 September 1533. But it was a girl, a princess: Elizabeth for the King's mother, not Henry for himself, nor Edward for his grandfather and a long line of male sovereigns stretching behind them.

The staggeringly unexpected nature of this event is demonstrated by the appearance of the official document in which Queen Anne had to break the news to the world.[49] Queens, by convention, did this. This document, addressed to her chamberlain Lord Cobham, was already prepared. It began with a great flourish: 'And where as it hath pleased the goodness of Almighty God, of his infinite mercy and grace, to send unto us, at this time, good speed, in the deliverance and bringing forth of a Prince . . .' It ended in similar style, 'Unto Almighty God, high thanks, glory, laud and praising; and to pray for the good health, prosperity and continual preservation of the said Prince accordingly.' It was sealed with a signet in the name of 'Anne the Quene'. But in both cases, a hasty 's' had to be inserted after the word 'Prince', to give 'Princes' (an acceptable sixteenth-century spelling of Princess). This noticeable alteration still attests to the surprise and displeasure caused by the birth of the future Queen Elizabeth I.†

---

* Elizabeth of York, in 1503, took to her chamber only one week before the birth of her child.[48]
† The document is in the Manuscript Room of the British Library.

Chapter 10

THE MOST HAPPY?

A.R. The Moost Happi. Anno 1534.

Inscription on portrait medal of Queen Anne Boleyn

For the christening of Princess Elizabeth, Queen Anne demanded a special 'triumphal cloth' which her predecessor Queen Catherine had brought with her from Spain for the purpose of baptisms. Predictably, Catherine refused. 'God forbid', she shuddered, that she should give any 'help, assistance or favour' either directly or indirectly, in 'a case so horrible as this'. It seems that on this occasion Catherine maintained her refusal successfully; unlike the previous year when a follow-up order from the King had resulted in the eventual surrender of her jewels. But apparently the King did not interest himself in triumphal cloths.[1] In any case the christening of this unexpected princess was a somewhat low-key affair: for instance the splendid joust already planned in honour of a prince was immediately cancelled.

Archbishop Cranmer played the role of godfather, as Cardinal Wolsey had done for Princess Mary. Godmother at the baptism was the matriarch of the Howard family, Agnes, Dowager Duchess of Norfolk (Queen Anne's step-grandmother), an appropriate enough choice: she had also been one of the sponsors for the King's elder daughter. At the confirmation which immediately followed it, however, Gertrude Marchioness of Exeter, Queen Catherine's loyal friend, was obliged to stand godmother and to present the baby princess with three engraved silver-gilt bowls. As a gesture, the invitation to Lady Exeter – which she could not refuse – was less crude perhaps than the request to Catherine for the christening garment. But the point being made was the same. Low-key as the christening might be, nevertheless the old order was finished, the old Queen set aside and officially forgotten, the elder princess no longer heiress-presumptive to her father, a position she had occupied since her birth in 1516.

The royal herald hammered home the change in status of the King's first-born daughter, when he proclaimed the new-born Princess Elizabeth as the King's first 'legitimate' child. Immediately, therefore, Mary appeared to be the loser from the birth of a healthy baby to the King's new wife. Although the formal dissolution of her parents' marriage at Dunstable in May 1533 had made Mary theoretically illegitimate, no steps had been taken so far to emphasize the fact. In canon law it was possible for the position of such children whose parents, like Henry and Catherine, had married in good faith, to be regularized: the church did not act severely in such situations. Besides, Queen Anne might be well advanced in pregnancy, but no one knew better than the King and his advisers – principal among them Thomas Cromwell – how great were the perils of childbirth and how frail the life of infants could be ... how foolhardy, then, publicly to bastardize a princess whose services might still, as it were, be needed.

Indeed, for this very reason, considerable caution had been exercised in handling Princess Mary in the two years following her mother's consignment to seclusion and before the birth of her half-sister. It was only in November 1533 that Mary's household under the Countess of Salisbury – that of a royal princess – was dissolved and she herself placed in the household of the infant Elizabeth, to whom she was officially inferior.[2] Throughout this period, her marriageability remained a factor: Mary at seventeen and a half in the summer of 1533 was already older than her mother had been at the first of her weddings. In January 1532, for example, the chamberlain of the Duke of Cleves had paid an exploratory visit to the English court, and Chapuys at least had thought that match a possibility. A few months later Chapuys reported that the princess's name was being linked once again with that of her first cousin the King of Scots (still unmarried, despite a series of on-off negotiations with the French).

There was another side to this: Princess Mary's prestige abroad. Of Mary, after all, it could be said, as it was once said of her mother, that she was descended 'from great kings'. She was not only the daughter of the King of England, she was also the cousin of the Emperor: if the former would not allow her claims to succeed him, who knew but that the latter would not enforce them? With Queen Catherine out of the picture, diplomatically speaking, Princess Mary came into stronger focus.

At home, there was also the intriguing question of King Henry's attitude to his daughter. Undoubtedly at the time of the 1533 divorce he was still very fond of her; he was an affectionate man, happy to dote upon his children – so long as they did not cross his will – and Princess Mary in youth had been a charming, submissive, loving little girl, his 'pearl' as Henry once described her. Mary's own adoration for the powerful central figure in her life (and that of the whole country), her father, had been all any patriarch could have wished. Just as Mary's claims to the throne could not be lightly dismissed before the birth of Elizabeth, so too the King's love for her could not be assumed to have died, along with his love for her mother. In October 1532 there was a pleasant encounter between father and daughter in the country (*aux champs*) which it has been suggested was not entirely coincidental. The King did not say much except to ask Mary how she was, and assure her that henceforward he would visit her more often.[3] Where Mary's relationship with her mother was concerned, the King was not resolutely harsh. Catherine and Mary were allowed to write to each other and in June 1533 when Mary was sick, the King allowed Queen Catherine's physician and apothecary to attend to her.

The vulgar threats said to have been made by Queen Anne towards Mary – 'she would make of the princess a maid in her household ... or marry her to some varlet', she boasted in April 1533[4] – were obviously rooted in jealousy of this paternal affection, potentially so dangerous to Anne's own position. Of course such stories lost nothing in the telling: no story about the tempestuous, challenging Anne Boleyn ever did. It is easy to understand how Chapuys' informers rushed away with glee to repeat the details of the latest outrageous explosion to him, certainly not minimizing them along the way. But if some of the details are perhaps altogether too vivid, the general picture of Anne Boleyn's neurotic obsession with Princess Mary is clear enough.

Now Queen Anne had produced her own heir for the King. In September 1533, everything was changed. Or was it? Did Princess Mary really find herself totally relegated to dynastic obscurity by the birth of Princess Elizabeth, as at first sight would seem to have been the case? It is at this point that the complication of the new royal baby's inconvenient gender comes into play. The bold words of the royal herald concerning Elizabeth as the King's first 'legitimate' child glossed over the awkward fact that the King now had two daughters. It was already arguable as to which one was actually legitimate: if the divorce and subsequent remarriage was not accepted as valid, then it was actually Elizabeth who was the BASTARD (as Chapuys sometimes termed her – on one occasion in block capitals – when he did not use the word *'la garse'* or brat; Dr Ortiz, the imperial agent at Rome, writing in Spanish, called her *'la manchuba'* – the wench).[5] What was unarguable was that Mary was the elder, so that if both princesses, by some sleight of hand, were held to be legitimate (as the provisions of canon law would have allowed) then Mary's claims to succeed her father were still superior. All this was quite apart from Mary's royal descent on her mother's side, which Elizabeth, for all Queen

Anne's carefully emphasized genealogy – she bore the arms of Lancaster on her shield – could never match.

On the surface therefore the problem of the Tudor succession had been solved by the birth of a real live child within a truly valid marriage, but beneath it, nothing had been changed. The need for a male heir remained as urgent as ever; in fact, it could be argued that the involuntarily threatening presence of poor Princess Mary made it even more important for Queen Anne to produce a son than it had been for Queen Catherine. Certainly Queen Anne herself felt so. A portrait medal thought to have been struck to celebrate her coronation – but actually dated 1534 – bears the motto round its rim: 'A.R. The Moost Happi', but it was difficult to see how this happiness could be complete with a mere daughter to support her. The strain did not suit Anne's volatile temperament and quick tongue which found it all too easy to erupt into highly quotable expressions of disgust: she would like to give Mary 'a good banging', she exclaimed at one point, for the bastard she was.

Ironically enough, not only Anne's, but Mary's position might actually have been better had Elizabeth turned out to be that longed-for prince. Mary would then have represented no real threat: for all her relationship to the Emperor, her supporters would have had to acknowledge the tacit supremacy of a male heir in such a situation. Mary could then have enjoyed a more placid existence as an English princess, for whom a suitable marriage – to one of the French princes if not James of Scotland – would be found. As it was, Mary had to endure a campaign of cruelty from which she would not be rescued for many years; with debilitating effects not only on her health but on her character at a crucial time of her life.

How cursed the Tudor family had turned out to be in its perennial lack of male heirs! King Henry VIII, now in his forties, 'bald like Caesar' in the words of the Venetian ambassador, was still no more secure in this respect than he had been when he ascended the throne as a hopeful golden-haired youth. Leaving aside his nonexistent son, where were the promising nephews to support the dynasty? The situation regarding the only son of his elder sister remained as it had been in the 1520s, except that James V was now an adult: the monarch of an alien, sometimes hostile land with all that implied.

His younger sister Mary Duchess of Suffolk died – after a long illness – in June 1533, and her only son would die the following March. Her husband married again, almost immediately, the young heiress actually affianced to this sickly boy.[6] This was Katherine Willoughby, daughter of Queen Catherine's loyal servant, Maria de Salinas, Lady Willoughby de Eresby. Katherine was aged fourteen and Suffolk seven years older than the King, but time had not dimmed the sex appeal that had made him the most desired man at the early Tudor court as he wielded his long lance at the joust, and Katherine, a girl of independent spirit as it turned out, did not object. But Suffolk's sons by Katherine would of course have no share of royal blood.

Under the circumstances, King Henry turned his attention to the girls. These might shore up his position – while not solving the central problem. The lively Lady Margaret Douglas (the best-looking Tudor girl of her generation), daughter of Queen Margaret by Angus, was a particular favourite of his; and the fact that she had been born in England might be held to give her or her children superior rights in the succession over her Scottish-born brother James V. In the autumn of 1533, following the death of her aunt Mary Duchess of Suffolk, Lady Margaret was the senior royal lady in England, after the Queen (ignoring Princess Mary), and as such she was immediately made first lady of honour in the new household created for Princess Elizabeth. As for the Brandon girls, Lady Frances and Lady Eleanor, daughters of Mary Duchess of Suffolk, the King had taken a personal interest in marrying off his elder niece at the age of sixteen to a suitably supportive bridegroom, Henry Grey, 3rd Marquess of Dorset, in May 1533; although Dorset was related to the King via Elizabeth Woodville, he had no actual royal blood and thus constituted no threat.

There were however two families in the shadows close to the throne whose members indubitably did have royal blood: the Courtenays (headed by the Marquess of Exeter) and the Poles (headed by Lord Montague, eldest son of Margaret Countess of Salisbury). As it happened, both families had connections to Queen Catherine. Conservative reactionary politics, a dislike of religious reform, made a dangerous mixture with royal blood. The spectre of conspiracy from these families, especially if they showed signs of uniting, would always haunt King Henry so long as he had no proper heir – and not necessarily without justification. Lord Exeter, a man in his thirties, was after all King Henry's 'near kinsman': their respective mothers, Elizabeth and Katherine of York, had been sisters. Furthermore by his wife, Gertrude, Queen Catherine's ally, Lord Exeter had that invaluable asset, a son and heir: Edward Courtenay Earl of Devon, born in 1526 and thus arguably available to be matched to Princess Mary. (See family tree 2)

The royal blood of the Poles was equally incontestable, if one generation further removed; whereas Lord Exeter was a grandson of Edward IV, Lord Montague and his brothers were the grandsons of his brother the Duke of Clarence. But the Poles were a flourishing family: Lord Montague, like Lord Exeter, had a son and heir, and Reginald Pole, now in his early thirties, was another potential bridegroom for Princess Mary – who would not have to wait for him to grow up. Indeed, it was believed that this bright young man, at this point not yet ordained as a priest, had been Queen Catherine's favoured bridegroom for her daughter ever since the debacle of the Emperor's suit.

The affair of the Nun of Kent, Elizabeth Barton, which culminated in her arrest in July 1533, was calculated to play upon the King's paranoia. This young woman – she was about twenty-seven at the time of her arrest – had become increasingly famous both for her fits which left her 'as still as a dead body' and for her prophecies: 'while lying unconscious she would utter mysterious words.' A professed nun, at first she found her mystical visions greeted with respect and she even met Cardinal Wolsey. She became, however, a violent opponent of the royal divorce, encouraged by her confessor, a monk at Canterbury. As the prospect of the King's remarriage grew nearer, her prophecies began to take a distinctly subversive turn.[7]

In 1532, for example, she had a vision of Christ recrucified by the King's adultery and of Anne Boleyn as a Jezebel whom dogs would eat. Dangerous rumours began to spread that the Nun, in the prophetic mood, had envisioned Lord Montague succeeding to the throne of King Henry. Elizabeth Barton certainly had connections to opposition circles. Queen Catherine, with her usual good sense, had steadfastly refused to grant her an interview when she was in a position to do so, and thus could not be implicated in her fall (to the considerable disappointment of Cranmer and Cromwell). But Thomas More and Bishop Fisher had both been in touch with her in some manner as had the convent at Syon, notoriously supportive of Queen Catherine.

For the New Year of 1534 Queen Anne gave King Henry a magnificent gift. This was a golden table fountain designed by Hans Holbein which incorporated her heraldic falcon – that gentle bird as white as curd of the coronation verses – into the design. But the real present that Henry VIII wanted from his new wife was that 'new son of the King's blood' which, to quote the coronation celebrations again, would bring about 'a golden world' for his people. Since this responsibility to provide a son was of course considered to be hers, it must have been with an extraordinary sense of relief that around the turn of the year Queen Anne did indeed find that she was pregnant. On 28 January 1534 King Henry triumphantly told Chapuys that he would soon be a father again.[8]

Between 8 March and 8 April work was done on the royal nurseries at Eltham Palace 'against the coming of the prince'. An iron canopy was made to go over the cradle, attention was paid to the setting of the glazing in 'the prince's lodgings' and the timber work of 'his' lodgings was painted with yellow ochre.[9] If we suppose Queen Anne to be roughly four months pregnant at the time the work was commissioned – as has been noted, that was the average period thought necessary for a pregnancy to be an established fact – then she had conceived in November, that is, some two months after the birth of Elizabeth. This was perfectly possible timing since like other royal or aristocratic ladies, Queen Anne did not breastfeed her baby (which might have inhibited conception).

For that matter, Queen Anne did not care for her child in anything like the modern sense, since it was thought commensurate with the rank of a princess (to say nothing of a prince) that she should have her own household. This makes Queen Anne's relationship with her little daughter peculiarly difficult to establish during the fleeting years in which she was alive to enjoy it. We know that Princess Elizabeth, having been moved to the care of Lady Bryan, was weaned (from her wet nurse) at the age of thirteen months.[10] But the order came from the King, and the formality of its language – 'with the assent of the Queen's grace' – attests to a way of life in which ceremonial emphasizing the child's rank was a prime consideration.

This is not to say that Queen Anne did not love her child; one should also beware of assuming that maternal affection is excluded altogether, just because a way of life is so unfamiliar. There are touching anecdotes from a more stressful period in Queen Anne's life, which, even if they became embroidered to please Anne's daughter (understandably enough), do at least attest to her basic tenderness as a mother. In one of these tales, Archbishop Matthew Parker was asked to see to the spiritual future of the little girl; in another, Queen Anne was seen holding out her child pleadingly to her angry husband. Nevertheless the King came first.[11] Queen Anne certainly interpreted her immediate duty at this time as being to please the King by giving him another child, rather than bringing up the one she had just borne – and all society would have agreed with her. It is significant that this new baby was indeed conceived at a moment when the King's passion for Anne had been manifestly renewed. A lady at court close to her heard the King say 'several times' that rather than abandon his new wife 'he would beg alms from door to door'. Anne had captivated him again. As a result, an informant at court was able to write to Lady Lisle at Calais on 27 April 1534 saying: 'the Queen hath a goodly belly'; he prayed 'Our Lord to send us a prince.' The Queen, God willing, would give birth to this prince in the high summer.[12]

Tumultuous events were taking place in England during the spring of this year, as the King and Cromwell, freed from foreign constraints, were able to pursue their remaking of the ecclesiastical structure of the country. Knowledge of his wife's pregnancy meant that the King had a satisfying emotional basis to it all: the plan God intended for England and himself was surely working. As he told Chapuys at the end of February, Princess Elizabeth would not be his heir for very long, since he expected the Queen to give birth to a son 'very soon'.[13] King Henry was certainly able to brush off the fact that in March 1534, even as the royal nursery was being prepared once again for Anne Boleyn's child, the Pope finally found for Queen Catherine. At long last he declared that her marriage to King Henry had been valid all along.

Like his bull against the King the previous July, the Pope's action availed Queen Catherine little. Who was to enforce her rights? The Emperor was fully occupied trying to handle the threat to his dominions, both in the east, represented by Suleiman the Magnificent, and in the Mediterranean, where corsairs loosely linked to the Sultan carried out a series of daring raids. King François with his eyes on a European situation which he intended to manipulate to his advantage (in 1536 he would conclude a treaty with Suleiman) had no wish to interfere in England. Clement VII died six months after declaring Queen Catherine's marriage valid. The following year, when the new Pope Paul III suggested that the French King might carry out his sentence against King Henry by force of arms, King François' reaction was to propose a possible marriage for Princess Mary with his third son, the Duc d'Angoulême – not quite the same thing.

Shortly before the birth of Princess Elizabeth, Queen Catherine had been moved to Buckden Palace in Huntingdonshire, the chief residence of the Bishops of Lincoln. It was not an unpleasant environment: there was a great hall built in the previous century, as well as a great tower, and commodious gatehouses; the domestic apartments were large. A moat passed between the tower and the adjacent church – which presumably prompted the choice of the place for the discarded Queen – but beyond that lay a small park.[14]

Queen Catherine however was not consoled by her new surroundings. From Buckden she maintained her furious rejections of her new title. To Suffolk in December 1533 she gave the same firm response as previously: 'in an open voice' she declined to be served or addressed as Princess Dowager. Her attendants muttered about the original oath to serve her as Queen: 'standing stiffly on their consciences' they questioned whether it might not even be perjury to serve her under any other name. As a result two of her chaplains were shut up in the porter's ward of the palace, leaving only Athequa, so that he could hear her confession in Spanish, 'in the which speech she is ever confessed' was the report 'and cannot be in any other so she saith'. Suffolk's final verdict to Norfolk was: 'we find here the most obstinate woman that may be'.[15] This defiance, from a little enclosed world far away from the court, was of small consequence in public terms compared to the tide of legislation now being enacted.

The Act of Supremacy, from the point of view of the country at large, was the most momentous of these. The powers claimed for the King under this act, as head of the church of England (*Anglicana ecclesia*) stretched as far as the definition of faith itself. In future the King of England was to enjoy not only 'the style and title' of Supreme Head of the Church, but all the prerogatives 'to the said dignity of supreme head of the same church belonging and appertaining.' But from the point of view of Queen Anne, Queen Catherine and Princess Mary, the Act of Succession – which symbolically if coincidentally had its third reading on 23 March 1534, exactly the same date as the Pope's decree in Catherine's favour – produced the more immediately revolutionary effect. The oath of support for this act now required from individuals presented partisans of the old order everywhere with a challenge which would not be easily surmounted.

The Act of Succession formally declared the validity of the marriage of King Henry and Queen Anne, together with the right of their lawful issue to succeed. Even now Princess Mary was not specifically named as illegitimate, although the terms of the act suggested that this must be the case. This omission was possibly a precaution taken by Cromwell; either because he remained wary on the subject of infant mortality, or because he sought, equally practically, to avoid harming Mary's prospects in the grandest marriage markets such as France. The value of a King's 'natural daughter' was, after all, a good deal less. For all that neglect, the title 'Princess' had been effectively taken from Mary, and she was not supposed to be addressed as such, any more than her mother should be greeted as Queen.

The new 'Lady Mary', who had borne the title of Princess since her earliest recollection, was humiliated. In addition, she was required to pay her respects to her baby half-sister Elizabeth: officially a *real* princess but to her merely the child of the hated concubine. Mary's health suffered. She no longer had her independent household but lived in the wake of Elizabeth. It was particularly intolerable to have to 'remove and follow the BASTARD', reported Chapuys, when Princess Mary was indisposed; it made her worse.[16]

Mary's servants, like those of her mother, felt the indignity of her relegation on her behalf, and also humanly found the whole thing difficult to remember. We find Lady Anne Hussey explaining rather desperately that the reason she had – wrongly, as she now saw – addressed 'Lady Mary' as Princess, was because she had always been accustomed to do so. Others in more public positions experienced the same difficulty: it is not always easy to adapt to new regimes however rigidly enforced. One can understand how the aged Bishop of Bath and Wells accidentally prayed for 'the lady Catherine the Queen' in Wells Cathedral in February 1535 although he followed it by naming 'my Lady Elizabeth Princess', her daughter. The Bishop – 'not much under eighty' – was astounded to receive a reproof, since he was quite unaware of what he had done. He hastened to apologize abjectly: 'I meant only Queen Anne, for I know no more Queens but her.'[17]

When Queen Catherine was brought the oath to swear at Buckden in May 1534 she was no more passive than before. She responded by reading aloud the Pope's judgement. The clerics – Archbishop Lee of York and Bishop Tunstall of Durham – found themselves not only exhausted but positively bored by her recitation of all her familiar arguments regarding the divorce 'in great choler, in agony, and always interrupting our words.' As they concluded: 'the specialities [details] whereof ... we do remit, for tediousness unto others to tell.'[18] They had heard it all before. The King had remarried. He was now head of the church of England. Wearily, they felt that it was up to her to make the best of her situation as the 'Dowager to Prince Arthur'. To Catherine, of course, with nothing else to think about (except her dispossessed daughter) the matter was as vivid and painful as on the dreadful day five years past when the Spanish ambassador had broken the news of the secret tribunal.

But Catherine's Spanish servants had to swear – or leave. According to Antonio de Guaras – who had close contacts in this household – some of them took refuge in a trick. They swore, in Spanish, that the King *'se ha hecho cabeza de Iglesia'* (has *appointed* himself head of the church of England) instead of *'sea hecho ...'* (the King may be *made* head ...). This equivalent of swearing with crossed fingers was said to have been the device of Queen Catherine. But some of her servants did leave rather than, in effect, perjure themselves: including Bastian, the Burgundian lackey who had served her for seventeen years. 'Now it pains me to be forced to leave so good a mistress', he told her as he knelt before her to say goodbye and Queen Catherine wept.[19]

Finally, however, the servants at Buckden were small fry. As for Catherine's personal safety, whatever Chapuys' oft-expressed fears, it can never have been the intention of the King to harm her. To put the situation at its most cynical, her health was already, by January 1534, giving rise to significant concern: the King told the French ambassador that she was 'dropsical and could not live long'.[20] (What would the implications be of her death? In more ways than one it might change the whole situation.) As for Mary, who naturally refused to swear, encouraged by her mother's example, the King's intention where she was concerned was to secure her submission, not hurt her.

When the Lady Mary was ill in September 1534 (exacerbated by that need to 'remove' with Princess Elizabeth), it seems that she was allowed a rare pleasure. Her father, as well as sending his own physician for her cure, 'permitted the Queen [Catherine] also to visit her' along with an apothecary. This apothecary was actually instructed to pay his respects to the one-year-old Princess Elizabeth, before attending to the patient. But this message got there too late, which must have been satisfying to Mary and Catherine. Nothing more is known about this visit, for which Queen Catherine had pleaded with Cromwell on behalf of her daughter – 'a little comfort and mirth, which she should take with me, should undoubtedly be half a health to her,' – although it provides further evidence that the King's heart was not absolutely closed to Mary.[21] (One may assume that no one was foolish enough to ask the 'obstinate' Queen Catherine to pay *her* respects to the little red-haired child who nominally presided over the household.)

Others were in a more perilous position. Where necessary the Act of Succession had the sharp teeth of a man – and woman – trap. Although refusing to swear the Oath of Succession which supported it merely carried a penalty of life imprisonment, any person who could be shown to have gone further and denied that the King was head of the church would suffer death. For such a refusal sought to deprive the King of his title – and that was now treason. These sharp teeth now closed on a series of individuals, as well as whole religious communities, who declined to swear the oath. Over the next years there were those who would perish by the axe as a result.

The Nun of Kent died at Tyburn, together with a priest, two monks and two friars, on 20 April 1534. (She was said to have recanted her subversive visions after examination 'because she knew her time had not yet come'.)[22] The Nun was not herself a victim of the Acts of Supremacy and Succession: for she was condemned for having prophesied the death of the King within a month if he married Anne Boleyn (one of the many prophecies of the time that did not come true). However when Sir Thomas More and Bishop Fisher were both arrested for refusing to take the oath, an attempt was made to link them to her case. In May and June of the following year Carthusian monks, leaders of communities which denied the King was head of the church, and a member of the Brigittine house of Syon (which Queen Catherine had particularly favoured) were put to death. The Pope's action in creating the imprisoned Bishop Fisher a Cardinal in May 1535 infuriated the King: Bishop Fisher went to the block on 22 June. On 6 July Sir Thomas More, after a year in the Tower of London in the course of which he worked on his *Dialogue of Comfort* and *Treatise on Passion*, followed him there.

Both men would go on to be canonized by the Roman Catholic church for their adherence to conscience and the true faith. At the time it was more relevant that such deaths – in the case of the Carthusians, barbarously

carried out, including disembowelling before death – added to the unpopularity of the woman who was blamed for them in the public imagination:
'Anne the Quene'. The troubled 1530s, with their revolutionary impact
on society at all levels, brought what have been described as a 'torrent of
prophecies and counter-prophecies', often based on the heraldic badges
and devices of great personages (a somewhat safer way of issuing criticism
than straightforward denunciation). In 1535 an old man recalled hearing
from his former master that 'the white Falcon would come of the North-
West and kill almost all priests'.[23] It was after all far easier to blame the
predatory white falcon – the 'concubine' with her inheritance of sinfulness
from Eve – than to accept that it was the King and the King's desires which
had brought all this about.

What a great expense it was for the King 'to continue his buildings in so
many places at once': thus Thomas Cromwell in 1534 saluted, somewhat
nervously, the explosion of refurbishment, reconstruction and new construction by Henry VIII, which commenced in the years of his marriage
to Anne Boleyn. It was as though the King, having made himself master
in his own house, metaphorically speaking, determined to hammer the
point home publicly by adding enormously to the number of his actual
houses. There is indeed something positively manic about his acquisi-
tiveness and extravagance in this respect. By the 1520s, most of the castles
in the south of England were in his hands (the attainder of Buckingham
resulted in the forfeiture of no less than twelve castles to the crown). In
1532 du Bellay, the French ambassador, described to his master how,
whenever he arrived at a royal property, King Henry would show him
round and tell him 'what he has done and what he is going to do.' The
dissolution of great abbeys, priories and other institutions – bringing the
King a further eleven palaces – provided other rich opportunities. At his
death Henry VIII would leave some fifty castles behind him: more than
any other English monarch before or since.[24]

There is something appropriately symbolic about the badges and initials
of his wife, represented in glass and stone and painted wood, which would
decorate these new palaces – as well as replacing those of Queen Catherine
in the old ones. (At Greenwich, for example, the house that Catherine had
loved, John Hethe, a London painter, was paid to remove those tactless
reminders of the past, the pomegranates, from the decorations of the King's
Privy Chamber and substitute Tudor roses; while in the windows the badges
of the new Queen replaced those of the former one.)[25] For Queen Anne
did stand for the new order, not only because, as has been noted, her
personal tastes in religion had always tended towards reform. Her very
presence by the King's side, jewelled and elegant, indicated that the King

had taken on the fight to make of England and its church an 'empire', subject to no one else's authority but his own – and won.

At Hampton Court, the elaborate replanning of the royal apartments, from 1534 onwards, placed those of Queen Anne on the same floor as that of her husband (Queen Catherine's had been on the floor above). Among the striking new embellishments were the formal gardens which stretched down from the palace to the river. Here the flowerbeds were edged with green and white railings (the Tudor colours) and huge heraldic beasts, which cost 20s each to colour, turned in the wind on weathervanes five or six feet high.[26] The leopards of Queen Anne (her secondary badge from her Brotherton ancestry) sprouting out of the flowerbeds, might look disconcertingly garish to the modern eye but they much impressed contemporaries; they signified her state and her supremacy as 'royally anointed' Queen.

Other details of this state supply further evidence of Queen Anne's love of graceful living – and her nervous temperament. There are payments for mirrors to be put in the roof of her apartments at Hampton Court, and a special 'breakfast table' made for her at Greenwich, one of two tables ornamented with inlaid tiles, which could be folded away, the other being 'for her grace to play upon'. But timber coops had to be made to contain the peacocks and pelican that had been sent to the King 'out of the new found land' (America) to keep them out of earshot of the Queen: 'by cause the Queen's grace could not take her rest in the morning for the noise of same.' Perhaps for the same reason – their agitation – Queen Anne disliked monkeys (although it is possible she was influenced by the fact that Queen Catherine, with memories of her southern childhood, loved them). But not all excitable creatures were banned: she did have a fondness for small dogs such as her 'little Purkoy'.[27] Here and there today – above the Provost's stall in King's College Chapel, Cambridge, completed in 1533 with the aid of a royal gift, or the doorways to the turrets of the gatehouse of St James's Palace – an H and an A entwined still provide mute witness to the brief and splendid era of 'Anne the Quene'.

In other ways, her love of music for example, Queen Anne was an appropriate consort for a Renaissance sovereign. One of her music books survives, consisting of thirty-nine Latin motets and five French *chansons* of the Franco-Flemish school (the first of which was perhaps composed for her coronation). The illustrations include a falcon furiously pecking at a pomegranate – another effective commentary on the new order in England. It has been suggested that this book was compiled for the Queen by a certain young musician called Mark Smeaton, a member of the King's chamber for the last four or five years, and a friend of her brother George Viscount Rochford.[28] Such a youth, a talented virginalist and organist and a 'deft dancer', was typical of the kind of company the Queen, with her artistic tastes, enjoyed. 'Master Weston' the lutenist was another. She herself had grown up amongst such young people dependent on the court for their living in Burgundy, France and, from the early 1520s, in England.

Dancing – of course – continued to take place. In 1533 Sir Edward Baynton, Queen Anne's vice-chamberlain, commented that there were 'never more pastimes' including specifically dancing, in the Queen's chamber. The fact that William Latymer in his *Cronickille* of Anne Boleyn's life (published in the reign of her daughter) would paint a picture of dance-less austerity merely shows how hagiography develops.[29] Latymer had been chaplain to Queen Anne and is thus in many respects a most important source; later he became chaplain to Queen Elizabeth and Clerk of her Closet, with the delicate problem, common to survivors of his generation, of handling the question of her mother's fate. His response was to stress all the most pious aspects of Queen Anne's character, blotting out the rest. But both sides could co-exist. Unlike Latymer, we can easily accept that a love of the arts, pleasure itself, is compatible with an interest in religion, in a woman of gifts and natural intelligence such as Anne Boleyn.

On the one hand, she wore the queenly robes, and magnificent evocative jewellery designed by Holbein and others, with the initials H and A entwined.* There is evidence that she patronized painters such as the Horenbout family from Ghent: Gerard, Lucas and Susanna.[30] Books in beautiful bindings, illuminated manuscripts, survive as testimony to an interest in literature to be compared with her love of music, and much rarer in a woman of that time, not educated to be a princess. All this was part of Anne Boleyn playing the role of Queen.

On the other hand we have Latymer's picture of a devout woman, obsessed by charity and the relief of the poor, and a strict supervisor of the morals of her household, with a special dislike of swearing, desiring 'a court inviolate'. But of course these activities – particularly the giving to the poor – were also an important part of a Queen's traditional role. As Whittington wrote of Anne in his grandiose panegyric:

> You are a faithful protector to paupers, widows and
>   orphans
> And your ear is open to the pleadings of the poor.
> You shine with pious religion like the Morning Star.

Since Queen Catherine had been notable for her generosity, and much loved in consequence, one has the impression that Queen Anne was

---

* The image by which Anne Boleyn is best known, displaying her with the letter B hanging from an elaborate pearl necklace, is generally seen in late sixteenth- or seventeenth-century copies: but it probably originates from her time as Queen.[31]

especially competitive with her predecessor in this area. Badges might be removed but, infuriatingly, sentimental memories were more difficult to erase. She was aware that the 'smocks and shirts' and flannel petticoats made by her own hands, which Latymer records her presenting to the poor, would be measured against those of 'good Queen Catherine'.[32]

Indeed, Latymer makes this very point over his account of the royal Maundy: that Queen Anne had been *more* generous than Queen Catherine. This was an ancient custom by which royal persons washed the feet of the poor, and presented a purse of money thereafter, in commemoration of the actions of Jesus Christ on the Thursday before his crucifixion. It was a practice that had fitted well with Queen Catherine's own belief in personal humility, and financial generosity. She continued to carry out 'the Maundy' in her enforced seclusion. She had evidently done so to all good effect – in terms of her continuing popularity – at Easter 1534, since the next year Sir Edmund Bedingfield, in charge of her household, was in a quandary about allowing the ceremony to take place yet again.

Catherine was clever enough not to use, for once, the argument that she was still Queen of England to enforce her claim. Instead she took her stand on the fact that Margaret Beaufort Countess of Richmond, 'the King's granddame' (who had never actually been queen consort), had kept 'a yearly Maundy'. Bedingfield recommended allowing 'my Lady Princess Dowager' her way, since what she was proposing would take place privately and at her own expense; otherwise Catherine might attempt to keep her 'Maundy' in the local parish church.[33] Latymer's lengthy description of Queen Anne's generosity at the Maundy is therefore aimed not only at building up his own subject, but also at denigrating her predecessor in exactly the area where she had been most beloved. A poor woman, for example, accustomed to receiving the maundy 'for four [previous] years' could not believe how much the increment had been increased, by the noble new Queen.

Queen Anne's patronage of evangelicals, her admittance of them to the ranks of chaplains, to which Latymer bears eloquent testimony, was however special to her; to take only one example, a known radical in religious matters, Nicholas Shaxton, appointed her almoner in 1533, became Bishop of Salisbury in 1535. (Queen Anne lent him £200 to pay his 'first-fruits' to the King.)[34] Her influence – that of a Queen Consort – should not be exaggerated: certain evangelicals were executed as heretics during her time; but the evidence of her household, combined with that of ecclesiastical appointments, shows that there was a real connection for those of reformist tendencies between the Queen's favour and preferment.

The love of spiritual reading including the Bible did not cease. Indeed, she liked to keep an English translation of the Bible in her chamber to which her ladies (who did not know French or Latin) were supposed to have frequent improving recourse. Latymer himself would travel abroad in search of books in spring of 1536 (returning in May, an awkward moment as it turned out). There were a great number of Cambridge scholars surrounding her, particularly from Gonville and Caius College, of which institution a more religiously old-fashioned cleric, Bishop Nix of Norwich, observed sourly: 'no clerk that cometh lately of that college but [he] savoureth of the frying pan.' An English Protestant woman of a younger generation, Rose Hickman, remembered her father – a merchant – telling her that as a young man going 'beyond the sea', he would run errands for Queen Anne Boleyn: she 'caused him to get her the gospels and epistles written in parchment in French together with the psalms'.[35]

Did Queen Anne also go down to the religious house at Syon and lecture the nuns there on 'the enormity of their liberty and wanton incontinence'? According to Latymer, after castigating them for reciting 'ignorant prayers from Latin primers' (which they could not understand), the Queen presented them with prayerbooks in English.[36] Although the nuns had apparently begun by trying not to admit the King's new wife – on the grounds that she was a married woman, and their rule did not permit them to admit such – they were quick to be found 'prostrate and grovelling' when she insisted on entering. And they ended by being duly grateful. It makes a good story and is certainly vivid reading. But since Latymer is not infallible, such a story should probably be placed in the scales against the wilder calumnies repeated by Chapuys and his ilk, neither necessarily true.

On one subject, however, Queen Anne's scriptural 'disputations' in the presence of the King, Latymer does provide a valuable sidelight, in view of what was to come. At some point Henry VIII decided that he did not like arguing with women – and thus women who chose to argue. It was far from being an exceptional view in the early sixteenth century for a man, let alone for a monarch; on the one hand biblical texts enjoined silence on the part of the female; on the other hand it was generally agreed that despite this prohibition most women had undesirably prattling tongues, possibly inspired by the Evil One himself. Nevertheless Henry VIII's exceptional dislike of disputatious women – or those who appeared to him to fall into this category – which he would evince in his later years, deserves further explanation.

Queen Catherine, in her prime, had been far too well-trained, and too clever, to allow herself to appear ungraciously argumentative; she had followed the pattern of a certain kind of intelligent woman throughout history, making her point without confrontation, well aware, as she told Chapuys, that it was better to persuade the King than to threaten him. The moment despair made her abandon this practice she aroused furious resentment in her husband just because she was clever enough to win most of the arguments. (As Anne Boleyn had pointed out – cruelly if accurately – in November 1529, the King should really not dispute with his wife, since she always won.)

At the beginning, the young Anne Boleyn's flashing, witty repartees had excited the King, and even her reproofs or sulks had ended in amorous reconciliation. These ups and downs had their own pattern; but they were very different from the kind of scene outlined by Latymer in his biography. Here, Queen Anne never dined with the King 'without some argument of Scripture thoroughly debated'. Her chamberlain – Lord Borough – and her vice-chamberlain Sir Edward Baynton would take part. According to Latymer (who as the Queen's chaplain was often present), King Henry took 'such pleasure' in all this that 'diverse and sundry times he would not only hear them but sometime would argue and reason himself'.[37] But perhaps his underlying feelings had been rather different. The King would specifically order his future wives to avoid argument. It seems likely therefore that female disputation became associated in his mind not so much with the sex in general, but with vanished, disgraced, contentious Queen Anne.

Latymer's picture of the pious Queen was completed by the strict morality which she enjoined on the young women who attended her. Given that she herself had waited on Queen Catherine and that she now had a girl called Jane Seymour in her chamber, one can either interpret this attitude as distasteful hypocrisy or practical vigilance. Certainly vigilance was justified. For the King was straying again – in so far as he had ever felt any particular royal duty to remain faithful to his second wife, whether pregnant or not. What the French ambassador called his 'amours' continued.

One of the girls in the Queen's chamber who was ticked off for frivolity was a certain Mistress Margaret (or Madge) Shelton. She was 'the concubine's first cousin' as Chapuys put it, since her mother, Lady Shelton, was sister to Sir Thomas Boleyn; Lady Shelton was now governess to her great-niece Princess Elizabeth, and her husband Sir John Shelton in command of the Princess's guard. Madge Shelton must have been extremely appealing; a few years later when the noted beauty Duchess Christina of Milan was being investigated as a possible royal bride, it was declared in the Duchess's favour that she 'resembleth much one Mistress Shelton', late of the Queen's chamber, with dimples – 'pits' – in her cheeks, 'very gentle of countenance' and 'soft of speech'.[38]

Madge Shelton was not only attractive, she was also spirited and flirtatious: the type of the cheerful Bessie Blount, perhaps, that had always amused the King. From Anne's point of view, however, she was the kind of girl – oh horrors! – who wrote 'idle poesies' in her devotional reading. A defaced book came to light. Once the culprit was discovered, Queen Anne 'wonderfully rebuked her' for inscribing 'such wanton toys in her book of prayers'. Human nature being what it is, it is surely not implausible to connect this incident with the King's dalliance with Mistress Shelton, dated by Chapuys from February 1535 onwards. In any case, Madge Shelton was not the first girl to attract the King's attention since the birth of Princess Elizabeth.

There had been 'a very handsome young lady' in the autumn of 1534, according to Chapuys. She had displayed an attachment towards 'the Princess' – by which Chapuys of course meant Mary not Elizabeth – at which point the fickle court began to treat Mary with more reverence too. Then there was Madge whose enjoyment of the royal favours seems to have lasted for about six months; for later in 1535, the King took another of his fancies, this time to Jane Seymour. Most likely the fancy was first taken while the King was under the roof of her father, Sir John Seymour, at Wolf Hall near Marlborough in Wiltshire. He stayed there, with the court, for about a week in early September, in the course of a progress which went as far south as Southampton before moving west as far as Bristol (the most westerly point he reached in his life).[39]

There is no way that the King could have met Jane Seymour for the first time at Wolf Hall.* The Seymours were a court family: Jane's eldest brother Edward was an Esquire of the King's Body. Jane Seymour herself had been at court since at least 1529 when she waited on Queen Catherine;[40] if she had not certainly been at Calais in 1532 (like her father and brother) she was unquestionably in attendance on Anne Boleyn before her coronation. Yet the pattern of the King's sudden passions was apparently unaffected by previous propinquity: Anne Boleyn had after all been at court for a least four years before she kindled the love light in the royal eye. Bessie Blount had been at court for five years before the romance which led to the birth of her son; Madge Shelton, his wife's cousin, can hardly have been a stranger.

All this was worrying for Queen Anne – how could it not be, considering

---

* Jane Seymour is not to be identified with the unnamed 'very handsome young lady' of the previous year, since Chapuys, who was acutely interested in these matters and reports on both relationships, does not make the connection.

the circumstances of her own rise to power? – but it was not necessarily disastrous. She had her own weapons with which to fight back. In the autumn of 1534, for example, she made a scene to the King about the 'very handsome young lady', complaining that she did not treat her with sufficient respect 'in words and deeds'. The King rushed away in a rage. But with the help of her sister-in-law Jane Viscountess Rochford, it was still easy for the Queen to get her rival sent away from court. The frivolous Madge Shelton who succeeded to favour does not seem to have presented a threat; because of the close relationship of the Sheltons to the Boleyns, it has even been suggested that Queen Anne pandered to the King in providing her pretty cousin for his delectation (although there is no proof of this, and it seems to fit uneasily with the Queen's proverbial jealousy).[41]

Queen Anne's temper remained erratic and her abuse colourful: she was said to have heaped more insults on her uncle Norfolk 'than a dog' so that he responded – but not to her face – by terming her *la grande putain* (the great whore). Even Thomas Cromwell came in for some of this, although their interests were apparently identified, both over the divorce and in their religious sympathies. In June 1535 he told Chapuys that Queen Anne had threatened to have his head off his shoulders, a challenge it was perhaps rather unwise to make at the Tudor court. This is not the type of incident which Chapuys would have exaggerated, since it was information of political importance, even if Cromwell himself was beginning to play a serpent's game by passing on the news. In the summer of 1535 the Venetian ambassador reported that King Henry was 'already tired to satiety of this new Queen'.[42]

And yet later that very year, Chapuys himself wrote to his master that Queen Anne was as powerful as ever: 'the King dares not contradict her'. As Chapuys had discovered, the character of the King was 'changeable', and in this respect 'the said lady [Queen Anne] well knows how to manage him'. The sexual magnetism she had once had for the King might be waning: at the age of thirty-five the dark gypsy looks, which had once been so striking, might be fading. About this time she was described by an English courtier as 'extremely ugly', worn out by constant exertion and anxiety (admittedly he made the remark to the hostile Dr Ortiz at Rome, who passed it on in Spanish: *'muy fea'*).[43] Anne was certainly no longer William Forrest's 'fresh young damsel' who could 'trip and go'. Nevertheless her 'craft', in Chapuys' phrase, remained; and King Henry, much as he disliked being argued with by women, had no objection to being managed by them – provided they did it gracefully and gently.

But Queen Anne's real weapon was what it had always been: her ability to provide the King with a male heir. After all, to put it at its crudest, Henry

VIII's alternative wife was Catherine of Aragon: now, as she approached her forty-ninth birthday, quite certainly past childbearing. (Although it is a credit to Chapuys' loyalty and tenacity that he attempted to argue this particular point with Cromwell: he named to him 'some women in this very country' who had been delivered at fifty-one, at which Cromwell himself acknowledged 'that his own mother was fifty-two when he was born'.) When Queen Anne drove away the 'very handsome young lady' from court, the King fulminated, telling her 'that she had good reason to be content with what he had done for her, which he would not do now if the thing were to begin and that she should consider from what she had come and other things.'[44] Nevertheless, rage, frustration, all this would be smoothed away if only Queen Anne, like the girl in the fairy story who promises to spin straw into gold in order to win the King, could produce a prince.

In this context, therefore, the failure of the pregnancy of 1534 was a sharp blow. The most likely end of it was a stillbirth: probably a month or so early, since the Queen had not retired to her chamber. Although no announcement was made of the fact, such mishaps were never the subject of official communiqués. Information about Queen Catherine's stillbirths comes from unofficial sources; the first of them, in January 1510, was not reported until May, in a private letter to her father. Queen Anne had 'a goodly belly' in late April 1534 and as 'fair a belly' as Sir William Kingston had ever seen on 24 June. She was sufficiently pregnant in the summer for the King to use it as an excuse for postponing a further meeting with King François 'on account of her condition'. (If she conceived in November, as is suggested, the baby was due in August.) Then comes silence. It was not until late September that Chapuys – out of touch with the court during its summer progress which he did not accompany – reported that the Queen was no longer with child.[45]

Although the theory has been advanced that this was a phantom pregnancy, brought about by Queen Anne's own desperate anxiety on the subject,* this is an unnecessary complication.[46] The only piece of evidence in its favour (apart from the unsurprising lack of official announcement) is a piece of gossip repeated by Chapuys which must be second- if not third-hand. King Henry's flirtation of the autumn of 1534 which angered Queen Anne was said to be due to his new doubts as to whether his wife had actually been *enceinte*. Such remarks, even if made, are easily understood in the context of King Henry's familiar desire to distance himself from any misfortune, and provide a justification for his own behaviour at the same

---

* Medically known as a pseudocyesis, it occurs in women desperate to have children, for obvious reasons; most famously in Queen Mary (Henry VIII's daughter) in the next reign but one.

time. They certainly do not weigh heavily against the previous positive evidence, including that of the King himself.

The most cogent argument of all that Queen Anne had been pregnant in 1534 and lost the baby – probably a son – belongs to the future. Then, another disaster in that area would be treated by the King as evidence that she too was incapable of bearing him a male heir; a disproportionate reaction if the birth of Elizabeth had been a solitary episode. It was after all the *repeated* tragedies of Queen Catherine that had convinced him that their union was against the law of God. Fortunately for Queen Anne, that grim sequence of events was hidden from her.

From the autumn of 1534 onwards, then, and for the first three quarters of 1535 Queen Anne sought her salvation in a third pregnancy. Almost certainly, by this time she was having to cope with the problem of her husband's periodic impotence; not a fortunate combination of circumstances. The King had assured his parliament at the beginning of the 1530s that he was not proposing to marry Anne Boleyn out of any kind of self-indulgent passion: 'for I am,' said he, 'forty-one years old, at which age the lust of man is not so quick as in lusty youth.' At the time, he was concerned merely to defend his abandonment of Catherine of Aragon. But maybe the words, hypocritical at the time, turned out to be all too true: not so much because the King was over forty, not for that matter because he was becoming increasingly corpulent (his grandfather Edward IV overcame this alleged disadvantage with zest), nor for any of the other myriad reasons which can be adduced to explain such a turn of events. Illness in the vital area may have contributed to the problem. (It has been pointed out that the King had bladder trouble in 1528 and himself recommended a cure for a tumour of the testicles.)[47] The truth was that Henry VIII never did have the kind of rampant priapic urge of, for example, a François I. By the standards of his time he was positively uxorious.*

As to Queen Anne's reaction to the King's marital performance, a bitter remark she was said to have made to her sister-in-law Jane Rochford would be quoted against her later: the King could not satisfy a woman, she exclaimed, in this vital respect he had neither *'vertu'* (skill) nor *'puissance'* (virility).[48] It is the kind of angry complaint that does have the ring of truth: Queen Anne after all was never one to mince her words. Here was

---

* There is an amusing saying – beloved of tourist guides – that Henry VIII is the only king who had more wives than mistresses. This may not be literally correct – who can be sure of the exact numbers of the women to whom Henry VIII made love? – nevertheless it is true that we have only three actual names of women plausibly supposed at the time to be the King's mistress, other than those of course that he subsequently married (Bessie Blount, Mary Boleyn and Madge Shelton). If we add to these, distinct if unnamed characters like the 'very handsome young lady' of 1534, the number still does not rise above six.

someone who was expected by the world to get pregnant, and getting blamed for a failure not of her own making.

We may suppose, however, that the King's attitude to his impotence, and the humiliation involved, was rather different. Nothing was ever a king's fault: no doubt he saw his failure as being not so much of his own making as hers. At the least, such troubles could not have endeared Anne to him; particularly if he continued to find other younger, less familiar women exciting, as seems to have been the case.

Queen Catherine was by now at Kimbolton Castle, near Huntingdon, to which she was moved shortly after the démarche at Buckden. In one sense her cause was not forgotten: during this summer of 1535, the King's Fool actually dared to perform a satire at court in which Queen Anne was termed the Bawd and Princess Elizabeth the Bastard. The King was angry and the Fool was punished; all the same, satire never digs its own foundations – of its very nature, it builds on those already laid. Furthermore, this was the season during which the Carthusians and others, including More and Fisher, were put to death.

As they surveyed the heads of the victims, set up at 'the gate of London', turning black in the sun according to a Spanish report (with the exception of Fisher's, which remained 'fresher'), people remembered good Queen Catherine. Yet Catherine's seclusion, at the orders of her husband, even more than her failing health, rendered her politically null: she could no longer be the symbol round which malcontents at home and abroad could rally. That function had now passed to her daughter Mary. (This explains, if it does not altogether excuse, Queen Anne publicly blaming her step-daughter for causing strife: 'she is my death and I am hers' she was fond of declaring dramatically at court in the autumn of 1535.*[49])

Kimbolton Castle had been built a mere sixty years earlier by the widow of the 1st Duke of Buckingham, but it was now in a state of great decay. Queen Catherine had not wanted to be taken there. Antonio de Guaras had friends in her household and, as we shall see, would come to visit it. From him we learn that nonetheless she comforted her servants at this latest development, adding that she trusted in the mercy of God that he would turn the heart of her dear husband 'so that he may see the error into which he has fallen'. But Kimbolton was at least better than Fotheringhay, not many miles away, or some of the other dank fortresses, such as Somersham, with which the Queen had been threatened. Arrival at Fotheringhay, part of her dowry from Prince Arthur, would have represented a tactical

---

* It is sometimes suggested that Anne Boleyn made this remark concerning Catherine of Aragon; but the imperialist report clearly names 'the Princess', ie Mary, not 'the Queen', ie Catherine, who was never termed 'the Princess' in such communications, since it was a matter of imperial policy that Catherine was still the only Queen of England.

defeat for this reason; the prospect of Somersham, set amid marshes (such plague-ridden situations were liable to hasten the deaths of the strongest) caused her to tell Suffolk that she would have to be dragged there with ropes.[50]

Not every outside contact was eliminated. Queen Catherine's two Spanish physicians, first Dr Fernando Vittoria and later Dr Miguel da Sá – 'the physician with her to her dying day' – not only looked after her health, but were able from time to time to correspond with Chapuys. The Observant friars paid visits to her various places of captivity, ostensibly to hear the confessions of her ladies and gentlemen; they were actually in a position to bear messages. But her maintenance was cut: having lived all her life in royal style she now had a manner of living which was less like that of a queen and more like that of the nun she had once refused to become. Of her former magnificent possessions she was now mainly surrounded by religious objects. Her jewels were long ago gone to Anne Boleyn: in her oratory – her closet – there were statues of St Barbara, St Margaret with a crown and a cross, St Catherine with her wheel, together with a crucifix of Spanish work. Only the silver-gilt holy water stoup, engraved with the initials H and C under a crown, served as a reminder of former glories – and her marriage.[51]

All this could be endured. The true hardship for Catherine lay in the refusal, now, to give her any chance to see her daughter, even when Mary was ill. Henry VIII's disgust at the unwillingness of either woman to bow her neck in submission had found its most effective form of expression. He pretended to believe that Catherine was 'so haughty in spirit' that she might take the opportunity of raising a number of men and making war 'as boldly as her mother, Isabella, had done'.[52] This was fantasy. The reality was the cruelty of a thwarted man, visited on an aging, sick woman.

Chapuys had never been allowed permission to visit his Queen. Increasingly worried about her health, he did make an ingenious attempt to do so in July 1534. He got together about a hundred Spaniards – including Antonio de Guaras – and rode with them in the direction of Kimbolton. Chapuys ignored a message from the King asking him to desist but did stop when Queen Catherine herself begged him not to disobey the King's orders. However, about thirty of the company rode on, including the ambassador's Fool: 'a very funny young fellow' who sported a padlock dangling from his hood. The serious purpose of the visit did not prevent a good time being had by the supporting players. The Fool, on seeing Queen Catherine's ladies at the windows of the castle, rushed into the moat up to his waist saying that he wanted to get at them; then he hurled his padlock into the window (the ladies were disappointed to find it did not contain a secret message). After that the ladies gave the Spanish gentlemen a hearty breakfast in the lower hall of the castle. The Fool however, miming the fact that he had toothache to the castle barber (responsible for such matters), got the barber to poke into his mouth; at which the Fool promptly bit him. Whereupon the barber screamed. And there were other japes.[53] Chapuys, cut off from all this, took care to travel home as ostentatiously as possible so that the Emperor's ambassador could be seen to have tried to visit the Queen. On the other hand, he had preserved a semblance of polite relations with the King for when a visit might be really urgently required.

That moment came eighteen months later. Throughout the autumn of 1535, Queen Catherine's condition deteriorated. By Christmas, she was reported to be sinking. Finally on 31 December Sir Edmund Bedingfield from Kimbolton informed Thomas Cromwell that 'the Princess Dowager' was 'in great danger of life'. Her doctor believed that even if she recovered for a short while, the end could not long be delayed.[54]

At court however, the traditional New Year's celebrations were joyous, particularly on the part of Queen Anne. It was not so much the mortal sickness of her predecessor that moved her with delight, but the fact that she was once more unquestionably pregnant: approaching three months at the turn of the year. In the first weeks of October 1535, shortly after the King's visit to the Seymours of Wolf Hall, Queen Anne had conceived a child. In spite of her husband's *'amours'*, his growing fancy for the demure Jane Seymour, Anne could rate herself once again 'the most happy'.

Part III

JANE SEYMOUR

Chapter 11

VERY MODEST

BEHAVIOUR

She has behaved in this matter very modestly.

Henry VIII on Jane Seymour, March 1536

The doctor who had predicted that if Queen Catherine recovered it would not be for very long, turned out to be right. She did rally at the beginning of 1536, long enough to receive the faithful ambassador Chapuys, who came rushing down to Kimbolton as did Maria de Salinas Lady Willoughby, and this time they were not stopped. Of course the Queen's daughter Mary was still far away (Catherine had not seen her for over two years): there was no mercy to be expected from the King in that direction.

It is doubtful whether Catherine of Aragon was ever reconciled to this separation, any more than she ever stopped loving the man she still considered to be her husband. She continued, however, to counsel submission to her daughter, 'save only that you will not offend God, and lose your Soul'. Otherwise, she urged Mary to avoid disputes as far as possible, 'obey the King's commandments, speak few words and meddle nothing.' Nor was this 'troublesome' time the right moment for Mary to get involved in negotiations for a husband. To her old friend Margaret Countess of Salisbury the Queen sent a message (of which the latter would all too soon stand in need): she prayed her to have a good heart 'for we never come to the kingdom of heaven but by troubles'.[1]

The Queen was not strong enough to write a last letter to the King in person: the text was dictated to one of her ladies. At the last, she remained concerned for his spiritual welfare. The letter began with a poignant touch of wifely admonition, as though Catherine were still somewhere in her mind reminding the King to thank God for the victory of Flodden, so many years before: 'My most dear Lord, King and husband, the hour of my death approaching . . . I cannot choose, but out of love I bear you, advise you of your soul's health which you ought to prefer before all considerations of the world or flesh whatsoever. For which yet you have cast me into many calamities, and yourself into many troubles.' But if the tone was wifely, who can blame her for this? Besides, it was too late for the King's rages, his outraged commands for her not to say her goodbyes, not to ask after his health ... And in any case: 'I forgive you all', the Queen dictated to her lady, 'and pray God to do so likewise'.[2]

Then she commended 'Mary our daughter' to the King, beseeching him to be a good father to her. The fate of her remaining maids – 'they being but three' – and their need for their marriage portions concerned her and she wanted all her servants to have a year's pay beyond their due. These anxious requests were characteristic of Catherine of Aragon: under English law, as a married woman she could not make a will, but she was allowed to leave a list of 'supplications' for her husband. But it is her final word to King Henry VIII which is the most affecting: 'Lastly, I make this vow, that mine eyes desire you above all things. Farewell.'

The rally was brief. The Queen's pains were so agonizing that she could not manage to eat or even drink. But she was able to tell Chapuys how much his visit meant to her: it would be a consolation to die in his arms and not 'totally abandoned like an animal' (*point désemparée comme une bête*). They talked for more than two hours; Queen Catherine, anxious as ever, was concerned whether the current 'heresies' of England were principally caused by the affair of the divorce. The ambassador reassured her. In the course of their conversation, he even got the Queen to smile once or twice: perhaps it was because he informed her, with more kindness than truth, that the King was sorry to hear of her illness. Later Chapuys would tell Erasmus that the Queen in her last days had derived much comfort from one of his works *De Preparatione ad Mortem* (ironically one of the works commissioned by Sir Thomas Boleyn, recently available in a new edition in England). When Chapuys rode back to London on the morning of 6 January, he was confident that she would, however briefly, recover.

That evening, however, the Queen had a relapse. Maria de Salinas had remained behind when Chapuys departed, and it was she who now held her mistress. At nightfall, the Queen could still manage to comb her own hair and tie it back – that 'abundant' hair which had once been her greatest beauty – without the help of her maids. But as the night hours passed, she asked her doctor, Don Miguel da Sá, to tell her the truth.

He replied with candour: 'Madam, you must die'. 'I know it' was the Queen's answer. Still, scrupulous to the last, she refused to have Mass said for her before dawn (the earliest hour permitted by the rules of the Catholic church); when her chaplain, Jorge de Athequa Bishop of Llandaff, suggested it, she quoted 'Latin passages' to the contrary. Finally in that dark mid-winter season dawn did come and the Queen did receive the sacrament. Accepting it, she said a prayer to her servants 'that would have broken any heart': she asked God's pardon for 'the King, her husband, for the wrong he had done her.' Yet she lingered. It was two o'clock in the afternoon before she died. When 'her hour came', she raised up her hands and placed her soul in the hands of God in the traditional words with which a pious Catholic, imitating Christ, hopes to die: *'In manus tuas, Domine, commendo spiritum meum'.* Then the Queen 'gave up her soul to God'.

It was 7 January 1536. Catherine of Aragon was just over fifty years old. She died in the arms of Maria de Salinas, who could remember the unhappy princess in the power of Henry VII, the radiant bride of the 1509 marriage ... and many other memories, decreasingly glorious, increasingly painful. Her body was placed in the chapel at Kimbolton and watched over by the three ladies of her household, Blanche and Isabel de Vergas and Elizabeth Darrell, as well as Maria herself.*

Almost immediately the rumours that King Henry had poisoned Queen Catherine began to spread. That was inevitable, given that much of the imperialist correspondence during her last years had been taken up with fears for her safety. In any case this was par for the contemporary course – the deaths of prominent persons whose removal was thought to be rather too convenient for their enemies were generally accompanied by such suspicions. The charge is ludicrous not only for the reason noted in the last chapter: God was likely to carry off Catherine soon enough without extra help. There is also the question of the character of Henry VIII. He regarded poison with moral repugnance: it was alien to him. The axe and rope, wielded in public, not secret poison were the weapons of his authority against those who defied the royal will, preceded if possible by the culprits' profound repentance at having crossed or betrayed him.

At first sight it is equally fanciful – if more romantic – to suggest that Queen Catherine died of a broken heart. The link between grief and mortal disease is after all indefinable. And yet, oddly enough, the autopsy performed on her body by the castle's chandler (one of his official duties) *did* reveal a large round black growth on her heart which was itself 'completely black and hideous'. He found all the other internal organs perfectly healthy and normal. In fact a late nineteenth-century specialist pointed out that Queen Catherine died of a form of cancer – melanotic sarcoma – then quite impossible for her physician to diagnose; the tumour

---

* Chapuys took great pains to get details of Queen Catherine's last hours from her servants, which he sent to Charles V with the important passages in cipher; other details came from Antonio de Guaras who would also have heard them directly from those present.

on her heart was almost certainly secondary, the chandler having missed the primary growth.[3] Nevertheless one notes that when Queen Catherine died, it was her heart that was most visibly affected. And that seems symbolic at least, if the connection is not medically sound.

'The very grievous, painful and lamentable news of the death of the very virtuous and holy Queen', in the words of Chapuys, was received by the ambassador in a message from Thomas Cromwell. King Henry VIII, according to popular legend, did not find the news so painful. He was said to have dressed himself in yellow – the colour of rejoicing – with a white feather in his hat (although Lord Herbert of Cherbury, in a seventeenth-century biography, wrote that the King wept at Catherine's last letter: both stories may of course have been true). Other sources attributed the tasteless yellow to Anne Boleyn, so that perhaps the royal couple radiated their 'joy and delight' in matching costumes; the two-year-old Princess Elizabeth for her part was displayed at court in her father's arms (one of her periodic appearances there) and taken publicly to church 'to the sound of trumpets'.[4]

Almost immediately royal avarice took over. Catherine's favourite Franciscan convent was not to receive her robes: the King decided that its members had quite enough already. Nor were they to tend to her funeral. As for burial in St Paul's (where Catherine had been married to Arthur, whom he formally regarded as her husband) that would cost more 'than was either requisite or needful'. The King also refused to comply with his former wife's other bequests of clothes and property until he had seen 'what the robes and furs were like'.[5]

It is however the careful notations on the official inventory of her belongings by Sir Edward Baynton that leave the strongest impression. It was thought worthwhile having hand towels of fine Holland cloth edged with gold and silken fringes 'Delivered to the King's highness' as were other garnished cloths and a desk covered in black velvet with gilt nails. A case of wooden trenchers, a crimson velvet coffer, and finally some of the 'Necessaries provided for the Princess Dowager, what time she lay in child bed', including fine Holland smocks, double petticoats and a cloth to cover a child, fringed with gold, were 'Delivered to the Queen'.[6]

The King's eventual choice of a burial place for Catherine – three weeks after her death – was the ancient and beautiful Peterborough Cathedral, about twenty miles from Kimbolton Castle. The hearse rested overnight on its ceremonial journey at Sawtrey Abbey. Obviously such a procession would attract less attention here in the midlands than for example on its way to St Paul's (as well as costing less money); even so the country people thronged the route to see the coffin of their 'good Queen Catherine' as it passed. The chief mourner appointed by the King was his younger niece, Lady Eleanor Brandon; the secondary mourner was the latter's youthful stepmother, Katherine Duchess of Suffolk, accompanied by her mother Maria de Salinas Lady Willoughby. Furthermore a concourse of poor men in black gowns and hoods, carrying black torches, was organized to attend, to give the occasion the dignity considered the due of the late Catherine of Aragon.

It was however the dignity due to a princess dowager, widow of a Prince of Wales, not a queen. For this reason Chapuys declined to attend. Perhaps that was just as well, since the preacher John Hilsey, Bishop-designate of Rochester (John Fisher's old see), announced in his sermon that Catherine herself 'had acknowledged that she had not been Queen of England'. This travesty of the truth was – for the time being – perpetuated on the tomb that was dug for her: on the orders of the King, the arms of Wales – not England – were quartered with those of Spain.

The position chosen for Catherine of Aragon's burial was in the northwest transept of the cathedral. William Forrest, who was present, described the funeral as stately; the wax figure in its robes on the hearse representing the late Queen (according to custom at royal funerals) was, he wrote, curiously lifelike. But Chapuys became indignant in his report to his master on the subject: the position was 'far removed from the high altar, and much less honourable than that of certain bishops buried there', he wrote. Such were 'the great miracles and incredible magnificence' which the English had given him to understand they would put forth in honour of her memory 'as due alike to her great virtues and to her kindred'. He cheered himself by believing they would compensate for it 'by making a becoming monument in some suitable place'.[7]

The removal of her rival – in the eyes of the world, if not in the affections of the King – should have ushered in the happiest period of Queen Anne's life. Instead it brought about her downfall. Her repeated wild remark concerning the King's daughter Mary the previous autumn – 'she is my death and I am hers' – had a frightening new significance where Mary's mother was concerned. As Chapuys commented drily, the marriage of 'the Concubine' had not become 'more valid and legitimate' as a result of Queen Catherine's death.[8] Henry VIII was now, by strict Catholic standards, a widower since his only wife in the eyes of the church had died; he was thus free to marry again whomsoever he chose. It hardly needs to be emphasized to the reader of this narrative how quickly any monarch who was a widower – particularly one without a male heir – regarded himself as not only free but bounden to marry again.

But of course by other standards – that of the new English church of

which he was the constituted head – the King was far from being free to
marry. His fancy for Jane Seymour might be intensifying, but his second
wife was pregnant, and that event for which the nation hoped – the birth
of his son – apparently set in motion once more. 'O lady Anne, O Queen
incomparable' ran the dedication in a poem by Clément Marot, 'may this
good shepherd with whom you find favour give you a son, the image of
his father the King, and may he live and flourish so that you may both see
him come to manhood.'[9] It is perfectly possible that the second half of this
pious hope might actually have been fulfilled – *both* parents of this putative
'prince' (who would have been born in the summer of 1536) would have
survived to see him 'come to manhood' – if only the child himself had lived
and flourished.

But it was not to be. At the end of January – the twenty-ninth is a
plausible date – Queen Anne miscarried.* It was 'a man child', something
over three months old. At the time, according to a contemporary account,
Queen Anne was hysterical with disappointment – and no doubt apprehension. The King had had a recent serious fall at jousting which had left
him unconscious for two hours. The Queen burst out that this dreadful
shock had caused the mishap, so great was her love for him. The plea and
the excuse fell equally on deaf ears. The King was supposed to have
remarked 'with much ill grace' that when the Queen had risen from her
bed of sickness, 'I will come and speak with you'. But a more ominous part
of the same story concerned the King's exclamation: 'I see God will not
give me male children'. George Wyatt's sympathetic biography of Anne
Boleyn, which although written many years later preserves the traditions
of her ladies-in-waiting, conveys the same impression of a chilling scene.
Here the King comes to Anne 'bewailing and bemoaning' the loss of his son,
only to have Anne herself break down and refer to his own 'unkindness'. The
King's last words were unmistakably threatening: 'he would have no more
boys by *her*'.[11]

Whether King Henry really greeted his wife's indisposition with such
lack of sympathy cannot be known for sure; but the invoking of God's will
does have a terrible plausibility to it, given the King's known tendency to
interpret his own misfortunes in the light of divine disapproval (of someone
else). In another contemporary account from the Exeters – for naturally
rumours on the subject ran rife at court – the King told an intimate in the

---

* This is the date given by Charles Wriothesley in his *Chronicle of England*. Wriothesley had been
created Windsor Herald at Christmas 1534 and was in a position to know the gossip: he heard the
Queen reckoned herself 'about fifteen weeks gone' with child when she lost it. Chapuys similarly
talked of 'three and a half months'. There was no mention of the condition of the foetus other
than the fact that it was male (and no reference to deformity). De Carles in his biography written
later in 1536 referred to 'a fine son' (*un beau fils*) born 'before term'.[10]

Privy Chamber that God was denying him a son. Most sinister of all was his own explanation for this: he had been bewitched by Anne Boleyn, 'seduced and forced into this second marriage by means of sortileges and charms'.[12] That was after all the ultimate denial of personal responsibility for everything that had occurred to make him leave his first wife – now safely departed.

At this point, the King's relationship with Jane Seymour took on fresh significance, with the first Queen dead, and the second Queen widely assumed to have an 'utter inability to bear male children'.* A passion which might under other happier circumstances – happier for Anne Boleyn, that is – have been enjoyable but transitory, became the focus for universal speculation. Chapuys indeed heard that it was news of the presents the King had recently given to 'Mistress Seymour' which had brought on Queen Anne's mishap. A story of a later date had Queen Anne finding Mistress Seymour actually sitting on her husband's lap; 'betwitting' the King, Queen Anne blamed her miscarriage upon this unpleasant discovery. There was said to have been 'much scratching and bye-blows between the queen and her maid'.[13]

Unlike the King's invocations of the divine will, however, there is no contemporary evidence for such robust incidents; the character of Jane Seymour that emerges in 1536 is on the contrary chaste, verging on the prudish. As we shall see, there is good reason to believe that the King found in this very chastity a source of attraction; as he had once turned to the enchantress Anne Boleyn from the virtuous Catherine. Yet before turning to Jane Seymour's personal qualities, for better or for worse, it is necessary to consider the family from which she came. That was after all how the young woman – any young woman who caught the King's eye – was viewed at the court of Henry VIII. Given the perennial state of what has been expressively termed 'faction' at the Tudor court, who would rise, who would fall if a Seymour captured that increasingly available matrimonial prize, Henry VIII?[14]

The Seymours were a family of respectable and even ancient antecedents in an age when, as has already been stressed, such things were important.[15] Their Norman ancestry – the name was originally St Maur – was somewhat shadowy although a Seigneur Wido de Saint Maur was said to have come over to England with the Conquest. More immediately, from Monmouthshire and Penbow Castle, the Seymours transferred to the west of England in the mid-fourteenth century with the marriage of Sir Roger

---

* It is this general assumption that suggests that Queen Anne was pregnant in 1534, and that she gave birth to a stillborn son, probably a few weeks early. Otherwise Queen Anne's gynaecological history consisted of only one birth – a healthy daughter; which does not seem sufficient evidence on which to base such a conclusion.

Seymour to Cecily, eventual sole heiress of Lord Beauchamp of Hache. Other key marriages brought the family prosperity. Wolf Hall in Wiltshire, for example, (scene of Henry's autumn idyll with Jane if legend is to be believed) came with the marriage of a Seymour to Matilda Esturmy, daughter of the Speaker of Commons, in 1405. Another profitable union, bringing with it mercantile links similar to those of the Boleyns, was that of Isabel, daughter and heiress of Mark William Mayor of Bristol, to a Seymour in 1424.

Sir John Seymour, father of Jane, was born in about 1474 and had been knighted in the field by Henry VII at the battle of Blackheath which ended a rebellion of 1497. From this promising start, he went on to enjoy the royal favour throughout the next reign. Like Sir Thomas Boleyn, he accompanied Henry VIII on his French campaign of 1513, was present at the Field of Cloth of Gold, attended at Canterbury to meet Charles V; by 1532 he had become a Gentleman of the Bedchamber. Locally, again echoing the career of Thomas Boleyn, he had acted as Sheriff of both Wiltshire and Dorset. It was a career that lacked startling distinction – here was no Charles Brandon ending up a duke – but one which brought him close to the monarch throughout his adult life.

Sir John's reputation was that of a 'gentle, courteous man'. That again was pleasant but not startling. But there was something outstanding about him, or at least about his immediate family. Sir John himself came of a family of eight children; then his own wife gave birth to ten children – six sons and four daughters. All this was auspicious for his daughter, including the number of males conceived at a time when women's 'aptness to procreate children' in Wolsey's phrase about Anne Boleyn, was often judged by their family record.

It was however from her mother, Margery Wentworth – once again echoing the pattern of Anne Boleyn – that Jane Seymour derived that qualifying dash of royal blood so important to a woman viewed as possible breeding stock. Margery Wentworth was descended from Edward III, via her great-great-grandmother Elizabeth Mortimer, Lady Hotspur. Indeed, in one sense – that of English royal blood – Jane Seymour was better born than Anne Boleyn, since she descended from Edward III, whereas Anne Boleyn's more remote descent was from Edward I. This Mortimer connection meant that Jane and Henry VIII were fifth cousins. But of course neither the Wentworths nor the Seymours were as grand as Anne Boleyn's maternal family, the ducal Howards. (See family tree 1)

The Seymours may not have been particularly grand, but close connections to the court had made them, by the generation of Jane herself, astute and worldly wise. Sir John Seymour was over sixty at the inception of the King's romance with his daughter (and would in fact die before the end of the year 1536); even before that the dominant male figure in Jane's life seems to have been her eldest surviving brother Edward, described by one observer about this time as both 'young and wise'.[16] Being young, he was ambitious, and being wise, able to keep his own counsel in pursuit of his plans. Contemporaries found him slightly aloof – he lacked the easy charm of his younger brother Thomas – but they did not doubt his intelligence. Edward Seymour was cultivated as well as clever; he was a humanist and also, as it turned out, genuinely interested in the tenets of the reformed religion (unlike his sister Jane).

As a boy, Edward Seymour had served as a page to the elder Mary Tudor as 'the French Queen'; he had been knighted in 1523 during Suffolk's campaign in France, and later served the King's son, Henry Fitzroy Duke of Richmond; in 1530 Sir Edward Seymour was made an Esquire of the Body to the King and as such went to Calais in 1532; at the coronation of Anne Boleyn, Seymour acted as official 'Carver' to Archbishop Cranmer. Now in his thirties,[17] he had already had a chequered marital career like so many of the courtiers surrounding the King (not only the monarch himself). Edward Seymour had repudiated his first wife, the heiress Katherine Fillol, for adultery and does not seem to have acknowledged the paternity of her offspring. His second wife was the formidable Anne Stanhope, whom Seymour had married in about 1534 – before Katherine Fillol's death. Anne Stanhope's imperious disposition would become a byword when she had an opportunity to display it – 'more presumptuous than Lucifer' wrote Antonio de Guaras – and she was widely believed to rule her husband (although this was the kind of misogynistic comment apt to be made about any vigorous woman). In 1536 it was more relevant that this combination of a calculating husband and a strong-minded wife made the Seymours a team to be reckoned with.

The vast family of Sir John Seymour began with four boys: John (who died), Edward, Henry and Thomas, born in about 1508. A few years later the King would speak 'merrily' of handsome Tom's proverbial virility. He was confident that a man armed with 'such lust and youth' would be able to please a bride 'well at all points'. Then came Jane, probably born in 1509, the fifth child but the eldest girl.[18] After that followed Elizabeth, Dorothy and Margery; two sons who died in the sweating sickness epidemic of 1528 made up the ten.

Apart from her presumed fertility, what else did Jane Seymour, now in her mid-twenties (the age incidentally at which Anne Boleyn had attracted the King's attention), have to offer? Polydore Vergil gave the official flattering view when he described her as 'a woman of the utmost charm both in appearance and character', and the King's friend Sir John Russell called her 'the fairest of all his wives' – but this again was likely to be loyalty to Jane

Seymour's dynastic significance. From other sources, it seems likely that the charm of her character considerably outweighed the charm of her appearance: Chapuys for example described her as 'of middle stature and no great beauty'. Her most distinctive aspect was her famously 'pure white' complexion.[19] Holbein gives her a long nose, and firm mouth, with the lips slightly compressed, although her face has a pleasing oval shape with the high forehead then admired (enhanced sometimes by discreet plucking of the hairline) and set off by the headdresses of the time. Altogether, if Anne Boleyn conveys the fascination of the new, there is a dignified but slightly stolid look to Jane Seymour, appropriately reminiscent of English mediaeval consorts.

But the predominant impression given by her portrait – at the hands of a master of artistic realism – is of a woman of calm good sense. And contemporaries all commented on Jane Seymour's intelligence: in this she was clearly more like her cautious brother Edward than her dashing brother Tom. She was also naturally sweet-natured (no angry words or tantrums here) and virtuous – her virtue was another topic on which there was general agreement. There was a story that she had been attached to the son of Sir Robert and Lady Dormer, a country neighbour, but was thought of too modest a rank to marry him (he then married a Sidney);[20] even if true, the tale brought with it no slur on Jane's maidenly honour. It was told more as a Cinderella story, where the unfairly slighted girl would go on to be raised triumphantly to far greater heights. Her survival as a lady-in-waiting to two Queens at the Tudor court still with a spotless reputation may indeed be seen as a testament to both Jane Seymour's salient characteristics – virtue and common good sense. A Bessie Blount or Madge Shelton might fool around, Anne Boleyn might listen or even accede to the seductive wooings of Lord Percy: but Jane Seymour was unquestionably virginal.

In short, Jane Seymour was exactly the kind of female praised by the contemporary handbooks to correct conduct; just as Anne Boleyn had been the sort they warned against. There was certainly no threatening sexuality about her. Nor is it necessary to believe that her 'virtue' was in some way hypocritically assumed, in order to intrigue the King (romantic advocates of Anne Boleyn have sometimes taken this line). On the contrary, Jane Seymour was simply fulfilling the expectations for a female of her time and class: it was Anne Boleyn who was – or rather who *had* been – the fascinating outsider.

We cannot be quite sure when the project to substitute Jane Seymour for Anne Boleyn was hatched among Anne's political enemies (and the enemies of her family). Obviously nothing could be fully fledged while Queen

Anne was pregnant but after her miscarriage events moved extremely fast, suggesting that news of the royal pregnancy had temporarily interrupted plots already laid. After all, the court can only have heard of this pregnancy a few weeks before it terminated, if then; for half of 1534 and virtually the whole of 1535, as Queen Anne desperately tried to work her magic on the resentful body of her husband, she would have been regarded by courtiers as possibly incapable of conceiving a further child.

That spring of 1536 the English court was an exciting place to be, awash with rumour of rise and counter-rumour of fall; unless of course you were Queen Anne Boleyn, when you felt not so much excited as beleaguered and probably endangered. This Queen, unlike her predecessor, had never had it in her range to build up a proper power base, other than her own relations (at least one of whom, the Duke of Norfolk, disliked her strongly and did not share her religious views), while temperamentally she preferred to challenge rather than to soothe.

At least her accounts show that Queen Anne had the bravado to keep up her royal state – and her royal spending.[21] During this period orange tawny silk was ordered for one nightgown (a loose *robe de chambre*, not a nightdress), and lengths of fine ribbon for rolling up her long hair. There were decorated leading-reins for the Queen's mules, green ribbons (the Tudor colour) for her clavichords and expensive caps for her 'woman fool'. Payments for the adorning of her 'great bed' – gold fringe of Venice and tassels of Florence gold – have however a particular poignancy, since it is unlikely that King Henry now cared to visit it.

Meanwhile, the anti-Boleyn faction at the English court advanced the cause of Jane Seymour to have her own richly ornamented great bed, which in this case the King would share. As it has been percipiently observed concerning the elaborate household arrangements of Henry VIII, nearness to the sovereign's person was nearness to power[22] – and who nearer to his person than his wife? Provided he visited her, that is.

This faction had come to include not only grandees like Lord Montague, heading the half-royal Pole family, and the Exeters, but some important members of the royal household network, jealous of the Boleyns. There was Sir Nicholas Carew, for example, the Master of the Horse, a man of about King Henry's own age who had sobered much since those madcap days of 1519, when as one of the notorious 'minions' he had roistered through the streets of Paris, and been reproved by Cardinal Wolsey. The King was extremely fond of Carew: he was a skilled jouster, always a passport to Henry's friendship, as well as being a man of great charm and polish; he was by now an experienced diplomat, with a good knowledge of France, both its court and its language. His wife Elizabeth was the daughter of Sir Thomas Bryan who had been vice-chamberlain to Queen Catherine and

Margaret Lady Bryan, governess to the King's children. Lady Carew's sister had been married to Sir Henry Guildford, that Comptroller of the Royal Household sympathetic to Queen Catherine who died in 1532. The influential Bryan connection was completed by Lady Carew's brother, the poet Sir Francis Bryan, another royal intimate, who was also a skilled diplomat.

To the intricacies of English politics and in-fighting were now added international pressures. If there was to be an accord between Spain and England – as the English diplomatic weather-vane turned once again away from France – then the Emperor had somehow to swallow the insult to Spain posed by the treatment of his aunt. The death of Queen Catherine, followed by heavy hints that 'the Concubine' herself might be replaced, produced a generally benevolent atmosphere for this. Although the Emperor's public demands for King Henry to acknowledge once more the authority of Rome were somewhat unrealistic, given that King Henry was even now helping himself to the rich pickings of the former Catholic church in England, his privately stated position was a good deal more pragmatic.

In this context, a crucial conversation took place between Chapuys and Thomas Cromwell on 31 March.[23] It was an after-dinner visit. From the first, Cromwell struck a cordial note by expressing his strong personal desire for friendship between his master and the Emperor; the recent gracious letters of Maria of Hungary, Queen-Regent of the Netherlands, had found much favour.* Chapuys for his part was equally amiable; seven years of experience at the English court had not been wasted. Courteously he explained why he had kept away from Cromwell for some little time, recollecting the story of Anne Boleyn's angry tirade against Cromwell the previous summer and not wishing him to incur her further displeasure. Under the circumstances, 'I could not but wish him a more gracious mistress', went on the Spaniard sadly, 'and one more grateful for the inestimable services he had done the King . . .'

Then Chapuys passed on to the heart of the matter. How much another marriage would be to King Henry's advantage – if it were true that he was considering one! Here was a king 'who had hitherto been disappointed of male issue and who knows quite well that this [present] marriage will never be held as lawful'. Chapuys' remarks on the subject of Princess Mary were equally pointed: although the birth of a legitimate son to the King would inevitably affect the princess's position (at present she was the King's sole legitimate child – at least in the opinion of the Spanish) nevertheless Chapuys still welcomed the prospect, such was the affection he bore for

---

* She was the sister of Charles V. The previous Regent, his aunt the Archduchess Margaret, had died in 1530, at which point Maria, the twenty-five-year-old widow of King Louis of Hungary, took over; she was another of the intelligent, charming women in which the Habsburg family abounded.

everyone in England. He also emphasized that he bore no 'hatred' for Anne Boleyn – which must have surprised Cromwell.

Cromwell's answer was equally amiable – and equally economical with the truth. For his part, he had never been the cause of the King's marriage to Anne 'though seeing the King wanted it, he had helped smooth the way'. Nevertheless the marriage had turned out to be a solid one. It was true that his master was 'still inclined to pay attention to ladies', yet Cromwell believed he would 'henceforth live honourably and chastely, continuing in his [present] marriage'. At this point, wrote Chapuys in his report to Spain, the King's secretary 'leaned against the window, putting his hand before his mouth' either to stop himself smiling or to conceal the fact he was doing so. Casually, Cromwell added that if the King *did* take another wife, it would certainly not be a French princess (as usual, any rumour of this upsetting possibility served to torture the Spaniards).

At this moment, not only did Chapuys know perfectly well the situation regarding Jane Seymour – that was precisely why he had raised the subject of the King's marriage – but Cromwell knew that he knew. For that matter, Chapuys knew that Cromwell knew that he knew. Such were the delights – the unchanging delights, one might almost say – of diplomacy. But this cheerful galliard danced by both men should not distract from the important message which Chapuys had delivered to Cromwell: the price of the Emperor's friendship was not in fact Henry VIII's submission to Rome, but getting rid of 'the Concubine'; nor were the rights of Princess Mary going to prove an obstacle. This was the third step in the destruction of Anne Boleyn, the death of Queen Catherine and her own miscarriage constituting the first two.

As Chapuys penned his report of the interview for despatch to Spain, he received an urgent message from those two industrious supporters of the late Queen Catherine, the King's first cousin the Marquess of Exeter and his wife Gertrude. It concerned Jane Seymour, a royal gift, and her rejection of it, the King's increased infatuation ... All this was heady stuff. But as a matter of fact, Chapuys had already heard of this remarkable episode from another source and the knowledge may well have influenced his tone to Cromwell.

A week or so before the Chapuys interview, King Henry had had the unpleasant task which sometimes falls to distinguished lovers, even monarchs, of explaining to his sweetheart that their relationship had not escaped popular attention. (Sir Edward Seymour had recently been made a member of his Privy Chamber by the King – an honour which could not fail to indicate the way the royal wind was blowing.) To Jane, his 'dear friend and Mistress', the King counselled calm. 'Advertising you that there is a ballad made lately of great derision against us, which if it go much abroad and is seen by you, I pray you pay no manner of regard to it.' But he sweetened the blow by enclosing a present of golden sovereigns, while promising that as soon as the author of this 'malignant writing' was discovered, the culprit would be punished 'straitly'. The King ended his letter with one of those gallant flourishes that Anne Boleyn would have recognized: 'Thus hoping shortly to receive you in these arms, I end for the present your own loving servant and Sovereign. H.R.'[24]

But Jane Seymour refused to accept his gift. On the contrary, she flung herself on her knees, and kissing the royal missive, begged the King (via his messenger) to remember that she was 'a gentlewoman of fair and honourable lineage without reproach'. Since she had 'nothing in the world but her honour, which for a thousand deaths she would not wound', she must return the sovereigns. 'If the King deigned to make her a present of money, she prayed that it might be when she made an honourable marriage.' Far from being put off, the King was still further enchanted by his rejection. Such blushing reticence on the part of Mistress Seymour inflamed his ardour – an ardour popularly thought to be flagging these days at least in physical terms – much as the saucy words of Anne Boleyn had once done. 'She has behaved in this matter very modestly', he said. In order to let it be seen that his intentions and affections were honourable, he intended in future 'only to speak to her in the presence of some of her relatives'.

Did Polonius – here represented by Edward Seymour and his associates – coach their Ophelia in this pretty maidenly speech to her middle-aged prince? (Chapuys referred to her as having been well taught by those 'intimate with the King, who hate the Concubine' not to comply with the King's wishes 'except by way of marriage'.)[25] Perhaps: on the other hand did Jane Seymour herself really need teaching to stand 'quite firm' on this important point? Once again, it is not necessary to believe that the girl herself was playing a role – an uncharacteristic one – just because the results of her withdrawal were so successful. Jane Seymour was the perfect bait just because she represented without artifice that purity a sentimental older man – and Henry was certainly sentimental at the start of his love affairs – was likely to admire.

There was another charge levelled against the new favourite: Jane was supposed to have been coached to tell the King that his subjects 'abominated' his second marriage, because they regarded it as illegitimate. But this was hardly an outrageous point of view and probably represented her own genuine opinion. The future would reveal that Jane Seymour did not hold the kind of Lutheran religious views that would lead her to support the Boleyn marriage, but clung to the old ways. Similarly, most people of England in their heart of hearts had always regarded the unpopular match as against the law of God. Only now was it possible to express such views without fear. Jane Seymour was as conventional in this as she was in other matters.

Equally, her point about her 'honour' was not so much coy as soundly practical since already the satirists were threatening her reputation. Anne Boleyn's lamentation on the same subject in the autumn of 1529 will be recalled: how she had missed the opportunity for 'some advantageous marriage' through waiting on the King. Jane Seymour, like Anne Boleyn, was not an heiress, and the famous gold sovereigns would indeed provide a useful dowry for some less exalted, but more secure match. Such gifts for young ladies of the court on marriage were a constant preoccupation on the part of everybody concerned. Catherine of Aragon, having been obsessed by her duty in this respect early on as a Princess of Wales, mentioned it in her will at the last. Since Jane Seymour could hardly expect a dowry from *her* mistress – Queen Anne – she displayed prudence rather than hypocrisy by handling the King's offer in this manner. After all, one of King Henry's first-known flirts, the girl to whom he played his lute-pipe while in Flanders at the court of the Archduchess Margaret, had written a year later to claim the 10,000 crowns he had promised her on marriage. Meanwhile Jane Seymour, like many future heroines of the English novel, guarded her precious good name, as being the only thing she currently had to sustain her.

A few weeks after this episode – on Easter Tuesday, 18 April – Sir Edward and Lady Seymour, chaperoning his sister, moved into the apartments at Greenwich hastily vacated for this purpose by Thomas Cromwell. This was an official indication that Cromwell had decided to join with them for the purposes of getting rid of Anne Boleyn at least. (Conveniently enough the King could reach these rooms 'by certain galleries without being perceived'.) Cromwell would say later that this was the moment at which he realized that the presence of Anne as Queen threatened the safety of the kingdom – and his own as secretary.[26] But his mind had surely been tending that way for some little time. It was hardly a difficult decision for a man of Cromwell's subtle political sense to make. Since the days of Wolsey, it had been apparent that one of the important if unacknowledged duties of the King's chief servant was to provide him with the wife he wanted at the time that he wanted her; should such a servant forget his duty, there was always Wolsey's fate there to remind him (Chapuys had made a delicate allusion to the subject in his interview). For Cromwell therefore, there was everything personal to gain by helping the King's 'honourable' affection towards fruition, and everything political as well – both at home and abroad.

From now on, therefore, Cromwell took the lead in what became open season for the destruction of Anne Boleyn.

*

Queen Anne herself was helpless. One can only feel sympathy for the desperate woman. After all, what crime had she actually committed (other than the dreadful crime of not producing a son). So she watched her future slip away from her amid the splendid rituals of the court: rituals which she of all people understood only too well how to interpret. In March her 'intense rage' concerning the King's love affair had been reported. Now she turned to softer methods. Chapuys had declined to come to court when the Queen was there and greet her with the formal kiss due from an ambassador. But when, on the same day that the Seymours moved into Greenwich, he attended Mass at court, the Queen treated him with great courtesy: 'for when I was behind the door by which she entered, she returned, merely to do me reverence'. But Chapuys, a sophisticated courtier who understood the language, responded with the coldest possible bow. Even more pathetic – in the sense that they were doomed to failure – were the Queen's last-minute attempts to establish a more friendly relationship with her step-daughter Mary, reported by Chapuys. Understandably, 'the Lady Mary' was not disposed to soften now and acknowledge, as she put it, 'any other Queen' but her late mother.[27]

On 23 April a ceremonial occasion offered the first outward sign of the inward revolution that was taking place. Sir Nicholas Carew was chosen as a new candidate for the Order of the Garter, instead of Queen Anne's brother, George Viscount Rochford, who had been widely expected to receive the honour. Such appointments were keenly scrutinized as a public indication of the royal favour: much as the line-up at a military parade on May Day in the Soviet Union would be inspected during the Cold War. Everyone knew that Carew was 'counselling' Jane Seymour. That appointment was for public show. Privately, on 24 April, at the instigation of Cromwell, King Henry signed a crucial document. This appointed Lord Chancellor Audley, some judges and a number of nobles, including incidentally both the Queen's uncle Norfolk and her father, to investigate certain unspecified activities, which might result in charges of treason.

As a result, Mark Smeaton, the musician and 'deft dancer' in the King's chamber, was lured away from the court at Greenwich and arrested on Sunday 30 April. Possibly he was tortured. This was no nobleman, to be treated with circumspection, but a young man of humble origins (perhaps Flemish – his name may have been originally de Smet or de Smedt). Smeaton had nothing to support him except his musical talent – the royal accounts show payments for his shirts, hose and shoes, and 'bonnets' since 1529 – that, and the fact that by a general agreement he was 'a very handsome man'. If a story of a rope knotted round his head and twisted with a cudgel is implausible, there was another story 'that he was first grievously racked.'[28] But in any case such a small frightened animal stood

Jane Seymour
m 1536

Badge of Jane Seymour showing a phoenix rising from a castle from which sprout Tudor roses.

Screen at King's College, Cambridge, showing H and A, for Henry and Anne Boleyn, and her crowned falcon badge (overlooked at her death).

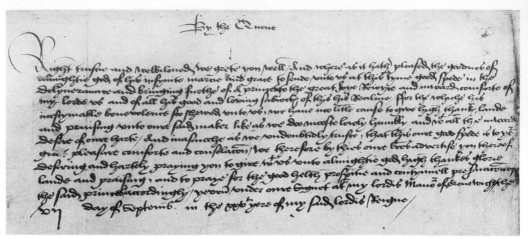

Announcement of the birth of Elizabeth 'by the Quene', showing that the letter 's' had to be inserted twice (on lines 3 and 11) to make 'princes' (i.e. princess) rather than 'prince' because a male heir had been so confidently expected.

Clock supposedly given by Henry VIII to Anne Boleyn: on the weights the letters H and A are engraved, together with lovers' knots, and their respective mottos, 'Dieu et Mon Droit' and 'The Most Happi'.

1534 medal of Anne Boleyn with her motto, 'The Moost Happi'.

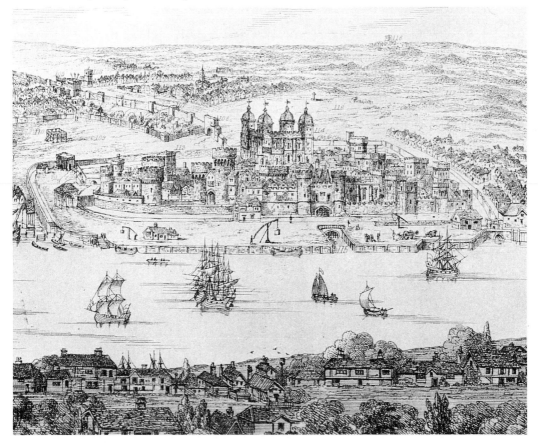

Sixteenth-century view of the Tower of London.

Henry VIII aged 45, painted about the time of his marriage to Jane Seymour.

Elizabeth Seymour, sister of Jane Seymour (incorrectly identified as Katherine Howard in the late nineteenth century); the resemblance to her sister is notable, especially in nose and chin. She wears widow's weeds after the death of her first husband; she subsequently married Gregory, son of Thomas Cromwell, and the Marquess of Winchester.

Jane Seymour painted by Holbein about the time of her wedding, 1536.

John Fisher, Bishop of Rochester.

Cardinal Thomas Wolsey.

Thomas Cranmer.

Thomas Cromwell.

Holbein's design for a gold cup for Jane Seymour, incorporating her motto, 'Bound to obey and serve'.

Designs for jewellery by Holbein, incorporating the initials H and I (J).

little chance against the power of the state. Mark Smeaton made a confession.

The action now moves back to Greenwich where Monday, May Day, was being celebrated by the traditional tournament watched by both King and Queen. A feature of it was to be the joust between Lord Rochford and Sir Henry Norris, Keeper of the Privy Purse and the betrothed of the King's former fancy, Madge Shelton. Unexpectedly, the King received a message. Its contents can only be guessed, but whatever they were, they caused him to rise and leave the tournament taking Norris with him. He did not give any explanation to his wife. Just as he had gone hunting from Windsor without saying goodbye to Queen Catherine, he now left Greenwich without bidding Queen Anne farewell. He never saw her again.

On his journey back to London, the King taxed Norris with certain revelations made by Smeaton; despite Norris's incredulous denials, he was taken to the Tower of London. Even more chilling to those watching the tragedy unfold – and doing their earnest best not to be involved in it – was the arrest of Lord Rochford. If the Queen's brother was to be brought down, who could count themselves safe who had ever enjoyed her patronage, let alone her courtly favour?

It was on Tuesday 2 May that the Queen herself was arrested at Greenwich and taken before the commissioners who had held the investigation, under her uncle Norfolk, to hear the accusations against her. These included not only adultery but incest (the penalty for which could be burning at the stake) and most heinous of all, surely, conspiracy to murder the King. After this, Queen Anne was taken by water from Greenwich to the Tower. The journey took about two hours.[29] How different now was her progress from that other great May morning, a mere three years before, when the minstrels had vied vainly with the artillery, and nothing could be seen for four magnificent miles but bravely decorated boats and barges! Then she had come to London to have a crown placed on her head. Now she had the whole sombre route on which to ponder the very different fate that might await her. It was little wonder that Queen Anne was on the point of collapse by the time she reached the Tower.*

At the sight of the Tower, into whose dungeons so many unfortunates had vanished, the Queen began screaming. She was heard to cry out: 'I was received with greater ceremony last time I was here'. The Constable of the Tower, Sir William Kingston, a just and kindly man, tried to comfort her. He assured her that she would not be housed in some dungeon (Queen Anne at this point was probably unaware just what other important

---

* She would not have been received at 'Traitor's Gate', then still known as the Watergate, but at the Barbican Gate with its wharf and special steps about fifty yards away.[30]

prisoners were held in the Tower) but in the lodging she had occupied before her coronation. She rewarded him by kneeling down and crying out, 'it is too good for me', then wept, then 'fell into a great laughing'.[31]

After this, the Queen managed to pass through the court-gate, but then her strength appeared to give out. She sank to her knees. In front of her escort of lords, she prayed to God to help her 'as she was not guilty of her accusement'. Then she begged the assistance of the lords themselves; would they implore the King 'to be good unto her'?

But King Henry was far away from such a distasteful scene, revelling in dreams of his future life with the delightful, modest Jane Seymour. (The young lady herself remained discreetly absent, protected first by her brother and his wife and then by the King's trusted friend, Sir Nicholas Carew, in his house at Croydon.) King Henry could leave the problem of his disgraced wife – a witch? a whore? a potential murderess? – to others.

Chapter 12

THE THIRD

MARRIAGE

This the third marriage was confirmed by them all to
be good and lawful.

Chronicle by a monk of St Augustine's, Canterbury, 1536

The trial of Queen Anne Boleyn was a cynical operation, intended to have only one result: her death. This death was necessary so that the King could achieve a third marriage as free from stain as the reputation of his new sweetheart. In this respect Queen Anne's trial was completely different from the ordeal endured by Queen Catherine in 1529: then at least, at Blackfriars, there had been a genuine spirit of enquiry – or at any rate some genuine confusion – about the validity of her marriage to King Henry. But no one was in any doubt, either during the trial of Anne Boleyn's alleged lovers, or during her own, that a guilty verdict was expected to be reached, and that it would be reached. It was a case of Norfolk's saying writ large: *Indignatio principis mors est* – the anger of the sovereign means death, even when the object of the rage is a wife.

Why was it considered essential to dispose of Queen Anne so completely? The answer to this lies in the behaviour of her predecessor. Once upon a time the King and his advisers had envisaged a dignified withdrawal from the stage by Queen Catherine, possibly into a convent. Instead they had faced seven years of protest, taking forms as various as imperialist threat from outside and personal support for Catherine from within the country. Anne Boleyn was not going to be given the same opportunity. Dismissal with what was in effect another divorce would have saddled the King with yet another ex-wife, only a few months after he had been freed by death from the first one. The timing of Queen Catherine's death had accelerated the downfall of Queen Anne: now once again, the influence of the dead woman stretched from beyond her grave in Peterborough Cathedral to pull down the woman who had supplanted her.

Very likely Cromwell did not even tell his master what he intended to do. There is a comparison to be made with the four knights who murdered Thomas à Becket in 1170; hearing Henry II cry out against 'this turbulent priest' they thought they knew the royal mind and acted accordingly without further consultation. The King's disgust with his second wife was public property ever since those ominous royal rumblings about witchcraft and the like following her miscarriage. His conscience was once again uneasy and it was absolutely necessary for Henry VIII to feel that 'God and his conscience were on very good terms' – as he had assured Chapuys that they were over the dissolution of his marriage to Catherine.[1]

It is true that the workings of the King's conscience followed the dictates of his heart amazingly conveniently. But this did not mean that he did not *have* a conscience. On the contrary, it was a lively and important part of his nature. This coincidence between passion and conscience was more apparent to outsiders than it was to him, a useful capacity for self-deception being another of his attributes.

In the past he declared that he would gladly restore Catherine to her place beside him – if only their marriage was valid. Now any nagging feelings of guilt about the lonely death of that sad, sick woman at Kimbolton who had loved him to the last were easily transferred into rage against Queen Anne: she who had personally lured him, by magic or otherwise, away from 'good Queen Catherine'. In tears the King told the young Duke of Richmond that Anne Boleyn was 'a poisoning whore' who had planned to kill both the boy and his half-sister Mary: what a lucky escape they had had! They all 'owed God a great debt'.[2] To the wilful self-deception in Henry VIII's character was added a strong dose of self-pity which in his case always ended by turning to anger.

This is not to absolve Henry VIII of guilt concerning his second wife's destruction, let alone the deaths of the innocent courtiers, some of them his close friends. On a rational level, the sovereign who agreed on 24 April to sign the commission of investigation into unknown treasonable conspiracies must have had a fair idea of what was going on. And even if that signing could be regarded as a purely routine administrative matter, the King went on a few days later to sign the documents necessary for summoning parliament (needed to ratify the changes that were envisaged concerning the succession).[3] That should have raised some questions in the mind of a man who was no fool, and certainly never the unwitting tool of his servants. It is merely to observe that Henry VIII found it easy enough to absolve himself.

Certainly, any possible connection between his original need for a divorce and the mighty reorganization of the church's structure that was currently going on in England, as the monasteries were dissolved, had long ago vanished from his mind. The woman who had once so boldly installed an English Bible in her own chamber for the edification of her ladies who could not read Latin, a gesture in advance of its time, was now immured in the Tower of London.

Queen Anne was probably housed in the so-called Royal Lodgings in the Inner Ward, to the south of the White Tower which she had occupied before her coronation, since this was what had been promised to her by Sir William Kingston; the Queen's apartments lay in a range running north from the Lanthorn Tower.* The terms of her confinement were not harsh. She took her meals with the Constable, as was the custom with state prisoners, and the presence of four or five ladies set to attend her proved that she was still to be treated as a queen. Nevertheless Queen Anne remained in the state of collapse precipitated by the suspense of her journey and her awe-inspiring arrival. She had always been highly strung, easily moved whether to anger or tears. Her laughter in the old days had sometimes been a little too loud for the occasion, or not quite appropriate. At a banquet at the end of 1534, for example, Queen Anne had much offended the French ambassador by suddenly laughing in his face: her explanation – that the King had forgotten to fetch an important guest, distracted by another lady he met on the way – was hardly deemed sufficient by the affronted envoy.[4]

Now the Queen seems to have broken down completely. (It is not irrelevant that she had suffered a miscarriage, under the most distressing circumstances, at the end of January; its after-effects, mental as well as physical, must have been still with her.) Kingston reported to Cromwell that she kept alternating between fits of weeping and fits of laughter, just as she had done at her first reception at the Tower. Her sayings became wild and incoherent, more like ravings than the polished witty conversation with which she had once beguiled the King.

Her words were however industriously noted down by her ladies. Queen Anne would later refer to these women angrily as 'wardresses'. Certainly they were women whose first allegiance was to the King (and Cromwell), not to their mistress: one of them was Anne's aunt Lady Shelton, who had already occupied the responsible position of governess to Princess Elizabeth; they included Lady Kingston as well as Mrs Margaret Coffin, wife of the Queen's Master of the Horse, and a Mrs Stoner.

---

* The Royal Lodgings, adapted by the Office of Ordnance, were finally demolished in the late eighteenth century. There is a tradition that Anne Boleyn was the first state prisoner to be housed in the Lieutenant-Governor's Lodgings (now known as the Queen's House, since the time of Queen Victoria). This is probably not correct, since it does not fit with Kingston's promise. Although the first payments for this black-and-white timber-framed Tudor building were made in 1533, it was not completed until 1540.

Mrs Coffin shared the Queen's bedchamber. Their instructions were to pass on everything the Queen said to the Constable and so to Cromwell. Out of this fragile tissue of a madwoman's fears, a solid tapestry of evidence was to be woven.

Even in her moments of sanity, Queen Anne was badly frightened – and with good reason. She had no idea what the precise foundation for the charges laid against her might be. The notion that the Queen had conspired with Sir Henry Norris to 'imagine' the death of the King was ludicrously improbable – what would either of them gain from that? – but the most outrageous charges can be the most difficult to combat, as experience of state trials, not only in the sixteenth but in the twentieth century, has demonstrated. Further courtiers were arrested whom it was decided had been imprudently connected with the Queen. On 4 May Sir Francis Weston and William Brereton, Groom of the Privy Chamber, were taken in: although there was some official perturbation, as Sir Edward Baynton wrote, 'that no man will confess anything against her, but alone Mark [Smeaton] of any actual thing'.[5] On 8 May Anne Boleyn's old admirer Sir Thomas Wyatt was arrested, although subsequently released. There was a dragnet out, instigated by Cromwell, to pull in anyone against whom scurrilous gossip and seamy revelation would add up to proof of treason with the Queen.

The cool processes of the law continued in the outside world. The machinery of the Tudor state might produce tyrannical effects, but it did exist, and the outward impression of tyranny was carefully avoided. Indictments for treason were laid before grand juries in both Middlesex and Kent: this was to cover the geographical areas where the various offences were supposed to have taken place.

What was so frightening for the Queen, conspiring, like her health and the shock of her arrest, to produce her deluded ramblings, was the sheer intimacy of the court positions of those who had been arrested. There was a constant history of close encounters with the four men – Smeaton, Norris, Weston and Brereton – who were put on trial first. How could there not be? And with close encounters went gallantries – the sort of romantic but unconsummated gallantries that the King had cheerfully permitted himself from the beginning of his marriage and, following his lead, were part of the custom of a Renaissance court. In a sense such involvements were a traditional way of passing the time during the endless court festivities, rather like jousting – except that during these bouts, men tilted gracefully against women and vice versa. Poetry, music and dance were woven into the fabric of such 'tournaments', wistful amorous declarations perhaps, vows, sighs, but not sex – and certainly not something as specifically dangerous as sex with the King's wife.

For the trial of Smeaton, Norris, Weston and Brereton which took place in Westminster Hall on 12 May, there is a contrast between the long list of charges read out, adulteries and conspiracies at Hampton Court, Greenwich and York Place (Whitehall), and the gossip purveyed then and ornamented later. The former frequently have an absurd quality: for example the Queen is supposed to have committed adultery with Norris within weeks of the birth of Princess Elizabeth at a time when she was still in seclusion at Greenwich before her official 'churching' (the religious ceremony which released a woman back into the world after childbirth).[6] As for the latter, none of the gossip constitutes any kind of proof. But the stories, preserved in hostile biographies, do have a domestic flavour, as though some of these words might have been spoken in a different context, flirtatiously, even provocatively – but innocently.

So the handsome young musician Mark Smeaton was accused of being in love with the Queen as well as receiving money from her. His fine clothes had aroused jealousy, considering his poor background and slender allowance from the King. (Weston was also accused of receiving money from the Queen – but then she gave to many young courtiers, part of her traditional role as patroness.) Perhaps Smeaton was in love with her. That was not in itself a crime. But there was certainly no evidence that the Queen had returned his love. The story of Antonio de Guaras, that Anne Boleyn had been in her turn madly in love with Smeaton, stands for many such slurs by those who were, like de Guaras, by definition hostile to the woman who had supplanted Catherine of Aragon. If Smeaton did profess himself romantically in love with the Queen (under better circumstances, that could be a good career move), then Queen Anne may have rebuked him for his presumption. That was the tenor of another tale which had the Queen reproaching him with his jealousy and pointing out that she could not be expected to have too much conversation with one who was not nobly born. 'A look sufficeth for me', Smeaton was supposed to have replied, 'And so farewell'.[7]

Sir Francis Weston was supposed to have made similar – if more well-bred – advances to the Queen a year earlier. Weston's flirtation with the Queen's first cousin, Madge Shelton, now betrothed to Sir Henry Norris, had annoyed the Queen and she reproved him for it. (Although her real annoyance may have been with the girl herself, who had not only caught Weston's eye, and that of the King, but also behaved frivolously over the matter of a prayer-book; in short, for a variety of reasons, an unsatisfactory type.) Weston daringly excused himself by saying that he really came to the Queen's chamber to see quite another person – 'It is yourself'. But at this, the Queen, 'defied him', that is to say, forbade him to advance further with his lance in this courtly joust.

The charges against Brereton were never made clear. But it is interesting to note that the most damning charge against Sir Henry Norris also touched upon the subject of Madge Shelton. It was proposed that his betrothal to Madge was hanging fire because of his passion for her mistress. In this connection the Queen was supposed to have made an extraordinarily reckless remark to Norris. The damning words were these: 'you look to dead men's shoes, for if ought came to the King but good, you would look to have me.' Yet the kernel of such a story could have been any kind of light-hearted exchange, in which the on-off rivalry of the two first cousins, Anne Boleyn and Madge Shelton, may have been the real point. The addition of that spicy detail about the death of the King brought with it the fatal tang of treason.

None of these considerations affected the jury empanelled to sit in Westminster Hall on 12 May as a result of returns sent in by the grand juries of Middlesex and Kent. By the rules of justice of the time, defending counsel were not permitted against charges of treason. All four men were condemned to die at Tyburn, with the extreme penalties of the law: to be cut down while alive, disembowelled, castrated and finally have their limbs quartered.

On Monday 15 May, the trial of Lord Rochford and Queen Anne took place in the Great Hall of the Tower of London. It was not a secret trial. Chapuys estimated that 2,000 people attended the spectacle, for whom special stands were erected.* The twenty-six peers who took part in the judgement were none of them strangers to the brother and sister, and some of them were closely connected. Their uncle the Duke of Norfolk presided as High Steward. Lord Rochford's father-in-law, Lord Morley, took part. Even the Queen's youthful swain Lord Percy, Earl of Northumberland since the death of his father, was among the peers present, although he did plead sudden illness and left before the end of the proceedings.

There was no novelty in this public repudiation of close ties, remembering how two of Buckingham's sons-in-law had sat in judgement on him. Thus solidarity with the royal will was demonstrated, and relatives avoided the frightening taint of suspicion about their own loyalty. Although Thomas Boleyn Earl of Wiltshire was excused the task of condemning his own children, there is no suggestion that the man who had been a faithful royal servant all his adult life (and intended to go on being so) made any attempt to question the events leading up to their inevitable doom. Indeed, he carefully denounced the actions of the alleged conspirators against the

---

* Like the Royal Lodgings, the Great Hall has been demolished; but the stands erected for spectators at the trial could still be seen 250 years later.[8]

King, if not his own kindred. In this he was less of a callous father – although he can hardly be described as a very tender one – than a man of his age. As for Norfolk, he wept – 'the water ran in his eyes' – but he presided.[9] To most people the sovereign was like a basilisk and his glittering stare, whether animated by favour or fury, held all but the strongest (Thomas More and John Fisher come to mind) in a hypnotic state of agreement.

The Queen was tried first.[10] She arrived in a calm frame of mind. According to the herald Charles Wriothesley who was present, she gave 'wise and discreet answers to her accusers', excusing herself with her words so clearly 'as though she was not actually guilty'.[11] But then the evidence presented was hardly of such a convincing nature as to bring about a volte-face and a confession.

One truncated note in the legal report of the trial has sometimes been thought to indicate that she was genuinely guilty of sexual relations with Mark Smeaton at least. There was a question of a deathbed confession by a certain Lady Wingfield a few years back 'who was a servant of the Queen and shared the same tendencies', passed on by the woman who listened to it.[12] But this kind of hearsay, which somehow emerged so miraculously just when it was needed, was really no more plausible than the other imaginative charges that Queen Anne had tried to poison Queen Catherine and her daughter, or wished to kill the King. The real measure of her wisdom and discretion, the source perhaps of her dignified composure – after all she was a Queen by achievement if not by training – was to realize that there was no purpose now in struggling against her fate.

She was certainly not guilty.[13] Queen Anne herself never admitted to any offence and the evidence to the contrary was a patchwork of half-truths and outright lies. All this, however, is less cogent than the sheer psychological improbability of the Queen endangering her position by adultery, let alone attempting to destroy the one man on whose favour she was totally dependent – the King. The sexual fascination of Anne Boleyn, to which her career bears witness, was not founded on indiscriminate sharing of her favours, rather on her ability to manage herself – and her own attractions. Tantalizing mystery, even withdrawal, can after all exert as much fascination as sexual generosity, if not more. As a young girl, her behaviour was never recklessly promiscuous but, if anything, calculating (Lord Percy had been one of the most eligible young men in England). There is no evidence that Anne Boleyn changed once she became Queen.

As for the death of the King, the monarch had the power to make her (as he had once done) or break her (as he now intended to do). Anne Boleyn was no princess of Spain, no daughter of Isabella the Catholic, no aunt to an Emperor. She had never had any real power, except insofar as the King had allowed her to exercise it. It was her destruction, not that of the King, which had always been the issue, ever since her failure to fulfil her, proper role as the mother of the King's son.

The trial of Lord Rochford followed that of the Queen. Here the evidence against him of incest with his sister was little short of pathetic. Character-assassination which came much later suggested that the Queen 'much wanting to have a manchild to succeed, and finding the King not to content her' used her brother (among others) to beget a child. That was of a very different order from evidence actually produced at the time. The worst that happened was some kind of allegation from Rochford's wife Jane about 'undue familiarity' between brother and sister. To this Rochford himself was supposed to have exclaimed bitterly to his judges: 'On the evidence of only one woman, you are willing to believe this great evil of me'. Otherwise there was vague talk about Lord Rochford being 'always in his sister's room' – hardly a lethal offence, and hardly, one would have thought, proof of incest. There was no attempt to prove conspiracy to murder. As a result George Constantine, servant to Sir Henry Norris, talked of 'much money' being laid, and 'great odds' being taken that Lord Rochford would actually be acquitted.[14]

The gamblers were reckoning without the real purpose of the arraignment of Lord Rochford, which was to blacken the name of his sister to the point where her malevolent nature became an article of faith. On the one hand such a creature deserved to die; on the other hand, none of her own vicious charges was to be taken seriously. The question of the King's impotence, about which there was a good deal of private speculation – Chapuys at this point thought it doubtful that Jane Seymour or anyone else would have a chance of conceiving a royal child – could be used neatly to get rid of the superfluous Queen Anne. It was now that the fatal words of Queen Anne to Lady Rochford were produced: *'que le Roy n'estait habile en cas de soy copuler avec femme, et qu'il n'avait ni vertu ni puissance'* (that the King was incapable of making love to his wife and he had neither skill nor virility). The words were actually written down in court, although Lord Rochford, with some spirit, read them out.[15] This was far more damaging than the nonsense talked about incest, because it was far more likely to be true.

The motives of Jane Lady Rochford remain obscure: her father Lord Morley had been a devoted adherent of Queen Catherine, and she herself may have been intending to help the cause of Catherine's daughter Mary. Alternatively, and more simply, she may have hoped to remain on the winning side (as actually happened) despite the disadvantage of her husband's 'guilt'. At all events, the effect of such frightful words was to damn Queen Anne most efficiently. No one could abuse the monarch in such a devastating and intimate way and live (especially if there was a disquieting possibility the charge might even be true).

The sentence, pronounced by Norfolk, was the same in both cases: the Queen and her brother were to be burnt or executed according to the wish of the King. Lord Rochford had denied that he was guilty, following the sentence, and Queen Anne did likewise. Thereafter they both formally admitted that they deserved punishment. This was in accordance with the conventional procedure of the time, and provided a suitable frame of reference for asking for pardon; as well as, if appropriate, avoiding the forfeiture of property. Finally Lord Rochford accepted the prospect of death with what has been described as 'oriental fatalism': since the state had judged him guilty, then he could no longer be innocent.[16] Similarly Queen Anne bowed her neck meekly beneath the weight of the royal justice, her best chance – her only chance – of avoiding bowing that same neck to the axe of the executioner.

Mercy might be sought but it would not be found. Two days later, 17 May, the five condemned men were executed on Tower Hill, their sentences commuted from the fearful penalties to be paid at Tyburn by the wish of the King. All five died with professions of loyalty to their master on their lips, although only Smeaton asked for pardon for his 'misdoings'. Lord Rochford, exercising the condemned man's privilege of addressing the large crowd which always gathered for such popular entertainments, kept up his stoicism to the last. This custom was sometimes negated, in the case of supposed subversives, by the rolling of drums to drown the prisoner's words. But Lord Rochford did not abuse it.

'Masters all', he began in a ringing voice, 'I am come hither not to preach and make a sermon but to die, as the law hath found me, and to the law I submit me.' Then he recommended his audience to trust in God, and not in the 'vanities of the world'.[17] These sentiments of resignation and piety found much approval among those who only a short while before had been placing bets that he would be found not guilty – since he happened to be innocent.

Queen Anne now lived in hourly expectation of her death. After the firm dignity of her conduct at her trial, she reverted to more erratic behaviour. She might be 'very merry' and eat 'a great dinner', or she might be in floods of tears. At times, said Kingston, the Queen positively longed to die and 'the next hour much contrary to that'. She veered between talk about retreating to a nunnery – 'and is in hope of life' – and discussing her own execution.[18]

The latter prospect caused the Queen to make a black joke. The 'hangman of Calais' had been specially summoned (at a cost of £24) since he was an expert with a sword; thus, in Anne's case, the sharp efficient 'sword of Calais' was going to be substituted for the axe. This was a favour to the victim since her despatch was likely to be swift (the use of the axe could sometimes mean a hideously long-drawn-out affair).* When the Queen learned this, she told Kingston that she had 'heard say the executioner was very good' which was just as well since she had 'a little neck'. Then she circled it with her hand – that 'ivory neck ... raised upright' once praised by an admirer as her special beauty. All the time, according to Kingston, she was 'laughing heartily'. Kingston added that he had seen 'many men and also women' executed who had all been 'in great sorrow', whereas 'this lady has much joy and pleasure in death'.[19]

But Anne Boleyn was not in fact to die as a Queen, that title for the sake of which she had kept the King in play for seven long years – and had incurred the hostility of nearly the whole country. Before the time came for her to die, a bizarre ritual had to take place: a *second* divorce was secured for the King. That is, Anne Boleyn's marriage to Henry VIII was pronounced to be invalid by Archbishop Cranmer. It is not known for certain why this judicial farce was thought necessary. (The logic of it is another matter: for if Anne Boleyn had never been properly married to the King, she could hardly have committed adultery as his wife.)

One suggestion is that the King intended to legitimize Henry Duke of Richmond, now aged just on seventeen, and make him his heir.[20] For two reasons, this does not seem very likely. First, the health of the boy whom the King had once loved more than his own soul, was already giving serious concern; he was suffering from tuberculosis, and would in fact die two months later. Even more cogently, the King would not take the trouble to legitimize his bastard at the very moment when he might confidently expect to be provided with a new heir by a new wife. That was the way to store up trouble in the future. Taking into account the King's dynastic dreams, it is more reasonable to suppose that the King's aim by this last-minute divorce was to brand Princess Elizabeth a bastard, rather than legitimize the Duke of Richmond. That way Elizabeth, like Mary, could not hope to challenge the position of the King's children by any third marriage: that glorious string of sons that Jane Seymour, herself one of a family of ten, would surely produce.

The grounds which satisfied Cranmer that he could lawfully declare the King's marriage to Anne Boleyn invalid can also only be guessed.[21] Possibly Anne confided to Cranmer in an interview on 16 May that she had been

---

* There is no record of who made this decision. Presumably the authorities were anxious to avoid an embarrassingly botched-up event for propaganda reasons; they wanted justice, not some horrific rite, to be seen to take place.

not only precontracted to Lord Percy but also secretly married to him; alternatively that their relationship had been consummated, following betrothal (which would have had the same effect of making it a binding union). In this, Anne Boleyn may have been exaggerating to save her life, or she may, as was noted in chapter seven, have been actually telling the truth – now that it was in her interest to be frank. Her situation as regards Percy had apparently been ambivalent enough to warrant a dispensation from the Pope in late 1527 to cover it; while Percy's subsequent wife certainly took the line that her husband had been precontracted to Anne Boleyn, even though he himself solemnly denied it.

There is no reason to believe, as is sometimes suggested, that Archbishop Cranmer tricked Anne Boleyn to secure a confession: that he falsely held out the prospect of survival in return for it. Anne Boleyn's periodic hopes 'for life' belong (like her manic laughter) to the general pattern of her disturbance, as Kingston's detailed accounts show. The Archbishop's beha- viour in all this was inglorious enough without an added burden. He had been the creature of the Boleyns, and as such raised from comparative obscurity. He had been the King's man in bringing about the divorce from Catherine; immediately afterwards he placed the crown on Anne's head. Now he annulled the marriage he had helped to create. A letter to the King written on 3 May indicates the subservience of spirit which enabled Cranmer to take this step without apparent trouble to his conscience.

On the one hand, wrote Cranmer, 'I never had better opinion in woman, than I had in her' (Anne Boleyn) 'which maketh me to think, that she should not be culpable'. On the other hand, 'I think your Highness would not have gone so far, except she had surely been culpable'. It is a fine example of the effects of the stare of the basilisk. In his own words, 'Of all creatures living' Cranmer had been 'most bounden' to Anne Boleyn – 'next to the King', that is.[22]

The decree of nullity was dated 17 May, the official copy signed on 10 June and subscribed by both houses of parliament on 28 June, a week after it was introduced to convocation. The marriage of the King and his second wife was now officially dissolved. But by this time the former Queen Anne Boleyn was long dead. They came for her early in the morning – about eight o'clock, on Friday 19 May. She had made a full confession to Archbishop Cranmer the day before and received the sacrament – incidentally steadfastly maintaining her innocence of the charges against her but humbly professing her love for the King.*[23]

---

* Cranmer never directly revealed the contents of Anne's confession; this is the construction put upon the report given by the Scottish reformer Aless to Anne's daughter Elizabeth (admittedly twenty-three years later) that Cranmer told him on the morning of Anne's execution, she would shortly become 'a Queen in Heaven'.

There had been some concern about the public nature of the erstwhile Queen's execution. It was based on worry about what she might say to the crowd in her farewell address; could she be trusted to follow the excellent example of her brother? Kingston for one suggested to Cromwell that 'at the hour of her death' Anne might 'declare herself to be a good woman for all men' with the exception of the King.[24] This irritable remark was no doubt prompted by Kingston's recent experience of his captive's volatile nature. It was decided to hold the execution, not on Tower Hill, where there was free public access, but on the green inside the Tower which was, as it happened, conveniently adjacent to a chapel. An added advantage of using this more private spot was the fact that the gates of the Tower were habitually locked at night, so that entry could be controlled.

In this way the gathering on Tower Green was a comparatively small one that Friday morning – although it was still in no sense a secret ceremony. Thomas Cromwell was there, to oversee the successful accomplishment of his plan, and Lord Chancellor Audley, accompanied by the herald Wriothesley. The Dukes of Norfolk and Suffolk were both there; so was the sickly young Duke of Richmond whom Anne Boleyn was supposed to have tried to poison. Then there was the Lord Mayor of London and his sheriffs. After that came the inhabitants of the Tower, virtually a small town with its multiple dwellings. Antonio de Guaras for example, who lived nearby and had friends living within the Tower, managed to get in the night before, and was thus able to give a first-hand account of the execution in his *Spanish Chronicle*, despite the care of the authorities that imperialists should not be allowed to be present.[25] (Chapuys' servant was 'put out'.) And the ravens were there, traditional scavengers in the Tower since time immemorial, then as now clustering round the site.

De Guaras thought that Anne Boleyn showed 'a devilish spirit' as he watched her walk, followed by four young ladies, the short distance, about fifty yards, slightly uphill from the Lieutenant's Lodgings to the green. She looked 'as gay as if she was not going to die'. It is more likely however that this gaiety represented not so much indifference as a positive welcome to her fate – joyful release at last from her troubles. Other witnesses concurred that Anne Boleyn met her death with 'much joy and pleasure' as she had convinced Sir William Kingston that she would. De Carles heard that in her dignity and composure she had never looked more beautiful. The tears and hysteria were all over now.

Anne Boleyn wore a mantle of ermine over a loose gown of dark grey damask, trimmed with fur, and a crimson petticoat. She had a white linen coif holding up her hair beneath her headdress. She had promised to say 'nothing but what was good' when she begged for leave to address the people and she kept her word. She spoke simply and affectingly. 'Masters,

I here humbly submit me to the law as the law hath judged me, and as for mine offences, I here accuse no man. God knoweth them; I remit them to God, beseeching Him to have mercy on my soul.' Then she called on Jesus Christ to 'save my sovereign and master the King, the most godly, noble and gentle Prince that is, and long to reign over you'. She spoke these words, wrote Wriothesley, 'with a good smiling countenance'.[26]

Anne Boleyn now knelt down. Her ladies removed her headdress, leaving the white coif to hold up her thick black hair away from her long neck. One of her ladies put a blindfold round her eyes. She said: 'To Jesu Christ, I commend my soul' (the same words spoken by Catherine of Aragon – but in Latin). To watchers it then seemed that 'suddenly the hangman smote off her head at a stroke' with his sword which appeared by magic, unnoticed by anyone including the kneeling woman. In fact the famous 'sword of Calais' had been concealed in the straw surrounding the block. In order to get Anne to position her head correctly, and stop her looking instinctively backwards, the hangman had called 'Bring me the sword' to someone standing on the steps nearby. Anne Boleyn turned her head. The deed was done.

Afterwards one lady-in-waiting covered the head with a white cloth and the others helped with the body. Both were conveyed the twenty yards to the Chapel of St Peter ad Vincula. There the disgraced woman was quietly interred.

Anne Boleyn, thirty-five or -six at the time of her decease, had been Queen for nearly three and a half years but it was a mere four months since the death of the King's first wife. As though in anticipation of the usurper's execution, the wax tapers round Queen Catherine's tomb in Peterborough Cathedral were said to have 'kindled themselves' at Matins the day before; equally mysteriously, they were 'quenched' without human aid at the *Deo Gratias*.[27] Elsewhere in the country, however, people swore that they had seen hares running – the hare, the sign of the witch – and would continue to do so on the anniversary of the execution of Anne Boleyn.

The secret betrothal of Henry VIII and Jane Seymour took place at Hampton Court early in the morning of 20 May, twenty-four hours after his previous wife's execution. Perhaps the betrothal might even have taken place on the actual day of Anne Boleyn's death. Certainly sentiment did not hold it up. But it was thought prudent to secure a dispensation for the marriage between a couple 'in the third and third degrees of affinity', that is, either of second cousins, or those who stood to each other as second cousins, through some sexual relationship. (Since the King and Jane Seymour were actually fifth cousins, it has been supposed that one of the King's mistresses must have been second cousin to Jane Seymour.)

Archbishop Cranmer, ever industrious in his master's cause, signed this dispensation – 'T. Cantuarien' – on 19 May, the date of the former Queen's death.[28]

During the tumultuous events of recent weeks Jane Seymour had first been housed 'in almost regal splendour' at Sir Nicholas Carew's house at Croydon; by 15 May, however, she was installed in a house looking on to the river within a mile of Whitehall. Here Sir Francis Bryan kept her in touch with the workings-out of the royal will. First he brought her news that Queen Anne had been condemned. Then he visited her after the execution and formally apprised her it had taken place. (Her reaction is not recorded.) From here she was conveyed by water to Hampton Court for the betrothal.

After that Jane Seymour may well have gone to her family home, Wolf Hall in Wiltshire, and the King may even have gone with her,* although he was absent from her side on Ascension Day – 25 May. On this occasion he took the opportunity to assure the French ambassadors that he was absolutely at liberty to marry since his wife's death (the implication being: to marry a French princess). However diplomatic such an assurance might be, it did show a certain cheerful disregard for the fact that the English King had been betrothed to Jane Seymour five days previously. The King and Jane were both in London by 29 May.

On 30 May the marriage between the King and Jane took place, quickly and quietly, Cranmer having dispensed the need for banns, in 'the Queen's closet' at Whitehall. It was of course a 'Queen's closet' which had been so named for the previous consort. The use of the phrase (by one of Lord Lisle's correspondents on 31 May, keeping him up to date in Calais with the court news) draws attention to the considerable confusion now caused by the simple use of the words: 'the Queen'. During the year 1536 there were actually *three* Queens in England, or at any rate three women who might, officially or unofficially, be referred to as such. A monk at St Augustine's, Canterbury, made this entry for 1536: 'The same year the first and second marriages of the King, by the assent of all the parliament house, were annihilate and found unlawful. But [t]his the third marriage was confirmed by them all to be good and lawful.'[30] The simplicity of this statement masked the hard labour of revisionism which now had to take place, in terms of public attitudes and public display. And it had to take place speedily.

It was one thing for Miles Coverdale, who had been about to dedicate

---

* But they were neither betrothed nor married at Wolf Hall, however pleasant such a tradition may be: it is clear from the contemporary accounts that these two events took place respectively at Hampton Court and Whitehall.[29]

his translation of the Bible into English to Anne Boleyn, to have the name of Jane Seymour hastily printed across it instead. That was easily accomplished. Heraldry proved more expensive. Let us take the example of Dover Castle, to which the King would take his third wife in the course of a progress that summer, in order to inspect the fortifications (a favourite pursuit). As it happened Galyon Hone, the King's glazier, had only just been paid nearly £200 for inserting 'the Queen's badge' in various windows in the royal lodgings within the castle; since these payments took place between 16 April and 14 May, they must refer to the badges of Anne Boleyn, official consort at the start of this period, still alive but in the Tower at the end of it. They presumably replaced those of Catherine of Aragon, with the summer's progress in mind. However timing was everything: for between 2 July and 30 July substantial payments had to be made to Galyon Hone for once again removing 'the old Queen's badges' and replacing them with those of Jane Seymour.[31]

At Ampthill, once the refuge of Queen Catherine, then refurbished with the badges of Queen Anne by Galyon Hone, yet more glass and more badges of the new Queen's arms had to be commissioned from the same source. At Greenwich, also, the badges of Anne Boleyn, which had once supplanted those of Catherine of Aragon, were now in turn replaced by those of Queen Jane Seymour. Once again Galyon Hone did the work. By his marital career, Henry VIII proved himself to be the glazier's friend at least.

Under the circumstances, it was fortunate that Anne Boleyn's heraldic leopard proved easy to transform into Jane Seymour's heraldic panther 'by new making of the heads and tails'.[32] (Was the choice of the panther an example of Jane's innate tactfulness, perhaps?) All the same, badges of the previous incumbents were sometimes overlooked and lingered like awkward memories of the past – unless they were interpreted as grim reminders of the instability of the present. However, such was the ostentation of the King's new-found happiness – a 'good and lawful' marriage at last! surely no one deserved it more – that stability rather than instability seemed the order of the day.

The King showed off his new bride, using the traditional Whitsun festivities of the City to introduce 'Jane the Quene' to his subjects. On the eve of their wedding, they walked together to the Mercers Hall to watch the setting of the City Watch. This contemporary version of the modern Lord Mayor's Show involved a torch-lit procession of 2,000 men and hundreds of constables in scarlet cloaks, as well as morris dancers and elaborate tableaux. On 7 June King Henry and Queen Jane came by water from Greenwich to Whitehall. The procession of barges, those of his lords preceding that of the King, made a brave sight, and as the royal barge passed the boats lying in the Thames 'every ship shot guns'. A notable sign of the times was the presence of Chapuys, standing by a tent with the imperial arms on it, surrounded by his gentlemen dressed in velvet, to watch the King and his new wife go by. When the royal barge drew level, Chapuys sent his trumpeters and musicians to row round it giving a mighty musical fanfare 'and so [they] made a great reverence to the King and Queen'.[33]

Another sign of the times was the colourful display of streamers and banners draped in salute all over the walls of the Tower of London; within these gaudy walls the body of Anne Boleyn lay in the grave in which it had been placed less than three weeks earlier, but no one now thought of that. So the King passed through London Bridge with his own trumpeters blowing sonorously before him. It was 'a goodly sight to behold', wrote the herald Charles Wriothesley.[34] The next day Queen Jane watched from the new gatehouse of the Palace of Whitehall sited directly over the Charing Cross to Westminster highway as the King rode to open parliament. This was the assembly which would formally confirm the invalidity of King Henry's marriage to Anne Boleyn; preparations for it had been begun at the end of April.

The celebrations went on, in harmony with the great summer feasts of the church. There was another magnificent procession to celebrate the Feast of Corpus Christi on 15 June. This time the King and Queen together rode to Westminster Abbey, the King first, the Queen with her ladies following. Within the abbey Queen Jane's train was held up by King Henry's niece Lady Margaret Douglas. Fourteen days later, the Feast of St Peter was marked by a pageant on the Thames, a joust at Whitehall, watched by King and Queen, and a triple wedding of young lordlings and ladies, scions of the families of de Vere, Neville and Manners.

At this latter event, the King appeared masked, surrounded by eleven attendants and wearing richly embroidered 'Turkish' garments. It was all quite like the old days, except that the general surprise when 'the King put off his visor and showed himself' must have been even more difficult to maintain for his wife and courtiers than it had been in the heady days of his youth when he was merely a giant of 6 feet 2 inches. For the King was rapidly becoming enormously fat.

There were no more tributes to his 'angelic' appearance. Holbein, now in his service as the King's painter, shows him in a picture probably painted to celebrate his third marriage as having a face already enlarged to spade shape, a tight little mouth, tiny eyes and a beard vainly attempting to conceal the loss of a chin. A hat hides the head which had become 'bald like Caesar's'; the beringed fingers are chubby, to put it at its kindest. With his great height and commensurate girth the King was on his way to becoming, in physical terms at least, the most formidable prince in Europe, as he had once been the handsomest. And there was more to come.[35]

There is however no indication – at this point – that his weight increase caused him any mortification (as we shall see, this changed). King Henry was extremely happy in personal terms during the summer of 1536 and one of the things that brought about this happiness was the conciliatory, affectionate character of his third wife. He had made the right choice. Everything Queen Jane did seemed to confirm that.

Her treatment of her step-daughter Mary was especially sensitive. Well in advance of Jane Seymour's marriage, she was believed to be 'well-disposed' towards the proud, unhappy girl seven years her junior; given the difficulties of their respective positions, some kind of tentative friendship may have already grown up. Mary was extremely dependent on female friendship, robbed of contact with her mother for many years before the latter's death. Masculine relationships were in contrast dangerous, not only in terms of a strict upbringing but because she was determined not to prejudice the question of her marriage, in which her whole future was bound up. In their correctness, sense of duty, and piety, the two young women, Jane the Queen and Mary the erstwhile princess, were indeed not that unalike.

Now Queen Jane was generally credited with having caused the King to 'reinstate' his elder daughter. How much was she in fact responsible? In one way it is difficult to evaluate the Queen's precise influence in this. One can hardly believe that the new insecure Queen would have single-handedly secured a reversal of policy against her husband's real wishes. The King's patience with advice which he had no wish to hear, or petitions he did not wish to receive had not grown with the years. It had always been in King Henry's best interests to secure the submission of Mary to such humiliating concepts as the invalidity of her own parents' marriage. While court gossip predicted that Mary would be reinstated as her father's heir – to the King's fury when he heard about it – reality was very different. The King was prepared to threaten his daughter with the Tower and even execution in order to secure her obedience. Finally Mary gave in and agreed to everything. On 14 June she wrote her father a letter of self-abasement: 'I beseech your Majesty to countervail [balance] my transgressions with my repentance for the same' and the next day another one where his 'mercy' and 'benignity' were contrasted with her 'offence' and 'sinfulness'. She told the King that she prayed daily to God 'that it may please him to send you issue'.[36]

On the other hand, Queen Jane's quasi-maternal desire to reconcile father and daughter was obviously quite genuine. Maybe the real importance of Queen Jane's intervention on behalf of her step-daughter was in the pleasing light it cast on her character in the eyes of her husband: she had shown herself in the most womanly light as one prepared to plead on behalf of the helpless. There was one story that King Henry reacted to the Queen's supplications for Mary by saying that she must be out of her senses to think of such a thing: 'she ought to study the welfare and exaltation of her own children, if she had any by him, instead of looking out for the good of others'. But Jane's reply was a model of sweet serenity. In soliciting Mary's reinstatement she thought she was asking not so much for the good of others as for 'the good, the repose and tranquillity of himself, of the children they themselves might have and of the kingdom in general'.[38]* Such a Queen – such a wife – who was always on the lookout for the good of others was not such a bad thing to have (and one notes that she listed the King's 'good, repose and tranquillity' first).

From now, as regards the rehabilitated Mary, 'kind and affectionate behaviour' was to be the order of the day. On 6 July the King and Queen spent the day visiting her at Hunsdon. Queen Jane took the opportunity to present a 'very fine' diamond ring, and the King a cheque for 1,000 crowns, with instructions that she should ask for anything else she wanted. The royal accounts bear witness to a constant stream of gifts exchanged between Queen Jane and her 'most humble and obedient daughter and handmaid'. There were all manner of things, not only rich jewels, but intimate little luxuries: touching smaller presents included fresh cucumbers sent from Mary to the Queen and further presents to Queen Jane's gardener at Hampton Court.[39]

'The Lady Mary' was rather like a plant herself, in need of proper care and attention to flourish. She was still very short, like her mother and, like the late Queen Catherine, had that odd, gruff voice which contrasted with her tiny stature; but she was not plump as Catherine had been in youth: 'thin and delicate' was the verdict. Yet Mary was certainly not plain: 'more than moderately pretty' was one description; a few years later, she was said to possess 'a pleasing countenance and person'.[40] What she needed was happiness: now it seemed likely that under the benevolent auspices of Jane Seymour, she stood a chance of finding it.

The real keynote to Queen Jane's character was, however, her submissiveness. That was indicated from the start by the motto she had chosen: 'Bound to obey and serve'. (With hindsight there was something disquietingly bold about that of Anne Boleyn which proclaimed herself to

---

* A colourful (but second-hand) story was spread much later: how the pregnant Queen urged the King to receive Mary, calling her 'your chiefest jewel of England' at which King Henry patted her belly, exclaiming, 'Nay, Edward, Edward'. The incident cannot literally have taken place, since Mary was reinstated immediately after the marriage when Queen Jane was certainly not pregnant; but it does incarnate the tradition that she was sympathetic to Mary, especially since the original source for the story was said to be one of Mary's own gentlewomen.[37]

be *'La plus heureuse'*: the most happy.) Chapuys courteously referred to the contrast as he continued to pay reverence to the young Queen. He was invited to her chamber by the King after Mass where he 'kiss'd her and congratulated her on her marriage' to Henry's evident satisfaction. Her predecessor had borne the device *'La plus heureuse'*, declared Chapuys, but Queen Jane would bear 'the reality' of the happiness.[41]

Queen Jane's 'good and virtuous' reputation spread abroad: where of course the contrast with the late Anne Boleyn was hardly to her detriment, particularly in view of the latter's known 'Lutheran' sympathies. The King's cousin, Reginald Pole, youngest son of Margaret Countess of Salisbury, was in Venice. When he was summoned back to explain the writing of a work critical of the religious changes in England – *Pro Ecclesiasticae Unitatis Defensione* – he declined to come. But on 14 July he did refer with enthusiasm to 'the goodness of God' which had rid King Henry of 'that domestical evil at home . . .' – by which he meant Anne Boleyn – 'the cause of all your errors' with 'her head I trust, cut away.' Pole was sure the King would soon see the light of God again. He was particularly confident of such a happy outcome 'because I understand already, that in place of her, of whom descended all disorders, the goodness of God hath given you one full of goodness, to whom I understand your Grace is now married.'[42]

On the occasion of Chapuys' interview, the King left him with the Queen, while he talked to some other ladies. But he seems to have returned in time to hear Chapuys wish for her to obtain the honourable name of 'pacific': one who was the author and conservator of peace. The King's protective instinct was at work. He wished to excuse his wife who must not be overtaxed in her new duties: Chapuys was the first ambassador to whom she had spoken and 'she was not accustomed to it'. However, he was delighted with Chapuys' suggestion of the name 'pacific'. He could quite believe that the Queen desired to obtain it, he said complacently, for 'besides that her nature was gentle and inclined to peace, she would not for the world that he were engaged in war, that she might not be separated from him'. Here was a contented man.

Queen Jane for her part was equally contented with her corpulent, middle-aged (the King was now forty-five) but mightily royal husband. There is no reason to suppose otherwise. People died in obedience to the King's orders – and they also loved. From Jane Seymour's point of view, marriage was merely another way of submitting 'to the law' as Anne Boleyn had finally done, another way of acknowledging that the King was 'the most godly, noble and gentle Prince that is' as Anne Boleyn had put it in her last address. Nor was Jane Seymour's fate an unenviable one according to the expectations of the time, leaving aside the basic satisfaction to a kindly nature in bringing happiness to her step-daughter as well as her husband. We should be careful not to wish upon her the romantic pre-occupations of a later age; and in so doing forget her vast dowry – 104 manors scattered through nineteen counties, five castles and a number of chases and forests, including Cranborne Chase, and the Paris Garden in London.[43] Above all, she was now Queen. In short, because Jane Seymour had a sympathetic nature, it did not mean that she was without conventional aspirations.

It was the duty of a young woman to secure, or have secured for her, the most advantageous match possible, one that would help her family up the perilous ascent to the top in Tudor society. Jane Seymour had been wafted up to the summit. As a result, her family went up too. Sir Edward Seymour was created Viscount Beauchamp a week after his sister's wedding. That would be only the beginning, if Queen Jane could fulfil her only other female duty, produce a son, and in so doing make her brother the uncle of the future King. For this would be not simply a blood relationship when a King was past his prime, and thus liable to die before his son reached his majority. Such an uncle would have a good claim to act as Regent, either officially, or unofficially in the Queen's name.

As to the prospect of this all-important conception, the general satis-faction of the King with his new wife would suggest that those problems of impotence which had plagued the end of his marriage to Anne Boleyn were cured. Perhaps the famous modesty – the sexual innocence – of Jane Seymour was reassuring; she would have no expectations on these matters. She was certainly not the kind of woman to deliver a cutting remark about such a delicate situation, of the sort that Anne Boleyn was alleged to have flung at Jane Lady Rochford. In this connection, it is significant that preparations were soon put in hand for her coronation. As mentioned earlier, there was a particular link between the coronation of a queen consort and the likelihood of her bearing her husband's heir. There had been murmurs at the time of the King's third marriage that he would never succeed in procreating again: 'there was no fear of the occurrence of any issue of either sex'. Now the murmurs died away. Instead preparations went forward 'against the Coronation of the Queen'.[44]

The summer progress of the King and Queen saw them at Rochester, Sittingbourne and Canterbury, as well as Dover Castle. There were numer-ous hunting expeditions – twenty stags were killed on 9 August alone. Meanwhile work was being done for the future coronation, and payments recorded in the royal accounts of the King's surveyor James Nedham already totalled over £300. One projected date was Michaelmas – the Feast of St Michael and All Angels on 29 September – to coincide with the festivities which always took place around this time. But Wriothesley believed it would be a month later, at the end of October. Chapuys heard that the King intended 'to perform wonders' for this latest wife (no doubt in the hopes of obliterating popular memories of another coronation three years before).[45]

Then there was a severe outbreak of the plague. The King's notorious sensitivity to this threat meant that preparations for the coronation were immediately suspended. The event was only postponed. There would surely be another day for the crowning of 'Jane the Quene'. Perhaps by then she too, like her predecessor, would be pregnant. For God was so manifestly smiling on this union, which might appear to be the King's third marriage, but was actually in the firm view of Henry VIII his first 'good and lawful' one. Queen Jane's personal badge – apart from her heraldic leopard – consisted of a castle from which a phoenix surrounded by flames (and Tudor roses) issued forth. King Henry had every confidence that his dynasty, like the phoenix, would be reborn from the troubles of the past.

Chapter 13

ENTIRELY BELOVED

Our most dear and most entirely beloved wife, the
Queen, now quick with child, for the which we give most
humble thanks to Almighty God . . .

Henry VIII to the Duke of Norfolk, summer 1537

Henry VIII would look back on Jane Seymour as the wife with whom he had been uniquely happy; forgetting perhaps those early years with Catherine of Aragon, the charming young Spanish princess so eager to please him. Queen Jane's state was to be commensurate with his esteem: the speedy matrimonial turnover of May making it particularly important to emphasize her high position. Thus the chamberlain to the new Queen was to be the King's cousin, sharing Plantagenet blood, Thomas Manners Earl of Rutland, whereas Anne Boleyn's chamberlain at her coronation had been a peer of a mere four years' standing, Lord Borough.[1]

Wonderful jewels were fashioned for the new Queen, with H and I (for the Latin Ioanna) replacing the previous Hs and As, much as the stained-glass leopards had given way to the panthers. An emerald-centred pendant, dropping with pearls, was designed by Holbein. And Holbein too was the designer for a magnificent gold cup, presented by the King to the Queen, weighing $65\frac{1}{2}$ ounces. Here were featured medallions of antique heads, dolphins and cherubs holding up the Queen's arms under a crown imperial, as well as the initials H and I entwined in a true lover's knot. Furthermore that motto, 'Bound to obey and serve', which had made such a favourable impression on everyone, was inscribed prominently on the cup not once but twice.*

The court of Queen Jane, if it was to be splendid, was also to be decorous. She was, for example, strict about the dress of her ladies.

---

* The cup, made to Holbein's design, was found in the royal inventories until the reign of Charles I when the King had it melted down with the rest of his plate to pay for his fight against the parliamentary forces.[2]

Obviously, the contemporary desire to install a young woman in the Queen's household was unaffected by the change of mistresses there: indeed, it could be argued that a place at a court where already two ladies-in-waiting had risen to the rank of royal consort was likely to be more advantageous than ever. Lady Sussex had just managed to infiltrate Lady Lisle's daughter Anne Basset (failing with her other daughter Katherine) when a message came from the Queen that Mistress Anne's 'French apparel' would not be suitable.

At first the Queen agreed that Mistress Anne should wear out her clothes, so long as she added a bonnet and frontlet (forehead band) of velvet to them. Lord Lisle's agent in London, John Husee, wrote to Lady Lisle in Calais that he had seen Mistress Anne the day before in the velvet bonnet which Lady Sussex altered for her 'which I thought became her nothing so well as the French hood, but the Queen's pleasure must be done'.* But two weeks later the affair of Mistress Anne's foreign clothing was still rumbling on. Now 'the Queen's pleasure is that Mistress Anne shall wear no more of her French apparel' but must equip herself with suitable gowns of black satin and velvet; furthermore her cloth for smocks (chemises wearable by day and night) was being censured as being too coarse, and she needed 'chests' (fill-ins at the neckline). The condemned 'French apparel' was relegated to making two years' worth of petticoats.[3]

Consciousness of her own non-royal origin was probably responsible for Queen Jane's insistence on uniformity: not an unusual reaction. We should remember that Queen Anne Boleyn endeavoured to iron out frivolity among her maids, both ladies being as it were poachers turned gamekeepers. It was probably not irrelevant that Mistress Anne would be described a few years later as 'a pretty young creature' who had caught the King's eye. Queen Jane's love of gardening, a thoroughly English taste to which the royal accounts attest, puts her in a more sympathetic light: she had a celebrated gardener at Hampton Court called Chapman. Equally a passion for eating red deer buck and quails – which, at 12d for six dozen, were ordered repeatedly from Calais – points to the earthy woman within the kindly but staid figure painted by 'Hance' (Holbein) in the season following her marriage.[4]

The kindness itself was, however, genuine. Queen Jane's fondness for her step-daughter Mary continued. As for Elizabeth, although Antonio de Guaras gleefully related a tale in which Queen Jane begged the King that the daughter of the wicked Anne Boleyn should be downgraded in rank, this must be regarded as wish-fulfilment on the part of the partisan

* French hoods, perched on the back of the head, and revealing much more hair, certainly look far more becoming to the modern eye.

THE SIX WIVES OF HENRY VIII ·

Spaniard. There is no other evidence for it:[5] as will be seen, the King and the King alone decided on the degree of his daughters. Queen Jane's role was to be that benevolent 'mother' to both princesses (the word stepmother was not used) which indeed she showed herself.

For the vexed subject of the succession had been temporarily settled in a satisfactory manner – to the King. The new act, passed by parliament in June, gave him extraordinarily wide powers. The future children of his latest marriage were, naturally, to be the heirs to the kingdom. Should however there be 'a lack of lawful heirs of your body', parliament empowered Henry VIII to 'give, dispose, appoint' the crown 'to such person or persons ... as shall please your Highness'. The King himself was to nominate the councillors who were to rule the kingdom, should he be succeeded by a minor. This second Act of Succession, replacing that of 1534, was never to be repealed or altered 'by any act heretofore made or hereafter to be had done.'[6]

This new act meant that Elizabeth as well as Mary was now illegitimate. But the relative positions of the two girls at this point were very different. With Mary's rehabilitation, the question of her marriage (she was now twenty) naturally loomed up again; with that, came the further question of her precise status. Given Mary's grand connections there was some talk of her being recognized as her father's heiress-presumptive until a son came along. Chapuys would of course have liked this, and Cromwell at least seemed to have dangled the prospect of the Lady Mary's claims being recognized after those of her father's 'lawful issue'. But Elizabeth, with no connections worth mentioning, for the time being simply shared in her mother's disgrace, since her marriageability – she was three on 7 September 1536 – could scarcely be regarded as a matter of urgency.

All this meant in effect that the King had both his daughters perfectly under his control. He could, if he wished, at any time ask parliament to remove the stain of bastardy, and he could even, if he wished, allow Mary, as the elder, the coveted position of heiress-presumptive. But he could not – would not – be 'directed or pressed' to do so, as he told Richard Pate Archdeacon of Lincoln in April 1537. If the conduct of his 'natural daughter' Mary continued to be satisfactory, 'we shall not only know her for our daughter, but use her besides in all things as to the degree of the daughter of so great a Prince'; but this elevation must come from 'the inclination of our own heart'.[7]

Under the circumstances the King, prompted by Queen Jane, was prepared to be extremely affable. Thus 'Madame Marie' was said by the French ambassador to be 'first [at court] after the Queen' in October 1536, and given the honour of presenting the napkin for washing to the King and Queen at the end of the state banquet (the Marchioness of

Exeter proffered the water). As for Elizabeth, the King was described as being 'very affectionate' towards his little 'Madame Ysabeau': the verdict of the court was that 'he loves her very much'.[8] And for all his refusal to grant his 'natural' children proper status, it was notable that the King allowed them to take precedence over their lawfully born cousins, the Ladies Frances and Eleanor Brandon, children of his dead sister. When all was said and done Mary and Elizabeth were still the daughters of 'so great a Prince' – himself. Thus the royal bets continued to be hedged.

Outside the court, however, there was a challenge to the royal will more difficult to control than a young woman or a little girl: rebellion in the north. If the King's domestic life was essentially restful from the summer of 1536 onwards, its tranquillity was in marked contrast to the tempestuous nature of the problems which faced him elsewhere. The Pilgrimage of Grace, as the multiple northern risings came to be known, was in essence a huge popular demonstration of disgust. It was a disgust which contained many different elements. There was for example the gathering indignation of the great northern lords, who found their historic independence threatened by Cromwell's new central (and southern) organization; some of these magnates, Lords Darcy, Hussey and Dacre, had been in touch with the imperialists for some time. Then there were people who were simply oppressed by Cromwell's novel taxes and disliked the King's new 'low-born' counsellors in consequence.

Above all there were those who deeply resented the religious changes also imposed from the centre, hated Archbishop Cranmer, loathed the new Bible, no matter what Queen it was dedicated to, and wanted their old customs back – including their old feast days, now being banned or discouraged, especially during harvest time (although the court continued to celebrate them). Yet even within these forces of religious conservatism, there were disparate elements; some wanting the authority of Rome restored, others accepting the royal supremacy and concentrating on the restoration of ancient practices.[9]

In particular the forcible dissolution of the monasteries by the King's commissioners, a highly visible operation affecting the whole structure of a community, provided a focus for such widespread discontent. But the King was quite cut off from such feelings. For one thing, he had never visited the north and for another he envisaged the dissolution in quite different terms as a means of getting prodigiously much richer – by lawful means. For parliament had recently passed an act dissolving all small religious houses with an annual income of less than £200 – quite apart from the wealthy abbeys and monasteries which would be suppressed over the next few years. So the King did benefit – to the tune of hundreds of thousands of pounds – and benefited even more when he proceeded to sell off the great abbeys to his courtiers (apart from making free grants to the favoured).

The news of a rising in Louth, in Lincolnshire, on 1 October 1536, which began with the seizure of two tax-collectors, and swelled to 30,000 people, was therefore greeted by the monarch with an explosion of disgust of his own. (The tax-collectors were put to death: one lucky fellow was hanged, but the other was sewn into a cowskin and given to dogs to devour.) Not only the mere fact of rebellion but the rebels' specific demands infuriated the King. These included the plea for different priests and more aristocratic counsellors to advise their sovereign.

On 10 October Henry issued an 'Answer to Petitions of Traitors and Rebels [in] Lincolnshire'. It began: 'considering choosing of counsellors, I never have read, heard nor known that princes' counsellors and prelates should be appointed by rude and ignorant common people; nor that they were persons meet, or of ability to discern and choose meet and sufficient counsellors for a prince.' Having carried on in this vein of mingled indignation and contempt, rejecting all demands, the King ended by adjuring the rebels to go away and sin no more, above all 'remember your duty of allegiance, and that ye are bound to obey us, your King, both by God's commandment and the law of nature'.[10]

But these majestic sentiments did not prove persuasive. On the contrary the rising spread like wildfire, including not only 'rude and ignorant common people' but gentlemen and even nobles who acted as their leaders. Robert Aske, a Yorkshire man who happened to be passing through Lincolnshire at the time of the first revolt, returned home and raised a huge body of 'pilgrims'. About 40,000 of them marched on York in what they termed 'our Pilgrimage of Grace* for the restitution of Christ's Church', singing and carrying banners of Christ crucified on one side and the communion chalice and wafer on the other. They entered the city on 16 October.

Afterwards there would be much dispute as to which of the nobles and gentry had freely joined the rebellion (as Lord Darcy was believed to have done) and which had merely done so under duress, fearing for themselves and their families, while secretly continuing to favour the government. This was the position of the northern magnate John Neville Lord Latimer, for example – or so he maintained. He had been taken hostage by Aske and forced to act as his mouthpiece beneath the very eyes of his children and third wife, a young woman twenty years his junior whose maiden name had been Catherine Parr. Latimer would argue that he had never intended

---

* The origin of the overall name given to the various different risings.

any disloyalty.[11] But at the time there was no doubt that the crisis was profound and that in the composite Pilgrimage of Grace, soon raging in almost all corners of the north, the King faced the sternest test of his reign so far. While the Duke of Suffolk and the Earl of Shrewsbury, at the King's orders, managed to restore order in Lincolnshire, they faced superior numbers in the north (Shrewsbury had only 7,000 men). In the meantime royal money was in short supply which meant that, in an age before a standing army, loyal forces were not easy to raise, while the slowness of sixteenth-century communications made it difficult for anything to take place at speed.

The King's personal indignation swelled. An answer to the Yorkshire rebels, dated 2 November 1536, was drawn up in his own hand.[12] Faith – and the King's own credentials as a theologian – were touched upon. He marvelled 'not a little that ignorant people will go about or take upon themselves to instruct us (which sometimes have been noted to be learned) what the right Faith should be'. How could they be 'so ungrateful and unnatural to us, their most rightful King?' As to the dissolution of the monasteries, once again he was amazed that his subjects should wish 'a churl or two' (by which he meant the monks) to enjoy the profits of the monasteries 'in support of vicious and abominable life' rather than their prince, in support of his 'extreme charges due for your defence'. But the rebellion continued.

Given the King's angry mood, he would have liked it to have been forcibly quelled. It was the practicalities of the situation, coupled with the advice of the Duke of Norfolk, entrusted with the pacifying of the north, which led to a less bellicose solution. He was persuaded to grant a general pardon to those north of Doncaster for all offences committed before 7 December 1536. The King did so reluctantly, attempting to exclude the ringleaders from pardon. But in the end, for the sake of a necessary peace, there were no exceptions.

It must have angered the King additionally that the fate of the monasteries produced a tiny temporary blot on the serene surface of his new marriage. The French ambassador heard that, at the beginning of 'the insurrection', Queen Jane had thrown herself on her knees before her husband and 'begged him to restore the abbeys'. But the King had not got rid of Anne Boleyn and married Jane Seymour to listen to these kinds of pleas. He told his wife to get up. 'He had often told her not to meddle with his affairs', he said, and made a pointed allusion to 'the late Queen' (Anne). As the French ambassador commented, writing on 24 October, that rebuke was enough to frighten a woman, 'who is not very secure'. In December the Bishop of Faenza gave what may well be another version of the same story.

Queen Jane had said to the King that 'perhaps God permitted this rebellion for ruining so many churches; to which he replied by telling her to attend to other things, reminding her that the last Queen had died in consequence of meddling too much in state affairs'.[13]

The incident (or incidents – although it is difficult to believe that any woman was foolish enough to try her luck twice in exactly the same way with Henry VIII) is however interesting. It provides confirmation of Queen Jane's own religious conservatism; she shared the feelings of the majority of her husband's subjects who preferred the old ways. In later years Jane Seymour would be regarded as a Protestant heroine, due to a false identification with other male members of her family who did become keen Protestants – an example of historical patriarchy, perhaps. But the evidence of her own time is quite clear: unlike Anne Boleyn she was not in any way 'Lutheran' but rather the reverse. Indeed Luther himself heard in September that the new Queen was 'an enemy of the gospel' as he put it.[14]

Furthermore the gossip of ambassadors and others is backed up by the suggestion that Queen Jane did attempt to prevent the suppression of at least one religious house. When the Prioress of the condemned Cistercian convent at Catesby wrote to Thomas Cromwell asking for his help, she reminded him that 'the Queen' had 'moved the King's majesty for me', i.e. pleaded with him, offering the King 'recompense' if the house at Catesby was spared. The Prioress wanted Cromwell's assistance 'that the Queen's grace may obtain her request that it [the convent] may stand.'[15]

In fact Catesby did not escape suppression: it vanished before the end of 1536, for all Queen Jane's pleading. Feminine lectures and admonitions had always sat uneasily on the King, even when he was young, as Queen Catherine had known and Queen Anne may have known but ignored. Anne Boleyn was the last woman the King would permit to speak challengingly to him with impunity. If he was to be troubled in any way, then he could either hint or point straight out to the fate of 'the late Queen'. Every queen following the execution of Anne Boleyn was on sufferance, with a dreadful penalty awaiting her if she failed the test; just as every queen was in another sense on sufferance following the casting-off of Catherine of Aragon, with the lesser penalty of divorce to be feared if she failed to meet the King's requirements.

At the same time Queen Jane was not expected to be a complete cipher. Nor should we regard her as such just because she was frightened of the King (as most people were by this time, and with good reason). One notes that the King's outburst referred to the fact that he had 'often' warned her against meddling; she had simply gone too far on this occasion and on a particularly sensitive matter. In May of the following year, Don Diego Hurtado de Mendoza arrived as a special envoy from Charles V, charged with negotiating a suitable marriage for Mary – Don Luis, heir to the throne of Portugal and brother of Charles V's wife Isabella, was being suggested. Chapuys, on leaving the King's presence, went on to present a warm letter addressed by the Emperor to the Queen. According to the ambassador, Queen Jane 'showed great pleasure, and said that she would always do her best to advance the Emperor's affairs and those of the Princess [Mary]'. She then told Chapuys that she had tried to persuade the King to abandon his old friendship with France and seek that of the Emperor 'that very night at supper.'[16]

Whether Queen Jane was being strictly truthful in her assurances to Chapuys we cannot know for sure: she may have been merely exercising the fine old art of diplomatic flattery (which shows that she had advanced from her bashfulness of twelve months previously). What is clear is that Queen Jane regarded it as normal to discuss political matters with her husband six months after the King's rebuke. For a woman to be married successfully to Henry VIII was to conduct an elaborate game of Grand-mother's Footsteps – with the King as a gigantic Grandmother. There could be cautious advances: but there must also be swift retreats at the sight of the terrifying royal frown.

Queen Jane Seymour understood the rules of the game. Was she not bound to obey and serve? And now, in the most vital way, she showed herself to be the perfect spouse. For early in January 1537, at the end of the New Year and Twelfth Night festivities at Greenwich – oh wondrous event! – King Henry succeeded in getting his third wife pregnant.

These inspirational celebrations were held in icy weather. The river Thames was frozen over, so that the ceremonial procession of boats from London to Greenwich for Christmas could not take place. Instead the King rode, from Westminster, with Queen Jane and his daughter Mary beside him, first to St Paul's, and then on to Greenwich itself. Abbots in rich copes incensed the head of the Anglican church and his wife as they passed. Queen Jane was unable to go to the funeral of her father, Sir John Seymour (who had died on 21 December) in view of this public commitment. But then the King was anxious to demonstrate that his regal authority was undiminished by recent insalubrious events in the north: he needed the royal family about him, as a symbol of security.

If the weather was unwontedly cold, another strange aspect of the Greenwich Christmas was the presence of the prominent rebel, Robert Aske, who was there at the invitation of the King. Aske was granted a safe conduct until 5 January by a monarch in a mellower mood, apparently convinced that Aske was truly repentant of his offences. And the seeming mellowness continued throughout the season, as King Henry outlined to

Aske gracious plans for a reconciliatory northern progress the following summer. Queen Jane, as yet uncrowned, might have her coronation in York Minster, for example. And Robert Aske believed his king. For that matter King Henry may well have believed himself.

It was not to be. New risings in the north in January under Sir Francis Bigod and Lord Conyers, unconnected with Aske, gave the excuse for a general policy of repression. Furthermore the King's anger and apprehension were fuelled by the behaviour of the Pope in seeking to support his malcontents with aid from abroad. The Pope had created the King's cousin Reginald Pole a cardinal of the church just before Christmas; now he despatched him as papal legate to François I in Paris and Maria of Hungary in Brussels to urge them to take action against Henry. But both rulers feared to drive England into the opposite camp by offending the King. Although King Henry was balked of his true aim of luring the Cardinal to England and punishing him there, Pole had to flee. He first took refuge with the neutral Bishop of Liège, then made his way by degrees (through Germany) back to the safety of the Holy City.

But there was no refuge for the rebels within England. By the end of February the King was issuing a cold-blooded order to the Duke of Norfolk, his lieutenant in the north, regarding 'Our pleasure' for that region. Norfolk was to cause 'dreadful execution' to be done upon a good number of inhabitants of every town, village and hamlet that had taken part in the rebellion. Very few of these had been active in rebellion after the general pardon of the previous December, but were executed on trumped-up pretexts for deeds done before this date. Some were to be hung up on trees; others were to be cut in quarters. 'The setting of their heads and quarters in every town, great and small ...' was to be 'a fearful spectacle to all other hereafter that would practise any like matter'. This was to be done without pity or discrimination. In this manner, 'the terror of this execution' would remain in 'the eye of their [the northern people's] remembrance' for ever more.[17]

So the north was left to stink – literally – of carnage and decay, while families and neighbours were left to contemplate – literally – the dreadful fate of those who had defied the King. In May the leading rebels were brought south to the Tower of London for trial. These included Aske, who had helped suppress the Bigod rising and whose subsequent guilt was highly doubtful, as well as Lords Darcy and Hussey. (Lord Latimer, however, husband of Catherine Parr, escaped for lack of evidence.) Aske was among those who were returned north after their condemnation, to be put to death on the site of their offence: so he was returned a prisoner in chains to York, the city which he had once entered a chanting pilgrim, and hanged on 28 June. But others were executed in London.

All this was in grim contrast to the happy progress of Queen Jane's pregnancy. (Those quails from Calais turned out to be a craving.) The comparison was indeed made by Wriothesley in his *Chronicle*. He wrote – without irony – of the streets reeking of death as the rebels were drawn from the Tower of Tyburn, and heads were nailed up on London Bridge and elsewhere, while at the same time a solemn *Te Deum* was being sung for the joy of the 'quickening' of the Queen's baby. The occasion called for bonfires to be lit all over the city; a hogshead of wine was set up at each fire, which the poor were allowed to drain to the last drop. 'I pray Jesu, and it be his will, send us a prince' was Wriothesley's predictable conclusion.[18]

The Queen's condition was made known in March, although she must have been aware of it in late February when she stood godmother to the son of her brother Edward Seymour Viscount Beauchamp and his second wife Anne Stanhope. Thanks to the irregularity in Edward Seymour's earlier marriage – he had disowned his offspring by his first wife, Katherine Fillol – this baby was actually the heir to the new Beauchamp title: it had been created at the time of his sister's wedding with special remainder 'to his male heirs born thereafter'.[19] The ceremony took place at Chester Place (the site of the modern Somerset House, named for a subsequent Seymour title), recently acquired from the Bishop of Chester. A further indication of the rise of the house of Seymour was the fact that besides the Queen, Cromwell and the King's daughter Mary acted as godparents.

Ever since his sister's marriage, Edward Seymour's ascent, that of the senior royal brother-in-law, had indeed been up a shining path. The day after his elevation to the peerage he had received the grant of numerous manors in Wiltshire and elsewhere, including Ambresbury and Easton Neston. Then he was made Captain of the Isle of Jersey, after that joint Chancellor of North Wales. The queen's pregnancy – the possibility of a future King – conferred a further blessing on her relatives who would also be the relatives of this putative sovereign. Edward Seymour was made a Privy Councillor on 22 May 1537. In August he was granted the land including the suppressed priory of Maiden Bradley in Wiltshire where the grant was valued at nearly £160 per year, but the fortunate recipient had only to pay the King rent of £16 – the statutory tenth.[20]

Edward was not the only Seymour to be honoured. Of his other surviving brothers, Henry preferred to live a quiet country life, but the handsome and high-spirited Thomas was made a gentleman of the Privy Chamber, following his sister's marriage. In October 1536 he received the stewardship of Chirk Castle and other border castles in Wales, and the next year the manor of Holt in Cheshire. Elizabeth Seymour, one of the Queen's younger sisters, completed the *galère* of Seymours who played a role at court: after the death of her first husband, she married (some time before 1538) Gregory Cromwell, son and heir of Thomas, Baron Cromwell since his elevation to the peerage in July 1536.

The news of the 'quickening' of the Queen's child was celebrated on Trinity Sunday, 27 May: that is, when she was roughly four and a half months pregnant, working the date backwards from that of her baby's birth. Some of the expressions of delight were positively biblical. The Convocation of Oxford University found three reasons to rejoice. First, God had given them a prince who had delivered them from the yoke of the Bishop of Rome; secondly, 'the rascals' raised up against him in the north by the Devil had been routed. 'The last and greatest benefit' lay in the fact that 'our most excellent lady and mistress Queen Jane, our noble and godly princess, King Henry the Eighth's wife, had conceived and is great with child, and upon Trinity Sunday ... like one given of God, the child quickeneth in the mother's womb'.[21]

The Duke of Norfolk, still in the north cleaning up after 'the rascals', sent his congratulations to the future father. In reply, on 12 June, the King took the opportunity to cancel that northern progress which he had outlined so expansively to Robert Aske at Christmas. The reason was the condition of 'our most dear and most entirely beloved wife, the Queen, now quick with child, for the which we give most humble thanks to Almighty God'. He had decided, and his Council agreed, to make a progress which never took him further than sixty miles away from her side, for fear that 'being a woman' she might take fright at 'some sudden and displeasant rumours and bruits that might by foolish or light persons be blown abroad in our absence'. The results might be damaging to her pregnancy 'which God forbid'. At the same time, King Henry, master in his own house, took pains to emphasize that this decision was his own, not his wife's. Queen Jane, he assured the Duke of Norfolk, was 'in every condition, of that loving inclination, and reverend conformity, that she can in all things well content, satisfy, and quiet herself with that thing which we shall think expedient and determine':[22] in other words, bound to obey and serve.

It might be cynical to suggest that the King, whose courage was never at its height when there was a threat to his own person, be it from disease or the discontented, welcomed such a valid excuse for avoiding the inhospitable north. After all, a great deal did depend on the 'prosperity' of the Queen's health 'both for our own quiet and for the commonwealth of our whole nation' as the King correctly pointed out to Norfolk. He even added that the Queen's pregnancy was a 'thing of that quality, as every good English man will think himself to have a part in the same': could royal generosity go further?

Nevertheless the fact that the King saw fit to mention Queen Jane's doubts about the actual date of her baby's birth – she might be a month or two further advanced than had been previously thought – does hint at his real reluctance to venture north. In the event the Queen had not mistaken her dates. Maybe she genuinely thought she had, maybe her ladies allowed her to believe so. New instructions issued for the Queen's coronation, to take place in the last week of October, with Knights of the Bath created on 21 October, suggest an earlier date of birth may indeed have been anticipated.[23] A third possibility is that the King simply decided to be anchored in the south by an imminent birth, and it would have been a brave female who would have contradicted him. 'Loving inclination, and reverend conformity' certainly dictated otherwise.

As in the case of those many bygone royal pregnancies, now officially erased from the popular imagination, everyone knew that the coming baby would be a boy. The Queen took to her chamber in late September. By October the people were said to 'look daily for a Prince'. As for the King, it has been suggested that Holbein's great Whitehall mural of three generations of the Tudor dynasty (surviving now only in a partial cartoon and later copies), with the initials H and I once again entwined in true lover's knots, may have been inspired by the impending birth of his heir.[24] The King even had a Garter stall made ready for his son in St George's Chapel, Windsor. Once again there were astrologers on hand to assure Queen Jane quite positively that the King's instinct was correct. Then on the afternoon of 9 October the Queen went into labour. She lay in the recently refurbished royal apartments at Hampton Court, where the leopards had been turned to panthers, and the falcons replaced with phoenixes.

Her ordeal was not quickly over – nor indeed was that of the expectant country. After two days, a solemn procession was mounted through the City 'to pray for the Queen that was then in labour of child'. Finally, at two o'clock in the morning the next day, 12 October, the child was born.[25] The prophets had got it right. The King would not have to dismantle his son's Garter stall; as he had had to cancel the tournament planned for 'the prince' expected to be born to Anne Boleyn four years earlier. It was a boy.

The child was named Edward, for his great-grandfather, but more especially because it was the eve of the Feast of St Edward. Antonio de Guaras heard that the King wept as he took his baby son in his arms.[26] It is a touching story and certainly believable: what better cause could Henry VIII, an emotional man, find for his tears? At the age of forty-six, he had achieved his dream. God had spoken and blessed this marriage with an heir male, nearly thirty years after he had first embarked on matrimony.

Despite the length of labour – two days and three nights – the baby was not delivered by Caesarean section, as was rumoured later. The operation had been known since ancient times, probably deriving its name from the Roman law *Lex Caesarea* concerning the burial of women who died while pregnant (not from the birth of Julius Caesar as sometimes suggested). But at this date there was still no question of a woman surviving it. It was employed solely for women dying in advanced pregnancy, in order to save the child: a Venetian law of 1608, for example, required it in such a situation. A tale of a Swiss pig-gelder, who was said to have carried out a Caesarean operation on his own wife in 1500, probably relates to an extra-uterine pregnancy, since the woman went on to have several more children by natural means; there is an authentic account of another operation of 1610, but the mother died of infection.[27]

The tradition that the operation was performed is preserved in a ballad, 'The Death of Queen Jane', found in a collection of ballads by nineteenth-century editors who heard it in 'the singing of a young gypsy'. Here the Queen herself demanded a surgeon after being 'in travail, for six weeks or more'. But she was already dead – or moribund – when the operation was performed:

> He gave her rich caudle
> But the death-sleep slept she
> Then her right side was opened
> And the babe was set free.
>
> The babe it was christened
> And put out and nursed
> While the royal Queen Jane
> She lay cold in the dust.

Another story had the King deliberately sacrificing the life of the Queen by ordering the baby to be cut free.[28]

Of this ruthlessness however King Henry was not guilty. For one thing, there is no reference to such an operation in the elaborate accounts of the prince's birth by officials. But what makes it quite clear that no such operation was performed is the fact that Queen Jane, far from sleeping 'the death-sleep', was alive and well enough after the birth to receive guests after the baby's christening three days later. Wrapped in velvet and fur, she was placed in the antechamber of the Hampton Court Chapel, where she carried out the consort's customary duty – as Elizabeth of York had done with Prince Arthur – until well after midnight.[29] This would have been inconceivable in a woman who had just had 'her right side . . . opened And the babe . . . set free'.

*

In the meantime the whole world, or so it seemed, went mad with joy. The *Te Deums*, the bonfires, the hogsheads flowing with wine in the direction of the ever-present poor to 'drink as long as they listed', the bells which sounded from morning till night from every church, the noise of the guns – 2,000 shot from the Tower – which drowned them, all this may be imagined. Then there were the ecstatic congratulations put forward by all parties; for not only 'every good English man' in the King's generous phrase felt himself involved in this wonderful result, but every good English woman. As the Dowager Marchioness of Dorset, exiled at Croydon owing to possible infection with the plague, explained: not only had it 'pleased God so to remember your Grace with a prince' but also 'us all, your poor subjects'. Bishop Hugh Latimer lost his head further: in referring to the event in a letter to Cromwell he started to make outright comparisons to the birth of St John the Baptist. 'Thanks to our Lord God, God of England', he went on, 'for verily he hath shown himself God of England, or rather an English God', before adding, ruefully, 'But what a great fool am I.'[30]

The Queen herself made the official announcement of the birth, according to tradition. This time, just as the tournament celebrating a son did not have to be cancelled, the wording which referred to 'a Prince' did not have to be altered. 'Jane the Quene' had been 'brought in childbed of a Prince conceived in most Lawful Matrimony between my lord the King's Majesty and us.' The circular letter was sealed in the margin by the Queen's signet, in which the royal arms of France and England impaled the six quarterings of Seymour under a crown.[31]

The christening, on 15 October, was sumptuous. In the absence of the Marchioness of Dorset at Croydon, Gertrude Marchioness of Exeter carried the baby, assisted with her precious burden by her husband and the Duke of Suffolk. The train of his robe was borne up by the Earl of Arundel, Norfolk's son. Among the gentlemen of the Privy Chamber holding up the canopy over the baby's head was his uncle, Thomas Seymour. Edward Seymour, however, had a more weighty duty: he carried the Prince's four-year-old half-sister Elizabeth, on account of 'her tender age'.[32] As for Mary, she acted as godmother to the child who had at last supplanted her – even in the eyes of her most devoted adherents – as the heir to the English throne.

On 18 October, the baby was proclaimed Prince of Wales, Duke of Cornwall and Earl of Carnarvon.[33] On the same day, the yet-further-enhanced prospects of the Seymour family were recognized. Edward Seymour Viscount Beauchamp was created Earl of Hertford, with the same proviso in favour of the sons of his second marriage as before. The King granted him lands worth over £600 a year – compared to the £450 a year he had inherited from his father. Thomas Seymour was knighted, and would subsequently receive grants of Coggeshall in Essex and Romsey in Hampshire.

Only the sister who had made all this possible failed to flourish. About the same time as her brothers' elevation, Queen Jane fell ill of puerperal fever. This 'child-bed fever', if it turned to septicaemia, was the great cause of maternal mortality before the nature of hygiene and the course of infection were properly understood. For a time she struggled, and on the afternoon of 23 October was reported by her chamberlain Lord Rutland to be slightly better thanks to 'a natural laxe'. But the rally did not last. Septicaemia did set in and with it delirium: Cromwell referred afterwards to the Queen's 'fantasy in her sickness', blaming her condition on those who allowed her to have the wrong things to eat or who let her take cold.[34] But for Queen Jane (and for myriads of other women including the King's mother Elizabeth of York who had died in a similar manner) her fate was inevitable, whatever the treatment.

By eight o'clock on the morning of 24 October, the Queen, who had been 'very sick' all night, was failing; her confessor was sent for, and the sacrament of extreme unction prepared. Cromwell was informed by Sir John Russell from Hampton Court that the King had intended to go on a hunting trip to Esher that day but had put it off. Nevertheless he would go to Esher on the morrow: 'If she amend, he will go; and if she amend not, he told me this day, he could not find it in his heart to tarry'. There is a dreadful disbelieving weariness about the report. The Duke of Norfolk for his part urged Cromwell to come down to Hampton Court next day 'to comfort our good master, for as for our mistress, there is no likelihood of her life'. Indeed, he doubted whether the Queen would still be alive when Cromwell read the letter of his 'sorrowful friend, T. Norfolk', written at eight o'clock at night.[35]

Norfolk was right. Queen Jane died before midnight on 24 October, just twelve days after the birth of her son. She was twenty-eight years old and had been Queen of England for less than eighteen months. The same churches which had celebrated the birth with such enthusiasm were now draped in black. Sad and solemn Masses for the repose of 'the soul of our most gracious Queen' replaced the jubilant *Te Deums*. As King Henry told the King of France who was congratulating him on the birth of his son: 'Divine Providence has mingled my joy with the bitterness of death of her who brought me this happiness.'[36]

The burial of Queen Jane was planned for 12 November. Well before this date, the question of a new Queen had already been discussed. Cromwell in fact used a single letter to Lord William Howard, the English ambassador in France, to break the happy news of the prince's birth ('in good health and sucketh like a child of his puissance'), the tragic news of the Queen's death ('departed to God' – he blamed her attendants), and the interesting news that the King must once more be regarded as in need of a wife ('his Council have prevailed on him for the sake of the realm'). In a business-like manner Cromwell then proceeded to review the possibility of a French princess – yet again. There was for example Madame Marguerite, the King's daughter, or Marie de Guise, widow of the Duc de Longueville, 'whom they say the King of Scots doth desire' . . .[37]

This does not mean that the King's own grief was not sincere. 'Of none in the realm was it [the Queen's death] more heavily taken than of the King', wrote Edward Hall in his *Chronicle* and that was surely true.[38] His only rivals in mourning would have been his daughter Mary who became 'accrazed' (mad) with sorrow following the death of her beloved step-mother and of course the Queen's family, whose sadness must have been tinged with worldly disappointment. Everything points to the fact that Henry VIII mourned Jane Seymour with a genuine sense of loss, the 'entirely beloved' wife who had presented him with his heart's desire, at the cost of her own life.

Others, like Dean Aldrich, the Registrar of the Order of the Garter, might talk of Queen Jane's triumph: *'Mater in caelo gaudeat'* – Let the mother in heaven rejoice – as she looks down on the son she has left below. The homily of Sir Richard Morysine on the subject was even more outspoken: he talked of 'comfortable consolation, wherein the People may see how far greater causes they have to be glad after the joyful birth of Prince Edward than sorry for the death of Queen Jane'. But King Henry was left with a permanent sentimental recollection of a pale and pliant young woman who had been the perfect wife. He would remember her for the rest of his life, continuing nostalgically to visit her family home at Wolf Hall where their romance had begun. In his last testament Jane Seymour was enshrined as his 'true and loving wife'.[39]

King Henry left the arrangements for Queen Jane's burial, according to the custom, to the Duke of Norfolk as Earl Marshal and Sir William Paulet as Treasurer of the Household.[40] The King himself 'retired to a solitary place to see to his sorrows'. The functionaries had to send for Garter Herald 'to study precedents', since although there was a certain experience in burying former Queens recently, a 'good and lawful' Queen had not been interred since Elizabeth of York nearly thirty-five years previously.

First the wax chandler 'did his office' of embalming, then the Queen's corpse was 'leaded, soldered and chested' by the plumbers. After that, ladies and gentlemen in mourning, with white kerchiefs hanging over their heads and shoulders, kept a perpetual watch around the royal hearse in 'a chamber of presence' lit by twenty-one wax tapers until 31 October, the Vigil of the Feast of All Saints, when the entire Hampton Court Chapel and the great chamber and galleries leading to it were hung with black and 'garnished with rich images'. The hearse, after being incensed, was then processed by torchlight to the chapel itself where Lancaster Herald, in a loud voice, asked all present 'Of their charity' to pray for the soul of Queen Jane.

After that priests watched in the chapel by night and the Queen's ladies by day until 12 November when the hearse was taken in solemn procession to Windsor, borne on a chariot drawn by six horses, and accompanied by nobles and heralds with banners. 'The Lady Mary' had sufficiently recovered from her first grief which had prostrated her to play the role of chief mourner, and rode at the head of the procession on a horse with black velvet trappings. The poor who watched the hearse pass were presented with alms; at Eton College the Provost and boys saluted it 'with caps and tapers in their hands'. The coffin was accordingly installed within St George's Chapel and the next day solemnly buried in a vault beneath the centre of the choir: 'and all finished by twelve o'clock that day.'

A magnificent monument was now planned for the grave which the King intended to share with Queen Jane in the fullness of time: there was to be a statue of the Queen reclining as if in sleep, not death, and children were to sit at the corners of the tomb, with baskets from which red and white roses, worked in jasper, cornelian and agate, enamelled and gilded, would scatter forth. The late Queen's own jewels including beads, pomanders and 'tablets' were distributed among her step-daughters and the ladies of the court (Mary was a principal beneficiary). Chains and brooches of gold went to the Queen's brothers, Thomas and Henry Seymour. Queen Jane's jointure and dowry, however, went back into the King's hands.

How long would it be before the Council, if not the King, found another use for them? King Henry kept Christmas of 1537 at Greenwich in 'mourning apparel': he did not in fact leave off his black until the day after Candlemas, 3 February 1538.[41] By this time Cromwell's business-like enquiries about French princesses immediately after the Queen's death had turned into a hunt on an international scale for a new woman to share the English King's marriage bed.

John Hutton, ambassador in the Netherlands, was one of those ordered to draw up a list. He did so groaning as he told Cromwell: 'I have not much experience among ladies, and therefore this commission to me is hard'.[42] Those proposed ranged from a fourteen-year-old girl waiting on the French Queen 'of a goodly stature', to the widow of the late Count of Egmont who was described as being over forty but not looking it. The presumed fertility of both ladies was extremely important ('goodly stature' was thought to indicate 'aptness to procreate children', and a continuing appearance of youth was another helpful sign). This was because the Council, quite as much if not more than they wanted a new Queen, wanted 'a Duke of York', that is, a second son for the King. Prince Edward, pale like his mother, was not a particularly robust baby; and in any case experience showed that two sons was really the minimum needed to keep a monarch secure about his succession.

Hutton particularly commended the sixteen-year-old Duchess Christina of Milan: 'an excellent beauty', tall for her age, with 'a good personage of body'. The daughter of Christian II of Denmark and Charles V's sister Isabella, Christina had been married at thirteen to the Duke of Milan and widowed without children a year later. She was in fact the great-niece of Catherine of Aragon, but such difficulties as affinities were the last thing on King Henry's mind when he heard about the delicious Christina. With her pretty smiling face and her dimples, two in her cheeks and one in her chin 'which become her rightly well', she was said to resemble Madge Skelton. The young Duchess now lived in the Netherlands at the court of her aunt, the Regent Maria of Hungary. The King's excitement grew. Would it be possible to get her portrait? And he would like to know more of the current crop of French princesses . . .

Hutton also mentioned a certain 'Anna of Cleves', daughter of the ruler of that country, a dukedom on the edges of France and the Netherlands whose main significance derived from its strategic position. But Hutton added, 'I hear no great praise neither of her parentage nor her beauty'. Naturally the King felt no particular excitement on that score.

Part IV

ANNA of CLEVES
and
KATHERINE
HOWARD

Chapter 14

AN UNENDURABLE

BARGAIN

His Grace, prudently considering how that marriage is
a bargain of such nature as must endure for the whole
of life of man, and a thing whereof the pleasure and
quiet, or the displeasure and torment of the man's
mind doth much depend ...

Message from Henry VIII, 1538

The quest for a new Queen of England began in earnest at the beginning of 1538. There were three ways of looking at it. On a purely domestic level, the English court, having enjoyed the continuous presence of a consort at the King's side since 1509, suddenly felt the lack. It was not so much that maids wanted a mistress who would criticize their dress, more that everyone wished for the existence of a Queen's household in which maids (and others more senior) could find remunerative places. The numbers of people employed in this manner had after all been impressive in the past: Catherine of Aragon had begun with 160 people, Anne Boleyn with nearly 200 and Jane Seymour not many fewer. Now chamberlain and cook equally lost their livelihood. When Mistress Anne Basset (she of the saucy French hoods) wrote to her mother in Calais, 'I trust to God that we shall have a mistress shortly', she spoke for the whole court.[1]

Secondly, there was the diplomatic angle. Cromwell, acting in his master's best interests, saw in the quest a heaven-sent opportunity to forge some new European alliance. The moment was certainly propitious for it, from England's point of view. Signs that the feuding between François I and Charles V – always the best security for England – might draw to an end brought with them the corresponding threat of English isolation. The aggressive policies of Pope Paul III, he who had created Reginald Pole a Cardinal and sent the money for the succour of the northern rebels, were only likely to be encouraged by any such Franco-imperial truce. Under the circumstances, marriage – or at least marriage negotiations – with one side or the other would serve to keep England in the game.

Thirdly, there was King Henry's own need for a helpmate – and bedmate. Paradoxically, the King in his late forties, gross, no likely object of desire, was far more difficult to please than that handsome boy of 1509, ready to fall in love where policy directed him, whom any girl might easily love in return. In the selection of a wife, as in so many other matters, Henry VIII had grown used to having his own way. He had chosen two out of his three wives himself, and for romantic reasons. This was unusual and set him apart from his contemporaries: Charles V's marriage to his cousin Isabella of Portugal had been dictated by policy, and François I had married twice, his predecessor Louis XII's daughter and the Emperor's sister, out of the same considerations.

The previous exercise of choice also set the King apart in the assumptions he was likely to make about any new bride. In 1538 Henry VIII wanted – no, he *expected* – to be diverted, entertained and excited. It would be the responsibility of his wife to see that he felt like playing the cavalier and indulging in such amorous gallantries as had amused him in the past. (How else was the conception of 'a Duke of York' – another responsibility of the wife – to be ensured?) At the same time the King allowed his ambassadors to proceed in the time-honoured manner with the ritual inspection of suitable candidates, not seeing that there might be some innate contradiction between the demands of diplomacy and those of a romantic but by now deeply self-indulgent nature.

There is a further point to be made. As a husband, the King of England did not have an altogether savoury reputation in Europe at this time. A later age may perhaps wonder what all the fuss was about in the late 1530s: the King had after all merely divorced one aging wife amid international protest, married his mistress, her lady-in-waiting, had her head chopped off for adultery, married *her* lady-in-waiting ... In short, only half the folk rhyme had been achieved: 'Divorced, beheaded, died'. This of course is with the benefit of hindsight. The execution of Queen Anne Boleyn had left a worrying impression upon those very royalties who, related to Catherine of Aragon, had deplored the marriage. Jokes about the King's marital career were already current as he sought a fourth wife. Even if the young Duchess Christina of Milan did not actually remark that if she had two necks, the King should have one of them, the wisecrack was a significant piece of contemporary myth-making.[2]

Returning to the international scene, at first the basic choice for Henry VIII seemed to be the same as had faced his father when designing a marriage for his heir half a century before: France or Spain (now enlarged to the Empire). Where France was concerned, Europe happened to be rich in princesses who would be regarded for diplomatic purposes as representing a French alliance. There was the French King's surviving daughter, fifteen-year-old Marguerite de Valois. (Her sister, Madeleine, briefly married to James V of Scotland, had died of tuberculosis in June 1537). Of the French King's cousins, Marie de Guise was rumoured to be betrothed to James V as a substitute for Madeleine, but she had two younger sisters, Louise and Renée de Guise. Two further cousins of François I, Marie de Vendôme and Anne of Lorraine were also available.

King Henry was not immediately disposed to accept the fact that Marie de Guise, a tall striking young widow who had already produced a son, was in truth debarred to him. 'Would you have another man's wife?' enquired the French ambassador. But Marie de Guise's betrothal to his nephew – twenty years the King's junior – merely added a certain spice to Henry VIII's interest. So did reports of her voluptuous figure. He himself was 'big in person', said the King, and had need of 'a big wife'. In short, how could this splendid creature prefer 'the beggarly and stupid King of Scots'?[3] To this Marie de Guise was supposed to have replied that she might be a big woman, but she had a very little neck: either her own joke, or another significant piece of contemporary folklore.

In any case, the Scots did not linger over the betrothal: Marie de Guise set sail for her new country and was married to James V on 9 May 1538. The English King was left hopefully suggesting that some kind of parade of the remaining French princesses should be organized for him at Calais. This encouraged Castillon, the French ambassador, to indulge in some saucy Gallic badinage. If the ladies were to be paraded like ponies, would not the King like to go further and mount them one after the other, retaining for himself the best ride? At this point, even King Henry had the grace to laugh and blush.[4]

There were in fact two conventional methods of selecting an eligible princess, and neither of them involved a parade in front of the potential bridegroom. One was a personal visit of inspection by a trusted envoy, either the ambassador on the spot or someone specifically entrusted with this delicate task. The other method was complementary: it consisted of commissioning a special portrait in order to check up on the diplomatic reports. This was a practice of long standing: when Henry VI, for example, was interested in the daughter of the Count of Armagnac, he sent his own artist to her father's court.[5] Sometimes the mission was secret: at the end of the fourteenth century Charles VI of France, hearing of the beauty of Egidia, daughter of Robert II of Scotland, despatched his painter privately, only to find that she had married before he arrived; after which the French King sent 'a most expert painter' to various European courts as a result of which he chose Isabella of Bavaria, and married her. Although it was generally the men who received the pictures of the ladies, Charles V's sister, Isabella of Austria (mother of Duchess Christina), had been shown a portrait of Christian II of Denmark before she left the Netherlands to marry him.

In this way Hans Holbein, as King's painter, was in for a busy time in 1538, much as the King's glazier Galyon Hone had been busy in 1536. Holbein's first task was however to depict not a French princess but the most suitable candidate from the imperial side: the sixteen-year-old Duchess of Milan. From a worldly point of view, she had many advantages, quite apart from her all-important status as the niece of Charles V. There was the question of her dowry, what she would derive from the duchy of Milan; while with her sister she had further possible rights involving her father's Danish kingdom (from which he had been ejected). But once again what the King really hankered after was an opportunity for a personal inspection at Calais.

His envoy Sir Thomas Wyatt was told his views on the subject: 'His Grace, prudently considering how that marriage is a bargain of such nature as must endure for the whole life of man, and a thing whereof the pleasure and quiet, or the displeasure and torment of the man's mind doth much depend.' (On that score, Henry VIII could certainly already claim to speak from experience.) Under the circumstances, was it not common sense for the pair actually to meet? They could then, if necessary, without 'dishonour or further inconvenience' break off the alliance.[6] The imperial court was however no more disposed to ignore the conventions in this matter than the French had been. So the King had to trust to portraiture – although in view of what was to come, one cannot help feeling real sympathy for his prescient if clumsy attempts to play the Doubting Henry and trust only to the evidence of his own senses.

The imperial court despatched its own picture. But by tradition, the enquiring country always preferred to place its trust in its own artist who had no motive to err on the side of flattery. So before the first picture had been received, Holbein had already set off for Brussels with the King's special envoy Sir Philip Hoby. On 12 March the Duchess stood for Holbein from one o'clock to four o'clock in the afternoon. Despite the limitations of 'but three hours space', the English ambassador John Hutton was enthusiastic about the results: Holbein had shown himself to be 'the master of that science [drawing] for it is very perfect'. Compared to Holbein's work, indeed, that of the Netherlands artist was 'slobbered' (slapdash) and Hutton sent a servant to intercept it before it reached London. Holbein was back in London with his own drawing by 18 March.[7]

King Henry was enraptured. Holbein's picture 'singularly pleased' him, confirming as it did the lively description of Christina, smiles, dimples and all, that he had already received. He had also heard of her tastes – she loved hunting for example. Then there was her 'modesty' (shades of Jane Seymour!). Of course, that could be due to 'simple ignorance' which would be a pity, but on the other hand it could be a proof of her natural wisdom; and from her card-playing, Christina was to be rated 'very wise'. Her height – gratifying to a man who had been denied the splendid Marie de Guise – was constantly stressed. (She towered over the English envoys, as they admiringly reported.) Against this, Christina's only possible physical disadvantage – a slight sallowness of complexion which was 'a little brown' – scarcely seemed to matter.[8]

The court had been a gloomy place since the death of Queen Jane, and in mid-March it had not been much more than a month out of mourning. Now the King was reportedly 'in a much better humour than he ever was, making musicians play on their instruments all day long.' Chapuys also noted that there had been numerous masques ever since: 'a sign that he proposes to marry again'. In her dark widow's dress, with her dignified air belied by a mischievous curling mouth, the Duchess looked as if she might combine the royal graciousness of Catherine of Aragon with the liveliness of the young Anne Boleyn. The King immediately commissioned a full-length portrait in oils from Holbein.* And on hearing that Christina was being mooted as a wife for William, young heir to the Duke of Cleves, King Henry wrote off indignantly to Sir Thomas Wyatt in Brussels. After all, 'it might perchance come to pass' that *he* might decide to honour 'the said Duchess by marriage, her virtues, qualities and behaviour being reported to be such as is worthy to be much advanced.'[9]

Negotiations for the King's union with this paragon were however maddeningly protracted. What was now envisaged was a double yoking of the King to the Emperor's niece, and his daughter Mary to the Emperor's brother-in-law, Don Luis of Portugal. But the Spanish commissioners who arrived in London in February to bring all this about were a disappointment: the King referred bitterly to their 'gay words' which concealed a lack of any real authority. As the usual wrangling went

---

* The resulting picture is now in the National Portrait Gallery, London, where the Duchess is described as Christina of Denmark (her country of origin); looking at it today, one can still appreciate the King's delight.

on about dowries and jointures, the King boasted of the future he could provide for his new family. Although he already had an heir, he intended to provide dukedoms for 'our younger sons': the titles of York, Gloucester and Somerset were mentioned.[10] Yet by June, the arrival of such a string of baby dukes seemed as far away as ever. The King, his Council and his various envoys were beginning to make statements such as 'time lost cannot be recovered', which amounted to the obvious fact that the royal bridegroom was not getting any younger . . .

These languid imperialist overtures raise doubts as to whether the Emperor ever really intended the marriage to go through. It was true that there was a genuine problem of affinity – at any rate from the imperialist point of view, since Christina was 'near kinswoman' (great-niece) to the woman they considered to have been King Henry's wife, Catherine of Aragon. Yet King Ferrante of Naples, in 1496, had been given a dispensation to marry his own father's sister, something specifically forbidden by Leviticus (and they were actually linked by blood not marriage).[11] It will be remembered that more recently King Manuel of Portugal had married the niece of his first two wives (who had been sisters). As has been noted, such things could be overcome when both parties desired to do so.

It seems likely therefore that the Emperor's true intention was to scupper the French negotiations, which were of course similarly proceeding, rather than to marry off his niece and thus formally favour England. In June Holbein and Hoby set off again to the continent to paint Madame Marguerite, daughter of François I, and another princess, possible Marie de Vendôme. The travellers were back again in August, to capture Renée and Louise de Guise at Joinville (the King had been encouraged by the French ambassador to believe that these two were even lovelier than their eldest sister Marie, now Queen of Scotland, although Renée was actually designated to be a nun). After that it was on to Nancy to draw Anne of Lorraine. The unofficial nature of such expeditions was underlined by the fact that Renée was absent, and Louise in bed with a fever – although a drawing was still undertaken. The Duchesse Antoinette de Guise wrote a report of the various visits to her daughter Marie in Scotland: 'If the worst comes to the worst, if you do not have your sister for a neighbour, it may well be your cousin'[12] (Anne of Lorraine).

Holbein had wasted his French journeys. Marie de Vendôme died in September; Anne of Lorraine married the Prince of Orange in 1540 and Louise de Guise the Prince de Chimaix in 1541; Renée de Guise went on to become the Abbess of St Pierre de Reims. In any case the King's real desire – to 'honour the said Duchess' Christina by marriage – remained undiminished. He was however about to receive a singular check to his hopes, both personally and publicly.

On 17 June 1538 the Emperor Charles V and King François I declared a ten-year truce at Nice, through the mediation of Pope Paul III. The feasting which followed, at a summit meeting at Aiguesmortes, was seen by the Pope as a celebration of Christian unity against the encroaching Turks. For Charles V it represented an unpleasant necessity: a series of unsuccessful imperial campaigns, contrasted with French successes, all in the shadow of the Turkish threat to Italy, made such a peace essential to his security. For Henry VIII however, the spectacle of his brother kings feasting together in new amity symbolized the dangerous isolation of England. The marriage negotiations at Brussels continued: but it would be an optimist who really expected them to succeed. The following February Wriothesley was received by the delightful Duchess, admiring her red lips and pink cheeks in her 'marvellous good brownish face' as well as her wisdom and her wit. He was permitted by her aunt, the Regent, to ask Christina directly whether she was 'minded' to marry his master – he had heard to the contrary. But the Duchess firmly denied expressing any such opinion. '"As for my inclination", quoth she, "what should I say? You know that I am at the Emperor's commandment"'. And she repeated the words.[13] They were certainly true enough.

At this point it may be felt that Wriothesley pushed his luck. For he told the Duchess that if she were matched to his master, 'you shall be matched with the most gentle Gentleman that liveth; his nature so benign and pleasant, that I think till this day no man hath heard many angry words pass his mouth'. At this Duchess Christina smiled, and according to Wriothesley, might even have laughed but for the needs of dignity: she behaved 'like one (methought) that was tickled'. And so in a sense the sixteen-year-old girl may have been.

In the summer of 1538, the threat to English security was a real one.[14] The Pope's success in uniting France and Spain gave him the confidence to propose more public action against a country which had defied his authority. The bull of excommunication of 1535 had been issued but not executed. Now the Pope considered issuing a bull of deposition against King Henry; Cardinal Pole was sent as papal legate to Spain in order to encourage the Emperor to invade England and bring the country into the fold of the Catholic church once more. As for Scotland – ever a worrying neighbour in times of England's trouble – the Pope ostentatiously made the Scot David Beaton a cardinal, just as he had elevated the Englishman Reginald Pole two years previously.

There was little for the Pope's comfort regarding religious affairs in

England. Shrines and cathedrals were being pillaged of their treasures: an emerald cross was taken from Winchester and three caskets of jewels from Chichester. Most painful of all was the news that the famous shrine of St Thomas à Becket at Canterbury had been looted in September: chests of jewels were carried away so heavy that 'six or eight strong men' were needed to lug one box, and twenty carts to carry them away.[15] (The cult of St Thomas was hardly one that Henry VIII was likely to endorse, with comparisons between his own behaviour and that of Henry II too close for comfort.) On 17 December, the Pope would proclaim that the bull of excommunication originally issued in 1535 should now be put into effect.

Meanwhile the mood of the King of England was increasingly paranoid; given his hereditary preoccupation with the subject of the Tudor dynasty, it was hardly surprising that his paranoia took the form of a many-pronged attack on his cousins of royal blood living in England: the Courtenay family headed by the Marquess of Exeter, the Poles headed by Lord Montague. (See family tree 2) If he could not silence the egregious Cardinal Reginald Pole, author of that damnable book *Pro Ecclesiasticae Unitatis Defensione*, emissary of the Pope to England's enemies, he could at least see that his relations suffered. As for Thomas, Baron Cromwell, with his cold, wary eyes fixed on any potentially over-powerful group at court, the fall of such rivals was welcome. Alleged plotters among the courtiers also suffered, including Sir Nicholas Carew, he who had once pandered to the King and protected his sweetheart Jane Seymour.

Sir Geoffrey Pole, second son of Margaret Countess of Salisbury, was arrested in August 1538 and taken to the Tower. There, like many another terrified prisoner, he babbled away. The matter of what Sir Geoffrey repeated was not in itself particularly damning, but given the King's determination to destroy the family which menaced him (or so he told the French ambassador) it was enough to secure the arrest of his eldest brother Lord Montague, and the Marquess of Exeter.[16] Women and children came next. Gertrude Marchioness of Exeter and her twelve-year-old son, Edward Courtenay Earl of Devon, were taken to the Tower in November. Lord Montague's little boy was also arrested – in his case he vanished into the Tower's maw, for he never emerged from it, dying at some unrecorded point a few years later.

The most shocking arrest was that of Margaret Countess of Salisbury. Now 'aged and feeble', here was a lady whom the King had 'once venerated no less than his own mother' for the piety 'in which she had grown old'. These words would be written later by her son the Cardinal. The Countess of Salisbury had in fact written letters specifically denouncing his book but once again servants' gossip was dredged up to justify her interrogation. Aged she might be, but it turned out that even now the Countess of

Salisbury was not exactly feeble. She endured long, relentless, brutal examinations, sometimes all day, yet her interrogators were obliged to report: 'though we used her diversely' (a sinister phrase) 'she protested her innocence'. They were minded to pay her that ultimate compliment once given to Catherine of Aragon in a similarly desperate situation: 'we may call her rather a strong and constant man than a woman'.[17]

It is highly unlikely that the Countess was guilty of conspiracy. It was true that in religion she clung to the old ways – she was rumoured to have forbidden her servants to read the New Testament in English[18] – but that was hardly a crime in someone who, having been twelve years old at the Battle of Bosworth Field, was in fact a mediaeval survivor. Way beyond childbearing age, she constituted no threat in herself to the King. As the Cardinal wrote, the real crime of this 'most innocent woman' was to be 'allied to him in blood'. For the time being the Countess was kept under house arrest, and transferred the following year to the Tower of London.

As for Exeter, Cromwell would later assure the French ambassador that he had planned to marry the young Earl of Devon (his heir) to Mary, kill Prince Edward and thus 'usurp the kingdom'. Of such a lethal and well-thought out plan, no evidence was ever produced. Instead, there were reported remarks such as these from Exeter: 'I like well the proceeding of Cardinal Pole' (in July 1536), or (said to Montague), 'I trust to see a merry world one day'. Exeter was supposed to have been 'melancholy' on the birth of Prince Edward. Montague too was alleged to have accused Lord Darcy at the time of the Pilgrimage of Grace of acting like a fool; he should 'first have begun with the head', i.e. attacked the King.[19] Nevertheless, despite the lack of proper evidence, both men, Exeter and Montague, were found guilty and executed on 9 December 1538.

Their real crime was of course to stand too close to the trunk of the English royal family tree. Montague in addition was tainted by his brother's conduct. At the same time, the threat represented by Exeter, the King's first cousin, was not entirely imaginary. His power base in Devon and Cornwall in particular made him potentially dangerous if that Catholic invasion urged by the Pope ever materialized. Exeter was a man of substance, a grandee, that adult male of authority ever preferred on the throne to a delicate baby. If Exeter never planned to 'usurp the kingdom' in the lifetime of King Henry, talk of what would happen after the King's death was another matter. As the King approached fifty, and his health (and weight) gave cause for concern, such discussions – discreet or otherwise – were inevitable. All this inspired King Henry and Thomas Cromwell to see the value of what has been described as a 'pre-emptive strike' against these royal relations, the sort of men (and apparently women too) that the King had been educated since boyhood to fear.[20]

It was in this hysterical atmosphere of judicial deaths at home and fear of invasion from abroad that Cromwell decided to resurrect a matrimonial project for his master that had previously attracted little real enthusiasm. Dreams of the lovely Christina on one level and the imperial alliance on another had distracted attention from the possible suitability of the duchy of Cleves to provide the new Queen. If anything, it had been the ruling family of Cleves who made the running: in 1530, for example, Duke John III, known as 'the Pacific', had proposed a marriage between his son and Mary; in 1532 his chamberlain had visited the English court. The existence of some unmarried daughters in the dukedom meant that their names had been mentioned in the flurry after the death of Queen Jane; although Ambassador Hutton's slighting comments on Anna of Cleves' 'parentage' and her 'beauty' will be recalled. In June 1538 a double marriage of Mary to William, heir to the dukedom of Cleves, and King Henry to some unspecified relation was briefly floated.

Now, at the beginning of 1539, as the King reviewed troops in London – over 16,000 men marched by him as he stood at the gatehouse of Whitehall – Cromwell considered that the Cleves marriage might be an idea whose time had come. And lo and behold! such were the magic properties of diplomatic need, that the Lady Anna of Cleves was suddenly found to be the acme of nobility and even loveliness. For at least one person involved, it was to prove a fatal transformation scene.

Cleves belonged to the intricate world of the Lower Rhine: a maze of duchies, electorates and bishoprics at first sight far removed from the great game being played out elsewhere between mightier powers. There had been Counts of Cleves since the eleventh century;* a romantic legend told of the knight who had appeared to the heroes of Cleves in a boat guided by swans – hence the family's later use of the swan device; they were transformed into dukes at the beginning of the fifteenth century under the ruling family of Mark. Then Duke John III of Cleves-Mark's marriage to Maria, heiress to the nearby duchies of Jülich and Berg, brought all these territories together in 1521, with Düsseldorf as their capital.[21]

Four children were born to the ducal couple. Anna, born on 22 September 1515, was the second, three years younger than Sybilla; after Anna, in July 1516, came William; lastly Amelia, born in 1517. The ancestry of Anna of Cleves was certainly not undistinguished. She could claim English royal descent on her father's side from Edward I and his first wife Eleanor of Castile, whose daughter Margaret had married the Duke of Brabant. But despite her drop of English blood, the names in her family tree recalled

---

* The name is preserved today in the town, Kleve, fourteen kilometres south of the modern Dutch border, in the German state of North Rhine-Westphalia.

in the main the geographical area in which Anna of Cleves had been brought up: from her mother the line of German princesses stretched back to Sybilla of Brandenberg, Sophia of Saxony and Adelaide of Teck. Such lineage, if not particularly impressive to the English, did at least recall one popular queen – Philippa of Hainault, consort of Edward III, who had pleaded mercy for the burghers at Calais in 1347.

The next step in the territorial aggrandizement of Cleves came in the summer of 1538 when Duke John's heir William was recognized by the inhabitants of Guelderland as their new Duke, taking his claim from his Jülich-Berg mother. This succession was however a controversial subject, especially since Guelderland provided vital access to the Zuyder Zee seaboard. If William was successful in maintaining his position, the house of Cleves now looked like controlling a strategic portion of the Lower Rhineland: the inland duchies of Jülich, Berg and Cleves and now Guelderland with its coastline as well. The development of this bloc was naturally most unwelcome to Charles V in his role as a Netherlands territorial prince.

It was however the interplay of religion, territory and revolt which made Cleves not so much a provincial threat to Charles as a potentially exciting ally for England: this was what Cromwell had grasped. The autumn of 1530 had seen the foundation of a League of 'all Protestant princes and free cities' headed by Johann Frederick 'the Lion-hearted' of Saxony and Philip 'the Good' of Hesse, and the Treaty of the Schmalkaldic Alliance, including seven princes and eleven cities, followed. The persistent Turkish menace, coupled with the danger that the League would join with France, meant that the Emperor was not secure enough at this point to take it on and suppress it as he would have wished.

But it is important to realize that not every Germanic princely house was Lutheran Protestant.[22] The real influence at the Clevian court of Duke John III, a well-educated and cultivated man, was Erasmus not Luther. Many of the chief men there were close associates as well as admirers of the Dutch scholar and theologian. Duke John's church regulations of 1533 were taken to Erasmus for consultation and approval; in April Duke John granted him a pension. It was on the recommendation of Erasmus that the humanist scholar Konrad von Heresbach was made tutor to the young William of Cleves. Duke John's instinct for balance is illustrated by the fact that in 1527 he married his eldest daughter Sybilla to Johann Frederick of Saxony who would later head the Schmalkaldic League; but Duke John, bearing in mind his cognomen of 'the Pacific' perhaps, did not join the League himself. In many ways, therefore, the court at Düren, the hereditary seat of the Dukes of Jülich on the Ruhr river, might seem to have provided the ideal background for raising an English Queen for the 1540s: fundamentally liberal, but serious-minded, theologically inclined, profoundly Erasmian, as the court of Catherine of Aragon had once been.

Unfortunately Maria of Jülich-Berg was no Isabella of Castile; nor were the exciting ideas of the Renaissance concerning the education of women (or at least princesses) allowed to hold sway here. It seems that Duchess Maria was herself a strict Catholic, not subject to the liberal reforming notions of her father and husband; her confessor was the well-known writer Dom Joannes Justus Lanspergius, prior of a (Catholic) charterhouse. Be that as it may, she was certainly strict, and had strict ideas on the upbringing of her daughters – 'one that looketh very straitly to her children' who were never allowed 'far from her elbow'. If William of Cleves was tutored by Konrad von Heresbach, his sister Anna, separated from him by birth by only ten months, could not read or write in any language other than her own.[23] This was the dialect called *deutsch* or *dietsch*, known as Dutch to the English, who found it oddly grating on their ears.

The court of Cleves was another world from that of Renaissance Spain (or England). It was true that its inhabitants were reputed to love a drink: 'good cheer'. But on investigation, there was no evidence that Anna herself indulged. On the contrary, it was said of her that 'she occupieth her time mostly with her needle'. Of course a propensity for needlework was not in itself a disaster, remembering Catherine of Aragon's wifely determination to continue sewing her husband's shirts through thick and thin. It was just that the master of the English court had been accustomed to wives who could do all this and a great deal more. Above all music was of the greatest importance to him. A gifted musician himself, Henry VIII's love of song and dance was part of the air he breathed; he took it for granted that his consort would possess musical accomplishments (for which reason he had proposed to examine those French princesses on the quality of their singing).

But no one could examine the Lady Anna of Cleves on her singing – or her playing for that matter. She could not sing. Nor could she play on any instrument. Once again the contrast with previous consorts was vivid: in vain would be sought the graceful training of the young Catherine, the artistic talents of Anne Boleyn which even Catherine's supporter William Forrest had praised (to say nothing of Catherine's Latin studies and Anne Boleyn's fluent witty French). As the envoy Nicholas Wotton wrote back to England, in Germany it was 'a rebuke and an occasion of lightness' if a great lady was able to sing or play, let alone be 'learned'.[24] At the age of twenty-three, shy, ignorant and humble – 'of very low and gentle conditions' – poor Anna of Cleves was ill-equipped for the contentious, sophisticated world which lay somewhat beyond her mother's elbow. She certainly did not possess the arts to enchant a corpulent testy husband, uncertain of his own virility, nearly twenty-five years her senior (Henry VIII was in fact exactly the same age as Anna's mother, Duchess Maria).

But then no one at either court was looking at things in that realistic light – except possibly Duchess Maria. There is some suggestion from her later correspondence that she was unwilling to let her daughter go to England. This may have been maternal solicitude: the Duchess loved this daughter particularly and was 'loath to suffer her to depart from her'.[25] But given the contemporary standards for marriage, when a match with a king was an approved destiny, whatever his age or person (Christina of Milan would have married Henry VIII, if so instructed), it was perhaps rooted in religious scruples about 'Protestant' England.

In England, however, the alliance, the bulwark against the Empire, was everything. It was encouraging news to the English that Charles V himself was infuriated by the idea of the Cleves match: in November it was reported that 'he greatly stomacheth it', that is, dislikes it. When the Emperor was moved to suggest that Duchess Christina might come back into play, that seemed to the English further proof of the match's suitability.

In February 1539 Duke John the Pacific died, leaving the Cleves-Guelderland territories now welded together in the control of his twenty-two-year-old son, William. It was a loss: at least to Cleves. Duke William, despite his Erasmian education, had none of his father's pragmatic good sense. Ambitious for the future, he dreamt of a great marriage that would bolster him up in order to maintain his claim to Guelderland which the Emperor rejected.

In the meantime negotiations between England and Cleves ran merrily along, with good reports of the Lady Anna reaching Cromwell. On 18 March, for example, he was able to tell King Henry that 'she excelleth as far the Duchess [of Saxony, her sister] as the golden sun excelleth the silver moon'. Perhaps his next words sounded a note of caution: 'Every man praiseth the good virtues and honesty, with shamefastness [modesty] which appeareth plainly in the gravity of her face'.[26] But then Cromwell was after all merely repeating what he had heard from Christopher Mont, the English agent of the court of Saxony; while virtue and modesty had been the chief characteristics of the late lamented Queen Jane.

The reception of the English envoys who came to inspect Anna and her sister Amelia, two years her junior, was, it is true, slightly disconcerting. The 'daughters of Cleves' were produced for them wrapped up in such 'monstrous habit and apparel' that they could see neither their figures nor their faces properly. When, conscious of their duty to their King, the envoys protested, the Chancellor of Cleves showed similar indignation to that of the French ambassador earlier. 'Why?' he said, 'would you see them naked?'

It was clearly a case of filling out descriptions with portraits. Pictures were promised for England, and very possibly despatched.[27] Since the painter to the Duke of Saxony – Lucas Cranach the Elder – was ill, some other Flemish artist was selected. In the meantime Holbein, on England's behalf, was to be once again employed, and of course, expense apart, that was really the preferred option. So Holbein set out on his third mission in pursuit of his master's fourth marriage in August 1539.

He arrived at Düren, expenses already paid, including £13 6s 8d 'for the preparation of such things as he is appointed to carry with him'. It has been suggested that this meant that Holbein was put in the unusual position of painting on the spot (under the inspection of court officials), instead of making sketches, to be worked up into paintings later with the aid of his excellent memory.[28] The result was certainly on parchment, mounted on canvas, which would have made transport of a proper painting easier.* Whatever the stringency of Holbein's working conditions, Wotton, the English envoy, who knew the ladies concerned, found that the artist had 'expressed their images very lively', that is, in a very lifelike manner.[30]

For all Cromwell's desire for an alliance against the Empire with the Lutheran princes in Germany – in which category Cleves, with its connection to Saxony, counted – England itself had recently lurched away from any kind of Protestant extremism. In June 1539 the new parliament passed the so-called Act of the Six Articles on the subject of heresy, specifying for the first time that certain opinions constituted heresy (a matter hitherto left to the discretion of the ecclesiastical courts). Carried out ostensibly in the interests of moderation and uniformity, these were clear and savagely punitive measures of religious conservatism: denial of the real presence in the sacrament, for example, was to be punished by death by burning; those who denied the efficacy of private confession and private Masses were to be hanged; former priests and nuns who broke their vows of celibacy by marrying were also to be hanged unless they remedied their situation before the Act became law. Whether intended to defuse that Catholic crusade envisaged by the Pope or to placate a country still looking nostalgically to the old ways, the Six Articles certainly represented a blow to men of reforming zeal like Cranmer (who was obliged to put away his wife) and Cromwell.

Yet in terms of foreign policy, the Cleves alliance continued to be seen

---

* This portrait is now in the Louvre. It is not known what happened to the portrait of Amelia of Cleves; the focus all along had been on Anna, as the elder. Amelia of Cleves never married. The interesting picture of Anna of Cleves in St John's College, Oxford, has recently been discovered to be contemporary, by an unknown Flemish artist from the workshop of Barthel Bruyn the Elder in Cologne, or even Bruyn himself, not a seventeenth-century copy. It may have been that picture promised in July 1539.[29]

as part of an offensive against the Emperor. If the passing of the Six Articles represented a reverse for Cromwell, such a German Protestant-oriented treaty would represent a positive gain for him. Holbein was back in England by the end of August: his works were shown to the King on his summer progress at Grafton. The King liked what he saw – or at any rate, since his reaction is not recorded, he did not dislike it. If the picture of Anna of Cleves did not make him call for musicians and masks as that of Christina of Milan had done, he was content for the details of the alliance to be hammered out. Besides, his envoys had been enthusiastic.

It was true that there had been a precontract involving the Lady Anna; in 1527 her father had contemplated marrying her to the son of the Duke of Lorraine, part of his planned campaign of across-the-board alliances, otherwise expressed in the marriage of Sybilla to Johann Frederick of Saxony. Anna of Cleves was then twelve, but Francis of Lorraine merely ten, beneath the age of consent: so that it was assumed these were spousals *de futura*, rather than *de praesenti* (that is, spousals without the force of marriage). Given the death of Anna's father, it was not quite clear at this point how and when these spousals had ended – except that they *had* ended. The Clevians firmly maintained that the Lady Anna 'was free to marry as she pleased'.[31] This being what the English currently wanted to hear, the marriage treaty, which had been brought to England at the end of September, was signed on 4 October.

As Duke William engaged to collect his sister's modest dowry from his various territories, it was Cromwell who now turned his attention to music. The need to jollify the English court, after its two-year span without a mistress, was keenly felt. Cromwell sent for musicians from Venice: the Bassano family. The choice was a diplomatic as well as a cultural one. The Bassanos were Jews, and could therefore be trusted not to act as agents of the papacy; at the same time unofficial refuge in England (whence the Jews had been expelled in 1290) away from the decrees of the Inquisition suited them well. The Bassanos arrived in 1540 bringing with them their violas as well as a new instrument. For it is one of the pleasant footnotes to the Cleves marriage – some might regard it as the only positive gain – that in this manner the violin first reached England (its earliest recorded use here is in 1545).[32]

The English desire for a new Queen to further the dynasty now looked like being satisfied – if not in that imperialist direction which had generally been expected. In August a conversation had taken place between George Constantine (formerly servant to Anne Boleyn's 'lover' Sir Henry Norris) and the Dean of Westbury during a journey to South Wales. Constantine reported the court gossip of the summer: the Duchess of Milan was said to be demanding certain 'pledges', before she would marry the King. When the fascinated Dean enquired further, Constantine explained: 'Marry, she sayeth that the King's Majesty was in so little space rid of the Queens, that she dare not trust his Council though she durst trust his Majesty; for her Council suspecteth that her great-aunt was poisoned, that the second was innocently put to death, and the third lost for lack of keeping her in childbed.' As Constantine explained: 'he was sorry to see the King so long without a Queen when he might yet have many fair children' and he added, helpfully, that his own father was ninety-two, and yet had ridden over thirty miles before 2 pm. 'Is the King now lusty?' asked the Dean. Constantine's reply was, yes, he was lusty although 'it grieveth me at heart to see his Grace halt so much upon his sore leg.'[33]

It remained to be seen whether Constantine's – in the main – hopeful analysis was correct. Meanwhile in the royal apartments and elsewhere, the usual rite of passage was taking place: the initials of Queen Jane Seymour were being altered to those of the future Queen Anna. Conveniently enough, in certain places medallions with the initials of H and A, left over from the regime of the last Queen – but one – could simply be enamelled. In the ceiling of the Chapel Royal at St James's Palace the heraldry, ciphers and mottoes of the King and the new Queen were joined together.[34]

The journey of Anna of Cleves to England where the King was impatient to receive his bride was now the subject of some delicate discussion. The Lady Anna was to travel alone – except for her cortège – since mourning for Duke John precluded both her mother and brother from travelling. Heaven alone knew what might happen to a sheltered girl, who had never travelled by sea, at such a 'tempestuous' time of year! She might take cold 'or other disease'; and since they were dealing with a girl who was 'young and beautiful', there was the further danger that the sea journey might 'alter' her complexion.[35] Under the circumstances, it was suggested by her officials that she should travel by land to Calais, in order to make the shortest sea journey possible. Although the King had envisaged a voyage from Holland, a passport was duly sought from the Regent of the Netherlands on 30 October.

As for the situation in the Netherlands, the problems of the Emperor in his own dominions had recently been compounded by rebellion in Ghent. At least the Peace of Aiguesmortes between France and Spain meant that Charles V could travel unmolested through French territory in order to sort out his restless burghers. The coincidence that Charles V set out, initially, for France, and Anna of Cleves set out for England at roughly the same time was to prove an important factor in the young woman's story – more important indeed than the damaging action of the sea air and spray on her complexion.

The Lady Anna travelled from Düsseldorf to Cleves, and on to Antwerp.[36] Here she was received with joy by fifty English merchants in 'velvet coats and chains of gold' although the noblemen in her own cortège wore black, being in mourning; the merchants escorted her to her 'English lodging' with torches although it was still daylight. Proceeding down the coast, at Gravelines she was greeted with 'a shot of guns'. She finally reached the frontier of Calais – English territory – between seven and eight o'clock in the morning on 11 December, where the future Queen was formally received by Lord Lisle as Governor.

At Calais the Lady Anna made the acquaintance of the other important lords and gentlemen of the Privy Chamber, many of them with connections to the previous Queen. They included Gregory Cromwell, husband of Elizabeth Seymour, Edward Seymour Earl of Hertford who had been made commander of the fortifications of Calais and Guisnes in February, and Sir Thomas Seymour (wearing a valuable chain 'of a strange fashion'). Then there was one Thomas Culpeper, a great favourite of the King's, in the Privy Chamber. The merchants of Calais hastened to present their future Queen with a gift of one hundred marks in gold; the mercantile character of Calais was further emphasized when on her way to her lodging, the Lady Anna passed through lines of merchants as well as soldiers. Only the smoke sent up by the ordnance fired off slightly marred the occasion: none of her train could see each other.

Nevertheless the Lady Anna was determined to please: everyone remarked on that, including Lady Lisle in her report to her daughter back in England, Anne Basset. It was true that fifteen Clevian ladies had arrived too, threatening the places reserved for the English; nevertheless the lady herself was gracious and would prove easy to serve. The Lady Anna remained indeed sweet-tempered even though the weather now became 'tempestuous', much as had been predicted in Cleves.

She looked at the royal ships and 'much commended and liked the same' (a taste likely to endear her to the King). Via her steward, Hoghesten, and envoy, Olisleger, she asked to learn the kind of card games which would amuse the King: she was taught 'cent' (a game later known as picquet). The Earl of Southampton, a veteran courtier of the King's own age who had carried out many diplomatic missions for him, reported that 'she played as pleasantly, and with as good grace and countenance as ever in my life I saw any noble woman.' Since cards – like music – were important at the English court (Anne Boleyn had been wont to gamble with the King) all of this was a good sign. The Lady Anna even went so far as to persuade the slightly reluctant English courtiers to demonstrate 'the manner and fashion of Englishmen sitting at meat', after they had declined to dine with *her* in 'the manner of her country' on the grounds of etiquette. Although

Southampton was slightly worried about the sitting-down, he was able to pronounce the Lady Anna's manners those of 'a princess'.[37]

Southampton was also in a position, thanks to the delay, to conduct a significant, if informal conversation with Hoghesten and Olisleger. In it, he stressed the King's 'most godly desire and affection to have more children' in case 'God fails us in my Lord Prince [Edward]'. In the sad eventuality of the boy's death, he told the Lady Anna's representatives, they would at least have another prince 'of your side ... to reign over us in peace'. So the time passed, with the Lady Anna demonstrating both her natural curiosity and her wish to please, while the courtiers dreamt of a healthy Anglo-Clevian dynasty.

Unfortunately it was not until 27 December that Anna of Cleves was able to make the crossing from Calais to Deal. By this time the King had been waiting at Greenwich far too long – including the Christmas season – and the patience of this notoriously impatient man had worn thin. Furthermore – another factor in the story of Anna of Cleves – with the passing days his imagination had begun to run riot. This was after all a new experience for him: the arrival of an innocent and unknown young bride. Anne Boleyn and Jane Seymour were two ladies familiar to him before marriage; as a boy he had grown up with Catherine of Aragon before he married her.

Escorted by fifty ships, the vessel carrying the Lady Anna arrived at Deal at five o'clock in the evening. Having changed her dress, she was received by the Duke and Duchess of Suffolk, and then taken to Dover Castle to rest: the weather remained icy, and if no longer tempestuous, at least very windy. From here the Lady Anna started off in the direction of Canterbury, to be met at Barham Downs by the Archbishop and other bishops, who conducted her to the Canterbury abbey of St Augustine's for the night.

This building had been suppressed as an abbey in 1538 and was now destined to be 'the King's Palace'. Conversion, however, had had to be rushed through at the news of the latest consort's arrival. Under the direction of James Nedham, the King's surveyor, there had been a great deal of furious work in the period since October, with nearly 350 men working on the site, and thirty-one dozen candles ordered for night work – Nedham at least was delighted with the bad weather which had delayed the Lady. Galyon Hone had of course been employed once more on five 'arms of the King's and [new] Queen's and eleven badges of theirs': Anna of Cleves choosing the swan as one of her devices, from the supporters of her family crest and the legend of the Knight of the Swan. In spite of the expenditure and care taken, the Lady Anna only spent one night at St Augustine's: but then it was expected she would be back – with her husband.

On 31 December she reached Rochester, where she was conducted to the Bishop's Palace.[38]

It was at this point that the King's thin patience snapped; alternatively his boyish romantic nature – on which he prided himself – got the better of him. In order to 'nourish love', as he told Cromwell, he decided to pay a visit to his affianced bride the next day, New Year's Day. In true fairy story fashion, the King proceeded to ride from Greenwich to Rochester, attended by some of the gentlemen of his Privy Chamber, all dressed alike in hooded 'cloaks of marble colour' (that is, multi-coloured).[39] On arrival, he sent Sir Anthony Browne, his Master of the Horse, up to the Lady's chamber, to say that he had a New Year's gift to deliver to her.

Sir Anthony Browne said – afterwards – that from the moment he set eyes on the Lady Anna, he was immediately struck with dismay. Whether that was true or not, what was quite sure was that the Lady's next visitor, a certain anonymous gentleman in a multi-coloured cloak, was deeply disappointed by what he saw. His friend of many years, Lord Russell, bore witness that 'he never saw His Highness so marvellously astonished and abashed as on that occasion'.[40] The interview itself did nothing to assuage the royal feeling of being let down. Lady Anna, who was in truth probably bewildered (she spoke no English at all at this point), gave the fatal impression of being bored. She had been watching the New Year's Day bull-baiting out of her window when these mysterious visitors began to appear. Beyond the common courtesies, she saw no reason to interrupt her spectator sport further.

Suddenly – as it seemed to her – her unknown visitor embraced her. He showed her a token the King was supposed to have sent his betrothed for a New Year's gift. All this left the Lady Anna in her turn thoroughly 'abashed'. Her only recourse after a few words (in her grating *deutsch*) was to continue to look out of the window. The King was left to retire to another room, and assume the purple velvet coat of royalty, which left the attendant lords and gentlemen bowing deeply (they were well trained when to recognize and when not to recognize their master). Thus, more majestically garbed, the King returned to the Lady Anna.

Reports vary as to what happened next. According to Wriothesley, the Lady Anna now 'humbled herself lowly', the King saluted her all over again, and so they 'talked lovingly together'. But this is probably the herald's tactful gloss on what had been a ludicrously misjudged scene on both sides. The important comment was that made by the King to Cromwell after he had left the Lady Anna. 'I like her not', said Henry VIII.[41]

The question must now be raised as to what the King saw, compared to what he had expected to see: was there a deception and if so by whom? There are after all a number of candidates, not only Holbein, but the

English agents and envoys abroad. Let us take the actual appearance of Anna of Cleves first: for this we are fortunate in having a first-hand description, written only a few days later by the French ambassador, Charles de Marillac, who was not prejudiced in either direction, towards her beauty or her ugliness. Anna of Cleves looked about thirty, he wrote (she was in fact twenty-four), tall and thin, 'of middling beauty, with a determined and resolute countenance.' The Lady was not as handsome as people had affirmed she was, nor as young (he was of course wrong about that), but there was a 'steadiness of purpose in her face to counteract her want of beauty'.[42] This in turn seems to fit well with Christopher Mont's careful reference to the 'gravity in her face' which went so well with her natural modesty.

The 'daughter of Cleves' was solemn, or at any rate by English standards she was, and she looked old for her age. She was solemn because she had not been trained to be anything else and the German fashions did little to give an impression of youthful charm in a court in love as ever with things French, or at any rate associating them with fun and delight. Although Henry VIII never actually 'swore they had brought over a Flanders mare to him',* the apocryphal story does sum up, as apocryphal stories often do, the profound cultural gap between the two courts of Cleves and England. Turning to Holbein's picture, one finds this solemnity well captured: a critic might indeed term it stolidity. Besides Wotton, in his report, had confirmed that Holbein, generally regarded as the master of the 'lively' or lifelike (not the flattering) in his own time, had indeed captured Anna's 'image' very well.

Of course a beautiful young woman, however stolid or badly dressed, would still have been acceptable. Anna of Cleves was not beautiful, and those reports which declared she was were egregious exaggerations in the interests of diplomats – to this extent, the envoys are the real culprits, not the painter. But was Anna of Cleves actually hideous? Holbein, painting her full-face, as was the custom, does not make her so to the modern eye, with her high forehead, wide-apart, heavy-lidded eyes and pointed chin. There is indirect evidence that Anna of Cleves was perfectly pleasant-looking from the later years of Henry VIII. When Chapuys reported Anna of Cleves as rating her contemporary, Catherine Parr, 'not nearly as beautiful' as herself, this expert observer did not choose to contradict her;[44] so that the boast was presumably true, or at least true enough not to be ridiculous.

---

* The story comes from Bishop Burnet at the end of the seventeenth century, with no contemporary reference to back it up. Horace Walpole, in his eighteenth-century *Anecdotes of Painting in England*, gave it further credence: Anna of Cleves was 'a Flanders Mare, not a Venus, as Holbein had represented her by practising the common flattery of his profession'.[43]

Anna of Cleves
m 1540

Badge of Anna of Cleves, showing the ducal coronet of Cleves.

Coins of Henry VIII showing HK (for his first wife) and HI (for Ioanna or Jane Seymour).

The Great Gatehouse of Hampton Court Palace.

BELOW AND OPPOSITE *Selection of jewels and ciphers designed by Holbein showing the Queens' initials entwined with that of the King.*

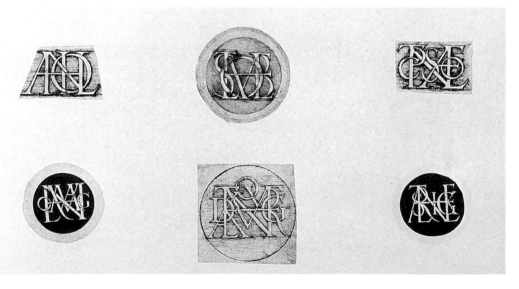

Richmond Palace by Wyngaerde.

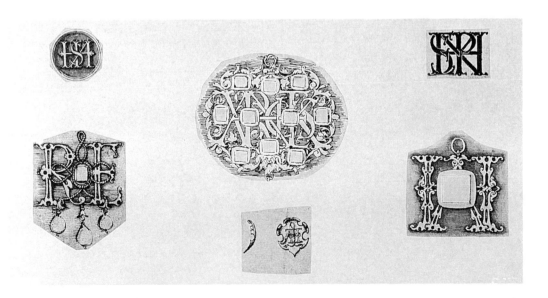

The Emperor Charles V.

*Christina of Milan by Holbein whom
Henry VIII, on the basis of this portrait,
hoped to marry.*

François I, King of France.

James V of Scotland.

Anna of Cleves by Holbein: the portrait that persuaded Henry VIII to send for her as his bride.

Chart showing Anna of Cleves's projected journey to England in the autumn of 1539.

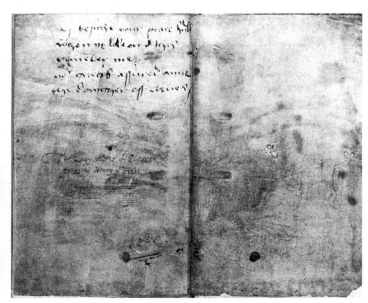

Dedication on a blank leaf at the back of a Book of Hours, printed in Germany about 1533, given by Anna of Cleves to Henry VIII: 'I beseech your grace humbly when you look on this remember me. Your grace's assured Anna the daughter of Cleves.'

Anna of Cleves: a contemporary portrait from the workshop of Barthel Bruyn the Elder in Cologne, and possibly by Bruyn himself; recent x-rays have revealed a longer nose under the paint.

But it may be that in giving this frontal view, intended to prevent the concealment of defects, Holbein unintentionally minimized one of Anna's. Recent X-rays of that other contemporary portrait, from the workshop of Barthel Bruyn the Elder (or Bruyn himself), have revealed a considerably longer nose underneath the paint.[45] Holbein's nose is not short – but nor is it excessively long, no longer for example than that of Jane Seymour. Even though long noses were not the disfigurement they are considered in the age of photography, a slightly bulbous nose may be one explanation of the King's disappointment.

Then there is the question of Anna of Cleves' complexion. It may be that this was a problem: her own officials' protests about the damage to be done by a long sea voyage may have been a tactful way of handling it. When the King roared at his courtiers that he had been misinformed – by them amongst others, since they had seen her at Calais – the only explanation which could be stammered out was that her skin was indeed rather more 'brown' than had been expected.[46] (Southampton's observation that the Calais encounter had not seemed the right time to disparage the Lady Anna 'whom so many had by reports and paintings extolled' was probably nearer the truth.) In any case the same 'brownness' had been attributed to the Duchess Christina; while Anne Boleyn had been 'Brunet' – and that had proved no impediment to her progress, even if the contemporary ideal was to be 'pure white'.

Even allowing for all this we are still left with something mysterious in the whole episode, and the sheer immediacy of the King's disappointment (followed by his indignation – which was, however, never directed at Holbein). The explanation must therefore lie in something equally mysterious, the nature of erotic attraction. The King had been expecting a lovely young bride, and the delay had merely contributed to his desire. He saw someone who, to put it crudely, aroused in him no erotic excitement whatsoever. And more intimate embraces lay ahead: or were planned to do so.

Now that the gap between expectation and fulfilment had proved total there was one crucial question. Since this marriage would so manifestly be for the King's 'displeasure and torment' rather than for his 'pleasure and quiet', was it indeed a bargain that must endure?

Chapter 15

THAT YOUNG GIRL
KATHERINE

*They [the noblemen and citizens of England] had
perceived that the King's affections were alienated
from the lady Anna to that young girl Katherine
Howard, the cousin of the Duke of Norfolk.*

Richard Hilles to Henry Bullinger, summer 1540

On Twelfth Night, 6 January 1540, the marriage took place at
Greenwich between Henry VIII, a widower of forty-eight with
three children, and Anna of Cleves, a foreign-born (and foreign-
speaking) 'maid'* half his age. The ceremony took place in 'the
Queen's closet', where incidentally King Henry had also married Jane
Seymour. Around the bride's 'marrying ring' ran the words 'God send
me wel to kepe': a pious hope which she at least expected to be
fulfilled. Afterwards the royal couple went on 'a procession' together,
the new Queen Anna dressed in cloth of silver 'hanging' with jewels
and 'being in her hair', that is, with her hair flowing loose to indicate
her unmarried state, surmounted by a coronet of pearls and precious
stones interwoven with rosemary, traditional emblem of love and
fidelity in marriage. It was, wrote one observer, 'a goodly sight to
behold'.[1]

But the King did not find it so – and he had already made that quite
clear. After that disastrous meeting at Rochester the King had returned
in a mood of childish disappointment and grown-up anger to Greenwich.
The Lady Anna was then received formally in a pavilion set up at Shooter's
Hill by a group including the Earl of Rutland who was to be her Lord
Chamberlain as he had been that of Queen Jane. Having changed into

---

* The word then generally used for an unmarried woman and a virgin; 'spinster' derives from the
seventeenth century.

cloth of gold, Anna was then conducted to Blackheath for her official meeting with her future husband, similarly dressed in gold. In this manner they had ridden together to Greenwich.

Cloth of gold made no difference. In the days before the wedding, the King remained in a mood of resentful despair. To Cromwell he cried out that if he had known what he now knew, the Lady Anna 'would never have come within the kingdom'. 'By way of lamentation', he added, 'What Remedy?' Cromwell, according to his own later testimony, replied, 'I know none', and that he was 'very sorry therefore'; subsequently he expanded this, 'And so God knoweth I was, for I thought it a hard beginning.' So Cromwell veered between trying timidly to speak up for the Lady Anna – 'I thought she had a Queenly manner' – and bewailing that his master was 'no better content'. The King, while admitting that Lady Anna was 'well and seemly', harped monotonously on the fact that she was 'nothing so fair as she had been reported'.[2]

In this crisis, it was still just possible that the King would be saved at the eleventh hour. The question of the Lady Anna's precontract with Francis of Lorraine had never been examined very thoroughly; in the autumn, the representatives of Cleves had merely declared the Lady Anna to be free, on their authority. Now the King's Council, 'much astonished and abashed' in their turn, were asked to investigate it. The result was unsatisfactory: 'A revocation' had indeed been made, they found, and besides 'they were but spousals' (that is, *de futura*). The ambassadors of Cleves were equally unhelpful. They dealt once again with the whole subject remarkably cavalierly and 'only by words made a light matter of it, saying it was done in their [the young couple's] minority and had never after taken any effect.' No dispensation from the precontract was produced; the most they would do – on 5 January, the eve of the wedding – was to promise to produce authentic copies of the necessary documents within three months.[3]

As it happens, the representatives of Cleves were never able to do this. The best that they could produce was a notarized statement – on 26 February following – concerning a certain report in the Cleves archives, dated five years previously. On 15 February 1535, when Anna was twenty, the Clevian Chancellor Groghroff had simply announced *'der hilich aff sy'* – the spousals (with Lorraine) were off; or as Hoghesten and Olisleger now put it, 'they were not going to take their natural course'. The actual papers – above all the dispensation – were never produced, making the existence of the dispensation extremely doubtful. It is therefore one of the paradoxes of the marital career of Henry VIII that the marriage he entered with such reluctance may well have been genuinely invalid from the start.*

On 5 January 1540, however, the Lady Anna merely made a formal declaration of her freedom; and that avenue of escape was closed. 'I am not well handled', was the King's reaction, words which should have cast a chill into many hearts and no doubt did. He spoke further of the need 'against my will, [to] put my Neck in the Yoke'. Just before the ceremony, he told Cromwell: 'My Lord, if it were not to satisfy the world, and my Realm, I would not do that I must do this day for none earthly thing'.[5]

In view of King Henry's manifest gloom – and let us not forget that the wedding night still lay ahead – the question must be raised as to why the ill-omened marriage ever went through. For what it was worth, it was hardly a popular alliance in the country. Anna of Cleves herself was for the time being a mystery; so xenophobia was able to hold full sway, she being a representative of 'these Germans, a sort of beggarly knaves.' For that matter she was not a magnificent Princess as Catherine of Aragon had been: Cleves itself was seen as being neither rich nor powerful, and her own dowry was small, since in his haste to bind the Duke of Cleves to him, King Henry had been uncharacteristically magnanimous in that respect. A servant of the Bishop of Durham was arrested for putting this disgruntled reaction into words: 'we have no help now but from the Duke of Cleves, and he is so poor that they cannot help us.' Furthermore, Anna of Cleves was envisaged (inaccurately) as the kind of virulent Lutheran who would not come to England 'so long as one Abbey is standing'. (A devout Protestant put it more favourably but equally inaccurately: the new Queen was believed to be 'an excellent woman and one that fears God' with great hopes of an extensive propagation of the gospel by her influence.)[6]

King Henry's own explanation for the marriage is probably the correct one. It was 'for fear of making a ruffle in the world; that is ... to drive her Brother into the hands of the Emperor, and the French King's hands, being now together'. As Suffolk explained, the King would have been glad 'if the solemnization could have been avoided' but without appearing himself to reject the Lady. Charles V's journey towards rebellious Ghent had been marked by an amicable encounter with his new brother the French King. This was no season, Cromwell calculated, to upset England's carefully calculated foreign policy, and lose her one ally –

---

* H. A. Kelly, in *The Matrimonial Trials of Henry VIII*, suggests that the original spousals between Anna and Francis of Lorraine may actually have been *de praesenti* (that is, with the force of marriage) despite the bridegroom's youth; this did happen before the age of consent, as in the case of Henry himself and Catherine of Aragon, and would have needed a proper rebuttal. However, even spousals *de futura*, which unquestionably took place, needed a valid dispensation.[4]

Cleves – who might cause the Emperor a deal of trouble. So Henry VIII found himself in the unlikely role of sacrificial victim of his secretary's manoeuvres. Charles V's journey through France, coupled with the Lady Anna's delayed journey, had brought about a fatal accident of timing. As King Henry would correctly declare at a later date: 'I never for love to the Woman, consented to marry'.[7]

Under these circumstances, it was hardly surprising that the wedding night did not go well. If the King had entertained faint hopes of experiencing an access of lust at the appropriate moment – after all his bride was quite 'seemly' – they were not fulfilled. One thing is quite clear about the encounter: it was a complete failure from the King's point of view. When Cromwell rashly enquired the next day, 'How liked you the Queen?', the King replied succinctly: 'I liked her before not well, but now I like her much worse.'[8]

Naturally he was quick to blame the Lady rather than himself. Her body, not her beauty, was now the issue. For example he told Sir Anthony Denny, a member of his Privy Chamber, that his wife was not only 'not as she was reported, but had breasts so slack and other parts of body in such sort that [he] somewhat suspected her virginity'. The King's verdict was this: 'he could never in her company be provoked and steered to know her carnally.' Cromwell was given the same message and the King imparted it privately to two of his doctors, Dr Chamber and Dr Butts: 'her body [was] in such a sort disordered and indisposed' that it could not 'excite and provoke any lust in him.' It had, in short, a 'loathsomeness' he could not overcome. Dr Butts was given further details of the 'hanging of her breasts and looseness of her flesh'.[9] There were various other testimonies, but they all added up to the same thing: the King was not able to consummate his marriage.*

This unhappy state of affairs did not alter. Eight days after the wedding – on 14 January – Cromwell informed the Duke of Suffolk that 'the Queen [Anna] was then a maid' since their master 'misliked her body and the disposition thereof'. In February the King repeated the same melancholy message to Cromwell. Even though he lay with his wife 'nightly' or every second night, yet 'she was still as good a Maid ... as ever her Mother bare her' for anything the King had 'ministered' to her. There was however no question of his own virility; he told Dr Butts that he had had *duas pollutiones nocturnas in somno'* (two nocturnal ejaculations) in the same period. No, the reason for his failure was that the King had now

---

* Although these all-too-vivid testimonies were made later, they are remarkably unanimous in their tenor and in any case fit the known facts of the King's behaviour in the spring following his marriage to Anna of Cleves.

settled into 'mistrusting' his wife's virginity, as he informed Sir Thomas Heneage, 'by reason of looseness of her breasts and other tokens'. As a result of this, he had not the appetite to do 'what a man should do to his wife.'[10]

These unattractive charges tell us, of course, more about King Henry than Queen Anna; the King's suspicion of her virginity certainly need not be taken seriously. It is in direct contradiction to the known strictness of Anna's upbringing (by her mother) and her character as displayed both before her wedding and after it. It must simply be seen as part of the King's speedy campaign to rid himself of his unwelcome new wife – at no blame to himself.

But these charges do serve to remind us that a wedding night involves two sets of reactions, not one. It is true that King Henry VIII does deserve pity (some of that pity, indeed, which he liberally bestowed upon himself). When he 'lamented the state of princes ... in marriage' to Cromwell, so much worse than that of the poor, since 'princes take as is brought to them by others, and poor men be commonly at their own choice and liberty',[11] he stated an obvious but nevertheless distressing fact (if you happened to be a prince). But what of the fate of the princesses? What did Queen Anna herself feel about these unsuccessful gropings and fumblings? And had she any realization that her own physical attributes were being blamed for this lack of success?

Fortunately for Queen Anna's peace of mind, she seems to have been wonderfully protected from humiliation by a complete ignorance of what are now known as the facts of life. Her senior English ladies conducted a conversation with her on the subject some months later; they included Lady Rutland and Jane Viscountess Rochford, veterans of the royal bed-chamber. These ladies suggested to the Queen that she was in fact still 'a maid'. In response Queen Anna described the procedure which had succeeded the earlier more energetic efforts. (According to Dr Butts, the King did all he could – in vain – for four nights, and then continued merely to visit his wife. Dr Chamber had urged him 'not to enforce himself' for fear of making things worse.) 'When he [the King] comes to bed', declared Anna, 'he kisses me and taketh me by the hand, and biddeth me, "good-night sweet heart" and in the morning, kisses me, and biddeth me, "Farewell, darling". Is not this enough?' she enquired innocently.[12]

To this Lady Rutland replied firmly: 'Madam, there must be more, or it will be long ere we have a Duke of York which all this realm most desireth.' She also wondered whether the Queen had not discussed these delicate matters with Mother Lowe, known as 'the mother of the Dutch [that is, German] maids'. 'Marry, fie, fie, for shame, God forbid', exclaimed the scandalized Queen Anna.

Such ignorance was not a universal condition. On the contrary most girls grew up (as we shall see) with a good healthy knowledge of these matters, imparted in fairly frank language. Furthermore, it was generally considered the duty – the holy duty – of a mother to prepare her daughter for what to expect on her wedding night; otherwise, as St Bernardino of Siena had vividly expressed it in the previous century: 'it is like sending her to sea with no biscuit'.[13] But Anna of Cleves was different. Her closeness to her mother's elbow in Germany had denied her a proper worldly education, since the strait-laced Duchess Maria evidently saw no need for what St Bernardino called 'biscuit'. In England, however, her ignorance protected her from undue personal mortification.

In these early days of the new marriage at least the court was happy with the restoration of a Queen's household. Queen Anna of Cleves was granted a household totalling 126 – not a great deal less than that enjoyed by Queen Catherine of Aragon in 1509. There were some 'Dutch' ladies (hence Mother Lowe's position), although King Henry had anxiously demanded in advance that any attendants brought over should be 'fair', much as his father had laid down the law concerning Catherine's Spanish ladies forty years earlier. Queen Anna, however, was allowed to employ her compatriots, without specification, in certain important positions: Dr Cornelius, her doctor, was a Clevian, gynaecological needs dictating this delicacy with foreign princesses; then there was Master Schulenberg, her cook, and her footman, Englebert.

Where the English were concerned, jockeying for positions had been going on since the autumn, when the Cleves marriage treaty was signed. If the match itself was the 'reforming' Cromwell's triumph, then at least the fecund Howard family, with Norfolk as their calculating and 'reactionary' patriarch, had managed more mundanely to place two of their number among the six maids-in-waiting to the new Queen. One of these was a pretty bubbly little girl, newly brought to court for this purpose, called Katherine Howard. It would not be long before this placing would be seen as a 'reactionary' triumph comparable to the Cleves marriage. But at the time it was merely part of the endless process of place- and marriage-broking which occupied all families in and around the Tudor court.

On 4 February the King took his new wife from Greenwich to Westminster. This was in one sense a familiar ceremony by which the King presented the Queen to the capital. However, in this case – unusually – there was to be no triumphant state procession through the City of London itself, on the way to Westminster. The great trail of richly decorated barges, all hanging with escutcheons, set forth up river, first the King with his nobles and gentlemen, then the Queen (in a separate barge) with her household.

The shops on the Thames duly saluted the procession as it passed and a thousand 'chambers of ordnance' were shot off within the Tower of London by its guns, which 'made a noise like thunder'. But the procession passed on beyond the Tower, and Queen Anna was finally helped ashore at Westminster itself. The omission may well have been a sign of the King's dissatisfaction with the situation in which he found himself.[14]

Meanwhile the international situation in 1540 did not provide that justification for the new marriage which might have comforted the King. When Charles V arrived in the Netherlands in February, following his untroubled crossing of France, he was able to make short work of the Ghent rebellion; the city's privileges were revoked and thirteen people were executed. As for Duke William of Cleves, his eyes had veered away from the King's daughter Mary towards another princess who was a far more exciting possibility as a bride. This was the twelve-year-old Jeanne d'Albret, daughter of Marguerite d'Angoulême by her second marriage to the King of Navarre, who was not only the heiress to that kingdom, but also the niece of the King of France.

England did, however, have the possibility of a real Lutheran ally among the German princes. While King Henry waited anxiously at Greenwich for the tempestuous seas which divided him from the Lady Anna to die down, his twenty-three-year-old daughter Mary had found herself in the unexpected position of entertaining a suitor of her own. Duke Philip of Bavaria, nephew of the Elector Palatine (the Palatinate being a more powerful princedom than Cleves), arrived on his own initiative to court her. While the pious Catholic Lady Mary did not particularly relish her suitor's Lutheran religion, she conversed with him graciously enough in Latin, and in German through an interpreter. The excited French ambassador actually thought kisses had been exchanged in the wintry gardens of the Abbot of Westminster; he commented that 'No lord of this kingdom has dared to go so far' since the death of Exeter, who was supposed to have planned to marry Mary to his son; that had horribly illustrated the perils of any conspiracy, imaginary or otherwise, involving marriage to the King's elder daughter.[15] According to her recent practice, Mary indicated that she would submit to her father's wishes, whatever the religion of her putative bridegroom, so that when the King made Duke Philip a Knight of the Garter, and bestowed gifts upon him, there seemed a distinct possibility of a Lutheran link with England. Once again, this was liable to cause gratifying annoyance to the Emperor, who would also not be best pleased at the bestowal of his cousin's hand in such a direction.

Yet on the surface all the turbulence of the spring of 1540 in England seemed to relate to religious matters, and their impact on politics, rather than the King's personal life or diplomatic intrigue. It has been recently commented that the events of this period confused even those who lived through them, 'so shifting were political fortunes, and so uncertain was the prospect of reform or reaction'.[16] On the one hand Bishop Stephen Gardiner, the most prominent 'reactionary' prelate, attacked the reformers: he had recently returned to the Council, having been ambassador in France for three years. On the other hand reformers such as Dr Robert Barnes, Thomas Garret and William Jerome fought back with energy. In a dispute concerning the nature of grace, free will and penance, the King himself was consulted (his continuing pride in his own theological expertise – as a person 'which sometimes have been noted to be learned' – will be recalled in his angry dismissal of the Pilgrims of Grace). Barnes, Garret and Jerome ended up in the Tower 'by the King's commandment': they would be executed on 30 July. Yet on 30 July, equally, three priests, long-term supporters of Queen Catherine and of course the Pope, Thomas Abel, Richard Featherstone and Edward Powell, would also be put to death.

As for Cromwell, there were mixed signals here too. In April observers might legitimately have thought that his star was still in the ascendant: on 18 April, he was further ennobled from Baron Cromwell to Earl of Essex (a county in which he had considerable property) and on the same day created Lord Great Chamberlain. As for the royal marriage that he had been instrumental in bringing about, the bill confirming the dower for the Queen Anna was also passed through parliament in April. But appearances were once again confused and deceptive. As spring turned to summer, the important star in the ascendant was not Cromwell's but that of the young girl who had first come to court to serve Queen Anna: Katherine Howard.

No confirmed authentic picture of Katherine Howard survives.* (Although, as we shall see, there may be a tantalizing glimpse of her, in profile, in a window of King's College Chapel, Cambridge.) The fact that Katherine Howard is the only one of Henry VIII's wives for whose appearance we must rely properly on contemporary descriptions, gives her career an appropriately evanescent quality. The same mistiness surrounds her date of birth. She was eighteen or nineteen when the King's roving eye first fell upon her: that is, roughly thirty years younger than he was.† Despite his growing size the King had evidently given up his desire for 'a

---

* 'Hopeless mislabelling' has resulted in a portrait of quite another lady being associated with her name; in fact this picture, in its various versions, probably depicts Elizabeth Seymour, sister to Queen Jane and daughter-in-law to Cromwell. She wears widow's black, appropriately enough since she was a young widow before she married Gregory Cromwell; she also bears a sisterly resemblance to Queen Jane, especially the nose and chin.[17]

† Lacey Baldwin Smith, in *A Tudor Tragedy* (the major study of Katherine Howard and the events surrounding her), gives 1521 as a plausible date; this fits with the statement of the French ambassador that Katherine Howard was eighteen in 1539.[18]

big wife', for Katherine was not only small, as Catherine of Aragon had been, but diminutive: *parvissima puella* – a really tiny girl. If King Henry was about thirty years older than Katherine, he must have been well over a foot taller. We need not speculate further about their respective weights. The French ambassador rated her beauty as only middling (the same phrase he had used for Anna of Cleves, incidentally), but he did praise her gracefulness, and he found much sweetness in her expression;[19] her habit of dressing *à la française* (as opposed to Anna of Cleves' Germanic fashions) no doubt commended itself to him.

Even if Katherine Howard was not a beauty, she must have had considerable prettiness and obvious sex appeal (as well as – or perhaps because of – her youth) since we know that she captivated the King instantly. As her step-grandmother Agnes Duchess of Norfolk would state later: 'the King's highness did cast a fantasy [fancy] to Katherine Howard the first time that ever he saw her'. This may have been at a banquet given by Bishop Stephen Gardiner, ally to the Norfolk party in his religious conservatism; at any rate Gardiner was said to have 'very often provided feastings and entertainments' for the King and his new sweetheart after that, while London citizens got used to seeing the King crossing the Thames by boat to visit her – sometimes as late as midnight.[20] It was tempting afterwards to see Katherine Howard planted as some kind of decoy duck to lure the aging King.

In a sense this was of course true of Katherine, as it was true of every young woman who obtained those coveted places in the Queen's household. Time had not dimmed the lessons of the past. Thomas Boleyn, Earl of Wiltshire, had recently died, but he died in dignity (to be splendidly interred in the parish church at Hever), having profited from the rise of his daughter but avoided the taint of her disgrace. The careers of the Seymour brothers, as uncles to Prince Edward, were evidently flourishing, having overcome the check caused by the death of their sister. Ever since the King's disgust with Anna of Cleves had been made clear to his intimates, there was obviously some kind of opportunity here. But in another sense, the Howard family found themselves with a slightly unexpected candidate for consort – or at least titular mistress and patroness, as Anne Boleyn had been for so many years – in little Katherine.

Here was no intelligent adult woman, wise in the ways of the world – and of course courts, as both Anne Boleyn and Jane Seymour after years of observant service in royal households had been in their different ways. Katherine Howard was a child compared to these two – and she was in fact some four or five years younger than either lady had been at the moment when she attracted the King, as well as being born a generation later.* She

* Katherine Howard was some twenty years younger than Anne Boleyn; twelve years younger than Jane Seymour; six years younger than Anna of Cleves.

was not illiterate as is sometimes suggested: her ability to read and write (after a fashion) put her into a very small category of women of her time, noble or otherwise. Katherine Howard was in contrast, for example, to Lady Lisle's daughter Anne Basset, who when she wanted to write a letter sent for a man to do it for her.[21] But being literate did not mean that Katherine Howard was in any way at all educated; in this lack she was absolutely typical of the girls of her time.

Her real education had been in the school of life as represented by her step-grandmother's household: and there the lessons were, as we shall see, very different from the courtly arts imbibed by Anne Boleyn in Burgundy and France, the virtuous prudence fostered in Jane Seymour by her courtier father, and later by her brother and sister-in-law. In the full flush of promoting Victorian values, the nineteenth-century author of *Lives of the Queens of England*, Agnes Strickland, found in the career of Katherine Howard 'a grand moral lesson, a lesson better calculated to illustrate the fatal consequences of the first heedless steps in guilt, than all the warning essays that have ever been written on those subjects'.[22] A less moralistic age will feel more sympathy for the girl whom the freak wave of the King's desire threw up so cruelly ill-prepared on the exposed shore of history.

Katherine Howard was brought up poor, despite the grandeur of her Howard lineage, tracing royal descent from Edward I via the Mowbray Dukes of Norfolk.[23] (See family tree 1) It was in fact the same royal descent as that of her first cousin, Anne Boleyn, but if the two girls shared half their blood (Katherine's father and Anne's mother were brother and sister) their respective backgrounds were very different. Compared to the hard-working, ambitious Sir Thomas Boleyn, conscious that he had his way to make at court, Lord Edmund Howard was feckless and rather lazy, inhibited (as he saw it) by his aristocratic birth from making the efforts suitable to those of a lesser degree. He fought bravely enough at Flodden, when his father commanded the English field, although his was one of the few actions which was unsuccessful. He was knighted in 1515. But his career never amounted to very much, given his opportunities, owing perhaps to the King's lack of enthusiasm for him, or perhaps to some mole of nature which had caused that lack of enthusiasm.

Towards the end of his life Lord Edmund would complain that 'If I were a poor man's son, I might dig and delve for my living': instead he found himself 'small friended ' and 'beaten by the world'. As for being beaten, his third wife was sufficiently irritated by Lord Edmund to strike him, when medicine for voiding gravel caused him to lose control, with the angry words: 'it is children's parts to bepiss their bed'. His life was punctuated by appeals to others to relieve his poverty, starting with Cardinal Wolsey, and going on to the point when he was compelled to hide himself away to avoid the bailiffs. Granted the post of Controller of Calais in 1534 – possibly through the influence of his niece Anne Boleyn – he was removed from it a few years later for reasons which are mysterious, and died soon afterwards in March 1539, that is, before his daughter Katherine came to court.

His real importance for Katherine was to place her within a vast sprawling network of cousins. The Howards were indeed an amazingly prolific family: Lord Edmund had twenty-two brothers and sisters, of whom nine lived long enough to marry. By 1527 he himself was responsible for ten children. Some of these he seems to have inherited: for his first wife and Katherine's mother, Jocasta (Joyce) Culpeper, was already the widow of Ralph Legh, with Legh children, when Lord Edmund married her in about 1515.

Joyce Culpeper was the daughter of Richard Culpeper of Oxenheath in Kent. The Culpepers were a reputable Kentish family with many ramifications: Joyce was for example a distant cousin to that Thomas Culpeper in the King's Privy Chamber (not to be confused with her brother, also called Thomas Culpeper). As the wife of Lord Edmund Howard, Joyce gave birth to another six or seven children, before dying when her daughter Katherine was still quite young. Although it is impossible to disentangle exactly which of Lord Edmund's notional ten children were his and which were his wife's by her first marriage, the point is immaterial in the history of Katherine Howard. Unquestionably her father's daughter, she was born low down in the family order, and formed part of a crowd from birth.

Katherine may have spent her childhood at Oxenheath, by now the home of her maternal uncle. The significant moment in her life, however, was that when she was taken into the household of her step-grandmother Agnes Duchess of Norfolk at Chesworth near Horsham, and Lambeth. Katherine's mother was already dead and Lord Edmund Howard proceeded to marry twice more, on both occasions to widows, Dorothy Troyes and Margaret Jennings (she who so cruelly humiliated him over his accident) without having any more children – or for that matter solving his economic situation. But the practice of sending girls (and boys) away from home to be raised elsewhere was independent of family circumstances. It was a custom whose value obviously depended on the nature of the household concerned: the choice being nothing to do with the moral values, and everything to do with the nobility of the household in question. In this way the King's grandmother, Margaret Beaufort, royal, pious, widowed and in love with learning, had earlier proved the ideal president for an educative establishment and many noble striplings passed through her care.

In the case of Katherine Howard, the household of Agnes Dowager Duchess of Norfolk was the obvious selection, quite apart from the family relationship. For this remarkable, tough old woman in her sixties – she was

a contemporary of Margaret Countess of Salisbury, now in the Tower –
could bid to be the senior English matriarch. This was especially true after
her step-daughter-in-law Elizabeth Stafford Duchess of Norfolk separated
from her husband in 1534. (She took exception to his flagrant relationship
with a member of her household, Bess Holland, rudely described by the
furious Duchess Elizabeth as 'that harlot . . . the washer of my nursery'.)[24]

Born Agnes Tylney, the older Duchess was the second wife of the 2nd
Duke of Norfolk, whose first wife had also been a Tylney (so that a
dispensation in the second degree had to be sought for the marriage).
Together with her own children, Duchess Agnes had a vast family of step-
children, who were also her own relatives, to raise. The Duchess had
certainly been a prominent figure at court for the last forty years: to the
fore of all the great ceremonies. She had, for example, been attendant upon
Catherine of Aragon at her wedding night to Prince Arthur in 1501; she
was one of the godparents to Princess Mary in 1516; she bore the train of
her step-granddaughter Queen Anne Boleyn at her coronation and a few
months later acted as godmother once more to Princess Elizabeth.

Like other great ladies of her time, Duchess Agnes believed in the direct
administration of medicine, not delegation, and prided herself on her
remedies. We find her recommending this treatment for the dreaded sweat-
ing-sickness to Cardinal Wolsey: 'I give them treacle and water imperial,
which doth drive it from the heart,' she informed him, 'and thus have
helped them that have swooned divers times, and [those] that have received
the sacraments of the church [that is, in danger of death]; or vinegar,
wormwood, rosewater and crumbs of brown bread under the nose in a
linen cloth'.[25] Afterwards, vultures hovering round the carcass of Katherine
Howard's reputation would suggest that Duchess Agnes had kept something closely approaching a high-class brothel, but the true comparison
was to a high-class finishing school in which some quietly prospered and
others more daringly looked round to exploit its opportunities (or were in
their turn exploited).

Certainly Duchess Agnes was considered to be a responsible figure, quite
apart from her rank, to whom the care of the young could be safely
entrusted, as the lists of those to whom she was made guardian (such as
Elizabeth Knyvet or the three children of the Countess of Bridgewater)
demonstrates. But of course the comparison to a large school occurs once
again when one considers the enormous size of the Duchess's household –
over one hundred people at Lambeth – and the scandals which might take
place as a result. (The Duke of Norfolk had certainly taken advantage of
the size of his household in his long-term liaison with Bess Holland.)

Katherine's first romance took place while she was still in the country, at
the Duchess's house Chesworth near Horsham in Sussex. A neighbour

called Henry Mannox was hired to teach music there in 1536. The bold young man proceeded to try to seduce the fifteen-year-old girl in between the virginal and lute lessons, although if we are to believe Katherine's subsequent confession about her original admirer, full sex did not take place: 'at the flattering and fair persuasions of Mannox being but a young girl I suffered him at sundry times to handle and touch the secret parts of my body which neither became me with honesty to permit nor him to require'.[26]

Since Katherine would confess to greater intimacies with another, this account is probably accurate, with the penitent tone added later. Mannox himself, while admitting 'he felt more than was convenient' when meeting Katherine 'in the dark evening' in the Duchess's chapel, also swore that he never knew her 'carnally'.[27] Mannox followed Katherine to London, and attended the Duchess's house at Lambeth. No one seems to have taken this behaviour among young people particularly seriously: the trouble with Mannox was not his morals but the fact that, as a mere music teacher, he was no kind of match for Katherine, the Duke's niece.

Katherine's next romance, with Francis Dereham, a gentleman-pensioner in the Duchess's Lambeth household, was much more serious. There is every reason to suppose that, unlike her relationship with Mannox, it was fully consummated. Since the couple were also in the habit of addressing each other as 'wife' and 'husband' one can go further and suggest that Katherine and Francis Dereham were actually precontracted to each other, their private vows reinforced by full sexual union.

This romance took place in the great house, approached by a fine gateway off 'the King's highway leading from Lambeth Town to St George's Fields', that is, the Lambeth Road. Although the Lambeth house was by the standards of the time a suburban residence, it was a magnificent one. Here in the warren of galleries large and small and chambers occupied by the Duchess's numerous attendants, or in the broad garden which extended to the south the whole length of the building, Katherine and Francis were able to pursue their love affair. Katherine later limited the affair to three months in the autumn and winter of 1538 (when she was seventeen), which she called 'the whole truth'. It may not have been quite that: for she was sufficiently involved with Dereham for him to entrust her with £100 to keep for him when he went off to Ireland – a further proof of the seriousness of the relationship. However, her account of it is certainly explicit enough: 'Francis Dereham by many persuasions procured me to his vicious purpose and obtained first to lie upon my bed with his doublet and hose and after within the bed and finally he lay with me naked and used me in such sort as a man doth his wife many and sundry times but how often I know not.'[28]

Others would give more lubricious details of the goings-on at Lambeth

in the room where the young women slept communally (like all people of
their age and time) just as the young men shared another dormitory. Two
gallants, Dereham and Edward Waldegrave, a gentleman in waiting on the
Duchess, found a way of calling secretly at night on Katherine and another
girl, Joan Bulmer. Dereham and Waldegrave would lie on the girls' beds
in the night hours up to dawn; as for what went on then, there were tales
of how Katherine and Dereham would 'kiss and hang by their bellies as if
they were two sparrows', and a certain 'puffing and blowing' going on in
the dark which to those that heard it surely denoted sex. Love tokens were
exchanged: satin and velvet gifts from Dereham, an armband for his sleeve
from Katherine, and an embroidered friar's knot.[29]

At this point Mannox was jealous enough to warn the Duchess by means
of an anonymous note, sent with a friend, and left in her chapel pew.
The Duchess discovered Katherine embracing Dereham and was 'much
offended', hitting out – literally – at everyone in sight, including Joan
Bulmer who was also present. Yet however scabrous all this might sound,
related later by those who were in dreadful fear and anxious to distance
themselves from these events by condemning them, it still does not amount
to more than Katherine's own confession: there was a relationship, in which
Dereham 'used [her] . . . as a man doth his wife' – and seeing that Katherine,
an unmarried girl, probably at this point considered herself betrothed to
Dereham, even her submission to his advances had nothing so very terrible
about it by the standards of the time.

But Dereham, if better born than Mannox, was not a great match, and
Katherine appears to have cooled towards him during his absence in Ireland,
especially when she transferred closer to the court, at her uncle Norfolk's
house, and even more so when she made the acquaintance of the gallant
Thomas Culpeper, in the King's Privy Chamber. Katherine's early feelings
for Culpeper can only be gauged by her behaviour to him at a later date,
but from her welcoming attitude to him then, one suspects that she was
genuinely in love with him in the autumn of 1539. Then that momentous
event took place which was liable to make her fortune – and transform that
of her family: the King fell in love with her. So this was Katherine Howard,
susceptible, sexually attractive to men from an early age, partially seduced
by Mannox when she was fifteen, a process completed by Dereham two
years later. By the time she was appointed to the household of Queen Anna,
she was certainly experienced: in her own words, she had learned 'how
women might meddle with a man and yet conceive no child unless she
would herself'.[30]

It is this record of Katherine's past which makes it more likely that the
Howard family made the most of their good luck when the King fell for
her, rather than deliberately pushed her – and her alone – in this way. She

was not an ideal candidate for Queen. Norfolk's twenty-year-old daughter Mary might have been more suitable if the affinity with the King, her father-in-law, could have been sorted out: she was the widow of his son the Duke of Richmond, but still 'a maid' since the marriage had never been consummated, owing to the bridegroom's delicate health. Mary Duchess of Richmond was both intelligent and attractive, and there is reason to believe that the King admired her. Katherine had not been wildly promiscuous – many girls of that time, if their private lives were exposed in any kind of brutal examination, would prove to have had similar experiences, especially when they expected to marry the man concerned. (One must remember that Anne Boleyn had had some kind of precontract with Lord Percy, and quite possibly consummated it into the bargain.) On the other hand she was certainly not innocent. But the real awkwardness lay in the fact that Katherine had been in some form precontracted.

Once the King declared his interest, all this was conveniently forgotten. The Norfolks – Duke and Dowager Duchess – could hardly be expected to point out the unsuitability of the King's choice, still less the stained feathers in the plumage of their little goose who had turned out to be a swan. For one thing, it was against human nature to spoil their own triumph, and for another it would have been extremely frightening, more than experienced courtiers would have risked, to have deliberately provoked the monarch's wrath in the cause of revisiting a young girl's past. In the spring of 1540, where romance was concerned King Henry VIII was a recently disappointed man: no one cared to make him suffer another disappointment.

There were dangers in this policy, of course: one of the dangers lay in the fact that Katherine's earlier Dereham relationship had not exactly been conducted secretly, 'but many knew it'.[31] Another danger lay in the nature of the goose-turned-swan herself: did she really possess that mixture of nerve and calculation which had brought Jane Seymour as well as Anne Boleyn to the royal bed? Perhaps the very youthful sensuality which enchanted the King – reckless and promising – should have made her adult sponsors uneasy.

Instead Duchess Agnes coached Katherine on 'how to behave to the King' as once the Seymours and Sir Nicholas Carew had coached Jane Seymour. The royal passion grew. The first official indication of the King's feelings was the granting of lands, confiscated from a felon, to Mistress Howard on 24 April. In May, she received twenty-three gifts of quilted sarcanet, paid for by the King. At some point around this time, mid-April perhaps, the King made love fully to his sweetheart. Although there was naturally no official announcement of this happy event, the fact that it took place can be deduced from the change in the King's treatment of Queen

Anna. At Easter (that year in late March), he was still lamenting his situation and parliament, as has been noted, duly confirmed Queen Anna's dower in April. But after Whitsun – in mid-May – the pace changed. The King felt an urgent need to get rid of Queen Anna, and the reason was surely that since the relationship had been consummated there was a possibility – at least in his mind – of Mistress Howard being pregnant (a rumour to the effect that she was 'already *enceinte*' was repeated by the French ambassador Charles de Marillac in July).[32]

Queen Anna's last ceremonial appearance in her role as royal consort was at the May Day celebrations of 1540.* This month also saw the formulation of questionnaires concerning the precise nature of an individual's faith – with emphasis on belief in the sacraments – in which, as the French ambassador noted, the King, wearing his theologian's hat, took a personal interest. At first sight, it was this new concentration on heresy that enabled Norfolk and his allies to trap the recently ennobled Earl of Essex – Thomas Cromwell. On 10 June the King was apparently so convinced of Cromwell's lack of proper orthodoxy – 'sacramentarian heresy' – that he ordered the arrest of the most powerful man in the kingdom (after himself) who had served him faithfully for over ten years. Marillac received a message from the King to the effect that Cromwell had been about to suppress 'the old preachers' and enforce 'new [Lutheran] doctrines' upon him 'even by arms'.[33]

The arrest was accompanied by a distasteful scene when the grandees took the opportunity to punish the upstart who had kept them for so long from what they considered their proper positions of power. In particular, they robbed him of the symbols of the Order of the Garter. The Duke of Norfolk pulled the hanging figure of St George from round Cromwell's neck, while the Earl of Southampton tugged the Garter off his knee.

For all Cromwell's defiance – he threw his own bonnet on the ground and challenged them to name him a traitor – the magic spell that had for so long protected him, the confidence of the King in his servant's supreme abilities, had been fatally weakened by the whole affair of the Cleves marriage. It was Norfolk who had gone on a special embassy to France in February, and if England turned on its axis once again in that direction, then the whole of Cromwell's German imbroglio would be rendered at a stroke unnecessary and even rather dangerous. It was Norfolk's beguiling little niece who had rejuvenated the King where Cromwell's candidate, Anna of Cleves, with her 'Queenly manner', her shyness and her ignorance, had failed.

---

* Coincidentally, these were the very celebrations that had marked the beginning of the end for Queen Anne Boleyn.

Although the precise details of Cromwell's fall remain mysterious, as more than one historian has described them,[34] the influence of the personal on the public in the life of King Henry VIII is never better illustrated than by the whole episode. On the one hand, Cromwell's misjudgement over Anna of Cleves made him politically vulnerable, although the precise nature of his misjudgement was one he could scarcely have anticipated; on the other, the King's unexpected *coup de foudre* – his sudden 'fantasy' for Katherine Howard – gave the 'reactionary' party of Norfolk and Gardiner their opportunity to triumph politically and religiously over the rival 'reforming' faction in a way that was highly welcome but which, once again, they could scarcely have anticipated in 1539. So the two young women, Anna of Cleves and Katherine Howard, came to stand as symbols of different religious and political power groups. Anna of Cleves lost and Katherine Howard won – or so it seemed at the time.

Cromwell was taken by water to the Tower of London, his house sealed up and guarded by archers, his money and plate confiscated by the King. Piteous letters did not save him from his fate. God knew 'what labours, pains and travails' he had taken on his master's behalf, Cromwell wrote. Furthermore, if it were now in his power 'as it is [in] God's, to make your Majesty to live ever young and prosperous, God knoweth I would ...' A particularly pathetic note was struck when he referred to King Henry, if it would not offend His Majesty, as having been to him 'more like a dear father ... than a master'.[35]

But Cromwell's dear father was in ferocious mood. Cromwell was to be sentenced to death – by an Act of Attainder: there was to be no trial. Ironically enough it was a novel method of procedure he himself had suggested for dealing with Margaret Countess of Salisbury, who was, however, still languishing in the Tower. Cromwell was therefore to be the first person to die in this way, his crimes being high treason and heresy. Included in the Act of Attainder were the charges that Cromwell had sworn to marry the King's daughter Mary in 1538 and himself usurp the throne – which must surely have strained the credulity of even the most loyal courtier. There was however a last service he was able to perform for the King: from the Tower, he deposed all those conversations on the vexed subject of the King's fourth marriage, the wedding night and thereafter, which would be helpful to the King's case for nullity. Two days before his arrest, Cromwell had shown himself well aware of the problem when he told his protégé Sir Thomas Wriothesley details of the unhappy situation, with a sigh: 'Ah, but it is a great matter'. The next day, according to his own account, Wriothesley sagely observed that if some relief were not found, they would all 'smart for it' some day.[36]

The King had in effect two possible grounds on which to divorce Anna of Cleves. There was the question of the precontract, although that might prove difficult to establish if the amicable mood of Cleves was disturbed by the mention of separation. An envoy was sent to confer with the English ambassador in France, Sir John Wallop, as to whether the Cardinal of Lorraine might provide further information regarding the earlier contract between his nephew Francis of Lorraine and 'the Queen here' (Anna). What was really wanted was 'a true copy of the said pact'; although Wallop was urged to act discreetly in the matter, 'as it appear not that it do proceed from Us'.[37] It does not seem that this mission was successful: the precontract remained a good argument, but not a clinching one.

Then there was the question of non-consummation: in itself this was the clearest cause of nullity by the rules of the church, but it was one that was inevitably difficult to establish – with the need to prove a negative. This was especially true when a couple had indisputably shared a bedchamber all night on more than one occasion. As there were those who insisted Prince Arthur must have consummated his marriage to Catherine of Aragon on these grounds, scoffers would be bound to look askance at the King's convenient avowals of impotence. As the English merchant Richard Hilles would write scornfully to the leading Protestant Henry Bullinger in Zürich about the notion of the Lady Anna being still 'a maid' when the King had had her alone for five or six months: 'a likely thing, forsooth!' It had all come about because 'the King's affections were alienated from the lady Anna to that young girl Katherine Howard', whom he described as 'a cousin [actually a niece] of the Duke of Norfolk'.[38]

Each of the arguments had its weakness. But by combining them – he had not been able to consummate the marriage because it was unlawful in the first place – the King was able to occupy that territory to which he was so partial in these situations, the moral high ground. Furthermore it made it possible to see any future marriage – to Mistress Howard for example – as a dynastic duty, since, as Cromwell expressed it, 'you [the King] should never have any more children, for the comfort of the realm, if you should so continue' with Queen Anna.[39]

The next step was to secure the cooperation of Queen Anna herself. This was vital if the matter was to be settled satisfactorily (and the King had all too vivid experiences of how matters might go wrong if the lady concerned did not cooperate . . .). It would not help England if the Duke of Cleves, unnecessarily courted to be an ally as it turned out, was equally gratuitously turned into an enemy by the rejection of his sister. A great deal depended on how Anna of Cleves took the news of her dismissal; her agreement to the facts of non-consummation was especially important since, however much the King could lament and swear his impotence, his situation remained extremely complicated if his wife told another story.

So far as can be made out, Queen Anna had really no inkling of the fate awaiting her. That summer, life for her seemed to be getting more pleasant rather than less: she was gradually learning English; furthermore the English people were taking to her. The French ambassador at least testified that she had gained their love, and that they 'esteemed her as one of the most sweet, gracious, and humane queens they had had';[40] this view, even if an exaggeration, acts as a corrective to the conventional cruel picture of Anna of Cleves as Henry VIII's clumsy and inadequate Flanders mare. When the Queen was transferred away from the court to Richmond Palace on 24 June, on the excuse of the threat of plague, she had no reason not to enjoy life in the pleasant riverside palace built by Henry VII at the turn of the century. However, the next day she received a rude awakening. A deputation came to her and informed her that the King had discovered their marriage to be invalid.

According to one account, Queen Anna fainted at the news. But the commissioners who confronted her told another story to the King. They had informed her 'by mouth of an interpreter' – there were to be no false impressions about this message – 'who did his part very well'. As for the Queen, she listened to them 'without alteration of countenance'. One is inclined to believe the commissioners; although her composure may have been due to shock rather than indifference. Anna was certainly in a frightening as well as a bewildering situation for a young woman in a foreign country without proper advisers. The knowledge that King Henry had had one unsatisfactory wife executed must surely have played its part in her submission. (Her brother the Duke of Cleves would say later that he was glad his sister had fared no worse.) For submit she did. The Queen 'made answer', wrote the commissioners, 'the effect of which tendeth to this, that she is content always with your Majesty'. It was significant that in her formal letter of submission, she signed herself 'Anna, daughter of Cleves' rather than presuming to herself the style or name 'Queen'.[41]

Whether by luck – out of sheer terror – or by instinct – having observed her husband's wilfulness – Anna of Cleves had managed to return that answer most likely to gratify the King. And she presented him, furthermore, with a deeply pleasing image: that of a submissive woman, accepting his will, his decisions in all things, casting herself on his mercy. Under such circumstances, Henry VIII had always shown himself capable of being generous. He was generous now to 'the daughter of Cleves'.

She was to have precedence over all the ladies in England, except the Queen, the King's daughters by any future marriage, and his existing daughters. She was to receive a handsome settlement of manors and estates 'in divers counties', some of which had been recently forfeited by Cromwell, worth some £3,000 a year (an enormous sum). All this was for the lifetime of the Lady Anna on one condition – that she did not pass 'beyond the sea': instead she was to be naturalized as the King's subject and lead a new, prosperous and happy life as the King's adopted 'good sister'. This condition was of course essential for damage limitation where Cleves was concerned: the English could not have a disgruntled Lady Anna at liberty to stir up trouble abroad. Instead, as an English subject, she was like any other subject, committed 'wholly unto Us [the King], to remain and continue with Us ... as We should dispose of her within our Realm.' (Another foreign-born princess, Catherine of Aragon, had argued strongly that she was *not* the King's subject if her marriage was invalid; which probably accounted for the care taken on this point with the Lady Anna.)

The various steps needful for the King's latest divorce were now set in motion. The obedient findings of the clergy were that there had *both* been a precontract *de praesenti*, insufficiently investigated at the time of the marriage, *and* that the union had not been consummated; furthermore the marriage was void because Henry had acted under duress – from Cromwell. On that basis, the King's latest 'great matter' was passed by convocation on 9 July: 'there had been no carnal copulation between Your Majesty and the said Lady Anna, nor with that just impediment interceding, could it be possible.'[42] It was approved by parliament four days later. Throughout this process, the fiction – for so it manifestly was – that the clergy had themselves become uneasy about this latest marriage and petitioned the King to have it examined was blandly maintained. So Anna of Cleves was formally removed from the position of Queen of England which she had occupied for six months and a few days: an even shorter period than the tragic Jane Seymour who had been Queen for a year and a half.

Even before the dissolution of the marriage a special act concerning impediments had been passed through parliament, which declared that after 1 July 1540 any marriage contracted and consummated should be valid, whatever unconsummated precontracts existed. It is sometimes suggested that Katherine Howard had confessed something of her past and was seeking to be freed of any bonds to Dereham; but since there is no other evidence that Katherine did any such thing (on the contrary she seems to have allowed the doting King to believe happily in her complete innocence), this act has been more plausibly viewed as an extra piece of caution on the subject of the Cleves divorce.[43] The consummation of the King's projected marriage to Katherine would have the force of nullifying his (unconsummated) union with Anna of Cleves, whatever the circumstances of their break-up.

There was a relevance to Katherine's situation in the statute but it lay in her close blood relationship to Anne Boleyn rather than her past. The statute sanctimoniously denounced the former profitable practices of the

Roman church which for the sake of making money out of dispensations had added unnecessarily to the prohibitions surrounding marriage. Among cases listed – now to be free of the need for dispensation – were 'kindred or affinity between cousin germans [first cousins]' and 'carnal knowledge of any of the same kin or affinity'. So that neatly took care of that. The King and Katherine were free of the ghost of Anne Boleyn.

There remained the problem of Duke William of Cleves and his reaction. No one wanted to press him into the arms of the Emperor out of mortification. The general opinion of the King's advisers was that it would be best if the King's 'good sister' broke the news to him herself. At first even the docile Lady Anna seems to have objected to this: she agreed to respond favourably to her brother's communications but preferred not to have the humiliating task of explaining the circumstances which had led to her rejection. But on 13 July the King directed Suffolk (a veteran of this kind of mission) and others to press the Lady Anna to write the actual letter. A draft of what she should say was enclosed.[44] Furthermore, her original letter of submission to the King (in English) was to be translated by her into 'her tongue' and signed once more. Otherwise people might suggest that she had agreed 'ignorantly, not understanding whereunto she did subscribe'. Suffolk was to offer a heavy hint that whereas agreement would be regarded as evidence of 'plain and sincere dealing' on the Lady Anna's behalf, 'refusal might arouse the King's suspicions . . .'

Above all, the Lady Anna was not to be encouraged, as it was expressed, to 'play the woman'. The royal instructions ended on a sternly misogynistic note. If the Lady Anna's subscription to all this was not gained in writing, 'all shall remain uncertain [dependent] upon a woman's promise to be no woman' – that is, not to behave as women generally did. It was felt hardly likely that the Lady Anna would be capable of such restraint, just as 'the changing of her womanish nature' was downright impossible. But for all the pessimism of the English, the Lady Anna did not 'play the woman', if that meant being changeable or tricky.

She wrote to the King again on 16 July, reiterating her promise to be 'Your Majesty's most humble sister and servant'. To her brother she wrote meekly as dictated: 'I account God pleased with [what] is done, and know myself to have suffered no wrong or injury.' She was still a maid: 'my body preserved in the integrity which I brought into this Realm.' There was fulsome praise of King Henry. Even if she could not 'justly have [him] as my Husband,' nevertheless she found him to be 'a most kind, loving and friendly Father and Brother, and to use me as honourably, and with as much humanity and liberality as you, I myself, or any of our Kin or Allies could wish or desire . . .' Anna of Cleves also pressed her brother to continue his friendship with England. Merely in a few final words did she indicate the reality of her position: 'Only I require this of you, That you so use yourself in this Matter, [that] I fare not the worse; whereunto I trust you will have regard.'[45]

Still, the English felt some anxiety about the reaction of Cleves – not unmixed with the irritability of those who have behaved badly and know it. The instructions to the envoys sent there display this. For example, the Duchess Maria might well make a fuss, as mothers do: if she was not satisfied 'and such like' the envoys must simply make their excuses politely and leave. As for the Duke of Cleves, on no account was he to receive any financial recompense, since the King was treating his sister so liberally. In the event Duke William received the news, and the Lady Anna's letter, 'with no very good cheer'. But later that evening Olisleger came unbidden and supped with the English; he assured them that despite the Duke's concern, there would be no breach between the two countries. It was true that the Duke was anxious for his sister's return to 'her own country ... for the people here would gladly have her, and would grudge every inch at her tarrying there', that is in England.[46] To this the envoys smoothly replied that the Lady Anna was staying in England of her own free will.

So the King's fourth marriage formally ended, to the general amazement of Europe. When King François was told that King Henry had got rid of his Queen, he repeated incredulously: 'The Queen that now is?' On being assured, yes, that Queen, he merely gave a deep sigh: 'Ah'. After the amazement came the disgust. The English ambassador at the imperial court told the Duke of Norfolk that there had been a good deal of adverse gossip about the divorce and 'obloquies' showered on the King's name.[47] (Although Charles V was sharp enough to perceive that his confrontation with Cleves was now much eased – as indeed proved to be the case.)

None of this impeded the smooth progress of the preparations for the King's fifth marriage, which parliament had obediently requested him to make for the sake of further royal heirs (although the name of the bride was omitted). In other quarters, however, there was no mystery about that name. On 12 July, for example, Joan Bulmer, she who had shared Katherine's nocturnal romps at Lambeth, despatched a letter stating she had heard of her friend's great destiny, and would she, Katherine, now please send for her to court?[48] It was a letter which on the surface at least was typical of the kind of plea any future mistress of a royal household might receive. Time would show whether some of these merry companions of Katherine's girlhood pleasures might not come back to haunt her.

For the present 'that young girl Katherine Howard' was riding secure in the King's affection. The weather was extremely hot and dry: no rain had fallen since the beginning of June (and would not fall again until early

October).[49] In this torrid season, on 28 July, Henry VIII married his latest sweetheart: choosing the very day on which Thomas Cromwell was executed at the Tower of London.

The ceremony took place at Oatlands Palace in Surrey. It was a moated palace of medium size which the King had acquired in 1537, and the Queen's apartments there had been decorated for a woman who never lived to occupy them – Jane Seymour. Now he had a very different wife to grace his court at Oatlands and elsewhere. In her marriage vows, which the King already had good reason to believe that she would carry out, Katherine swore to be 'bonair and buxom in bed'. She also swore to live with her husband in sickness and in health 'till death us depart'.[50]

Chapter 16

OLD MAN'S JEWEL

*Thinking now in his old days, after sundry troubles of
mind which have happened to him by marriages, to
have obtained such a jewel for womanhood and very
perfect love to him ...*

**The Privy Council on the King's marriage to Katherine
Howard, 1541**

To Henry VIII, Katherine Howard was his 'blushing rose without a
thorn'.[1] He was besottedly in love with her. Now that he had married
his innocent young flower (Katherine took as her personal emblem the
rose crowned), the King could hardly keep his hands off her. His constant
public caresses of his bride led several observers to the conclusion that
King Henry loved this particular wife more than he had 'the others'.
Cranmer's secretary, Ralph Morice, wrote: 'The King's affection was so
marvelously set upon that gentlewoman, as it was never known that he
had the like to any woman'.[2] Whatever the comparisons to the past, the
King's passion certainly aroused general comment. It was regarded with
gratified complacency by Katherine's relations. While those at court who
were not quite so pleased by this elevation of the Howards held their
peace – for the time being.

Just as the King lavished affection on his young wife, he showered her
with rich gifts. The girl who had been brought up as a member of a large
impoverished family, a poor relation to the grandees about her, was now
the recipient of a stream of magnificent jewels, gold beads decorated
with black enamel, emeralds lozenged with gold, brooches, crosses,
pomanders, clocks, whatever could be most splendidly encrusted in her
honour. At the New Year of 1541, for example, spent at Hampton Court,
Queen Katherine received among other presents 'an upper habiliment
containing eight diamonds and seven rubies' and a necklace of 'six fine
table diamonds and five very fair rubies with pearls in-between'; a muffler
of black velvet furred with sables, hanging from a chain of thirty pearls,

was further ornamented with rubies and pearls strung on chains of gold.[3] The cornucopia was seemingly bottomless.

Naturally, the usual transformation scene had to take place, courtesy of Galyon Hone, with badges removed, new badges supplied: at Rochester, for example, that former monastic priory converted for the King's use, where Anna of Cleves had slept on her bridal journey towards London, Katherine Howard's badges were supplied. Elsewhere, the exceptionally rapid turnover of Queens meant that some quick decisions had to be made. For instance, there was the question of the dedication of an English obstetric work called *The Byrthe of Mankind*, drawing on the Latin of Rhodion's *De Partu Hominis*. This has been described as 'perhaps the most interesting work on Midwifery in the English language', being 'the head and source of English literature' (previous works on the subject in English had been in manuscript only); its illustrations are also among the first copperplate engravings in England. The author-translator was Richard Jonas – and he had come to England in the train of Anna of Cleves.[4]

Obviously the dedication had been originally intended for his then mistress, but there was fortunately just time for Jonas to substitute as his dedicatee: 'the most gracious and in all goodnesse most excellent vertuous Lady Quene Katheryne'. *The Byrthe of Mankind* went through many editions down to 1676, but this dedication to Queen Katherine Howard (the only known dedication of a book to her) is peculiar to the 1540 edition and had vanished by the edition of 1545; another piece of symbolic evanescence in the career of Katherine Howard.

But there is one permanent monument to this May-and-December marriage of 1540 which has been discerned: in the great east window of King's College Chapel, Cambridge. The initials H and K can be seen in the tracery among other Tudor royal emblems proclaiming the supremacy of the Tudor dynasty in state and church.* Similarly, in a side window of about the same period, a deliberate resemblance to Henry VIII himself has been discovered in the face of King Solomon, probably painted by Galyon Hone. In which case, it may well be that the figure of the Queen of Sheba, seen in profile with her short nose and full lips, sensual and suppliant, presenting gifts to Solomon, preserves, however fleetingly, the likeness of Katherine Howard.[6]

At the time, the status of Queen Katherine as consort was further underlined by the castles, lordships and manors granted to her, many of which had belonged to Queen Jane Seymour in the past, and some, more

---

* The K cannot refer to Catherine/Katherine of Aragon since the work is attributed to Dierick Vellert, in the period after his return from Constantinople in 1533.[5]

recently, to Thomas Cromwell. The King's attitude to Katherine was summed up by the French ambassador: he was 'so enamoured' that he could not 'treat her well enough'. As for Katherine's own state of mind, the motto she chose to go with her emblem of the crowned rose went as follows: *'Non autre volonté que la sienne'*, 'No other wish but his.'[7]

This was certainly a politic motto: one likely to bring comfort to an elderly husband sexually entranced by his new young wife. But at the time of Katherine's marriage, it was not necessarily insincere. Nor should one assume that Katherine Howard lacked all feelings for King Henry, just because he was older – much older than her – fat and sometimes sick, while she had already shown herself to be a flighty young thing with an eye for a handsome young man. As with Jane Seymour, the real clue to Katherine Howard's wifely emotions lay in the office of King and the enormous, awed respect it evoked. The two young women were of totally different character; nevertheless they had both been brought up since birth to bow without question before the great royal sun which blazed at the centre of every courtier's life.

One should see Katherine as an impressionable girl – if not an innocent one in the conventional sense of the word. Some time later she would be revealed as believing that the King actually knew what sins were spoken in the confessional, just because he was the King: for whatever was said 'surely the King, being supreme head of the church, should have knowledge of it'.[8] This reminds us that the King's ecclesiastical title, claimed when Katherine was barely in her teens, gave a whole new quasi-religious dimension to the conventional notion of royal might, for the generation growing up in the 1530s. Such a level of naivety, such a belief in his omnipotence, made it easy for Queen Katherine to regard King Henry with bedazzled reverence; and then there was gratitude for his generosity.

Her emotions were not of course strictly speaking to do with love, let alone that romantic love so generally despised by the pundits of the time; but they were quite as much as many contemporary wives felt for their husbands, especially those – not a few – with a considerable disparity of age between them. At the same time, the experience of reverence and gratitude did not mean that Katherine Howard had radically changed her character when she became Queen. She remained pleasure-loving as she had been in her previous short existence, to atone for its rigours.

As Queen, however, she had new ways of enjoying herself: the exercise of patronage, for example. By mid-November she was arguing with Archbishop Lee about the advowson, or right of presentation, of the archdeaconry of York, which she wanted for one of her chaplains, Mr Lowe, when it should fall vacant through death. (The Archbishop disapproved of an advowson hanging over the head of a man thought likely to die: 'this uncharitableness is so discrepant to the order of priesthood'.)[9] Members of her family were duly advanced according to the expectations of those whose candidate had won the royal matrimonial lottery. Katherine's brother Charles Howard was placed in the Privy Chamber. The following year, an interesting appointment was made in the Queen's own household, apparently at the instigation of Duchess Agnes. Francis Dereham, Katherine's erstwhile fiancé, to use the modern term, was made her secretary.[10] With hindsight, it was not a very wise appointment by those who surely wished to seal away the incriminating past; on the other hand the intention may have been to shut Dereham's mouth with what was in effect a handsome bribe. In any case, when the appointment was made, in August 1541, it caused no particular comment; it was simply part of the conventional pattern of a Queen's patronage in which friends as well as relatives naturally found a place.

In other ways Queen Katherine enjoyed her position and was determined to maintain it. Her youth made her especially sensitive to possible slights from her step-daughter the Lady Mary who was five years her senior. She complained that Mary did not treat her with sufficient respect, compared to Mary's favourable attitude towards Queen Jane Seymour and Queen Anna of Cleves. Piqued, Queen Katherine exercised her new powers to have two of the Lady Mary's maids removed. There may have been something in Katherine's resentment, since Chapuys, reporting on the matter, thought it was important that 'means to conciliate ... the new Queen' should be found, and then the maids would probably be allowed to remain.[11]

This kind of girlish hauteur on the part of Katherine is perhaps pardonable, given that the husband whose will she had vowed to make her own was, at this stage of his life, no desirable older man like his contemporary the Duke of Suffolk (also with a young wife), but rather closer to an obese monster – if a doting monster. It is clear that King Henry suffered a violent increase in his weight – already vast enough – in the year 1540. Frederick Count Palatine had visited England in September 1539, as the brother-in-law of Christina of Denmark, in a last-minute attempt to stave off the Cleves commitment; seeing a recent picture of the English King in October 1540 he asked the English ambassador, Richard Pate, whether his master had not 'waxed fat'. Pate tactfully ducked the question; he merely assured the Count that the King was as merry and lusty as ever, 'lauded be God', and 'as well enseamed' (that is, fit: the term used for hawks in prime condition for being worked).[12] Merry and lusty King Henry might be – especially following his summer marriage to Katherine – but with his 54 inch waist and 57 inch chest, measurements attested by his armour made in 1540, he can hardly be described as being in prime condition.*

Various elements contributed to these proportions. The first was hereditary: the King's grandfather Edward IV, another tall man, had been heavily overweight in his last years – and he had died at forty-one; Henry VIII was nearly fifty. Then King Henry, like most of his contemporaries, loved to eat and drink; his appetite has come to be regarded as excessive because it led to an excessive physique, but in fact the regular demolition of huge meaty repasts washed down with wine and beer (no one drank water) was the rule not the exception. As a big hearty man, with a big frame to fill, he was certainly greedy, but that in itself was not uncharacteristic of the age in which he lived. The real trouble was one common to many who have been athletes in youth and then find themselves unable to fulfil the same punishing routine, so that muscle turns to fat, and in King Henry's case, yet more fat.

The King's health was now giving serious cause for concern. He had been a wonderfully healthy young man, 'well enseamed' indeed, until the check of that jousting accident in 1524. But in the late 1520s he began to suffer from varicose ulcerations of his legs – the first one probably occurred in 1528 – which in time became chronic. Gradually the inflamed veins became thrombosed, and the next stage was the cruelly painful swelling of the lower legs, causing intermittent bouts of fever, a condition liable to cause rage and frustration in a far more moderately tempered man than Henry VIII.† Added to which, the King's second dangerous fall, in January 1536, which left him unconscious for two hours, had seriously impaired his general state. His legs gave him a lot of trouble in the summer of 1537, again in 1539, and yet again in September 1540. It was a vicious circle. Naturally the King's expanding weight did not help the condition of his legs; at the same time the condition of his legs frequently prevented him taking the exercise which would have been therapeutic.

The fact that the King went on a special regime in December 1540 –

---

* This set of armour, its borders based on a design by Holbein and made under the master armourer Erasmus Kyrkenar at Greenwich, is erected as a colossal standing figure in the Royal Armories at the Tower of London; it still makes a commanding – and menacing – impression upon the visitor 450 years later.

† The theory that the King suffered from syphilis has been rejected in recent years. Sir Arthur Salusbury MacNalty in *Henry VIII. A Difficult Patient*, 'The Diagnosis of King Henry's "Sorre Legge" ', points out that a syphilitic ulcer would have been recognized by Tudor surgeons and treated with mercury, but mercury was not prescribed for the King. It has recently been suggested that the King's problems were due to 'a lack of ascorbic acid' in his diet, that is, scurvy; but this condition was common to his contemporaries: the King's personal weakness was his 'Sorre Legge' and its side effects.[13]

inspired no doubt by his passion for Katherine – is in itself evidence, not untouching, of his concern about his problem. This 'new rule of living' as the French ambassador called it, specially designed to cure corpulence, meant that the King would rise between 5 and 6 am, hear Mass at 7, then ride till 10, which was his dinner hour. Marillac duly reported that the King was feeling much better as a result, certainly better than during the previous winter when his leg had kept him largely inactive.[14]

Regrettably, the new rule could not stave off a serious attack of fever in the early spring of 1541. One of the ulcers kept open to maintain health suddenly closed, to the King's 'great alarm'. The danger was considered extreme, and the King's temper matched the danger. Marillac reported that his mood swings were extraordinary and savage. Although pain was of course the excuse, and one that should be treated prima facie with sympathy, the fact that the King was now muttering away about the execution of Cromwell ('the most faithful servant he ever had') as having been brought about by his ministers 'upon light pretexts, by false accusations' shows that sympathy should also be extended to those who had to tend upon him. He formed, wrote Marillac, 'a sinister opinion of some of his chief men in his illness'. Nor were the King's more remote subjects treated with any more tenderness. 'He had an unhappy people to govern', he shouted, whom 'he would shortly make so poor that they would not have the boldness nor the power to oppose him'.[15] In his agony, the King's two most unattractive qualities were well in evidence. First there was his self-pity – everything was someone else's fault – and then there was his self-will – no one must oppose him on anything at any time ever. No wonder the courtiers trembled.

Those in attendance on the sick-bed did not include the young Queen. This was at the King's own request: understandably he did not want his fresh romantic relationship clouded with images of illness, swollen suppurating legs and so forth. Thus King Henry went at least ten or twelve days in March 1541 without seeing his wife. It seems likely that this was the period when Queen Katherine began to wonder whether she might not combine the substantial joys of being Queen with the more light-hearted pleasures of her previous existence.

One of the bizarre aspects of the court of King Henry and Queen Katherine must have been the visits of the King's 'good sister', the Lady Anna of Cleves. At New Year 1541, for example, a year to the day since her first unfortunate encounter with King Henry, the Lady Anna celebrated by flinging herself down on her knees before Queen Katherine Howard, 'as if she herself were merely the most insignificant damsel'. She had already despatched her gifts for the occasion: two huge and magnificent horses caparisoned in mauve velvet. The placatory presents of Anna of Cleves to her 'good brother' would indeed continue to be a feature of their relationship, as though the Lady Anna was determined never to be out of mind, even if she was temporarily out of sight. Examples of the signature of Lady Anna of Cleves have been described as 'excessively rare': one of them is to be found in a hand-illuminated Book of Hours, *Hore ad usum Sarum*, printed in Germany in about 1533, given by the Lady Anna to the King.* These dedicatory words are written on a blank leaf at the end: 'I beseche your grace huble when ye loke on this rember me. Yor graces assured anne the dowther off cleves'. ('I beseech your grace humbly when you look on this remember me. Your grace's assured Anne the daughter of Cleves.')[16]

At the 1541 banquet, which followed the former Queen's obeisance to the present incumbent, it was noted that the Lady Anna looked as happily unconcerned 'as if there had been nothing between them' (herself and the King). Anna of Cleves, aged twenty-five, ended the evening dancing with Queen Katherine Howard, aged nineteen, while the old King stumped off to bed, because his leg was hurting him. This arrangement was evidently a great success. The next day all parties had dinner together again, with much 'conversation, amusement and mirth'; as before the evening ended with the young ladies dancing together after the King retired.

Such cheerful intimacy had no precedent: the King's previously divorced wife, Catherine of Aragon, had been kept in seclusion, and as 'Princess Dowager' was certainly never allowed near the court to confront the new Queen. The case of the Lady Anna was however very different for two reasons. First, the King had a vested interest in proving to a disconcerted, if not scandalized Europe, that the lady in question fully agreed with the dissolution of their union. When the theologian Melanchthon referred to 'the English Nero', it was a reassuring rebuttal to welcome the Lady Anna at court – as a sister if not a wife. (We do not know whether that 'marrying ring' with its hopeful inscription 'God send me wel to kepe' was still on her finger, but if so, it had magically become the gift 'of a loving brother'.)[17]

Since King Henry always felt bonhomous towards those who bowed to his will, he was fully prepared to be on the best of terms with his ex-wife. Indeed, so jolly were King Henry and Lady Anna together at the beginning of August that rumours began to spread that he was about to restore her to her previous position. This was of course nonsense, but the fact that these rumours continued to surround the Lady Anna for the next few years shows how incomprehensible the putting aside of a princess with

---

* This handsome Book of Hours is now in the Folger Shakespeare Library, Washington. The dedication is not dated, but from the signature must belong to the period following Anna of Cleves' divorce, rather than the short period of her marriage when she would have signed herself in the style of preceding consorts, 'Anna/Anne the Quene'.

connections, in favour of a chit of a girl, was to most outsiders. Furthermore, these rumours were nearly always attended by sexual innuendoes; as though the explanation given for the divorce, the non-consummation of the marriage, was equally incomprehensible. And yet for once it was the truth.

There was a second good reason for all this cordiality. The Lady Anna herself was extremely anxious to take the King's promise that there should be nothing but friendship between 'her brother' and herself at its face value. Observers were divided into those who thought it 'stupidity' on her part to accept her dismissal with such bovine equanimity: 'she did not understand'. There were others who thought 'this is marvellous prudence on her part'.[18] The latter were surely right. The Lady Anna was not a fool: she had been bewildered at first by what happened to her but once she assessed the situation, she conducted herself not only with dignity but also with shrewdness.

Anna of Cleves had come to like England and, speaking a little more of the language, to like the English, as well as being liked by them (as Marillac testified). Of the royal family, she seems to have been especially fond of the little Elizabeth, nearly seven at the time of this divorce;[19] she was also on excellent terms with Mary, who was her own age, and whose religious attitudes she shared. What was the alternative? She could make a humiliating return to Cleves – from where she had set forth so proudly to be a queen of a great country – and find herself once more under the care of a strict mother while her brother negotiated another marriage for her, to be made once again for (his) reasons of state. In making such a return, she would, incidentally, sacrifice the handsome settlement the grateful King had made upon her.

Here in England, on the other hand, she had an honourable position at court, no rejected woman, but the first lady after the Queen and the royal daughters. Like a rich widow (ever a favourable position for any woman untroubled by grief) she had a household, a large income and property, untrammelled by any need to bow before any male authority except that of the English King, who manifestly did not wish to exercise that authority in any of its more trying aspects. It is true that she would lack the experience of sex, but then she would also lack the dangerous side to that, the potentially lethal experience of childbirth; quite apart from her unrecorded reactions to the King's earlier efforts to consummate his marriage which may not have filled her with desire to repeat such an experiment.

So the Lady Anna took refuge in a good-natured and, it must be said, endearing hedonism. She began to enjoy a drink, as Chapuys noted, abandoning her previous abstinence. She spent her money freely, in Marillac's words, taking 'all the recreation she could in diversity of dress and pastime', without any man to stop her. Not only were there a great many women at

Katherine Howard
m 1540

Crowned rose badge of Katherine Howard.

Window of the Queen of Sheba, King's College Chapel: the face of the Queen of Sheba may be a portrait of Katherine Howard (of whom there is no authenticated likeness).

Thomas Howard, 3rd Duke of Norfolk; uncle to both Katherine Howard and Anne Boleyn.

Detail of the Window of the Queen of Sheba.

Henry VIII about 1542.

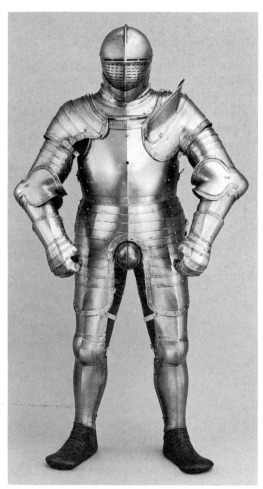

Armour made for Henry VIII in 1540, the year he married Katherine Howard.

PARVVLE PATRISSA, PATRIÆ VIRTVTIS ET HÆRES
ESTO, NIHIL MAIVS MAXIMVS ORBIS HABET.
GNATVM VIX POSSVNT COELVM ET NATVRA DEDISSE,
HVIVS QVEM PATRIS, VICTVS HONORET HONOS.
ÆQVATO TANTVM, TANTI TV FACTA PARENTIS,
VOTA HOMINVM, VIX QVO PROGREDIANTVR, HABENT
VINCITO, VICISTI. QVOT REGES PRISCVS ADORAT
ORBIS. NEC TE QVI VINCERE POSSIT, ERIT.

Edward, Prince of Wales, son of Henry VIII and Jane Seymour.

Elizabeth, daughter of Anne Boleyn and Henry VIII, aged about 13, attributed to William Scrots.

Miniature of Mary, daughter of Henry
VIII and Catherine of Aragon.

Mary, by Holbein.

The Lady Mary after Queen.

The only known letter by Katherine Howard addressed to 'Master [Thomas] Culpeper': it expresses her desire – 'for I never longed so much for anything as I do to see you' (line 5 from top) – and is signed (short line on the right, near bottom of page) 'yours as long as life endures', then 'Katherine' immediately underneath it.

The Chapel of St Peter ad Vincula, at the Tower of London, showing the execution site of Katherine Howard and Anne Boleyn in the foreground. Both Queens were subsequently buried in the Chapel.

Edward, Prince of Wales, aged about 6.

Katherine Willoughby, Duchess of Suffolk, by Holbein.

this time who were far worse off but one might go further and argue that the Lady Anna of Cleves was, for the time being, one of the happiest women at the Tudor court. No wonder that while the Clevian envoy Olisleger was 'disconsolate' at the relegation of his country's position as represented by the divorce, the words generally used to describe the Lady Anna herself, indifferent to those concerns, were 'cheerful' and 'gay' and 'joyous'.[20]

Queen Katherine Howard certainly faced a more challenging destiny. After he recovered from his illness, the King decided to take her with him on an important progress – that northern tour which he had so far never made, since the pregnancy of Queen Jane Seymour had caused it to be postponed. It is possible that a northern coronation was planned for the new Queen, as four years earlier it had been intended to have Queen Jane crowned at York Minster, or so King Henry had told Robert Aske.

In the popular imagination, the crowning of Queen Katherine was strictly linked with her production of a second son for the King. In Marillac's report to France of 10 April, he wrote that 'this Queen is thought to be with child, which would be a very great joy to this King, who, it seems, believes it, and intends if it be found true, to have [her] crowned at Whitsuntide'.* Embroiderers were said to be working on furniture and tapestry, using copes and ornaments stripped from the churches: 'moreover, the young lords and gentlemen of this court are practising daily for the jousts and tournaments to be then made'. When the King took his richest tapestries, plate and dress away with him to the north, Marillac was convinced that the reason was the future coronation of 'this Queen', which was generally hoped to be at York just as the people of York themselves hoped for 'a Duke'.[22]

It may well be that if Queen Katherine had succeeded in becoming pregnant either on the eve of her journey to the north or in the course of it, York would indeed have witnessed that act symbolic of a nation's prosperity, the coronation of a pregnant queen. That did not happen. Nevertheless encouraging and interesting reports of the Queen being 'unwell' while with her husband at Grafton Regis in mid-July, quite apart from Marillac's prognostication, indicate that a royal pregnancy was at least a possibility. This in turn suggests that, despite his recent dangerous illness, the King was still able from time to time to make love to his wife: his rose crowned.

The previous year he had, after all, given his doctor specific details to

---

* Conversely, certain English people were said to feel 'a scruple' over the fact that Queen Jane, mother of Prince Edward, had never been crowned; this of course strengthened the position of Mary, whose mother had been crowned.[21]

support the notion that he could still make love – if not to Anna of Cleves. Furthermore, on delicate subjects like fertility (and potency), one should beware of hindsight. Although the King had not fathered a child for four years, during this time his then wife, Queen Jane, had been pregnant for nine months, he himself had been a widower for over one year, and he had then been trapped (his version) for six months in a physically impossible marriage. The procreation of 'a Duke of York' by the King was certainly not out of the question.

Yet at some point in the spring, probably in the period immediately following the King's illness, Queen Katherine renewed her involvement with Thomas Culpeper. Why did she do so? And why did Culpeper agree? Taking the Queen's point of view first, it seems right to seek an explanation in Katherine's fatal lightness of temperament rather than in some more Machiavellian intention. Katherine Howard's character was reckless, not devious (except when, like any young person, she tried to hide her conduct from her elders). She was the sort of girl who lost her head easily over a man, a girl who agreed generally with what men suggested. In short she was the reverse of calculating.

It might be thought that Queen Katherine took up with Culpeper in order to provide the King with a healthy living (secretly bastard) child. But this is to misread both relationships – Katherine's with Culpeper, and Katherine's with the King. The one was intended to be a romantic dalliance – within certain limits: Katherine was, on her own admission, one who knew how to 'meddle with a man' without conceiving a child. The other was based on the duty of a consort to a husband of whom she stood in awe. If Katherine dallied with Culpeper to please herself, she in turn made it her business to please the King. Naively – Katherine Howard was extremely naive – she saw no harm in combining these two things, so long as she could get away with it undetected. In a sense, she did succeed in combining them, at least for a good while. As we shall see, the contented King had no inkling of what was going on, and on 1 November would give 'most humble and hearty thanks' for 'the good life' he led now and 'trusted to lead' in the future with the Queen.[23]

Culpeper's point of view was rather different. Here was the kind of young man all too easily thrown up by the Tudor court: ambitious, ruthlessly using his personal attractions to further his career. Although distantly related to Katherine Howard through her mother Joyce Culpeper (they were sixth cousins), Thomas Culpeper had not known Katherine as a child, let alone seduced her early on, as scandalmongers liked to pretend later. He himself seems to have begun life as a page (his brother, also called Thomas Culpeper, as was Katherine's mother's brother, had been one of Cromwell's servants).[24] Our Thomas Culpeper had worked his way up to his envied position in the King's Privy Chamber at least two years before these events took place; in this capacity he had been at Calais to greet the Lady Anna of Cleves.

Culpeper was now in his late twenties; his charm was an important part of his armoury. It was however the charm of Don Giovanni rather than that of Sir Lancelot. There was a story of Thomas Culpeper's assault on the wife of a certain park-keeper. Three or four of Culpeper's men had held her down in a thicket in the park, while Culpeper ravished her. He then killed one of the villagers who tried to deliver the wretched woman. This sordid tale ended with the King pardoning Culpeper for what was evidently, from the King's angle, considered merely as the sexual peccadillo of a high-spirited young buck.[25]

One might compare Culpeper to the young Charles Brandon, thirty years earlier, working his way up to wealth and a dukedom through royal favour. The difference was that, in the early years of the reign of Henry VIII, the ambitious sought to be boon companions to the King. Now it was probably more far-sighted to seek the favour of the Queen. There were rich pickings to be had there during the King's lifetime and then there was a question of what would happen next. The King's recent dangerous illness had emphasized the fact that it was no longer a question of 'if the King dies' (as it might have been, for example, in 1524, or even in 1536), but 'when the King dies'. The sight of the sovereign, on the eve of his fiftieth birthday, monumentally overweight, painfully crippled by his ulcerated legs, reminded every courtier daily of the royal mortality.

In the spring of 1541, Prince Edward was only three and a half years old, so that the question of a regency – whose claims were the strongest, those of blood or rank? – which come to dominate much secret thinking and manipulation in the 1540s. But a Dowager Queen had also by tradition a strong position; in the English past, the man who married or controlled the Dowager had often significantly improved his own fortunes. When Queen Katherine started to show Thomas Culpeper 'great favours', includ-ing the gift of a 'chair and a rich cap',[26] her cavalier both took the profits and looked to the future – his future.

In April Queen Katherine wrote a love letter to Culpeper (that this should be the only one of her letters to survive is sadly appropriate). The first eighteen words, in another hand, are innocuous enough: 'Master Culpeper, I heartily recommend me unto you, praying you to send me word how that you do'. After that Katherine herself weighed in. The spelling is execrable, as most ordinary girls' spelling was at this time – those that could write at all – as bad if not worse than that of the foreign-born Anna of Cleves. Even so Katherine clearly had to labour over it. Towards the end of the letter, she writes: 'I would you were with me now that you might see what pain I take in writing to you'.* But the passion is unmistakable, and comes across as clearly through the misshapen words, as the King's love for her was signalled to his courtiers by his caresses. Katherine was entranced by Culpeper, as once she had been entranced by Mannox and Dereham.

'I heard that you were sick and never longed so much for anything as to see you', writes Katherine. 'It makes my heart die to think I cannot be always in your company.' She urges him to come when Lady Rochford is in attendance 'for then I shall best leisure to be at your commandment'. Then she thanks Culpeper for promising to be good to 'that poor fellow, my man, for when he is gone there is no one I dare trust to send to you'. She adds: 'I pray you to give me a horse for my man for I have much ado to get one and therefore I pray send me one by him.' It is signed – touchingly perhaps but how indiscreetly! – 'Yours as long as life endures – Katheryn'.[28]

Henry VIII baptized his northern progress in blood. On the flimsy excuse of feared insurrection – the Tower was to be cleared of state prisoners – he ordered the execution of Margaret Countess of Salisbury, held there for the last two years. This can claim to be the most repulsive piece of savagery ever carried out at the King's wishes. Here was a woman he had long revered for her piety and decency, who had stood to him over the years almost as a mother figure, who had – an amazing feat – trod her way through the intricacies of the Tudor royal maze without stumbling. Lady Salisbury had stoutly denied any charges against her, despite fierce interrogation, at the time of her arrest in November 1538. Her real crime was of course to be the mother of one who sided with the Pope and was beyond the King's vengeance: Cardinal Pole. She had never been tried: her conviction and attainder had been by act of parliament. Now, on 27 May 1541, she was told she was going to die.

To those who came for her – as usual it was early in the morning – Lady Salisbury merely commented that it was very strange, since she knew not what crime she had committed. She then walked quietly to the block. But her ordeal was not over. About 150 persons, including the Lord Mayor, watched as 'a blundering *garçonneau*' (Chapuys' phrase for the youth standing in for the official executioner who was away) attempted to carry out his task. Despite Lady Salisbury's physical frailty – she was nearly seventy – the boy-executioner did not find it easy to finish her off: demonstrating how fortunate Anne Boleyn had been to receive the 'mercy' of

---

* 'I wode you war wythe me now that you mouthe se wat pane I take yn wryteg to you' is how Katherine rendered the above words; although the spelling is corrected above, the original letter (now in the Public Record Office) is reproduced as an illustration.[27]

that expert swordsman from Calais. He 'hacked her head and shoulders to pieces' before the old lady was finally pronounced dead. Cardinal Pole, relating the horrifying news to a correspondent, exclaimed that he would 'never fear to call himself the son of a martyr'.[29] He added: 'which is more than any royal birth'. But of course it was because of her royal birth that Margaret Countess of Salisbury was finally a martyr, like her father the Duke of Clarence when she was a child and her brother Edward Earl of Warwick when she was a young woman. Hers was the last and bloodiest death in the bloodstained history of the house of Clarence.

Freed from the fearsome danger presented by the continued existence of such a satanic enemy as this old lady, King Henry set forth for the north with Queen Katherine. His political aims included not only the settlement – by his dominating presence – of northern England, where some of the old religious ways were obstinately retained, but also some kind of accommodation with his nephew the King of Scots. There was danger here: the Scots had the ability to stir up the discontented English on their borders as well as linking to other Irish malcontents. The two kings had never met, but perhaps King James, now nearly thirty, could on this occasion be lured south. So the King of England – and Queen – solemnly progressed on from Grafton Regis, to Lincoln, and so to Pontefract and York.

There was great ceremony at all stages of the journey. The King had to be seen to reign, and Katherine Howard of course had to be seen to be his royal consort. At Lincoln for example, entered on 9 August, the King and Queen began by going into a tent in order to change their clothing of green and crimson velvet respectively for cloth of gold and silver. Then they set off again on horseback in procession for the cathedral, where a carpet, stools and cushions of cloth of gold awaited them. They stood side by side – they must have presented a startling contrast, the enormous King and his tiny Queen – as they were 'censed' (incense was swung over them) before going in to receive the sacrament while the choir sang a *Te Deum*. Piety was not the only note struck. There was also sport – or at least liberality. Two or three hundred deer had been enclosed, and greyhounds were now sent in amongst them to bring them down, so that there was enough meat to be bountifully shared round.[30]

At York in mid-September the royal couple lingered. It was here if anywhere that Henry might have received James; but the Scottish King declined to be tempted even by a hint that he might receive that official recognition of his place in the English succession so far denied to him. For one thing King James V was himself without direct male heirs at this point, his two baby sons by Marie de Guise having died in April; the Scots were understandably wary of risking his person in the hands of the English.

By the beginning of October the King had moved on to Hull, where he occupied himself with a favourite pursuit, inspecting and designing fortifications. The tone of his orders made it clear that the old attitudes towards England's northern neighbour, the proverbial mixture of contempt and hostility, was dominant: 'Item, to have a regard to the avoiding of Scots and vagabonds from time to time'. From Hull, the King and Queen travelled slowly south. While at The More, in October, the King presented Katherine with a gold brooch set with thirty-five diamonds and eighteen rubies, together with a depiction of 'the story of Noah' as a demonstration of his continuing love for her.[31] It was on 1 November, when the royal entourage had reached Hampton Court, that the King made that solemn thanksgiving for the happiness which the Queen had brought him.

That was his last moment of pure joy where Katherine was concerned. There had been a dark sub-text to the shared northern journey. The insubstantial nature of the King's happiness was about to be revealed to him. Just as plots – and the King's desire – had brought Katherine to the throne, so plots – and the envy of others – would now destroy her. With her wanton past (as it might be perceived) and her indiscreet present (to put it at its mildest) she was all too vulnerable a target.

When the crisis came, it came very suddenly. That is the clear impression of all the various reports on the subject of the fifth Queen's fall. To outsiders – like Chapuys – one moment Katherine was the beloved consort, the next moment her coffers and chests were sealed, Archbishop Cranmer had 'charge of everything', and the Queen herself was held apart (and incommunicado) from her husband. In the first instance, what brought this crisis about, so startling, so unexpected, was a visitation from the past, in the shape of a tale told by one John Lascelles.[32] He came to Cranmer with details related to him by his sister, Mary Hall, who as a chamberwoman to Dowager Duchess Agnes had known Katherine in the old days at Lambeth.

What Lascelles told Cranmer was enough to convince the horrified Archbishop of three things, all in their different ways extremely unpalatable. First, the young Queen's life before marriage had been far from irreproachable. Secondly, she might well have been precontracted as a girl; although in a sense this condoned her behaviour, nevertheless it presented an immediate problem of the validity of her marriage to the King. Thirdly – Cranmer would not have been human if he had not found this the worst prospect of all, at least in the short term – he had to break the news of the thorns surrounding his little innocent rose to the adoring King. As his secretary Ralph Morice wrote, given the King's love of his wife 'no man durst take in hand to open him that wound'.[33]

What inspired Lascelles to make these revelations? The most convincing explanation lies in the fears of Lascelles, and others, for further triumphs of the 'reactionary' religious party in England, due to the paramount influence of Katherine's uncle, the Duke of Norfolk. Lascelles' record shows him to have been 'a convinced reformer' in the words of Cranmer's biographer; one who had lamented the fall of Cromwell, and denounced Norfolk publicly.[34] (He would end up being burnt at the stake for heresy five years later.) Lascelles does not seem to have been animated by any particular malice towards Katherine; as we might say today, it was nothing personal, just (religious) business.

On 2 November – All Souls' Day – the Archbishop confronted his duty. At Hampton Court, during a Mass for the dead at which he was not the celebrant, he slipped a paper bearing details of Lascelles' charges into the King's hand. It was as he feared. At first the King seemed 'much perplexed'. He 'loved the queen so tenderly' that for the moment he honestly believed the paper must be a forgery.[35] Such calumnies against prominent people were common enough to justify such a reaction: as we shall see, Anna of Cleves remained a target for them. Although this proved to be the calm before the raging storm, the fact that such a paranoid character as Henry VIII did not harbour any brooding suspicions concerning his young bride indicates either the genuine nature of his happiness with her or the depths of his self-deception (or perhaps both). For the time being, at any rate, the matter was to be kept utterly private.

It should be noted at this point that all Lascelles' revelations, and those subsequently related by Mary Hall herself, concerned Queen Katherine's behaviour *before* marriage. But of course details of what Katherine had been up to in the north (and elsewhere), while the King slept off his exhaustion at reviewing his fortifications, were ticking away like a time bomb. As with Katherine's behaviour before marriage, there had been witnesses – all too many of them. For the time being it was Dereham who was hauled off to the Tower, along with various waiting women, and Dereham who was tortured. Culpeper on the contrary was still 'merry a-hawking'. His merriment however was not destined to last long since, in the general flood of revelation which followed, Dereham himself took care to implicate Culpeper: hoping to save himself by stating (correctly enough) that Culpeper had followed him in the Queen's affections. So now Culpeper too was arrested, and Culpeper too was tortured.

As the hideous truth emerged – this was no calumny, the Queen was not innocent – the King's 'perplexity' gave way to an orgy of self-pity. He blamed his Council – who else? – for 'this last mischief'. He lamented his misfortune in having a succession of such 'ill-conditioned' wives. After that his mood turned to mighty anger, in view of his Queen's ingratitude, the monstrous betrayal she had brought about. He called for a sword to go and slay her 'that he loved so much'. He vowed that all the pleasure 'that wicked woman' had had from her 'incontinency' (wantonness) should not equal the pain she should feel from torture. And finally 'he took to tears'. Some of his courtiers thought he had actually gone mad.[36]

But this reaction was hardly proof of madness. The fact, the unbearable fact was that the King had been tricked in the first place to accept as a virgin one who was anything but that, and since then he had probably been cuckolded. He knew it and so did everybody else. (If one compares his carefree attitude to the revelations concerning Anne Boleyn's so-called 'lovers' in 1536 one realizes how little he had actually believed those charges.) His madness was in fact the natural outrage of the tyrant who found there were areas of human behaviour that even tyranny could not regulate.

In the meantime Queen Katherine herself had to be brought to make a confession, and Cranmer was the man to do it. She collapsed completely when confronted by him. His account of his conversation with her makes pitiful reading; nor indeed was he himself unmoved by her condition.[37] 'I found her in such lamentation and heaviness, as I never saw no creature, so that it would have pitied any man's heart in the world, to have looked upon her.' Her attendants talked to him of her wild and vehement moods, which only the Archbishop's return served to calm. Cranmer himself mentioned 'frenzy'. However, what really calmed the Queen was the fact that Cranmer was instructed by the King – finally – to signify his 'most gracious mercy'. This unlooked-for concession was intended to follow an exaggerated denunciation of her faults and a relation of what the Queen should rightly suffer by law. Understandably, poor Katherine was a great deal more 'temperate and quiet' when she heard this message of 'grace and mercy'; it was indeed far more than she could have possibly expected, as she told the Archbishop.

It was not pure humanity which dictated this order of events. Cranmer was not a cruel man but he was a frightened one, and remained so where his royal master was concerned (remembering how he had cravenly abandoned the cause of Queen Anne Boleyn, his patroness, to whom 'of all creatures living' he had been 'most bounden'). He now conceived it to be his duty to extricate his master from his marriage to the unfortunate Katherine with as much speed and decency as possible. It was not an experience he can have relished, particularly when the scandal over the dismissal of Anna of Cleves, murmured against by Protestants in Europe, had scarcely died down.* But on this occasion the question of the Dereham

---

* Katherine Howard was the fourth royal consort whose rejection Cranmer had to manage in some way; he had handled the divorce of three previous Queens, Catherine of Aragon, Anne Boleyn (on the eve of her execution) and Anna of Cleves.

precontract seemed momentarily heaven-sent to solve everyone's difficulties. The King's fifth marriage could be pronounced as having been invalid from the start. Katherine herself would simply be disgraced and put away since her behaviour with Dereham was excused by the precontract. (Dereham himself was another matter.) For this Cranmer needed Queen Katherine's confession. And for such a confession, the Queen must not be driven by fear into 'some dangerous ecstasy'.

When she could manage to speak, Queen Katherine stammered out her gratitude and her self-abasement: 'Alas, my Lord that I am still alive, the fear of death grieved me not so much before, as doth now the remembrance of the King's goodness' and the thought of what 'a gracious and loving Prince I had'. By six o'clock in the evening she was 'quieted'. Then the forlorn Queen suddenly recollected it was the hour at which Thomas Heneage used to bring her news of the King. She 'fell into another pang' at 'the remembrance of the time'.

As a result of what the Queen confessed to him, Cranmer felt he did have enough evidence of a precontract, especially since 'carnal copulation following' reinforced a shaky betrothal and gave it proper force. One of the problems, however, now and later, was that the devastated Queen, her brains addled by sheer terror, kept failing to grasp the point that a precontract, if proved, was more likely to save her than condemn her. Instead she took refuge in excuses which showed yet again how young and foolish she was. She talked of Dereham's 'importune forcement' of her and his 'in a manner, violence'.[38] Katherine Howard had always lacked the natural intelligence of her cousin Anne Boleyn, quite apart from her lack of education; now there was no one to advise her, just a number of scared people who would do anything to save their own skins.

In any case, it may have been that the King would not finally have allowed the (valid) excuse for the Queen's behaviour of the precontract to stand. He never saw Queen Katherine again after her arrest on 12 November. As ever, he distanced himself physically from the crisis. On 5 November he left Hampton Court 'suddenly after dinner', without explanation, and went to Whitehall in his small barge; he did not return to Hampton Court until the Queen had been removed – on 14 November – to Syon.* As the arrests and interrogations and shocking revelations proceeded, distance scarcely lent enchantment to his contemplation of his wife's behaviour nor that of

---

* The so-called haunted gallery at Hampton Court, originally built by Wolsey to link the chapel with his state apartments, is where a desperate Queen Katherine is said to have tried to reach her husband and plead her innocence before being dragged away by her attendants; a white-clad woman is supposed to haunt the spot, shrieking as she gradually vanishes. The original incident is unconfirmed; in any case a recent reconstruction of the first floor of the Tudor palace shows that Queen Katherine could not have reached the chapel from her own apartments in this manner.[39]

his predecessor in her embraces, Dereham. Discovering the marriage to be invalid might have the effect of leaving the Queen alive – and it would also, logically, absolve Dereham.

Time would show that the King continued to harbour a special resentment against Dereham, presumably as the 'spoiler' of his bride, even greater than that against Culpeper, who was after all accused of the greater crime of adultery. By accusing both Dereham (in his period as secretary to the Queen) and Culpeper of an adulterous liaison, treason could be invoked – adultery with the King's wife was treason – and death could satisfactorily follow.[40] One of these deaths would be that of Katherine. But here the King could simply take his stand on the law. Let justice be done.

Maids, waiting-women, gentlemen and other terrified informers were now pouring out their salacious stories of life after dark during that northern progress, quite apart from stories of Katherine's past. Torture was used on others: Robert Damport, for instance, a friend of Dereham, was stretched on a rack callously nicknamed 'the Duke of Exeter's daughter' (so-called from the Duke who had introduced it into England in the reign of Henry VI).[41] Even if only a half of what was now related was true – the introduction of torture makes it difficult to be certain about the absolute truth of every detail – then Queen Katherine had behaved with such wild folly since her marriage as to make the question of her actual adultery a purely technical one.

Perhaps that was the answer. Perhaps the Queen had not – technically – committed adultery. She may have stopped somewhere just short of having full sex with Culpeper, using the most common contemporary method of birth control, *coitus interruptus*, as Anne Boleyn and King Henry had once done. There were other practices too which could be enjoyed without the danger of conception, as Katherine knew well from her uninhibited life before marriage. Culpeper continued to deny full 'carnal knowledge' even under torture, and the Queen, in her various confessions, held to her innocence. (However, she indubitably lied in sexual matters in her attitude to the Dereham affair – he had not forced her – so that perhaps not a great deal of reliance should be placed on the word of a shattered girl, who could not yet quite take in the appalling consequences of her own recklessness.)

Nevertheless the repeated confessions and reports of clandestine meetings between a man notorious for his gallantry and a woman who was already sexually awakened really do not admit of any other explanation than adultery. Queen Katherine can have been innocent of the charge only if the narrowest possible interpretation of the word is used. After all, what else did she do with Culpeper, out of her chamber two nights running and up the backstairs at Lincoln, until two o'clock in the morning? (This was the report of her cousin Mistress Katherine Tylney: so much for the demure little figure who had stood beside the King that very morning in front of the cathedral, while sanctifying incense wafted over her.) The interrogations of the minor figures produced a host of circumstantial evidence like this. It was one thing for one Margyt Morton to assert that she saw the Queen look out of her chamber window on Master Culpeper at Hatfield, in such a way as she, Margyt, thought 'there was love between them'.[42] That could be a piece of post hoc invention. But remorselessly, the detailed stories piled up to confirm what Culpeper – and the Queen – admitted, of stolen rendezvous by night at places which included Greenwich, Lincoln, Pontefract and York.

Many of the charges involved the Queen's attendant, Jane Viscountess Rochford, a bird of ill omen where English Queens were concerned (it was she who had also been in waiting on Queen Anne Boleyn, her sister-in-law, and damned her for an incestuous relationship with her husband). Lady Rochford attempted to paint herself as an innocent bystander who had somehow been at the other end of the room where the Queen was meeting Culpeper, without knowing what was going on. Katherine on the other hand reversed the image and described a woman, like Eve, who had persistently tempted her with seductive notions of dalliance; while Culpeper too took the line that Lady Rochford had 'provoked' him into a clandestine relationship with the Queen. 'Little sweet fool', Lady Rochford was supposed to have said fondly about Culpeper when he (according to Katherine) refused to end their meetings, 'Yet must you [Katherine] give men leave to look, for they will look upon you'.[43] Once again, as with the technicalities of the Queen's adultery, absolute truth – and thus relative blame – is impossible to establish. One can however assert definitely that Lady Rochford, Queen Katherine and Culpeper were all in their different ways involved up to the hilt in something that none of them should actually have countenanced for a moment.

The case of Dereham is rather different. There is no proof, or even likelihood, that he was intimate with the Queen following her marriage. That appointment to the secretaryship, however unwise it turned out to be – handy live ammunition for the Queen's accusers – was more likely, as noted, to have been intended to keep his mouth shut about the past. Yet he would suffer torture and then, on 10 December, the full barbaric death accompanied by disembowelling and castration while still conscious, demanded by the law of treason. The King could have granted mercy from these extreme penalties at least. But for Dereham he did not. The fact that he chose to do so for Culpeper – who died on the same day simply by having 'his head stricken off' – may have been due to a vestigial affection for him. As Marillac wrote to King François, Thomas Culpeper had been brought up in the English King's chamber from childhood 'and ordinarily shared his bed' (he had 'apparently wished to share the Queen's bed too', added the Frenchman wittily).[44] Culpeper's rank was also higher than that of Dereham: these things counted in such matters. Finally, however, the King may have preferred Culpeper to Dereham because Culpeper at least had not been the first lover of the wife 'he had loved so much'.

The Queen's removal to the palace of Syon (once the site of that convent much favoured by Catherine of Aragon) left a number of high-born ladies in effect homeless. The Lady Mary was taken off to the household of the young Prince Edward. The King's daughter-in-law Mary Duchess of Richmond, Katherine's first cousin, but not otherwise linked to her, was taken to Kenninghall in Norfolk. The young girls-in-waiting, who had been so proud of their appointments, were instructed to return to their relatives: with the exception, one notes, of pretty Mistress Anne Basset for whom the King intended to provide, considering 'the calamity of her friends'.[45]

At Syon, arrangements for Queen Katherine's reception were punitive, although not excessively so. She was to be held in rooms 'furnished moderately as her life and conditions hath deserved' with only 'a mean number of servants' – yet there were to be rooms, not a cell, and there were to be servants, four gentlewomen of her choice and two chamberers, not jailers. As usual at the Tudor court, dress was the medium to convey the message. Sir Thomas Seymour was deputed to confiscate all the Queen's jewels and bring them to the King. She was to be allowed six of her favourite becoming French hoods – but they were to be edged with gold, not gems. Satin, damask and velvet kirtles were all permitted, so long as they were not adorned with pearls or precious stones. Marillac pointedly compared her treatment to that of Anne Boleyn before her execution; this Queen also was leading a sober and secluded existence as though in preparation. 'Whereas before she did nothing but dance and rejoice ... now when the musicians come they are told there is no time to dance.'[46] His words constitute a sad commentary – sadder than perhaps Marillac intended – on the fall of Katherine Howard.

The action was taking place elsewhere. In mid-November the Council had to issue some embarrassed communiqués to the English ambassadors abroad to explain this latest development in the long-running series, the matrimonial history of their King. Sir John Paget, in France, was informed how the King had chosen Katherine Howard when pressed to marry again by his Council: 'thinking now in his old days, after sundry troubles of mind which have happened to him by marriages, to have obtained such a jewel for womanhood and very perfect love to him, as should have not only been to his quietness, but also brought forth the desired fruit of marriage.' Now all this joy was turned to extreme sorrow in view of the Queen's 'abominable' behaviour (the word generally used to describe Katherine's conduct). When the French King was informed of all this, his delighted private comment was: 'she hath done wondrous naughty'. Officially, however, he sent his 'good brother' of England a solemn little sermon (which must also have given him some pleasure). He referred to 'the lightness of women' not affecting 'the honour of men'; and 'the shame' being confined to 'those who commit the crime'.[47]

On 24 November Katherine Howard – whom the Council had formally demoted from the title of Queen two days earlier – was indicted for having led 'an abominable, base, carnal, voluptuous and vicious life' before marriage 'like a common harlot with divers persons . . . maintaining however the outward appearance of chastity and honesty'. So she had led the King 'by word and gesture to love her' and thus 'arrogantly coupled herself with him in marriage'. She had also concealed the contract she had had with Dereham 'to the peril of the King and of his children to be begotten by her' (who might have found themselves bastards). After marriage she had again shown Dereham 'notable favour', while inciting Culpeper to carnal intercourse, telling him she loved him above the King.[48]

In December a number of important persons were taken into the Tower of London: their crime was 'misprision of treason', that is, advance know-ledge that someone else intended to commit treason, in other words, concealing the secret of Katherine's guilty past. Other servants and 'light young men . . . privy to the naughtiness of the Queen and Dereham, besides advancing Dereham to her service' were arrested.[49] They included her step-grandmother, old Duchess Agnes, who pleaded sickness frantically but in vain (the recent execution of Margaret Countess of Salisbury can scarcely have encouraged her to believe that her age would pardon her). Then there were Duchess Agnes's step-children, the Countess of Bridgewater, Lord William Howard and his wife – 'a very simple woman' – one of Katherine's brothers, Henry Howard, and his wife, and a pack of unfortunate children belonging to these prisoners. The Tower of London was so crowded that the Royal Apartments had to be pressed into use.

The fall of the house of Howard would indeed have satisfied its most resolute enemy – had it not been for the obstinate survival of the head of the house, Thomas Duke of Norfolk. The grovelling letter he sent to his sovereign, referred – with what true anguish! – to 'mine ungracious mother-in-law, mine unhappy brother and his wife, with my lewd sister of Bridg-water' and above all to 'abominable deeds' done by two of his nieces. Norfolk referred to himself as 'prostrate at the King's feet'.[50] Certainly he had adopted metaphorically the most recumbent position possible. And so he survived.

*

New Year at court was a gloomy business, as sombre as that mournful New Year which had followed the death of Queen Jane but for a very different reason. King Henry was described by Marillac as 'little joyous, and his ministers pensive and melancholy'.[51] It was not only a case of the absent Queen Katherine. The clean sweep of Howards taken off to the Tower in December (and still languishing there – the King relented and released them by degrees over the next ten months) left some remarkable gaps at court. Those who remained, contemplating these absences, could not help feeling fearful for themselves.

As a matter of fact, rumour had it that Queen Katherine, at Syon, was herself actually 'making good cheer'. Marillac now heard that she was plumper and prettier than ever, worrying about her clothes and her appearance, and 'more imperious and troublesome to serve than even when she was with the King'. As a Frenchman, Marillac had never been a friend to Katherine Howard (he continued to praise the dignified Anna of Cleves), so that one should treat his remarks with reserve. Yet when he reported that the Queen accepted she would die, but hoped it could be in secret, he probably did capture the unthinking blitheness with which Katherine regarded her fate, incapable still of grasping the reality of her situation.[52]

On Friday 10 February, however, Katherine was ordered to be transferred to the Tower. Then at last, as she was being taken to the small sealed barge which would convey her there, the truth came home. Katherine struggled and had to be forced aboard. Escorted by Suffolk – in a much bigger barge, stuffed with soldiers – Katherine was now taken to the prison which had struck horror into so many hearts before hers. Here, however, she was at least accorded the honours due to a Queen (despite the Council's formal removal of the title) and so, dressed in the black velvet of impending mourning, she was escorted to the Queen's Apartments in the Tower. But her queenly state did not console her. Katherine Howard now wept and cried out and tormented herself 'miserably without ceasing'.[53] There was indeed no more time left to dance, as the musicians had been told in the autumn, and very little time left to live.

Katherine was brought to the Tower in response to the Act of Attainder which had been first read in the House of Lords on 21 January, and finally passed through both houses, receiving the King's assent on 11 February. Its passage had, however, caused certain anxieties. The Lord Chancellor's elaborate speech at the opening of parliament, regarding the Bill, took more than an hour. Delegates of both houses were proposed to go down to Syon to examine the Queen further and 'take away her womanly timidity' (presumably to get more of the truth out of her).[54] In the end, however, they did not go but listened instead to an address from the King on 6 February.

The worry in these earnest minds was a legitimate one: of what exactly was the Queen guilty? She had never confessed to adultery – and nor had Culpeper or Dereham. Culpeper had actually been put to death for *intent* to commit adultery (as Buckingham had been put to death for intent to commit treason). The whole question of the precontract remained a delicate one. It was however the King's will that Katherine should suffer under an Act of Attainder which proved her treason. So Katherine too was condemned to die for the 'violent presumption' that she had committed adultery.

On the Sunday Katherine was informed that she was going to die. Perhaps the horror of the clumsy death of Margaret Countess of Salisbury had communicated itself to her. She asked to have the block brought to her in advance 'that she might know how to place herself' and 'make trial of it'. The next morning, Monday 13 February, members of the Privy Council came for her at seven o'clock, with the exception of Norfolk (family feeling or what passed for it presumably kept him away) and Suffolk who was ill. According to Marillac, she was 'so weak that she could hardly speak', but confessed in a few words that she had merited a thousand deaths for so offending a King who had treated her so graciously.[55] Katherine Howard was then executed – cleanly – on the same block and in the same place as her cousin Anne Boleyn not quite six years previously.

It was now the turn of Jane Viscountess Rochford. Marillac heard that, unlike the trembling Katherine, she made 'a long discourse' on her faults. There were of course a great many onlookers at this fascinating spectacle (so much for Katherine's desire to die secretly – as difficult in such an age as to live secretly, which she had not managed either). Among them was one Otwell Johnson who wrote an account of it all to his brother John, a merchant in Calais.[56]

The two ladies, wrote Johnson, 'made the most godly and Christian end'. They had uttered 'their lively faith in the blood of Christ only' so that he believed their souls were now with God. 'With goodly words and steadfast countenances, they desired all Christian people to take regard unto their worthy and just punishment with death.' Such a punishment had been merited by their offences against God, and 'also against the King's royal majesty very dangerously'. Both Katherine and Lady Rochford ended by praying heartily for the preservation of the King. In view of Marillac's report of Katherine's weakness, most of this Johnson probably took from Lady Rochford rather than the Queen, although Katherine's intention was obviously the same.* Lady Rochford was now executed in her turn on a block still wet and slippery with her mistress's blood.

* Reliable contemporary accounts make it clear that Katherine's famous touching final speech beginning: 'I die a Queen, but I would rather die the wife of Culpeper' was certainly never made;

Both bodies – that of the decapitated Queen and of the lady who had certainly not served her wisely, if too well – were taken like that of Anne Boleyn to the nearby Chapel of St Peter ad Vincula and there interred. At the time of her death, Katherine Howard had been Queen of England for just over eighteen months, and may still not have reached her twenty-first birthday.

---

her mood was very different. We have the Culpeper speech on the authority of Antonio de Guaras only (who on this occasion was not present). In any case in his chronicle, he reverses the order of Anna of Cleves and Katherine Howard as consorts, making Cromwell still alive at the time of Queen Katherine's death.[57]

Part V

CATHERINE PARR

Chapter 17

NECESSITY AND THE
WIDOW

Not so much choice as necessity, put [the King] on
marrying a widow about two years after this

Bishop Burnet, *The History of the Reformation of the Church*
of England

Chapuys likened the King's grief after the fall of Katherine Howard to that of a woman crying more bitterly at the loss of her tenth husband than she had over the deaths of all the other nine put together: 'the reason being that she had never buried one of them without being sure of the next, but that after the tenth husband she had no other one in view, hence her sorrow and her lamentations'.[1] It was certainly true that after five wives and over thirty years of matrimony, the King – for once – had no one in view. It was also correct that this was unlike any previous situation King Henry had faced: he had actually married Anne Boleyn *before* he divorced Catherine of Aragon, got rid of her to marry Jane Seymour within days, and equally rid himself of Anna of Cleves for a more-or-less instant wedding with Katherine Howard. Even the unexpected decease of Jane Seymour had found the Council discussing their master's matrimonial plans for the future in the very letters abroad which broke the tragic news.

In the spring of 1542 matters were significantly different. It was not a coincidence that some economy was practised over the removal of Katherine Howard's badges from Rochester: those badges inserted by the King's glazier Galyon Hone in the previous spring. Now a mere local workman was employed in 'taking out of the Lady Howard's arms' from the various chambers since no new Queen with her own heraldic demands was expected.[2] The change in the situation was a question of certain additional clauses in the act which condemned Katherine Howard to death.

Ostensibly intended 'to avoid doubts for the future', these clauses actually had quite the contrary effect. Anyone who knew anything 'incontinent' (wanton) about the queen now had to reveal it under pain of treason. Furthermore, if the King – or his successors – should propose marrying any woman 'whom they took to be a pure and clean maid' but was not, there were the same dire penalties for those involved. The deceitful woman herself would be guilty of high treason 'and all who knew it and did not reveal it were guilty of misprision of treason'.[3]

It was these last words which cast a chill over the court. The merry game of inserting a young girl into the King's affections was over: for who could tell if she was actually as chaste as she pretended? And if not, then the Tower at best and the axe at worst awaited her unlucky family and friends. Such provisions were indeed grossly unfair. How could old Duchess Agnes who 'had bred her of a child' be expected to tell tales against Katherine? Demanding by law that a wife reveal her own 'incontinence' was also a piece of grievous tyranny especially with the King 'of so imperious a temper'.[4] Nevertheless while they were in force – springing no doubt from the King's rebarbative rage against the young wife he had loved and trusted – no one cared to risk advancing an unmarried girl.

By the end of January, the King was said to have cheered up a little, although his health remained poor and his weight in consequence increased. But he did at least enjoy 'a great supper' with twenty-six ladies at his table and another thirty-five at a table nearby. Among those singled out by his attentions were Sir Anthony Browne's niece, Lord Cobham's sister, and Mistress Anne Basset. Of the latter, Marillac commented sourly that she was 'a pretty young creature with wit enough to do as badly as the other if she were to try'.[5]

That was the point. Would Sir Anthony Browne, or Lord Cobham, or Mistress Basset's relations wish to place themselves in danger? As for the women themselves, they knew 'in what a slippery estate they were, if the King, after his receiving them to bed, should, through any mistake, declare them no maids'. (That was a complicated subject in its own right where the King was concerned. He had after all decided that Anna of Cleves was not a virgin on her marriage while he had believed Katherine Howard to be one: he was almost certainly wrong in both cases.) The rotting heads of Culpeper and Dereham fixed on spears to one of the turrets of London Bridge served as a perpetual reminder of the dangers of that game – and would continue to do so. A Greek traveller, Nicander Nucius, visiting the English court in 1546, noted the heads were still to be seen, although 'denuded of flesh'.[6]

As for marrying abroad, there were obvious difficulties there. One candidate from the past was no longer available. Duchess Christina of Milan had been married to Francis of Lorraine the previous year: so the marital carousel continued to revolve since he was that heir to the duchy of Lorraine to whom Anna of Cleves had – or had not – been pre-contracted. In the meantime the suppressed giggle with which Duchess Christina had greeted the English envoy's reference to his master's 'benign and pleasant' nature – 'the most gentle Gentleman that liveth' – might have turned to irrepressible laughter in view of the fact that Henry VIII had now executed two of his wives, as well as divorcing two others.

Where foreign alliances, cemented by marriage treaties, were concerned, it was more to the point these days that King Henry had three marriageable children to play with: the Lady Mary at twenty-six, whose prospects always improved in the absence of a Queen who might bear further children to push her away from the succession, the Lady Elizabeth, rising nine, and Prince Edward, whose position as undoubtedly legitimate heir made him ripe for these kind of negotiations, despite his tender age. Yet a King, however decrepit his health, however terrifying his temper, still needed a Queen. The problem was not easily solved.

There was one convenient option open to him of course: the King could take back the Lady Anna of Cleves. That at least was the opinion of her supporters. The French ambassador commended her 'rare' patience in such a difficult situation: 'all her affairs could never make her utter a word by which one might suppose that she was discontented', which he put down to the 'singular grace of God'. Furthermore, he had heard reports that the Lady Anna was 'half as beautiful again since she left court'.[7]

Unfortunately patience was not enough to protect the Lady Anna from scandalous innuendoes. The oddity of her 'unmarried' situation in England continued to tease the popular imagination. In the winter, two London citizens, Richard Taverner and Francis Lilgrave, had been imprisoned for describing Queen Katherine's disgrace as a judgement on the King for having put aside Anna of Cleves; as for the latter, she was alleged to have been confined of one child in the summer and to be once more *enceinte*. The truth was probably that Anna of Cleves' previously 'thin' figure had filled out with good food and because she was 'fond of wine' – hence her increased desirability, by the standards of the time.[8] Chapuys indeed was prepared to run the two things together: he accepted stories of her lack of chastity, simply because of her taste for tippling.

And patient as she might be, the Lady Anna had not managed to conceal her own pleasure at the downfall of her supplanter – and former dancing partner – not so much out of spite, as because the position of Queen was once more so clearly vacant. Her household went further. Two of her ladies, Jane Rattsey and Elizabeth Basset (another sister of Mistress Anne), were summoned before the Council and subsequently committed to prison for such indiscreet remarks as these on the subject:

'What! Is God working his own work to make the Lady Anna of Cleves queen again?' The ladies believed that 'It was impossible that so sweet a queen as the Lady Anna could be utterly put down'. Elizabeth Basset went further, expressing what many must have felt: 'What a man is the King! How many wives will he have?'[9] These were small fry, although it is notable how the King took care to have their wagging tongues checked, and continued to keep a watchful eye on such rumours in the future.

The gossip and criticism were not confined to England. John Paget, the English ambassador in Paris, sent the King an anonymous French publication condemning the King's 'just proceedings' (as he put it) against Anna of Cleves which took the form of an impassioned (if fabricated) 'Remonstrance' from the Lady herself. It was actually written by John of Luxemburg, Abbot of Ivry, probably with the intention of stirring up trouble between the English King and the German Protestant princes. Paget protested to King François, who in a fraternal spirit promised to stop the printing of this annoying work, and recover any copies already made.[10] Even so, the real tiresomeness suffered by the King and Council – at what was undeniably a delicate moment in his matrimonial fortunes – was the persistence of Cleves, as represented by its envoy Olisleger, in raising the question of a reconciliation between King Henry and the former Queen Anna.

Olisleger, on instructions, absolutely refused to take the original royal 'no' of July 1540 for an answer. He beavered away despite Cranmer's discouragement. The Archbishop found it very strange that the Lady Anna should want to be taken back 'and so trouble the succession': meaning that any child born subsequently would have its legitimacy seriously in doubt, what with the Lady Anna's precontract to Francis of Lorraine, and the dissolution of her marriage to the King. Finally the English Council had to issue a formal refusal, begging Duke William of Cleves never to issue such an embarrassing request again. The King had fully determined never to restore his 'sister' to his bed since 'what was done was founded upon great reason, whatever the world might allege'. Olisleger held his peace for the time being, for fear of any deterioration in the treatment of the Lady herself. But he did lobby Marillac, to see if the French King would intercede. Marillac's cynical advice was that King François should either do nothing, or else put the case for the Lady Anna to the English with sufficient diplomatic ambiguity as not to offend them – and drive them into the arms of the Emperor.[11]

Marillac's reference to the Emperor was made with good reason. That worrying Habsburg-Valois alliance had proved mercifully short-lived (from the Tudor point of view). The renewal of hostilities between France and the Empire in July 1542 meant that England was once more in a position to choose between them. For Henry VIII, the choice was not a difficult one to make. As France was England's natural enemy, the Empire was her natural friend: the unhappy figure of Catherine of Aragon was no longer present to trouble the counsels of Henry VIII and, as it turned out, her ghost did not have the power to haunt her nephew Charles V either. In February 1543 a secret treaty was made between them for the purposes of an invasion of France.

When this became known, there was much moral indignation from the other side. One French ambassador – to the Signory of Venice – expostulated: 'What but the design of subjugating Christendom could make a revengeful prince like the Emperor forget the insult done him by the King of England, in the person of his aunt?' The Pope too would rebuke the Emperor for such a league with the monarch who had 'injured him' through 'the repudiation' of Catherine of Aragon.[12] The truth was that realpolitik was more important to both sovereigns. Charles V was delighted to believe that England would match him by sending 42,000 troops against France, attacking Boulogne while he marched through Champagne. As for King Henry, he needed to make sure that the troublesome Scots were not aided, as so often in the past, by the French. There was a further personal consideration. A manly zest for war, as it was generally seen at the time, had characterized him in youth. Now with advancing years, he returned to the idea of such martial adventures, which might prove more properly rejuvenating than marriage with a wanton young wife.

As France and the Empire prepared to fight each other, English levies were drawn up on the borders of Scotland. James V was then presented with what was in effect an ultimatum from his stronger neighbour (and uncle): he was commanded to sign a treaty acknowledging King Henry's suzerainty, and also to abandon Scotland's traditional pro-French and pro-papist policies, as advocated by Cardinal David Beaton. Not surprisingly, King James rejected this. English raids followed under Norfolk as Lieutenant of the North and Captain-General of the army: hoping no doubt by the ferocity of his public spoliation of Scotland to atone for his nieces' 'abominable behaviour' in private. A Scottish counter-attack met with disaster when the Scottish army was routed at Solway Moss on 24 November. A number of leading Scottish nobles, including Lords Cassilis, Glencairn and Maxwell, were captured and taken south.

The Scottish King himself did not survive. His fate provided a painful echo of the Flodden tragedy. James V was not actually slain on the field of battle, as his father had been, but he collapsed, a broken man. There was some consolation in the fact that his wife Marie de Guise was in an advanced state of pregnancy: it was hoped that a son and heir would replace those two baby princes who had died the previous year. But the heir to the throne proved to be an heiress: 'the young suckling' born on 8 December who would be known thereafter as Mary Queen of Scots. Six days later James V died at the age of thirty.

He was supposed to have greeted the news of his daughter's birth with the melancholy prophecy: 'Adieu, fare well, it came with a lass, it will pass with a lass': an allusion to the marriage of the heiress Marjorie Bruce and Walter Stewart which had founded the Stewart dynasty.[13] Certainly the English regarded it as an example of divine intervention that the crown of Scotland had now passed to a very young female, while the heir to the crown of England was a young male, conveniently five years her senior. The Scottish problem looked like being solved in the happiest possible way from the English point of view – a marriage – and for once it was the Scots not the English who were faced with the problem of an heiress conveying her inheritance to her husband. The Scottish captives, primed with English money, returned home having secretly promised to bring this about.

No wonder courtiers noticed a new zest and energy in the English King early in 1543, as though the black shadows of the previous year had at last been cast off. Feasts were held again at which the King's daughter the Lady Mary 'in default of a Queen' presided.[14] Military victory over the troublesome Scots was one kind of tonic. But the King also had another private reason to feel contented. While plots were being laid for the future marriage of Prince Edward to Mary Queen of Scots, he himself was contemplating matrimony rather sooner. If he had not exactly fallen in love again – it is doubtful whether this rampant emotion, responsible for so many of the cataclysmic events of his life, troubled him further after the debacle with Katherine Howard – he had at least viewed with affectionate approval an English lady now at court. The woman in question was now known as 'my lady Latimer' but she had been born some thirty-one years before as Catherine Parr.

Of all the good qualities Catherine Parr Lady Latimer possessed to fit her for being the King's sixth consort, none was more satisfactory than the fact that she was a widow. After all, even the most paranoid of sovereigns could hardly expect Lady Latimer, a woman previously married (as it happened, more than once), to be 'a pure and clean maid' in the sense of being a virgin. So her supporters and relations could safely advance her cause, without fear of reprisals under the notorious provisions of the 1542 Act of Attainder. It was as Bishop Burnet, in his *History of the Reformation*, neatly described it, 'not so much choice as necessity' that put the King on to marrying a widow.[15]

Catherine Parr was the eldest child of Sir Thomas Parr of Kendal and Maud

Greene, a Northamptonshire heiress. The year 1512 is the most likely year for her birth; a brother William was born on 14 August 1513 and a sister Anne in 1514.[16] The Parrs were a distinguished northern family in origin, even though their lives had mainly been led in the south since the late fifteenth century. Catherine's grandfather Sir William Parr of Kendal had been allowed to marry the great heiress Elizabeth FitzHugh, daughter of Henry Lord FitzHugh and Alice Neville, with lands in Yorkshire and Northumberland, as a reward for his services to Edward IV. After his death, she remarried Sir Nicholas Vaux of Harrowden Hill, and so brought her family south. Nevertheless the existence of northern estates, and Kendal Castle in Westmoreland, visited by the male Parrs from time to time, maintained the connection. It would be right therefore to see Catherine Parr as having northern blood, even though she did not have a northern upbringing.

It was to her grandmother Elizabeth FitzHugh that Catherine owed that remote but genuine royal descent which now proves to be one of the few things that all six wives of Henry VIII had in common.* Catherine Parr, like the King's father, could trace her descent from Edward III's fourth son John of Gaunt, and like Henry VII, she was descended from a Beaufort, offspring of his slightly dubious third union with Katherine Swynford. This Beaufort connection meant that Sir Thomas Parr and Henry VIII were fourth cousins, Catherine Parr being the King's fourth cousin once removed.†

Sir Thomas Parr – knighted at the coronation of Henry VIII – was a companion-in-arms of the young King and, like Sir Thomas Boleyn and Sir John Seymour before him, present at the Field of Spurs in France in 1513. Maud Lady Parr was attached to Catherine of Aragon as a lady-in-waiting: it is possible at least that her first child was actually named for her mistress and that Catherine of Aragon even stood godmother to Catherine Parr.[18] At all events Maud Parr was imbued with a lifelong loyalty to the first Queen Catherine. Then what looked like two promising careers at court were cut short when Sir Thomas Parr died in 1517. Maud Parr was left with three young children whose prospects in life – which meant,

---

* This should be seen as a reflection of the narrowness of aristocratic society in a world of small population, rather than as some unconscious desire on the part of the King to commit a form of incest, as has been suggested.[17] The ladies in question were not closely related to each other (or the King) with the exception of the first cousins Anne Boleyn and Katherine Howard, which, following Anne's disgrace, was never considered a point in favour of Katherine, quite apart from the problem of affinity. (See family tree 1)

† Henry VIII and Jane Seymour were in a roughly similar relationship to each other being fifth cousins, but they were related on his maternal (Yorkist) side; Catherine Parr had on the contrary Lancastrian blood.

basically, securing them good marriages – she now made her chief concern, to the extent that she never married again.

Given the early death of her father, it is very likely that Catherine Parr was mainly brought up in Northamptonshire with her relations. In later life, she would show much devotion to her uncle, another Sir William Parr, subsequently created Lord Parr of Horton, and his daughter, another Maud, later by marriage Lady Lane. There, too, she would have been educated – up to a point. There is an optimistic theory that Catherine Parr was educated along with Catherine of Aragon's daughter Mary, possibly by the great Vives himself, and as a result learnt 'fluent' Latin as a girl. On the one hand, the age gap between herself and Mary – four years – makes this extraordinarily unlikely (there is no reference to Catherine Parr in the quite detailed accounts of the then Princess Mary's youth). On the other hand it is clear from Catherine Parr's own later history that she was by no means fluent in Latin in 1543 when the King's eye fell favourably upon her. As late as 1546 the nine-year-old scholar Prince Edward – who had a didactic streak in his nature where his older female relations were concerned – sent Catherine Parr a letter solemnly approving her efforts in this direction and 'her progress in the Latin language'.[19] (The only Latin letter in existence under her own name is not actually written in Catherine's hand.)

One should therefore view Catherine Parr more as an Isabella of Castile – who valiantly learnt Latin after she was grown up – than as a Catherine of Aragon, so well-instructed as a child, at the specific orders of the mother who had lacked such an education herself. Catherine Parr would certainly display herself in adulthood as a person with a deep and genuine love of learning: she prized it among her intimates such as Katherine Duchess of Suffolk and members of her household such as Lady Jane Grey, noted from an early age for her intellectual tastes. The fact that Queen Catherine Parr had a desire for self-improvement, not having been granted the exceptional education of a princess, makes her in fact more admirable (and more interesting) rather than less.

It was not altogether surprising that Catherine Parr showed herself to be a remarkable woman. She had a remarkable mother in Maud Parr. Lord Dacre, aiding her in one of her matrimonial projects, referred to 'the wisdom of my said Lady [Parr] and the good wise stock of the Greenes whereof she is come' as well as 'the wise stock of the Parrs of Kendal, for all of which men do look when they do marry their child, to the wisdom of the blood of that they do marry with'. First, Maud Parr battled away on Catherine's behalf for a match with Lord Dacre's grandson, the heir of Lord Scrope of Bolton in 1523 (when Catherine was not yet twelve years old).[20] She failed, for all the wisdom of her own stock and that of the Parrs, because she could not offer a sufficient dowry for Catherine and at the same time bring off an even more exalted match: that of William, her only son, to Anne Bourchier, of Plantagenet descent, and only daughter and heiress to the last Bourchier Earl of Essex.

Great sums could not be spent in both directions. In 1527 Maud Parr secured the glittering marriage for her boy but had to look elsewhere for her girl. Catherine Parr was finally married at the age of seventeen, in 1529. Two years later Maud Lady Parr died, leaving a chain with an image of St Gregory to her daughter, and her family, as she hoped, thoroughly established since her younger daughter Anne Parr was destined for a place at court.

There is another myth about Catherine Parr, that she had been already married to two old and sickly men before 1543, the first of them actually insane. In fact her first bridegroom was a young man, probably not much older than his bride, and certainly not insane even if his health was poor: Edward Borough, son of Thomas, Lord Borough, chamberlain to Queen Anne Boleyn.[21] With him she went to the family estates in Lincolnshire. Catherine did not spend long there. Edward Borough died in 1532, the year after Maud Lady Parr. Catherine was now a childless widow of twenty, with a moderate jointure derived from estates in Kent; her brother had been absorbed into the Essex household of his father-in-law. It was clear that Catherine's destiny was another marriage.

This time her bridegroom was indeed an older man. John Neville, Lord Latimer, of Snape Castle in Yorkshire, was a northern grandee who had already been widowed twice, leaving him with a son, also called John, and a daughter Margaret. Lord Latimer was now about forty – only two years younger than the King. This Latimer marriage, concluded in 1533 about the time of the coronation of Queen Anne Boleyn, marked the real beginning of the upward mobility of Catherine Parr. At the age of twenty-one, she was now in charge of running an extremely large household, as well as the care of a step-daughter: in both cases she succeeded triumphantly. Margaret Neville, far from resenting Catherine for her youth, proved to be the first in the long line of younger women who would respond to her maternal warmth and friendship. In her will of 1545, Margaret Neville wrote: 'I was never able to render her grace [Catherine] sufficient thanks for the godly education and tender love and bountiful goodness which I have ever more found in her.'[22]

Nevertheless, it was not to prove an easy life. Catherine Lady Latimer was obliged to develop other qualities while in the north: that 'prudence' on which all observers commented was first forged at the time of the Pilgrimage of Grace, when her husband was among the lords torn between the local threats of Robert Aske and his duty to the southern government.

It will be remembered that Lord Latimer was taken away hostage by Aske, in front of his wife's eyes, and 'sore constrained' by Aske. Under the circumstances, he acted for a while as Aske's mouthpiece, only to enrage the King, who demanded that Lord Latimer reject Aske 'and submit . . . to our clemency'. In December 1537, Latimer went south and tried to explain that he had acted under duress, leaving his wife and children unprotected in the north.[23]

This time it was Catherine and her Neville step-children who were put under house arrest by the rebels to secure Latimer's return. Latimer rushed back north. Between threats of death to his family, and accusations of treason directed against himself, Latimer – and Catherine too – had to tread a delicate path. In the end Latimer was among those who survived, since there was not enough evidence against him, but his health never really recovered from these horrible excitements. In the last years of her husband's illness, Catherine spent more and more time in her London house in Charterhouse Yard, and less in the north.

Here she renewed her connections to the court where her sister Anne had been in waiting on Queen Katherine Howard. Anne was now the wife of a fellow courtier William Herbert, the illegitimate grandson of the Earl of Pembroke. Then there was a friendly connection to the Lady Mary which had its origins not so much in any shared education, as in the remembered devotion of Maud Lady Parr to Mary's mother (always a touchstone of affection where Mary was concerned). In contrast, Catherine was also beginning to be in touch – in a mild way – with those interested in the more evangelical aspects of the Anglican religion. That was something that would obviously commend her more to the reforming Archbishop Cranmer than to the reactionary Bishop Stephen Gardiner of Winchester: but it was not thought worthy of note at the time of the King's courtship.

'My lady Latimer's' interests were not entirely intellectual. At some point during the final stages of her husband's long-drawn-out mortal illness, she also fell in love with Thomas Seymour. For Catherine was a more complicated character than observers, obsessed by the stereotype of the prudent woman and virtuous widow, realized and her nature was by no means devoid of passion. She had been married briefly to a young weakling, and for ten years to a man twenty years her senior, also an invalid for much of that time. Now she had in mind taking the great wealth which would now come to her, and using it to make at last a marriage according to her own desires. At this point – still before the actual death of Lord Latimer – the King began to express an interest in her. The shadow of this vast cumbersome galleon, royal pennant flying, fell across plans which would certainly have been on a personal level far more agreeable.

The King's first presents to 'my lady Latimer' were dated 16 February, two weeks before Lord Latimer died on 2 March. Later, Catherine Parr would be quite candid about what happened next. She was, in the time-honoured fashion of a romantic heroine, torn between love and duty. In the end duty won. She told Thomas Seymour: 'As truly as God is God, my mind was fully bent ... to marry you before any man I know. Howbeit, God withstood my will therein most vehemently for a time, and through his grace and goodness, made that possible which seemed to me most impossible; that was, made me renounce utterly mine own will, and to follow his will most willingly'. But clearly duty did not win without quite a severe struggle. 'It were long to write all the process of this matter', Catherine told Seymour.[24]

Thomas Seymour dropped back, with what – if any – assurances for the future cannot be known. The triumphant Parrs stepped forward. By 20 June, Lady Latimer and her sister Anne Herbert constituted a conspicuous presence at the court, then at Greenwich. Three weeks later a licence for marriage without banns was issued for King Henry 'who has deigned to marry the lady Catherine, late wife of Lord Latimer, deceased'. It was a ceremony which could now lawfully take place in 'any church, chapel or oratory'.[25] The venue actually chosen, however, was a familiar one to the King where marriages were concerned. It was 'the Queen's closet' at Hampton Court where he had already married Jane Seymour and Anna of Cleves (but not Katherine Howard).

Here, on 12 July, Henry VIII and the twice-widowed Lady Latimer were married. Unlike certain of his weddings it was not a secret ceremony. On the contrary, both the King's daughters were bidden to be present, as well as his niece Lady Margaret Douglas and others, including Anne Herbert. When Bishop Gardiner asked if anyone knew of any impediment to the match, it was a case of 'none opposing but all applauding'. The Ladies Mary and Elizabeth had recently undergone a pleasant reverse in their fortunes: a new act of parliament on 14 June restored them officially to the succession, after Prince Edward and his future direct heirs born thereafter, although it was in fact done without legitimizing them. This arrangement was described as being 'convenient' if the King were to go abroad on a military campaign.[26] Their presence at the ceremony was a sign of a new harmony between these erstwhile princesses and their father.

As for the King himself, it was remarked that as Bishop Gardiner pronounced the now familiar words of the marriage service, an expression of real happiness crossed that bloated face. (To judge from the terrifying Matsuys' portrait of about this date, backed up by contemporary seals, it was a face that grew more like a vast potato marked with eyes and mouth to resemble a man, with every year that passed.) So the King replied 'Yea' to the formal question as to whether he wished to marry Catherine. As for her, 'the lady also replied that it was her wish'.[27]

The woman who brought about this cheerfulness, the new Queen Catherine Parr, was herself never described by anyone as a beauty: even the term 'of middling beauty' used for both Anna of Cleves and Jane Seymour by Marillac was not applied in this case. 'Pleasing' and 'lively', 'kind' and 'gracious' were the most flattering epithets ascribed to her. It is true that a difference of age and status may have been responsible for this lack – widows of over thirty were not expected to be beauties – but when Anna of Cleves indignantly exclaimed that the new Queen was 'not nearly as beautiful as she', Chapuys, passing on the comment, did not see fit to contradict it.[28]

Queen Catherine Parr's only known authentic likeness, attributed to William Scrots, shows an amiable face rather than an intriguing one; the nose is short, the mouth small, and the forehead broad rather than domed in the way that contemporaries admired. Her hair was rather similar in colour to that of Catherine of Aragon: light auburn, tinged with what Agnes Strickland in the nineteenth century would call 'threads of burnished gold'.[29]*

But if the new Queen Catherine was not a beauty, she was neither dull nor austere. She enjoyed dancing. The Spanish Duke of Najera reported that in 1544 when the Queen was 'slightly indisposed', she still came out of her room to dance 'for the honour of the company'. She was well set up – the tallest of King Henry's wives – and her height would have enabled her to cut a regal figure since her conception of her role as queen consort also included a great deal of ornate dressing-up.† Her first recorded presents from King Henry included the making of Italian gowns with 'pleats and sleeves', and other gowns in the French and Dutch styles, as well as French hoods (the King paid the tailor's bill). The Duke of Najera noticed how magnificent her costume was: the brocade kirtle beneath an open robe of cloth of gold, the sleeves lined with crimson satin, the train more than two yards long. Two crosses hung from her neck, as well as a jewel composed of fine diamonds, and there were more diamonds in her headdress; pendants hung from her golden girdle.[30]

Quite apart from the clothes that she commissioned for herself, Queen Catherine inherited a vast collection of the dresses of the late Queen Katherine Howard, stored at Baynard's Castle (the traditional wardrobe-storehouse of the Queen Consort). This, which may seem macabre to us

---

* This was not pure Victorian fantasy. Agnes Strickland saw a lock of it, only a few decades after her tomb was opened and a lock of hair cut from the corpse. In 1990 the same relic at Sudeley Castle still preserved chestnut and golden lights.

† Her coffin was found to measure 5 feet 10 inches overall which suggests a good height.

and redolent of Bluebeard's household arrangements, was in fact a perfectly practical measure in the sixteenth century, when rich gowns were pieces of valuable property. When a messenger had to ride to London to fetch certain of 'the Queen's Grace's furred gowns from Baynard's Castle' back to the court which was on progress, he may well have returned with one of the splendid robes Katherine Howard was forced to leave behind when she went to Syon: there was no embarrassment on the subject.[31]

Like Queen Anne Boleyn, Queen Catherine Parr sent for silks for her dresses from Antwerp, where her silk woman was married to the King's financial agent there. Virtuous as she might be, Queen Catherine Parr was not always prompt in paying: 'the Queen owes me much money' was the comment upon one occasion. Shoes were a real passion: forty-seven pairs ordered in one year, in crimson, white, blue and black, all trimmed with gold at 14s a pair, with black velvet a shilling cheaper, corked shoes lined with red and 'quarter shoes' (which could be thrown away) at 5s each.[32]

Queen Catherine, like many of her husband's preceding wives – and the King himself – was fond of music, and had her own consort of viols, with musicians from Venice and Milan, paid 8d a day. Painting, at least portraiture and especially miniatures, were a more unusual interest. She had John Bettes limn the royal portraits and probably patronized the Dutch-born painter Hans Eworth if he is to be identified with 'Hewe Hawarde' – the name Eworth gave the English a lot of trouble – to provide miniatures of herself and the King at 30s each. Her own portrait was painted by a female artist, Lucas Horenbout's widow Margaret (unless the 'Item to Lucas' wife' in Queen Catherine's accounts referred to Margaret as her husband's executrix).[33]

In other ways, with her love of her greyhounds (fed on milk), her parrots (fed on hempseed), her feeling for flowers and herbs, her affection for her dwarf jesters and her female jester, 'Jane Foole' as she was known, with a special 'red petticoat' bought for her, Queen Catherine Parr comes across as someone who enjoyed the small pleasures of life. Whatever the ailing King's moods, it must have been a relief to the courtiers that their new Queen was of friendly disposition. As a family tradition, passed down by her cousin and attendant Sir Nicholas Throckmorton had it:

> She was dispos'd to mirth in company
> Yet still regarding civil modesty.[34]

From this latest royal marriage, there was one loser as well as many gainers among the Queen's own relatives. That was the Lady Anna of Cleves, who seems to have allowed herself to believe her own publicity, that the King would take her back. She gave way to 'great grief and despair', made the derogatory comment on Catherine Parr's looks quoted earlier, and added for good measure that there could be 'no hope of issue' since Queen Catherine (four years her senior) had been married to two husbands without bearing a child. Even if Anna of Cleves did not actually say, 'A fine burden Madam Catherine has taken upon herself,' describing the King as 'so stout' that 'three of the biggest men that could be found could get inside his doublet', there is no doubt that she felt far more the woman scorned now than ever she had felt in 1540, at the King's marriage to Katherine Howard.[35]

All in all, the summer of 1543 was a bad time for Anna of Cleves. She might now have wished to return home, as Chapuys heard, 'in her shirt (so to speak)' and forget her handsome maintenance in England. Unfortunately the moment for that had passed. In the Netherlands the Emperor Charles swept to triumph over her brother Duke William who was forced to beg pardon 'on his knees'.[36] The Treaty of Venloe was concluded in September, by which the Duke abandoned his alliance with France, and surrendered Zutphen and Guelderland. With Catholicism restored to the Low Countries, it made sense for Duke William himself to renounce the Protestantism which had briefly animated him: his marriage to Jeanne d'Albret, niece of François I, went the way of his previous religious convictions and was annulled by the Pope. The imperialist takeover was completed when a Catholic Duke William married Maria of Austria, another niece, but the niece of Charles V.

The Lady Anna, whose own marriage to the King of England was, like that of Duke William to Jeanne d'Albret, a relic of a diplomatic past nobody now cared to remember, could not even expect to find comfort from the mother who had cherished her. For the Duchess Maria had died shortly before the Treaty of Venloe, allegedly heartbroken over the occupation of Guelderland, which had been her own inheritance. Marginalized in Europe by these events, in England equally the Lady Anna was swept off again to the edges of English court life: but no one now remarked on her jollity.

As for the Parrs, they were the gainers on many different levels. Anne Herbert, also praised by Roger Ascham for her learning, was placed in her sister's household, as was Queen Catherine's cousin, Maud Lady Lane, and her step-daughter Margaret Neville. Her uncle William, created Lord Parr of Horton, was to be her Lord Chamberlain. This distinguished veteran, now about sixty, had been Esquire of the Body to Henry VII, before serving Henry VIII; he survived for four years to enjoy the triumph of the Parrs, something which the early death of Edward IV had denied to his father. Her brother-in-law William Herbert entered the Privy Chamber, was knighted, and was set on his way to build a massive fortune centred round the lands of the former Abbey of Wilton, and other estates in Wales.

Queen Catherine's brother, William Parr of Kendal, had found favour with the King already: he had come to court with a recommendation from the Duke of Norfolk in 1537, and his uncle Sir William Parr of Horton had also asked Cromwell to find him a place in the Privy Chamber. In 1539 he was created Baron Parr of Kendal (the FitzHugh barony of his grandmother's family would have been preferred but there was trouble over the title). In April 1543 – when his sister's rise had already begun – he was given various appointments in the north, as well as being made a Knight of the Garter.

There was no doubt that William Parr was a most genial man. People paid tribute to his 'florid fancy and wit'. His delight was said to be 'music and poetry, and his exercise war' (an agreeable order of priorities), which no doubt explained why 'his skill in the field answered not his industry, nor his success his skill'. Unfortunately this geniality did not serve to keep his heiress wife Anne Bourchier by his side. She had run off some time before Catherine Parr's marriage 'and said openly she would live as she listed'; although she had no children by William Parr, she now produced some 'bastards', in much the same way as Edward Seymour's first wife had done.[37] However, by the laws of the time, none of this impeded William Parr from receiving the Bourchier inheritance for which he had married her: Anne Bourchier Lady Parr was merely granted an allowance. After the death of her father his Essex title had been briefly held by Thomas Cromwell; in December 1543 William Parr himself was created Earl of Essex.

As Queen Catherine Parr had fulfilled her duty to her own family by marrying the King, she was now bound to fulfil her duty to the King by tending to his family. She had taken as her motto: 'To be useful in all I do'. It is greatly to her credit that she managed to establish excellent loving relations with all three of her step-children, despite their very different needs and ages (the Lady Mary was twenty-one years older than Prince Edward). Of course she did not literally install them under one roof: that is to misunderstand the nature of sixteenth-century life when separate households were more to do with status than inclination. At the same time, the royal chidren were now all together on certain occasions, under the auspices of their stepmother: as in December 1543 when Maria of Hungary asked the English ambassador about the health of Queen Catherine, as well as 'my Lord Prince [Edward], my Lady Mary and my Lady Elizabeth,' and whether, with the King, they continued still in one household. But the real point was that Catherine was considered by the King – and the court – to be in charge of them, an emotional responsibility rather than a physical one. When the King, away from his sixth wife's side, wrote to her a personal postscript, 'Give in our name our hearty blessings to all our children', he expressed that truth.[38]

Queen Catherine's relationship with Elizabeth developed fully a few years later. Having attended the wedding of her father, the girl did not see her stepmother for a year; missing her at court in June 1544 she wrote Queen Catherine a letter (in Italian) deploring that fact. Her previous joint household with the Lady Mary having been disbanded by December 1542, the Lady Elizabeth for the time being joined Prince Edward's establishment. Similarly the real tenderness which Prince Edward 'the noble imp' displayed for his stepmother found more expression as he grew older. The Lady Mary however came to court under Queen Catherine's wing, having formed part of Queen Catherine's household from the beginning. She was 'retained to be with the Queen', for the rest of King Henry's life.[39]

The Lady Mary's health had not been proof against her various reverses of fortune: even though she was now officially confirmed in the succession, Mary from now on suffered from a series of colics, and other unspecific internal illnesses, all of which required a good deal of medicine – as well as periodic blood-letting. Yet it would be wrong to view the twenty-seven-year-old 'maid' entirely in terms of a boot-faced and frustrated spinster: she was for example passionately fond of gambling (like her father) and like Queen Catherine had a taste for clothes and jewels, as well as music and dancing. Equally, it is possible that the Lady Mary's natural interest in learning, encouraged years ago by her own mother, played its part in this Queen Catherine's efforts at self-improvement.

The aging Chapuys, in failing health, viewed with satisfaction at last the lifestyle of the unhappy girl who had been his protégé since the death of her mother. All of it he ascribed to the kindness of Queen Catherine 'who favours the Princess [Mary] all she can'.[40] Chapuys, like virtually all the commentators on the King's sixth marriage with the exception of Anna of Cleves, had an unqualified admiration for Catherine Parr.

Another duty of the Queen Consort, beyond being the titular mother of the royal family, was to act as Regent of the realm in her husband's absence – if the situation demanded it (and her qualities justified the appointment). On 7 July 1544 the minutes of the Privy Council recorded that 'The Queen's Highness [Catherine Parr] shall be regent in his grace's absence; and that his highness' progress shall pass and bear test in her name, as in like cases heretofore hath been accustomed'.[41] Despite the King's plethora of wives, the only precedent in his reign was in fact that of Catherine of

Aragon. She had acted the part with considerable verve when King Henry went to France in 1513, and the Scots were troubling the borders.

In 1544, King Henry was once again taking to a French campaign, and the Scots were once again obdurately refusing to understand that their finest destiny must lie in submitting to England, rather than favouring France. It was no longer a glorious young prince who was to lead his Englishmen towards Boulogne, in accordance with his treaty with the Emperor, but an unwieldy invalid who had to be winched aboard his horse with his armour cut away from around his swollen leg.[42]

The troubles of the King with his legs continued; he had been ill shortly before embarkation, and there is a touching vignette of Queen Catherine Parr sitting with his painful leg in her lap. She also moved into a small bedroom next to his, out of her queenly apartments, emphasizing the fact that many a man on his sixth wife must be assumed to stand in need of a nurse and for this role the widowed Lady Latimer was well-equipped. Her apothecaries' bills reveal lists of cures, from suppositories made from olive-oil ointment and liquorice pastilles to cinnamon comfits, as well as plasters and sponges for the administration of fomentations. About this time the King took to wearing reading-glasses with gilt frames: it has been suggested that the Queen may have suggested this improvement in the quality of her husband's life.[43]

By now a nurse was probably a greater necessity than a bedmate. As the King made his preparations for the campaign, he saw to it that parliament acknowledged the place of Catherine Parr's children in the succession, if any: that is, after Prince Edward and his issue, but before the Ladies Mary and Elizabeth. (The Queen was referred to as one 'by whom as yet his majesty hath none issue, but may full well when it shall please God'.) But this must be regarded as an optimistic piece of legislation at best by the 1540s. No coronation appears to have been suggested for Queen Catherine Parr. Certainly, in the course of the King's sixth marriage, references to 'a Duke of York' died away, while the practical importance of the Lady Mary noticeably increased: 'having but one Boy between her and the inheritance', as the King himself told the French ambassador in 1542, angling after a marriage for his daughter to a French prince.[44]

As a good wife, Queen Catherine saw her husband off at Dover. Thereafter she continued to send him a stream of affectionate letters. It is interesting to compare their tone with that of the first Regent Queen Catherine of Aragon thirty years earlier: both ladies dip their pens deep in honey (Cordelia-like restraint would hardly be appropriate when dealing with King Henry) but the slightly bossy note struck by Queen Catherine of Aragon – herself the daughter of two monarchs, and the senior to this particular King by six years – is altogether absent from the correspondence of Queen Catherine Parr. Submissiveness to duty is the keynote here (as in her explanation of her royal marriage when she really wanted to marry Thomas Seymour).

'Although the discourse of time and account of days neither is long nor many, of your Majesty's absence', she begins, 'yet the want of your presence, so much beloved and desired of me, maketh me, that I cannot quietly pleasure in anything until I hear from your Majesty.' On the one hand her 'love and affection' compel her to desire his presence, on the other hand 'the same zeal and love forceth me also to be best content with that which is your will and pleasure'. The Queen goes on: 'This love maketh me in all things to set apart my own commodity and pleasure, and to embrace most joyfully his will and pleasure whom I love. God, the knower of secrets, can judge these words not to be only written with ink, but most truly impressed in the heart.'[45]

In return for what she called her 'scribbled' letter (actually remarkably well-written), the Queen received a communication from her husband addressed to his 'Most dearly and most entirely beloved wife' which was dictated. He excused himself – 'we be so occupied, and have so much to do in foreseeing and caring for everything ourself, as we have almost no manner rest of leisure to do any other thing' – but of course King Henry hated writing letters himself. The famous love letters to Anne Boleyn had been born out of a whirlwind of romantic love. As he filled in the wise and kindly Queen-Manager at home with details of military matters, he felt no such inclination to pick up the pen himself, beyond a quick postscript concerning his children, as the letter was being closed up: 'No more to you at this time, sweetheart, both for lack of time and great occupation of business, saving we pray you to give in our name our hearty blessings to all our children.'[46]

The councillors with which Queen Catherine, as Regent, was surrounded were the actual administrators of the realm: on 25 July, for example, in a postscript of her own, she assured the King of their 'diligence'.[47] Yet although her importance in matters of government was certainly a good deal less than that of Queen Catherine of Aragon had been, it was also a good deal greater – officially – than that of any other consort. And her signature, which included the initials of her maiden name, was affixed to all documents.

The Scottish situation was the real bugbear that councillors and Queen had to face. Dreams of a marriage treaty between Prince Edward and Mary Queen of Scots, although confirmed by the Treaty of Greenwich of 1 July 1543, had been rudely dispelled shortly afterwards. Scottish popular indignation at the Treaty was vocal. Now the pro-French party in Scotland, including Cardinal Beaton and the widowed Marie de Guise, swung the country back in that direction. (Scotland's vacillating Governor, the Earl of Arran, hitherto pro-English, swung too.) As so often in the history of this period, the birth of a particular royal baby on a particular date was of crucial significance: in January 1544, Catherine de' Medici, wife of the heir to the French throne, gave birth to a son, François, after ten childless years. To many Scots it now made much more sense to link the baby Queen to a French prince, rather than an English one.

England under the command of Prince Edward's senior uncle, Edward Seymour Earl of Hertford (his first independent command), responded with a ferocious attack on southern Scotland, including the firing of Edinburgh and Holyrood Palace itself, to which the cynical but appropriate oxymoron 'the Rough Wooing' was applied. (Hertford, who was ordered to see that 'the upper stone may be the nether and not one stick stand by another', took his responsibilities seriously.)[48] If Arran had defected from the English cause, other Scottish nobles joined it: the Earl of Lennox, with the prospect of becoming another pro-English Governor of Scotland, married Lady Margaret Douglas about the time that King Henry travelled to France.

Queen Catherine was able to write to the King in France with satisfaction about Lennox's successes. On 9 August 1544, she decided that he was enjoying 'good speed' just because he was now 'serving a master whom God aids', that is the English King; under his former master, the King of France, Lennox had not done half so well. In general Queen Catherine proved herself a loyal helpmeet where the necessities of the Rough Wooing were concerned. In July she gave thanks to all those 'who served in the late journey' in her capacity as Regent; while she herself penned a prayer for 'men going into battle' for the troops in France (of a rather more merciful nature than Hertford's instructions). 'Our cause being now just, and being enforced to enter into war and battle, we most humbly beseech Thee, O Lord God of Hosts, so to turn the hearts of our enemies to the desire of peace, that no Christian blood be spilt; or else grant, O Lord, that with small effusion of blood and to the little hurt and damage of innocents, we may to Thy Glory obtain victory.'[49]

Archbishop Cranmer may have helped the Queen over her prayer – in the framing of it, if not the actual sentiments, so characteristic of this essentially conciliatory woman. The King was back in England by October. (Boulogne had agreed to surrender on 13 September, but the King did not then pursue his campaign as far as Paris, despite promises to Charles V to do so.) By this time Cranmer and the Queen had been in close contact over matters to do with the regency for three months: Cranmer being a member of the Council. Together, accompanied by those members of the Privy Council who had stayed in England, they had made a progress through Surrey and Kent, where some of the Queen's jointure properties were situated, and stayed together in Cranmer's former palace at Otford. Money was spent on refurbishing at both Leeds Castle and Chobham where 'the Queen's Chambers' needed repair.[50]

King Henry did not expect that such propinquity would have any effect on the character and belief of such an admirably balanced woman as his newest wife: his mind did not work like that. Still less did it occur to him that there was more than one way in which his authority might be challenged by a Queen. So far as he was concerned, in late 1544, following the terrible debacle with Katherine Howard, vice in a Queen was strictly connected to adultery; and of that there was certainly no danger from his dutiful spouse.

There was a story going round – repeated by Antonio de Guaras – that King Henry had announced his impending sixth marriage to his Council as follows: 'Gentleman, I desire company, but I have had more than enough of taking young wives, and I am now resolved to marry a widow ...' The King then sent for the lady in question and announced, rather in the manner of King Cophetua to the beggar maid: 'Lady Latimer, I wish you to be my wife'. At this, Catherine knelt before him. 'Your Majesty is my master, I have but to obey you'.[51] Time would show whether the submissiveness of Queen Catherine Parr was to be relied upon completely.

Chapter 18

OBEDIENT TO

HUSBANDS

Children of Light ... If they be women married, they
learn of St Paul to be obedient to their husbands ...

Queen Catherine Parr, *The Lamentation of a Sinner*

'Her rare goodness made every day like Sunday, a thing hitherto unheard of in royal palaces': thus Francis Goldsmith, chaplain to Queen Catherine Parr, expounded on the subject of his royal mistress's household.[1] If one allows for his hyperbole – after all at least four of King Henry's consorts had also attempted to create suitably decent environments – there is no doubt that the household of Queen Catherine Parr was seen at the time as standing for exceptional piety. (There was no conflict perceived with her enjoyment of dancing and 'mirth in company', which were after all connected to her primary role – to please the King by acting as a gracious consort.) Her court stood however for evangelical piety. Just as Catherine, the widow of Lord Latimer, had seethed with passion for Thomas Seymour beneath her calm surface, so Catherine, the consort of Henry VIII, harboured surprisingly subversive views despite an outward appearance of conformity.

The chaplains appointed, not only Goldsmith but reformers such as John Parkhurst and Anthony Cope, Miles Coverdale later, the high-born ladies such as Anne Countess of Hertford and Jane Lady Denny who formed an important part of it, held opinions very far from those of the Catholic and reactionary party in the Privy Council. One of these ladies – Katherine Duchess of Suffolk – was especially influential. Like Archbishop Cranmer, with whom Queen Catherine had spent those significant months on royal progress in the King's absence, Duchess Katherine had both the opportunity and the inclination to encourage the new Queen in her natural tendencies towards reform and it was probably she who introduced the Queen to the reforming erstwhile Bishop Hugh Latimer (recently deprived of his bishopric for opposing the Act of the Six Articles).[2]

The Duchess, born Katherine Willoughby, was the heiress-daughter of the favourite lady-in-waiting of Catherine of Aragon, Maria de Salinas. She had been married off at fourteen and was even now only in her late twenties (about seven years younger than the Queen). But as the power of the once 'hardy' Duke of Suffolk, King Henry's old jousting companion and trusted servant, waned, that of his young wife waxed. As she grew up Duchess Katherine showed herself to be something of a tigress: 'a lady of sharp wit and sure hand to thrust it home and make it pierce when she pleased'. Duchess Katherine was credited with having influenced Suffolk in the direction of the reformers before his death. More fulsomely, John Parkhurst eulogized her in Latin verse, as having 'the endowments ... of mind' which placed her on a level with 'men of the highest distinction'.[3]

Suffolk died in August 1545 at the age of sixty-one: faithful to the last, he attended a meeting of the Privy Council in his final days. Two years after her husband's death, Duchess Katherine was said to rule all Lincolnshire (where his estates lay).[4] Her religious opinions were those of the new generation – certainly far from those of her mother or the Queen her mother had served.

So far as it can be ascertained, the views of these chaplains and ladies were also removed from those of King Henry himself; although in the remaining years of his life no one ever knew absolutely for sure what the old King's real religious views were, perhaps because, in a state of constant pain and thus irritability, he did not quite know himself. We are however on much firmer ground with the religious beliefs of Queen Catherine, for she left behind a modest but interesting body of devotional writings. It is a mistake to overlook the importance of these works just because they are often derivative: apart from the scriptures, *The Imitation of Christ* by Thomas à Kempis was one source, and *The Mirror of the Sinful Soul* by Marguerite of Navarre (Marguerite d'Angoulême) another.[5] Queen Catherine's writings should be seen in another context: that of the sheer paucity of works by any woman in this period.

It has been pointed out that Queen Catherine Parr is one among only eight women who had books published in the sixty-odd years of the reigns of the first Tudor monarchs, Henry VII and Henry VIII.[6] Quite apart from the fact that the Queen chose to use the prominent position granted to her by marriage to write these works, the way she exercises her authorial voice is also significant. Thomas à Kempis' *The Imitation of Christ*, for example, takes the form of a dialogue between a male deity – 'Jesus', 'Sire', 'Lord' – and an author addressed as 'my son', but Queen

Catherine, with unconscious eloquence, transposes everything into the (genderless) first person so much more suitable to her own aspirations.[7] It was no wonder that her humble little manuals, so suitable also for female suppliants in a thousand chapels and oratories throughout the country, proved to be extremely popular, and went through many editions.

Prayers and Meditations, first published in 1545, was intended in Queen Catherine's own words to 'stir' the mind 'patiently to suffer all afflictions here, to set at nought the vain prosperity of this world, and always to long for the everlasting felicity'. It includes that 'Prayer for men to say entering battle' quoted in the previous chapter, as well as the 'Prayer for the King'; its main thesis is the redemptive nature of the Passion of Jesus Christ. Beyond that, the tone is one of simplicity and sincerity, devoid of any kind of radicalism. Certainly Queen Catherine's *Prayers and Meditations* were sufficiently anodyne to go through nineteen editions by the end of the sixteenth century, undeterred by the doctrinal changes of the various reigns which followed.* Such sentiments as these: 'Teach me Lord to fulfil thy will, to live meekly, and worthily before thee, for thou art all my wisdom and cunning, thou art He that knowest me as I am' found their way to many hearts.[8]

The precociously erudite Lady Elizabeth had selected Marguerite of Navarre's work, of which a French edition had appeared in England in 1531, to translate for her stepmother as a New Year's gift in 1544; presumably because she knew it to be a favourite volume. The Lady Elizabeth had the translation bound in a charming cover of her own design, which is still extant. The following New Year, at the age of eleven, Elizabeth went one better and proceeded to translate her stepmother's own *Prayers and Meditations* into three languages, French and Italian as well as Latin, for presentation to her father.[9]

But *The Lamentation, or Complaint of a Sinner, made by the most vertuous and right gratious Ladie, Queene Catherine* would not have been an acceptable New Year's gift for Henry VIII. Nor was it in fact printed during his lifetime, but first published in 1547 under the auspices of the Queen's brother William Parr, Duchess Katherine and William Cecil. The latter referred to it as the work of a woman 'by marriage most noble, by wisdom godly ... renowned Catherine, a wife to him that was king to realms'.[10] It is not difficult to see why it was not thought fit to present *The Lamentation of a Sinner* during the last years of the King's life.

---

* A manuscript version, supposedly in Catherine Parr's handwriting, although missing the last fifty-nine verses of the printed versions, is in Kendal Town Hall. Measuring only 5 by 3 centimetres, it is written on parchment, ornamented with touches of gold and colour, and bound into a silver casing. It was presented by the Queen to Elizabeth Tuke, daughter of the Treasurer of the Chamber of Henry VIII, and remained with her family until the late seventeenth century.

This was a time of feverish uncertainty where doctrinal matters were concerned, further complicated by the struggle for dominance among the King's advisers, in which religion, politics and feuds among the nobility were inextricably enmeshed.

Once again *The Lamentation of a Sinner* is marked by simplicity and sincerity. But it does have a distinct doctrinal slant. King Henry – 'my most sovereign favourable lord and husband' – is paid tribute, not only for being 'godly and learned', but also for being 'our Moses' who 'hath delivered us out of the captivity and bondage of Pharaoh [Rome]'; while the 'Bishop of Rome' is denounced along with 'such riff-raff' as he planted 'in his tyranny'.[11] (For this reason the book was temporarily suppressed during the Catholic reaction under Mary.) Anti-papalism apart, however, the strongest message of the book is the crucial need for the laity to benefit from personal study of the Bible.

The Queen inveighed against those who criticized reading the Bible on the grounds that it would lead to heresy: surely such criticisms might in themselves be a form of blasphemy against the Holy Ghost. 'Is it not extreme wickedness,' she wrote, 'to charge the holy sanctified word of God with the offences of man? To allege the Scriptures to be perilous learning; because certain readers thereof fall into heresies?' Did people deny themselves food, just because some people overate? Or avoid using fire just because they watched a neighbour's house burn down? 'O blind hate!' she exclaimed. 'They slander God for man's offence.' In the meantime, without direct biblical enlightenment, 'we, that be unlettered, remain confused, without God, of his grace'.

Yet in May 1543 the Council had decided that the 'lower sort' did not benefit from studying the Bible in English. The Act for the Advancement of the True Religion stated that 'no women nor artificers, journeymen, serving men of the degree of yeomen or under husbandmen nor labourers' could in future read the Bible 'privately or openly'. In a sermon in the City of London the next year, it was suggested that the study of the scriptures was making the apprentices unruly.[12] Women (in the sense of women of the people), yeomen and apprentices – all these led lives far removed from the court where Queen Catherine was apparently in the habit of holding study groups among her ladies for the scriptures and listening to sermons of an evangelical nature. Although a later clause in the 1543 act did allow any noble or gentlewoman to read the Bible (in contrast to 'the lower sort'), this activity must take place 'to themselves alone and not to others'.

It remained to be seen whether such innocent aloofness from the consequences of her actions could be successfully maintained. In her emphasis on the individual, her ignoring of the effects of grace through the sacraments, and her concentration on salvation through Jesus Christ alone, Queen Catherine had travelled a long way down the road to heresy – even if she did not actually cross the boundary: 'Yet we may not impute to the worthiness of faith or works our justification before God,' wrote Queen Catherine, 'but wholly to the merits of Christ's passion'.

While the persecution of heresy was intermittent in the last years of Henry VIII's reign, it could never be assumed to be in abeyance, so long as it suited the book of one particular faction to drag down representatives of another by this means. The tough provisions of the 1539 Act of Six Articles on the subject of heresy still existed. There was another aspect to all this. In *The Lamentation of a Sinner*, Queen Catherine referred to the so-called 'Children of Light', those who were 'so pure and holy' that they could simply read the scriptures without need for further instruction. She added a rider: such holy people, if they were 'women married', should learn from St Paul 'to be obedient to their husbands, and to keep silence in the congregation, and to learn of their husbands at home.'[13] In her own conduct, Catherine Parr, whose husband was the 'godly and learned' Henry VIII, would be wise to practise what she so modestly preached.

Of other works ascribed to Queen Catherine Parr, two anonymous translations into English, one of Savonarola and one of Erasmus, are probably not hers; whereas another translation from the Latin, *Psalms or Prayers taken out of Holy Scripture*, with which she is not generally credited, has been convincingly traced to her.[14] 'Books of the psalm prayers, gorgeously bound and gilt on leather' by Thomas Berthelet in May 1544, for which the Queen paid, were possibly her presentation copies of the work, which was later frequently bound in with her *Prayers and Meditations*. The translations may have been a form of Latin exercise, as evinced by another payment of the spring of 1544 for 'a primer for her grace in Latin and English with epistles and gospels unbounded'.

Beyond authorship, Queen Catherine's role as a patroness recalls that of Queen Anne Boleyn. She encouraged the translation of Erasmus' paraphrases of the scriptures, if she did not carry it out personally. Nicholas Udall, he who had written the coronation ode for Queen Anne, benefited from this encouragement. He dedicated his translation of the Gospel of St Luke to her, which was completed in 1545. Udall trusted that King Henry would now see fit to let it be published 'to the same use that your Highness Queen Catherine hath meant it, that is to say, to the public commodity and benefit of good English people now a long time sore thirsting and hungering [for] the sincere and plain knowledge of God's word'.[15] But the King did not see fit. The publication of this translation (the Gospels and Acts of the Apostles) would have to wait for 1548, when St Luke's Gospel was still dedicated to Catherine, with an overall dedication to the new King.

Like Queen Anne Boleyn, again, Queen Catherine exercised her influence to protect reformers who had got into trouble. In 1544, for example, she sent her own servant Robert Warner to plead for the reforming schoolmaster Stephen Cobbe before the Court of Aldermen in the City of London. It seems that she saved him on this occasion, although he ran into further difficulties the next year.[16] She also encouraged reformers not only in her own household but in that of Prince Edward, such as John Cheke, Anthony Cooke and William Grindal, with obvious significance for his character and the future of the country.

It is clear that Queen Catherine Parr, far more than Queen Jane Seymour, deserves that title of the Protestant Queen sometimes erroneously granted to the latter. Had Queen Catherine succeeded in producing the 'many sons' hoped for by John Leland the antiquary in a dedication of about this time,[17] or even just one of them to succeed Jane Seymour's son on the throne, no doubt it would have been given to her. Motherhood of a Protestant King would have achieved a reputation which personal example and devotional writings could not.

Around 1545, Henry VIII commissioned an enormous picture to symbolize the glory of the Tudor dynasty. It is a remarkable work for two reasons. First the relative sizes and positioning of the figures are guided by their dynastic importance. On the outside, divided from the inner family by pillars, stand the King's two daughters; they are of more or less equal size, except that the Lady Mary occupies the foreground of her panel, while the Lady Elizabeth is receded slightly into the background. The central group consists of the mighty King on his throne, shapely – not swollen – legs and ankles well displayed, as they might have been in his heyday as a jouster. The heir to the throne, Prince Edward, is positioned on his right hand, surprisingly well-grown for a seven- or eight-year-old with his face almost adult-sized.

The second remarkable feature is the presence in this inner group of Queen Jane Seymour painted life-sized and the dominating female figure. There is no sign of Queen Catherine Parr, who at the time when this picture was executed had been the King's 'most beloved' consort for two years, had acted as his Regent and now presided over his court. To the King it was an evocative representation of the male succession he had struggled so hard to establish, including the 'entirely beloved' Queen Jane who had finally enabled him to do it. To later eyes it may convey a further message: the significance of any woman, including a queen like Catherine

Parr, was in the end defined by her ability to fulfil her husband's philo-progenitive desires.

A series of struggles for power within the Privy Council and at court generally marked the last years of Henry VIII: once more Howards vied with Seymours. But now it was the regency of the future King rather than the marriage of the present one which was the fundamental issue; although, as we shall see, all hope of manipulating King Henry via his affections – for a mistress if not a wife – had not been abandoned. In these struggles, the Howards, not only the Duke of Norfolk but his son, the soldier-poet the Earl of Surrey, were represented as before by the 'Catholic' party headed by Bishop Gardiner. The Seymours headed by the Earl of Hertford and including his younger brother Sir Thomas Seymour, and Archbishop Cranmer, tended towards reform.

The Parrs also favoured reform, not only the Queen but William Lord Parr of Kendal and the Herberts. But whereas the Duke of Norfolk – the premier duke in England – could claim to represent the most distinguished family in England, and the Earl of Hertford was indubitably the blood-uncle of the future King (as well as having much enhanced his military reputation in Scotland and France), the Parrs could advance neither claim to make them major players in this game: Queen Catherine was missing from the dynastic picture. This very fact might have kept her and her family free from hostility. Unfortunately it was not to be. Her own religious views made her an excellent target for attack, in order to mount an indirect assault on the reformers in the Privy Council.

In the complicated diplomatic manoeuvres of these years, Queen Catherine was similarly not a major figure. She was recognized to be a reformer, but nobody thought she had the kind of influence that had been attributed to Catherine of Aragon with her Spanish connections (or for that matter the dominating Anne Boleyn). Tributes to her graciousness drew attention to her true role in the King's life as Queen-Manager, a smoother-over of tricky situations, not a maker of policies. In the meantime the Anglo-imperial alliance began to fall apart, with accusations on both sides that promises had not been fulfilled. In the summer of 1545 Queen Catherine tactfully assured the new imperial ambassador Van der Delft of King Henry's 'sincere affection and goodwill';[18] but in fact the Emperor's determined neutrality in the face of King François' aggressive campaigns to recover Boulogne infuriated King Henry.

All in all, this summer was a testing time for the English King. The Scots had managed to inflict a defeat on him at Ancrum Moor in the early spring. Now the French avenged the loss of Boulogne by sailing along the south coast of England, landing on the Isle of Wight, with the declared purpose of invasion, ending King Henry's tyranny and restoring the rights of the church. The King was present on the south coast himself, at Portsmouth, where he arrived on 15 July, with the Queen, to oversee defences. There, four days later, he had the appalling experience of watching his favourite ship the *Mary Rose* suddenly heel over and sink in front of his eyes (and those of his court), probably due to an ingress of water when its gunports were open, ready for action. Nearly all the 700 men on the *Mary Rose* perished, their drowning cries reaching the ears of the King on land. Although the invasion was held off despite this disaster, the French were still able to harry the Sussex ports. This gave a hollow ring to the King's boast of the previous year, made 'very loudly', that the French had been 'whipped by land and by sea'.[19]

Equally it was for such unsuccessful manoeuvres that his subjects endured inflation, levies and taxes, a debasement of the coinage (in 1544), their plight compounded by a series of bad harvests. In the pursuit of that military glory which had brought him such happiness in his youth, this new Henry V spent nearly two million pounds in his last years – and wasted in effect the vast revenues he had derived from the dissolution of the monasteries. Peace with France was not made until June 1546, when King Henry agreed at last to surrender Boulogne, provided King François paid him an enormous price for it phased over a number of years.

The King added to the complication caused by his various diplomatic initiatives by his usual Byzantine manoeuvres with regard to the marriages of his three children. Did he really intend to mount some kind of new Protestant alliance with the German princes? The Duke of Holstein was to be offered one of his daughters, whose place in the succession was emphasized. On the other hand there were negotiations for a marriage between Prince Edward and a Habsburg princess. It was agreed that the young prince, as heir to the English throne, was 'the greatest person in Christendom, meet for any such offer'; the name of one of the Emperor's nieces was mentioned.[20] (Charles V was well supplied with nieces since his brother King Ferdinand of Hungary had eleven daughters, one of whom had just married Duke William of Cleves.) Familiar arguments about the dowry were indulged in on both sides, with the English via Bishop Gardiner suggesting that the dowry should be commensurate with the bride's status as the Emperor's niece, and the imperial ambassador pointing out – with some truth under the circumstances – that the Emperor had many nieces. None of these marriage treaties were fulfilled in the King's lifetime, the intention being diplomatic temptation rather than consummation.

As for 'the greatest person in Christendom' himself – Prince Edward – at home in England he led a life whose outward state was appropriate to that description. But at least he now had a stepmother in Queen Catherine able to cast a little glow into it by that 'tender love' which her step-daughter

Margaret Neville had praised. The young prince's correspondence shows that in his relationship with the Queen he evinced a warmth and liveliness not elsewhere displayed by this formal princeling. She is *'Mater Charissima'*, 'my dearest mother' – his familiar form of address for her – and held 'the chief place in my heart'. Although a number of letters have survived from both prince and Queen, there must have been many more. For it is clear that the correspondence was both regular and frequent: at one point the Queen pardons Edward for not having written 'for several days', understanding that his affection for her is constant, and his studies engrossing.[21]

Prince Edward, a pedagogue in the making, takes a keen interest in his stepmother's progress in Latin (so much slower than his own), 'on which account I feel no little joy'. He gives her little lectures like this, in which one suspects that the Queen's own enjoyment of life may be the target, rather than his sister's: 'pardon my rude style in writing to you, most illustrious Queen and beloved Mother, and receive my hearty thanks for your loving kindness to me and my sister. Yet, dearest Mother, the only true consolation is from Heaven and the only real love is the love of God. Preserve, therefore, I pray you, my dear sister Mary from all the wiles and enchantments of the evil one, and beseech her to attend no longer to foreign dances and merriments which do not become a most Christian Princess.'[22] (Prince Edward was eight and a half when he wrote this.)

From 1546 onwards, Queen Catherine was also in direct charge of the twelve-year-old Lady Elizabeth, who was brought to court and listed for the future among those 'accustomed to be lodged within the King's Majesty's house'. It is unlikely that the Lady Elizabeth could remember her real mother, a Queen to whom no one now referred: she had been just over two and a half when Anne Boleyn was executed and in any case had been brought up separately (according to royal custom). After that she had encountered a series of stepmothers whose main concentration had been on forging bonds or otherwise with her half-sister Mary (with the honourable exception of the briefly installed Anna of Cleves who had taken a fancy to the wary, intelligent seven-year-old child). Now in Queen Catherine Parr Elizabeth found not only an experienced adoptive parent (whose 'care and solicitude' for her health she treasured), but one whose intellectual interests and reforming tendencies fitted with her own: the 'fervent zeal your Highness hath towards all godly learning.'[23]

Presenting her translation of *The Mirror of the Sinful Soul*, Elizabeth had politely asked her stepmother to 'rub out, polish and mend ... the words (or rather the order of my writing) the which I know in many places to be rude'.[24] Even if it was more likely to be Queen Catherine's own writings that needed polishing and mending – her accomplishments could never match those of her step-daughter – Elizabeth's words were a gracious acknowledgement of a relationship which (for the time being at least) was uncomplicated and pleasing on both sides.

In 1546 the pace of persecution towards heretics gathered speed. Sir Thomas Wriothesley, now Baron Wriothesley, had succeeded the milder Lord Audley as Lord Chancellor in May 1544: he was now ardent in his pursuit of those heretics with connections to the court. Wriothesley was one of those who had hailed Catherine Parr on her marriage as 'a woman in my judgement, for virtue, wisdom and gentleness most meet for his Highness; and sure I am', he went on, 'His Majesty had never a wife more agreeable to his heart than she is.' Those days were long gone. He now belonged to the party of those who were happy to disturb His Majesty in this harmonious relationship, if in so doing the reformers could be cast down. George Blagge, for example, was a courtier and minor poet who narrowly escaped being burnt alive for heresy that summer for allegedly denying the efficacy of the Mass. In the end the King's personal favour saved Blagge, but while under sentence he wrote fiercely of his religious enemies painting their 'Roman Church' with the 'rose colour of persecuted blood'.[25]

There were rumours about the instability of the Queen's position. On the one hand it is difficult to know how much weight to attach to them; the idea, floated abroad, of the King getting rid of Catherine Parr to marry Katherine Duchess of Suffolk is an unlikely one, and the rumour-monger himself admitted that the King showed no alteration in his behaviour towards his wife. Similar rumours persisted about the Lady Anna of Cleves, who was alleged to have borne two children by the King in May 1546, simply because she was one who came and went to the court 'at her pleasure' and had an 'honest dowry' to support her. A prophecy in June by one Robert Parker 'that the Queen should not long reign and there must be another Queen' was part of the rich coinage of prediction of which there were many examples, few of which ever came true. On the other hand, Queen Catherine herself was said to be much angered by the rumour about her friend Duchess Katherine and one can understand that in her position this kind of talk, even if groundless, was not always easy to bear.[26]

A key arrest from Catherine's point of view was that of Anne Askew on 24 May. She was a young woman in her early twenties, of strongly reformist views – with a love of biblical studies like the Queen's. Undeniably she had many connections to the court. Anne Askew's sister was married to the steward of the late Duke of Suffolk; her brother Edward had a post in the King's household. She had been briefly married in her native Lincolnshire and borne children, but had come to London after her husband apparently expelled her for crossing swords with local priests. (One of the accusations against her was that she had abandoned her married name – Kyme – for her maiden name of Askew.) In 1545 Anne Askew had already been cross-examined for heresy and had responded to her accusers with vigour. She survived the experience. She could not survive the renewed assault of 1546, although she never gave in to her male accusers. Addressed – constantly – by the Lord Mayor as 'Thou foolish woman', she retorted: 'Alack, poor mouse'. Her remarkable spirit, maintained even under the torture which was illegal for a woman of her degree, did at least gain her reverence as a Protestant heroine of the next reign.[27]

At the time, immured in the Tower of London, Anne Askew was endlessly pressed on the subject of the great court ladies whose religious views were suspect to Wriothesley and his aide Richard Rich. This pair actually operated the rack themselves, infuriated by her obstinate silence, when the Lieutenant of the Tower shrank from doing so. She would admit to receiving presents of money – shillings – from the servants of Anne Countess of Hertford and Jane Lady Denny, but absolutely declined to go further and give the essential lead to their husbands (or the Queen).[28] On 16 July Anne Askew, still horribly crippled by her tortures but without recantation, was burnt for heresy. Alongside her died, also for heresy, John Lascelles: he whose scandalous revelations had led to the imprisonment and death of Queen Katherine Howard.

It remained to be seen whether Queen Catherine Parr would follow her predecessor to the Tower of London: if for a very different reason. Ironically, it was Queen Catherine herself who contributed the vital missing element, enabling her religious enemies to attack her standing with her husband. The King's health – 'the anguish of a sore leg' – made him extraordinarily 'forward' (irritable) at this time, as even his smoothest supporters had to admit. In an emollient version of the events of that summer of 1546 Lord Herbert of Cherbury simply related how, in his agony, the King 'lov'd not to be contradicted' in his opinions, especially as he said, in his old age and by his wife. It is clear from this, as from the account by the Protestant martyrologist John Foxe which is the real source for the story, that Queen Catherine had indulged in the impermissible where Henry VIII was concerned: she had lectured her husband, and had even 'in the heat of discourse gone very far'.[29]

She should have known better; after all she had been married to another older man in poor health. Queen Catherine's nursing skills were part of her charm where King Henry was concerned, and remained so. As Bishop Burnet described it, the King put up with the existence of those radical preachers in her apartments, because in every other way Queen Catherine behaved so admirably; above all she showed 'that wonderful care about the

King's person, which became a wife that was raised by him to so great an honour'.[30] It was no part of a nurse's duty to contradict a difficult patient.

And perhaps in her heart of hearts Queen Catherine did know better. Perhaps that impulsive side to her, so much at variance with her outwardly correct conduct, seen previously in her love for Thomas Seymour, simply did not allow her to remain silent on the subject of her own religious views. The earnest Christian in her overcame the nurse. 'The Children of Light ... If they be women married, they learn of St Paul to be obedient to their husbands', she had written. That was the counsel of perfection, but Catherine Parr, despite being hailed as the ideal consort, a respectable reliable widow no longer in her first youth, was no more absolutely perfect than any other human being, male or female.

On 4 July the Privy Council ordered the Queen's auditors to produce her estate books. That probably meant that the charges to be brought against her were completed, since it indicated that her extensive properties might shortly be forfeited.[31] Publicly the King's mood continued to vary: he paid a visit to the Queen when she in turn fell ill, and treated her very graciously; yet experienced courtiers knew that along with his explosive rages, King Henry also possessed a delusive ability to extend politeness to those he was about to destroy, notably Cardinal Wolsey. Those who had drawn up the charges were certainly convinced that the King would go with their plans to eliminate his sixth wife.

Then at the last minute, everything was thrown into confusion again. The King confided to his doctor, Thomas Wendy, a favoured servant, what was about to take place. A copy of the charges was subsequently dropped by an anonymous councillor outside the passage in the Queen's chamber. Whatever the King's real intentions at this point, there is no doubt that the Queen herself was devastated by this revelation of what lay in store: not surprisingly for one married to a man who had demonstrated several times his ability to punish recalcitrant wives. But she did not panic. Instead, she took that particular way out which was open to her as a woman (and denied to a man) involving complete self-abasement combined with acknowledgement of her sex's weakness; much as Gertrude Marchioness of Exeter had once pleaded for herself over the affair of the Maid of Kent, on the grounds that her 'fragility and brittleness' made her 'easily seduced ... and brought into abusion and disbelief'.[32]

Rushing to the King, the Queen found him in the mood to set about a discourse on religion. This was a test – a crucial test. Queen Catherine did not flunk it. In Foxe's account she declined to take part in the discourse but answered instead 'that women by their first creation were made subject to men'. She went on, 'Being made after the image of God, as the women were after their image, men ought to instruct their wives, who would do all their learning from them'. She herself had an extra reason to wish 'to be taught by his Majesty, who was a prince of such excellent learning and wisdom.' The whispering ghosts of Catherine of Aragon, Anne Boleyn and Jane Seymour (all three of whom had learnt in their various ways of the King's impatience with female argument) would certainly have counselled this tactful allusion to that theological expertise on which the King prided himself.

The battle was not quite won. 'Not so by St Mary', replied the King. 'You are become a doctor [of the Church] able to instruct us and not to be instructed by us.' But this pointed reference to her previous heated discourses was met with an inspired explanation by the Queen. It seemed that the King 'had much mistaken the freedom she had taken to argue with him'. She had only done it to distract him from his pain, and of course to take the opportunity to learn from him herself, from which she had greatly profited.

'And is it even so?' asked the King. 'Then Kate, we are friends again.' He embraced his wife affectionately, and gave her 'very tender assurances of constant love'.

The next day when Lord Chancellor Wriothesley came with forty guards to arrest the Queen, he was met with an outburst of the royal temper and cries of 'Knave!' 'Fool!' and 'Beast!' Queen Catherine Parr lived to breathe again. More than that, her position was strengthened by the failure of the attack. At the August reception of the French ambassador, following the peace treaty, she was prominent in the ceremonies of the court; the pious – but not unworldly – Queen was also loaded with new jewels which were the visible expression of those tender assurances the King had given her in mid-July.[33]

In view of the happy outcome of this episode, it cannot be known for certain how much danger really threatened Queen Catherine, although she certainly believed in it herself, as any prudent woman would have done, given her husband's career of marital destruction. In another incident, most plausibly placed in the autumn of 1545, the King had allowed himself to be drawn into a ploy against Archbishop Cranmer which was not dissimilar in its outcome: at the moment when the arrest of the Archbishop was sought, he freed himself on the King's authority by waving a ring especially sent to him by his master for that purpose.[34] Such little games, however terrifying for the victims – and Queen Catherine was undoubtedly terrified – were one way of keeping the Privy Council on its toes; since no one could be absolutely sure that he possessed the King's authority, no one would find it easy to usurp it. At the same time, there was always the danger that the relaxation of the King's angry mood would be too late to save the victim from his or her fate – as had happened in the case of Cromwell. One would not wish to take risks in such circumstances.

Queen Catherine's abandonment of her heated discourses was wise enough. Across the water, the Duchesse d'Étampes, mistress to François I, had Lutheran tendencies herself, but according to the English ambassador she let the French King believe 'that he is god on earth, that no one can harm him and that those who deny this are moved by selfish interest'.[35] That was certainly a successful formula for dealing with self-willed monarchs, as the Duchesse's long reign demonstrated.

Nevertheless Queen Catherine's complete withdrawal from her previous assertive position was not merely expedient – although no one could have blamed her if it had been. Along with her intellectual curiosity, she also continued to demonstrate the modesty suitable to a female: even where learning itself was concerned. In February, before her troubles, she had answered a request from the University of Cambridge for her intercession with the King (they had asked for a stay of their possessions and it seems the Queen was successful in securing it). The terms of her answer would have satisfied the most tyrannical husband that she did not set herself up as 'a doctor'. Derogatory references to her own lack of education abounded.[36]

In particular she professed herself both surprised and flattered that they should have addressed her in Latin. They might easily have expressed 'their desires and opinions, more familiarly' in 'the vulgar tongue' (English) so much more suitable for her intelligence. Evidently the university had formed 'rather partially than truly' its high opinion of her progress in learning. She added: 'for this Latin lesson I am taught to say of St Paul: *Non me pudet evangelii* [The gospels cause me no shame]'. As for her little homily that Cambridge should not overdo its 'hunger for the exquisite knowledge of profane learning ... forgetting our Christianity', there was nothing at all subversive about that.

The submissiveness of Queen Catherine, the more conventional side of her nature which enabled her to live – mainly – at ease with the demanding King, was also genuine. It merged with her religion, her sense of the infinite if sometimes mysterious mercies of God. In this frame of mind, she urged Lady Wriothesley to accept the death of her little boy: 'put away all immoderate and unjust heaviness ... that the Father in heaven may think you are most glad and best contented to make him a present of his spiritual and your only natural son.'[37] Although even here Queen Catherine sympathetically recognized the terrible tug of human love: after all the Virgin Mary herself had given way to 'a sorrowful natural passion' for her son's death.

When Queen Catherine had given up her plan of marrying Thomas Seymour in 1543, she had interpreted the will of the King as being the will of God. Three years later, it was not difficult for the same woman to make the same equation, and abandon her new-found taste for theological discussion as being not only dangerous but also contrary to the divine order of things.

With the contender in her extinguished, Queen Catherine's role was now predominantly that of nurse. There was plenty of scope for it. A fever in the spring of 1546 had shaken the King badly; observers noted how terrible he looked. About this time, he annotated a passage in the Bible about old age: *'Dolens dictu'* ('A painful saying'). That expressed the weariness of his mood and the pain of his body. In September the threatening fever recurred, although officially termed a cold. The King's apothecary's bill for August included payments for two 'urynals' sent to Hampton Court as well as 'eyebright' water for his eyes, liquorice for his hands.[38] Although the King was hardly moribund at this point – he was able to take outdoor exercise as late as 7 December – none of the ambitious courtiers who surrounded him, their keen eyes bent on the future, were in any doubt that his days were numbered.

On about 10 December King Henry fell dangerously ill again. Publicly the Privy Council did not admit the gravity of the situation. Wotton, for instance, the ambassador in France, was carefully instructed to play it down. It was true that the King had had a fever 'upon some grief of his leg', but he was now 'thanks be to God, well rid of it,' and his health was such that they trusted His Majesty would continue to flourish 'for a great while'. This was for Wotton to pass on: 'in case any light brute [rumour] may rise to the contrary'.[39]

The reality was different. The King was dying: but he was dying very slowly. On the actual timing of his decease a great deal depended in the inner world of the Privy Council in which the religious radicals were now rising. These were headed by Hertford and John Dudley recently created Viscount Lisle (son of Henry VII's servant executed for extortion): by December Van der Delft, the imperial ambassador, was referring to Hertford as having 'obtained authority with the King'.[40] More than that hung on the exact moment of King Henry's death. It turned out that this reign, so bloodily stained with the judicial murders of the King's close relatives, ancient colleagues and lifelong servants, would end with yet more deaths – unless the King himself died in time for them to be saved.

On 2 December Henry Howard Earl of Surrey, Norfolk's son, was arrested on charges concerning his 'fidelity' to the King. As a poet Surrey was a perfect courtly knight, but as a man he was both arrogant and reckless – not for nothing was he Buckingham's grandson – and, at the age of thirty, still acted the 'foolish proud boy'.[41] Surrey could write:

> ... The things for to attain
> The happy life be these, I find:
> The riches left, not got with pain;
> The fruitful ground, the quiet mind ...

But he showed no signs of following his own prudent advice.

The crime with which Surrey would be officially charged was one of 'improper' (and thus treasonable) heraldry: he had used the arms of Edward the Confessor (from whom he was descended), a privilege which belonged 'only to the King of this realm'. Surrey was sent to the Tower, where his father, unable for once to avoid the taint of treachery, followed him. Improper heraldry was one thing: Surrey's real mistake was surely to have quarrelled violently with Hertford, who took over his command in France and whose military triumphs aroused Surrey's jealousy. He made no secret of his dislike of the 'upstart' Seymours – he was supposed to have said that 'these men love no nobility and if God called away the King they [the true nobility] would smart for it.' In the context, his 'improper' use of the royal arms could be construed by his rivals as a deliberate advancement of the superior Howard claims to the regency.[42]

Certainly Surrey believed in the superiority of his family over the Seymours, but he was charged with treachery to the King, and here the evidence, which like that against Buckingham depended on a great deal of lethal gossip, is far more doubtful. The controversial use of the royal arms had actually been granted to an ancestor in 1473; the version of them produced at Surrey's trial may have been merely 'heraldic doodling'.[43] Unfortunately the Howards were a family united against themselves, quite apart from their outside enemies. Some of this sprang from Norfolk's rejection of Surrey's mother, Elizabeth Stafford, in favour of his mistress Bess Holland. Surrey's sister, Mary Duchess of Richmond, also bore a grudge against her father for not pursuing the matter of her jointure with the King (as the widow of his late son). Norfolk's motive had as usual been a desire to avoid trouble with his master.

Mary Richmond revealed under interrogation that her father had proposed in 1544 that she should first marry Thomas Seymour, and from that position of advantage become the King's mistress, so that she might 'the better rule here as others had done'. She had refused this insulting offer. Her brother Surrey was also said to have suggested she should become the King's mistress, acting the part of Madame d'Étampes towards King François, so as to advance her family in the government of the kingdom. Such spiteful damaging charges were impossible to disprove (or prove). The long history of the Howards trying to rule the King through his affections makes it possible that these conversations took place, although one should remember that Mary Richmond, in understandable terror, was intent, like so many other witnesses in the past, on saving her own skin, rather than sinking with her father and brother. Some of this does seem to have penetrated the King's imagination and fired up his paranoia; at any rate he underlined certain passages among the accusations in a hand which was by now very shaky. One of these was: 'if a man were to advise his sister to become a harlot thinking thereby to bring it to pass and so would rule both father and son.'[44]

At Christmas, Queen Catherine, and the Ladies Mary and Elizabeth, were to be sent away to celebrate the season at Greenwich, leaving the King in London, busy with these wearing and – if one credited them – horrifying revelations. The Queen departed on Christmas Eve. She never saw her husband again. The royal party returned to London by 10 January, and the King could still receive ambassadors six days later, but he did not send for his wife. On 10 January the King of France was told that although King Henry's health had improved, neither the Queen nor the Lady Mary could see him; nor were any plans being made for them to do so.[45]

On 19 January Surrey was executed, leaving Norfolk still in prison, condemned to follow him to the block, despite his frantic discourse to the Privy Council from the Tower on his sufferings: 'never gold was tried better by fire and water than I have been'. As for his wretched past, those abominable Queens, Norfolk referred again to 'the malice borne me by both my nieces whom it pleased the King to marry', which was 'not unknown to such as kept them in this house'.[46] (The house in question was the Tower of London.) Once again however the Duke of Norfolk was to survive. His master fell into a coma before Norfolk could be executed; under the circumstances it was not thought prudent to carry out the sentence, and Norfolk was left for the time being to languish under attainder in 'this house'.

King Henry VIII died in the small hours of the morning of 28 January 1547. He was fifty-five years old and had reigned for nearly thirty-eight years. Obscurity surrounds his actual deathbed. In his last days only members of the Privy Council and the gentlemen of his Privy Chamber had been permitted to see him. We know that Archbishop Cranmer, his loyal servant, reached him when he was already beyond speaking, having been sent for, at the King's request, by Sir Anthony Denny. However, when the Archbishop asked the King to give some sign, either with his eyes or his hand, that he trusted in the Lord, the King managed to press Cranmer's hand.[47] We do not know for sure who else was present – except that the Queen was not – nor indeed whether he asked for his wife at the

last, before his speech failed. For Queen Catherine was kept firmly away.
King Henry may perhaps, as consciousness failed too, have called for an
earlier wife, the dream-wife, the mother of his son, Queen Jane Seymour,
or as the memories of vigorous youth sometimes return at the last he
may even have imagined himself still married to Catherine of Aragon,
who had been his spouse seven times as long as any other wife.

We cannot know this because the speedy exercise of power by the now
ruling Seymours had begun. This included the 'doctoring' of the King's
will by the use of the 'dry stamp' (a stamp not needing the King's
signature) which enabled members of the Privy Council to obtain hugely
increased bequests by use of the expedient phrase: 'unfulfilled gifts' (from
the King). The public announcement of the sovereign's death was delayed
for two days at the orders of the Privy Council, as part of this policy of
securing power and holding on to it. At which point Hertford also
deemed it necessary to tidy up another aspect of the King's past: 'If you
have not already advertised my Lady Anna of Cleves of King Henry's
death, it shall be well done if you send some express person for the
same'.[48]

An enormous chest, containing the dead King, now sat in the middle of
his Privy Chamber for five days while the chapel was made ready for his
hearse. This was installed on 2 February, and surrounded with eighty tapers.
Two days after that Edward Seymour Earl of Hertford became Duke of
Somerset and a rash of other titles broke out: his brother Thomas, for
example, became Lord Seymour of Sudeley, having been made a Privy
Councillor in the last days of the King's life; William Lord Parr of Kendal
was created Marquess of Northampton. Somerset, as he will be described
in future, now assumed, with the help of his supporters, the title of Protector
of the Kingdom, reigned over by his nine-year-old nephew King Edward
VI; even though the King's will had appointed sixteen executors who were
all to be equal regents for the boy.

It was under the auspices of the new Protector that the King's funeral
was now arranged to take place in St George's, Windsor. That was the site
King Henry had designated for his burial 'when the most high God called
him out of the world' as long ago as 1517; he was then still married to his
first wife, whom he had envisaged sharing his grave. In 1529 the King
began to have adapted for his own use the spectacular tomb commissioned
by Cardinal Wolsey from Italian craftsmen, for which the Cardinal had
earmarked a disused chapel. In his will, however, the King expressly desired
his 'Body, which when the soul is departed, shall ... so return to the Vile
Matter it was made of' to be placed with the bones of 'our true and loving
Wife Queen Jane'. (He also indicated that he would have preferred a simple

burial, but that was impossible, given 'the Room and Dignity which God hath called us unto . . .')[49]

So Queen Jane's tomb, halfway between the high altar and the choir stalls, was opened up again after nine years. On 16 February, following a sermon by Bishop Gardiner on the text 'Blessed are the dead which die in the Lord', the King's enormous coffin was let down into it 'in a vice' with the help of sixteen yeomen of the guard of exceptional height and strength. The officials broke their staves over the grave to indicate that their employment with one King was over, while Garter King of Arms proclaimed King Edward 'with a loud voice' and all close by cried out *'Vive le noble Roy Edward'*. Then the trumpets sounded 'with great melody and courage, to the comfort of all them that were present'.

The spectators who were thus comforted by the noise of trumpeters did not include the nine-year-old King. By custom, he was not present, but remained in London. Queen Catherine, however, was there; she watched the proceedings by which her husband's body was carefully lowered by sixteen giants down into the tomb of his third wife from the so-called Queen's closet above, first named in honour of Catherine of Aragon.

Her feelings of grief were no doubt sincere. Nevertheless they may be compared to those of Hamlet's mother after the death of Hamlet's father, an event which she soon learnt to regard philosophically with the comforting reflection: 'all that lives must die, Passing through nature to eternity'. For like Queen Gertrude, Queen Catherine, a woman who believed in being 'obedient to husbands', would shortly be looking to another one.

Chapter 19

FAREWELL
ADMIRABLE QUEEN

Vale, Regina veneranda.

Edward VI to Queen Catherine Parr, February 1547

On 7 February 1547 the new King Edward VI wrote a letter of condolence in Latin to his 'very dearest mother'. He referred to the great sorrow common to them both; the only consolation being that the late King was by now enjoying 'happiness and eternal beatitude'. For with a confidence that did him credit as a son, Edward VI expressed his conviction that, after such a reign as his, Henry VIII's earthly journey must swiftly terminate in heaven. He ended the letter *Vale, Regina veneranda*: 'Farewell, admirable Queen'.[1] The next day every church in the City held a solemn dirge for the dead King, tolling a knell and celebrating a Requiem Mass in Latin. It was virtually the last time in this reign that the parishes – showing less confidence than King Edward in his father's immediate assumption above – would pray for a soul in purgatory.

The admirable Catherine Parr was now the Queen Dowager of England, but until her stepson Edward married – for all his father's negotiations, not an immediate prospect for a nine-year-old boy – she was still the first lady in the land. This precedence over all others, including the King's daughters, had been explicitly granted to the Queen by statute. She was also left handsome provision in the will of this, her third husband, to add to her Latimer inheritance: ten thousand pounds' worth of plate and jewels and household stuff, as much 'apparel' as she wanted to take away as well as what she possessed already, and 'one thousand pounds in money'; an extremely substantial sum. All this, on top of her liberal royal jointure which included properties at Hanworth and Chelsea, was a reward, in the words of the late King, for Queen Catherine's 'great love, obedience, chastity of life, and wisdom.'[2]

If Queen Catherine was still the first lady in England, the position was purely symbolic: she had no other role in the new government of the country. For she was not included in the regency Council headed by the Protector, Edward Seymour Duke of Somerset; although both her position and her performance as Regent in 1544 entitled her to expect it. This effective marginalization – as a childless and thus superfluous Dowager – was not something to which Catherine Parr (whose motto was 'To be useful in all I do') was accustomed. It may well have played its part in urging her towards the embraces of Thomas Seymour, while he for his part found her position as the admired stepmother of the young King powerful enough to attract him, to say nothing of her vast wealth (infinitely greater than it had been in 1543). The relationship on which the Queen and Seymour embarked after the old King's death had therefore in it something of advantage to both: for Catherine a role to play, for Seymour self-aggrandizement. At the same time the evidence suggests that something beyond mere worldliness drew them together.

Thomas Seymour was now approaching forty, about four years older than the Queen. Unlike Catherine, he had never been married although, as was seen, his name had been linked with that of Mary Duchess of Richmond. Gifted with charm and intelligence as well as a handsome appearance ('one of the prettiest men of the court'), Seymour had been a favourite of the old King, his brother-in-law, who had made him Lord High Admiral of England in 1544. In 1545 Seymour was given Hampton Place, near Temple Bar. Later he would be much attacked: a servant would refer to Seymour's 'slothfulness to serve and his greediness to get' (although another employee called his service 'ever joyful'). But in 1547 he showed no greater greed than the rest of the nobility round him. Seymour's real weakness was his morbid jealousy of his elder brother Somerset, whose military victories had first marked him out before his position as Protector raised him up.[3]

This subsequent offensive – when Seymour was in disgrace – also suggested that he had tried to marry in turn both the Ladies Mary and Elizabeth, before turning to the Queen Dowager. But there is no evidence in the records of the Privy Council that Seymour made any such applications. The Lady Mary would point out that she had never actually spoken to Seymour although she had seen him. The evidence for Seymour's attentions to Elizabeth (in the period before his marriage to Catherine) depends on some letters, printed later and now discredited, and gossip: Elizabeth was told by her governess Katherine Ashley that Seymour 'would have me afore [he had] the Queen'. Another tradition had Seymour himself withdrawing from a proposition that would have advanced him so dangerously close to the throne: 'I love not to lose my life for a wife', he was supposed to have explained. 'It has been spoken of but it cannot be.'[4] What militates against this, quite apart from the lack of real evidence, is the timing of Seymour's courtship of Queen Catherine.

Seymour's name and the Queen's were never linked during the years of Queen Catherine's marriage; Seymour had been much abroad while Catherine, in the words of the King's will, had been famed for her 'chastity of life' in a court where malicious tongues would certainly have reported otherwise. This does not preclude the possibility that in 1543 Catherine, while resigning herself to God's will and a royal marriage, may have been woman enough to wonder just how long God would wait before gathering King Henry to 'happiness and eternal beatitude' in Heaven. The same thought, in more robust terms, may have occurred to the ambitious Thomas Seymour. If words were exchanged on the subject, Catherine Parr and Thomas Seymour were discreet enough to keep that to themselves. One can only say that such practical pledges were not unknown in an age when marriages were quite frequently arranged between old unhealthy men and women many years their junior (as witness the promise King Henry gave to his sister Mary, packed off to wed the doddery King of France).

However the situation had been left in 1543, with feelings dormant perhaps rather than extinguished, in 1547 passion rapidly flared up between the pair again. The word passion is used advisedly, since it is clear that a full-blooded love affair began between this Gertrude and this Claudius very shortly after the King's death. King Edward was crowned on 20 February; Thomas Seymour was among those who held his nephew's train. The next day he was foremost among the challengers at the jousts (shades of the Duke of Suffolk wielding his lance beneath the lovesick eyes of the then Queen Mary!). That evening Lord Seymour was the host at a feast in his house which was voted 'a goodly supper'. By 17 May, less than four months after the King's death, Thomas Seymour was able to describe himself to Queen Catherine at the end of one letter as 'him whom you have bound to honour, love, and all things obey' and in another as 'him that is your loving and faithful husband during his life, T Seymour'.[5]

These are clear references to a marriage which had either taken place already, or would do so very soon, since such language is equally compatible with marriage and with a solemn if secret betrothal, especially one which had been further validated by sexual union. The exact date of the wedding of Thomas Lord Seymour and the Queen Dowager cannot be known for certain: on balance of probabilities it took place at the end of May. (The news would reach the ears of the imperial ambassador a fortnight later.) In an age before registration existed, such dates did not need to be revealed if circumstances dictated prudence. As Anne Boleyn's advancing pregnancy had led to secrecy over her marriage to Henry VIII, so the delicate matter of Catherine Parr's all-too-recent bereavement suggested a similar discretion.

From the Queen's slightly coy reference in their correspondence, it seems that Thomas Seymour made the running. He pressed the Queen to an early date, when convention would have dictated a much longer mourning period such as she herself advocated. 'My lord', wrote Catherine, 'whereas you charge me with a promise with mine own hand to change two years into two months, I think you have no such plain sentence written with mine own hand'. She suggests lightly that Seymour may be 'a paraphraser', that is, one 'learned in that science [by which] it is possible you may of one word make a whole sentence'.[6]

The convention of a royal widow's mourning was one that could have a practical significance: it was possible that the widow of a King might prove to be pregnant by him, and should not therefore marry until the matter had been settled, lest the paternity of the King's posthumous child be called in question. For this reason Henry VIII's sister Mary, as the widow of Louis XII, had been examined by physicians at the French court to make sure she was not pregnant: since if Mary had borne a posthumous son, François I would have been disinherited. In this case, given the general assumption of Queen Catherine's infertility after three childless marriages, the matter was more one of principle than genuine expectation of some miraculous royal offspring. Besides, the speed served as a stick to beat Thomas Seymour by those who were already angered by the presumption of the match.

If we do not know the precise date of the wedding, we do know some of the details of the courtship. It took place, romantically enough, by starlight in the riverside gardens of the Queen's Chelsea Manor. (One should not for this reason regard Thomas Seymour and Queen Catherine as exceptionally hardy outdoor types given the average temperatures of an English spring; the lack of domestic privacy in the sixteenth century meant that the garden was often a convenient rendezvous for such clandestine meetings.) It was a house that King Henry had acquired from Lord Sandys in 1536, and had been granted to Queen Catherine in 1544 as part of her jointure. To judge from the engravings – it was pulled down about 1700 – Chelsea Manor, although sometimes described as a palace, was not particularly grand. But it did have beautiful gardens with their river setting, on which a great deal of money and labour had recently been spent: twenty-nine gardeners had been paid for planting cherry trees, nut trees, peach trees and damask roses as well as privets and whitethorn.* Henry Russell, the royal gardener at Westminster, supplied two banks of rosemary and six borders of lavender.[7]

Catherine gave her lover instructions about his arrival which leave little doubt about the nature of their relationship: 'When it shall be your pleasure to repair hither, you must take some pains to come early in the morning, that you may be gone again by seven o'clock. And so, I suppose, you may come without suspect. I pray you let me have knowledge overnight at what hour you will come, that your portress may wait at the gate to the fields for you.' She signed herself: 'By her that is and shall be your humble and true and loving wife during her life. Kateryn the Quene. K P'. Seymour on his side thanked her for her 'goodness' to him 'shown at the last being together' and asked for a letter from her every three days – even three lines – as well as 'one of your small pictures' (the miniatures Queen Catherine delighted in).[8]

Some of the Queen's friends were of course in the secret. Her sister Anne Herbert teased Seymour at court and made him 'change colours'. But he took it in good part. 'By her company (by default of yours)', he wrote gallantly to Catherine, 'I shall shorten the weeks in these parts, which are each of them three days longer than they were under the planets in Chelsea'. Anne's husband, now Lord Herbert, was also aware of what was going on, as was Duchess Katherine of whom Seymour was happy to report: 'I perceive I have my lady of Suffolk's goodwill touching my known desire of you.' (The strong-minded Duchess was clearly in favour of romantic second – or in this case fourth – marriages: six years later the great lady would marry her gentleman-usher Richard Bertie.) It was Duchess Katherine whom the Queen would quote at the end of her letter in which she poured out her heart on the subject of her previous love for Seymour, her submission to God's will (and the King's) and now her wonderful newfound happiness: 'I can say nothing', Catherine concluded, 'but as my Lady of Suffolk saith "God is a marvellous man!"'[9]

The approval, the connivance even, of Queen Catherine's friends and relations was one thing; breaking the news to the titular ruler of England, King Edward, and its effective governor, the Duke of Somerset, was another matter. It is clear that the Protector was not inclined to encourage the 'tender love' between the Queen Dowager and her stepson, just as he was not disposed to admit her to the regency Council: to him she was a woman without any overt power, whose influence must therefore be curtailed. On the eve of his father's death, Edward had thanked his stepmother for her New Year's gift, framed miniatures of herself and the

* Chelsea Manor was situated by the modern Chelsea Pier and where Cheyne Walk is bisected by Chelsea Manor Street.

King, adding that to see them in person – as he expected to do shortly – would be even better 'than something in chased gold'. But by May Edward was explaining why he had not written to Catherine as he used to do: he kept being assured that he *would* see her face to face since the Queen was now living very near to him – except that the meetings were always put off.[10]

Since the actual marriage was still a secret, the first idea was to pretend that Seymour was still at the stage of wooing the Queen. For this the help of the Lady Mary – who had left Catherine's household in mid-April – was enlisted. Seymour wrote to her, diplomatically as he supposed, asking her to plead his cause. He received an extremely frosty reply. On 4 June Mary described the proposed alliance as 'strange news'. She declined altogether to be 'a meddler in this matter' considering, she wrote pointedly, 'whose wife her Grace was of late'. As for persuading Queen Catherine to accept him, Mary told Seymour that 'if the remembrance of the King's Majesty my father' (still so 'ripe' with Mary herself) would not suffer Catherine 'to grant your suit' there was nothing she Mary could do to help. Mary's final disengagement from this distasteful subject showed her a worthy daughter of the dignified but not unacerbic Catherine of Aragon: being only 'a maid' herself, she was 'nothing cunning' in such affairs between men and women.[11]

It was time to turn to the young King, already disposed to be fonder of this generous, rollicking uncle than he was of the austere Protector. This time the method employed was rather more subtle. John Fowler, servant to King Edward (who would admit later that he had received money from Seymour for supplying information about the royal household as early as June 1547), was to be the double-agent.[12] Fowler prepared the ground by wondering aloud: 'I marvel my Lord Admiral [Seymour] marryeth not'. He then proceeded to ask of the King: 'Could your grace be contented he should marry?' When Edward, falling into the trap, replied; 'Yes, very well', Fowler instantly asked the prepared question: 'Whom would his Grace like to his uncle to marry?'

But at this point matters looked like going wrong – with the stepson as well as the step-daughter. 'My Lady Anna of Cleves,' answered Edward innocently, already aware of the problems of the expensive family incubus. And when he thought about it a little more, he got the answer wrong a second time: 'Nay, nay, wot [know] you what? I would he married my sister Mary to turn her opinions'. Fortunately, with tact and time, the boy was brought round to see the match between his uncle and stepmother as something he himself had initiated to solace her bereavement. On 25 June he wrote an affectionate letter to Queen Catherine which contained this official blessing: 'We thank you heartily, not only for the gentle acceptation of our suit moved unto you [to marry Seymour] but also for the loving accomplishing of the same, wherein you have declared a desire to gratify us'.[13]

The Protector and his wife were under no such pretty illusions. As King Edward recorded succinctly in his journal: 'The Lord Seymour of Sudeley married the Queen, whose name was Catherine, with which marriage the Lord Protector was much offended'. Any offence the Lord Protector felt was compounded by the reaction of his Duchess. Anne Stanhope, formerly Countess of Hertford, now Duchess of Somerset, had needed the patronage of Catherine Parr in the reign of King Henry; as when Catherine had interceded for Hertford at his wife's instigation, to get him back from Scotland in time to join the King in France.[14] Their shared religious sensibilities had seemed to be a further bond. Unfortunately Duchess Anne had one of those imperious natures – the word often applied to her by her contemporaries – which found memories of previous inferiority intolerable.

She now openly 'jostled' with Queen Catherine for precedence on the grounds that as the wife of the Protector she was the first lady in England. There was absolutely no justification for this. Not only had Queen Catherine been explicitly granted this precedence by statute, but the Ladies Mary and Elizabeth and even the Lady Anna of Cleves had the right to follow her before the Duchess of Somerset. Not content with jostling in doorways – the introduction of Spanish farthingales in the 1540s, skirts held out wide by circular hoops of wood or whalebone, must have made this an interesting spectacle – Duchess Anne also refused to carry the train of the woman married to 'her husband's younger brother'. She was said to have observed, with a shrewishness that belied the grandeur that she claimed: 'If master admiral teach his wife no better manners, I am she that will'.[15]

This ludicrous struggle was merely the visible manifestation of the series of rows that broke out between the Somersets and the Seymours (although of course Catherine would be referred to as Queen for the rest of her life and served with the state due to a Queen). Jewels were one topic for heated discussion as the Protector attempted to distinguish between what was Catherine's own, and the jewels of state (which he kept), while his brother furiously rebutted his claims. The Protector actually hung on to Queen Catherine's wedding ring, presented to her by King Henry. Other than that, the ownership of those jewels given to Queen Catherine by King Henry to wear at the visit of the French ambassador in the summer of 1546 continued to be disputed for the rest of Catherine's life – and even beyond it. Some months after her death Seymour would write to the Lady Mary trying to get her confirmation

Catherine Parr
m 1543

Badge of Catherine Parr: a crowned maiden rising out of a Tudor rose.

William Parr, Marquess of Northampton, brother of Catherine Parr, by Holbein.

Thomas Seymour, fourth husband of Catherine Parr.

Henry VIII and his family, painted by an unknown artist in about 1545; he is flanked by his daughters Mary and Elizabeth, and accompanied by his son Edward and Edward's mother, Jane Seymour, who was, however, dead when this portrait was painted. (Catherine Parr, not depicted, was Queen Consort at the time.)

*Engraving of Henry VIII in his last years
by Cornelius Matsuys.*

Medal of Henry VIII as 'defender of the faith', 1545.

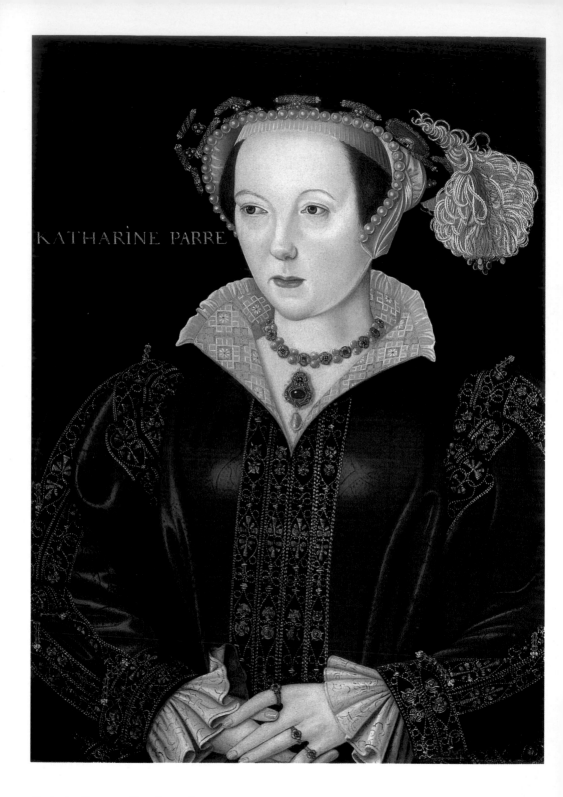

KATHARINE PARRE

Catherine Parr, attributed to William Scrots.

A manuscript version of Catherine Parr's Prayers and Meditations, *supposedly in her handwriting, now in Kendal Town Hall.*

Sudeley Castle.

The slab of marble marking the grave of Catherine of Aragon, in the north presbytery aisle, Peterborough Cathedral.

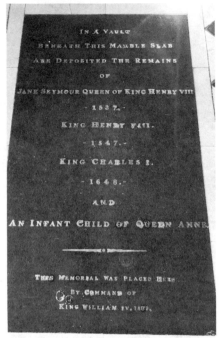

Slab marking the vault beneath the floor of the choir of St George's Chapel, Windsor, in which Jane Seymour and Henry VIII are buried.

Plaque in the floor of the Chapel of St Peter ad Vincula marking the burial place of Anne Boleyn.

The tomb of Anna of Cleves showing the initials
AC beneath a ducal crown, on the south side of the
High Altar in Westminster Abbey.

Plaque in the floor of the Chapel of St Peter ad Vincula,
Tower of London, marking the burial place of
Katherine Howard.

The tomb of Catherine
Parr in the Chapel of
Sudeley Castle: created
during the restoration
of the Chapel in the
nineteenth century by
Sir Gilbert Scott.

The Queen's Closet, St George's Chapel, Windsor, named for Catherine of Aragon whose pomegranates can be seen among the ornamentation; from this closet Catherine Parr watched the funeral of Henry VIII.

From Thomas Bentley's Monument of Matrones, *1582, showing Queen Catherine Parr lying in her tomb (centre) and (above left) being received by God the Father.*

that the Queen had not been expected to return these gems 'after the Triumphs finished'. This time Mary did not answer.[16]

Catherine's letters to Seymour show that the 'admirable Queen' had by now been more or less swallowed up by the ardent woman, at any rate in private. Duchess Anne was referred to as 'that Hell'. In a row over the Queen's property, let by Somerset to a Mr Long, Catherine told Seymour: 'My Lord, your brother hath this afternoon made me a little warm [angry]. It was fortunate we were so much distant for I suppose else I should have bitten him'.[17] This was not exactly the language of submission. She who had assured the late King Henry that women were created subject to men, had been subsumed into the other Catherine Parr who became thoroughly heated in argument.

And then an extraordinary thing happened. Queen Catherine at the age of thirty-five – 'past middle age, which barren was before' – conceived her first child. It was not only extraordinary but unlooked-for: one hopes that the happy surprise compensated for Seymour's less than satisfactory career after their marriage. As jealous in his own way as Duchess Anne was in hers, Seymour allowed his differences with his brother to cloud his judgement. Now the laziness and greed mentioned by his servant did play their part. He failed to command the fleet against the Scots in 1547 and 1548, preferring his country estate at Sudeley. Even more inexcusably he made pacts with the very pirates in the English Channel he should have been eliminating, in order to share the booty.[18] The Queen however expected to spend the months of her pregnancy – the child must have been conceived at the end of November 1547 – tranquilly enough at her properties of Chelsea and Hanworth near Hampton Court, as well as at Sudeley.

She was not without companionship of the sort she had always enjoyed: younger women she could mother. One of these was the Lady Jane Grey, the eleven-year-old daughter of Lady Frances Brandon and Henry Grey, Marquess of Dorset: a girl whose dynastic importance had been notably increased by the last will of Henry VIII. Here the late King had specified that the descendants of his younger sister Mary should follow his three children (and their heirs if any) in the succession; thus ruling out the descendants of his elder sister Margaret, most prominently represented by her granddaughter Mary Queen of Scots. This omission – if sustained – would cause much heart-burning in years to come, as the adult Mary Queen of Scots attempted to establish her blood-right to succeed Queen Elizabeth I. In 1548 it simply meant that Lady Jane Grey, as the senior grandchild of Mary Duchess of Suffolk (there were no grandsons living) was fourth in line to the throne, supposing none of the King's children left any heirs. Such universal barrenness did not look likely at this point.

If King Edward was too delicate for fatherhood, and Mary, in her early thirties, doomed to be 'a maid', then there was always Elizabeth, in her fifteenth year, attractive and graceful, and surely nubile.

The Lady Elizabeth was also under the wing of the Queen Dowager. One of those who already appreciated her appeal was her stepmother's husband Thomas Seymour. Boisterous by nature, conscious of the effect of his charms on women – he still had the 'lust' the King had praised as calculated to please a woman if the 'youth' had fled – it may have seemed natural to Seymour to indulge in sexy horseplay with his wife's young charge. By Whitsun of 1548 (mid-May) when matters came to a crisis, Queen Catherine would have been nearly six months pregnant; given her condition, Seymour may have also found it natural to look for diversion elsewhere. But if these were Seymour's natural instincts, then his reason should have restrained him, the reason of a man long at court, familiar with the gilded corridors of Tudor power. For an unmarried man, it was perilous enough to approach in this way the next-but-one heiress to the throne; for a married man it was not only perilous but a source of scandal.

But Seymour formed the habit of entering the girl's room before she was fully dressed, patting her 'upon the back or on the buttocks familiarly', snatching kisses, and even pocketing the key of the room so she could not escape. Then he would appear himself bare-legged and clad only in a short night-gown (dressing-gown). Elizabeth's servant Katherine Ashley would tell tales of the Lord Admiral flinging back Elizabeth's bed curtains to bid her 'good morning' while the girl herself burrowed back (whether in modesty, ecstasy, or a combination of the two, Elizabeth never revealed). On one occasion at Hanworth, Catherine, with the 'mirth and good pastime' for which she had been noted during her marriage to King Henry, joined in. She held the girl down while Seymour cut her black gown into a hundred pieces.[19] Of all these incidents – including that involving the Queen herself, however light-hearted – one can only repeat the verdict on the midnight rendezvous of Katherine Howard, Culpeper and Lady Rochford: all those concerned (except possibly Elizabeth) should have known better.

It was Queen Catherine who finally decided that enough was enough and sent the girl away. Elizabeth went to Cheshunt where she was put in the care of Sir Anthony Denny. Katherine Ashley gave as a reason the Queen's dismay at finding Elizabeth in Seymour's arms, but later withdrew the story. Since Catherine and Elizabeth remained on affectionate terms afterwards, the Queen was probably animated as much by concern for her charge's reputation as by jealousy. That is certainly the impression left by a letter from Elizabeth to Catherine. The younger woman had obviously received a lecture on the subject of decorum and had decided on consideration that her stepmother was right: 'I was replete with sorrow to depart from your highness, especially leaving you undoubtful of health ... I weighed it more deeply when you said you would warn me of all evils that you should hear of me, for if your grace had not a good opinion of me you would not have offered friendship to me that way.'[20]

The true measure of Elizabeth's continuing devotion to her step-mother's memory is seen in the treatment of Queen Catherine's character during Elizabeth's reign. For example, Thomas Bentley's pious work, *The Monument of Matrones*, printed in 1582, showed Queen Catherine being received by God Himself, with the line from Revelation round the picture: 'Be thou faithful unto the death; and I will give thee a Crown of Life'. Queen Catherine was allowed to be depicted as one of the 'virtuous Queens' of history along with Queen Esther, St Margaret of Scotland and Queen Elizabeth herself.[21] Queen Elizabeth I was not noted for her advancement of the female sex. No other consort of Henry VIII – and certainly not the sovereign's mother Queen Anne Boleyn – was thus honoured.

Fear of the plague drove Queen Catherine from Chelsea to her estate at Hanworth in June 1547. From here she exchanged cheerful – and frank – letters on the subject of her advancing pregnancy with her husband. 'I hear my little man doth *shake his bell*', wrote Seymour, referring to the news of the quickening of his child. 'I do desire your Highness to keep the little knave so lean and gaunt with your good diet and walking, that he may be so small that he may creep out of a mousehole'. Catherine responded in kind: 'I gave your little knave your blessing who like an honest man stirred apace after and before. For Mary Odell being abed with me had laid her hand upon my belly to feel it stir. It hath stirred these three days every morning and evening so that I trust when you come it will make you some pastime'.[22]

Later that month the Queen retired to Sudeley Castle in Gloucestershire where she intended to give birth, taking with her Lady Jane Grey. The presence of the clever, solemn little girl provided solace for the Queen, now that Princess Elizabeth, her companion for the last two years, had left her. For Seymour, however, Jane represented something more material – an heiress. Her father, the Marquess of Dorset, had thought of removing Lady Jane from Chelsea at the news of the Queen's remarriage, but Seymour's will had prevailed and she stayed. Seymour saw himself as negotiating a profitable marriage for Jane – possibly to King Edward himself – in exchange for a proper payment from her father.

Another guest in Queen Catherine's household was the result of benevolence on her part: she agreed to take into her custody her erstwhile sister-in-law Anne Bourchier, Countess of Essex and now, for want of a divorce from William Parr, Marchioness of Northampton. As an accused adulteress – a charge certainly true – Anne Bourchier would otherwise have faced a far more unpleasant fate.

Sudeley lay in one of the most beautiful parts of England and had royal connections which stretched back as far as the time of King Ethelred the Unready. The castle to which Queen Catherine repaired had, however, been mainly built in the middle of the fifteenth century.* In turn Edward IV and his brother Richard, as Duke of Gloucester, owned it; Henry VII granted it to his uncle Jasper Duke of Bedford, but it was crown property once more by 1509. Henry VIII and Anne Boleyn visited it for a week in July 1535, in the last year of their marriage. By the time King Edward granted Sudeley to his uncle, it was in that state of disrepair (needing expensive renovation) into which neglected castles so easily fell. Seymour however was determined to maintain proper state here, not only for himself but for the Queen Dowager. A verse celebrated this as follows:

> Her house was termed a second court, of right,
> Because there flocked there still nobility;
> He spared no cost his lady to delight
> Or to maintain her princely royalty.[23]

Many of the Queen's own arrangements consisted of elaborate preparations for the nursery. This child stood to receive a substantial inheritance from both father and mother one day; it would also be first cousin to the King on its father's side, Thomas Seymour having been the brother of Queen Jane, and for that matter, of course, related to the Protector's own family. When the Duchess of Somerset gave birth to a fine boy at St James's Palace (where King Edward was also lodged) on 19 July, a message came from the young King to his uncle hoping that 'the Queen will have another'. For this quasi-royal infant, tapestries illustrating the twelve months of the year were installed, with a chair of state covered with cloth of gold, cushions of the same material and a gilded bedstead. An inner chamber featured further hangings, costly plate and a rich cradle with three down pillows and a quilt.[24]

On 30 August Queen Catherine went into labour. The child was born and it was a girl. She was named Mary for the Queen's step-daughter, although it was Lady Jane Grey, present at Sudeley, who stood godmother. On 1 September Seymour received an amiable communication

---

* Sudeley today, wonderfully well-tended, still constitutes one of the most vivid evocations of the style of early Tudor royal or semi-royal living.

from his brother who expressed himself glad that 'the Queen, your bedfellow' had had 'a happy hour', and escaping all danger (she was after all no longer young and this was her first child) had made Seymour a father of 'so pretty a daughter'. The conventional sixteenth-century regrets followed: 'And although (if it had so pleased God) it would have been both to us, and we suppose also to you, a more joy and comfort if it had been thus, the first, a son', the Protector nevertheless hoped for 'a great sort of happy sons' in the future.[25] But by the time this letter arrived, Queen Catherine had fallen, like Queen Jane Seymour before her, desperately ill of puerperal fever; and the prospect of those happy sons would shortly be gone forever.

In her fever, Catherine's delirium took a painful (but not unusual) form of paranoid ravings about her husband and others around her. This cast a terrible blight over the last days of a marriage which had originally been made, in some sort on both sides, for love. Catherine accused the people around her of standing 'laughing at my grief'. 'I am not well handled,' she cried. When Seymour tried to soothe her by lying down at her side and saying gently, 'Why, Sweetheart, I would [do] you no hurt', the poor deluded woman answered, 'No, my Lord, I think so' and whispered in his ear about the many 'shrewd taunts' she had received.[26] This distressing episode allowed those accusations of poison – so familiar to this period over any unexpected death – to be brought against Seymour afterwards. But the charge was quite untrue: mercifully for Seymour at the time, the Queen's own behaviour at the last gave it the lie.

For as the Queen began to sink towards death, her fever fled. She dictated her will calmly, revealing that same attitude of trust and loyalty towards Seymour, not only her 'married spouse and husband' but the great love of her life, which she had always felt. Queen Catherine, 'sick of body but of good mind', left everything to Seymour, only wishing her possessions 'to be a thousand times more in value' than they were.[27] She died on 5 September, six days after the birth of her daughter. Catherine Parr was thirty-six years old. She had been consort to King Henry VIII for three and a half years (the same period as that very different Queen, Anne Boleyn) and married to Thomas Seymour, her fourth husband, for fifteen months.

Lady Jane Grey acted as chief mourner at the Queen's funeral, after which her body was buried in St Mary's Church, adjoining Sudeley Castle. According to custom Seymour, the widower, was not present. Miles Coverdale, the Queen's almoner at Sudeley, preached the sermon at the obsequies. He made the sternly Protestant point that the traditional offering of alms was not to 'benefit the dead' (that is, to pay for Masses for the soul in purgatory) 'but for the poor only'. Furthermore the tapers which were carried at the funeral and then 'stood about the corpse' were for the 'honour of the person and for none other intent or purpose'.[28] But then Catherine Parr, the true Protestant Queen, would have approved.

The baby Mary Seymour lived on for a while. The attainder and execution of her 'covetous, ambitious, seditious' father in March 1549 put an end to Mary's prospects as a great heiress since his properties were forfeit to the crown. Instead, she led the life of a poor little royal girl, whose rank as 'the Queen's Child' (as she was always known) demanded the kind of state which there was no money to support. As a result Mary Seymour lived under the care of Katherine Duchess of Suffolk. The Duchess did not try to disguise the fact that the endless servants deemed necessary for this one little girl were a great burden to her. First their incessant prattle – 'maids, nurses and others' – drove her mad, and secondly the cost was fearful: 'whose voices mine ears may hardly bear but my coffers much worse', as she put it in her usual caustic manner.

A letter of complaint from Duchess Katherine to her friend William Cecil referred feelingly to the silver plate in 'the Queen's Child's' nursery in 1548. The following year Duchess Katherine protested that she really could not maintain this expense much longer without a pension to help her. She would transfer the onerous household to Mary's maternal uncle William Marquess of Northampton, except that he was equally poverty-stricken: having 'as bad a back for such a burden as I have'. One hopes that the fact that Duchess Katherine was prepared to look after the child but not 'her train', indicates that she showed kindness to the orphan Mary herself if not to her 'maids, nurses and others.'[29]

An act of parliament removed the attainder on Mary Seymour on 21 January 1550 (although Sudeley was not restored to her). Mary Seymour was still alive that summer, on the eve of her second birthday, but after that there is no record, either of her life or death. An eighteenth-century tradition that Mary Seymour married one Sir Edward Bushel (a gentleman of that name was found in the household of Queen Anne of Denmark at the beginning of the next century) and left descendants by the name of Johnson and Drayton cannot be sustained.[30] A wealthy 'Queen's Child' who lived to adulthood in the 1560s would not have escaped remark. It can safely be assumed that the contemporary curse, death in early childhood, provided its own solution to the short sad life of Mary Seymour.

King Henry was dead, King François died two months later at the end of March 1547. The Emperor Charles V now rode high in a Europe which he had for over thirty years shared with the other two members of the royal triumvirate. Then in 1555 he too departed – but voluntarily – from the great stage, when he renounced his crown in favour of his son Philip; he died as a monk, three years later. By this time the boy King Edward VI was dead too, in July 1553 of tuberculosis, three months before his sixteenth birthday. Mary Tudor, the unhappy daughter of Henry VIII and Catherine of Aragon, succeeded to his throne: she married her cousin Philip of Spain, eleven years her junior, the following year.

Through all this, there was one relic of the past who lived on and on, the Lady Anna of Cleves. She was the witness to those events in England which toppled heads during the reign of King Edward, recorded by the boy himself laconically and without emotion in his journal for January 1548: 'Also the Lord Sudeley, Admiral of England, was condemned to death and died the March ensuing'. Three years later the Protector himself fell victim to a power struggle. On 22 January 1552, the King wrote: 'The Duke of Somerset had his head cut off upon Tower Hill between eight and nine o'clock in the morning'.[31] Anna of Cleves was still there in England when the axe claimed a fresh victim, Lady Jane Grey, at the beginning of the reign of Mary. The crime of Jane Grey was to have allowed her father-in-law John Dudley Duke of Northumberland (who followed Somerset as Protector) to claim the crown for her, on the grounds that King Edward had left it to her – the senior grandchild of Mary Duchess of Suffolk – and away from his sisters in his will.

On 30 September 1553 Anna of Cleves rode in a coach with the Lady Elizabeth at the coronation of the triumphant Queen Mary at which 'there was one blowing of the trumpet all day long'. The new Queen's carriage went first, drawn by horses 'trapped with red velvet', while she herself wore 'blue velvet furred with powdered ermine'. The royal ladies followed her in 'a rich chariot covered with cloth of silver', with the Lady Elizabeth facing the front 'and at the other end with her back forward, the Lady Anna'.[32] This coupling with Elizabeth continued at the state banquet that evening. The two of them sat together at the end of the table, Elizabeth now heiress-presumptive to the throne, and Anna of Cleves' precedence moved up to that of the third lady in the land.

The Lady Anna's reaction to the execution of Somerset gives a clue to how she herself regarded these remarkable ups and downs of royal and courtly fortune. 'God knows what will happen next!' she wrote to her brother Duke William of Cleves, 'and everything is so costly in this country that I have no idea how to manage the running of my household'.[33] Like many widows – as in a sense Anna of Cleves was, since the death of 'her brother' King Henry had removed her male protector – she became obsessed by money and servants, the money servants cost, the money she did not have to pay them, the money she was owed, the servants she needed, the money ... the servants ... Her frequent letters to the Council during the reign of King Edward became a doleful litany.

After Mary ascended the throne, Anna of Cleves even attempted to resurrect her long-buried marriage to Henry VIII and get it declared 'legitimate' so that she might enjoy the treatment, especially in the realm of finance, of a Queen Dowager. She would also be able to get her dowry paid 'even if absent from England'. This of course would have superseded the careful arrangement made at the time of the divorce in 1540 by which the dowry was conditional on her not going 'over the seas'. The Lady Anna was simply told that there were too many other pressing matters for the Council's attention.[34] So she continued to petition, and worry, and write anguished letters back to the country she still regarded as her home.

The worst row occurred over the Lady Anna's 'cofferer', a Clevian named Jasper Brouckhusen. Originally, Dr Cruser, an envoy from Cleves who tried to unravel all these complaints, had formed the impression that Brouckhusen and his fellow Clevian Dr Cornelius were the only members of Anna's household genuinely devoted to her interests. So Cruser had Brouckhusen promoted to his position of cofferer. Now Brouckhusen struggled to institute savings among servants, for whom, as he grumbled, 'the beer was never good enough, the bread never delicate enough, the meat was never juicy enough'.[35] Among other economies, Brouckhusen suggested the Lady Anna's servants should be given their own hide of land on which to grow food.

Not surprisingly this well-meant proposal for self-help was resented within the household itself; while Brouckhusen's battles on his mistress's behalf with the Privy Council earned him enemies on that side as well.[36] More seriously, a cousin of Anna of Cleves who had held a minor position at the court of King Henry, Count Franz von Waldeck, took to visiting her, possibly with the aim of becoming her heir; at any rate he installed himself with eight grooms of his own in attendance. In so doing he cut across the cost-paring Brouckhusen, whose authority the well-born Waldeck in turn resented. Waldeck managed to get Brouckhusen dismissed for dishonesty – embezzlement – and secured the sacking of other supposedly loyal servants. Brouckhusen, however, was undefeated. He returned to Cleves where he defended himself so ably that he was able to come back to England.

Throughout this, the Lady Anna herself took her cofferer's part on the grounds that he had genuinely tried to help her. But on the Clevian side (thanks to the mischief-making of Count Waldeck) this partisanship was seen as further evidence of Brouckhusen's intrigues. In truth Brouckhusen had probably tried to carry out a difficult task to the best of his ability, if not always with tact. Nevertheless in September 1556 the *coup de grâce* was administered to him, and some other servants. Duke William of Cleves asked King Philip to intervene on the grounds that Brouckhusen, his wife and one Bastard of Wylick had driven his sister mad by their 'pernicious doctrines and marvellous impostumes'. The Council investigated the matter discreetly, the Queen (Mary) 'willing us to have special care of this matter'. Finally it was considered that the wishes of 'the noble prince the Duke' should be carried out, but with 'as little offence to the said Lady Anna as may be'.[37] A few days later Brouckhusen and his supporters went.

It is obvious that the Lady Anna's real desire was now to return to Cleves, a feeling that had been growing on her since the King's insulting marriage to Catherine Parr. In April 1551 she wrote wistfully (in *deutsch*) about the prospect: 'And so I might come to life again among my friends. For as I think my friends down there have by now all forgotten about me, I should think that I will re-enter their memories again, once my friends' eyes have seen me'. A year later, as she outlined her poverty to her brother and begged him to send her some money, she assured him that he would not find it 'a hindrance' if she were to return.[38] But nobody was prepared to rescue this princess from her predicament, as superfluous a female in her own way as Catherine Parr had been as a Dowager. Her brother persuaded the English Council to pay some of her debts but no more.

The best Anna of Cleves could hope for was the occasional visit to the English court. She had always enjoyed good relations with Mary who seems to have remained genuinely well-disposed to her for her own sake, not only in memory of her father. So Anna would send beseeching letters, like the following, dated August 1554 and addressed to Queen Mary and her husband. Anna described how desirous she was 'to do my duty to see your Majesty and the King [Philip]', while wishing them both 'much joy and felicity, with increase of children to God's glory, and to the preservation of your prosperous estates'.* It was signed 'From my poor house at Hever, Your Highness' to command, Anna the Daughter of Cleves.'[39]

To the English Council on the other hand, Anna of Cleves was an ungrateful pensioner, forever whingeing about a way of life which was quite lavish enough in the councillors' opinion – even too lavish, given that the reason for it had vanished with the death of King Henry. Besides, she was not even native-born in the first place; as she herself wrote to Duke William: 'England is England, and we are foreigners'. When the Lady Anna complained that the pensions for her servants had not been paid in the summer of 1552 the Council blandly announced that King Edward was on a progress – which lasted from the beginning of July till the middle of September – and during this time had 'resolved not to be troubled with payments'. When it was decided that the King should take possession of

---

* But this wish was not granted. Queen Mary would die childless four years later at the age of forty-two.

Bletchingly which belonged to the Lady Anna, in exchange for Penshurst, the deal was simply communicated to her (leaving poor Anna to enquire: 'Where is Bletchingly?').[40]

At the same time the English were right to think that the Lady Anna did live in considerable state. She was allowed Richmond Palace (where the news of Henry VIII's wish for a divorce had been broken to her) till her death. Penshurst, which had passed from the Duke of Buckingham to the custodianship of Sir Thomas Boleyn, was an enviable palace. Hever Castle, another castle with even stronger Boleyn connections, also in Kent, had been granted to her in 1540. From her correspondence, Anna of Cleves spent a good deal of time at Hever where tradition has it that she chose a room from which she could watch the gate and oversee the goings-on of the household. Hever remained hers till her death, after which it was bought by the Waldegrave family.

Another Kentish palace, Dartford, was given to her in exchange for lands in Surrey. A house of Dominican nuns since the reign of Edward III, Dartford nunnery was dissolved in 1539. Its position on the main road to the Kentish coast made it a natural royal acquisition, and a handsome palace was developed out of the small priory, at a total cost of £60,000 (including 15s for gilding the arms of the current Queen – Katherine Howard). Then there was Anna of Cleves' London establishment. In 1556 she apparently rented the house of Sir Thomas Cawarden, since he put in a claim for expenses that she had incurred there and failed to pay. Apart from numerous tapers for her chantry (the Catholicism Anna of Cleves had learned from her mother was, under Queen Mary, the restored religion of England), there were spices as well as sheep for the kitchen, at 7s the piece, earthen pots for the scullery, and wood and rushes in profusion. But it is the list of the 'good cheer' to be installed before the Lady Anna's arrival which confirms the description of the Lady Anna's household as 'a Rhenish principality' in miniature. There were to be two hogsheads of beer of a ton each, three hogsheads of Gascon wine in the cellar, as well as ten gallons of Malmsey wine, and ten gallons of sack; while further hogsheads were to be carted up from the country.[41]

Lastly, Anna of Cleves was allowed the use of Chelsea Manor, that small but delightful 'palace' where Thomas Seymour had courted Queen Catherine Parr 'under the planets'. It was here that she fell ill in the spring of 1557 and here that she spent the months of her decline. She died on 16 July 1557. Anna, the daughter of Cleves, was in her forty-second year. She did not live to see the accession of King Henry's last child, Elizabeth, the girl whom she had once petted, on 17 November 1558.

Given the lingering course of the Lady Anna's illness, cancer seems a likely cause of her death. But no particular explanation was felt to be needed for the decease of a woman of her age. She had indeed exceeded the life expectancy of her sex, so often laid low by the peril she never had a chance to endure: child-bearing. Anna of Cleves had outlived Henry VIII, the man to whom she had been 'married' for six months, by ten years.

The last will and testament of Anna of Cleves dating from shortly before her death fully justified the reputation granted to her by Holinshed in his *Chronicles*: 'a good housekeeper and very bountiful to servants', whatever the problems they had caused her during her lifetime. First she asked her executors to be 'good lords and masters' to her 'poor' employees. An extremely long list of bequests followed; all the gentlewomen in her Privy Chamber were remembered by name, the Clevian Katherine Chayre, as well as numerous Englishwomen, and others right down to her laundresses and 'Mother Lovell for her attendance on us in this time of sickness'. Then Dr Symonds was rewarded 'for his great pain and labours'; her gentlemen, like her ladies, were listed in detail, down to the 'children of the house' and the grooms who got 20s apiece.[42]

Queen Mary was asked to see that the 'poor servants' would get their fair recompense, while the Lady Elizabeth was left some jewels with the hope that she would take on one of the Lady Anna's 'poor maids' called Dorothy Curson. Grander connections, such as her brother Duke William, her unmarried sister Amelia of Cleves and Katherine Duchess of Suffolk, received various rings ornamented with rubies and diamonds. 'Alms children' were left money for their education; the poor of Richmond, Bletchingley, Hever and Dartford were remembered.

The Privy Council – 'whereas it hath pleased almighty God to call to His mercy the Lady Anna of Cleves' – issued orders for the funeral which was intended to pay suitable tribute to the anomalous but nevertheless distinguished position she had occupied.[43] The funeral took place on 4 August, the body being brought by water from Chelsea to Charing Cross the night before and then carried to Westminster Abbey. The procession, lit by a hundred torches, was totally enveloped in black, from the heralds and their horses, to the beadsmen in their black gowns new for the occasion.

At the door of the abbey, those on horseback alighted and 'the good lady', that is to say the corpse in its coffin, was received by the Lord Abbot and the Bishop of London in their copes 'incensing her'. Candles burnt all night in the abbey, as the coffin lay beneath its great hearse, which according to Henry Machyn, a furnisher of funeral trappings, had needed the labour of seven principal carpenters. It was placed between the high altar and the choir, painted with her arms and the motto of the house of Cleves: *'Spes meo in deo est'*, beneath a canopy of black velvet. At each corner heralds bore banners: of the Trinity, the Virgin Mary, St George and St Anne.

The next day at the Requiem Mass, the role of chief mourner was carried out by another connection to the royal past, 'my Lady of Winchester', who was in fact Elizabeth Seymour, sister of the late Queen Jane, once married to Cromwell's son, and now on her third marriage, to the Marquess of Winchester. The text chosen by the preacher, the Abbot of Westminster, for his sermon, was that of Dives and Lazarus: bearing in mind Dives' gluttony, he exhorted his audience to 'amend your lives while you have time'. After the coffin had been lowered into its grave (between the choir and the west transept) and the staves and rods of the Lady Anna's officers had been broken and thrown into it, a pall of cloth of gold and the hearse were placed on top, together with a cross, which remained for ten days. But the mourners, despite the sermon they had just heard, 'went to the abbey to dine, where there was prepared for them a sumptuous dinner at the cost of the executors'.

It had been a brave show, or brave enough. Only the weather provided a slight difficulty. It was extremely hot, even for the early August season. The poor, who would generally have flocked to the service in order to receive the alms traditionally dispersed, were warned from the pulpit in advance to stay at home. No 'dole' would be handed out on this occasion. So that the poor in their enthusiasm would not be tempted to disobey the instructions (hot weather always brought the fear of plague, to say nothing of hygiene), it was announced that the 'dole' would be brought to them later at home.

Afterwards a fine tomb of black and white marble was made for Anna of Cleves in Westminster Abbey. The design was in the Grecian style and 'executed in a masterly manner'. A native Clevian, Theodore Haeveus, a minister in Caius College, Cambridge, who designed there for Dr Keys, may have been responsible.[44] Two tiers of panels ornamented the sides of the tomb. The upper tier contained innocuous medallions with the initials A.C. surmounted by a ducal coronet (for Cleves). But the lower tier revealed a series of skulls, with crossbones, on a black background. In this appropriately sombre manner, the fourth wife and last surviving consort of Henry VIII was commemorated.

EPILOGUE

Chapter 20

WHAT THE KING

LUSTED

It is seductive to regard the six wives of Henry VIII as a series of feminine stereotypes, women as tarot cards. Thus Catherine of Aragon becomes The Betrayed Wife, Anne Boleyn is The Temptress, Jane Seymour The Good Woman; Anna of Cleves is The Ugly Sister, Katherine Howard The Bad Girl; finally Catherine Parr is The Mother Figure ... There are elements of truth, of course, in all of these evocative descriptions, yet each one of them ignores the complexity and variety in the individual character. In their different ways, and for different reasons, nearly all these women were victims, but they were not willing victims. On the contrary, a remarkably high level of strength, and also of intelligence, was displayed by them at a time when their sex traditionally possessed little of either.

Catherine of Aragon, Anne Boleyn and Catherine Parr possessed real intellectual ability, give or take their very different educational opportunities; indeed, the fact that Catherine of Aragon was the cleverest, followed by Anne Boleyn and finally Catherine Parr, directly reflects these opportunities. Neither Jane Seymour nor Anna of Cleves was stupid, according to those who observed and reported upon them. Poor Katherine Howard, whose single surviving handwritten document is an illicit love letter to Thomas Culpeper ('I heard that you were sick and never longed so much for anything as to see you') is of course the odd one out in this respect; although one should remember that the ability to scrawl even her own words of love put Katherine ahead of many of her female contemporaries.

The strength of these women proved relevant to the unfolding of their story. Much is made of the vigour (or obstinacy) of Catherine of Aragon in refusing to grant her husband a divorce; but Anne Boleyn, 'The Lady', otherwise 'La Concubina' or more crudely still 'the King's goggle-eyed whore', also showed herself to be made of steel. Anne Boleyn is a character whose independence of mind and behaviour, as a woman, make her curiously modern. They justify the recent attention which has been paid to her place in the Protestant development of England; although one should beware of forgetting that Anne Boleyn captivated the King by her grace, wit and a pair of sparkling black eyes, not by her religious opinions (which he did not share). Born to a comparatively minor station in life, she had the tenacity to hold out for the highest role of all – that of the King's wife – and achieve it.

Whether Jane Seymour was the tool of the Concubine's scheming enemies, or a bright young woman who saw her family's chance and took it, or somewhere between the two, either way her comportment during those fraught months of 1536 was a model of discreet wisdom. In the year of three Queens, she was able to emerge as Queen Jane, five months after the death of Queen Catherine, eleven days after the death of Queen Anne, an object of universal welcome and even admiration. As for Anna of Cleves, it is time to rescue her from the cruel sobriquet of 'the Flanders Mare' which Henry VIII never actually applied to her. Her behaviour during her bewildering short marriage and the many confusing years in a foreign land which followed, displayed a touching dignity; she deserves sympathy not derision.

It has been emphasized that Catherine Parr was very far from being a passive character. We have our first glimpse of her as a youthful Lady Latimer at the time of the Pilgrimage of Grace, watching her middle-aged husband being taken hostage by Robert Aske; she remained behind to guard his properties and children. Her behaviour as Queen, whether promoting religious causes in which she believed, or saving herself from the fatal taint of heresy, was spirited rather than submissive. After the King's death it was passion which guided her.

Nor was Catherine Parr the only Queen to be swayed in this way. The story of Henry VIII and his six wives is familiarly interpreted as a tale of the overweening royal lusts and their consequences. That is certainly one way of looking at it. In this narrative it has been suggested that King Henry, a romantic man, for better or for worse, married four of his six wives for love and even managed to fall in love with Anna of Cleves' picture before being daunted by reality. But one can also view these events from the other side of the mirror: this is also the story of six passionate women.

At the Blackfriars court in 1529 Catherine of Aragon suddenly flung herself on her knees before the King and to the general amazement – and admiration – sobbed out, in her strong Spanish accent, the words that Shakespeare would later adapt for immortality:

> Sir, I desire you do me right and justice;
> And to bestow your pity on me; for
> I am a most poor woman, and a stranger,
> Born out of your dominions . . .

Here she was acting not so much as 'the most virtuous woman I have ever known' as Chapuys described her on her death but as 'the highest hearted' – that is, of the greatest spirit.[1]

If Catherine of Aragon loved her husband, then two of King Henry's other wives – Katherine Howard as well as Catherine Parr – had been in love with other men when he chose to raise them up as his consort. Katherine Howard certainly experienced passion, although she remained to the end of her life the kind of young woman, like a charming amoral butterfly, incapable of seeing that the gratification of her sexual instinct might lead her into a net of destruction. As for Anne Boleyn, there is no reason to suppose that she did not reciprocate the attentions of Lord Percy in those distant secret days at court, when he was in waiting on Cardinal Wolsey and she a young woman of little fortune but much grace, in waiting on the Queen. After she was Queen, her continued dangerous ability to attract masculine desire – even if, as is argued here, she did not choose to satisfy it – played into the hands of her enemies as they plotted her downfall.

Yet, in a sense, the strength and courage of these women only serves to emphasize the fact that they were ultimately helpless in face of the central force in their lives: the embodiment of power, which was of course male (like all real power in this period), in the shape – the increasingly gigantic shape – of the King. Or as Catherine Parr hastened to assure King Henry, in order to soothe his anger (and save herself): 'women by their first creation were made subject to men'. It was a point of view expressed after her death by her friend and admirer William Cecil, when he described her as a woman 'by a mighty King [created] an excellent Queen, by a famous Henry [created] a renowned Catherine'; her greatest role, for all her godly wisdom, being as 'a wife to him that was a King to realms'.

This ultimate helplessness reaches its most poignant form in the events of the executions of Anne Boleyn and Katherine Howard. To modern ears, the most grisly aspect of these scenes is the resignation of the women concerned: Anne Boleyn referring to 'the most godly, noble and gentle prince that is'; Katherine Howard, so weak she could hardly speak but still praying heartily for the King, who was about to provide her with her 'worthy and just punishment'. To their contemporaries, however, such words had nothing gruesome about them: references to the mercy and gentleness of the prince were not only conventional but absolutely necessary, remembering how a mere lady-in-waiting was put in prison for reportedly asking the simple question: 'How many wives will the King have?' (He had just had his fifth wife put to death.)

The reverse was also true: Jane Seymour and Catherine Parr (and for that matter Katherine Howard) were equally helpless in face of the King's love. As for Anna of Cleves, she found herself with no alternative but to relinquish her position in words of fulsome praise for the man to whom she had fondly imagined she was married. If she could not have King Henry as a husband, she told Duke William, nevertheless she held him to be 'a most kind, loving and friendly Father and Brother'. Only in her last sentences to her real brother did she significantly underline the vulnerability of her position: let him take care to behave in this affair '[that] I fare not the worse; whereunto I trust you will have regard'. It took the spirited sixteen-year-old Christina of Milan, secure at Brussels under the protection of her uncle, the most powerful man in Europe, to stifle a giggle behind her hand when King Henry's envoy referred to his master as 'the most gentle Gentleman that liveth'.

Leaving aside strength, passion and helplessness, there is another bond that links together every one of the six wives. To a greater or less extent, each Queen was created or destroyed by her biological destiny. Let us imagine that the first of Catherine of Aragon's sons, Prince Henry, born on New Year's Day 1511, had lived, instead of dying of some nameless infant disease at seven weeks. It was for this child that a great tournament was staged, presided over by Catherine in the character of 'Noble Renown, Queen of the Realm' while Henry, as 'Cœur Loyal', thundered down the lists again and again in front of her doting gaze. This Prince Henry – five years older than Princess Mary – would have been marriageable in the late 1520s, could have provided his father with grandsons by the 1530s, and would have been approaching thirty-six at the time of his father's death. Even if her other sons had not survived, it is inconceivable that Catherine, as the mother of the heir, would have been discarded. Noble Renown would surely have continued to preside over the realm of which Cœur Loyal was King, until the day of her death.

This is not to say, baldly, that the English Reformation would not have taken place if the son or sons of Catherine of Aragon had lived: that is far too simple a statement, ignoring the complex processes which make up any revolutionary change. The abuses and malpractices within the English

Catholic church, the irritations of a papal authority often exercised as part of most unspiritual diplomatic intrigues, the limitations (or otherwise) of the royal power within the kingdom where the clergy were concerned ... these were matters for which solutions would inevitably be sought, as they were sought throughout Europe. What we can say with confidence is that King Henry would not have divorced Catherine of Aragon if her biological destiny had been different; thus the nature and course of the English Reformation would not have been the same. One may even dream that the destruction of a great cultural heritage represented by the dissolution of the monasteries (whose treasures went to fund the King's martial ambitions) would not have taken place.

Catherine of Aragon's supplanter, Anne Boleyn, also fell victim to her inability to provide the King with a son. One recalls the astonishment and the disappointment evinced at the birth of her only full-term child, Elizabeth – that announcement in which prince had twice to be altered to princess, so optimistic had everyone been of the desired outcome. It is indeed impossible to exaggerate the absolute preoccupation with a male heir – preferably two – which possessed England during the sixteenth century. Unfortunately, the royal Tudors proved not to be philoprogenitive as a family; it was their cousins who all too often were able to supply themselves with sons, and thus – at any rate in the royal view – threaten the fragile succession.

Undoubtedly, one cannot understand the marital career of Henry VIII without taking into account this obsession. In the first instance, it was rooted in terrible folk memories of the civil wars of the previous century. It was received wisdom that 'for quiet repose and tranquillity of our realm', in the words of Henry VIII to François I in 1533, the King must have a son. It was true that the King himself had 'received the principal title to his realm through the female line', as Chapuys once tactlessly pointed out to Henry.[2] (Chapuys presumably referred to King Henry's mother Elizabeth of York, but of course his father's hereditary claim to the throne also passed through *his* mother, Margaret Countess of Richmond.) But the fact that female descent occurred and re-occurred throughout the family tree made no difference to the prevailing feeling of the time. The ideal heir was 'a 'noble man', who would be 'a royal ruler'.

Nor was Henry VIII unique. Men – not only kings but nobles and others further down the property-holding classes – wanted sons to continue their own true line, as they perceived it. When Protector Somerset condoled with Thomas Seymour on the birth of a daughter and hoped for 'a great sort of happy sons' to come, he was expressing the conventional sentiments of his time; or as John Husee put it to John Basset: 'by God's Grace at the next shot to hit the mark'.[3] At the heart of the matter were the rules of property and inheritance by which the husband assumed not only the wealth but the rights of his heiress wife.

Naturally this kind of feared takeover found its most extreme form where kingdoms were at stake. King Henry hung back from wedding his daughter Mary to her first cousin James V of Scotland in 1524 lest the inferior kingdom seize the opportunity to swallow up its superior (as the English saw the situation). Twenty years later the Scots in turn hung back from allowing the child Mary Queen of Scots to be married to Prince Edward. 'If your lad were a lass and our lass were a lad (and so be King of England), would you then be so earnest in this matter?' asked the Scots, reasonably enough.[4] That mellow period in the 1520s, when Henry VIII did envisage Mary as his heiress, was dominated by his wish to marry her to her other first cousin, the Emperor Charles V. Dreams of a world dynasty, and his future grandson ruling over a vast empire, made up to him for the lack of his own son. Charles V's rejection of Mary, which occurred shortly before Henry VIII fell in love with Anne Boleyn, was a crucial psychological element in Henry's rejection of Mary's mother.

Thereafter the language of the divorce proceedings, and all correspondence pertaining to it, was heavily laced with allusions to the King's need for male issue; while Cardinal Wolsey's promotional letter regarding Anne Boleyn referred to her 'apparent aptness' to bear children (by which sons were of course implied). But Anne Boleyn did not manage to produce these sons. A nursery was prepared at Eltham for the prince who was expected to be born in the summer of 1534; this baby probably died during a birth which was slightly premature. Another chance came with her pregnancy of late 1535; but in January 1536 Queen Anne miscarried a male foetus at three and a half months. Had she continued healthily pregnant throughout that spring and early summer, it is inconceivable that her downfall would have been plotted as it was, let alone her virtue impugned: the danger of casting a shadow on the legitimacy of the impending royal issue was one no wise courtier would have risked. The King's infatuation with Jane Seymour would have fallen into place as part of the pattern of little romances which beguiled him from time to time. In June Queen Anne Boleyn would have been the triumphant mother of the King's male heir, a few weeks after the date on which the failed progenitoress was in fact executed.

Jane Seymour and Catherine Parr were both victims of their biological destiny, albeit in a different sense. The statistics of women who died of puerperal fever following childbirth at this time are impossible to ascertain; estimates – guesses – vary from ten per cent to thirty per cent. The fact that a third of the King's wives died in this manner, however, underlines the point that privilege did not mean protection. On the contrary, royal and aristocratic women were in greater danger in this respect than women of the people. Breast-feeding went some way towards protecting the latter from repeated pregnancies, whereas aristocratic women, their infants with entire households to look after them as well as wet-nurses, had to return to their duty of providing further heirs as soon as possible.[5]

The intensely high rate of infant and child mortality meant that no one – and especially not a king – could feel secure with only one son. Henry VIII himself was a second son who had succeeded a delicate elder brother. François I was the fortunate father of 'a fair joyous Dauphin' and several other sons by his first wife Queen Claude; but one notes that the succession in France eventually had to go to his sister's grandson Henri IV. Jane Seymour, who had 'showed so great hope of much fruit to come from her body' as Bishop Tunstall wrote after her death, had in fact only managed to produce one son. Moves to supplement the King's male issue were therefore immediate on her decease. Negotiations for the King's fourth marriage openly discussed this question of a second son, 'a Duke of York', and if possible several more (future 'Dukes of Gloucester and Somerset' were mentioned to the representatives of Christina of Milan).

The two marriages of 1540 which took place six months apart – the winter wedding of discomfited royal strangers and the high-summer union of an aging man with his thornless rose – can both be seen in this philo-progenitive light. Anna of Cleves was rejected because she could not arouse the King to his necessary royal duty. When she innocently described the King's nocturnal behaviour to her ladies as quoted in Chapter Fifteen, 'he kisses me and taketh me by the hand, and biddeth me, "goodnight sweet heart" and in the morning, kisses me', Lady Rutland's reply was absolutely to the point: 'Madam, there must be more'. Otherwise 'it will be long ere we have a Duke of York which all this realm most desireth.' The King's short (and – until its conclusion – happy) married life with Katherine Howard granted him at least some fresh opportunities to try to bring about what all the realm desired. As it happens, he did not manage to do so. Henry VIII too was a prisoner of his biological destiny.

In a memorable phrase, Martin Luther observed of the English King (at the time of his first divorce): 'Junker Heintz will be God and do whatever he lusts'.[6] But even Junker Heintz, lust as he might, could not secure a string of sons. And by a fine piece of historical irony, this man who sacrificed so much (and so many) for a son, did have one child who brought glory to his dynasty – but it was a daughter, Elizabeth I.

The six wives of Henry VIII have left no descendants.* The King's three

---

* Queen Elizabeth II is not descended from Henry VIII but from Henry VII; the line passed via his daughter Queen Margaret of Scotland and her grand-daughter Mary Queen of Scots, to the latter's son, James VI of Scotland, I of England. (See family tree 2)

children all died without issue and no credence can be given to the story that Queen Catherine Parr's daughter by Thomas Seymour lived to marry and leave offspring. Nevertheless lingering traces of them remain.

Inevitably the majority of these recall the King's first marriage. This is not entirely because he was joined to a powerful Spanish princess with a royal descent of her own to commemorate in badges, on his armour and in glass, although this played its part. The pomegranates of Granada were still to be seen on the uniforms of the men who drowned on the *Mary Rose* in 1545. There was a solemn double portrait of Henry and Catherine as King and Queen, including her patron St Catherine of Alexandria and the ubiquitous pomegranates in the tracery (now in the East Window of St Margaret's, Westminster); it seems to have been installed at one point in the chapel of the King's Palace of New Hall, regardless of who it commemorated.[7]

But the timescale of the King's various marriages was also heavily weighted in favour of his first to a degree that sometimes causes surprise. That is to say, King Henry was married to Catherine of Aragon for twenty-four years, if one takes the end point as his divorce in May 1533; in effect that was half of her lifetime, and approaching half of his (they had been married twenty years before the tribunal was set up at Blackfriars).* The entire sum of Henry VIII's other five marriages reached a mere ten and a half years: Anne Boleyn and Catherine Parr were both married to the King for three and a half years, Jane Seymour and Katherine Howard for eighteen months and Anna of Cleves for six.

Of these later wives, the traces are more random. There are initials which the revisionists forgot to remove: an H A for Henry and Anne Boleyn above the Provost's Stall in King's College Chapel for example. The K in the great East Window of the same chapel refers, from its date, to Katherine Howard. The heraldic mottoes and arms of another consort who flourished briefly, Anna of Cleves, are still to be found in the Chapel Royal of St James's Palace.

There are portraits (of five out of the six wives). There are jewels, with the letters K (or C), A and I (for J), interwoven with that of the unchanging H. There are relics. The bed of Queen Jane Seymour – that 'great rich bed and belongings to it' which she was said to have embroidered herself – remained in the royal family until the belongings of Charles I were sold off during the interregnum when her brother's great-grandson bought it for £60.[8] It featured in the will of his widow the Duchess of Somerset in 1674 who left it to her grand-daughter the great heiress Elizabeth Countess of

---

* The King's youngest wife, Katherine Howard, born about thirty-six years after Catherine of Aragon, was young enough to be her grand-daughter.

Ailesbury; this souvenir of the industry of a sixteenth-century Queen may –
who knows? – be somewhere extant.

Then there are the graves.

In Prague Cathedral the four wives of the Holy Roman Emperor Charles
IV, the fourteenth-century ruler of Bohemia, are buried – in a single
sepulchre – beside the Emperor himself; their sculptures also adorn the
triforium of the cathedral next to his. But these queens all died natural
deaths, none was rejected, none was despised. There is no such evidence
of serial domestic harmony to be found in the burial arrangements of Henry
VIII and his six wives. On the contrary, a moving pilgrimage may be made
to five resting-places which evoke anew the poignant circumstances in
which these women died and is a proper tribute to their memory.

The only two who do lie close together, sharing in effect a grave – the
first cousins Anne Boleyn and Katherine Howard – do so because they were
executed by the sword and the axe at the same block within the Tower of
London. Thereafter the decapitated bodies of the disgraced Queens were
conveyed to the nearby Chapel of St Peter ad Vincula and buried in
unmarked graves in the chancel, with other state prisoners who had similarly
died. In the case of Anne Boleyn, Queen Elizabeth I never sought to
rehabilitate her mother's reputation, let alone make some more fitting
acknowledgement of the burial-place of the woman who had borne her.
To the end of her reign, she remained 'Great Harry's daughter' – and his
alone – in her public utterances; by such an emphasis, she pointed to the
source of her own royal authority on the one hand, and distanced herself
from the murky circumstances of her mother's death on the other. (The
1536 Act of Succession which had declared Elizabeth a bastard was never
actually repealed; since she was able to succeed under the terms of her
father's will, such a repeal would have been another intrusive reminder of
old unhappy far-off things.)

As for Katherine Howard, childless and scarcely out of her own uncared-
for childhood, her relations led the field of those who considered that an
unmarked grave was by far the most suitable place for her to lie, once her
brief span as the King's 'perfect jewel of womanhood' was over. So Norfolk's
'two false traitorous nieces' – whom he disowned for their 'abominable
deeds' – vanished from memory as they had vanished from sight, into an
anonymous interment.

The late nineteenth century brought a more charitable attitude. In 1876
the Chapel of St Peter, built in its present form in the early years of Henry
VIII's reign, was restored. With the approval of Queen Victoria, the remains
unearthed in the nave were placed in the crypt; but the bones found in the
chancel, including those which could be identified as belonging to Anne

Boleyn and Katherine Howard, were reburied beneath the marble pavement before the altar.[9]

There two octagonal plaques now commemorate the graves; they are simply inscribed with names, coats-of-arms and dates of death. It is notable that the royal title which was stripped from each woman, Anne Boleyn by divorce on the eve of her execution, Katherine Howard by order of the Council, has been restored to them both in death. So the lettering reads: 'Queen Anne Boleyn. MDXXXVI' and 'Queen Katherine Howard. MDXLII'.

Services are held regularly in this beautiful tranquil church, Sunday Matins and christenings of the families of the yeoman warders (beefeaters) who live within the Tower itself. Visitors regard the plaques respectfully. The yeoman warders who act as guides are inclined, like the present writer, to regard Anne Boleyn as innocent (of adultery) and Katherine Howard as guilty; but their sympathies are directed in both cases towards the woman, rather than the man to whom she was married, Henry VIII. Only a few yards away, the site of the block is still marked and the ravens are still there to scavenge.

In contrast, the grave of Jane Seymour receives little attention as such, despite the fact that it lies at the heart of St George's Chapel, Windsor, the site of many royal ceremonies today, including those of the Order of the Garter. This is because the fame of King Henry's 'true' and 'entirely beloved' wife is obliterated by that of the monarchs with whom she shares her burial-place; it is as though the 'very modest' behaviour which was prized in her lifetime has been perpetuated in death.

The magnificent monument King Henry had planned for them both, had as its basis the great tomb intended by Cardinal Wolsey for himself which the King had seized as booty. It turned out to be an ill-omened piece of commemoration. None of the King's three children who followed him on the throne showed any interest in completing it (although we should acquit Queen Mary of the malicious and unsubstantiated charge of having her father's heart secretly burnt in revenge for her mother's sufferings: this would have been quite out of character with the dignified reverence she actually displayed towards him).[10] The tomb was looted at the time of the civil war and parts of it sold off, although the marble sarcophagus remained at Windsor until it was ejected at the orders of George III; it has ended up housing the remains of Nelson in the crypt of St Paul's Cathedral: an interesting example of unintentional continuity in history.

The royal vault in the centre of the choir of St George's, where Queen Jane and King Henry were buried in turn, was opened again a hundred years after his death, to admit the decapitated corpse of King Charles I. In 1696 one of the many children of Princess (later Queen) Anne who died as an infant was buried there. Then, in 1813, the vault was discovered by accident; the lead coffin of Henry VIII had been inadequate for its task and had gaped open, revealing his awesome skeleton. In the presence of the future George IV, then Prince Regent, the coffin of 'the Martyr King' Charles I was cut open. But the coffin of Jane Seymour, the original inhabitant of the vault, sad victim of a far more commonplace death, excited no particular interest and so was left untouched.

A large oblong piece of black marble now marks the site in the choir. The 'Queen's closet', from which Catherine Parr watched the body of her husband being winched down into the vault by sixteen gigantic soldiers, looking down from the fine wooden oriole window, still bears the pomegranates associated with the woman for whom it was created, Catherine of Aragon. The black oblong carries this inscription: 'In A Vault Beneath This Marble Slab Are Deposited The Remains of Jane Seymour Queen of Henry VIII. 1537. King Henry VIII. 1547. King Charles I. 1648. [By modern reckoning, 1649.] And An Infant Child of Queen Anne.' Finally: 'This Memorial Was Placed Here by Command of King William IV. 1837.' So, decorous to the last, Jane Seymour is buried under a description which, apart from being perfectly accurate – the truth if not the whole truth – is also a fine example of patriarchal economy: 'Queen of Henry VIII.' Queen Jane was after all the mother of the King's son, unlike the other five women with claims to be regarded as 'Queen of Henry VIII', hence her presence, honoured if inconspicuous, in the royal vault.

In the case of Anna of Cleves, who spent six months as the King's wife, and over seventeen years as a 'good Sister', the burial-place is even more magnificent, the practical obscurity which surrounds it even deeper. That fine, possibly Clevian-designed tomb, with its skull-and-crossbones, has lain untouched in Westminster Abbey ever since it was installed. It is in fact located on the south side of the high altar itself: part of the actual sanctuary of the abbey where the coronation ceremonies take place. (At the coronation of Queen Elizabeth II, the box to contain the royal family as spectators, including the Queen Mother and Prince Charles, was built right on top of the side altar which houses Anna of Cleves.)

At the same time the tomb manages to be quite unnoticed. Already by 1625, hangings were shrouding it. Today a large Italian painting of the Madonna and Saints, over a vast tapestry said to have been used in the Latin plays of Westminster School, above the altar's slab of marble which cost £7 in 1606, all combine to distract attention from the tomb, despite its august situation. A small reddish portion of the tomb is visible to the public (who are not admitted to the high altar) from the back, somewhat dwarfed by the vast adjacent white marble monuments to male dignitaries. Letters of dull gold painted here read: 'Anne of Cleves. Queen of England.

Born 1515. Died 1557.' Once again the description is tactfully terse – the truth but certainly not the whole truth. So the paradox of the life of Anna of Cleves is well-illustrated. She lies at the heart of Westminster Abbey. And she is forgotten.

The coffin – and even the corpse – of Catherine Parr did not find proper repose at Sudeley for nearly 300 years. There were some unexpectedly upsetting incidents, and a parallel may be seen with the career of the woman herself, so much less serene than her nursing role to elderly husbands would suggest.

The beginning was peaceful enough, the peace of neglect. For a while after her agonizing deathbed, Queen Catherine lay in an unmarked grave in the chapel at Sudeley. The execution and attainder of Seymour less than a year later meant that her commemoration languished more by default than with the positive efforts at obliteration extended to Anne Boleyn and Katherine Howard. Sudeley Castle, however, had the ill fortune to be a royalist stronghold in the civil war; as a result of which the victorious parliament condemned it to be 'slighted', that is, rendered unusable as a fortress in 1649. Thereafter deterioration of the structure was rapid, chapel as well as castle. By 1752 George Ballard, an antiquarian writing the lives of women celebrated for their learning, recorded that the burial place of Catherine Parr was unknown: 'a circumstance', he found, 'somewhat extraordinary'.[11]

In 1782, however, her coffin was disinterred by chance. A Mr John Lucas, who occupied the land which included the ruins of the chapel, then proceeded to rip open the lead; although at least one observer was 'much displeased' by his presumption: 'it would have been quite sufficient to have found it [the coffin]'. To his amazement Lucas found the whole body 'uncorrupted'. No proper attempt seems to have been made to give this amazingly preserved body a decent reburial, since a year later it was reported that the flesh was now quite fetid and there was a reference to 'the stench of the corpse'. However, a stone slab was now placed upon the coffin to discourage further curious sightseers. In spite of this, a party of drunken men submitted the body to a further ordeal ten years later; having roistered round the coffin, they decided to dig a new grave for it as part of their escapade, but were so drunk that they interred it upside down.[12]

The final interruption was more respectful. In 1817 the Rector of Sudeley, together with a local antiquary, searched out the disintegrating coffin. (By now it was clogged full of ivy.) The lead was firmly nailed together to prevent further intrusions.[13] The two of them also located the original inscription which had been on the coffin, copied it out (the egregious Lucas having given quite a false account of it) and replaced it. So at last Queen Catherine Parr's grave became a fine and private place.

After 1837, when the Dent family purchased Sudeley and carried out extensive rehabilitation, the chapel too was restored, under the direction of Sir George Gilbert Scott. An impressive altarpiece was then erected on the northern side of the sacrarium to the memory of Catherine Parr, with an effigy, rendered as lifelike as possible with the use of her portraits. A replica of the plate found on her coffin is engraved nearby: 'KP Here lyethe quene Kateryn, Wife to Kyng Henry the VIII And Last the wife of Thomas Lord of Sudeley high Admyrall of England and onkle to Kyng Edward the VI dyede September mccccc xl viii'. So, with her hands clasped devoutly in prayer, Catherine Parr has ended her days encased in smooth white marble; after a few adventures along the way, she is finally commemorated as the submissive Queen of the Victorian (and her contemporaries') imagination.

Of the six wives of Henry VIII, it is Catherine of Aragon who has ended up with the most appropriate royal resting-place; interred in a great cathedral – Peterborough – with the makings of a shrine for those who care to pay their respects to her memory there. She has triumphed in death, as she failed to do in life; but then that is the natural Christian outcome.

The manner of Catherine of Aragon's funeral itself was not auspicious and displeased the faithful ambassador Chapuys. 'They do not mean to bury her as Queen', he wrote, declining to attend; instead the rank of Princess Dowager was used which Catherine had so furiously rejected, and the banners of Wales (not England) displayed with those of her native Spain. Her daughter tried to ameliorate this at the end of her short reign. Queen Mary left instructions in her will for the body of 'my most dear and well-beloved mother of happy memory' to be removed from Peterborough as soon as possible after her own burial and laid beside her; 'honourable tombs or monuments' were to be provided 'for a decent memory of us'.[14] But her successor Queen Elizabeth did not see fit to encourage such a conjunction of the Catholic Queens, any more than she had busied herself with the memory of her own mother. Finally, it is Elizabeth herself, not Catherine the 'well-beloved mother', who lies side by side with Queen Mary in Westminster Abbey; the two half-sisters share an 'honourable' (and impressive) tomb.

The wooden hearse of Catherine of Aragon, with its banners and its black velvet pall, where the wax tapers were said to have kindled themselves at the execution of Anne Boleyn, was still visible in 1586. The following year Mary Queen of Scots was buried in Peterborough Cathedral following her execution at nearby Fotheringhay Castle, although later removed to Westminster Abbey. (The same gravedigger, known as Old Scarlett, attended to both Queens, whose deaths were separated by a span of fifty-one years.) The civil war brought riotous iconoclasts to Peterborough.

An eyewitness, Francis Standish, reported how 'the rabble', among other depredations, snatched the black velvet pall from Queen Catherine's grave, overthrew her hearse and took it away.[15]

By 1725 Queen Catherine's grave was needing repair; a prebendary of the cathedral supplied it at his own cost, together with a tiny plate of brass. The gravestone vanished during the course of the unsentimental eighteenth century – at a time when the Catholicism of Catherine of Aragon was also proscribed as a religion – and is believed to have formed part of the Dean's summerhouse. Once again the Victorian age proved more charitable. It was the major restoration of the cathedral, starting in 1891, which led to the proper installation of a respectful memorial. When the marble pavement in the choir was laid, and its foundations made secure, the vault containing the Queen's coffin was uncovered (as it had evidently been, briefly, in 1781 before being reburied).[16]

Thereafter a slab of Irish marble was placed above her grave in the north presbytery aisle just outside the sanctuary. It was inscribed with her arms, pomegranates and a cross and paid for by public subscription of the 'Catherines/Katherines' of England, Scotland, Ireland, Australia and America.* The banners were those she would have wanted: that of an infanta of Castile and Aragon, and of a queen consort of England, the gift of another foreign princess married to a man who would become King of England: Mary of Teck, consort of George V. Gold lettering on the grille above her grave reads (once again as she would have wished) 'Katharine Queen of England'.

This was only the beginning of the ecumenical celebration of Queen Catherine of Aragon. In January 1986, the four-hundred-and-fiftieth anniversary of her burial, a ceremonial coffin was carried from Kimbolton, correctly stopping at Sawtrey Abbey on the way. A banquet was subsequently held by Spaniards, and English, both Anglicans and Catholics. The Spanish ambassador presented a brilliant new royal standard, on which can also be seen the Queen's personal emblem of the pomegranate. A tablet was erected by the citizens of Peterborough on 29 January 1986 to this effect: 'A QUEEN CHERISHED BY THE ENGLISH PEOPLE FOR HER LOYALTY, PIETY, COURAGE AND COMPASSION'.

It is rare to find the Queen's grave without fresh flowers placed upon it. Nothing is known about those who over the years have performed this touching act of respect. One can however safely assume that, whatever their own religious views, they agree with this estimate of the character of Catherine of Aragon: loyal, pious, courageous and compassionate.

---

* Although her age at her death is wrongly given as forty-nine; Queen Catherine was fifty on 16 December 1535, three weeks before she died on 7 January 1536.

REFERENCES

Details of books, documents, etc, given here in abbreviated form, will be found in the list of Reference Books.

Chapter 1

1 In 1494. Elliott, *Imperial Spain*, p. 65.
2 Wood, *Letters*, I, p. 114.
3 Mattingly, *Catherine*, p. 15.
4 Cit. Claremont, p. 49.
5 Cit. Dowling, *Humanism*, p. 16.
6 Cit. Fernández-Armesto, p. 118.
7 Scarisbrick, p. 13.
8 Elliott, *Spain and Its World*, p. 31.
9 Fernández-Armesto, p. 41.
10 McConica, p. 19.
11 Elliott, *Imperial Spain*, p. 73; Prescott, II, p. 325.
12 Gwyn, p. 356.
13 Anglo, *Spectacle*, p. 19.
14 Chrimes, p. 50 and note 5; Wood, *Letters*, I, p. 118.
15 CSP Spanish, I, passim.
16 CSP Spanish, I, p. lxiii; but Chrimes, p. 280, gives March 1488.
17 Mattingly, 'De Puebla', p. 29 and note 1; Mattingly, *Diplomacy*, p. 141.
18 CSP Spanish, I, p. 4; p. 6.
19 CSP Spanish, I, p. 7.
20 de Iongh, p. 72.
21 Mattingly, *Catherine*, p. 21.
22 CSP Spanish, I, p. 213.
23 CSP Spanish, I, p. 146.
24 CSP Spanish, I, p. 156; p. 164.
25 CSP Spanish, I, p. 176.
26 CSP Spanish, I, p. 209.
27 BL Egerton MS, 616, fols 10; 11; 12; Wood, *Letters*, I, p. 121ff.
28 CSP Spanish, I, p. 235.
29 CSP Spanish, I, p. 240; p. 250.
30 Cit. Prescott, II, p. 331.
31 CSP Spanish, I, p. 256.
32 *Anglica Historia*, p. 123; *Harpsfield*, p. 28; CSP Spanish, I, p. 262.
33 Mattingly, *Catherine*, p. 32.
34 CSP Spanish, I, p. 264; p. 265.
35 Cit. Paul, p. 9.
36 Forrest, p. 27.
37 Hume, *Wives*, p. 28.
38 Anglo, *British History*, p. 32 and note 2.
39 Hume, *Wives*, p. 27.

Chapter 2

1 CSP Spanish, I, p. 523.
2 For details see Anglo, *Spectacle*, p. 54ff; Claremont, pp. 86–7.
3 King, *Iconography*, pp. 36–7; p. 41.
4 Colvin, III, Part II, p. 50.
5 Anglo, 'Heron Accounts', p. 370. The first carriage or coach as we understand the term appeared in London in 1555.
6 Cit. Hume, *Wives*, p. 151, note 1.
7 CSP Spanish, I, p. 176.
8 CSP Spanish Supplement, p. 10.
9 CSP Spanish Supplement, p. 1; p. 9.
10 CSP Spanish Supplement, p. 1.
11 Wright, p. 39; p. 50.
12 Hall, I, p. 165.
13 Nicolas, *Elizabeth of York*, p. lxxxviiff.
14 Harris, *Buckingham*, p. 79.
15 Cit. Lockyer, p. 89.
16 Cit. Paul, p. 15.
17 Nicolas, *Elizabeth of York*, p. 103.
18 CSP Spanish, I, p. 262.
19 CSP Spanish, I, p. 271; p. 272; p. 302.

20 CSP Spanish, I, p. 301.
21 See Mattingly, 'De Puebla', pp. 34–40.
22 CSP Spanish, I, p. 322; Scarisbrick, p. 8.
23 CSP Spanish, I, p. 306.
24 Scarisbrick, p. 13 and note 2.
25 CSP Spanish, I, p. 295.
26 Chrimes, p. 287, discounts 'this improbable allegation'.
27 Fernández-Armesto, p. 55.
28 CSP Spanish, I, p. 386.
29 CSP Spanish, I, p. 376.
30 Cit. Scarisbrick, p. 9.
31 CSP Spanish, I, p. 386; Gairdner, p. 285.
32 CSP Spanish, I, p. 411.
33 CSP Spanish, I, pp. 434–5; p. 440.
34 CSP Spanish, I, p. 359.
35 BL Egerton MS, 616, fols 27; 29–30; 32; 34–7.
36 CSP Spanish, I, pp. 422–3; p. 432.
37 See Claremont, p. 109ff; p. 138.
38 CSP Spanish Supplement, p. 19.
39 CSP Spanish Supplement, p. 15.
40 CSP Spanish Supplement, p. 25.
41 Mattingly, 'De Puebla', p. 36ff; Castro, p. 523 and note 119.
42 CSP Spanish, II, p. 2.
43 Mattingly, Catherine, p. 82.
44 Paul, p. 30.
45 Armstrong, Charles, I, p. 12.
46 CSP Spanish, I, p. 469.
47 Chrimes, p. 297.

Chapter 3
1 Claremont, p. 139; Mattingly, Catherine, p. 97.
2 Scarisbrick, p. 188, note 3; CSP Spanish Further Supplement, p. 450; L & P, VI, p. 169.
3 Williams, Residences, p. 37; L & P, I, p. 38; Hall, I, p. 70.
4 Cit. Marius, p. 53.
5 King's Jewel Book, p. 160.
6 Miller, Nobility, p. 93.
7 Cit. Starkey, Reign of Henry VIII, p. 37.
8 Elliott, Essays, p. 31; p. 34.
9 Hall, I, p. 4.

10 L & P, I, pt. 1, pp. 23–4.
11 L & P, I, pt. 1, p. 59; Mattingly, Catherine, p. 197, agrees with this conclusion, but see Starkey, Reign of Henry VIII, p. 48, for the view that 'most of all' Henry wanted the support of Ferdinand against France.
12 Cit. Clive, p. 78; CSP Spanish, I, p. xlviii.
13 Cit. Chambers, pp. 70–71; L & P, III, pp. 142–3 and note.
14 Nicolas, Henry VIII, p. xxiii; Giustinian, II, App. II, p. 312; cit. Starkey, Reign of Henry VIII, p. 41.
15 Davey, p. 95ff; Trefusis, passim.
16 Hall, I, p. 70.
17 L & P, I, pt. 1, p. 60; Cavendish, p. 11.
18 King's Jewel Book, p. 169; p. 171; p. 174.
19 King's Jewel Book, p. 179; Colvin, IV, p. 26.
20 Hall, I, p. 49; Nichols, Inventories, p. xi; Williams, Henry VIII, p. 65ff.
21 Nichols, Regulations, pp. 137–207; Furnivall, p. 66; p. 109.
22 Colvin, IV, p. 10ff; Williams, Henry VIII, p. 30ff.
23 Mathew, p. 54.
24 Starkey, 'Representation', p. 211.
25 Cit. Marius, p. 83.
26 CSP Spanish, II, p. 24.
27 CSP Spanish, II, p. 38; although Catherine told Ferdinand on 27 May the mishap had occurred 'a few days ago', this cannot be true, since the new baby born on 1 January 1511 must have been conceived on about 1 April 1510. The birth of this new baby also makes nonsense of Fray Diego's claim that Catherine miscarried at the end of May 1510, a daughter who had possibly 'lingered' in the womb after the debacle of 31 January 1510; CSP Spanish Supplement, p. 34; Dewhurst, 'Miscarriages', p. 51.
28 Ellis, 2nd Series, I, p. 180.

29 L & P, I, pt. 1, p. 37ff; p. 381; Hall, I, p. 27.
30 L & P, I, pt. 1, p. 75.
31 L & P, I, pt. 1, p. 10; Mattingly, *Diplomacy*, p. 134.
32 Cit. Starkey, *Reign of Henry VIII*, p. 40.
33 Knecht, p. 33; Kingsford, p. 199.
34 Hall, I, p. 95.
35 CSP Spanish, II, p. 248.
36 See L & P, I, pt. 2, p. 959; p. 968; p. 974; p. 988.
37 L & P, I, pt. 2, p. 1027.
38 Cit. Lewis, p. 121; L & P, I, pt. 2, p. 1016.
39 Armstrong, *England*, p. 104.
40 Ellis, 1st Series I, pp. 84ff.
41 CSP Venetian, II, p. 139; Hume, *Wives*, p. 83.
42 Cit. Mattingly, *Catherine*, p. 123.
43 Hall, I, p. 129.
44 See Gunn, passim, especially p. 28; p. 86; pp. 93–6.
45 Wood, *Letters*, I, p. 187; Gunn, p. 36.
46 Loades, p. 13, note 4; CSP Spanish, II, p. 273; Mattingly, *Catherine*, p. 110.
47 CSP Venetian, II, p. 139; L & P, I, pt. 2, p. 1349 and note; she may have been the daughter of a lady of the court of Henry VII who signed herself 'C La Baume' in a Book of Hours, BL Add. MS, 17,012 fol. 80b.
48 Harris, *Buckingham*, p. 51ff; but see Bernard, 'Compton', p. 756ff for the view that Henry wished 'to sleep with both sisters'.
49 Cit. Marius, p. 104.

Chapter 4
1 Madden, p. xx; Loades, pp. 14–15; cit. Brigden, p. 289.
2 Cooper, *Cambridge*, I, p. 292; p. 298; Giustinian, I, p. 182.
3 Cit. Claremont, p. 161; *Excerpta*, p. 287.
4 Knecht, p. 45; Seward, p. 64.
5 CSP Venetian, III, p. 248; p. 529;

p. 560; IV, p. 287.
6 CSP Venetian, IV, p. 287; cit. Dowling, *Humanism*, p. 19.
7 Dowling, 'Woman's Place', p. 38; G. R. Elton's remark, cit. Marius, p. 200, as having 'the smack of truth'.
8 Ridley, *Statesman*, pp. 100–112; Dowling, *Humanism*, p. 37ff.
9 Hall, I, p. 179.
10 Hall, I, pp. 175–7.
11 Mattingly, *Catherine*, p. 143; McConica, p. 60.
12 Pugh, pp. 437–40; Dowling, *Humanism*, p. 25.
13 Gray, p. 64; Cooper, *Cambridge*, I, p. 304.
14 Mattingly, *Catherine*, p. 140; Dowling, 'Support for Katherine', p. 49, note 26.
15 Cit. Cooper, *Margaret*, p. 6; Jones and Underwood, p. 184.
16 Clifford, p. 73.
17 Clifford, p. 58.
18 Giustinian, II, App. II, p. 312.
19 Forrest, p. 28.
20 Mattingly, *Catherine*, p. 133ff; CSP Venetian, III, p. 385.
21 L & P, II, pt. 2, p. 1263; p. 1305.
22 L & P, II, pt. 2, p. 1326; p. 1328; p. 1354.
23 L & P, III, pp. 142–3. CSP Venetian, III, p. 480; Giustinian, II, p. 237; L & P, II, pt. 2, p. 1263.
24 Gwyn, p. 101.
25 Cit. Richardson, p. 106; although her date of birth is not known, she must have been very young since in 1519 her father was only 36; Nichols, *Inventories*, p. xi.
26 Nichols, *Inventories*, p. ix; see Harris, *Buckingham*, p. 265, note 12.
27 L & P, III, pt. 1, p. 500.
28 Cit. Mattingly, *Catherine*, p. 158.
29 Cit. Hare, p. 63; p. 120.
30 Russell, *Field of Cloth of Gold*, is the authoritative study of the episode, from which the following details (unless otherwise acknowledged) are taken.

31 Cit. Gwyn, p. 359; p. 356.
32 Ives, *Boleyn*, p. 40, believes she must have been present.
33 Cit. Russell, p. 5.
34 Mattingly, *Catherine*, p. 159.
35 *Chronicle of Calais*, pp. 28–30.
36 Cit. Dowling, *Humanism*, p. 19.
37 Colvin, III, pt. 1, pp. 221–2; Morshead, p. 49 and note a.

Chapter 5
1 CSP Venetian, III, p. 104.
2 MacNalty, *Henry VIII*, p. 162; Dewhurst, 'Miscarriages', pp. 49–54.
3 Cit. Strickland, II, p. 523.
4 See Harris, *Buckingham*, p. 179ff.
5 CSP Venetian, II, p. 561.
6 Ellis, 1st Series, I, p. 177.
7 Harris, *Buckingham*, p. 202; Gwyn, p. 161, also describes the evidence of 'treasonable thoughts' as 'damning'.
8 Hall, I, p. 223; CSP Spanish, II, p. 365.
9 Scarisbrick, p. 128 and note 1.
10 Cit. Knecht, p. 160.
11 Madden, p. xxvi; CSP Spanish, III, pt. 1, p. 108.
12 Colvin, III, pt. 2, p. 55; CSP Venetian, III, p. 236; Mattingly, *Catherine*, p. 162.
13 CSP Spanish, Further Supplement, pp. xxxiv–v.
14 CSP Spanish, Further Supplement, p. 84; p. 135.
15 CSP Spanish, Further Supplement, p. 103; p. 108.
16 Cit. Mattingly, *Catherine*, p. 171.
17 Noreña, *Vives*, p. 71; p. 76; p. 79 and note 16; p. 82.
18 Cit. Watson, *Vives and Education*, p. 137ff.
19 Cit. Watson, *Vives and Education*, p. 29.
20 Cit. Scalingi, p. 59; cit. Marius, p. 227.
21 Reynolds, p. 222; L & P, III, pt. 2, p. 1539; G. E. C., VI, p. 627, note e (Hunsdon); the date of this

marriage is sometimes erroneously given as 1520.
22 Ives, *Boleyn*, p. 33 and note 25; Wood, *Letters*, II, p. 194.
23 Kelly, *Trials*, p. 48.
24 Hall, I, p. 306.
25 Eaves, p. 89; p. 128; p. 163; Mary's most recent biographer describes the Scottish marriage as 'often ignored' but for a short while 'a real option', Loades, pp. 25–6.
26 Hall, II, p. 21; L & P, XVIII, p. 175.
27 SP, IV, p. 113; p. 243; p. 292.
28 Hay, p. 123.
29 CSP Spanish, Further Supplement, pp. 5–9; p. 42.
30 Hall, II, pp. 29–30.
31 CSP Spanish, III, pt. 1, p. 108.
32 CSP Spanish, III, pt. 1, pp. 108–112; p. 121.
33 CSP Spanish, Further Supplement, p. xxxvii; p. 443; CSP Spanish, III, pt. 1, p. 122; p. 129.
34 Ridley, *Henry VIII*, p. 136.
35 Gunn, p. 97.
36 CSP Venetian, III, p. 455.
37 CSP Venetian, III, p. 454; Nichols, *Inventories*, p. xv; Watson, *Vives and Education*, p. 151.
38 Skeel, p. 285, App. I.
39 Henry Brandon was the second child to bear that name; the first, born in 1516, died before 1522, G. E. C., X, p. 830, note f (Richmond); CSP Venetian, III, p. 448.
40 SP, I, p. 162.
41 Cit. Watson, *Vives El Valenciano*, p. 75.

Chapter 6
1 Ives, *Boleyn*, p. 3; this birthday is derived from Jane Dormer who describes her as '*not quite* twenty-nine' at the time of her execution on 19 May; she would have heard this from her mistress, Anne's stepdaughter Mary; see Clifford, p. 81.
2 Cit. Paget, p. 163 and note 9.
3 Camden, p. 2; Paget, p. 163ff and

note 10 summarizes the debate and the sources; Ives, *Boleyn*, accepts Paget's thesis; Warnicke, *Boleyn*, p. 16, challenges it, and in so doing has Anne as six when she goes to France.

4 Friedmann, I, p. 37–8; p. 128 and note 1; Byrne, *Letters*, p. 63.

5 See Franklyn, passim.

6 McConica, p. 61; G. E. C., X, p. 137 (Ormond); Ives, *Boleyn*, p. 11ff.

7 G. E. C., X, p. 130, note f (Ormond).

8 Paget, p. 164; Ives, *Boleyn*, p. 21; G. E. C, VI, p. 628, note e (Hunsdon).

9 G. E. C, X, p. 139, note j (Ormond).

10 Paget, pp. 163–4; p. 166.

11 Written in 1536, first printed in 1545, de Carles, p. 231ff; Cavendish, p. 29; Dowling, *Latymer*, p. 37.

12 Forrest, p. 53; de Carles, p. 234.

13 SP, VII, p. 565.

14 L & P, III, pt. 1, p. 369; p. 372; pt. 2, p. 749 (wrongly calendared as being Mary Boleyn); Ives, *Boleyn*, p. 45–6.

15 L & P, VI, p. 485; Sander, p. 25; Ives, *Boleyn*, p. 50.

16 CSP Venetian, IV, p. 236; CSP Spanish, IV, pt. 2, p. 473; Ives, *Boleyn* p. 51, note 12.

17 Sander, p. 25 and note 1; *Original Letters from Zürich*, II, p. 552; Wyatt, p. 182; Scarisbrick, p. 148.

18 Cit. Elton, *Police*, p. 137; *Oxford English Dictionary*.

19 Agnolo Firenzuolo, *The Beauty of Women*; cit. Richardson, p. 103; de Carles, p. 234; cit. Ives, *Boleyn*, p. 52; Sander, p. 25.

20 Starkey, *The Independent*, 23 April 1991; Starkey, *Henry VIII: European Court*, p. 92.

21 Wyatt, p. 18.

22 Whittington; Forrest, p. 53.

23 Cavendish, p. 36.

24 Furnivall, p. xvi.

25 Cavendish, p. 30ff.

26 Cavendish, p. xxvi.

27 See Kelly, *Trials*, p. 52ff.

28 See Ives, *Boleyn*, pp. 83–99 for an analysis of these texts; Wyatt, p. 184.

29 Cit. Ives, *Boleyn*, pp. 91–2; Lewis, p. 229.

30 Mattingly, *Catherine*, p. 182, and Ives, *Boleyn*, p. 108, agree on Shrovetide 1526; Warnicke, *Boleyn*, p. 55ff, whose timescale is quite different, proposes spring 1527.

31 By Lucas Horenbout; CSP Venetian, IV, p. 287; Simon Grynaeus to Martin Buler, 1531, *Original Letters from Zürich*, II, p. 552.

32 Byrne, *Letters*, p. xv.

33 Ridley, *Letters*, p. 13–18.

34 Cit. Ridley, *Letters*, p. 41.

35 Cit. Ridley, *Letters*, p. 37.

36 Cit. Ridley, *Letters*, p. 53.

37 Cit. Ridley, *Letters*, p. 49 and note 1; Savage, p. 39 and note 1 suggests 'O' instead of 'B', ie O.N.R.I. (Henri) de R.O.M.V.E.Z., 'a name possibly found in romances', but in fact 'B' looks far more likely than 'O'.

38 Hall, II, p. 80, p. 195; cit. Madden, p. lii.

39 Cit. Madden, p. clv, see Madden, App. II, p. clxxiii.

40 See Scarisbrick, p. 152ff.

Chapter 7

1 Gunn, p. 95; Warnicke, *Women*, p. 51.

2 Friedmann, I, p. 48.

3 SP, IV, p. 385; p. 272; Byrne, *Letters*, p. 65.

4 Seward, p. 21; Richardson, p. 99.

5 Mattingly, *Catherine*, p. 179; *Harpsfield*, p. 6.

6 Schnucker, pp. 657–9.

7 Cit. Claremont, p. 181, note 2.

8 Ridley, *Letters*, p. 37.

9 CSP Spanish, IV, pt. 2, p. 84; V, pt. 2, p. 28; Ellis, 1st Series, III, p. 42.

10 Scarisbrick, p. 151 and note 2; Behrens, p. 163.
11 Cit. Claremont, p. 181; cit. Paul, p. 78.
12 Kelly, *Trials*, pp. 21–9; Loades, p. 53, note 24.
13 Surtz and Murphy, pp. ix–xiii.
14 Scarisbrick, p. 163ff.
15 Kelly, *Trials*, p. 31.
16 Mattingly, *Catherine*, p. 186; Hume, *Wives*, p. 121 and note 1.
17 Neither Scarisbrick, p. 153ff, nor Gwyn, p. 506ff, hold Wolsey to be the author of the divorce; although see Mattingly, *Catherine*, p. 178; SP, I, pt. 1, p. 194; L & P, IV, pt. 2, p. 1467; pp. 1470–71.
18 Brigden, p. 138; p. 169.
19 Surtz and Murphy, p. iii; Ridley, *Letters*, p. 35.
20 Kelly, *Trials*, p. 38ff.
21 Ridley, *Letters*, p. 43.
22 Cit. Scarisbrick, p. 201.
23 Byrne, *Letters*, p. 63; Ridley, *Letters*, p. 61.
24 See Dowling, 'Boleyn and Reform', p. 30ff, for 'extensive evidence' of her protection and advancement of reformers.
25 Brigden, pp. 116–17 and note 173; BL Harleian MS, 6561; L & P, IV, pt. 2, pp. 126–7; Dowling, 'Boleyn and Reform', p. 30.
26 Brigden, p. 128; L & IV, pt. 3, p. 197; Dowling, 'Boleyn and Reform', p. 37.
27 Dowling, 'Boleyn and Reform', pp. 35–6.
28 Dowling, 'Boleyn and Reform', p. 36; Nichols, *Foxe*, pp. 1–59.
29 Knowles, 'Wilton', pp. 92–6; Ridley, *Letters*, p. 59.
30 Ridley, *Letters*, p. 57; p. 39.
31 Ridley, *Letters*, p. 65.
32 Ridley, *Letters*, p. 69; p. 71.
33 Ridley, *Letters*, p. 67; p. 45; CSP Spanish, III, pt. 2, p. 784.
34 CSP Spanish, III, pt. 2, p. 789; Hall, II, p. 145.
35 Cit. Hume, *Wives*, p. 151, note 1.

36 CSP Spanish, III, pt. 2, p. 841.
37 See Kelly, 'Kinship', pp. 72–3; SP, IV, pt. 2, p. 2210.
38 SP, IV, pt. 2, p. 2210.
39 Madden, p. lii; Hall, II, p. 195.
40 Hall, II, p. 195; Madden, p. lii, note 3; *Harpsfield*, p. 83.
41 Cit. Ives, *Boleyn*, p. 136.
42 Watson, *Vives and Education*, p. 90ff; Noreña, *Vives*, p. 104, note 129; p. 104, note 103; p. 106, note 4.
43 Kelly, *Trials*, p. 62.
44 Kelly, *Trials*, pp. 62–3.
45 Cit. Hume, *Wives*, p. 160.
46 Hall, II, pp. 145–7.
47 Cit. Claremont, p. 190 and note.
48 Cit. Hume, *Wives*, p. 160.

Chapter 8
1 BL Royal MS, 20, B, XVII; Dowling, 'Boleyn and Reform', p. 33.
2 L & P, IV, pt. 3, p. 2379.
3 Kelly, *Trials*, p. 59.
4 Kelly, *Trials*, p. 86.
5 CSP Venetian, IV, pp. 219–20; Cavendish, p. 79.
6 Hume, *Wives*, p. 162; Roper, p. 71.
7 Cavendish, pp. 80–82 and note 15; App. pp. 268–71; L & P, IV, pt. 3, pp. 2525–6.
8 L & P, IV, pt. 3, p. 2526.
9 Cavendish, pp. 87–8; p. 229, note 87.
10 Kelly, *Trials*, p. 90.
11 Cit. Kelly, *Trials*, p. 123; L & P, IV, pt. 3, pp. 2576–82; CSP Spanish, IV, pt. 2, p. 211.
12 CSP Spanish, IV, pt. 1, p. 232; Cavendish, p. xxvi; L & P, IV, pt. 3, p. 2679.
13 Ives, *Boleyn*, p. 137, ascribes it to Anne's hostility; and Ridley, *Henry VIII*, p. 164, points out that all contemporary writers blame Anne; but see Gwyn, p. 581, for the theory that it was not due to Anne, but to Henry's failure to get a divorce; and Scarisbrick, p. 229, for

'a putsch' by various nobles, due to Henry resenting this failure.

14 SP, I, pt. 1, p. 351; Friedmann, I, p. 127.
15 CSP Spanish, IV, pt. 1, p. 115; for Chapuys see Mattingly, 'Ambassador', p. 179ff.
16 CSP Spanish, IV, pt. 1, p. 220; p. 225.
17 CSP Spanish, IV, pt. 1, p. 225.
18 CSP Spanish, IV, pt. 1, p. 275; L & P, VI, p. 168.
19 CSP Spanish, IV, pt. 1, p. 117.
20 CSP Spanish, IV, pt. 1, pp. 351–2.
21 CSP Spanish, IV, pt. 1, p. 833.
22 CSP Spanish, IV, pt. 1, p. 762.
23 CSP Spanish, IV, pt. 2, p. 3.
24 CSP Spanish, IV, pt. 2, p. 33.
25 Cit. Ives, *Boleyn*, p. 173.
26 CSP Spanish, IV, pt. 2, p. 177.
27 Ives, *Boleyn*, p. 175; Friedmann, I, p. 128, note 3.
28 Hume, *Chronicle*, p. xix; p. 14; Hume, *Wives*, p. 271, note 1.
29 Cit. Brigden, p. 169; CSP Venetian, IV, p. 304; CSP Spanish, Further Supplement, p. 450.
30 Cavendish, p. 79; Ellis, 1st Series, II, p. 42.
31 Elton, *Police*, p. 11.
32 *Original Letters from Zürich*, II, p. 552.
33 Erickson, p. 189; 1 Kings 16:22–40.
34 Cit. Brigden, p. 211.
35 Ives, *Boleyn*, p. 175.
36 See Nicolas, *Henry VIII*, p. xxxii; p. 4; p. 13; p. 44; p. 47; p. 50; p. 72; p. 74; p. 90; p. 95; p. 101; p. 179; p. 183; p. 217; p. 222.
37 Colvin, IV, pp. 300–302 and note 3; *Henry VIII*, Act II, scene IV; Williams, *Henry VIII*, p. 113.
38 Cit. Williams, *Henry VIII*, p. 113.
39 CSP Spanish, IV, pt. 2, p. 385; p. 707.
40 Mattingly, *Catherine*, p. 235.
41 CSP Spanish, IV, pt. 2, p. 850.
42 Scarisbrick, p. 267ff.
43 CSP Spanish, IV, pt. 2, p. 63; p. 96.

Chapter 9
1 CSP Spanish, IV, pt. 2, p. 198; L & P, V, p. 161; Hume, *Wives*, p. 178; p. 181 and note 1.
2 CSP Spanish, IV, pt. 2, p. 487.
3 CSP Spanish, IV, pt. 2, p. 113.
4 CSP Spanish, IV, pt. 2, p. 113.
5 Scarisbrick, p. 290.
6 Colvin, IV, pt. 2, p. 164ff; cit. Mattingly, *Catherine*, p. 243.
7 Ives, *Boleyn*, p. 181, note 113.
8 Colvin, IV, pt. 2, p. 40ff.
9 Cit. Mackie, p. 355.
10 Ridley, *Cranmer*, pp. 50–51.
11 See Hamy, p. xiff.
12 Nicolas, *Henry VIII*, pp. 254–82; G.E.C., IV, p. 419 (Dorset).
13 CSP Spanish, IV, pt. 2, p. 487; p. 254.
14 Starkey, 'Representation', p. 197; L & P, V, p. 591.
15 See Arber, II, p. 35ff for 'Triumph at Calais'.
16 Arber, II, p. 39; Hamy, p. 72ff; the elevation of Thomas Boleyn to the Earldom of Wiltshire meant that his daughters could be termed 'Lady'.
17 Seymour, p. 37.
18 Knecht, pp. 227–8.
19 See Ives, *Boleyn*, p. 202 and notes 61–2, for Calais or even later in the year; Warnicke, *Boleyn*, pp. 100–101, suggests that Anne became Henry's mistress 'in the physical sense' after Archbishop Warham's death; Hume, *Wives*, p. 194, thinks the Pembroke creation was a reward; Scarisbrick, p. 309 and note 2, thinks Anne may have 'yielded' either before or after being made Marquess: 'we cannot know'.
20 *Chronicle of Calais*, p. 43ff; Nicolas, *Henry VIII*, p. 272.
21 Ridley, *Henry VIII*, p. 215.
22 Cit. Friedmann, I, p. 190, note 1.
23 Cit. Starkey, *Reign of Henry VIII*, p. 106.
24 Mattingly, *Catherine*, p. 246.
25 Cit. Ridley, *Cranmer*, p. 63.
26 SP, I, pt. 2, p. 398; Marius, p. 455.

27 Ellis, 1st Series, II, p. 39; Hall, II, p. 225; CSP Spanish, IV, pt. 2, p. 699.
28 Hume, *Chronicle*, pp. 12–13.
29 See BL Add. MS 6285 for 'Order of the Coronation'; Arber, II, p. 43ff for 'Triumphant Coronation'; Colvin, III, pt. 1, p. 265.
30 Hume, *Wives*, p. 205, note 1.
31 CSP Spanish, IV, pt. 2, p. 700.
32 Brigden, p. 211; Friedmann, I, p. 205 and note 2; Anglo, *Spectacle*, p. 258.
33 BL Add. MS 6285; Hume, *Chronicle*, p. 13.
34 Whittington.
35 King, *Iconography*, p. 196.
36 King, *Iconography*, p. 50ff.
37 Arber, II, pp. 52–60 for Udall, 'Coronation Verses'.
38 Brigden, p. 6; Arber, II, p. 48; Hume, *Chronicle*, p. 14.
39 Hume, *Chronicle*, p. 14.
40 Hall, II, p. 225; SP, I, pt. 2, p. 398.
41 SP, I, pt. 2, p. 398.
42 SP, I, pt. 2, p. 402ff.
43 Cit. Paul, p. 123.
44 CSP Spanish, IV, pt. 2, p. 789.
45 CSP Spanish, VI, p. 164; Book of Hours, BL Kings 9, fol. 66 & 231b; King, *Iconography*, p. 6.
46 CSP Spanish, IV, pt. 2, p. 789.
47 Nichols, *Regulations*, p. 125.
48 Nicolas, *Elizabeth of York*, p. 103; although both Warnicke, *Boleyn*, p. 164, and Ives, *Boleyn*, p. 212, suggest the baby was born before it was expected, the real point was surely the awkward fact that it had been conceived before its parents' marriage.
49 BL Harleian MS, Vol. 283, leaf 75; SP, I, pt. 2, p. 407, note 2.

Chapter 10
1 CSP Spanish, IV, pt. 2, p. 756; Ives, *Boleyn*, pp. 229–30; Mattingly, *Catherine*, p. 136.
2 Loades, p. 77.
3 L & P, V, p. 700; CSP Spanish, IV,

pt. 1, p. 527; Loades, p. 72.
4 CSP Spanish, IV, pt. 2, p. 630.
5 CSP Spanish, V, pt. 1, p. 551, and see Index; Hume, *Wives*, p. 243.
6 The boy's ill health may explain why Suffolk commandeered his bride, see Gunn, p. 132.
7 Knowles, *Religious Orders*, p. 182ff.
8 CSP Spanish, V, pt. 1, p. 21.
9 Rawlinson MS, D776, fols 94–104.
10 9 October 1534, SP, I, pt. 2, p. 426.
11 Cit. Ives, *Boleyn*, p. 272; p. 364.
12 CSP Spanish, Further Supplement, p. 4450; Byrne, *Lisle*, I, pp. 447–8, where the dating is corrected from 1535.
13 CSP Spanish, V, pt. 1, p. 19.
14 Langley, p. 3ff.
15 SP, I, pt. 2, pp. 415–17.
16 L & P, VII, p. 463.
17 Madden, p. lxiii; SP, I, pt. 2, p. 427.
18 SP, I, pt. 2, pp. 419–20.
19 Hume, *Chronicle*, pp. 40–41 and note 40.
20 Hume, *Wives*, p. 234.
21 Loades, p. 81, note 9; L & P, VII, p. 463.
22 Knowles, *Religious Orders*, p. 188–9; Neame, p. 198ff.
23 Thomas, pp. 398–9.
24 Colvin, III, pt. 1, p. 2, note 1; IV, p. 2; p. 5; Starkey, *Henry VIII: European Court*, p. 8.
25 Colvin, IV, pt. 2, pp. 104–5.
26 See Strong, *Renaissance Garden*, p. 25ff.
27 Colvin, IV, pt. 2, p. 241; Ives, *Boleyn*, p. 266–7 and note 54.
28 See Lowinsky, for analysis of the MS and this thesis.
29 See Dowling, *Latymer*, p. 30ff.
30 Ives, *Boleyn*, p. 286.
31 Strong, *Tudor Portraits*, I, p. 5–7.
32 Whittington; Dowling, *Latymer*, p. 53ff.
33 'Original documents relating to Katherine', pp. 572–4.
34 See Dowling, 'Boleyn and Reform', passim.

35 Dowling, 'Boleyn and Reform', p. 35; Dowling and Shakespeare, p. 97.
36 Dowling, *Latymer*, p. 61.
37 Dowling, *Latymer*, p. 61.
38 Friedmann, II, p. 56–8 and note 1; Latymer calls her Mary but she is generally referred to as Margaret or Madge: Dowling, *Latymer*, p. 62, note 33; SP, V, pt. 2, p. 7 and note 1.
39 CSP Spanish, V, pt. 1, p. 264; Seymour, p. 41ff.
40 Wriothesley, I, p. 43.
41 CSP Spanish, V, pt. 1, p. 344; Ives, *Boleyn*, p. 243.
42 CSP Spanish, V, pt. 1, p. 355; p. 311; p. 484; CSP Venetian, V, p. 27.
43 CSP Spanish, V, pt. 1, p. 571; Ortiz to Empress Isabella, 1 September 1535; cit. Friedmann, II, p. 138 and note 1.
44 CSP Spanish, V, pt. 1, p. 468; p. 264; p. 344.
45 Cit. Dewhurst, 'Miscarriages', p. 54; L & P, VII, p. 463.
46 Dewhurst, 'Miscarriages', p. 54; but both Ives, *Boleyn*, p. 286 and notes 4 and 11; and Warnicke, *Boleyn*, p. 175, accept that Anne was pregnant at this date; Warnicke points to between 26 June and 2 July as being the most likely period when she lost her child.
47 Hall, II, p. 209; Scarisbrick, p. 211.
48 CSP Spanish, V, pt. 2, p. 126.
49 L & P, IX, p. 294.
50 SP, I, pt. 2, pp. 415–17; Mathew, p. 50.
51 'Original documents relating to Katherine', p. 574.
52 CSP Spanish, V, pt. 1, p. 130.
53 Hume, *Chronicle*, p. 47ff.
54 SP, I, pt. 2, p. 451.

Chapter 11
1 Goldsmid, p. 6; Mattingly, *Catherine*, pp. 292–3, note 5, interprets this as referring to a husband although Loades, p. 78, note 5, thinks it refers to 'dubious male company'.
2 See CSP Spanish, V, pt. 2, pp. 10–24; Hume, *Chronicle*, for deathbed of Catherine.
3 CSP Spanish, V, pt. 2, p. 18; Sir Norman Moore, demonstrator of morbid anatomy at St Bartholomew's Hospital, later President of the Royal College of Physicians, 'Death of Catherine', p. 152; MacNalty, 'Death of Queen', p. 275.
4 Herbert, p. 555; Hall, II, p. 266; Clifford, p. 77; CSP Spanish, V, pt. 2, pp. 10–24.
5 Will of Catherine: BL Cotton MS Otho C, X fol. 917, Titus C, VIII, fol. 44; Herbert, p. 555.
6 'Wardrobe stuff of Katherine' in Nichols, *Inventories*, pp. 23–41.
7 Claremont, p. 253ff; L & P, X, pp. 102–4; Forrest, p. xii; p. 120.
8 CSP Spanish, V, pt. 2, p. 20.
9 Cit. Dowling, 'Boleyn and Reform', p. 43.
10 Wriothesley, I, p. 33; L & P, X, p. 104; de Carles, p. 242; Warnicke, *Boleyn*, p. 202ff, argues her case for the fall of Anne as following inevitably on the miscarriage of a deformed foetus, but there is no contemporary evidence for the deformity which would surely have been remarked had it existed (see Bernard, 'Fall', p. 586); Sander, writing in 1584, refers to 'a shapeless mass of flesh', words that could apply to any miscarried foetus.
11 Cit. Ives, *Boleyn*, p. 344; Wyatt, p. 444.
12 CSP Spanish, V, pt. 2, p. 28.
13 CSP Spanish, V, pt. 2, p. 20; Clifford, p. 79.
14 For the literature on 'faction', see esp. Ives, *Faction*.
15 See St Maur, p. 10ff; Seymour, p. 17ff.

16 Cit. Miller, *Nobility*, pp. 154–5.
17 His traditional date of birth is 1506, based on an inscription on a portrait, but his career suggests that around 1502 is more realistic.
18 SP, I, pt. 2, p. 577; sometimes incorrectly stated to be the eldest child, but St Maur, p. 20, leaves no doubt she was the fifth, with 1509 the most plausible date.
19 *Anglica Historia*, p. 337; Herbert, p. 575; SP, V, pt. 2, p. 7, note 1.
20 Seymour, p. 36.
21 Williams, *Henry VIII*, p. 142.
22 Starkey, 'Representation', p. 189; Starkey, *English Court*, p. 110.
23 L & P, X, pp. 242–5.
24 L & P, X, pp. 200–201; pp. 242–5; Ridley, *Letters*, p. 75.
25 L & P, X, p. 245.
26 L & P, X, p. 245; Ives, *Boleyn*, p. 361.
27 Cit. Hume, *Wives* p. 267; CSP, V, pt. 2, p. 10.
28 It was certainly rumoured that Smeaton was tortured as reported by George Constantine (Amyot, p. 64), although he could not find out for sure; Hume, *Chronicle*, pp. 60–61; Lowinsky, p. 192ff.
29 David Lyon, National Maritime Museum, to author.
30 Geoffrey Parnell, English Heritage, to author.
31 Wriothesley, I, p. 36ff.

Chapter 12
1 L & P, VI, p. 164.
2 CSP Spanish, V, pt. 2, p. 125.
3 But Ives, *Boleyn*, p. 361ff, thinks 30 April the crucial date.
4 CSP Spanish, V, pt. 1, p. 376.
5 See Ives, *Boleyn*, p. 374ff; Wyatt, p. 225.
6 See Ives, *Boleyn*, p. 390, who rightly calls it 'medically improbable'.
7 Cit. Hume, *Wives*, p. 272.
8 Ives, *Boleyn*, p. 386.
9 Amyot, p. 66.
10 See Ives, *Boleyn*, Ch. 17, for the fullest modern account of the trial, together with a detailed discussion of the sources.
11 Wriothesley, I, p. 38.
12 Ives, *Boleyn*, p. 377ff.
13 Ives, *Boleyn*, and Warnicke, *Boleyn*, share this view; but see Bernard, 'Fall', for the theory that Anne was guilty.
14 Clifford, p. 79; cit. Ives, *Boleyn*, p. 376; Amyot, p. 66.
15 CSP Spanish, V, pt. 2, p. 126.
16 Smith, 'Treason', p. 488.
17 Wriothesley, I, pp. 39–40; *Chronicle of Calais*, p. 46.
18 See L & P, X, pp. 381–2 and Ellis, 1st Series, Vol. II, pp. 52–68 for letters of Sir William Kingston concerning Anne in the Tower.
19 *Chronicle of Calais*, p. 46; Whittington.
20 Kelly, *Trials*, p. 244.
21 Kelly, *Trials*, p. 245ff.
22 Ridley, *Cranmer*, p. 104.
23 Ridley, *Cranmer*, pp. 109–11; a scornful letter from Anne said to have been written before her execution, referring to Jane Seymour, is certainly a forgery: the sentiments do not accord with her known utterances and the handwriting is totally unlike, BL Otho C, X fol. 218. Similarly the story of a book of devotions given at the last minute to Wyatt's sister dates only from 1745 and has been described as 'incapable of proof': see Marsham, 'Manuscript Book', p. 259–72.
24 L & P, X, p. 381.
25 See Hume, *Chronicle*, p. 70ff.
26 De Carles, pp. 269–71; Wriothesley, I, p. 41; Hamy, p. ccccxxxvii.
27 Ellis, 1st Series, II, p. 63.
28 Kelly, *Trials*, p. 259; L & P, X, p. 384.
29 Jackson, p. 144; L & P, X, p. 411; pp. 413–14.
30 L & P, X, p. 413; Nichols, *Foxe*, p. 283.

31 BL Add. MS 34,150, fols 47–52; Newcastle MS, Ne 01, unfoliated, for Account Book of James Nedham.
32 Colvin, IV, pt. 2, p. 45; p. 105; pt. 1, p. 27.
33 Wriothesley, I, p. 43ff.
34 Wriothesley, I, p. 42; p. 50.
35 CSP Venetian, IV, p. 287; Rowlands, p. 113.
36 CSP Spanish, V, pt. 1, p. 300; pt. 2, p. 124; SP, I, pt. 2, pp. 454–5; Goldsmid, pp. 4–190.
37 CSP Spanish, V, pt. 2, p. 124.
38 HMC Rutland, I, pp. 309–11.
39 CSP Spanish, V, pt. 2, p. 195; Wood, *Letters*, p. 262; Madden, pp. 6–8; p. 34.
40 Cit. Madden, p. clv.
41 L & P, X, p. 450.
42 Strype, I, pt. 2, p. 304.
43 Seymour, p. 43.
44 L & P, X, p. 447.
45 Wriothesley, I, p. 55.

Chapter 13
1 Miller, *Nobility*, p. 177.
2 Starkey, *Henry VIII: European Court*, p. 127.
3 L & P, XII, p. 254; p. 286.
4 L & P, XVII, p. 40; Rowlands, p. 114; Madden, p. 8; Savage, p. 71; HMC Bath, IV, p. 338.
5 Hume, *Chronicle*, p. 72.
6 Cit. Mackie, p. 381.
7 SP, VII, p. 685.
8 L & P, XI, p. 346.
9 See Ridley, *Henry VIII*, p. 285ff.
10 Byrne, *Letters*, pp. 141–3.
11 James, 'Kateryn', p. 110.
12 Byrne, *Letters*, pp. 150–54.
13 L & P, XI, p. 346; p. 510.
14 Starkey, *Reign of Henry VIII*, p. 117; L & P, XI, p. 188.
15 See Levine, pp. 120–21: since the King's Commissioners only wrote their favourable report for acquitting Catesby on 12 May 1536, when Queen Anne Boleyn was

already in the Tower awaiting trial, the Queen who pleaded for Catesby thereafter must have been Queen Jane Seymour, not her predecessor.
16 CSP Spanish, Further Supplement, p. 453.
17 Byrne, *Letters*, pp. 168–70.
18 Wriothesley, I, p. 64.
19 GEC. xii/i, p. 61, notes a and d (Somerset).
20 Miller, *Nobility*, p. 233ff.
21 L & P, XII, pt. 1, p. 600.
22 SP, I, pt. 2, p. 551.
23 L & P, Addenda I, pt. 1, pp. 430–31.
24 Cit. Chapman, p. 121; Rowlands, pp. 113–15.
25 Wriothesley, I, p. 65.
26 Hume, *Chronicle*, p. 73.
27 See Dewhurst, *Confinements*, p. 7.
28 'Queen Jane', scc Bell, pp. 113–56; Hume, *Chronicle*, p. 73.
29 BL MSS Catalogue, III, p. 504 (Cotton Julius XII).
30 SP, I, pt. 2, p. 571.
31 BL Cotton Nero C,X fol. 1; Nichols, *Edward the Sixth*, I, p. xxiii.
32 L & P, XII, pt. 2, p. 319.
33 Wriothesley, I, p. 68 and note d, who as a herald was unlikely to be mistaken; although Edward in his journal wrote that he was just about to be created when his father died, this presumably referred to his installation.
34 SP, VIII, pt. 2, p. 1; SP, I, pt. 2, p. 572.
35 L & P, XII, pt. 2, p. 339.
36 L & P, XII, pt. 2, p. 339.
37 SP, VIII, pt. 2, p. 1.
38 Hall, II, p. 280.
39 Nichols, *Edward the Sixth*, I, p. xxv, note a; L & P, XXI, pt. 2, p. 442; Smith, *Henry VIII*, p. 224; for will, see L & P, XII, pt. 2, pp. 372–4.
40 L & P, XII, pt. 2, pp. 340–41.
41 Hall, II, p. 280.
42 SP, V, pt. 2, pp. 5–7.

Chapter 14

1 Williams, *Henry VIII*, p. 174.
2 Hume, *Wives*, p. 315, note 1.
3 L & P, XII, pt. 2, p. 449.
4 Kaulek, pp. 80–81.
5 See Campbell, p. 197ff.
6 Byrne, *Letters*, p. 198.
7 Rowland, pp. 116–17.
8 SP, VIII, p. 15; p. 21; p. 59.
9 Byrne, *Letters*, p. 186.
10 Byrne, *Letters*, p. 192ff.
11 Kelly, *Trials*, p. 14.
12 Chamberlain, II, p. 149.
13 SP, VIII, pp. 142–6.
14 See Wernham, p. 142ff.
15 Cit. Mackie, p. 396.
16 Loades, pp. 120–21 describes the evidence as 'negligible'.
17 SP, VIII, p. xxxiv; p. 507; cit. Harris, 'Women', p. 278.
18 McConica, p. 178.
19 L & P, XIV, pt. 1, p. 15; p. 18; Miller, *Nobility*, p. 64–8 and note 142.
20 Miller, *Nobility*, p. 68.
21 See Bouterwek, p. 359ff; Isenburg, I, tafel 44; VI, tafel 17.
22 Iserloh, V, p. 523ff; Bouterwek, p. 339ff; Dolan, p. 9.
23 Mathew, p. 167; Bouterwek, p. 367; Ellis, 1st Series, II, p. 122ff.
24 Ellis, 1st Series, II, p. 123.
25 Bouterwek, p. 367.
26 SP, I, p. 605.
27 Chamberlain, *Holbein*, II, p. 178.
28 Rowlands, p. 117.
29 See Hacker and Kuhl, pp. 172–5; MacEntegart in Starkey, *Henry VIII: European Court*, p. 142 and Cat. xi, 2.
30 Campbell, p. 84ff; Pope-Hennessy, p. 321, note 41.
31 Bouterwek, App. A; Ellis, 1st Series, II, p. 121.
32 Peter Holman, BBC Radio 3, 23 June 1991.
33 L & P, XIV, pt. 2, p. 139ff.
34 Colvin, IV, pt. 2, p. 241.
35 Bouterwek, p. 374ff.
36 Bouterwek, p. 375; *Chronicle of Calais*, p. 167ff.
37 SP, VIII, p. 208ff.
38 Colvin, IV, p. 39.
39 Goldsmid, p. 6; Wriothesley, I, p. 109.
40 Strype, I, pt. 2, p. 455.
41 Wriothesley, I, p. 109, note g; Strype, I, p. 459.
42 Strickland, III, p. 48.
43 Burnet, I, p. 434.
44 L & P, XVIII, pt. 1, p. 513.
45 Campbell, p. 85; Hacker and Kuhl, p. 175.
46 Strype, I, pt. 2, p. 453.

Chapter 15

1 Hall, II, p. 302; Wriothesley I, pp. 111–12 and note c.
2 Goldsmid, p. 6.
3 Strype, I, pt. 2, p. 452; Goldsmid, *Rare Tracts*, p. 8.
4 Kelly, *Trials*, pp. 268–9.
5 Goldsmid, p. 8.
6 L & P, XIV, pt. 2, p. 280; *Original Letters from Zürich*, I, p. 627.
7 Goldsmid, p. 9; Strype, I, pt. 2, p. 454.
8 Goldsmid, p. 10.
9 Goldsmid, p. 10ff; Strype, I, pt. 2, p. 458ff.
10 Strype, I, pt. 2, p. 460.
11 Strype, I, pt. 2, p. 459.
12 Strype, I, pt. 2, p. 462.
13 Cit. King, *Women*, p. 41.
14 Wriothesley, I, p. 112 and note c.
15 Cit. Loades, pp. 127–8.
16 Brigden, p. 309.
17 See Strong, *Tudor Portraits*, I, pp. 41–4.
18 Smith, *Tragedy*, App., pp. 209–11.
19 Kaulek, p. 218; L & P, XVI, p. 5; cit. Strickland, III, p. 118.
20 L & P, XVI, p. 655; *Original Letters from Zürich*, I, p. 205.
21 Dowling, *Humanism*, p. 242.
22 Strickland, III, p. 98.
23 See Smith, *Tragedy*, pp. 37–71.
24 Cit. Harris, 'Marriage', p. 373.
25 Ellis, 1st Series, II, pp. 28–9.
26 J. M. Robinson, Librarian to the

Duke of Norfolk, letter to author; HMC Bath, II, p. 8.

27 Cit. Smith, *Tragedy*, p. 55.

28 Survey of London, XXIII, pt. 1, p. 138ff; HMC Bath, II, p. 8.

29 L & P, XVI, p. 618; Hall, II, p. 380.

30 Cit. Smith, *Tragedy*, p. 59.

31 Hall, II, p. 380.

32 L & P, XV, p. 254; p. 321; Smith, *Tragedy*, p. 124, suggests sex took place 'three months before' the marriage, which fits; L & P, XV, p. 446.

33 L & P, XV, p. 363.

34 See Scarisbrick, p. 423; and Starkey, *Reign of Henry VIII*, p. 123.

35 Goldsmid, p. 5ff.

36 Cit. Hume, *Wives*, p. 361.

37 SP, VIII, p. 372.

38 *Original Letters from Zürich*, II, p. 205.

39 Goldsmid, p. 12.

40 L & P, XV, p. 446; Williams, *Henry VIII*, p. 178ff; p. 196; Ellis, 2nd Series, II, p. 158.

41 SP, VIII, p. 395.

42 Goldsmid, pp. 16–22; Kelly, *Trials*, p. 273.

43 Kelly, *Trials*, p. 261.

44 SP, I, p. 638ff.

45 BL Cotton MS, Otho, C, X fols 232; 236; 238; fols 240–41; Burnet, 1, p. 446ff; Goldsmid, p. 24.

46 SP, VIII, p. 419.

47 SP, VIII, p. 412; L & P, XV, p. 61.

48 L & P, XV, p. 438.

49 Wriothesley, I, p. 123.

50 Williams, *Residences*, p. 179; cit. Smith, *Tragedy*, p. 123.

Chapter 16

1 *Rutilans Rosa Sine Spina* (Blushing rose without a thorn), cit. Strickland, III, p. 122 and note 2.

2 Nichols, *Foxe*, p. 260.

3 BL Stowe MS 559 fols 55–68.

4 Colvin, III, pt. 2, p. 234; Ballantyne, p. 297ff.

5 Wayment, *Kings College: Great Windows*, p. 38.

6 H. C. Wayment to the author; Wayment, *Kings College: Great Windows*, p. 21.

7 L & P, XVI, p. 5.

8 HMC Bath, II, p. 8ff.

9 L & P, XVI, p. 149.

10 Smith, *Tragedy*, p. 161.

11 L & P, XVI, pp. 148–9.

12 L & P, XVI, p. 60.

13 MacNalty, *Henry VIII*, pp. 159–65; for the theory of scurvy, see Kybett.

14 L & P, XVI, p. 148.

15 L & P, XVI, p. 284ff.

16 CSP Spanish, VI, p. 305; Folger Shakespeare MS 115/27 (STC 15982).

17 L & P, XV, p. 493.

18 L & P, XV, p. 446; cit. Strickland, III, p. 82.

19 Leti, *Vita di Elisabetta*, cit. Strickland, III, p. 81.

20 CSP Spanish, VI, p. 305.

21 CSP Spanish, VI, pt. 1, p. xix.

22 L & P, XVI, p. 550.

23 APC, VII, pp. 352–3.

24 The practice of two children within the same family bearing the same forename occurred when the first child was expected to die; the family name would be given to a newborn sibling, only to find the original bearer unexpectedly surviving. The existence of *three* Thomas Culpepers in some kind of relationship to Katherine Howard of course makes their biographical details remarkably confusing to disentangle.

25 See Smith, *Tragedy*, p. 162ff.

26 Hall, II, p. 313.

27 The letter is not dated, but Smith, *Tragedy*, p. 168, plausibly assigns it to this period when the Queen was already showing Culpeper 'marked favours', although the Public Record Office (PRO, SP.I, Vol. 167, fol. 14) puts it at August 1541.

28 PRO SP.I, Vol. 167, fol. 14.

29 L & P, XVI, p. 435; p. 507.
30 L & P, XVI, pp. 517–18.
31 L & P, XVI, p. 636.
32 Ridley, *Cranmer*, p. 220.
33 Nichols, *Foxe*, p. 260.
34 Ridley, *Cranmer*, p. 220.
35 Burnet, I, p. 493.
36 L & P, XVI, pp. 665–6.
37 L & P, XVI, p. 689ff.
38 L & P, XVI, p. 691.
39 *Hampton Court Palace*, p. 32; for example, Green, *Haunting at Hampton Court*, has Katherine hammering on the door: 'Henry, Henry, for God's sake see me'; for the reconstruction, Simon Thurley to the author.
40 Kelly, *Trials*, p. 275.
41 Strickland, III, p. 155.
42 L & P, XVI, pp. 617–18.
43 L & P, XVI, pp. 618–19; Wriothesley, I, p. 132.
44 L & P, XVI, pp. 630–31.
45 SP, I, p. 692.
46 Aungier, p. 90; SP, I, p. 691.
47 APC VII, pp. 352–6; L & P, XVI, p. 649.
48 L & P, XVI, p. 642.
49 L & P, XVI, pp. 570–72.
50 SP, I, p. 721.
51 L & P, XVII, p. 1.
52 L & P, XVII, p. 44.
53 L & P, XVII, p. 50.
54 L & P, XVII, p. i and note 1.
55 L & P, XVII, p. 44; p. 50.
56 Ellis, 1st Series, II, p. 128.
57 Hume, *Chronicle*, p. 86.

Chapter 17
1 CSP Spanish, VI, pt. 1, p. 411.
2 Colvin, IV, pt. 2, p. 234.
3 L & P, XVII, p. 13; cit. Burnet, I, p. 495.
4 Burnet, I, p. 496.
5 CSP Spanish, VI, pt. 1, p. 473.
6 Herbert, p. 677; Nucius, p. 48.
7 L & P, XVI, p. 614; XVII, p. 17.
8 CSP Spanish, VI, pt. 1, p. 408; p. 414.
9 Cit. Strickland, III, pp. 84–5.
10 See Macray, pp. 249–64; L & P, XVII, p. 52.
11 L & P, XVII, p. 676; SP, I, p. 716; Ridley, *Cranmer*, p. 225.
12 L & P, XIX, pt. 1, p. 369.
13 Pitscottie, I, p. 406.
14 L & P, XVIII, pt. 1, p. 29.
15 Burnet, I, p. 496.
16 See James, 'Kateryn', p. 12, and the fact that marriage negotiations were entered for Catherine first, although a date as late as 1514 (Martienssen, p. 18) has been suggested; we know that Catherine was born after July 1511, since her mother referred to her daughter as being under twelve years old in a letter 14 July 1523; William Parr must have been conceived in November 1512, which suggests earlier rather than later in 1512 for Catherine's birth (or even the winter of 1511); James, letter to the author.
17 J. C. Flugel, 'The Character and Married Life of Henry VIII' in *Psychoanalysis and History*; cit. Smith, *Henry VIII*, p. 65.
18 James, 'Kateryn', p. 108.
19 Martienssen, p. 24; James, 'Kateryn', p. 108, and letter to the author; Dowling, *Humanism*, p. 236; Nichols, *Edward the Sixth*, I, p. 16.
20 Cit. Martienssen, p. 34; but James, 'Kateryn', p. 108, implies Dacre's opposition despite this praise.
21 The confusion has arisen owing to the fact that young Edward's grandfather, another Edward (Lord) Borough, in his early sixties at this date, had become insane: he ended his life in care in the house of his son, where Catherine Parr spent her brief first married life; see James, 'Kateryn', pp. 108–9; G.E.C., II, pp. 422–3.
22 G.E.C., (Latimer) VII, p. 484 note a.
23 Cit. James, 'Kateryn', p. 110.
24 L & P, XX, pt. 1, p. 266; Dent-

Brocklehurst MS.
25 L & P, XVIII, pt. 1, p. 478.
26 L & P, XVIII, pt. 1, p. 483; Somerset, p. 14.
27 Auerbach, p. 20; L & P, XVIII, pt. 1, p. 483.
28 L & P, XVIII, pt. 1, p. 472; p. 513; XX, pt. 1, p. 65.
29 Strong, *Tudor Portraits*, I, App. 2, pp. 363–5; Strickland, III, p. 295.
30 L & P, XVIII, pt. 1, p. 266; CSP Spanish, VII, p. 55.
31 Williams, *Henry VIII*, p. 234; L & P, XIX, pt. 2, p. 688ff.
32 L & P, XVIII, pt. 1, p. 50.
33 Strong, *Eworth*, p. ix; Auerbach, p. 69, note 1 and 2.
34 Williams, *Henry VIII*, p. 35; L & P, XXI, pt. 1, p. 321; *Legend of Throckmorton*, p. 18.
35 Hume, *Chronicle*, p. 108.
36 CSP Spanish, VI, pt. 2, p. 447; SP, IX, p. 505.
37 G.E.C., IX, pp. 669–74, note a (Northampton); note b; note d; X, pp. 309–11 (Parr).
38 Nichols, *Edward the Sixth*, I, p. xxxviii; Byrne, *Letters*, p. 365.
39 Loades, p. 117.
40 CSP Spanish, VIII, p. 2.
41 SP, I, p. 763.
42 Scarisbrick, p. 486.
43 Williams, *Henry VIII*, p. 246.
44 Cit. Strickland, III, p. 214; Madden, p. xcii.
45 BL Lansdowne MS 1236, fol. 9; Strype, II, pt. 2, p. 331–2.
46 Byrne, *Letters*, p. 365–7.
47 SP, X, p. 13, note 2.
48 Hamilton, II, p. 326.
49 L & P, XIX, pt. 2, p. 58; cit. Martienssen, p. 180.
50 Ridley, *Cranmer*, p. 248; Colvin, III, p. 261.
51 Hume, *Chronicle*, p. 107.

Chapter 18
1 L & P, XVIII, pt. 1, p. 283.
2 Haugaard, p. 358.
3 Cit. Claremont, p. 159, note 2; cit.

Read, p. 42.
4 Harris, 'Women', p. 280.
5 James, 'Devotional Writings', p. 135.
6 Warnicke, *Women*, p. 95.
7 See Mueller, p. 177 for this 'degendering from explicit masculinist norms in the direction of a universalizing of the Christian gospel'.
8 Haugaard, pp. 354–5.
9 Haugaard, p. 347.
10 *Lamentation of Queene Catherine*, pp. 293–313 and note 3; James, 'Devotional Writings', p. 136.
11 *Lamentation of Queene Catherine*, p. 295ff.
12 Brigden, p. 347 and note 120.
13 *Lamentation of Queene Catherine*, p. 311.
14 See James, 'Devotional Writings', pp. 137–8.
15 Dowling, 'Woman's Place', p. 42.
16 Brigden, p. 359; Bindoff, III, pp. 550–51.
17 L & P, XX, pt. 1, p. 1.
18 CSP Spanish, VIII, p. 104.
19 Rule, p. 22; L & P, XX, pt. 1, p. 3.
20 SP, X, p. 715ff.
21 BL Cotton MS, Vespasian, F, III, 18 fol. 42; Nero, C, X 4, fol. 7; Strype, II, pt. 2.
22 Nichols, *Edward the Sixth*, p. 9.
23 Cit. Somerset, p. 13; Wood, *Letters*, III, p. 178.
24 Somerset, p. 13.
25 Cit. Martienssen, p. 15; Bindoff, I, pp. 440–41; Muir, p. 273.
26 L & P, XXI, pt. 1, p. 136; pp. 514–15; p. 436.
27 Read, p. 42; Starkey, *Reign of Henry VIII*, pp. 143–4.
28 Brigden, p. 370ff.
29 Herbert, p. 735; Foxe, *Book of Martyrs*, first published abroad 1559; first printed in England 1563; Burnet, I, p. 540.
30 Burnet, I, p. 540.
31 Martienssen, p. 215ff.
32 Foxe, pp. 553–61; Wood, *Letters*, II, p. 98.

33 L & P, XXI, pt. 1, p. 696.
34 Ridley, *Cranmer*, p. 396 and note.
35 Cit. Knecht, p. 411.
36 Strype, II, pt. 2, pp. 337–8.
37 Strype, II, pt. 2, p. 339.
38 Cit. Starkey, *Reign of Henry VIII*, pp. 133–4; L & P, XXI, p. 395.
39 SP, XI, p. 395.
40 L & P, XXI, pt. 2, p. 307.
41 Cit. Robinson, p. 49.
42 Williams, *Norfolk*, p. 9ff; Robinson, p. 49ff.
43 Robinson, p. 243, note 12.
44 Williams, *Norfolk*, p. 13; SP, I, p. 891 and notes 1 and 2.
45 L & P, XXI, pt. 2, pp. 359–60.
46 L & P, XXI, pt. 2, p. 282.
47 Smith, *Henry VIII*, p. 13; Starkey, *English Court*, p. 116ff; Ridley, *Cranmer*, p. 257ff.
48 See Miller, 'Unwritten Will', pp. 87–105; Tytler, I, p. 18.
49 L & P, XXI, pt. 2, pp. 320–21; *Foedera*, pp. 142–5.

Chapter 19

1 Strype, II, pt. 2, p. 517.
2 *Foedera*, pp. 142–5.
3 HMC Salisbury, I, p. 61; Hume, *Chronicle*, p. 158; Jordan, *Edward VI*, I, p. 368ff.
4 Seymour, p. 73; CSP Domestic, pp. 19–22; Jordan, *Edward VI*, I, p. 370.
5 Tytler, I, p. 64.
6 Ellis, 1st Series, II, p. 152.
7 Colvin, III, pt. 2, p. 64.
8 Ellis, 1st Series, II, p. 152.
9 Maclean, pp. 44–5; Dent-Brocklehurst MSS.
10 Nichols, *Edward the Sixth*, I, p. 41.
11 BL Lansdowne MS, 1236, fol. 26.
12 Jordan, *Edward VI*, I, p. 374ff.
13 Nichols, *Edward the Sixth*, I, p. 46.
14 Jordan, *Chronicle*, p. 6; L & P, XIX, pt. 1, p. 394.
15 Seymour, p. 222.
16 CSP Spanish, IX, p. 123; Seymour, p. 225.
17 Cit. Martienssen, p. 232.

18 *Legend of Throckmorton*, p. 18; Jordan, *Edward VI*, I, p. 369ff.
19 Cit. Williams, *Elizabeth*, p. 13ff.
20 Cit. James, 'Kateryn', p. 117.
21 Bentley, *Monument*, II, 'Fourth Lampe'; I, 'Second Lampe'.
22 Tytler, I, p. 102.
23 L & P, VIII, p. 989; *Legend of Throckmorton*, p. 18 (often misquoted as '*His* house …').
24 CSP Domestic, p. 9; Strickland, III, p. 278.
25 CSP Domestic, p. 11.
26 Tytler, I, p. 140.
27 Tytler, I, p. 140.
28 Cit. Martienssen, p. 237.
29 BL Lansdowne MS, 2, fol. 46; fol. 47; Harris, 'Women', p. 279, note 145; CSP Domestic, p. 21.
30 See Strickland, III, p. 295 and note 1.
31 BL Cotton, Nero, C, X fol. 10/13; Jordan, *Chronicle*, pp. 10–11; p. 107.
32 Nichols, *Machyn*, p. 45; p. 46; Nichols, *Chronicle*, p. 27.
33 Bouterwek, p. 139.
34 CSP Spanish, XI, p. 279.
35 Bouterwek, p. 140.
36 For Brouckhusen affair, see CSP Domestic, p. 87; p. 47; Macray, p. 264; Bouterwek, p. 146ff.
37 APC, New Series, V, p. 353.
38 Bouterwek, p. 139; Tytler, II, p. 433.
39 CSP Domestic, p. 63.
40 APC, New Series, II, p. 81; p. 471.
41 *Loseley MSS*, pp. 9–14; Colvin, IV, pt. 2, p. 73; Williams, *Henry VIII*, p. 178.
42 Cit. *Foedera*, XIV, pp. 709–14; *Excerpta*, pp. 295–302.
43 APC, New Series, VI, p. 128; Nichols, *Machyn*, p. 144ff.
44 Ayloff, p. 2; p. 15ff; *Excerpta*, pp. 303–13.

Chapter 20

1 Cit. Mattingly, *Catherine*, p. 310, note 18.

2 L & P, VI, p. 163.
3 Cit. Harris, 'Property', p. 615.
4 SP, II, p. 560.
5 See McLaren, pp. 22–46.
6 L & P, XVI, pp. 50–51.
7 Wayment, 'St Margaret's' pp. 292–8.
8 HMC Bath, IV, p. 371.
9 Hammond, *Tower of London*, pp. 34–5.
10 Morshead, p. 49, note a; Scarisbrick, p. 497, note 4.
11 Ballard, p. 69.
12 Garnett, p. 13.
13 Garnett, p. 15ff.
14 Cit. Loades, App. 3, p. 371.
15 Gunton, p. 57; p. 335; Swain, p. 42.
16 Barcroft, p. 45; Sweeting, p. 30.

REFERENCE BOOKS

Details of only those books, documents, etc, cited in abbreviated form in the References; a full bibliography is impracticable for reasons of space. The place of publication is London unless otherwise stated.

(APC) Acts of the Privy Council

AMYOT, THOMAS, 'Transcript of an original Manuscript containing a Memorial from George Constantyne to Thomas Lord Cromwell', *Archaeologia*, 22, 1831

The Anglica Historia of Polydore Vergil AD 1485–1537, ed. with a translation by Denys Hay, Camden Series, 74, 1950

ANGLO, SYDNEY, *Spectacle, Pageantry and Early Tudor Policy*, Oxford, 1969

ANGLO, SYDNEY, 'The *British History* in early Tudor propaganda. With an appendix of manuscript pedigrees of the Kings of England, Henry VI to Henry VIII', *Bulletin of the John Rylands Library*, 44, Manchester, 1961

ANGLO, SYDNEY, 'The Court Festivals of King Henry VII: A study based upon the account books of John Heron, Treasurer of the Chamber', *Bulletin of the John Rylands Library*, 43, Manchester, 1960

ANGLO, SYDNEY, 'The London Pageants for the Reception of Katharine of Aragon: November 1501', *Journal of the Warburg and Courtauld Institutes*, 26, 1963

ARBER, EDWARD, *An English Garner*, II, 1879

ARMSTRONG, C. A. J., *England, France and Burgundy in the Fifteenth Century*, 1983

ARMSTRONG, EDWARD, *The Emperor Charles V*, 2 Vols, 1910

AUERBACH, ERNA, *Tudor Artists. A Study of Painters in the Royal Service and of Portraiture on Illuminated Documents from the Accession of Henry VIII to the death of Elizabeth I*, 1954

AUNGIER, G. J., *The History and Antiquities of Syon Monastery*, 1840

AYLOFF, SIR JOSEPH, Bart.,'An Account of some ancient monuments in Westminster Abbey', in *Vetusta Monumenta quae ad Rerum Britannicarum Memoriam Conservandum*, Society of Antiquaries, 2 Vols, 1747

(BL) British Library MSS

BALLANTYNE, J. W., 'The "Byrth of Mankynde"', *Journal of Obstetrics and Gynaecology of the British Empire*, 10, 1906

BALLARD, GEORGE, *Memoirs of Several Ladies of Great Britain who have been celebrated for their Writings* ... (1st edn 1752) Oxford, 1775

BARCROFT, MICHAEL, '"Luckiest of All". An Insight into a crucial period of Peterborough history', 1983

BEHRENS, BETTY, 'A note on Henry VIII's divorce project of 1514', *Bulletin of the Institute of Historical Research*, 11, 1934

BELL, ROBERT, ed., *Ancient Poems, Ballads and Songs of the Peasantry of England*, 1857

BENTLEY, THOMAS, *The Monument of Matrones: containing seven severall Lamps of Virginitie*, 3 Vols, 1582

BERNARD, G. W., 'The fall of Anne Boleyn', *English Historical Review*, 106, 1991

BERNARD, G. W., 'The rise of Sir William Compton, early Tudor courtier', *English Historical Review*, 96, 1981

BINDOFF, S. T., *The House of Commons, 1509–1558*, 3 Vols, 1982

BOUTERWEK, A. W., 'Anna von Cleve, Gemahlin Heinrich VIII, König von England', *Zeitschrift des Bergischen Geschichtsvereins*, 4, 1867 and 6, 1869

BRANDI, C., *Charles-Quint. 1500–1558*, traduit de l'allemand par Guy de Budé, Paris, 1939

BRIGDEN, SUSAN, *London and the Reformation*, Oxford, 1989

BURNET, GILBERT, DD, *The History of the Reformation of the Church of England*, new revised edn by Nicholas Pocock, I, Oxford, 1865

BUSCH, DR WILHELM, *England under the Tudors*, I, 1895

BYRNE, M. ST CLARE, ed., *The Letters of King Henry VIII. A Selection with a few other Documents*, new edition, 1968

BYRNE, M. ST CLARE, ed., *The Lisle Letters*, Chicago, 1981

(CSP) Calendar of State Papers, Spanish

(CSP) Calendar of State Papers, Spanish, Further Supplement to Vols 1 and 2, ed. Garrett Mattingly, 1947

(CSP) Calendar of State Papers, Spanish, Supplement to Vols 1 and 2, ed. G. A. Bergenroth, 1868

(CSP) Calendar of State Papers, Venetian

(CSP) Calendar of State Papers, Domestic, 1547–1580

CAMDEN, W., *Annales rerum Anglicarum et Hibernicarum ...*, 1615

CAMPBELL, LORNE, *Renaissance Portraits. European Portrait-Painting in the Fourteenth, Fifteenth and Sixteenth Centuries*, 1990

CARLES, LANCELOT DE, 'Poème sur la mort d'Anne Boleyn', in Georges Ascoli, *La Grande-Bretagne devant l'Opinion Française, depuis la guerre de cent ans jusqu'à la fin du XVIe siècle*, Paris, 1927

CASTRO, AMERICO, *The Structure of Spanish History*, Princeton, 1954

CAVENDISH, GEORGE, *The Life and Death of Cardinal Wolsey*, ed. R. S. Sylvester, Early English Text Society, 1959

CHAMBERLAIN, ARTHUR B., *Hans Holbein the Younger*, 2 Vols, 1913

CHAMBERS, R. W., *Thomas More*, 1935

CHAPMAN, HESTER W., *The Last Tudor King. A study of Edward VI*, 1958

CHRIMES, S. B., *Henry VII*, 1972

The Chronicle of Calais in the reigns of Henry VII and Henry VIII to the year 1540, ed. N. G. Nichols, Camden Society, 1846

CLAREMONT, FRANCESCA, *Catherine of Aragon*, 1939

CLIFFORD, HENRY, *The Life of Jane Dormer Duchess of Feria*, ed. Rev Joseph Stevenson, SJ, 1887

CLIVE, MARY, *This Sun of York. A biography of Edward IV*, 1973

COLEMAN, CHRISTOPHER, and STARKEY, DAVID, eds, *Revolution Reassessed. Revisions in the History of Tudor Government and Administration*, Oxford, 1986

COLVIN, H., ed., *The History of the King's Works*, III, 1975; IV, 1982

COOPER, C. H., *Annals of Cambridge*, I, 1842

COOPER, C. H., *Memoir of Margaret Countess of Richmond and Derby*, Cambridge, 1874

DAVEY, HENRY, *History of English Music*, 1895

Dent-Brocklehurst MSS, Sudeley Castle, Gloucestershire.

DEWHURST, JACK, *Royal Confinements*, 1980

DEWHURST, JOHN, 'The alleged miscarriages of Catherine of Aragon and Anne Boleyn', *Medical History*, 28, 1984

DICKENS, A. G., *Thomas Cromwell and the English Reformation*, 1959

DODDS, M. H., 'Political Prophecies in the Reign of Henry VIII', *Modern Language Review*, 11, 1916

DOLAN, J. P., CSC., *The Influence of Erasmus, Witzel and Cassander in the Church Ordinances and Reform Proposals of the United Duchies of Cleve during the Middle Decades of the 16th Century*, Münster, Westfalen, 1957

DOWLING, MARIA, *Humanism in the Age of Henry VIII*, 1986

DOWLING, MARIA, 'A Woman's Place? Learning and the Wives of Henry VIII', *History Today*, 41, 1991

DOWLING, MARIA, 'Anne Boleyn and Reform', *Journal of Ecclesiastical History*, 35, 1984

DOWLING, MARIA, 'Humanist Support for Katherine of Aragon', *Bulletin of the Institute of Historical Research*, 56, 1982

DOWLING, MARIA, ed., *William Latymer's Chronickille of Anne Boleyn*, Camden Miscellany, 4th Series, 39, 1990

DOWLING, MARIA and SHAKESPEARE, JOY, 'Religion and Politics in mid-Tudor England through the eyes of an English Protestant Woman: the Recollections of Rose Hickman', *Bulletin of the Institute of Historical Research*, 54, 1980

EAVES, R. G., *Henry VIII's Scottish Diplomacy. 1513–1524. England's relations with the Regency Government of James V*, New York, 1971

ELLIOTT, J. H., *Imperial Spain 1469–1716*, 1969

ELLIOTT, J. H., *Spain and Its World. 1500–1700*, 1989

ELLIS, HENRY, *Original Letters illustrative of English History*, 1st Series, 3 Vols, 1825

ELLIS, HENRY, *Original Letters illustrative of English History*, 2nd Series, 4 Vols, 1827

ELLIS, HENRY, *Original Letters illustrative of English History*, 3rd Series, 3 Vols, 1846

ELTON, G. R., *Policy and Police. The Enforcement of the Reformation in the Age of Thomas Cromwell*, Cambridge, 1972

ELTON, G. R., *The Tudor Revolution in Government. A Study of Administrative Changes in the Reign of Henry VIII*, Cambridge, 1953

ERICKSON, CAROLLY, *Anne Boleyn*, 1984

Excerpta Historica, or, Illustrations of English History, Printed by Samuel Bentley, 1831

FERNÁNDEZ-ARMESTO, FELIPE, *Ferdinand and Isabella*, 1975

Foedera ..., ed. Thomas Rymer, VI, 1741, republished 1967

Folger Shakespeare MSS, Folger Shakespeare Library, Washington DC, USA

FORREST, WILLIAM, *The History of Grisild the Second: A Narrative in Verse, of the Divorce of Queen Katharine of Aragon*, ed. W. D. Macray, Roxburghe Club, 1875

FOXE, JOHN, *Book of Martyrs (Actes and Monuments of these latter perillous dayes ...)*, 1563

FRANKLYN, CHARLES A. H., *The Genealogy of Anne the Quene*, Brighton, Sussex, 1977

FRIEDMANN, PAUL, *Anne Boleyn. A Chapter in English History. 1527–1536*, 2 Vols, 1884

FURNIVALL, F. J., *Early English Meals and Manners*, Early English Text Society, 1931

GAIRDNER, JAMES, ed., *Memorials of Henry VII*, 1858

GARNETT, F. B., 'Queen Katherine Parr and Sudeley Castle', *Transactions of the Cumberland and Westmorland Antiquarian and Archaeological Society*, Kendal, 1894

G. E. C., ed., *The Complete Peerage*, 13 Vols, reproduced edn, 1982

GIUSTINIAN, SEBASTIAN, *Four Years at the Court of Henry VIII. January 12 1515 to July 26 1519*, trans. by Rawdon Brown, 2 Vols, 1854

GOLDSMID, E. and G., eds, *A Collection of Eighteen Rare and Curious Historical Tracts and Pamphlets*, Edinburgh, 1886

GRAY, J. H., *The Queens College of St Margaret and St Bernard in the University of Cambridge*, 1899

GREEN, NORAH, *Haunting of Hampton Court*, 1980

GUNN, S. J., *Charles Brandon, Duke of Suffolk 1484–1545*, Oxford, 1988

GUNTON, SIMON, *The History of the Church of Peterburgh*, 1686

GWYN, PETER, *The King's Cardinal. The Rise and Fall of Thomas Wolsey*, 1990

(HMC) Historical Manuscripts Commission, Bath Papers, II and IV (*Seymour Papers*), 1907 and 1968

(HMC) Historical Manuscripts Commission, Rutland Papers, 12 Report, Appendix, Pt. IV, I, 1888

(HMC) Historical Manuscripts Commission, Salisbury Papers, I, 1883

HACKER, PETER and KUHL, CANDY, 'A Portrait of Anne of Cleves', *Burlington Magazine*, March 1992

HALL, EDWARD, *Henry VIII*, introduction by Charles Whibley, 2 Vols, 1904

Hamilton Papers, ed. J. Bain, 2 Vols, Edinburgh, 1890

HAMMOND, PETER, *The Tower of London*, Department of the Environment, 1987

Hampton Court Palace, Department of the Environment, 1988

HAMY, P. A., SJ, *Entrevue de François Premier avec Henry VIII, à Boulogne-sur-Mer, en 1532. Intervention de la France dans l'Affaire du Divorce*, 1905

HARE, CHRISTOPHER, *A Great Emperor. Charles V, 1519–1558*, 1917

Harpsfield's Narrative of the Divorce, ed. Lord Acton, 1913

HARRIS, BARBARA J., *Edward Stafford, Third Duke of Buckingham, 1478–1521*, Stanford, California, 1986

HARRIS, BARBARA J., 'Marriage Sixteenth-Century Style: Elizabeth Stafford and the third Duke of Norfolk', *Journal of Social History*, 15, 1982

HARRIS, BARBARA J., 'Property, Power and Personal Relations: Elite Mothers and Sons in Yorkist and Early Tudor England', *Signs*, 15, 1990

HARRIS, BARBARA J., 'Women and Politics in early Tudor England', *The Historical Journal*, 33, 1990

Hatfield Papers, Hatfield, Hertfordshire

HAUGAARD, WILLIAM P., 'Katherine Parr: the Religious Convictions of a Renaissance Queen', *Renaissance Quarterly*, XXII, 1969

HAY, DENYS, ed., *The Letters of James V*, Edinburgh, 1954

HERBERT OF CHERBURY, LORD, *The History of England under Henry VIII*, 1870

HOGREFE, PEARL, *Tudor Women. Commoners and Queens*, Iowa, 1975

HUME, MARTIN, *The Wives of Henry the Eighth and the parts they played in history*, 1905

HUME, MARTIN, trans. with notes and introduction, *Chronicle of King Henry VIII of England, being a contemporary record of some of the principal events of the reigns of Henry VIII and Edward VI, written in Spanish by an unknown hand*, 1889

IONGH, JANE DE, *Margaret of Austria. Regent of the Netherlands*, trans. from the Dutch by M. D. Herter Norton, 1954

ISENBURG, WILHELM KARL PRINZ ZU, *Europäische Stammtafeln*, fortgeführt von Frank Baron Freytag von Loringhoven, Band I, Marburg, 1980; Band II, Marburg, 1984; Band VI, Marburg, 1978

ISERLOH, ERWIN, GLAZIK, JOSEPH and JEDIN, HUBERT, *Reformation and Counter Reformation. History of the Church*, V, 1980

IVES, E. W., *Anne Boleyn*, Oxford, 1986

IVES, E. W., *Faction in Tudor England*, revised edition, 1986

JACKSON, REV CANON J. E., 'Wulfhall and the Seymours', *Wiltshire Archaeological and Natural History Magazine*, 15, 1875

JAMES, SUSAN E., 'Queen Kateryn Parr. 1512–1548', *Transactions of the Cumberland and Westmorland Antiquarian and Archaeological Society*, 88, 1988

JAMES, SUSAN E., 'The Devotional Writings of Queen Catherine Parr', *Transactions of the Cumberland and Westmorland Antiquarian and Archaeological Society*, 82, 1982

JONES, MICHAEL K., and UNDERWOOD, MALCOLM G., *The King's Mother. Lady Margaret Beaufort Countess of Richmond and Derby*, Cambridge, 1992

JORDAN, W. K., *The Chronicle and Political Papers of King Edward VI*, Ithaca, New York, 1966

JORDAN, W. K., *Edward VI: (I) The Young King. The Protectorship of the Duke of Somerset*, 1968

JORDAN, W. K., *Edward VI: (II) The Threshold of Power. The Dominance of the Duke of Northumberland*, 1970

JOURDA, PIERRE, *Marguerite d'Angoulême. Duchesse d'Alençon. Reine de Navarre (1492–1549)*, Paris, 1930

KAULEK, JEAN, ed., *Correspondence Politique de M. de Castillon et de Marillac*, Paris, 1885

KELLY, H. A., *The Matrimonial Trials of Henry VIII*, Stanford, California, 1976

KELLY, H. A., 'Kinship, Incest, and the Dictates of the Law', *The American Journal of Jurisprudence*, 14, Indiana, 1969

KING, JOHN N., *Tudor Royal Iconography. Literature and Art in an Age of Religious Crisis*, Princeton, 1989

KING, MARGARET L., *Women of the Renaissance*, Chicago, 1991

King Henry VIII's Jewel Book, ed. Rt Rev Edward, Bishop Suffragan of Nottingham, Lincoln Diocesan Architectural Society, 17, 1883–4

KINGSFORD, C. L., ed., *The First English Life of King Henry the Fifth, written in 1513 by an anonymous Author known commonly as the Translator of Livius*, 1913

KNECHT, R. J., *Francis I*, Cambridge, 1982

KNOWLES, M. D., 'The Matter of Wilton in 1528', *Bulletin of Institute of Historical Research*, 31, 1958

KNOWLES, M. D., *The Religious Orders in England*, 1971

KYBETT, SUSAN MACKEN, 'Henry VIII: A Malnourished King?', *History Today*, 39, 1989

(L & P) Letters and Papers of Henry VIII

The Lamentation, or Complaint of a Sinner, made by the most vertuous and right gratious Ladie, Queene Catherine; bewailing the Ignorance of her blind life, led in Superstition: verie profitable to the Amendment of our Lives, The Harleian Miscellany, V, 1810

LANGLEY, R., *Buckden Palace. A Short Account*, 1932

The Legend of Sir Nicholas Throckmorton, ed. J. G. Nichols, 1874

LEVINE, MORTIMER, *The place of women in Tudor government in Tudor rule and revolution. Essays for G. R. Elton from his American friends*, ed. J. Guth and John W. McKenna, Cambridge, 1982

LEWIS, C. S., *English Literature in the Sixteenth Century excluding Drama*, Oxford, 1954

LOADES, DAVID, *Mary Tudor. A Life*, Oxford, 1989

LOCKYER, ROGER, *Henry VII, Seminar Studies in History*, 1968

The Loseley Manuscripts, ed. A. J. Kempe, 1835

LOWINSKY, EDWARD E., 'A music book for Anne Boleyn', in *Florigilegium Historiale*, ed. J. G. Rowe and W. H. Stock

MACKIE, J. D., *The Earlier Tudors 1485–1558*, Oxford, revised edn, 1966

MACLEAN, JOHN, F. S. A., *The Life of Sir Thomas Seymour, Kt, Baron Seymour of Sudeley, Lord High Admiral of England and Master of the Ordnance*, 1869

MACNALTY, SIR ARTHUR SALUSBURY, *Henry VIII. A Difficult Patient*, 1952

MACNALTY, SIR ARTHUR SALUSBURY, 'The Death of Queen Catherine of Aragon', *Nursing Mirror*, 28 December 1962

MACRAY, REV WILLIAM DUNN, 'The "Remonstrance" of Anne of Cleves', *Archaeologia*, 47, 1883

MADDEN, FREDERICK, *Privy Purse Expenses of the Princess Mary, daughter of King Henry the Eighth, afterward Queen Mary*, 1831

MARIUS, RICHARD, *Thomas More. A biography*, New York, 1984

MARSHAM, ROBERT, 'On a Manuscript Book of Prayers in a Binding of Gold Enamelled, said to have been given by Queen Anne Boleyn to a lady of the Wyatt family; together with a Transcript of its Contents', *Archaeologia*, 44, 1873

MARTIENSSEN, ANTHONY, *Queen Katherine Parr*, 1973

MATHEW, DAVID, *The Courtiers of Henry VIII*, 1970

MATTINGLY, GARRETT, *Catherine of Aragon*, 1942

MATTINGLY, GARRETT, *Renaissance Diplomacy*, 1955

MATTINGLY, GARRETT, 'A Humanist Ambassador', *Journal of Modern History*, 4, 1932

MATTINGLY, GARRETT, 'The Reputation of Doctor de Puebla', *English Historical Review*, 55, 1940

MCCONICA, J. K., *English Humanists and Reformation Politics under Henry VIII and Edward VI*, Oxford, 1965

MCLAREN, DOROTHY, 'Marital fertility and lactation 1570–1720', in *Women in English Society 1500–1800*, ed. Mary Prior, 1985

MILLER, HELEN, *Henry VIII and the English Nobility*, Oxford, 1986

MILLER, HELEN, 'Henry VIII's Unwritten Will: Grants of Lands and Honours in 1547', in *Wealth and Power in Tudor England, Essays presented to S. T. Bindoff*, ed. E. W. Knives, R. J. Knecht and J. J. Scarisbrick, 1978

MOORE, SIR NORMAN, 'The Death of Catherine of Aragon', *The Athenaeum*, 1885

MORSHEAD, SIR OWEN, *Windsor Castle*, 2nd revised edn, 1957

MUELLER, JANET, 'Katherine Parr's Prayers and Meditations', *Huntington Library Quarterly*, 53, 1990

MUIR, KENNETH, *Life and Letters of Sir Thomas Wyatt*, Liverpool, 1963

NEAME, ALAN, *The Holy Maid of Kent. The Life of Elizabeth Barton, 1506–1534,* 1971

Newcastle MSS, Nottingham University Library, Nottingham

NICHOLS, J. G., ed., *A Collection of Ordinances and Regulations for the Government of the Royal Household made in diverse reigns . . .,* 1790

NICHOLS, J. G., ed., *Chronicle of Queen Jane, and of two years of Queen Mary,* 1850

NICHOLS, J. G., ed., *Inventories of the Wardrobes, Plate, Chapel Stuff etc of Henry Fitzroy, Duke of Richmond and of the Wardrobe Stuff at Baynard's Castle of Katharine, Princess Dowager,* Camden Society, 1855

NICHOLS, J. G., ed., *Literary Remains of King Edward the Sixth,* Roxburghe Club, 2 Vols, 1857

NICHOLS, J. G., ed., *Narratives of the days of the Reformation chiefly from the manuscripts of John Foxe the Martyrologist,* Camden Society, 1859

NICHOLS, J. G., ed., *The Diary of Henry Machyn 1550–1563,* Camden Society, 1848

NICOLAS, N. H., ed., *The Privy Purse Expenses of Elizabeth of York . . . with A Memoir and Notes,* 1830

NICOLAS, N. H., ed., *The Privy Purse Expenses of King Henry the Eighth. November 1529 – end of December 1532,* 1827

NICOLAS, SIR HARRIS, ed., *Proceedings and Ordinances of the Privy Council of England,* VII, 1837

NOREÑA, CARLOS G., *Juan Luis Vives,* The Hague, 1970

NOREÑA, CARLOS G., 'Juan Luis Vives and Henry VIII', *Renaissance and Reformation,* 12, 1976

Notes and Queries

NUCIUS, NICANDER, *The Second Book of the Travels,* Camden Society, ed. Rev J A Cramer, 1841

'Original documents relating to Queen Katharine of Aragon', *Gentleman's Magazine,* New Series, Vol. 42, 1854

Original Letters relative to the English Reformation, Written during the reigns of King Henry VIII, King Edward VI and Queen Mary: chiefly from the archives of Zürich, ed., Rev Hastings Robinson, 2 Vols, 1846–7

(PRO) Public Record Office MSS

PAGET, HUGH, 'The Youth of Anne Boleyn', *Bulletin of the Institute of Historical Research,* 55, 1981

PAUL, JOHN E., *Catherine of Aragon and her friends,* 1966

PITSCOTTIE, ROBERT LINDSAY OF, *History and Chronicles of Scotland,* 2 Vols, 1899

POPE-HENNESSY, JOHN, *The Portrait in the Renaissance,* 1966

PRESCOTT, WILLIAM H., *Ferdinand and Isabella,* 3 Vols, 1838

PUGH, R. B., ed., *Cambridgeshire and Isle of Ely,* Victoria County History, III, 1959

Rawlinson MSS, Bodleian Library, Oxford

READ, EVELYN, *Catherine Duchess of Suffolk*, 1962

REYNOLDS, E. E., *Thomas More and Erasmus*, 1965

RICHARDSON, WALTER C., *Mary Tudor. The White Queen*, 1970

RIDLEY, JASPER, *Henry VIII*, 1984

RIDLEY, JASPER, *The Statesman and the Fanatic*, 1982

RIDLEY, JASPER, *Thomas Cranmer*, Oxford, 1962

RIDLEY, JASPER, ed. and with a new introduction, *The Love Letters of Henry VIII*, 1988

ROBINSON, JOHN MARTIN, *The Dukes of Norfolk. A Quincentennial History*, Oxford, 1982

ROPER, WILLIAM, *The Lyfe of Sir Thomas Moore, knighte*, ed. E. V. Hitchcock, 1935

ROWLANDS, JOHN, *Holbein. The Paintings of Hans Holbein the Younger*, Oxford, 1985

RULE, MARGARET, *The Mary Rose. The Excavation and Raising of Henry VIII's Flagship*, foreword by HRH the Prince of Wales, revised edn, 1983

RUSSELL, JOYCELYNE G., *The Field of Cloth of Gold, Men and Manners in 1520*, 1969

(SP) State Papers, King Henry the Eighth

SANDER, NICOLAS, *Rise and Growth of the Anglican Schism*, trans. with notes by David Lewis, 1877

SAVAGE, HENRY, ed., *The Love Letters of Henry VIII*, 1949

SCALINGI, P. L., 'The Scepter or the Distaff: The Question of Female Sovereignty 1516–1607', *The Historian*, 41, 1978

SCARISBRICK, J. J., *Henry VIII*, 1968

SCHNUCKER, R. V., 'Elizabethan Birth Control and Puritan Attitudes', *Journal of Interdisciplinary History*, 5, 1975

SEWARD, DESMOND, *Prince of the Renaissance. The Life of François I*, 1974

SEYMOUR, WILLIAM, *Ordeal by Ambition. An English Family in the Shadow of the Tudors*, 1972

SKEEL, C. A. J., *The Council in the Marches of Wales*, 1904

SMITH, LACEY BALDWIN, *A Tudor Tragedy. The Life and Times of Catherine Howard*, 1961

SMITH, LACEY BALDWIN, *Henry VIII. The Mask of Royalty*, 1971

SMITH, LACEY BALDWIN, 'English Treason Trials and Confessions in the Sixteenth Century', *Journal of the History of Ideas*, 15, 1954

SOMERSET, ANNE, *Elizabeth I*, 1991

ST MAUR, H., *Annals of the Seymours*, 1902

STARKEY, DAVID, ed., *Henry VIII. A European Court in England*, 1991

STARKEY, DAVID, ed., *The English Court: from the Wars of the Roses to the Civil War*, 1987

STARKEY, DAVID, 'Representation through Intimacy. A study in the symbolism of monarchy and court office in early modern England' in *Symbols and Sentiments, Cross-cultural studies in Symbolism*, ed. Ioan Lewis, 1977

STARKEY, DAVID, *The Reign of Henry VIII. Personalities and Politics*, 1985

STARKEY, DAVID, 'A head of her time', interview in *The Independent*, 23 April 1991

STOW, JOHN, *A Survey of London*, introduction and notes by C. L. Kingsford, 1908

STRICKLAND, AGNES, *Lives of the Queens of England from the Norman Conquest*, 8 Vols, reprint edn, 1972

STRONG, ROY, *Hans Eworth. A Tudor artist and his circle*, Leicester, 1965

STRONG, ROY, *The Renaissance Garden in England*, 1979

STRONG, ROY, *Tudor and Jacobean Portraits*, 2 Vols, HMSO, 1969

STRYPE, JOHN, *Ecclesiastical Memorials . . . of the Church of England under King Henry VIII*, 3 Vols, 1822

SURTZ, EDWARD, SJ and MURPHY, VIRGINIA, eds, *The Divorce Tracts of Henry VIII*, foreword by John Guy, Angers, France, 1988

Survey of London, XXIII. South Bank and Vauxhall. The Parish of St Mary Lambeth, Part I, 1951

SWAIN, E. G., *The Story of Peterborough Cathedral*, 1932

SWEETING, W. D., *A New Guide to Peterborough Cathedral*, 1893

THOMAS, KEITH, *Religion and the Decline of Magic*, 1971

TREFUSIS, LADY MARY, collected and arranged, *Songs, Ballads and Instrumental Pieces composed by King Henry the Eighth*, Roxburghe Club, Oxford, 1912

TYTLER, PATRICK FRASER, *England under the Reigns of Edward VI and Mary*, 2 Vols, 1839

WARNICKE, RETHA M., *The Rise and Fall of Anne Boleyn. Family Politics at the Court of Henry VIII*, Cambridge, 1989

WARNICKE, RETHA M., *Women of the English Renaissance and Reformation. Contributions in Women's Studies*, 38, 1983

WATSON, FOSTER, ed., *Vives and the Renascence Education of Women*, 1912

WATSON, FOSTER, *Luis Vives, El Gran Valenciano, 1492–1540*, Oxford, 1922

WAYMENT, HILARY, *King's College Chapel, Cambridge. The Great Windows*, Cambridge, 1982

WAYMENT, HILARY, 'The East Window of St Margaret's, Westminster', *The Antiquaries Journal*, 61, 1981

WERNHAM, R. B., *Before the Armada. The Emergence of the English Nation. 1485–1588*, paperback edn, New York, 1972

WHITTINGTON, ROBERT, *In laudem illustrissimae et formosissimae Heriones dominae Annae, Marchionissae penbrochiae . . . Carmen panegyriton*, Hatfield MSS, Hatfield, Hertfordshire

WILLEMENT, THOMAS, *Regal Heraldry*, 1821

WILLIAMS, NEVILLE, *Elizabeth I*, 1967

WILLIAMS, NEVILLE, *Henry VIII and his Court*, 1971

WILLIAMS, NEVILLE, *The Royal Residences of Great Britain. A Social History*, 1960

WILLIAMS, NEVILLE, *Thomas Howard, Fourth Duke of Norfolk,* 1964

WOOD, MARY ANNE EVERETT, ed., *Letters of Royal and Illustrious Ladies of Great Britain,* 3 Vols, 1846

WRIGHT, THOMAS, *Historical and Descriptive Sketch of Ludlow Castle,* Ludlow, 1924

WRIOTHESLEY, CHARLES, Windsor Herald, *A Chronicle of England during the Reigns of the Tudors, From AD 1485 to 1559,* ed. William Douglas Hamilton, Camden Society, 2 Vols, 1875

WYATT, GEORGE, 'Some particulars of The Life of Queen Anne Boleigne', in *The Life of Cardinal Wolsey by George Cavendish,* ed. S. W. Singer, 1827

INDEX

Abel, Thomas, 315
Act for the Advancement of the True Religion, 1543, 380
Act of Conditional Restraint of Annates, 1532, 181
Act of Restraint of Appeals, 1533, 187
Act of Six Articles, 1539, 300–1, 378, 381
Act of Succession, 1543, 208–10; 1536, 268, 425
Act of Supremacy, 1543, 207–8
Adrian VI, Pope, 23, 97
Aiguesmortes, Peace of, 1538, 293, 302
Ailesbury, Elizabeth, Countess of, 424
à Kempis, Thomas: *The Imitation of Christ*, 378
Albany, John Stewart, Duke of, 73, 103–4
Albret, Jeanne d' *see* Jeanne d'Albret
Aless, Alexander, 255n
Alfonso, Don, Prince of Portugal, 14
Alwaye, Thomas, 144
Ampthill, Bedfordshire, 181, 188, 259
Ancrum Moor, Battle of, 1545, 383
Andreas, Bernardus, 25
Angoulême, François, Duc d' (son of François I), 307
Angus, Archibald Douglas, Earl of, 73–4, 134
Anna of Cleves, 4th wife of Henry VIII: appearance, 1, 305–7, 368; religion, 1, 310; Katherine Howard waits on, 3; survival, 4, 409–11; name, 5; as prospective bride, 283, 296, 299; background and upbringing, 296–8; qualities and character, 298–9, 417–18; precontract with Francis of Lorraine, 301, 309, 310n, 325; portrait, 300–1, 306; travels to England, 302–5; meets Henry, 305–6; marriage, 308–11, 423–4; marriage uncon-

summated, 311–12, 325, 327, 338; innocence, 312–13; household, 313; and Henry's relations with Katherine Howard, 323–4; divorce and settlement, 324–9, 338, 410; popularity, 326, 338; visits Henry and Katherine, 336–8, 359; gifts to Katherine, 336–7; good relations with Mary Tudor, 338, 411; life-style in England, 338–9; proposed reconciliation with Henry after Katherine's execution, 359–60, 386; on Catherine Parr, 368–70; and Henry's marriage to Catherine Parr, 369–70, 372; relations with Elizabeth, 385; rumoured children by Henry, 386; and Henry's death, 394; life and money problems after Henry's death, 409–11; attempts to legitimise marriage, 410; and Brouckhusen, 410–11; wishes to return to Cleves, 411; properties, 412; death, will and funeral, 412–14; praise for Henry, 420; tomb, 427
annates, 181
Anne of Bohemia, Queen of Richard II, 193n
Anne Boleyn, 2nd wife of Henry VIII: appearance, 1, 122–4, 218, 307; Lutheranism and religious views, 1, 143–6, 177, 211, 263, 272, 418; waits on Catherine of Aragon, 3, 216; name, 5; and Field of Cloth of Gold, 87, 121, 186; Henry falls in love with, 115, 128–32, 136–7, 142–3, 170; birth and background, 115–17, 363n, 418; upbringing, 119–21, 317; character and qualities, 120, 124, 143–4, 169, 236, 247, 251, 298, 417–18; proposed marriage to James Butler, 121–2, 124–5; friendship with Marguerite d'Angoulême, 121, 184; liaison with Percy, 124–7, 135, 142, 251, 255,

Ghent, 302, 314
Giustinian, Sebastian, 54–5, 72–3, 81–2, 94
Glass of the Truth, A, (1532), 163
Goldsmith, Francis, 377
Grammont, Gabriel de, Bishop of Tarbes, 131, 135, 159
Granada (Spain), 11
Greenwich, 161, 211, 241, 259, 273
Greenwich, Treaty of, 1543, 374
Grey, Lady Jane, 403, 405–7; executed, 409
Grey of Powis, Edward, 4th Baron, 50
Grimaldi, Francesco, 47
Grindal, William, 382
Groghroff (Clevian Chancellor), 309
Grynaeus, Simon, 171
Guaras, Antonio de: on Anne Boleyn's unpopularity, 171; on Anne Boleyn's procession and reception in London, 191–2, 194; visits Catherine of Aragon in Kimbolton, 221–2; on death of Catherine of Aragon, 229n; on Anne Stanhope, 235; on Anne Boleyn's attachment to Smeaton, 249; at Anne Boleyn's execution, 256; hostility to Elizabeth, 267; and birth of Edward VI, 277; on execution of Katherine Howard, 354n; and Henry's marriage to Katherine Howard, 376; *Spanish Chronicle*, 191, 256
Guelderland, 297, 299, 370
Guildford, Sir Henry, 170, 173, 237
Guise, Duchess Antoinette de, 292
Guise, Louise de, 289, 292
Guise, Marie de *see* Marie de Guise
Guise, Renée de, 289, 293

Haevens, Theodore, 414
Hall, Edward: *Chronicle*, 51, 62, 96, 148, 151, 155, 190, 195–6, 281
Hall, Mary, 344–5
Hampton Court Palace, 212, 347 & n
Harpsfield, Nicholas, 135, 152
Hastings, Lady Anne, 70
Heneage, Sir Thomas, 312, 347
Henriquez, Juana, 46
Henry I, King of England, 94
Henry II, King of England, 10, 94, 246, 294

Henry V, King of England, 17, 26, 63
Henry VI, King of England, 289
Henry VII, King of England: secures throne, 9, 15–16; and son Arthur's marriage to Catherine of Aragon, 16, 18–20, 30; meets Catherine on arrival in England, 22–5; celebrates Catherine's arrival, 26–7; and Catherine's dowry, 31, 35, 40, 44; and Arthur's death, 33; fears over succession, 33–4; withholds financial support for Catherine, 36, 42, 44, 48; and Catherine's betrothal to Henry, 36–8, 52; widowhood, 38; marriage prospects, 39–41, 43–4, 47; treats with Philip, 41; and Juana's widowhood, 43, 47; gambling, 44, 55; death, 48, 51; appearance, 53; tomb, 90; genealogy, 423n
Henry VIII, King of England (*formerly* Duke of York; *then* Prince of Wales): weight increase and girth, 2, 220, 260, 288, 334–5, 358, 367; at Catherine of Aragon's wedding to Arthur, 27–8; and Catherine of Aragon's virginity, 29, 35–7, 49, 138, 140–1, 149, 153, 160–3, 167–8, 178, 196, 325; and Arthur's death, 33–4; betrothal to Catherine of Aragon, 35–8, 43, 47, 90; prospective marriage to Eleanor of Austria, 39, 41, 52–3, 90; repudiates betrothal to Catherine of Aragon, 39, 41; and Catherine's religious austerity, 41, 80; relations with Catherine, 42–3, 69–71, 266; appearance, 43, 53–5, 128, 260; accession and marriage to Catherine, 49–53, 57–8; gambling, 55, 173, 303; character and interests, 55–6; music, 55–6, 298; court life and pastimes, 57–60; love-making, 60–1; and birth and death of Prince Henry, 62; at war with France, 62–7, 96, 103, 361, 373–5, 383–4; and Flodden, 66; amours and romances, 70–1, 83, 101, 197, 216–17, 220n; and birth of Mary Tudor, 73; and European treaties, 75; humanism and learning, 76; and 'minions', 77–8; favours French alliance, 82, 84–6; and Charles V, 86; at Field of Cloth of Gold, 87–9; tomb, 90–1, 426–7; succession question, 93,

95, 202–4, 268; as Defender of the Faith, 97, 135; relations with Scots, 103; and Mary Tudor's proposed marriages, 104; and Charles V's repudiation of Mary Tudor marriage, 107; injured in joust, 107; falls in love with Anne Boleyn, 111, 115, 128–32, 136–7, 142–3, 170; letters to Anne Boleyn, 129–30; seeks divorce from Catherine of Aragon, 133–5, 137–41, 147–51, 167; dispensation and precontract with Anne Boleyn, 143–5; maintains conjugal relations with Catherine of Aragon, 151–2, 167; praises Catherine, 154–5; and divorce tribunal, 157–60, 162, 164; and fall of Wolsey, 165; meets Chapuys, 167; and Anne Boleyn's unpopularity, 171–2; appeals to universities over divorce, 175; as Supreme Head of English Church, 175–7, 181–2, 195, 206, 208–10; leaves Catherine of Aragon, 178, 180; rejects Rome inquiry into marriage, 179–80; meets François I in France, 183, 185–6; demands from Catherine of Aragon, 184–5; lovemaking with Anne Boleyn, 186–7; marriage to Anne Boleyn, 187–8; wins divorce from Catherine of Aragon, 190; and Anne Boleyn's coronation, 194–5; marriage relations with Anne Boleyn, 197–8, 218; relations with Mary Tudor, 201–2, 210, 261–2; and Act of Succession, 208–10; buildings and palaces, 211–12; dislike of disputatious women, 215–16; fondness for Jane Seymour, 217, 223, 232–3, 237–40, 244; and Anne Boleyn's failure to bear son, 219–20, 232–3; periodic impotence, 220–1, 252, 264; message from dying Catherine of Aragon, 227–8; and Catherine's death, 229–31; leaves Anne Boleyn, 243; and trial and death of Anne Boleyn, 246–7; betrothal to Jane Seymour, 257–65; and dissolution of monasteries, 269–70; and rebellions in north, 269–71, 274; and Jane Seymour's pregnancy and birth of son, 276–8; and Jane's death, 280–2;

search for new bride, 281–3, 287–93; Pope's bulls against, 293–4; purges rivals, 294–5; meets Anna of Cleves, 305; marriage to Anna of Cleves, 308–11; distaste for physical relations with Anna of Cleves, 311–12, 325; in love with Katherine Howard, 322, 324, 331–3; divorce from Anna of Cleves, 324–9; marriage to Katherine Howard, 330, 333; health decline, 335–6, 341, 358, 373, 391; on progress in north, 339, 342–4; lovemaking with Katherine Howard, 339–40; and fall and execution of Katherine Howard, 344–7, 350–2, 357; anti-French treaty with Charles V, 361; interest in Catherine Parr, 366; marriage to Catherine Parr, 367–8; religious beliefs, 378, 381; represented in dynastic painting, 382; and Catherine Parr's religious disputes, 387–9; and court power struggles, 392–3; death and burial, 393–5, 426–7; need for son, 421–3; portrait with Catherine of Aragon, 424; *A Glasse of the Truthe*, 147

Henry, Prince (son of Henry VIII and Catherine of Aragon), 61–2, 69, 420

Herbert, Anne, Lady (*née* Parr; Catherine's sister), 3, 363, 366–7, 370, 400

Herbert, Sir William (husband of Anne), 366, 370–1, 400

Herbert of Cherbury, Edward, 1st Baron, 230, 387

Heresbach, Konrad von, 297–8

Hertford, Anne, Countess of *see* Somerset, Anne, Duchess of

Hertford, Edward Seymour, 1st Earl of *see* Somerset, Edward Seymour, 1st Duke of

Hervet, Gentian, 78

Hethe, John, 211

Hever Castle, Kent, 411–12

Hickman, Rose, 215

Hiller, Richard, 308, 325

Hilsey, John, Bishop of Rochester, 231

Hoby, Sir Philip, 290, 292

Hoghesten (Anna of Cleves' steward), 303–4, 309

of Northampton and Earl of Essex),
363, 364, 371, 379, 383, 394, 406,
408
Pate, Richard, Archdeacon of Lincoln
(*later* Bishop of Worcester), 268, 334
Paul III, Pope, 207, 274, 287, 293–4
Paulet, Sir William (*later* 1st Marquess
of Winchester), 281
Pavia, Battle of, 1525, 105, 139
Penalosa (Imperial envoy), 108
Penshurst Place, Kent, 412
Percy, Henry, Lord: liaison with Anne
Boleyn, 124–7, 136, 165, 251, 255,
322, 419; marriage to Lady Mary
Talbot, 125–6
Percy, Lady Mary (*née* Talbot), 124–
6
Peterborough Cathedral, 230–1, 429
Peto, William, 172
Philibert of Savoy, Duke, 5, 38
Philip II, King of Spain, 107, 137n, 408–
10
Philip, Archduke of Austria, King of
Castile ('the Handsome'), 14, 38, 41–
3
Philip of Hesse ('the Good'), 297
Philippa of Hainault, Queen of Edward
III, 81, 297
Pilgrimage of Grace, 1536, 269–71,
275, 295, 365
Pole family, 204, 294
Pole, Arthur, 95
Pole, Edmund de la, 93
Pole, Sir Geoffrey, 294
Pole, Margaret, Lady *see* Salisbury, Mar-
garet Pole, Countess of
Pole, Cardinal Reginald: made *persona
non grata*, 95; teases Cranmer over
threat to Henry, 189; as potential
match for Mary Tudor, 204; made
Cardinal, 274, 287; papal mission to
Spain, 293; and Henry's purge of Pole
family, 295; mother executed, 342–3;
Pro Ecclesiasticae Unitatis Defensione,
263, 294
Pole, Sir Richard de la ('the White
Rose'), 32, 93, 105
Pole, Lady Ursula: marriage to Stafford,
94–5
Portugal, 14

Powell, Edward, 315
Praet, Louis de, 104
Princes in the Tower, The, 15
Puebla, Roderigo Gonzalva de, 16–20,
28, 36–7, 41, 43, 46–7
Pulgar, Hernando de, 11

Queen's College, Cambridge, 78

Rabelais, François, 121
Rattsey, Jane, 359
Renée, Madame (sister of Queen Claude
of France), 140
Rhodion: *De Partus Hominis*, 332
Rhys ap Thomas, 32
Rich, Richard, 387
Richard III, King of England, 28, 32
Richard, Duke of York, 16
Richards, Griffith, 161, 196
Richmond, Henry Fitzroy, Duke of
(illegitimate son of Henry VIII): mar-
riage, 30; birth, 83, 90; exaltation and
titles, 108–10; character, 111; Henry's
devotion to, 136; proposed as
husband for Mary Tudor, 151; in
France, 185; Edward Seymour serves,
235; and Henry's disavowment of
Anne Boleyn, 246; and Anne Boleyn's
divorce, 254; health, 254; at Anne
Boleyn's execution, 256
Richmond, Margaret Beaufort, Count-
ess of, 15, 19, 29–30, 66, 78–9, 214,
318, 421; death, 50
Richmond, Mary, Duchess of, 30, 170,
322, 350, 392–3, 397
Richmond Palace, 43n, 412
Ridley, Jasper, 129n
Rochford, George Boleyn, Viscount
(Anne Boleyn's brother): birth, 119;
in Henry's Privy Chambers, 131; and
Smeaton, 212; not appointed to
Garter, 242; arrested, 243; trial and
execution, 250, 252–3, 256
Rochford, Jane, Viscountess (*née*
Parker), 218, 220, 252, 264, 312,
342, 349; execution, 353–4
Rome: sacked (1527), 139, 143
Roper, Margaret (*née* More), 3, 100
'Rough Wooing, the', 375
Russell, Henry, 400

1540   2+